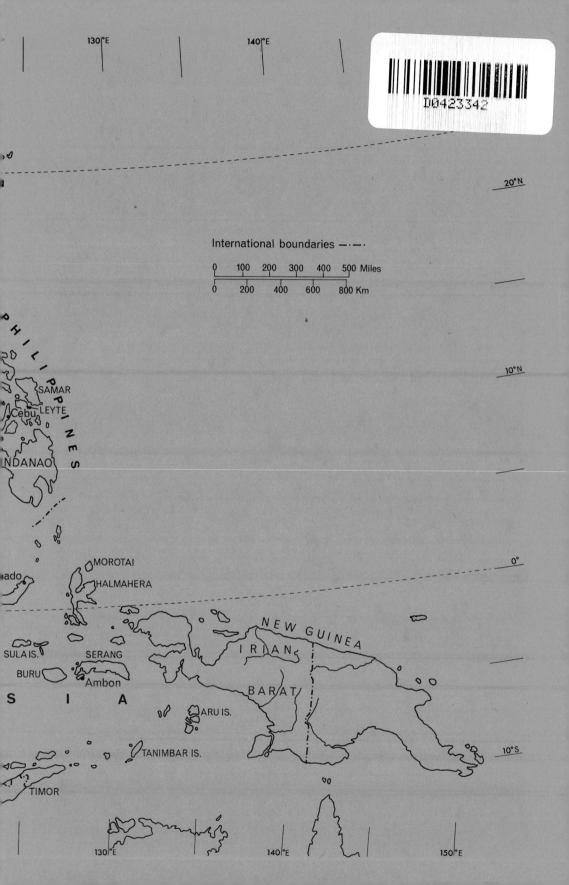

D0423342

130°E 140°E

20°N

International boundaries — · — ·

| 0 | 100 | 200 | 300 | 400 | 500 Miles |

| 0 | 200 | 400 | 600 | 800 Km |

10°N

PHILIPPINES

SAMAR

Cebu LEYTE

NDANAO

0°

MOROTAI

ado

HALMAHERA

NEW GUINEA

SULA IS.

SERANG

IRIAN

BURU

Ambon

S   I   A

BARAT

ARU IS.

TANIMBAR IS.

10°S

TIMOR

130°E 140°E 150°E

EMERGING SOUTHEAST ASIA
A Study in Growth and Stagnation

'*As we see nowadays in Southeast Asia or the Caribbean, the misery of being exploited by capitalists is nothing compared to the misery of not being exploited at all.*'
Joan Robinson, *Economic Philosophy*

McGRAW-HILL SERIES IN GEOGRAPHY
Edward J. Taaffe and John W. Webb, Consulting Editors

Broek and **Webb**   A Geography of Mankind
Cressey   Asia's Lands and Peoples
Cressey   Land of the 500 Million: A Geography of China
Demko, Rose, and **Schnell**   Population Geography: A Reader
Fryer   Emerging Southeast Asia: A Study in Growth and Stagnation
Fryer   World Economic Development
Murphy   The American City: An Urban Geography
Pounds   Europe and the Soviet Union
Pounds   Political Geography
Raisz   General Cartography
Raisz   Principles of Cartography
Starkey and **Robinson**   The Anglo-American Realm
Thoman, Conkling, and **Yeates**   The Geography of Economic Activity
Trewartha   An Introduction to Climate
Trewartha, Robinson, and **Hammond**   Fundamentals of Physical Geography
Trewartha, Robinson, and **Hammond**   Elements of Geography: Physical and
   Cultural
Trewartha, Robinson, and **Hammond**   Physical Elements of Geography
   (A republication of Part I of the above)
Van Riper   Man's Physical World

EMERGING SOUTHEAST ASIA

A Study in Growth and Stagnation

DONALD W. FRYER
Professor of Geography
University of Hawaii

McGRAW-HILL BOOK COMPANY
New York / St. Louis / San Francisco
Düsseldorf / Mexico / Panama / Toronto

EMERGING SOUTHEAST ASIA
A Study in Growth and Stagnation

Copyright © 1970 by Donald W. Fryer. All rights reserved.
Printed in the United States of America.
No part of this publication may be reproduced, stored in a retrieval system,
or transmitted, in any form or by any means, electronic,
mechanical, photocopying, recording, or otherwise,
without the prior written permission of Donald W. Fryer.

Library of Congress Catalog Card Number 75-105952

22587

1 2 3 4 5 6 7 8 9 0   Q B Q B   7 9 8 7 6 5 4 3 2 1 0

This edition is not for sale in the British Commonwealth
(excluding Canada), Dependencies and Trusteeships and the states of Burma, Egypt, Iraq,
Israel, Jordan, Kuwait, South Africa, Rhodesia, and Sudan.
An edition for sale in these areas is published by George Philip & Son Limited, London.

Dedicated to the staff and students
of the University of Malaya

PREFACE

For more than a decade Southeast Asia has forcibly obtruded itself on public attention in the West, rivalling the Middle East as potentially the most explosive quarter of the globe, and threatening on more than one occasion to bring the major powers of East and West into direct confrontation. Fortunately at the time of writing the danger that Southeast Asia's internal problems might escalate into major world conflict appears to be receding, and it is quite certain that the great majority of the region's population would much prefer to be left to work out their own destinies without external interference. But there are few overall reviews of the region available to the intelligent person seeking to broaden his understanding of Southeast Asia's pressing problems and their impact on the world at large, and the author hopes that this addition to the small stock of such studies will prove welcome to students, business men, public servants and others who require a work with greater attention to economic considerations than has been available so far.

Practical experience has taught the layman to have a healthy suspicion of economists and their arguments, but like it or not, at the present time most of us have to be economists of greater or lesser standing. Several of Southeast Asia's problems are of deep-seated origin and ultimately reflect basic cultural differences among its diverse populations, but it can scarcely be denied that the most pressing issues are largely economic in nature; apart from such obvious humanitarian considerations as the necessity for a major improvement in health and living standard, the future stability of the new states of the region and their continued adhesion to the largely free and open economy of the non-communist world are also at stake. Communists have always maintained the inherent superiority of their so-called 'socialist' societies over 'bourgeois' western ones, but in Asia their primary appeal has always been their total commitment to the cry from the countryside that the land must belong to those that till it. Although movements of agrarian protest have largely arisen spontaneously, the communists have moved swiftly, and all too often successfully, to capture them and to divert such protests to serving communist ends.

In countries with landlord-dominated governments, the fact that the voice of the peasant is often only heard by or through the local communist party is fraught with consequence. Yet in heeding the communist siren-song, the peasant accomplishes his own downfall; the communists have no effective solution to agrarian ills, nor indeed do they offer any real prospect of marked improvement in the lot of the urban worker. It is true that under certain conditions communist governments have shown an ability to generate a high rate of economic growth, but this has little to do with improving the general level of welfare; forced deliveries at depressed prices, rigorous rationing and prohibition of the right to strike are only some of the ways in which the masses are made to pay for building up economic and military strength in the communist world.

Most students of Southeast Asia firmly believe that the extension of communist rule over the region, which could only mean closer orientation towards Peking, would be a tragedy for Southeast Asia itself and for the world. But many also hold that partly through enormous and laxly-administered schemes of military and economic aid, which in practice have often turned out to be subventions to 'reliable' but locally discredited regimes, and partly through economic policies which tend to depress the prices of Southeast Asia's primary products and to discourage industrialization, the West is tending to channel local dissent towards the communists. On some occasions since 1950 it would not be difficult to show that these allegations contain a substantial germ of truth. Nevertheless, Southeast Asia is still largely master of its own fate, and in the words of one of its most talented and perspicacious leaders, Prime Minister Lee Kuan Yew of Singapore, 'the theory that history is on the side of the communists is bunk'. Almost uniquely in the Third World, Southeast Asia contains countries that accept that the world does not owe them a living, that incanting the shortcomings of colonialism will avail nothing and that modernization depends very largely on their own unaided efforts. Without the advantage of rapidly rising exports of petroleum or of other modern 'growth' minerals, the commonest causes of recent economic success in poor countries, and largely dependent on their traditional products for their foreign exchange, some countries of Southeast Asia over the past decade have achieved rates of economic growth that do not make such a bad showing against that of economic pace-setters such as Japan, and they have performed this feat under varying, though non-communist, forms of political organization.

Southeast Asia, in short, is essentially a region of hope, and a salutary example to the rest of the Third World that sensible, pragmatic economic policies work, and that forced-draft industrialization erected on totally unrealistic planning designed primarily to gratify the vanity and megalomania of charismatic heads-of-state, leads speedily to massive social and economic dislocation. To state this, of course, is merely to underline that what would appear to constitute sensible economic policy in some countries, may be politically out of the question, and an understanding of why this is so may well involve examination of issues dating far back into the colonial period or even earlier. Nations are often the prisoners of their history, but modernization demands that all such historical impediments to the developmental process be jettisoned. No attempt has been made to provide more than an introduction to such problems and to note the scars caused by the struggle to reconcile the old with the new.

As the dean of Southeast Asian geographers, Professor Karl Pelzer, has pointed out, study of Southeast Asia encounters difficulties that do not occur on anything like the same scale in South or East Asian studies. Southeast Asia does not possess a single cultural heritage as is the case with the two most populous major divisions of the Asian continent, and which is also true of much less densely populated Southwest Asia. Unlike East and South Asia which are composed of but two major states apiece and some minor appendages, Southeast Asia comprises a multiplicity of generally small states, among which are some miniscule ones; even the largest unit contains less than half the regional population, and has found the maintenance of national cohesion a matter of particular difficulty. Within each state plural societies and a variety of languages compound the difficulties facing the investigator, and although it may be true that some of these problems also occur in South Asia, virtually every government document in that region is available in English. Inevitably, therefore, it is impossible for any scholar, however protracted and diligent his field and library research, to be equally authoritative in each political unit or to familiarize himself with more than a small part of the region, and any overall survey must rely heavily on secondary sources. Thus the allocation of space in this study reflects primarily the author's own interests and field experience, but it has some logic, nevertheless. As the largest and most populous state of the region and that with by far the most massive developmental problems, Indonesia must assume a dominant position, and the lengthy analysis of Malaysia and Singapore appears justified by the fact that by the standards of the region the size of their joint economy is out of all proportion to their populations. Such outstanding success clearly merits detailed discussion, and it is scarcely necessary to apologize for the somewhat cursory account of Burma in view of that country's attempt to make itself as inaccessible as possible and to discourage strongly any attempt by the outsider to acquire the information to present to the world an impartial picture of the country.

The inexorable march of events must inevitably overtake publication of this book. It is hoped, however, that this picture of the region in the later Sixties will indicate in broad terms what are likely to constitute the major issues into the Seventies, and the probable lines of development in the region's component parts. Some events, such as the Indonesian recovery programmes and the sharp increase in communal tensions in Malaysia following the elections of May 1969, are still so close that any forecast can only be extremely hazardous; and over the whole region, the unresolved Vietnam war, to say nothing of the possibility of a major military confrontation between the USSR and China, continues to cast long shadows. One thing is certain, however; whether or not Southeast Asia is going to resolve its pressing problems of food production, rapid population growth and explosive city growth will be effectively decided over the coming decade, for no further time will be allowed it.

The rendering of Southeast Asian place-names into English frequently presents difficulties, and as in much of the Third World, new place-names continue to replace familiar old-established ones under the impact of nationalism. With but a few exceptions, the names used here are those of respective national volumes of the Official Gazetteers produced by the United States Permanent Committee on Geographic Names. Fortunately, territories formerly administered by English-speaking nations, Burma, Malaysia, Singapore and the Philippines, have generally retained the names and spellings established in the colonial period, although in Malaysia some familiar names have recently been replaced by new romanized Malay spellings, e.g. Melaka (Malacca), and all such official new spellings have been used here. It is possible that further Malaysian place-names may be altered following the resuscitation, after the end of 'confrontation', of the joint Malaysia-Indonesia committee on the transliteration of Malay and Indonesian names. In the wave of anti-Dutch feeling following the revolutionary war, when English replaced Dutch as the second language in the Indonesian school system, Indonesia declared its intention of replacing the Dutch system of transliteration by the English system used in the Malayan peninsula; but this policy was never rigorously implemented, and the country now seems to prefer its Dutch system, although for some names both Dutch and English versions have been officially used, and both may be recorded in the United States Official Gazetteers.

The transliteration of Thai place-names presents special difficulties, for in an independent country an official romanization was never necessary, although the need for one is increasingly felt and the Thai government has had to turn its attention to the problem. As a result, Western scholars, and indeed individual Thai ministries in their English publications, have used a variety of spellings. In rendering Thai places into English some writers have confined themselves to a strict transliteration of the Thai script, while others have endeavoured to provide an approximation to the Thai pronunciation. Use of the United States Official Gazetteer on Thailand has some disadvantages; many conventional spellings are set aside, nor is there always a coincidence with the names used in the standard geographic work on the country by R. L. Pendleton, *Thailand: Aspects of Land and Life,* for which English place-name spellings were produced by Dr. Walter Vella. The author is grateful to Dr. Vella for his advice concerning Thai place-names, but the United States Official Gazetteer has the advantage that its nomenclature has been adopted in most modern atlases. For international rivers such as the Mekong and Salween, conventional English spellings have been retained. In Vietnam, Laos and Cambodia, while many place-names used by the former French administration have remained unaltered, others have reverted to vernacular names which have always been used by the local inhabitants, and others still—generally arising from national development plans—are completely new. A particular problem arises in the case of the Red river of Tonkin. The name Songkoi (adopted here) or Song Koi represents customary usage and is widely employed in geographic writing (though a better transliteration could be Song Khoi or Song Hoi). The correct Vietnamese form, however, is Song Hong, but in fact the river is universally known in that country as the Hong Ha—a name which reflects that of the North Vietnamese capital, Hanoi (Ha Noi, literally, 'inside the river'). For their advice on this matter and on certain other names the author is grateful to his Vietnamese students.

In general the units of measurement are those of the United Nations Statistical Office and the FAO: these greatly facilitate international comparisons, and as these organizations' annual statistical publications are widely available, the student can easily update many of the tables provided here. For some commodities such as rubber and tin, however, where British interests have long been dominant, and for which there are official bodies with important statistical publications using British units of measurement, use of the latter has been preferred. In the national chapters also, local statistical units have been employed where this has been considered desirable for an understanding of agricultural problems, but in the case of former British territories the familiar British units have been retained.

The great part of this work was written while the author was Reader in Geography at the University of Malaya, Kuala Lumpur, and for the help he received from virtually all members of the staff of the Department of Geography the author wishes to record his deep gratitude; he is particularly indebted to Dr. James C. Jackson for his sustained interest and assistance over many years. The opportunity to spend a year in London with the Economic Planning Staff of the Ministry of Overseas Development greatly enlarged the author's comprehension of Southeast Asia's developmental problems, and he would like to record his thanks to Mr. R. S. Porter, then Director of the Geographic Division of the Ministry's Economic Planning Staff, for much useful advice and assistance. Thanks are also due to the following for the provision of photographic illustrations: Mr. Peter Jennings (pages 46, 49, 58, 76 *top,* 258, 302, 303, 304, 325, and 353) ; Mr. Wade Edmundson (pages 76 *foot,* 94 *foot,* 171, 181, 195, and 198) ; Mr. Edson Lott (pages 134, 135, and 158) ; Mr. T. C. Chiang (page 281) and for Fig. 6-8, page 282; Mr. Voon Phin Keong (page 240) ; the Department of Information and Broadcasting, Malaysia (pages 249, 272, and 275 *foot*) ; the Food and Agriculture Organization (pages 430 and 435) ; the Mekong Committee of ECAFE (page 124) ; Camera Press Ltd. (pages 381 and 422) ; and Paul Popper Ltd. (page 376). All other photographs are by the author.

DONALD W. FRYER

CONTENTS

MAPS AND DIAGRAMS

TABLES

SOME GEOGRAPHIC TERMS IN SOUTHEAST ASIAN LANGUAGES

BURMESE

aw	bay
chaung	stream
hka	river
kyaw	mountain
kyun	island
taunggyi	mountain
yoma	divide, range

INDONESIAN AND MALAY

air, ayer	stream
batang	stream
bukit	hill, mountain
gunung, gunong	peak, mountain
gunung api	volcano
kali	stream
kota	town
kuala	estuary
laut	sea
muara	estuary
permatang	dune, raised beach
pulau	island
sungei	river
tandjung, tanjong	cape
teluk, telok	bay, bend of river
ulu	headstream area, interfluve

CAMBODIAN

beng	lake, marsh
kas	island
kompong	village, town
phnom	hill, mountain
prek	stream, canal
stung	river

THAI

ban	village
doi	peak, mountain
dong	range, divide
ko	island
khlong	canal, stream
laem	cape
lam, lam nam	intermittent river
mae, mae nam, nam	river
muang	town, city
phra	pagoda, temple

VIETNAMESE

cho, chu	range, mountain
cua	estuary
hon	island
mui	cape
phu	range
song	river
xa, xieng, xom	village

EMERGING SOUTHEAST ASIA

A Study in Growth and Stagnation

CHAPTER ONE

Southeast Asia in the modern world

Before World War II Southeast Asia was scarcely even a geographic expression. For the West it was little more than an undifferentiated part of Monsoon Asia, the teeming eastern and southern margins of the great Asian continent; for Asians themselves, it had no significance at all. With but one exception, all of its component parts had been brought under imperial rule, but Siam, as the exception was then called, was scarcely a stronger or more cohesive unit *vis-à-vis* Burma or the Annamite lands, than mid-nineteenth century Afghanistan was in comparison with contemporary Khiva or Bokhara.[1] The great powers commanded the disposition of the resources of Southeast Asia just as they did those of South Asia and, to a very considerable extent, also those of the East Asian mainland. From Southeast Asia's mines and plantations a rich variety of foodstuffs, raw materials and mineral products flowed to the markets of Europe and North America, and to an increasingly significant degree, to those of Japan also. But this scarcely attached any special political significance to the lands of Southeast Asia, or invested them with any unique position in the eyes of the imperial powers; indeed, for the two greatest colonial empires, those of Britain and France, Southeast Asian possessions were of relatively minor significance.

So great have been the changes wrought in Asia since the Thirties that it is occasionally difficult to credit that they have all been crammed within scarcely three decades. But war is the most powerful of all agents of social change, and global war means global change; the apparently effortless overthrow of the imperial regimes in Southeast Asia by Japan undoubtedly helped to destroy their

---

[1] *The rise of Thai nationalism owed much to King Vajiravudh, or Rama VI (1910–25), a pamphleteer who attacked both the Chinese and slavish imitation of Western ideas and usages. The king held that only the monarch could ease Thailand's transition into the modern world, and that uncompromising loyalty to the throne must be the aim of every Thai patriot; but Vajiravudh's own wholesale borrowings from the West only underlined Thailand's ambivalence, and indeed, the essential contradiction of a hereditary absolute monarch in a modern society.*

capacity for survival in other parts of the world. An immediate consequence of
the Japanese success was the recognition of Southeast Asia as a part of the continent with a distinctive personality neither Indic nor Sinic, and with a claim to
be regarded as a major world region. First credited to the Indian historian K. M.
Pannikar, whose *Future of Southeast Asia* was published in 1943, the term
Southeast Asia was speedily adopted by the Allied Supreme Command, and by
the end of the war its use as a collective for the peninsulas between India and
China together with the Indonesian and Philippine archipelagos, was well
established.

Thus defined, Southeast Asia is not a very substantial portion of the earth's
surface; its total land area amounts to less than 1·6 million square miles,[2] but a
large submarine extension, much of which was land even in late Pleistocene times,
lies beneath the South China and Java Seas. But with merely 3 per cent of the
land area of the globe, Southeast Asia possesses some 7 per cent of its population,
and because the rate of population growth is much higher than in the world as a
whole, this proportion will rise to some 8 per cent by 1980 (*Table 1-1*). About
half of the region's total population is accounted for by Indonesia alone, but this
country has never realized the political and economic importance in Southeast
Asia that would seem to be implicit in such a proportion. Yet despite its rapid
population growth, heavy immigration before World War II suggested that the
region had a labour shortage, at least for capitalist forms of enterprise. Immigration from outside the region has now been reduced to a trickle and that largely
illegal, but in every country substantial internal migrations continue to take
place. Some of these migrations may be viewed as the latest of the successive
movements of peoples that have occurred in the region throughout history, but
the drift to the cities, from the economic standpoint the most important of all,
is part of a worldwide trend which since 1945 has proceeded apace everywhere
in the Third World. In Southeast Asia the urban revolution has progressed very
rapidly indeed, and in Malaysia and the Philippines particularly, the proportion
of the population living in urban conditions, particularly in cities with a population exceeding 100,000, is already high by Asian standards.[3]

These population movements have been superimposed on a remarkable
diversity of peoples, who, though possessing a broad underlying unity of material
culture, often reinforced by a general similarity of physical and psychical characteristics, for the most part show no great sense of personal attachment to the
nation states that have been created since 1945. There is, in truth, little reason

---

[2] *Excluding West New Guinea (Irian Barat), which in effect became part of Indonesia in
1963. See p. 291, footnote 3.*
[3] *T. G. McGee in* The Southeast Asian City, *G. Bell & Sons, London, 1967, p. 23,
claims that overall, Southeast Asia is one of the least urbanized regional blocs of the
Third World. The evidence is inconclusive, however, and there is probably little difference at the present in the relative sizes of the populations of India and Indonesia
living in big cities.*

Table 1-1 *Southeast Asia: estimated population at mid-year, 1937, 1950, 1965 and 1980 (millions)*

	1937	1950	1965	Percentage gain *1950–65*	Projected estimate 1980
Burma	15·6	18·5	24·7	*33·5*	35·0
Cambodia	3·0	3·9	6·1	*56·4*	9·8
Malaysia					
West Malaysia	4·1	5·3	8·0	*50·9*	12·7
Sarawak	0·4	0·5	0·8	*60·0*	1·4
Sabah	0·3	0·3	0·5	*66·7*	0·8
Brunei	0·03	0·05	0·1	*100*	0·2
Singapore	0·6	1·1	1·9	*72·7*	3·2
Laos	1·0	1·3	2·0	*53·8*	2·8
Indonesia	67·4	75·0	104·5	*39·3*	152·7
Philippines	15·4	20·1	32·3	*60·7*	55·8
Thailand	14·5	18·6	30·6	*64·5*	47·5
North Vietnam ⎱ South Vietnam ⎰	18·9	22·3	{ 19·0 16·1 }	*57·4*	46·4
Southeast Asia	**141·2**	**167·0**	**246·6**	***47·0***	**368·3**

Sources: United Nations, *Economic Survey of Asia and the Far East*, 1955; *Economic Survey of Asia and the Far East*, 1965; *World Population Prospects*, 1963

why they should have, for the real architects of independence were the leaders of the socialist and organized labour movements in the respective imperial homelands, not the minuscule élites who directed the so-called national revolutions. Only the former possessed the will, the resources and the experience to create genuine mass movements; the appeal of the nationalists, in contrast, was always to the middle class, the intelligentsia and particularly the student population, and to other privileged groups—an appeal, moreover, usually made in uncompromising communal, not national, terms, and which left the great mass of the population largely unaffected.[4] Every one of the new states possesses a population of mixed ethnic and geographic origin, each group in varying degrees maintaining its contacts with its original home or with similar groups in neighbouring states. In large measure this situation reflects the comparative ease with which successive waves of peoples have been able to penetrate into the region through the deep embayments of the Indian Ocean and the South China Sea, and although access

[4] *Reviewing the course of Indian history, Nirad Chaudhuri in his remarkable* Autobiography of an Unknown Indian, *Macmillan, London, 1951, pp. 492–3, finds no evidence that foreign rule was ever overthrown by any genuine indigenous opposition in a mass national resurgence. The real resistance to foreign rule, he claims, was never the people but the country and its oppressive climate. Quoted also in I. R. Sinai,* The Challenge of Modernization, *Chatto & Windus, London, 1964, p. 84.*

overland from the north is substantially more difficult, in no sense can the mountains and plateaus between the Songkoi and the Irrawaddy be considered an obstacle comparable with that formed by the Himalaya and the elevated Asian heartland.

The historian's comment that for almost every part of Southeast Asia at any time, connections with the wider world beyond the region have been of equal and often of greater importance than relations with Southeast Asian neighbours, is still largely valid. None of the areas enclosed within present national frontiers ever possessed any real unity save that imposed by the imperial power. With the achievement of independence the lack of basic cohesion has become patently obvious; nationalism, largely because it is virtually synonymous with communalism, has not been able to bind together the various peoples and parts of most states. As a result the implementation of national development plans has encountered formidable obstacles, and it is noteworthy that it is precisely the states with the greatest national cohesion, West Malaysia,[5] Thailand and the Philippines, that have achieved the greatest success in maintaining a high rate of economic growth.

While every country suffers to some degree from the centrifugal forces generated by multiracial and multicultural societies and their associated sectional and regional interests, the greatest disruptive influences are to be seen in Burma and in Indonesia, whose national revolutions gave an inordinately large degree of political power to particular ethnic groups, respectively the Burmans and the Javanese. In theory Burma is a Union, but in practice it is a unitary state in which Burmans dominate national policy. The imposition of Burman decisions continues to be unacceptable to most non–Burmans and has been a powerful factor in promoting the civil disturbances and insurrections from which the country has never been entirely free during the whole of its independent existence. In Indonesia regional economic interests reinforce ethnic and cultural diversity, and strongly pull the various parts of the country in different ways. President Sukarno's militant attitude over the West New Guinea (Irian Barat) issue for almost two decades was explicable not in terms of the value of this backward and isolated territory to a country that already possessed a superabundance of useless mountain and swamp, but because as virtually the only issue on which most Indonesians thought alike, it was a useful, indeed necessary tool in 'stirring the fires of national revolution,' to use the President's own pyrotechnic language. That Javanese dominance was long maintained arose from the inability of other ethnic or cultural groups to devise a common policy, for even on individual major islands the

[5] *In this work the term Malaya is used throughout in its geographic sense, to refer to the Malayan peninsula and its offshore islands, including Singapore. The state of Malaysia, created in 1963, originally included Singapore, but after the separation of August 1965 consisted of West Malaysia (formerly the Federation of Malaya) and East Malaysia (the ex-British Borneo territories of Sarawak and North Borneo, the latter being renamed Sabah). See also p. 211.*

different communities dislike each other almost as much as they do the Javanese jack-in-office, a shortcoming that proved fatal to the Sumatran regional revolt of 1957–58.

Overshadowing all Southeast Asia's external relations, and despite the virtual certainty that the region's best hopes of substantial increases in material welfare in the foreseeable future lie in continued close economic association with the West, are those with the Chinese colossus. True, for a time in the early Fifties, when its newly formulated policy of non-alignment enabled it to assume the role of spokesman for the uncommitted Third World, India exerted some influence in a region much of whose culture possessed an Indian origin, and where there was not only an old Indian imperial tradition but also numerous scattered Indian communities; the latter, however, are only of real significance in Malaysia. But India's status waned as the country failed to extract itself from a morass of pressing economic and political problems, while that of China waxed rapidly once Peking had demonstrated its formidable military strength and its apparent capacity for promoting rapid economic advance. Moreover, Southeast Asia had long been an area in which China had possessed major interests apart from a common frontier. Although Mongol excursions into Burma and Indonesia proved of no lasting significance, the extension of Chinese authority as far south as the Porte D'Annam, though thrown off in the tenth century, impressed on Vietnamese society an enduring Chinese stamp. But although Emperors continued to claim a vague sovereignty over the whole of Southeast Asia, the emigration of peoples from South China in large numbers to the *Nan Yang* (literally, southern seas) particularly during the nineteenth and early twentieth centuries, gave to Peking a much more significant interest in the region; by the end of the nineteenth century remittances from the overseas Chinese had begun to assume the proportions of a major item in China's balance of payments, and to mean the difference between life and death for many of its peoples.

The fifteen or so million of the Nanyang Chinese now represent only some 6 per cent of Southeast Asia's population and total no more than the equivalent of one year's increment of China's own population. But they are heavily concentrated in the urban areas so that most of the region's principal cities have a distinctly Chinese appearance, and they have a firm grip on many sectors of the respective national economies. At best they are viewed by indigenes with suspicion and mistrust, and the bloodshed that accompanied the expulsion of the Chinese population from the rural areas of Java in 1959 was merely incidental in a long series of pogroms and massacres which in Indonesia and the Philippines have extended over many centuries.

During the 'great leap forward' in 1958 Peking strongly supported the Indonesian Chinese, and offered to repatriate all who wished to return. With the disasters of 1959–61 Peking quietly dropped its championing of the Nanyang Chinese, and it became clear that it was not prepared to make an issue of their treatment with the governments of Southeast Asia; Peking probably regards the overseas Chinese as expendable in a major emergency, but clearly wishes them to continue to send back remittances so long as the respective governments allow them to do so. With China's recovery from the follies of the great leap forward and with the invasion of Assam in 1962, China's standing in Southeast Asia rose rapidly to its zenith. It would seem that the desire to discredit India completely in the eyes of Asia and to demonstrate quite clearly to its various governments that in future China intended to be the premier Asian power with whom it would be advisable to be on good terms, carried greater weight in prompting the Chinese attack than the dispute over the Tibetan border.

If this was Peking's intention, and the increasingly acrimonious quarrel with the USSR would give it added force, the attack was entirely successful. Burma, Cambodia and Indonesia, and outside the region Pakistan, hastened to affirm their determination to remain in Peking's good books; these countries, indeed, had already adopted a position which appeared rather more benevolent towards China than would seem to be required by strict non-alignment. Burma, which had long suffered from the depredations of the rump Kuo Min Tang army driven across the Shan border by the victorious People's Liberation Army, in 1961 implemented an agreement with China regarding boundary changes in the Wa states and in the so-called triangle of northern Kachin state, under which some 62 square miles of territory were transferred to China in return for the dropping of more extensive Chinese claims. Chinese aid to Burma was greatly stepped up; pressure on the 800,000 Indian and Pakistani residents was sharply increased, and in 1964 Burma began their systematic expulsion under conditions which ensured that they would return to their own countries as virtual paupers. Cambodia also accepted large Chinese credits and technical aid, and in 1963 terminated all aid agreements with the United States and requested the withdrawal of American aid personnel. Only Malaysia among Southeast Asian countries offered moral and financial support to India. Indonesia strongly supported the Chinese territorial claims against India, and in return received promises of assistance in Indonesia's 'confrontation' with the new Federation of Malaysia. Expanding like the frog in Aesop's fable, Indonesia declared that there were only two powers in Asia, China and Indonesia, and renamed the Indian Ocean *Laut Indonesia* (Indonesian Ocean), and the Straits of Malacca, the *Selat Sumatera* (Sumatra Straits).

Then, in one of the most dramatic reversals of fortune in postwar history, China's standing in the region evaporated almost overnight. The first shock came in Indonesia, where in mid-1965 President Sukarno was proposing a Djakarta-Phnom Penh-Hanoi-Peking-Pyongyang axis, and the Indonesian communist party (PKI) appeared on the eve of a complete takeover. But in October the *Gestapu* revolt, supported if not instigated by the PKI, was crushed, and inflamed Muslims throughout the country slaughtered the communists and their supporters in thousands. In 1967 President Sukarno was effectively relieved of his office, and the new *Ampera* cabinet moved gradually from coolness to an open breach with Peking. Indonesian Chinese were accused of assisting the PKI and attacks on Chinese and their property became widespread; in north Sumatra large numbers were rounded up to await transportation back to China.

Worse was to follow from the excesses of China's own 'cultural revolution' and the impact on the Nanyang Chinese of the 'little red book', the thoughts of Chairman Mao, and the activities of the Red Guards. By late 1967 China found itself without a friend in the region save North Vietnam, which itself looked increasingly to the USSR for military aid. Anti-Chinese riots in Rangoon led quickly to a total estrangement between Burma and China, and to the threat of Chinese assistance to the communist insurgents battling with the Rangoon government. China's other firm friend for so many years was also alienated by the activities of the Phnom Penh embassy, which according to Cambodia's Head of State constituted a gross interference in Cambodia's internal affairs, and only an apology from Peking prevented the termination of diplomatic relations between the two countries. Fear and suspicion of the local Chinese as a potential fifth column rose to a new height throughout Southeast Asia, and it began to appear that only through a fundamental reassessment of their position in national life could the Nanyang Chinese weather the storms ahead.

The situation of the region's Chinese population is further complicated by the existence of the Republic of China (Taiwan) which also bids for their loyalty, and which for this reason, among others, is regarded with almost as much distaste by governments of Southeast Asia as is Peking. The Nanyang Chinese are far from a homogeneous group, being divided most obviously by language (there are four major linguistic groups, Hokkien, Cantonese, Hakka and Teochiu, as well as several minor ones such as Hailam and Hokchiu) and economic interest, as well as by basic cultural differences; of the latter the most important is that between the China-born, the *totok* of Indonesia, and the locally born, the Straits Chinese of Malaysia and Singapore, and the *peranakan* of Indonesia. The locally born Chinese are generally more willing to accommodate to Western or indigenous institutions; the China-born remain uncompromisingly Chinese. While many of the Nanyang Chinese try to maintain a neutrality towards Peking and Taipei, and to pay lip-service to the government of the country in which they reside and which claims their first allegiance, overt or covert support for Peking is strongest among the urbanized semi-skilled and unskilled workers; such Chinese, however, are only really numerous in Malaysia and Singapore. But Peking also has a strong appeal for some sections of the Chinese youth, who find in an identification with the new China, indisputably a world power for the first time since the sixteenth century, a means of protest against their often real, but occasionally nominal, political and economic disabilities. Chinese High School students reject the use by their elders of devices to ingratiate themselves with the local population, such as adopting the role of the amiable buffoon—a guise that really fools nobody—as degrading; proud and defiant, the students insist on complete and immediate equality. As the Chinese High Schools have been among the favourite targets of communist infiltrators, their activities are under close surveillance by the governments of Southeast Asia, and in 1967 Indonesia closed down all Chinese schools.[6] Skilled workers, small business men, traders, owners of small estates and smallholders, to say nothing of the professional class and the *towkays* of industry and commerce, in short all those who have acquired a stake in their new country, generally have little sympathy for Peking, although their attitude is often tempered by the existence of relatives in China. The better informed certainly contrast the rapid economic growth of Taiwan and Hong Kong with the halting and laborious progress of the overstrained Chinese economy. They certainly have few illusions over the future of their enterprises should Peking extend its control over the lands of the south, and as immigrants from China's southern provinces they share the southerners' traditional hostility to the imperialists of Peking.

Over the whole of Southeast Asia like a dark shadow lies the possibility of Chinese involvement in the Vietnam war, and what would come in its train. A direct American attack on China itself appears out of the question, for not only has China been displaced as the principal source of military and economic aid to North Vietnam by the USSR, but it has been universally recognized that such an attack would be the quickest way of causing China's embattled factions to sink their differences in the face of a common enemy. But China's behaviour since 1965 has been anything but rational, and if the North Vietnam regime appeared in serious danger of military defeat, the danger of Chinese intervention might become very real. Thailand, the Philippines and Malaysia are already providing assistance to the American effort in Vietnam; but what these nations, and for that matter Burma and Indonesia, fear most is a greatly expanded campaign of infiltration and subversion by local communist groups, financed and encouraged by Peking. Despite all the efforts of the Russian aid programme, communism in Southeast Asia remains essentially China-oriented. China is almost certainly prepared to use whatever means are at its disposal, whether communist-inspired or not, to further its national ends, and its stated aim is the complete and final expulsion of every vestige of Western, particularly American, influence in Asia. Those who oppose continuing Western participation in the Vietnam war would do well to consider this fact.

Thus, whether it likes it or not, Southeast Asia has become that part of the

---

[6] *The ban may not prove permanent for the Suharto cabinet is believed to be anxious to curb excessive anti-Chinese feeling, as it realizes that Chinese capital and enterprise are essential for the country's economic recovery. In the Philippines, Chinese High Schools follow curricula laid down by Taipei, which itself keeps a close watch on schools' operations.*

world most closely involved in containing the Chinese revolution,[7] and the implications for the Nanyang Chinese are far-reaching. The liberal policies followed by the colonial regimes in this century resulted not in the Chinese becoming more assimilable, but less; the divisions between Chinese and indigenes, or Europeans, tended to harden as the Chinese were given the freedom to manage their own institutions, and in particular, a school system.[8] There now appears little future for the overseas Chinese as Chinese, as the leaders of Indonesia's community realize. To survive, the local Chinese must be prepared to give an undivided loyalty to their country of adoption and to abandon many practices and institutions dear to them, perhaps even the use of Chinese names. The new nations of Southeast Asia are no longer prepared to tolerate in their bodies large undigested Chinese minorities, and if the local Chinese communities cannot accept such changes, neither Peking nor Taipei can save them. The problem of readjustment is nowhere better exemplified than in the Malayan peninsula, where not only are the Chinese accorded a greater measure of political and social equality than is general in the region, but are numerically in the majority. Communal tensions were paramount in the separation of Singapore from Malaysia, and a Chinese Malaya is now unthinkable. The only future for the Chinese of West Malaysia is as Malaysians; even Singapore, an overwhelmingly Chinese city-state, finds it necessary to cultivate a distinctive Singapore image, stressing the multicultural origins of its society and that, for the Singaporean, being Chinese is purely incidental. The Chinese in Southeast Asia have proved a remarkably resilient group and their present status is largely the result of colonial policy; in all probability, they will adjust to the demands of nationalism just as they did to those of imperialism. Their enterprise and skill is sorely needed in the implementation of every country's development plans.

SOUTHEAST ASIA AND THE WORLD ECONOMY

Although a high rate of economic growth is not sufficient to enable Southeast Asia either to counteract pressure from the troubled giant of the north or to contain communist subversion from within, it must surely be judged basic for any hope of successful resistance. Fortunately, Southeast Asia already includes some countries whose rate of economic growth must be considered very creditable

---

[7] *Prime Minister Lee Kuan Yew of Singapore, one of Asia's most capable and respected politicians, strongly supported the West's involvement in South Vietnam on his visit to the United States in October 1967. Noted for his tough and capable handling of Singapore's own communists, Prime Minister Lee declared that a communist take-over in South Vietnam would be the end of Southeast Asia and 'if Vietnam goes, I am sure we will see armies of liberation moving westwards and southwards'.* The Times, *November 6th, 1967.*

[8] *Victor Purcell,* The Chinese in Southeast Asia, *Oxford University Press, London, 2nd ed., 1965, p. 468.*

by any standards, and which clearly demonstrate that a centrally planned economy and a rigid authoritarian society is not the only, nor, indeed, the best way for the Third World to improve its level of material welfare. The maintenance of these past performances in the economically successful countries, and the achievement of similar growth rates in other parts of the region, necessitate continued close commercial and financial relations with the West. The USSR is both unwilling and unable either to provide the enhanced capital requirements or to absorb the greatly expanded exports that such developments would involve; China is even less capable of providing such services.

It is significant that nearly all the newly independent nations created since World War II have maintained their adhesion to the largely free economy of the West. A few, either because of their political philosophies or because they have been dissatisfied with the prices received for their products, have diverted a substantial part of their trade towards the communist world. Their experience, on the whole, has been far from congenial; they have acquired Russian arms, and have received credits and technical assistance usually on rather tough terms and at the cost of mortgaging their exports for years ahead. To their chagrin, they have also seen Russian imports from them held in store, reaping the benefit of subsequent higher prices on the world market. Of the countries of Southeast Asia, only North Vietnam conducts nearly all of its trade with the Eastern bloc. Both Burma and Indonesia have from time to time made barter deals with communist governments, but by far the greater part of their respective foreign trade is still conducted with countries of the non-communist world. Indonesia's decision after 1963 to enlarge the share of its trade with the Eastern bloc and with the Third World materially hastened its progress towards bankruptcy.

Since 1963 when the Federation of Malaysia was formed, the West's only remaining territorial possession in the region has been Portuguese Timor; although by agreement with the governments concerned the West still retains a rather circumscribed use of military bases in the region, the West's principal interests in Southeast Asia are now economic. Though much investment has been lost through the expropriation by rapacious governments—notably those of Indonesia, Burma and North Vietnam—of mines, estates, factories, banks and other commercial and financial enterprises, an impressive Western capital stake remains in the region, and most governments are only too anxious for the flow of foreign capital into their territories to continue. Some broad idea of the status of Southeast Asia in the world economy can be obtained from its share of total world trade turnover (imports plus exports): in 1965 Southeast Asia accounted for just 2·6 per cent of the world total. This low figure might suggest that the region does not count for very much, and indeed, its status might even appear to be diminishing, for the corresponding proportions for 1928 was 4 per cent, and for 1962 a little over 3 per cent. This decline, however, reflects the overall deterioration of the role of foodstuffs and raw materials in world trade, which is becoming more and more concerned with the interchange of manufactures and machinery between countries at a high level of development. In the Sixties, low prices for primary products resulting from increasing competition from synthetic substitutes, and in part also from the deflationary policies adopted by many developed countries as a result of the growing world liquidity problem,[9] depressed export earnings of many Southeast Asian countries. In terms of 1966 prices Southeast Asia's exports have increased by about a third since 1928, and would have increased rather more had Indonesia been able to regain its prewar output levels of many agricultural products. For the world as a whole, however, exports more than doubled in value between 1928 and 1960, and the failure of Southeast Asia's export income to grow *pari passu* with the increase in world trade, as is the case generally in the Third World, has serious consequences for development programmes. The export performance of individual countries within the region, however, has been very uneven, and the record of Malaysia, Thailand and the Philippines contrasts markedly with that of Burma, Indonesia and the Indochinese states.

Directing attention to the part played by Southeast Asia in the trade patterns of the world's principal trading groups, to only one nation can the region be said to be of major importance, while to the world's three leading trade groups, the United States, the European Economic Community (EEC) and the European Free Trade Area (EFTA), Southeast Asia appears of little significance. In 1965 the region supplied some 3·7 per cent of the imports of the United States, and took 2·8 per cent of its exports; these small proportions involve, in absolute terms, a trade turnover of some $1,600 million, but Mexico alone is a more important trading partner of the United States than is the whole of Southeast Asia. To the EEC, the world's largest trading bloc, the region scarcely seems to matter at all; in 1965 it supplied only about 1·5 per cent of the Community's imports and took virtually the same proportion of the Community's exports. The region is of greater importance to West Germany than to France, particularly as an export market. Though trade with the EEC has tended slowly to increase, this has been of greater advantage to the Community, whose exports to Southeast Asia have been slowly increasing while imports from the region have stagnated; in large measure this reflects the difficulty experienced by Southeast Asia in selling its tropical products in competition with those from privileged former African possessions of France and Belgium, which under the Yaundé convention enjoy the status of associated states in the EEC. The continuance of close commercial relations between ex-possessions of EEC member-countries in Africa and the former administering power stands in marked contrast with the trade relations between Indonesia and the Netherlands; even in 1965, when the Dutch status in Indonesia had recovered considerably from its low-water mark of 1962, the Netherlands derived only 1·4 per cent of its imports from Indonesia. For several

[9] *See p. 444.*

years in the Sixties scarcely one per cent of Indonesia's exports were consigned
to the Netherlands, a great change from the trade pattern of the Netherlands
Indies, which regularly sent some 20–25 per cent of its exports to the mother
country.

Southeast Asia is of somewhat greater commercial importance to EFTA,
whose trade with the region is virtually monopolised by Britain; in 1965 the
latter derived about 1·6 per cent of its imports from the region and sent it nearly
3 per cent of its exports. Declining prices for tropical products in the Sixties were
mainly responsible for the fall in the share of Britain's imports derived from the
region since the beginning of the decade. But among major trading nations it is
to Japan, whose foreign trade has expanded enormously since 1945, that Southeast Asia has become of greatest importance. Japan received some 10·3 per cent
of its total imports from Southeast Asia in 1965, and in return sent it nearly 13
per cent of its exports. Nevertheless, even to Japan, Southeast Asia is a very much
less important trading partner than is the United States, and the reorientation of
Japan's trading links across the Pacific, instead of eastwards and southwards
across the Yellow and South China Seas, represents a major break with that
country's commercial and imperial traditions.

Yet all the evidence suggests that the region is likely to become even more
important to Japan in the future than it has been in the past. The world first
perceived Japan's interest in Southeast Asia during the Great Depression when,
with the advantages of very low labour costs and a depreciated yen, Japan flooded
South and Southeast Asia with cheap consumer goods, giving the *coup de grâce*
to several of the handicraft industries that had managed to survive competition
from European factory-made products, and despite the imposition of tariff
barriers in all dependent territories of the West, competing successfully with
manufactures from the mother country. But even before the Depression, Japan
had acquired large interests in natural rubber and abacá production in the region;
and as the Japanese economy was converted to a war footing as the Thirties wore
on, the Imperial High Command clearly saw that possession of the mineral
wealth, particularly in petroleum, and of the foodstuffs and raw materials of
Southeast Asia was indispensable to the realization of Japan's ambitions. In the
Thirties Japanese fishermen produced far more fish from Southeast Asian waters
than did indigenous fishermen, and combined this activity with espionage and
subversion.

Japan no longer specializes in the production of cheap consumer goods of
low quality, and it is now becoming a distinctly high-cost labour area. So far it
has been content to follow a mild, almost retiring policy in Asia and to adhere
strongly to its new association with the United States. There is some indication,
however, that Japan is now moving towards a reassessment of its relations with
the world, and it appears likely to adopt a policy in Asia more in keeping with its
new and enormous economic strength; evidence of this change is perhaps to be

seen in Japan's prominent role in the Asian Development Bank and its willingness to sponsor a special fund for the improvement of Asian agriculture. But although Japan has recognized its responsibility for the depredations and damage caused by its occupation of Southeast Asia during World War II, in practice it regards its reparation payments as development grants and uses them for the most vigorous promotion of Japanese exports. Southeast Asia now appears unlikely to become, as perhaps the Japanese once envisaged, a major source of minerals for Japan's booming industries; that role seems destined for Australia, which since 1960 has proved to possess the enormous ore bodies which make modern mechanized mining so profitable, and which are generally lacking in Southeast Asia. But the magnitude of Japanese investment in mining and manufacturing industries in some Southeast Asian countries has already given their governments concern; it is not the Japanese investment as such that is feared, but its share of total foreign investment. While any attempt to resuscitate the Greater East Asia Co-prosperity Sphere is unlikely, it does appear that Japan may have in mind using its capital and technical skill in conjunction with local low-cost labour to establish consumer-good industries in Southeast Asian countries, which will then provide a permanent market for Japan's sophisticated machinery and capital goods industries. In many ways such a policy makes good economic sense; but Japan's apparent determination to reserve for itself the capital-intensive complex industries and to foist off on neighbouring Asian countries the simpler manufactures in which Japan itself is increasingly uncompetitive, and yet to retain control of such industries overseas, is beginning to cause apprehension.

Although Southeast Asia does not assume any real importance from the standpoint of the direction of world trade, it nevertheless remains a dominant producer of several exceedingly important commodities. Moreover, while it is true that some of these commodities face difficult problems in the form of competition from synthetic substitutes, there is no lack of opportunities for improving competitive efficiency through cost reduction, or even for expanding output. This is an important consideration, for Southeast Asian countries must look mainly to an expansion in the exports of their primary products for acquiring the foreign exchange necessary to finance their national development plans. In 1967 Southeast Asia produced only some 1·8 per cent of the world's petroleum, by far the most important commodity entering world trade, but until the Sixties, when the large new fields of North and West Africa came into production, the expansion of output had kept pace with that of the world as a whole, and the region is still the only large producer east of the Persian Gulf. Of other minerals only tin is really important, the region normally supplying some 55–60 per cent of the world supply of new, or primary tin. Bauxite and iron are also of some local significance, although it now appears unlikely that the region will ever become a really large producer or exporter of either.

In many products of tropical agriculture, Southeast Asia holds a commanding position. It was the spices of the islands of the Banda Sea that first brought Europeans to the region over four centuries ago, and Southeast Asia still accounts for more than 80 per cent of world exports of pepper, cassia (cinammon), nutmeg and mace, and is virtually the only producer of cinchona bark, source of the drug quinine. Since the winding-up in 1960 of the World War II United States-sponsored plantings of abacá in Central America, Southeast Asia has been the sole producer of this cordage fibre, and it accounts for all but a minute proportion of world exports of kapok. It is also of major importance in vegetable oils; nearly 80 per cent of world copra exports originate in the region, which accounts for some 20 per cent by value of combined world net exports of vegetable oils. Although of much less importance than either South or East Asia as a rice producer, Southeast Asia nevertheless generates one half of world rice exports, and it is a significant exporter of coffee, tea, tobacco and sugar. Its most important export by far, however, is natural rubber; more than 85 per cent of the world output of natural rubber originates in the region, and all but a very small proportion of this output is exported.

But while it is true that there are opportunities for raising production levels of some of the region's primary exports, in several lines there are grounds for serious concern. With the important exceptions of petroleum and natural rubber, the production of most export-oriented products shows little tendency to expand, and there are many whose present output is now well below the prewar level. Products such as natural rubber, abacá, kapok and cinchona face increasingly severe competition from synthetic substitutes whose costs of production tend to depreciate as the scale of output rises. Newer producers of competitive natural products have also appeared. Under the stimulus of high domestic price support policies for cotton and soybeans, and the Agricultural Trade Development and Assistance Act of 1954 (Public Law 480) which makes possible sales of agricultural products abroad at concessional prices or under certain conditions as out-right gifts, the United States has become the world's largest producer and exporter of vegetable oils; in 1967 for the first time it became the world's largest exporter of rice. Technological change has also operated against some Southeast Asian products. Tin is unique among nonferrous metals in that demand over the great part of the postwar period has remained static. This is because part of world requirements are now met from secondary, or recovered metal, and partly because new techniques of electrolytic tinning have greatly economised in the use of tin in its principal employment, tinplate. As a packaging material, moreover, the latter has encountered growing competition from plastics and aluminium.

The poor prognosis of many export items is the direct consequence of World War II, when the entire region was occupied by Japan. It was the war emergency which was responsible for the creation, in little less than two years, of an enormous synthetic rubber industry, the development of new techniques of tin recovery, the production of synthetic anti-malarials, and the increasing use of man-made fibres in cordage. But these developments were merely accelerated by the war and it is certain that they would have appeared sooner or later. Moreover, the continued postwar growth of world production of synthesized products in part reflects the failure of producers to expand their output of natural products, to up-grade quality or to improve methods of marketing. That competition from synthesized products can be overstated is evidenced by the fact that regional exports of coffee, tea, sugar, tobacco and rice still stood below prewar levels in 1966; as other countries have been able to achieve substantial increases in the output and exports of these products, the reasons for the poor performance of Southeast Asia in these lines have largely to be sought within the region itself. Exports have stagnated because production has failed to grow; at the same time domestic consumption has tended to increase, thus reducing the exportable surplus.

The failure to expand output has generally a simple explanation. It is the direct result of government policies that discourage producer initiative by fixing prices at levels that do not compensate growers for the extra investment of labour and capital necessary for enhanced production, and these policies have operated against both large estates and indigenous smallholders alike. In part also, rampant inflation has so pushed up the costs of production in some countries that their products are no longer competitive in world markets with those from alternative suppliers; parts of the region, in effect, have been pricing themselves out of business. Even in the case of the two commodities whose output now stands well above that of prewar years, rubber and petroleum, what has been accomplished is probably only a fraction of what was possible. By discouraging for so long investment in new exploration by the international oil companies, Indonesia certainly deferred a very large future increase in output. The increase so far achieved in its oil output has been largely the fruits of investment made before the war in discovering and proving new oilfields, and Indonesia's production has been overtaken by many new producers outside the region, some of whom did not raise a barrel of oil in 1950. In Malaysia, it is true, major steps to preserve the competitive efficiency of the natural rubber industry have been taken, but elsewhere in the region the adoption of similar measures has been very protracted, and in Indonesia, the world's largest natural rubber producer until 1957, has scarcely begun. Without substantial new investment, Indonesia's present output of natural rubber cannot be sustained.

The adoption of policies that discourage production is one of the many irrational manifestations of nationalism. All newly independent states have been determined to transform the old colonial economy into a national one under indigenous control, but they have differed in the methods adopted to bring this about, from the essentially pragmatic approach of Malaysia to the dogmatic one of North Vietnam. It is significant, however, that disincentives to peasant production have been greatest in precisely those countries that profess an adhesion to some form of socialism. North Vietnam's socialized agriculture has suffered all the misfortunes that have invariably accompanied attempts elsewhere at implementing Marxist-Leninist doctrine in agriculture, and the preservation of a small private agricultural sector has so far proved essential. Burma professes a state socialism which finds the regaining of the prewar rice area a matter of the greatest difficulty. 'Socialisme à la Indonesia', to quote ex-President Sukarno, reduced the economy to one that might best be described as organized chaos, and led Dr Subandrio, former Foreign Minister, to urge the Indonesian people to overcome a chronic shortage of food grains and proteins by eating more tapioca and rats. It would probably be true to say that export performance in Southeast Asia has been inversely proportional to the degree of irrationality in each respective nationalism.

Southeast Asia shares with Central America the doubtful distinction of having the highest rate of population increase of any major world region, more than 3 per cent per annum; at such a rate, a population doubles itself in twenty-four years. In 1965 the population of Southeast Asia stood some 70 per cent above the prewar level, and as a result total domestic consumption of many foodstuffs formerly exported in large quantities, such as rice, coconut products, sugar, tobacco and spices, is now very much greater than before the war, even though per capita consumption of such products over large parts of the region has actually declined. Pressure on exportable surpluses could easily increase further, for there is little prospect of any immediate decline in the rate of population growth; indeed, the scope for the reduction of infant mortality over the whole of the region is so enormous that the successful execution of national development plans will result in the very much larger population for the region that is forecast by 1980 being realized even earlier than anticipated. All considerations, therefore, urge the adoption of policies that will result in increased production of exportable crops, and the abolition of pricing and procurement systems that discourage peasant initiative.

In Malaysia, Thailand and the Philippines, however, an open, largely free-enterprise economy has been preserved, in which within broad limits the pricing mechanism of a capitalist economy still operates. While it may be questioned whether such a form of economic society is best suited to the task of raising the general level of low-income countries with a high rate of population increase, the fact remains that these three countries have been conspicuously more successful in expanding production and raising export earnings than have their neighbours, who claim to have rejected capitalism. This is clearly visible from Table 1-2; and it cannot be claimed that the three countries concerned have enjoyed special advantages denied to other states in the region. The Philippine sugar and copra industries owe much, it is true, to their access to the protected American market, but nevertheless both the Philippines and Thailand have found that American surplus agricultural products sold under the concessional terms of PL 480 have greatly affected other markets for these two countries' traditional exports. Moreover, the regions's most important export, natural rubber, enjoys no privileged market at all; it has become the residual supply, meeting whatever unsatisfied world demand is left over after all the output of synthetic rubber in highly developed economies has been disposed of.

Table 1-2, nevertheless, conceals one fundamental change in the balance of national production within the region. In the Fifties, Indonesia was reaping the benefits of a very great increase in smallholder planting, largely unsuspected at the time, in the decade before World War II, but in the Federation of Malaya rubber production in the Fifties was still suffering from the effects of long inter-war restrictions on new planting. Prewar smallholder planting in Indonesia consisted entirely of unselected material, and though these trees are now producing at their maximum, productivity is only a fraction of that possible with modern material. Malaya on the other hand, has since 1952 carried out one of the most remarkable feats in the history of tropical agriculture as it has endeavoured to replace its stock of aged unselected trees; by 1966 about two million acres had been replanted or new planted to modern high-yielding material, and as this comes into bearing the yield per tapped acre will rise appreciably. Within a few years the national average yield will come to approach that on European estates, which already have a large proportion of their planted area under high-yielding material, and the gap between Indonesian and Malaysian production will then widen very rapidly. Only an immediate crash replanting and new planting programme, for which Indonesia appears to have minimal resources at the present, can save its natural rubber industry; as the age composition of its trees becomes progressively more unfavourable, output must decline.

The situation in respect of Indonesian vegetable oil production is almost as unsatisfactory. In 1965 palm oil output was still well below the level of 1939; many estates had suffered badly from neglect, some were entirely inoperative because of damage to the processing factory, and spare parts and machinery were virtually unobtainable. The resuscitation of the oil palm industry will require the investment of considerably more capital than the state-owned estate corporation appears likely to be able to countenance, and the establishment of a much higher degree of administrative efficiency and integrity, to say nothing of better labour discipline. In Malaysia, on the other hand, oil palm planting has boomed since 1956 when government grants for replanting old rubber-land also became available for replacing rubber by other crops. Indonesian copra production, very largely a smallholder activity, has been discouraged by compulsory purchasing by state agencies at prices well below those prevailing on the world market, and a very high proportion of the country's coconut palms are very aged or affected by disease.

The only striking increase in export-oriented production outside Malaysia,

Table 1-2   *Southeast Asia: production and exports of*
selected commodities, 1934–38 and 1965

	AVERAGE 1934–38			1965		
	A	B	C	A	B	C
	Southeast Asia	Malaysia Thailand Philippines	*Percentage B : A*	Southeast Asia	Malaysia Thailand Philippines	*Percentage B : A*
	thousand metric tons			*thousand metric tons*		
Rice (padi)	27,800	7,300	*26*	50,900	14,780	*29*
exports (milled rice)	5,760	1,760	*31*	3,770	1,950	*52*
Sugar (centrif.)	2,160	1,010	*47*	2,700	1,890	*70*
exports	1,850	810	*44*	1,250	1,100	*88*
Copra	1,350	770	*57*	2,020	1,590	*79*
exports	1,010	510	*51*	990	850	*86*
Natural rubber	910	510	*56*	2,100	1,170	*56*
exports	1,060	670	*63*	2,020	1,160	*57*
Palm oil	210	35	*17*	310	150	*48*
Tin concentrates	100	65	*65*	101	84	*84*
Petroleum	11,700	—	—	27,850	50	*0·2*
Bauxite	350	65	*19*	1,670	1,000	*60*
Iron ore	1,900	1,900	*100*	7,900	7,900	*100*

Sources: United Nations, *Statistical Yearbook*, 1966; FAO, *Production Yearbook*, 1966; FAO, *Trade Yearbook*, 1966

Table 1-3   *Southeast Asia: foreign trade, 1965 (million US $)*

	Exports, f.o.b.	Imports, c.i.f.	Turnover
Burma	226	247	473
Cambodia	105	103	208
Laos	1	33	34
Malaysia			
West Malaysia	1,104	852	1,956
Sarawak	142	158	300
Sabah	100	110	210
Brunei	64	36	100
Singapore	981	1,244	2,225
Indonesia*	688	621	1,309
Philippines	768	894	1,662
Thailand	627	726	1,353
South Vietnam	36	357	393
Total	**4,842**	**5,381**	**10,223**

* 1964

Source: United Nations, *Yearbook of International Trade Statistics*, 1965

Thailand and the Philippines, is provided by the Indonesian petroleum industry. This anomaly is largely explicable in terms of the enormous resources of the international oil companies, and the negotiating strength in dealings with the Indonesian government, gained by their clear determination to withdraw from production if operating conditions were made too difficult; unlike the estate companies, the oil companies could easily expand production elsewhere, and other host governments were only too anxious for them to do so. Nevertheless, the increase in output was less than might have been possible, and was partially offset by the almost complete collapse of the petroleum industry in Burma. The largest oil-producer in the British Empire in the early Thirties, Burma three decades later was producing scarcely enough petroleum products to meet its own very modest needs.

These changes in the national origin of export production within the region are summarized in Tables 1-2 and 1-3. In the years 1958–60 Malaysia and Singapore, Thailand, and the Philippines, with only 30 per cent of the region's population, earned over 55 per cent of its export earnings of nearly $3,000 million annually. Moreover, while other countries in the region were expropriating foreign capital assets, this group of countries were regularly receiving large capital inflows in the form of new foreign investment, which further improved their balance-of-payments position. Thus, with a high capacity for financing imports, Malaysia, Thailand and the Philippines were able to sustain high rates of economic growth, widening the economic gap that separated them from the remaining states. By 1965 the share of regional export earnings generated by the economically pragmatic group of countries had risen to over 75 per cent, and the implications of their disastrous economic policies appeared to be dawning slowly on Indonesia and Burma. With the political upheavals of 1965–67 in those two countries, the stage seemed set for the adoption of new policies which could make a higher rate of economic growth possible.

Table 1-4 *Southeast Asia: average annual rates of growth of gross domestic product at constant prices, 1955–65*

	AGGREGATE PRODUCT *percentage*		PER CAPITA PRODUCT *percentage*	
	1955–60	*1960–65*	*1955–60*	*1960–65*
Burma	5·7	2·3	3·7	0·2
Cambodia	8·2	5·0	5·9	2·7
Indonesia	3·9	2·6	1·8	0·2
West Malaysia	4·1	6·2	0·9	3·1
Philippines	4·5	4·6	1·4	1·2
Thailand	5·0	7·0	2·0	3·9

Source: United Nations, *Economic Survey of Asia and the Far East*, 1966

In Southeast Asia's import trade, Pan-Malaysia (i.e. Malaysia and Singapore), Thailand and the Philippines occupy an even more dominant position than in exports, accounting in the period 1960–65 for nearly 80 per cent of an average annual regional import bill of more than $4,000 million; some 40–45 per cent of this regional total was accounted for by Pan-Malaysia alone.[10] Analysis of the composition of imports reveals that for most countries the share of capital goods and materials for capital goods, an indication of the capacity for future economic growth, has averaged around 40 per cent, the figures for Thailand and the Philippines of some 45–50 per cent being distinctly above the regional average. Countries recording proportions significantly below the regional average include Laos, Indonesia and Malaysia, with averages of some 30–35 per cent. Laos is a long way from constituting a viable economy at present, and survives only through a Western aid programme that in relation to its population must be considered enormous. The Malaysian import pattern is complicated by the entrepot trade, but the country's imports of capital goods are in any case far larger than those of Indonesia, which has more than ten times its population. Malaysia, moreover, has a large food component in its import trade, all of which has to be purchased on commercial terms; unlike Laos or Indonesia, Malaysia has never received food on concessional terms either from the United States or from any other source.

THE TWO SOUTHEAST ASIAS

Examination of most economic criteria strongly suggests a division of Southeast Asia into two major economic units, Malaysia and Singapore, Thailand and the Philippines on the one hand, Burma, Indonesia and the Indochinese states on the other (*Table 1-4* and *Figure 1-1*). This division is also basic in the socio-political field. The first group consists of countries that, to use the term of Hla Myint, are 'outward looking'.[11] They recognize that they are part of a wider world to which they must make adjustments; they have been active in promoting schemes for regional cooperation and integration; and on all major world issues involving a confrontation of the Western and the communist powers, they have tended to support the West.[12] The second group consists of 'inward looking' countries;

[10] *The large entrepot trade of Singapore and Penang, however, makes some double counting unavoidable. Following the Indonesian confrontation of 1963, the entrepot trade with Indonesia officially terminated, but in practice appears to have been cut by about half. Confrontation ended in 1966, but the restoration of the entrepot trade to its level of the early Sixties appears a matter of some doubt. The future of the entrepot trade acquired heightened significance with the separation of Singapore from Malaysia in 1965.*

[11] *Hla Myint, 'The inward and outward looking countries of Southeast Asia and the economic future of the region', in* Symposium on Japan's Future in Southeast Asia, *Center for Southeast Asian Studies, Kyoto University, 1963.*

[12] *The exception has been over the Arab-Israel question, in which Malaysia and Indonesia, in theory Muslim nations, have strongly supported the Arab states. Laos, on the other hand, has supported Israel, as Singapore seems likely to do in the future.*

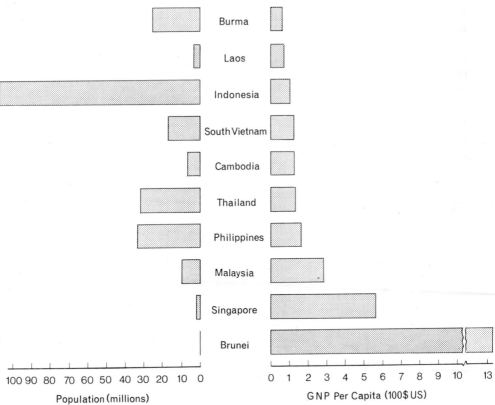

Fig 1-1 **Estimated population and gross national product, per capita 1966** (source: *World Bank Atlas*, 3rd edition, 1969)

The diagram suggests that in Southeast Asia large populations are synonymous with poverty, and that it is the smaller countries with low or moderate populations that enjoy the highest living standards.

economic growth has never been accorded a high degree of priority by their governments, which have tended to follow doctrinaire rather than pragmatic policies and have concerned themselves more with the preservation of existing cultural values than with accommodation to the modern world. Most of the states in this group, though claiming to be neutral, have often adopted a marked anti-Western position, and before 1967 at least, direct criticism of the communist powers was seldom, if ever, made. Whatever their political institutions, the problem of stagnating production must be faced sooner or later, and by 1967 both Burma and Indonesia had come to accept the necessity for Western aid, and to realize that fundamental changes in their economic policies were mandatory.

There is little in their respective physical backgrounds that helps to account for the markedly superior economic performance of the outward-looking group of countries. Thailand resembles its neighbours of mainland Southeast Asia much more closely than it does either Malaysia or the Philippines, and the closest physical similarities to the latter are to be found in the archipelagic state of Indonesia. Malaysia is unique, for its plains do not, as is generally the situation in mainland Southeast Asia, support the densest population and constitute the foci of national life; on the contrary, the most extensive plains of Malaya are either largely deserted, as is the case with the Pahang-Rompin lowland and the coastal plain of Sarawak, or else, as with the plains of Kedah and Kelantan, are areas where incomes per head are markedly below the national average. Nor do these three countries possess large areas of soils of above average fertility, or enjoy endowments of mineral riches largely denied to neighbours. The explanation for their greater economic progress is to be found in their respective social and institutional environments, which have enabled them to make better use of resources that are generally also available in the less affluent countries of the region.

It is difficult to resist the conclusion that it is largely to the preservation of a mainly free and open economy that Malaysia, Thailand and the Philippines owe their higher degree of well-being; there are fewer of the disincentives to production that operate so strongly in other states. What requires explanation is how such an economy has survived in these three countries in view of the general rejection of such a form of economic organization over very large areas of the Third World. This is by no means to suggest that Malaysia, Thailand and the Philippines have been unaffected by the postwar upsurge of nationalism in Asia; on the contrary, nationalism is as fundamental and vigorous in national life as in any other country of the developing world. The respective social environments of the three countries have caused nationalism to assume quite different forms from those generally encountered in Africa, Latin America, or in other parts of Asia, and because the charismatic leaders of newly independent African or Asian states can find little in Malaysian, Thai or Filipino nationalism to match their own experience, they have erroneously regarded the former as spurious. Moreover, because on most political issues they stand solidly in the Western camp and in all of them the communist party is banned, Malaysia, Thailand and the Philippines often find themselves accused of being little more than Western puppets.

Yet in view of their respective cultural backgrounds, each of the three countries concerned could hardly have developed in any other way. Thailand is unique in Southeast Asia in never having experienced colonial rule, and though its preservation as an independent state was fortuitous enough, it had far-reaching consequences. Nationalism was never primarily a device for overthrowing a foreign yoke, nor in fact was there ever any real conflict between traditional Thai values and those of the West. While it may have been correct to describe prewar Siam as an economic appendage of the British Empire in view of the fact that

Britain had by far the largest foreign investment in the country and that it was Siam's principal trading partner and held 37 per cent of its public debt,[13] the government was always careful to maintain a balance of dependence on the various powers, and contracts were often rotated among them. As with Japan, Thailand took what it wanted from the West, but in the process Western institutions and even Western products often underwent a substantial Thai modification, and by the time they had reached the population at large after filtering down from the court and the aristocracy, they were, in fact, no longer Western but Thai; semi-luxuries or conventional necessities such as cigarettes, for example, are commonly used as religious offerings. Thus in Thailand there has been no rejection of the West, because in the experience of the Thai population there was little specifically Western to reject. Thai nationalism is much more concerned with forestalling possible Lao separatism in the east and north, and is suspicious of the country's traditional enemies, particularly Cambodia, and of Thailand's large Chinese population.

The Philippines has also enjoyed the advantages of a longer consciousness of nationality than in most other states in the region. Filipinos believed that they were fighting for independence in the Spanish–American war of 1898, and though these early hopes were not realized, Filipino independence was virtually assured by the Jones Act of 1916 which provided for internal self-government. Complete independence would have been realized even without the intervention of World War II, through the operation of the Tydings–McDuffie Act of 1934, which provided for a ten-year transitional period of Commonwealth government. The few years of American control proved to have a far greater impact than the preceding three centuries of Spanish rule, and during this century many Filipinos came to accept many attributes of 'the American way of life', even though the majority were extremely poor by American standards. Although a major debate is in progress over the future of the American connection, this is largely conducted between privileged and wealthy Filipinos over the American stake in the exploitation of the Philippines' resources, and the possible continuation of the present privileged position of Filipino exports in the American market after the mid-Seventies, when the present trade treaty expires. While Filipinos have justly resented any description of them as 'little brown Americans', there is little anti-Americanism, and nationalism for the most part expresses itself in agitation against the Philippine Chinese. As with Thailand, the Philippines has also tried the widespread use of state-owned corporations as a means of stimulating a higher level of development, but as is so often the case, its public enterprises have been more public than enterprising; disappointed with the results achieved, the country has been wise enough to abandon public involvement in many lines of production to the private sector, which has shown itself more responsive to market stimuli. Capitalism in the Philippines, as in both Malaysia and Thailand, has few

[13] *Virginia Thompson*, Thailand, the New Siam, *New York, 1941, p. 167.*

of the political and emotional overtones that it possesses in much of the under-developed world.

Malaysia is in many ways the most remarkable state of all, for most economic criteria show that it has no peer in Southeast Asia; in particular, the occupational distribution of the working population, the level of urbanism, and per capita product, do not compare unfavourably with those of the poorer parts of south-eastern Europe. Malaysia is essentially a creation of the expanding world economy of the past century; it has no rich cultural or imperial tradition and has been carved out of the wilderness by immigrant peoples, an observation that largely holds true even for the Malay population itself, usually regarded as the indigenous inhabitants. Malaysia still retains many characteristics of a pioneering society, and indeed, pioneering is still in progress. In this development the immigrant Chinese came to be the largest ethnic group in the new Federation of Malaysia created in 1963 from a union of the old Federation of Malaya, Singapore, and the British Borneo Territories of Sarawak and North Borneo (renamed Sabah), although the new unit was put together to counter the Chinese majority in the Malayan peninsula itself. It was scarcely surprising that the new state proved incapable of meeting the strains imposed upon it; Singapore was separated off in 1965 and the future adhesion of Sarawak appears a matter of some uncertainty. Singapore's separation, moreover, did nothing to resolve the communal tensions in the peninsula, and indeed, only underlined them; nevertheless, Malaysia demonstrates a high degree of harmony and even equality in the everyday relations of its many peoples, and this is obvious even to a casual visitor. In many ways, Malaysia has much to offer the world as a model of race relations, and if communal issues can be restrained from further polarization, the country can look confidently to the future.

In external affairs, the three countries have tended to follow a common line; Thailand and the Philippines are members of the Southeast Asia Treaty Organiza-tion (SEATO), which also includes Pakistan, the United States, Britain, New Zealand, Australia and originally France, but Malaysia has remained outside. The three are also linked in the somewhat moribund Association of Southeast Asian States (ASA) founded in 1961, but estrangement between Malaysia and the Philippines over the question of Sabah, which the latter claimed for itself, destroyed any chance the organization might have had of promoting real economic cooperation. The Philippine claim is essentially a legal one, as befits a country in which law is the most respected of the professions, but whatever substance it may have, it is totally rejected by the peoples of Sabah themselves. During the Marcos administration, however, Philippine relations with Malaysia improved, and by 1966 ASA appeared likely to be reactivated. It was, nevertheless, promptly overshadowed by two new organizations, the Asia and Pacific Council (ASPAC) and the Association of Southeast Asian Nations (ASEAN). ASPAC was formed at Seoul in 1966, and includes Japan, Malaysia, the Philippines, South Korea,

South Vietnam, Taiwan and Thailand, together with Australia and New Zealand; although sponsored by Korea initially as a defence and anti-communist alliance, the organization also has social and economic aims. Southeast Asia itself is more likely to be concerned with promoting its development through ASEAN, an organization created at Bangkok in 1967, and which includes in addition to the founder members of ASA, Indonesia and Singapore. ASEAN's real purpose was to enable the new government of Indonesia to participate in an association for regional development and integration on equal terms with the ASA members. Singapore, which had also refused to join ASA, fortuitously enjoyed the same privilege, as it could scarcely remain aloof from any regional organization in which Indonesia took part, if only because the island state hoped to solve some of its own economic problems through helping to rebuild the shattered Indonesian economy.

With their markedly lower per capita products and per capita foreign trades, Indonesia, Burma and the Indochinese states constitute a different world. There can be little doubt that in view of its physical resources particularly in mineral wealth, the economically stagnant portion of Southeast Asia is potentially the richer of the region's two economic units; its present parlous economic condition reflects the failure, indeed the unwillingness, of its peoples to decide whether they want a modern society or a traditional one, an issue that is basic to the developmental problem of all newly independent countries. In such states traditional cultural values are often of supreme political importance, and their superiority over Western values has been proved by the success of the national revolution. As a result, militant nationalism often includes a large element of irrationality in economic policy, and its consequences are frequently ludicrous and occasionally tragic.

The dismal postwar performance of Indonesia, a country which contains about half the region's population, is the principal reason for the low standing of Southeast Asia in the world's economic league table. Yet Indonesia's pressing economic problems would almost certainly have proved tractable before 1966, had the government been prepared to leave the economy alone and to remove the disincentives to production. But this it was never able to do; its ceaseless tinkerings were essentially the means by which the regime endeavoured to ensure the loyalty of the privileged élites that constituted its main support. Indonesian independence had to be fought for, but apart from the damage to the sugar industry of Java there was little destruction of productive equipment, and the country began its independence at a most propitious time, with very high prices for all its primary products. Many Indonesians mistook the exceptional conditions of the Korean boom for the economic fruits of independence; but the prosperity was short-lived, and the government found it difficult to produce any real national cohesion except where it could focus discontent against aliens allegedly impeding the fulfilment of the revolution, above all through the use of the West New Guinea issue, and through legislation against the activities of Indonesian Chinese.

For a decade after 1956 Indonesia made no serious attempt to grapple with major structural defects in the economy; the main concern of government, which by then meant effectively President Sukarno, was to hold on to power by any means, irrespective of the effects on the economy, even if this led, in the President's own words, into 'an abyss of annihilation'. Continued appeals to traditional values in order to maintain revolutionary ardour, and, as a counterpoise to the growing political importance of the Army, the growth under Presidential protection of the PKI as the world's largest communist party outside the Eastern bloc, produced an increasingly hostile attitude to the West. Investment was discouraged and peasants concealed their output in order to avoid enforced sales to government agencies at less than market prices. Chronic inflation gradually priced Indonesian exports out of the world market and sapped at the foundations of society itself; only because such a large proportion of the population consists of a self-sufficing peasantry was the country able for so long to avoid complete economic collapse and bankruptcy. Acute balance-of-payments crises and periodic suspension of all imports had disastrous consequences for manufacturing industries.

The final folly was the 'confrontation' of Malaysia, and the placing of an embargo on all trade with that country. Confrontation was Indonesia's response to the accession to Malaysia of the British Borneo Territories, which President Sukarno coveted himself, or at least wished to have regarded as an exclusive Indonesian field of influence. Militarily and economically the policy was disastrous, and the abortive communist *coup* in Djakarta in October 1965 proved to be the beginning of the end of Indonesia's 'old order'; by 1966 the President's loss of his own charismatic appeal and the final depletion of Indonesia's foreign exchange reserves made change inevitable. Perhaps the best evidence of deterioration in Indonesia's living conditions is provided by the decline of per capita cereal, particularly rice, consumption, and without substantial American food aid, the decline would have been even more precipitate. Since mid-1966 a new government has been endeavouring to repair the ravages of two decades of neglect and mismanagement, and to use market incentives and Western aid to restore the economy.

In its economic and social policy, Burma is very reminiscent of Indonesia. Since the establishment of the Revolutionary Council by a military coup in 1962, Burma has tried to contract out of the modern world into a vacuum of its own creation; the government has endeavoured to insulate the country from all external corrupting non-Burman influences, though (somewhat illogically it would seem) Western technology is accepted, and to create a Burmese brand of state socialism. As in Indonesia capitalism was rejected, but the Burmans have been no more successful than others in finding a satisfactory alternative to the market as a means of allocating resources, and by the end of 1965 the nationalization of the entire commercial, financial and distributive machinery had led to an almost complete paralysis of distribution above the village level. Each succeeding month saw the national capital Rangoon, more decrepit, dirty and repulsive, a stark contrast to the burgeoning opulence of Singapore, Bangkok or Kuala Lumpur, and the city became avoided by almost all major international airlines.

Burma's rejection of the West is in some ways less comprehensible than that of Indonesia, for after 1937 Burma enjoyed a high degree of local autonomy and its independence followed swiftly upon that of India. Burma has been almost as much anti-Indian as anti-Western,[14] a reflection of the commanding position of its immigrant Indian population in many aspects of economic life before World War II. Much of the responsibility for Burma's present difficulties can be traced to the long civil war which broke out shortly after independence, and which has continued, punctuated by periods of relative quiescence, ever since. Even in 1967 large areas of the country lay outside the control of the central government, a situation that has led to the almost complete cessation of modern mining in the once important Shan plateau. But in the belief, which they share with Indonesians and with many Africans, that the rich natural endowment of their country will automatically produce an era of plenty once all forms of 'colonial exploitation' are removed, Burmans exhibit a pathetic political and economic naïveté. Burma is indeed fortunate in that in relation to its resource base its population can still be considered small, but these potential resources will not become tangible ones until Burma accepts that resources are man-made, and the expulsion of its Indian and Pakistani population and the nationalization of the entire economy outside the village sector have made the peoples of Burma poorer, not richer. The country's increasingly Marxist economic complexion and its tacit approval of virtually all that emanated from Peking, proved, however, a poor guide to future policy; the anti-Chinese riots in Rangoon and other cities in 1967 not only changed the political orientation of Burma but also served notice on the government that the populace was no longer prepared to tolerate the inconveniences and shortages that have accompanied Burma's socialist experiment. As with Indonesia, Burma has been forced to accept the necessity of producing a large and sustained increase in national output, and some revision of economic policy appears inescapable.

In Indochina, revolution and disturbances have been even more disruptive than in Indonesia and Burma, and fighting has occurred in some part or other without interruption since the end of World War II. Unfortunately for the French, the communists were in effective control of much of the country at the time of the Japanese surrender, and by securing an identification of communism with nationalism the Vietminh created an impregnable position for itself. The Geneva agreements of 1954 secured a division of the Vietnamese lands between a communist north and a non-communist south with eventual provision for a national election to decide the country's future, but this was little more than a face-saving device for the French, who had little doubt that the Vietminh would

[14] *A common Burman term for a European was ' white Indian'.*

sooner or later take over the whole country. But under the leadership of Ngo
Dinh Diem, and with growing American aid, a vigorous and temporarily successful attempt was launched to promote a South Vietnamese nationalism;
baulked of its prize North Vietnam reactivated its cadres in the south, and partly
in order to help solve its own intractable economic problems, endeavoured to
take over the south by force. After the assassination of Diem in the military coup
of 1963 it appeared that South Vietnam lacked many essentials to form a cohesive
state, and the unification of the country under the communists began to appear
a distinct possibility. Again the north was frustrated by massive American military and economic aid, but the political and economic rehabilitation of South
Vietnam has proved a long uphill struggle. Though rubber production increased
until 1965, the failure to establish effective control over the Mekong delta meant
that the rice trade, always the basis of the economy, has disappeared; South
Vietnam in fact, has become a major rice deficit area and the pensioner of the
United States. The distribution of American aid has been the subject of repeated
scandals, and it is difficult not to sympathize with the distaste that many of the
country's own intellectuals have felt both for the Diem regime and its military
successors. South Vietnam has still to show that it can form a viable state, but the
magnitude and laxity of the American aid programme scarcely encourages the
government to take the unpleasant and difficult steps necessary to bring this
about. North Vietnam, having acceded to the Eastern bloc, adopted a policy of
rapid industrialization and agricultural reform on the Chinese model, but as in
so many backward countries, it has proved very much easier to establish a modest
heavy industrial base *ab initio* than to revitalize an overpopulated and outworn
traditional agriculture. So far North Vietnam has not dared to eliminate the
private sector in agriculture by taking over the peasants' private plots, nor has it
attempted to up-grade the cooperatives into communes as in China.

Laos and Cambodia both owe their independence to the confusion following
the Japanese collapse in 1945, although both enjoyed special privileges in the
Union of French Indochina. Laos appears to lack almost every essential for a
modern state at present; it survives because the maintenance of a buffer state
along the Mekong suits the interests of the great powers. Culturally and linguis-
tically its affinities are with the Lao people of east and north Thailand across the
Mekong, and communist infiltration among the Lao, to say nothing of the occupation of more than half of Laos itself by the Pathet Lao, a communist body
sponsored and supported by Hanoi, makes Thailand highly suspicious of Laos
as a centre of Lao separatism. Laos has only a minuscule road system and its main
artery of communication is the Mekong; even with the improvements in navigation anticipated with the implementation of the Mekong Valley scheme,[15] any
substantial improvement in the level of economic activity is conditional upon
major additions to the transport system.

[15] *See pp. 122–5.*

Cambodia shares with Burma the advantage of having a relatively small population in relation to physical resources, and in Cambodia the disparity between population and resources is, perhaps, even more pronounced. The Cambodians' inability to exploit their endowment has been a major reason for Annamite or Vietnamese pressure from the east; Cambodia still lays claim to its lost territories of Cochinchina and has never accepted their incorporation into Vietnam. The encroachments by Thai and Vietnamese into a Cambodian state that some centuries ago extended from the Mae Nam (Menam) delta to that of the Mekong, colours all Cambodia's relations; intensely suspicious of its more populous and traditionally hostile neighbours, Cambodia is a state dominated by a determination to survive come what may, and to get solid guarantees of its territorial integrity from each of the great powers. Even before 1960 Cambodia had decided that China was the permanent and the West the temporary influence in Southeast Asia, and after that date the country moved towards a position of increasing accommodation to Peking. In 1963 further American economic aid was refused; border disputes with both Thailand and South Vietnam further eroded goodwill, and in 1965 diplomatic relations with Washington were broken off. The enthusiastic support given by Cambodia to General de Gaulle's plan for a neutralized Southeast Asia did little to endear the country to the United States, particularly as Phnom Penh continued to turn a blind eye to Vietcong bands using Cambodian territory as sanctuary. But despite its professed friendship for China, the events of 1967 showed that Cambodian policy is motivated by solid self-interest and that the country is nobody's puppet. Its trade, moreover, has always been mainly with the West, and its two major export items, rice and rubber, are still capable of further expansion. The freedom from war and insurrection won for Cambodia at Geneva by the obduracy of its Chief of State, Prince Norodom Sihanouk, has enabled the country alone of the Indochinese states to devote its major energies to economic growth and social development, and though there has undoubtedly been some statistical window-dressing, the Cambodian economic performance in the Sixties on the whole compares favourably with that of Malaysia, Thailand and the Philippines.

The division of Southeast Asia into two contrasting political and economic units finds a parallel in other parts of the Third World, particularly in Africa, where an economically pragmatic group including Kenya, Ivory Coast and Tunisia contrasts with doctrinaire Congo, Algeria and Tanzania. There is nothing inevitable about the continued economic advance of Thailand, Malaysia and the Philippines, and in all three countries underground communist organizations work for the downfall of the existing order; moreover, even if the communist menace can be contained, each country must find some solution to the basic social and economic problems confronting it which the communists are so adept in exploiting. In the Philippines, the gap between rich and poor widens perceptibly year by year; Thailand has major regional imbalances in the distribution of income and, though by far the richest state, Malaysia's communal problems could threaten total disaster. But given a decade more of peace and a containment of Chinese imperialism, these three countries could break through to economic 'take-off' and self-sustained growth. In 1965 it would still have appeared folly to suggest that these countries' superior economic performance would have any effect on their neighbours in persuading the latter to mend their ways. Nevertheless, China's cultural revolution and a growing public awareness in both Indonesia and Burma of the tremendous shortcomings of past economic policy, provide grounds for some optimism over the economic future of Southeast Asia.

CHAPTER TWO

The land and its utilization

Physically, Southeast Asia consists of two contrasting major regions of approximately equal area. Mainland, or continental Southeast Asia embraces Burma, Thailand, the Indochinese states and the Malayan peninsula, and has an area of some 807,000 square miles. Archipelagic, or insular Southeast Asia includes the political units Indonesia, the Philippines, East Malaysia (Sarawak and Sabah), Brunei and Portuguese Timor, which total some 754,000 square miles; but if West New Guinea, *de facto* part of Indonesia since 1963, is added, the area of insular Southeast Asia is raised to some 915,000 square miles. Both physical units have a structural complexity which belies their apparently simple arrangement of relief elements.

THE PHYSICAL BASE

From the Minya Gongkar massif in western Szechwan, mountain chains diverge rather like the fingers of a hand, suggesting an interaction of the predominantly E–W trend of the fold mountains of the Old World, and the predominantly N–S trend of the mountain systems bordering the Pacific basin. To the east of Minya Gongkar extends the Nanling of south China; to the southeast, the Annamite chain; to the south the Shan highlands, the mountains of west Thailand and their peninsular extensions into Malaya; and to the southwest, the Arakan Yoma of Burma. Each mountain system comprises several elements and only the Arakan Yoma presents any real barrier to communication. Apart from the northernmost portion of Burma adjacent to Tibet, absolute elevations are not very great, and only the Arakan Yoma attains summits of more than 10,000 feet. Recent uplift has produced a very rugged immature topography, and the thickly forested and highly malarious mountains are sparsely populated, contributing little to economic life except where mineral deposits occur.

Between these mountain systems are enclosed the great depressions which are by far the most significant feature of the human geography of mainland Southeast

Asia: the valley of the Songkoi, or Red river of Tonkin; the Mekong valley and the central depression of Thailand, separated from each other by the low Khorat plateau; and the Irrawaddy basin. These great river valleys form the cores of the national units of mainland Southeast Asia. But a substantial proportion of the lowlands also is thinly populated, for older alluvium is often much laterized, and such areas, as in the middle Mekong valley, contrast markedly with the densely populated newer alluvium of the deltas. Nowhere in mainland Southeast Asia nor on its submarine extension, the Sunda Shelf, are there any active or recently active volcanoes, whose ejactamenta replace the soluble minerals leached from the soil by downward percolating water.

Archipelagic Southeast Asia present perhaps the greatest structural complexity in the world; around the margins of two continental masses, the Sunda Shelf in the west and the Sahul Shelf in the east, are wrapped two great mountain systems, termed by van Bemmelen the Sunda and Circum-Australia systems. The Sunda Shelf extends to the coasts of Sumatra and Java and underlies all but the extreme north of the great island of Borneo, where structures akin to those of the Philippine archipelago appear. Mount Kinabalu in Sabah rises to the highest point of Southeast Asia if the snow-covered peaks of the Sukarno (Carstenz) range of West New Guinea, some 2,000 feet higher, are allocated to the Australian region. Much of the Sunda platform was land in late Pleistocene times, and a connection with Java via the Malayan peninsula, the Riau and Lingga groups, Bangka, Belitung and the Karimundjawa islands may well have existed until well into the Christian era.

It is, however, the islands arcs of the Sunda and Circum-Australia systems that give archipelagic Southeast Asia its highly distinctive geography, 'the most intricate part of the earth's surface' in the words of van Bemmelen. The islands are arranged in single or in double festoons, the inner arcs of which are strongly volcanic. Indonesia is the most active volcanic region in the world, Java alone having some 53 active volcanic centres, while the total for the country is almost 150. Seismic activity also occurs on a scale unmatched elsewhere. The great volcanoes vary greatly; some have very complex structures and clearly represent several cycles of activity and erosion, while others have a relatively simple form, rising as great circular masses to elevations approaching 10,000 feet. Even more importantly, they differ in the composition of their magmas and hence in their ejactamenta, a fact of vital significance to the distribution of population and land utilization. Volcanic activity is much more subdued in the Philippine archipelago, and in the east disappears in West New Guinea, to reappear with vigour in the Australian-administered eastern portion of the island.

The low latitudinal position of Southeast Asia, the broad extent of the intervening seas on its archipelagic fringes and the deep embayments of the mainland ensure a high degree of climatic uniformity. Fisher remarks that there is no other area in the world of comparable size with such a high degree of climatic homogeneity, or which receives as much rain over so wide an area.[1] Temperature exerts a negligible effect on the rhythm of biological and human activity in archipelagic Southeast Asia, nor is its influence very much greater on the mainland, where only Tonkin experiences an approach to a cool season. The agricultural cycle and the tempo of village life are thus largely determined by the rainfall regime.

Continuously warm and humid conditions typical of equatorial lowlands are experienced over a very large part of Southeast Asia. The Malayan peninsula as far north as about 7° N, the whole of Borneo and Sumatra, West Java, the northern Maluku (Moluccas) and the eastern Philippines receive copious rain at all times of the year. There are, it is true, considerable differences in the rainfall regimes of these various parts of equatorial Southeast Asia. South Sumatra, West Java and the eastern Philippines have much more rain in the period from October to March than in the middle months of the year; east Sumatra, Bangka and much of Borneo have a double maxima pattern in which October and November are usually the rainiest months; northern Maluku and nearby portions of Sulawesi have a double maxima pattern in which the earlier equinox is the wetter. But these differences have little real agricultural significance apart from their influence on the timing of operations in the cycle of rice cultivation, which is so arranged that the main harvest occurs at the end of the rainiest period of the year. There is always an excess of precipitation over evaporation and the soil remains permanently moist. From the standpoint of plant growth, there is no essential difference between climates of this nature and those with a definite dry season but with a precipitation in the rainy months so heavy that the soil is never able to dry out; climates of this latter type occur in both eastern and western peninsular Thailand, the Tenasserim, Tavoy and Arakan coasts of Burma, and in much of Cambodia, Sulawesi and Mindanao. With an annual rainfall of 80 inches and often very much more, those parts of Southeast Asia with permanently moist soils support an evergreen rain forest of a botanical complexity scarcely equalled elsewhere in the world.

The remainder of Southeast Asia experiences a dry season in which for a part of the year evaporation greatly exceeds precipitation, so that the soil can dry out to considerable depths. Yet the long and fierce dry season typical of much of the Indian region scarcely exists in Southeast Asia; very few stations record more than five dry months in the year, a dry month being defined by the Dutch soil chemist Mohr as one with less than 60 mm (2·4 inches) of rain. A precipitation of less than 60 inches is found only in rain-shadow areas on the mainland, such as central Burma, the Mae Nam plain of Thailand and part of the central plain of Cambodia, and in island Southeast Asia on the lee side of mountains athwart the oscillatory 'monsoons' of Java, Sulawesi and the Philippines. A precipitation of less than 40 inches is exceedingly rare, being confined to the Dry zone of Burma

[1] *Charles A. Fisher*, South-East Asia, *Methuen, London, rev. edn., 1966, p. 41.*

and to a few pronounced but limited rain-shadow areas in Java and Sulawesi. The severity of the dry season increases eastwards in the Sunda Ketjil islands of Indonesia as the Australian continent is approached; less than one inch of rain falls in northern Sumba between July and October, and this period is virtually rainless on the north coasts of Sawu, Roti and Timor. But even in areas with marked wet and dry seasons, rain comes largely as a result of intermittent frontal activity, and it is erroneous to conceive of the wet season as a continuous down-pour; throughout Southeast Asia the number of rainy hours per year are fewer than in Western Europe.[2] Orographical control of rainfall is strong, particularly at certain times of the year when windward slopes can trigger off powerful vertical movements. Many islands show striking differences both in the amount and in the distribution of rainfall between their northern and southern, and between their eastern and western coasts, as wind systems oscillate between the so-called Northwest monsoon (October–March) and the Southeast monsoon (April–September). Java and Sulawesi in particular, have very complex patterns of precipitation with pronounced variations in amount and in distribution within very short distances, a fact of major significance in land use.

Uniformly high temperatures and a heavy torrential precipitation result in a very rapid erosion and deep chemical weathering. Soils are generally very im-poverished, but in areas with a dry season there is a periodic check to leaching and capillary action may return some soluble minerals to the upper soil layers. The apparent contradiction between the luxuriant richness of the rain forest of low latitudes and the general poverty of equatorial soils has long been resolved and its significance is now becoming more widely appreciated; the forest contains within itself all the materials for its survival. It is possible that the equatorial rain forest originated at a time when weathering had not proceeded far and when soils were much richer in plant nutrients than at present, for the rain forest is of great geo-logical antiquity. Much of the original stock of plant nutrients is locked up in the forest itself and, with the rapid decomposition of plant waste under insect, fungoid or bacterial attack, is speedily released, to be reabsorbed by the growing vege-tation. Cutting and clearing of the forest interrupts this cycle and can quickly result in soil damage and accelerated laterization.

The most favourable soil conditions are thus encountered when minerals removed by leaching are periodically replaced, a development that eventuates in two ways. The more common is by the deposition of material in suspension in rivers and watercourses. The great river systems of mainland Southeast Asia have greatly enlarged discharges in the rainy season and flood extensive areas; many of them, moreover, have regular, predictable regimes, a factor of major signi-ficance to agriculture. The widespread practice of irrigation also assists in the maintenance of fertility through the deposition of suspended material, but irrigation, or more specifically, the impounding of water on fields by bunds or

[2] E. J. C. Mohr, Soils of the Equatorial Regions, *Edwards, Ann Arbor, 1944, p. 125.*

retaining walls, confers other benefits on the soil in all probability, whose full importance and origin is still imperfectly understood.[3] Alluvial lowlands subject to regular flooding or capable of being irrigated are thus the most attractive areas for agriculture, but the soils of the great rice-bowls of Southeast Asia are as much the product of human effort as of natural processes.

In archipelagic Southeast Asia, and in particular in Indonesia, the fall-out of volcanic material also operates to offset the effects of leaching and cultivation; volcanic fallout is transported both by wind and water, and much reaches the fields as suspended material in watercourses and irrigation channels. On the south coast of Java, volcanic material swept into the sea by the Seraju river is deposited along the south coast plain by the action of currents. Fallout derived from basic volcanic magmas is more beneficial than that derived from acidic magmas, and closely connected with magmatic composition, from the standpoint of cultivation, is the intensity of volcanic activity; volcanoes that are frequently in eruption have a greater ameliorating effect on the soils in their vicinity than have volcanoes with lengthy quiescent periods, or which indeed have been inactive since late Pleistocene times. In Central Java soil fertility and the distribution of population are closely related to the incidence of volcanic activity, and around Merapi, one of the world's most active volcanoes, population is densest on the eastern and southeastern flanks, which receive the greatest quantities of material from the prevailing west and northwest winds.[4] The correlation between areas of volcanic-enriched soils and high population densities is far from complete, however, for in eastern Indonesia several such areas support a low population density, and much depends on the material culture of the population.

It seems highly probable that except for certain relatively restricted areas where extreme soil conditions permitted only a specialized herbaceous vegetation, the whole of Southeast Asia must have been forested before the spread of agriculture. Even at the present a very large part of the region is still covered with forest of some kind; FAO estimates that some 63 per cent of mainland and some 65 per cent of archipelagic Southeast Asia are forested, and that the total forested area exceeds 270 million hectares, more than one million square miles (*Table 2-1*). But much of this forest has been greatly debased through the activities of man, and there are marked variations in the proportion of forest-land from country to country, ranging from Malaysia, which has almost 70 per cent of its land area in forests, to the Philippines, which has only some 40 per cent. There are also great variations in the regional distribution of forest within countries; much of the Philippines' remaining timber is located in Mindanao, Mindoro and Samar, and

[3] *Clifford Geertz*, Agricultural Involution, *University of California Press, Berkeley and Los Angeles, 1963, pp. 29–30.*

[4] *E. J. C. Mohr, 'The relation between soil and population density in the Netherlands Indies', in Honig, P. and Verdoorn, F.,* Science and Scientists in the Netherlands Indies, *New York, 1945, pp. 254–62.*

Table 2-1   *Southeast Asia: forests and forest utilization*

| | FOREST AREA | | REMOVALS 1953–55 AVERAGE | |
| | *million hectares* | | *million cubic metres* | |
	Total	In use	Industrial wood	Fuel wood
MAINLAND SOUTHEAST ASIA				
Burma	45·3	24·1	1·0	11·0
Cambodia	8·8	2·1	0·2	0·3
Laos	15·0	4·0	0·1	2·0
Malaya and Singapore	9·5	3·3	1·7	0·4
Thailand	29·9	19·1	1·7	1·4
South Vietnam	5·6 ⎱	9·3	0·4	0·5
North Vietnam	8·9 ⎰			
Estimate unrecorded			3·8	23·4
Total	**123·0**	**61·9**	**8·9**	**39·0**
INSULAR SOUTHEAST ASIA				
Brunei	0·4	0·2		
Indonesia	90·2	57·9	5·6	80·4
West New Guinea	31·0	0·1		
Philippines	13·2	4·1	3·6	0·1
North Borneo (Sabah)	6·3	0·4	0·5	0·1
Sarawak	9·3	1·3	0·5	
Estimated unrecorded			3·1	16·7
Total	**150·4**	**64·0**	**13·3**	**97·3**
Grand total	**273·4**	**125·9**	**22·2**	**136·6**

Sources: FAO. *World Forest Inventory,* 1958. United Nations and FAO, *Timber Trends and Prospects in the Asia-Pacific Region,* Geneva, 1961

although some 70 per cent of Indonesia is forested, the proportion falls below 30 per cent in Java and the Sunda Ketjil islands.

Two principal types of forest can be distinguished in Southeast Asia, although several genera are represented in both divisions. Wherever soils remain moist through the year the evergreen rain forest with its wealth of species, multi-storeyed structure and numerous epiphytes and woody scramblers reigns supreme; of major economic importance are the various species of Dipterocarpaceae such as *Balanocarpus, Shorea, Dipterocarpus* and *Drybalanops.* Where soils dry out for part of the year, the evergreen rain forest is replaced by a moist deciduous mon-soon forest, which although containing a lesser wealth of species, is also capable of forming dense stands under favourable conditions. In drier areas such as central Burma or western Thailand, the deciduous forest becomes more open, degenerating into a dry scrub and bamboo forest whose open and impoverished character is largely the product of burning and overgrazing. The monsoon forest also contains valuable dipterocarps such as *Shorea* (Sal), but its most valuable product is teak, a tree which is intolerant of waterlogged soils, and is therefore mainly associated with hilly or undulating limestone areas. Teak forests are best developed in Burma where they encircle the Dry zone, but they also occur in northern and eastern Thailand. Teak is also indigenous to Java, but the homogeneous teak forest of the limestone hills of Rembang and parts of the Southern mountains in East Java are artificial, having been planted in place of natural teak forests containing a large proportion of other species.

In both evergreen and monsoon forests alike the proportion of commercial species is very small. Teak forms only about 12 per cent of the growing stock of the forests of Burma and only 9 per cent of that of the northern provinces of Thailand. In the evergreen rain forest, the proportion of valuable dipterocarps and of other species of economic importance such as *Koompassia* and *Dyera* is smaller still.[5] Moreover, not all stems are of economic size; sawmills in Southeast Asia are generally crude by the standards of forest-product industries of Europe and North America, and demand large well-formed logs, rejecting smaller material that would be very acceptable to mills in those parts of the world where capital-intensive forest-product industries have necessitated scientific forestry and a very high degree of utilization of the total forest material.

The lowland rain forest is replaced in areas where surface water abounds by specialized swamp forests of various kinds, some of which also contain valuable commercial species, although exploitation of these forests presents many problems. Of greater importance are the coastal mangrove forests, which occur on gently shelving coasts without strong wave action of tidal scour. Extensive *Rhizophora* forests occur on either side of the Malacca Straits, in southern and western Borneo and in the Ca Mau peninsula of South Vietnam; the timber (*bakau* in Malaya and Indonesia, *bakauan* in the Philippines) is much used for charcoal burning and for the construction of offshore fishtraps. The many uses made of mangrove and the accessibility of mangrove forests have resulted in much over-cutting and deterioration. Nevertheless, all forest-conservation legislation has been difficult to enforce since the achievement of political independence.

At higher elevations the lowland forest gives way to an upland or montane forest with oaks and maples, and at elevations of over 3,000 feet conifers such as *Pinus merkusii*, *Pinus khasya*, and in the Philippines, *Pinus insularis* may appear, although always in limited stands. These softwoods have also been used in re-afforestation projects at lower elevations. Other conifers of the highlands include *Podocarpus* species, and in eastern Indonesia and New Guinea, *Agathis* (damar),

[5] *United Nations and FAO*, Timber Trends and Prospects in the Asia-Pacific Region, *Geneva, 1961, pp. 63, 69.*

and in the latter island also, *Araucaria* species occur. The proportion of conifers is exceedingly small, amounting to less than one per cent of the total forest of the region, but the elevation and latitudinal position of its northern extension combine to give to Burma a proportion approaching 10 per cent, the highest of any country in Southeast Asia. The consequent shortage of softwood is a serious handicap, particularly for the establishment of pulp and paper industries, and it is clear that a higher degree of utilization of local hardwood materials is mandatory if these important industries are to develop. One possible source of raw material for such industries is bamboo, a timber substitute with many uses in the region, and whose wide distribution in large measure reflects the hand of man. There are many species of these woody perennials in Southeast Asia and they form an important element in several types of forest. They are particularly well represented in monsoon forests, where their extension is encouraged by shifting cultivation and by burning, although of course, the more useful species are often deliberately planted.

Despite a forest wealth unmatched elsewhere in the world, per capita consumption of forest products in Southeast Asia is very low, being less than one-tenth that of economically advanced countries such as Britain or Australia. The productivity of the forest is only a fraction of what is known to be possible with good forest management; the principal product is, in fact, fuel wood, which accounts for nearly three-quarters of all removals from forests.[6] In archipelagic Southeast Asia almost as much fuel wood is produced from other sources as is derived from forests, a situation that is largely accounted for by a large production of wood from village garden-land in densely populated Java. Yet per capita consumption of fuel wood in Indonesia is estimated at only slightly over one cubic metre annually, and it is lower still elsewhere in the region. Moreover, a very large part of the total forest area is used only incidentally as a source of timber and is the domain of the shifting cultivator.

All evidence points to a greatly increased consumption of forest products with a higher level of development, and what is equally important, to a progressive shift from the production of primary forest-products such as sawn timber to that of the secondary forest-industries, plywood, board products, and above all, pulp and paper. The latter industries, which permit a much fuller utilization of the original forest material, scarcely exist in Southeast Asia at present. Although the larger part of the world's pulp production is derived from softwoods, the share of hardwood pulp is increasing rapidly, and modern pulp industries can make use of almost any kind of timber. A large per capita consumption of paper is the inevitable corollary of enhanced economic development, and foreign exchange shortages are a severe limitation to larger imports of paper. The very restricted use made of one of the world's major forest resources must clearly be modified if Southeast Asia is to gain the higher level of welfare that it so much desires.

[6] ibid, *p. 21.*

LAND UTILIZATION

The use made of the natural environment is a very important part of culture, and each of the many peoples of Southeast Asia have their preferred methods of making use of the land. Culture and the environment can conveniently be regarded as synthesized in ecosystems, and once established such systems are very resistant to change. Nevertheless, it is certain that the attainment of higher living standards in the region will be out of the question without far-reaching changes in traditional attitudes towards land and in the use made of it. Two markedly contrasting ecosystems are discernible in Southeast Asia, the *swidden* and the *sawah*; neither, however, is peculiar to it, and despite Sauer's belief that Southeast Asia is one of the hearths of agriculture,[7] there is no conclusive evidence that either system originated in the region.

Swidden agriculture

Over enormous areas of the humid tropics the dominant form of land use is a hoe or digging stick agriculture in which occupancy of the land for crop production is interrupted by lengthy rest periods in which the land is allowed to revert to 'bush' or secondary forest. This type of agriculture has usually been known as shifting cultivation, but it has a rich variety of regional names. The fields of the shifting cultivator are known as *caiñgin* in the Philippines, *rai* (ray) in Vietnam, *tam rai* in Thailand, *ladang* in Malaya and much of Indonesia, and *taungya* in Burma; these names however have many local variations, and strictly refer to a particular stage in the cycle of cultivation. The English dialect term *swidden* (burnt field) has been suggested as a generic name for this type of agriculture, and though by no means universally adopted has the advantage of emphasizing an essential feature of the system. Although most closely associated with undulating forest-land in Southeast Asia, it is also practised in more open grassland or savanna country, much of which represents debasement of the original forest cover.

Swidden agriculture is a means whereby the large store of plant nutrients locked up in the original forest material is released for acquisition by crops useful to man. In the process a sizeable proportion of the original nutrient endowment is rapidly lost, and this eventually compels the abandonment of cultivation. In time, and in the absence of further interference by man, the climax vegetation re-establishes itself and the original properties of the soil are restored; in practice, however, the time interval before the land is reoccupied for cultivation is seldom long enough for this to happen. Swidden agriculture, therefore, consists of a cycle of comparatively short periods of cropping punctuated by lengthy periods

[7] *Carl O. Sauer*, Agricultural Origins and Dispersals, *American Geographic Society*, *New York, 1952.*

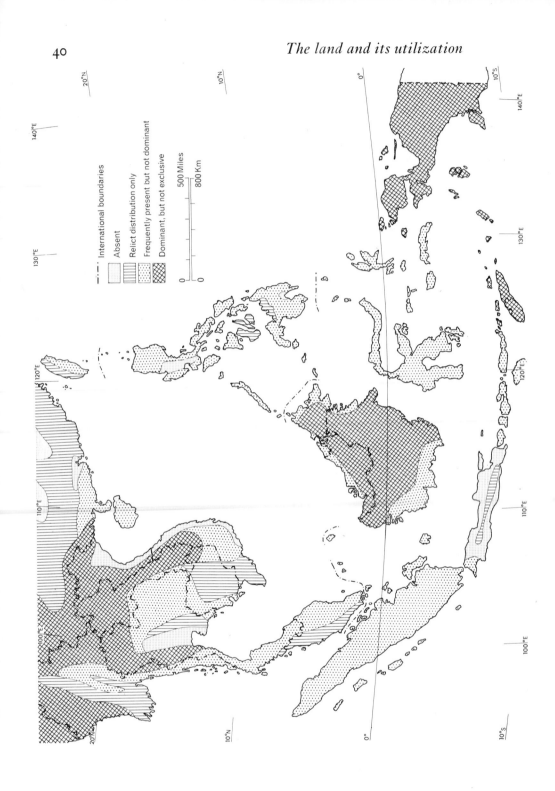

International boundaries

Absent

Relict distribution only

Frequently present but not dominant

Dominant, but not exclusive

0   500 Miles

0   800 Km

of fallow, commonly of some eight to twelve years' duration but occasionally extending to twenty years or more.

The transference of nutrients from the forest to cultigens (that is, plants completely dependent on man) is effected by clearing and burning, although in areas with a very heavy year-round rainfall burning may be impossible and the felled debris is allowed to decay as a mulch. Sites of swiddens are usually chosen to avoid the necessity of felling really large trees, so that secondary forest is usually preferred, and cutting is timed to give the felled material opportunity to dry out for a good burn, which is thus arranged to take place towards the end of the dry, or drier season. A proportion of the nutrients present in the forest material is lost in the gaseous products of combustion, and with the onset of the rains further losses result through the washing away of some of the ashes. It is therefore a matter of extreme urgency to get crops planted as soon as possible after the burn, so that they have the benefit both of early germination and the most favourable soil conditions. The soil is merely scratched with a hoe or digging stick, and the seeds either individually or in association are dibbled into the holes.

One of the most striking characteristics of swidden agriculture is the great variety of cultivated crops in each clearing. More than 400 cultigens are regularly grown by swidden cultivators of Mindoro in the Philippines, of which about a quarter may appear in any one swidden.[8] This multiplicity of crops is in part an insurance against natural hazard—some of the swidden crops will succeed whatever happens—but more importantly, it is a deliberate attempt, born of the profound ecological knowledge of the cultivator, to reproduce the very diverse plant variety of the forest itself, duplicating as far as possible its close canopy structure so that the soil is not subject to the rapid chemical and physical deterioration which inevitably follow on exposure to strong sunlight and heavy rainfall. Crops are thus not set out neatly in rows, but are sown here and there in apparently riotous confusion, and interspersed with herbaceous perennials such as pineapples or bananas, fruit trees, or occasionally preserved forest trees such as durian. The impression is false, however; crops are sown successively in precisely the environmental conditions proved best by immemorial experience, whether in first, second or third season clearings, around the margins of the swidden or towards the centre, in varying intensities of open sunlight or shade, on hearth ashes, or on termite mounds and in other specialized environments. In marked contrast to swiddens in Africa or in Latin America, dry rice (that is, rice grown as an ordinary field crop without impounding bunds or supplementary water) occupies an important place among swidden crops, and an even more fundamental role in the general culture of Southeast Asian swidden farmers. In terms of

[8] *H. Conklin*, Hanunoo Agriculture in the Philippines, *F A O, Rome, 1957, p. 147.*

---

opposite:

Fig 2-1   The distribution of shifting cultivation in Southeast Asia (after Spencer)

contribution to diet, however, it is much less significant than maize, and heavy reliance is also placed on roots and tubers such as tapioca (cassava), yams of many kinds, sweet potatoes and tuberous aroids of the taro family such as 'elephant's ear' (*Alocasia*) and *Colocasia* for much of the calorific intake. Legumes and leafy green vegetables in great variety are also conspicuous crops in new swiddens, as are such non-food crops as tobacco. But apart from poultry, animals are of minimal importance.

Swidden cultivators can obtain dry rice yields the equivalent of some 1,150–1,570 kg per hectare, a return which does not compare unfavourably with a regional average yield of somewhat less than 1,600 kg per hectare, and in respect of the return on labour input, swidden farmers can occasionally do better than sawah cultivators. But after the first cropping season yields commence to decline, and there comes a time when the return does not justify the labour of cultivation; this the swidden cultivator can forecast by the increasing vigour of weeds and by changes in the soil fauna. The cultivation of annuals is abandoned, but for some time still the swidden continues to produce from its perennials before being en-gulfed by regenerating secondary forest, termed *belukar* in much of Indonesia and in Malaya. Occasionally, tree crops able to compete with the volunteer vegetation may continue to yield for many years and to provide the cultivator with a cash income. This important commercial modification of the swidden cycle is further discussed below. Ultimately the swidden is abandoned, to be reoccupied after an appropriate period of years; yet the cultivator keeps no records whatsoever, and reoccupied swiddens seldom if ever have the same boundaries or size (the commonest size is between 0·5 and 1·5 acres) as their predecessors. The cultivator judges from his remarkable ecological knowledge when and whether a particular piece of land is suitable for reoccupation, and what crops can be grown.

It is obvious, therefore, that swidden cultivators require access to very large areas, even though their numbers form a very small proportion of the region's total population. FAO estimates that the shifting cultivators of Southeast Asia affect nearly 46 million hectares of forest land, and that some 4 million hectares of forest are cleared annually (*Table 2-2*). Despite this loss, much of which takes place in areas too inaccessible for commercial timber exploitation, many observers believe that, on balance, swidden cultivation is a satisfactory form of land use and that it is essentially conservative of resources. This is particularly so with 'true' swidden cultivators, those whose material culture is so firmly intertwined with the swidden system that they cannot be forced to take up any other kind of activity without complete social collapse. The mode of life of the true swidden cultivator makes the attainment of a high population density impossible, and so sufficient time is allowed for abandoned swiddens to be rehabilitated by natural processes.

But where such cultivators are constrained in their movements, either by pressure from other groups or by legislation aimed at forest conservation or water control, it can easily happen that the time available for natural recuperation of the soil in abandoned plots is inadequate, and accelerated deforestation and damage to the soil result. Moreover, in areas with a pronounced dry season, the recuperative powers of the vegetation and soil are much less than in continuously humid parts of the region, and correspondingly lengthier rest periods should be observed before reoccupation of abandoned clearings. A greater hazard, however,

Table 2-2 *Southeast Asia: extent of shifting cultivation*

	Population of shifting cultivators	Forest cleared annually	Total forest area under cultivation
	millions	*million hectares*	
Mainland Southeast Asia	7	2	26
Archipelagic Southeast Asia	6	2	20
Total	**13**	**4**	**46**

Source: United Nations and FAO, *Timber Trends and Prospects in the Asia-Pacific Region*, Geneva, 1961

arises from the activities of the 'false' shifting cultivator, the farmer who is essentially a tiller of permanent fields, accustomed to setting out crops in rows, to clean weeding and to ploughing. Under the pressure of rising population and stagnating yields on their tiny fragmented farms, the peasants of the region have been encroaching on forest-land wherever they can; the practical difficulties of enforcing forest conservation, discredited because of its association with former colonial regimes, and political disturbances and regional insurrections which have impeded normal distribution, have all helped to swell the attack on forest-land. In parts of Indonesia widespread food shortages have left many peasants with no alternative but to occupy whatever unused land they can to fend off starvation, and during the 'confrontation' with Malaysia from 1963 to 1966, Sumatran smallholders rediscovered a truth of the Japanese occupation—one cannot eat rubber. Indonesia's forest losses since independence have been prodigious, and amount perhaps to as much as half of the total losses of the inter-tropical world.

Thus in several parts of the region, conditions since 1950 have been conducive to accelerated impoverishment of vegetation and soil, and to an expansion of *Imperata* and *Eupatorium* grassland and scrub. *Imperata*, called *cogon* in the Philippines, *alang-alang* in Indonesia, *lalang* in Malaya, *tranh* in Vietnam, *va kha* in Thailand and *thatke* in Burma, is largely useless, and once established is exceedingly difficult to eradicate without mechanical equipment or chemical spraying. *Imperata* requires bright sunshine and when fired burns fiercely, but the underground rhizomes are very resistant so that natural or man-made fires assist its spread by reducing competition. The elimination of spear grass by natural means occurs through progressive shading by regenerating forest, but in a large grassland expanse this can only occur around the margins and the process can be extremely protracted; even in the absence of further human interference it would probably take upwards of 500 years to replace some of the extensive *coganales* of the Philippines, or the *alang-alang* wastes of eastern Indonesia. A reversal of the tendency of grassland to grow at the expense of forest—and already the proportion of the Philippines that is covered with *cogon* is variously estimated at between 20 and 40 per cent—will be clearly dependent upon sustained improvements in the productivity of the sedentary food-producing farmer. And of that, most countries in the region show all too few signs.

Sawah agriculture

Continuous cultivation of the more desirable annuals such as cereals on dry fields is a matter of great difficulty in humid tropical environments. The key to such permanent crop production is the *sawah*, an Indonesian word for an embanked ricefield, in which water derived either from natural precipitation or from a supplementary source, is impounded. The sawah's water covering protects the soil from the physical and chemical deterioration that afflict dry fields, and, in a manner still imperfectly understood, enables it to maintain a modest but constant yield year after year, sometimes two or three times a year, for century after century. Moreover, soils of very varying characteristics, even those exceedingly poor in plant nutrients, can be converted into sawahs; the essential condition is that there should not be loss of water underground through seepage, and given this sawahs soon acquire their own characteristics.

Two types of wet-rice, or padi, cultivation can be distinguished:[9] that dependent entirely on natural rainfall, the method employed in the Irrawaddy delta and in much of the Philippines, and that making use of supplementary water. The latter can originate either through the natural flooding of rivers, as in the Mae Nam plain of Thailand, the Palembang area of Sumatra, and along the lower Mekong in both Cambodia and South Vietnam, or by man-made irrigation systems of varying degrees of technical sophistication. There are, in fact, very few parts of the region where natural rainfall is either heavy or reliable enough to ensure a good crop in every season, and even in areas dependent on river flooding, the degree of hazard may be extreme; on the average, the Mae Nam plain before regulation had a satisfactory flood only one year in three. The use of irrigation techniques not only guarantees a satisfactory crop in every season, but it may also make possible the harvesting of two or more crops in the year; rice may thus succeed rice, though always of a different variety, or rice may be followed by rice substitutes or supplementary crops such as maize, sweet potatoes and legumes, or even rotate with sugar and tobacco. Irrigation, moreover, often results

[9] *Strictly padi is unhusked rice, but the term is often used to describe the method of cultivation.*

in an increment of fertility through the deposition of material in suspension. Yet even rain-fed sawahs have been able to maintain a stable yield over long periods, without benefit of green manuring or through the use of other soil-improving techniques. The fixation of nitrogen by blue-green algae, the decay of plant and animal material, the supression of weeds and the gentle movement of the water over the soil all probably help to contribute to the maintenance of the productivity of the sawah.

The use of irrigation has also permitted the conversion of sloping land into sawahs by means of terracing, of which Southeast Asia contains some most spectacular examples. The Ifugao people of Mountain Province of Luzon have constructed terraces whose walls may exceed 60 feet in height, but terraces rising tier upon tier up the sides of steep valleys also occur in West Java, Bali and in Tonkin. Indigenous irrigation techniques are generally crude and depend on simple earth or brushwood dams and short distribution channels, which confine irrigation to the upper and middle portions of valleys. Some peoples, however, have works of greater technical skill. The Balinese have excavated remarkable conduits to carry water from the slopes of Gunung Agung on to the southern plain, and the Tonkinese have created still more elaborate irrigation and drainage systems whose construction and maintenance could only have been possible to a well organized and disciplined 'hydraulic society'.[10] Many of the most stupendous terraces, however, were built long ago when real costs of construction were much cheaper than at present, and terracing, as with multiple cropping, is far from general. Indeed, many people are quite unable to cope with sloping land and possess little knowledge of irrigation; even bunds are uncommon on much of the flat Mae Nam plain, and the rising flood extends as far as the eye can see.

It was the introduction of European engineering techniques and the use of materials unknown to indigenous cultivators that permitted the unbroken extension of sawahs over the broad alluvial plains, whose higher portions in the past never received a sufficient flood to make rice cultivation possible except in years of very high floods, at which times the sawahs of the lowest lying areas were likely to be drowned, with consequent heavy crop losses. Drainage is an indispensable concomitant of irrigation, and in some parts of the region, notably in the Songkoi delta of Tonkin whose rivers possess erratic and unpredictable regimes, flood control has posed major problems. Even European irrigation systems, however, were largely diversionary and utilized only a small proportion of the total discharge. A higher incidence of multiple cropping will necessitate enlarged dams and storage facilities, and will inevitably entail a greater capital outlay on higher dams and more massive works.

[10] *Karl A. Wittfogel, in* Oriental Despotism, *Yale University Press, New Haven, 1957, distinguishes between hydro-agriculture, in which minor irrigation works are a purely local responsibility, and hydraulic agriculture necessitating major works organized by a centralized political authority.*

Rice terraces extend over the southern slopes of Gunung Agung, east Bali.

The drier northern flanks of Agung have fewer sawahs, and the *lontar (Borassus flabellifer)* is a conspicuous feature of the landscape. This palm is widespread in areas with a pronounced dry season, and usually supports a domestic sugar industry.

The rhythm of the sawah cycle is closely related to the oscillations of atmospheric circulation, but the many regional precipitation regimes, the existence of some 3,000 rice varieties with growing periods from as little as 60 to more than 300 days, and the widespread use of irrigation combine to produce countless variations of the system. The varieties grown reflect the accumulated experience of each particular district, but the choice also depends on local tastes, which may differ greatly even within short distances. Some peoples prefer glutinous rice for their own consumption. These varieties have a very soft grain and their protein content is lower than that of the hard rices; when steamed they become sweet and sticky and are thus much used in the preparation of cakes and pastries. Commercially, however, their importance is negligible.

There is a close connection between the yield and the amount of water available during the growing season; long-term padi gives a higher yield than rapidly maturing varieties. Over the greater part of mainland Southeast Asia, sawahs produce only one rice crop a year, but some countries such as Indonesia (particularly Java and Bali), Thailand and Vietnam, take a rice crop in every month of the year. But the most important harvest always occurs at the end of the rainy season, that is, the months of October and November in the mainland, and in April over much of Indonesia.

Cultivation techniques are considerably superior to those of the Indian region and broadcasting is usually only practised in areas of 'deep-water' rice, and when earlier transplanting has failed; but only in Tonkin do they reach the level of sophistication attained in the Far East. Although transplanting is almost universal, setting out the seedlings in regular rows to facilitate weeding is by no means so common, and in Indonesia, by far the largest rice-producer in Southeast Asia, the practice only became widespread with the introduction of Japanese push hoes in the Thirties. Generally little or no fertilizer is used apart from that applied to the seedling nurseries, but in the past large quantities of nitrogenous fertilizers were used on sawahs in Central and East Java in connection with the sugar industry. In Malaya the use of artificial fertilizer has been greatly stimulated by the post-independence rural development programme. Farmers in the Tonkin delta make use of a wide range of organic materials as manures to dress their fields, and are especially skilled in the use of green manures; the propagation of one such manure, *Azolla*, was the prerogative of a few famous villages, particularly La Van and My Loc, which alone had discovered the art of keeping the plant alive during the hot season.[11] Green manuring is also widely practised in many parts of Java, where a variety of leguminous crops is employed for this purpose; unfortunately, with increasing population pressure and the necessity of pushing up food production at all costs, the practice is almost everywhere tending to decline. Nevertheless, over wide areas of the region there is a growing awareness among ordinary farmers of the value of chemical fertilizers, and their use is increasingly accepted;

[11] *Pierre Gourou*, Les Paysans du Delta Tonkinois, *Mouton & Co., Paris, 1965, p. 393.*

indeed, in some countries fertilizers change hands at fancy prices, and the peasant is frequently unable to obtain all that he would like.

Many writers have commented that although sawahs employ a large proportion of the rural work-force, they cover only a minute fraction of the total national territory. Only a very small proportion of the terrain is in any case suitable for conversion to sawahs, but this situation also reflects the important fact that cultivators have long been aware that investment in improved water-control often yields a higher return than investment in extending the sawah area. Large extensions have indeed been made over the past century, but comparable future additions will, it is clear, entail a very heavy capital outlay. As the productivity of existing sawahs is well below what is known to be possible, investment in raising yields on the present area offers the best solution to most countries' food problems. Multipurpose water projects involving the generation of hydro-electricity and industrial development will in any case lead to some further extension of the sawah area, and such investment appears a better proposition than attempts to make rice-bowls of the vast areas of still unreclaimed swampland such as those of south Kalimantan and east Sumatra, a development that long dazzled the Indonesian government. It is vital, however, that such new investment, which will mainly involve a very large increase in the consumption and production of chemical fertilizers in conjunction with the use of rice varieties of proved high response, is not again nullified by population increase, as has been the case with every previous technical innovation of the sawah system.[12]

In most parts of Southeast Asia the villages of sawah farmers rise as darker green islands out of a sea of rice; often the houses are completely invisible at a distance, being concealed by a multiplicity of fruit trees, herbaceous perennials and bamboos. Fruits and vegetables produced from the house lots, which are often heavily manured, make a very valuable contribution to the diet of sawah farmers, and provide much of the vitamin, protein and mineral intake. Perhaps as much as 15 per cent of the cultivated land of Java and Madura is occupied by such gardens, termed in Indonesian *pekarangan*, and as the size of the farm holding diminishes, so the share of the garden plot and the intensity with which it is worked, tend to increase.[13] Although fruit and vegetable production is overwhelmingly for immediate local consumption, a few districts in each country have acquired a reputation for certain kinds of fruits, and in the vicinity of the great cities fruit production from *pekarangan* or *dusun* (Malaya) can become an important local industry, as in Pasar Minggu south of Djakarta, Gombak north of Kuala Lumpur and Bangkok Noi on the right bank of the Mae Nam Chao Phraya opposite Bangkok. In a few limited areas at high elevations the cultivation of temperate vegetables for urban markets may also be undertaken, as occurs

[12] *Geertz*, op. cit., *p. 146.*

[13] G. J. A. de Terra, ' *Mixed garden horticulture in Java* ', Malayan Journal of Tropical Geography, *vol. 4, 1954, p. 39.*

in the Priangan highlands of Java, on the Toba highlands in Sumatra, around Da Lat in South Vietnam and in the Cameron Highlands of Malaya. These activities, however, are always the province of specialists, usually Chinese, and even where carried on by indigenes, Chinese middlemen and dealers have a firm grip on production.

Many rice farmers also possess some land which for one reason or another cannot be converted into sawahs; and in Java, the area of such dry fields, or *tegalan*, had virtually come to equal that of sawah by 1930, and is now very much more. In limestone areas, sawahs cannot usually be constructed at all except in favoured spots, but in some of the limestone areas of Java, and even more strikingly in Madura, which has very little irrigable land, techniques of dry-field cultivation have reached a high level of refinement; sloping land may be elaborately terraced and the walls faced with stone or protected by *Paspalum* (buffalo grass) or by low hedges of *Leucaena*. Crop rotations and sowing in association are also practised, together with the use of green manures, vegetable composts, and, on fields used to grow such crops as sugar cane, large quantities of buffalo manure. Such meticulous cultivation of dry fields, however, is very unusual from the standpoint of the region as a whole, and dry fields are more often located on slopes provided with little or no erosion control, and receive little manure.

Among crops grown on dry fields are dry, or upland rice, of which there are

Sawah landscape in East Java. The villages are invisible in the islands of palms, bamboos and fruit trees.

also several varieties; maize, which in many parts of Central and East Java, in Madura, Cebu and in much of eastern Thailand is the chief cereal for human consumption; sweet potatoes, groundnuts, soybeans, chickpeas and other legumes, and tapioca. But with rapidly increasing population there is a strong tendency for this last crop to become of increasing importance, evidence of the impoverishment of both the land and its people. Tapioca, or cassava, is in fact a perennial and will grow into a sizeable tree; its roots are not ready for harvesting until at least twelve months, but it can be grown on soils that are too poor for other crops. The roots contain very little fat or protein and consist largely of starch, so that a diet with a large tapioca content is much more deficient than diets based on maize or polished rice, which can be productive of the deficiency diseases pellagra and beriberi. In the poorest parts of Java, such as the south Seraju hills, *sega ojek* (tapioca gruel) has become the staple food; rice, though produced on a few sawahs, is far too costly to be used for everyday consumption.[14] The final stage in the degeneration of the land is an eroded and *Imperata*-covered waste, on which a wretched peasantry has to depend increasingly on a debased and illegal shifting agriculture to supplement the miserable return on its fragmented permanent fields.

The limited role of livestock in Southeast Asian agriculture has received frequent comment. Sawah agriculture depends heavily on its work animals, oxen and water buffaloes to maintain the cycle of cultivation, but in the most congested parts of Tonkin all operations may be performed manually, as indeed is also the case in many areas of terracing; work animals cannot be taken up the steep hillsides and the terraces themselves are often too narrow to permit their deployment. Physical and cultural factors alike retard the development of livestock industries. Apart from religious tabus and the heavy costs of giving up crop-land for fodder production, the establishment and maintenance of good pastures is a matter of the greatest difficulty in a hot and humid environment; moreover, legumes, which have so materially improved the productivity of pastures in temperate latitude farming, have little of their usual beneficial effect in the humid tropics. Few tropical legumes have root nodules with large concentrations of nitrifying bacteria, and some introductions such as the touch-sensitive *Mimosa pudica* have become major nuisances. Guinea grass (*Panicum maximum*) has proved successful in research stations, but its maintenance is expensive and its use is confined to a few exotic developments.[15] On sandy soils the legume *Stylosanthus gracilis* (Townsville, or Tropical, lucerne) has proved a very satisfactory feed, and as its cultivation can be combined with coconut growing it may ultimately become more popular. Other useful fodders are *kudzu* (*Pueraria javanica*) and *alabang* (*Pollinia fulva*). But all of these fodders cannot stand over-grazing, so that it

[14] *Koentjaraningrat (ed.),* Villages in Indonesia, *Cornell University Press, Ithaca, 1966, p. 259.*

[15] *Guinea grass pastures are grazed by the dairy herd of a European company producing costly but high-quality liquid milk for the expatriate Singapore market.*

Everyday scene throughout lowland Southeast Asia. The essential task of bathing the buffaloes at the end of the day's work is invariably left to children.

is not possible to allow animals to forage for themselves, and hand cutting is necessary. Nevertheless, all livestock owners are in any case obliged to cut and carry fodder from odd patches of land too distant or too inaccessible for animals to graze directly. Roadsides, railway embankments, irrigation channels (though the grazing of these by animals is usually illegal), other patches of waste and the stubble after the rice harvest all provide some grazing, but the principal fodder is in fact *Imperata*, which when young can be eaten by most bovoids. For this reason periodic burning to produce flush growth is practised throughout Southeast Asia, an operation which has been noted as strongly retarding the regeneration of forest.

As few farmers have any deep experience of livestock, little care is taken of animals, which in large measure have to fend for themselves. All the great ricebowls, in fact, have continually to import animals from other areas to maintain the cycle of rice production, for the working life of an animal is short. Some districts, notably the Khorat plateau where buffaloes and cattle are bred for sale to the Mae Nam plain, the island of Sumba whose sturdy small horses are still much used for transport in Java, and parts of Cambodia, have tended to specialize on livestock breeding, but the general lack of interest in livestock is evidenced by the fact that it was not until 1960, and largely through an expansion of numbers in Thailand, that the region regained the level of buffalo numbers it possessed at the outbreak of World War II, and in some countries the prewar buffalo herd had not been regained even by 1965. Smaller livestock such as pigs and poultry which can largely be left to forage for themselves and can make use of the poorest land, and which reproduce easily and quickly, lend themselves well to sawah agriculture. Nevertheless, their productivity under such conditions is very low, the output of eggs per hen being less than half that achieved in Western Europe. Little or no control is exercised over breeding, and losses through easily preventable diseases are severe. Some idea of the enormous increase in productivity possible may be gathered from the experience of Singapore, not usually considered a place of any great agricultural significance; through the introduction of some of the new methods of breeding and feeding that have transformed the poultry industry in advanced economies, and a rigorous policy of vaccination against Ranikhet disease, by 1963 Singapore had pushed up the level of poultry numbers to over 20 million, not far short of that of the Federation of Malaya at the time, and had developed a substantial export trade in eggs to the mainland. Broadly similar techniques had also proved extremely successful in pig production. It is true that modern techniques of low-cost livestock production are best suited to units of large size, but there is no question that even backyard farmers can achieve major increases in their livestock output.

Sawah agriculture has also been involved in export-oriented cash crop production, most notably in Java, where European and Chinese companies rented village rice-land for the production of sugar, tobacco and even for rice. But it is insufficiently appreciated that in some parts of the region sawah agriculture itself is considerably commercialized, even if the majority of rice farmers are subsistence farmers in that they sell less than half of their total output. In the three great deltas of the Mae Nam, Mekong and Irrawaddy, a well-organized procurement and marketing system gathers rice in comparatively small lots from a very large number of small farmers, and mills and markets the produce for sale on the domestic market and overseas. Traditionally this trade has been largely in the hands of aliens and especially the Chinese, although in Burma large numbers of Indian merchants were also involved. In most countries however, since 1945 state marketing boards working in conjunction with state-assisted cooperatives have greatly reduced, even if they have not entirely eliminated, the role of the middleman. Nor is it correct to regard sawah agriculture universally as a 'veritable human ant-hill', as Gourou described the agricultural economy of the Tonkin delta.[16] There are wide variations in labour inputs in padi production in Southeast Asia, and in fact, sawah agriculture cannot provide regular and continuous employment for all those many millions dependent on it; few rice farmers work more than 150 days in the year. A defective agrarian structure, moreover, is not unique to sawah agriculture, and further consideration of this issue is deferred until other major systems of land use have been reviewed.

[16] *Pierre Gourou*, Land Utilization in French Indochina, *Institute of Pacific Relations, New York, 1945, p. 250. (Originally published as* L'Utilisation du Sol en Indochine Française, *Presses Universitaires de France, Paris, 1940.)*

The rice economy of Southeast Asia The rice situation of each particular country is discussed in the national surveys of Parts II and III but a brief review of the regional rice situation appears appropriate here. The high proportion of the total cultivated area under rice is, unquestionably, the most remarkable feature of the agriculture of Southeast Asia; for the region as a whole the proportion is slightly in excess of 50 per cent, a higher proportion than that of the world's two leading rice producers, China (about 35 per cent) and India (some 25 per cent). Only in two countries, Indonesia and Malaysia, does the percentage of the cultivated land under padi fall appreciably below half, and even in the former, padi occupies nearly half the total cultivated area of Java and Madura, although this proportion is fast falling (*Figure 2-2*). It is only in Malaysia that rice is not the principal crop, and despite its political importance to the Malays in that multiracial country, it is unlikely ever to become so. The unique position of rice in the economy of Southeast Asia is abundant testimony to the value placed on the crop by local cultures; rice is the preferred food even of peoples who can find little place for it in their own agriculture.

Over the space of some three decades since the outbreak of World War II, Southeast Asia has expanded its rice output by some 75 per cent (*Figure 2-3*), but population grew by an almost equivalent amount, so that despite a substantial reduction in the volume of rice exports, per capita consumption has almost everywhere stagnated or declined. In sharply increasing their per capita consumption, Thailand and Burma, traditionally the two great rice-surplus countries of Asia, are thus highly anomalous. For several years after the war rice yields remained virtually stationary, but in the later Fifties investment in national development plans in the form of improved water-control, fertilizer plants, fertilizer-distribution schemes, improved seeds and even in some mechanization of agriculture, slowly produced dividends, and yields augmented perceptibly (*Table 2-3*). Significantly, yields are highest in West Malaysia, where physical conditions appear far from optimum for rice cultivation; this is the result of a major government effort in investment in rural development, particularly in irrigation, improved varieties and fertilizer application, supported by effective extension services. Then follow the two Vietnams, which have inherited much of the Chinese technology of maintaining soil fertility, and Indonesia, Thailand and Burma. Yields are lowest in the Philippines, Cambodia, Laos and Sarawak, a reflection of the absence in these countries of extensive irrigation facilities and a high degree of dependence on natural rainfall, although in Sarawak rice cultivation is scarcely of any real significance at present. The low level of the Philippines is particularly disturbing, but Laos and Cambodia, with their large untapped water resources, have the potential for large gains in yields.

Such national figures, of course, obscure wide regional variations in yields within them; the best-performing rice area of West Malaysia on the Selangor coast achieves a yield between two and three times the national average, and the

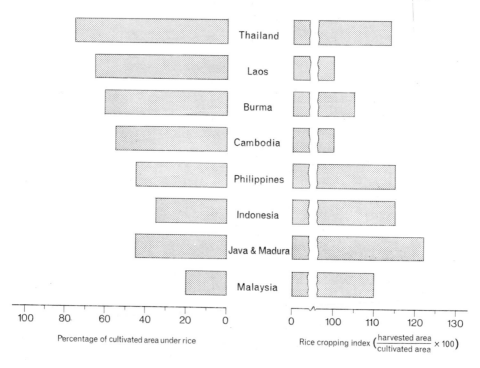

100 80 60 40 20 0   0 100 110 120 130

Percentage of cultivated area under rice   Rice cropping index $\left(\dfrac{\text{harvested area}}{\text{cultivated area}} \times 100\right)$

Fig 2-2   Percentage of cultivated area occupied by rice, and rice cropping index, average for late 1950's

Under the pressure of growing population food production is being pushed into progressively less favourable areas, and the share of the total cultivated area occupied by rice trends slowly downwards; government schemes of crop diversification, as in Thailand, exert a similar effect. The rice cropping index, on the other hand, is slowly increasing as a result of improvements and extensions of irrigation systems in national development plans.

best sawahs in Java yield over four times the average for the island. In Thailand, rice yields are substantially higher in the north and in the east coast of the peninsula than they are in the Mae Nam plain. If the general level of yields in each country could be brought up to those of their best-performing areas, the region's pressing food and agricultural problems would be virtually solved, but there is little prospect that such an increase in efficiency will ever prove possible. Over many millions of acres wide variations in yield are inevitable. Yet on a planted area only marginally greater than that of the Philippines, Japan achieves an average yield more than twice that of West Malaysia, thus giving the country a larger rice output than Indonesia, and almost equivalent to that of Burma and Thailand combined.

These facts might appear to indicate an enormous potential for improved

Table 2-3 *Southeast Asia: area, yield and production of padi, 1952–56 and 1961–65*

	AREA		YIELD		PRODUCTION		Contribution of yield
	1952–56 Average	1961–65 Average	1952–56 Average	1961–65 Average	1952–56 Average	1961–65 Average	to increased production
	thousand hectares		*kilograms/hectares*		*thousand metric tons*		*per cent*
Burma	3,990	4,750	1,500	1,640	5,980	7,780	37
Cambodia	1,720	2,280	970	1,080	1,660	2,460	31
Indonesia	6,490	7,040	1,700	1,800	11,070	12,640	44
Laos	530	730	930	830	490	610	—
West Malaysia	280	330	1,970	2,540	550	840	65
Sabah	30	35	1,670	2,290	50	80	72
Sarawak	80	110	1,060	950	90	105	—
Philippines	2,690	3,150	1,200	1,260	3,230	3,960	26
Thailand	5,340	6,200	1,360	1,510	7,240	9,370	43
South Vietnam	2,290	2,670	1,280	1,880	2,940	5,030	77
North Vietnam	2,120	2,340	1,610	1,930	3,420	4,520	68
Southeast Asia	**25,560**	**29,640**	**1,440**	**1,600**	**36,720**	**47,400**	**44**

Source: Calculated from F A O, *Production Yearbook*, 1966. Figures have been rounded

efficiency in rice production, but this is not the case; while there is undoubtedly still scope for major improvements in yields, it is beginning to appear that Southeast Asia does in fact make reasonably good use of the resources available to it in rice production. Physical and biological factors make the attainment of Japanese rice yields over much of Southeast Asia quite impossible. In a reassessment of the agricultural potential of the humid tropics, Chang points out that the attenuated solar radiation, persistently high night temperatures, lack of seasonality and high rainfall all combine severely to limit potential photosynthesis, and that the attainment of the potential yield prescribed by the thermal and radiative regime is greatly retarded by such factors as the intense leaching and oxidation of the soil, the absence of nitrogen-fixing legumes, the scarcity and high cost of fertilizers, the problems of weeds and the wide prevalence of pests and diseases. Chang is of the opinion that rice yields in the humid tropics could be raised from the present average of about 1,570 kg per hectare to about 2,000 kg per hectare through economically practical improvements, but that further increases will prove very difficult unless new varieties with greatly improved photosynthetic capacities, better dry-matter distribution within the plant and other desirable genetical features can be introduced.[17] Such fundamental biological advances appear unlikely. It is true that Chang's study relates to constantly moist tropical climates

[17] *Jen Hu Chang, 'The agricultural potential of the humid tropics'*, Geographical Review, *vol. 58, 1968, p. 351.*

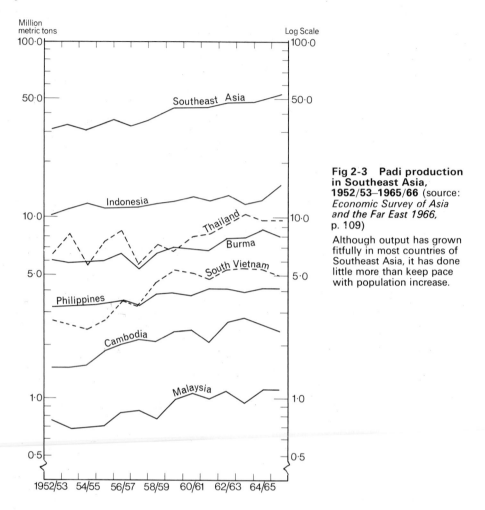

Fig 2-3 Padi production in Southeast Asia, 1952/53–1965/66 (source: *Economic Survey of Asia and the Far East 1966,* p. 109)

Although output has grown fitfully in most countries of Southeast Asia, it has done little more than keep pace with population increase.

(Koeppen Af type) and that agricultural conditions are somewhat more favourable in tropical monsoon and wet-and-dry climates (Koeppen Am and Aw types);
but a large part of Southeast Asia experiences constantly humid climatic conditions, or what is its equivalent, constantly moist soil conditions. Significantly,
rice yields are already highest in the more equatorial portions of Southeast Asia,
which may therefore have comparatively little potential for further increase in
the productivity of the soil. It is against much sobering considerations that the
extravagant claims being made for such introductions as the Philippine 'miracle'
rice IR-8, must be judged.

The real test of economic efficiency, output per worker or per man-day,
tells a very different story (*Table 2-4*). Although the quality of the soil, the use of

fertilizers or manure, and the varieties grown all affect the issue, productivity per farm worker is in large measure a reflection of the amount of land and capital at his disposal; diminutive holdings, a shortage of work animals and crude cultivating equipment are invariably associated with a low return to the worker. Thus North Vietnam, despite its relatively high rice yield, is unspeakably wretched; as Dumont says, 'unproductive techniques, less efficient than those of an African economy, are everywhere forced on the peasant by poverty and necessity'. There is little evidence that the Hanoi regime has led to any marked improvement in the peasant's lot.

Table 2-4 *Labour requirements for padi cultivation*

	Number of work days necessary	
	per hectare	*per metric ton*
South Vietnam		
Single transplanting	70	33·2
Double transplanting	75	34·0
Floating rice	77	40·5
North Vietnam		
Double-cropped fields,		
Dry season 5th month (June)	255	134·0
Wet season 10th month (Nov.)	177	84·6
Philippines		
Single-crop fields	52·8	28·7
Double-cropped fields,		
Dry season	54·3	28·7
Wet season	57·8	27·8
Japan		
Animal plough team	63	14·9
Hand tractor ploughing	27·4	6·5
United States		
Fully mechanized	5·0	1·2

Note—The above are selected samples only, and refer to varying dates. They must not be considered as national averages.
Source: A. Angladette, *Le Riz*, p. 748

Few studies have been made of input and output on the farms of Southeast Asia and to use such studies as a basis for generalization is distinctly hazardous; nevertheless, they are better than nothing. In Tonkin, where before 1939 some 40 per cent of all holdings were less than 0·8 hectares and where there was one draft animal for every 2·5 hectares, it took some eleven days' labour for a farm distinctly larger than average to produce 100 kg of rice, while on a 0·8 hectares farm more than twenty days were needed, a return inferior to that obtained by swidden farmers in many parts of Africa, and almost certainly well below that obtained by the neighbouring hill people on their *rai* clearings in the Annamite

Rice harvesting with the *ani-ani* (repeating knife). This laborious
method is encountered in many parts of Indonesia and the Malayan
peninsula, and is practised in order not to offend the rice spirit.

chain.[18] At the other extreme, in the central portion of the Mae Nam plain of Thailand, where the mean of farm size is more than 4 hectares and where most farms possess not only two buffaloes of the largest and strongest breed in Southeast Asia but also two oxen in addition, it appears to require only four days' labour to produce 100 kg of padi.[19] In the more favourable parts of the Mekong delta, real labour costs in rice production appear to be almost the same as those in central Thailand.[20] Between these two limits the other countries can be arranged, Burma and possibly Cambodia towards the more efficient extremity with Thailand; Java towards the lower; the Indonesian Outer Islands, Malaysia, the Philippines and South Vietnam somewhere in the centre. Certainly Thailand and Burma are the lowest-cost producers in the region; costs in Malaysia are almost twice as high, despite a national average yield not far short of double that of Thailand. The high costs of rice production in Malaysia reflect the alternative occupations in the country, all of which offer a larger reward to labour than padi cultivation. This observation, of course, applies *a fortiori* to Japan, which despite its high yields and high productivity per worker, is also a high-cost producer.

The rice economy of Southeast Asia from the standpoint of the return to the worker thus appears a singularly inefficient one. This may perhaps be best appreciated through a comparison with the United States, where almost two million acres, almost twice the rice area of Malaysia, are under rice. To produce 100 kg of rice in Louisiana requires merely 2·2 man-hours, and in California only 1·6 man-hours. An increase in the productivity of the rural worker is essential if Southeast Asia is to advance towards self-sustained economic growth.

With an annual rate of increase in demand that has exceeded the rate of growth of rice production, rice exports from the region have had to be sharply reduced from the prewar level to prevent a major decline in per capita consumption. Thus with the advent of new competitors in the international rice trade, Southeast Asia, traditionally the world's leading rice surplus area, has seen its share of world rice exports fall substantially (*Table 2-5*). However, this decline also owes much to balance-of-payments problems resulting from national development plans in traditional importers, and to the competition from surplus American wheat and other grains under the concessional terms of Public Law 480. Significantly also, there has been a marked shift in the destination of the region's rice exports. Before 1914 the rice trade looked mainly to Europe and to more distant markets, but in the interwar period, Asia, particularly the Indian region, came to be of greatest importance. Since 1945, however, Southeast Asia itself has become an increasingly large importer, and by 1962 had come to account

[18] *René Dumont*, Types of Rural Economy, *Methuen, London, 1957, pp. 138–40.*

[19] *K. O. Janlekha*, A Study of the Economy of a Rice Growing Village in Central Thailand, *Dissertation Series No. 15, University Microfilms, Inc., Ann Arbor and London, 1958, p. 246.*

[20] *James B. Hendry*, The Small World of Khanh Hau, *Aldine Publishing Co., Chicago, 1964, p. 87.*

Table 2-5 *Southeast Asia: rice exports and imports,
1934–38, 1952–56, 1961–63 and 1965*

	Average 1934–38	Average 1952–56	Average 1961–63	1965
INDIGENOUS EXPORTS *(thousand metric tons)*				
Burma	3,070	1,440	1,660	1,360
Thailand	1,390	1,280	1,420	1,850
South Vietnam ⎱			190	—
North Vietnam ⎬	1,320	170	10	10
Cambodia ⎰			240	470
Total, Southeast Asia	**5,780**	**2,890**	**3,520**	**3,690**
Percentage of world total	*68*	*53*	*56*	*50*
RETAINED IMPORTS *(thousand metric tons)*				
Indonesia	260	450	1,070	200
Malaysia ⎱	540	320	330	260
Singapore ⎰		130	180	190
Philippines	30	40	150	570
South Vietnam	—	10	20	240
Total, Southeast Asia	**830**	**950**	**1,750**	**1,460**
Percentage of world total	*10*	*19*	*29*	*20*

Source: FAO, *Rice Bulletin,* August 1966

for a quarter of total world rice imports. On the face of it, there appears to be some substance in the arguments frequently advanced in Malaysia, traditionally the largest rice importer in the region (although this position has been held by Indonesia since 1960), that reliance on a continuing surplus in neighbouring countries is potentially dangerous; by 1980 or even earlier, there could very well be no overall rice surplus at all. Nevertheless, the maintenance of a high volume of rice exports is fundamental to the economic development of most mainland states, particularly Burma, which has yet to regain its prewar rice area, an achievement that successive economic consultants have declared a *sine qua non*.

Plantation crop agriculture

Although in Southeast Asia the cultivation of crops largely or exclusively for export is usually associated with European enterprise, such crops were being grown for the European market long before Europeans themselves became directly involved in production. Moreover, early European planters were no more successful than other cultivators. Success came late, and in several lines of production such as coconuts, coffee and natural rubber, indigenous farmers or small-holders continue to provide a large proportion of total output.

At first European traders merely made use of local institutions as they found them, working with local rulers or sultans for the supply of the products they needed. Shortage of supply was seldom a problem; indeed, it was frequently difficult to find markets for all the pepper that native growers could offer, and at several times in the seventeenth century there was a marked oversupply of this commodity. But difficulties did arise when Europeans requested the production of crops not indigenous to the region, or that demanded much heavier inputs than pepper, which fitted well into the swidden system. The establishment of political control enabled the system of supply by native growers to be stabilized, and in Java the Culture System (1830–70) solved the problem of producing exportable annual and herbaceous perennial crops such as sugar, indigo and cotton, by attaching their production to sawah land; indeed, rice itself was an exportable crop and in the seventeenth century Java was an important exporter. Under this system the cultivation of exportable crops for delivery to the state was enforced on the peasant in exchange for remission of taxes; while it may have arisen in part through the inability of Dutch private enterprise to exploit Java's resources, through its use of compulsory labour a broad infrastructure was created which provided the foundations for the successful deployment of private capital in the so-called Liberal period after 1870.[21]

Some European-introduced perennials such as coffee, and much later *Hevea* rubber, did however prove suitable for incorporation in swiddens; these crops could be planted towards the end of the productive life of the swidden and thereafter left to fend for themselves. Their planting involved virtually no capital cost, and on reaching maturity the trees continued to provide an income for several years with little further labour input. This development, however, was clearly dependent on the availability of transport, so that it was effectively confined to the margins of navigable rivers at no great distance from the coast. But with the improvements in transport facilities in the present century, and particularly the construction of roads (much of which was in connection with the development of mining enterprises and the expansion of capital-intensive estate agriculture), rapid expansion of smallholder production became possible. In Sumatra the swidden cultivator tended to become a smallholder, and food production was often relegated to a subsidiary role. The cultivation of perennials, particularly rubber, by smallholders, many of whom had no previous experience of food production, also occurred in the Malayan peninsula and Borneo. This creation of a very large area of commercial crops with peasant part-time and spare-time labour represents a feat of autochthonous capital accumulation so far unmatched by any modern 'up by the bootstraps' scheme of economic growth.

Outside Java, particularly in the islands to the east of Sumatra and in Malaya —in short, wherever it was possible to obtain access to one of the main nineteenth-century entrepots, Penang or Singapore, the Chinese created a very profitable

[21] *Geertz*, op. cit. p. 63.

niche, first in acquiring produce from indigenous farmers for sale to Europeans, and later, as the market continued to expand, in engaging in production themselves. Indeed, but for the heavy disabilities repeatedly imposed upon them, the Chinese could have continued to perform a like function in Java itself; they were active in sugar production in the vicinity of Batavia in the seventeenth century, and in the eighteenth had begun, in effect, to rent land for rice and sugar production from the rulers of what were later to become the Native States (*Vorstenlanden*, or Principalities) of Central Java. The cultivation of quickly maturing herbaceous perennials lent itself admirably to speculative exploitation perfectly attuned to Chinese cultural characteristics. The Chinese in Southeast Asia had, and still have, neither the peasant's traditional attachment to the land, nor indeed, the European concept of land ownership as a source of prestige and power. For them the land was a resource to be used as long as it was profitable to do so, and to be abandoned as soon as it was not; they were interested in quick returns, and hence in quickly maturing crops with simple processing requirements. Their social organization enabled them to overcome the problems of land, labour and capital, and in effect, gave to Chinese agricultural enterprise some of the characteristics of the corporation, the device that finally enabled Europeans to reach a dominant position in plantation crop production.

Basic to Chinese agricultural enterprise were the social institutions giving it cohesion, the clan, *kongsi*, and above all, the secret society. These provided the capital for financing the acquisition of land from native rulers, organized the import of immigrant *sinkhek* labour from China for the work of cultivation, kept the labourers supplied with provisions including the indispensable opium, and marketed the produce. All the participants were rewarded with a share of the profits if any (thus anticipating a system of estate wages linked to the current price of the commodity produced by the estate), less expenses incurred on their behalf, which in the case of the labourers who were debited with the cost of their provisions and opium, were very substantial. But inevitably the lion's share of the profits went to the merchants of Singapore or Malacca (now Melaka) who in effect provided the entrepreneurial functions, and to the semi-feudal headmen or *kangchus* who performed the managerial functions.

The crops particularly associated with such Chinese enterprise were pepper, gambier, tapioca and sugar, although the last required rather special conditions of soil and climate. It was, in effect, a system of shifting agriculture on a grand scale. From the local ruler or chief, or in the case of Malacca from the British administration, the group would obtain access to a large area of land adjacent to a river, which provided the means of transporting produce in and out. Such concessions for pepper and gambier production were known in Johor as *kangkars*. Only part of the land would be planted, for the timber of the uncultivated land was essential for processing the crops. Pepper and gambier were planted simultaneously, usually in the ratio of one acre of pepper to ten of gambier; the gambier provided a cash return before the pepper came to maturity and the boiled gambier leaves were used as a fertilizer for the pepper vines. This system also ensured a more uniform deployment of labour throughout the year, but as soon as yields declined the land was abandoned, and cultivation moved to another block of the kangkar. The end result of such an ephemeral system was, of course, the replacement of high forest by a *lalang* waste, and eventually such apparently wasteful and speculative methods were heavily frowned upon by the British administration. But in a very scantily populated area of apparently limitless forest it was nevertheless a sensible method of land use whose long-term effects were undoubtedly strongly developmental. It helped to provide the capital for later Chinese investment in mining and estate enterprise, it assisted the immigration of large numbers of thrifty and hard-working Chinese to whom Malaysia undoubtedly owes a very large part of its present relative prosperity, and though on a smaller scale, it played its part with tin-mining in creating a restless frontier type of society in which innovation was encouraged. All of this contrasts strongly with the social and economic ossification of Java under the Culture System, which, with but perhaps the minor difference that it was operated on behalf of private interests in place of the state, in effect continued into the so-called Liberal and Ethical periods, and indeed, into the life of the Indonesian Republic itself.

In contrast, direct European attempts at export-crop production for long failed to equal the success of Chinese enterprise. Europeans were greatly handicapped by their lack of knowledge of tropical soils, the processes of plant growth, their ignorance of insect, fungoid and virus pests and their insistence on the traditional European practices of deep ploughing, wide planting and clean weeding as the essence of good husbandry. No more effective way of damaging or destroying the soil could be imagined; but they were at least as hamstrung by psychological attitudes also inherited from Europe. The planter looked upon the land in the manner of the typical country gentleman as a physical asset giving prestige and power, and destined to be handed on to his heir with the original properties of the soil intact; it could never be abandoned in the speculative cavalier fashion of the Chinese shifting cultivators. Only gradually did it become apparent that the land itself had no value whatsoever apart from that of 'the permanently exportable products derivable from the durable plants and trees actually growing upon it. Divest the land of this permanency in its products, and the capital is lost.'[22]

Unfortunately, European methods of cultivation often made 'permanency' out of the question. Nor were the planters ever able to match Chinese enterprise in supplying the other factors necessary for production; perpetually short of capital and seldom able to obtain or maintain an adequate labour supply, the

[22] Singapore Free Press, *November 25th, 1841; quoted by James C. Jackson in* Planters and Speculators, *University of Malaya Press, Kuala Lumpur, 1968, p. 118.*

early European planters struggled along with a succession of crops—pepper, cloves, nutmeg, cinammon, tea, tobacco, indigo, sugar and coffee—scraping by in times of high prices and selling out to some credulous or optimistic buyer in the inevitable ensuing slumps. This was the pattern in the Malayan peninsula; in Java, however, the forced labour of the Culture System proved so successful with coffee cultivation on previously unoccupied hill-lands, or *Woestegronden*,[23] that eighteenth- and early nineteenth-century attempts at establishing a European estate industry were never really consolidated, and coffee cultivation still remains almost exclusively a smallholder industry.

The decisive factor in the rise of European enterprise to a dominant position in export-crop production was the intervention of that extraordinarily flexible, permanent, impersonal yet supremely competent institution, the corporation or joint-stock company. Initially the corporation was not an agricultural innovator, and moved into agricultural enterprise, typically from trading or financial activities, only when a few private planters had already clearly demonstrated the possibility of profitable production. Some of the latter were even able to float their own companies, and in this way one of the most famous of all estate companies, the Deli Maatschappij, grew from the pioneer venture of Jacob Nienhuys in tobacco planting in east Sumatra in the Sixties of the last century. The political environment, moreover, was increasingly favourable. Towards the end of the century, the British administration in Malaya finally decided on a policy of providing positive encouragement to the establishment of permanent, large-scale European agricultural enterprise as a major instrument of economic development, and although in what was to become the Netherlands Indies the early planting companies had been able to get better terms from the then independent rulers of east Sumatra than from Batavia, after 1870 conditions became increasingly congenial for the establishment of corporate agricultural enterprise. After the turn of the century the Netherlands Indies administration was in many ways even more generous to such enterprise than that of Malaya; it did not levy export taxes, nor did it discriminate between Dutch and non-Dutch capital.

Thus all the difficulties confronting the pioneer European planters were at last resolved. A benevolent government provided land on extremely favourable terms, encouraged agricultural research and, in part, financed it from public funds, and in Malaya even provided loans to planters. Through their ability to tap the resources of the world's major money markets, the joint-stock companies could withstand the lengthy years of gestation inseparable from tree-crop production, and were not entirely dependent, as were the early planters, on the earnings of catch-crops to cover their heavy overheads; they could also more easily meet the expense of installing costly processing machinery in the search

[23] *These lands, though uncultivated, had been used from time immemorial by villagers for a variety of purposes, and in claiming them as state lands the government inflicted a material hardship on the rural population.*

for greater efficiency. Finally, the perpetual labour shortage was resolved through government regulations and control of immigrant labour recruitment from abroad, or, as in the case of the Netherlands Indies and French Indochina, by the organized recruiting of labour from congested parts of the domestic territory. The state in return required the estate companies to comply with regulations regarding the conditions of employment, and the provision of housing and of other social services for their workers. The charge that the planting companies were able to force governments to do their bidding cannot be substantiated in either Malaya or in the directly administered parts of the Netherlands Indies. Nevertheless, the planters of east Sumatra who had obtained their concessions before the establishment of a Dutch administration, used the legal weapon of the sanctity of their contracts with the native rulers to thwart many of Batavia's plans for the protection of estate workers and of the indigenous population. In the sugar districts of Java also, and particularly in the *Vorstenlanden*, the planting companies found numerous ways of defeating regulations aimed at protecting the rights of the peasant, or *tani*.

Although capital from the administering power predominated in each dependent territory, the huge profits made in estate operations during the great rubber boom of 1908–12 attracted capital from many sources. Heavy British investment was made in the Netherlands Indies as well as in Malaya; American investment, however, on the whole preferred the Netherlands Indies to Malaya, a decision which with the advantage of hindsight was clearly wrong. Franco-Belgian capital moved into Malaya before venturing into estate production in Indochina. Danish, Swiss, Swedish and Italian capital also participated in the formation of estate companies, as did that from Hong Kong, Shanghai and Japan. The concentration of estate interest in the continuously humid or equatorial portion of the region is striking, the only important industries in areas with a pronounced dry season being the production of sugar and tobacco on rented sawah land in Java, and the sugar industry of Negros and Luzon in the Philippines.

In large part this concentration reflects the requirements of *Hevea* rubber, by far the most successful of all estate crops so far. Rubber can stand even a pronounced dry season, although at such times the yield is so low that it may not be worth tapping; but the year-round harvesting possible with perennials in areas with no dry season greatly facilitates an even deployment of labour and equipment throughout the year, materially reducing overheads. Apart from rubber, other crops permitting continuous harvesting are oil palm, now experiencing a mild boom in Malaysia, and at elevations above 3,000 feet, tea. Year-round picking and low labour costs gave to the prewar Javan tea industry the world's lowest costs of production. It is striking that arborescent or herbaceous perennials with markedly seasonal yields have in large part tended to remain a smallholder preserve, and this is increasingly true of sugar and tobacco, in which there has been a large estate interest.

Nevertheless, certain parts of equatorial Southeast Asia were unattractive for estate industries; in both Thailand and the Philippines political difficulties stood squarely in the way. Anxious to preserve its independence in a period of colonial expansion, the Thai government was unwilling to allow large numbers of foreigners to insinuate themselves either in a labouring or technical capacity into the country and its economy; moreover, the traditional difficulties facing estate enterprise, such as the lack of transport and labour shortages, also directed European interest away from Thailand towards the dependent territories. A German group did obtain a concession in the Chanthaburi district of southeast Thailand in 1908, but the venture never prospered. It was not until the rubber-restriction schemes of the Twenties that Thailand began to acquire a substantial stake in the natural rubber industry, and then largely through plantings in the peninsula by smallholders of Chinese or mixed Chinese-Thai ancestry. In the Philippines, large estates existed in the Spanish period, but they were typically collections of tenancies, and although American capital became interested in the sugar industry, the Philippines had to compete with Hawaii, Cuba and Puerto Rico for such investment. American capital was very willing to invest in an estate rubber industry in Mindanao where physical conditions were very suitable, but Filipino nationalists persuaded the new American administration that the injection of large quantities of capital into an isolated part of the country would cause acute social strains, and delay the integration of its predominantly Muslim population into the Philippine nation.

Moreover, although in the Philippines, as elsewhere in Southeast Asia, the services provided by Chinese have in the long run proved indispensable, Chinese immigration has long been severely restricted and the Chinese population subject to many disabilities. Thus having failed to obtain an estate rubber industry, the Philippines, unlike Thailand, failed to acquire a smallholder one. Rubber planting did not seriously begin in the Philippines until the Thirties, an effort that must be judged too little and too late. That it was always possible to circumvent the laws aimed at preventing acquisition of land by non-Filipinos and at limiting the size of holdings, is clearly evidenced by the large Japanese-owned and operated estate abacá industry in the Davao area, which from chance beginnings before World War I experienced almost continuous expansion until 1940; nevertheless, the total abacá area remained largely unchanged for almost forty years. Thus, out of respect for nationalist feelings, the Philippines took no part in what has undoubtedly been the most spectacular success story in tropical agriculture in the present century. Burma's relative lack of interest in rubber planting is explicable partly in terms of the less favourable physical environment and the isolation of the part of the country most suited to production, and partly because of administrative inconvenience; until 1937 the country was administratively part of India, and final control rested in far away New Delhi. For British capital, Ceylon and Malaya had much more to offer.

Out of a total of nearly 20 million acres under plantation crops in the region, natural rubber accounts for over half; the area planted to rubber is more than twice as large as that of coconuts, the next most important such crop in terms of area, and one whose local consumption, in contrast to rubber, is very large. This concentration on natural rubber, of which Southeast Asia accounts for over 85 per cent of the world's supply, reflects the extraordinary virtues of the crop for large and small producer alike (*Table 2-6*). As more than half the content of natural rubber latex consists of water, and all but a small fraction of the remainder comprises polymerized unsaturated hydrocarbons produced from elements drawn from the air, the rubber tree, *Hevea brasiliensis*, makes minimum demands on nutrients and can be grown on a wide variety of soils, even on land abandoned by other crops; it is very successful on undulating land and even does well on flat alluvial land if drainage is satisfactory. It is as economical in its demands on labour as it is on soil; it gives a year-round yield, although when the tree is devoid of leaves during the short 'wintering' period this may fall low enough to make tapping unprofitable, and in a working day of some six to eight hours one tapper can handle about 4 acres on the 'half spiral alternate daily' or other common systems of tapping. If prices are unremunerative tapping can be suspended, and such resting is usually very beneficial to the tree, which responds with a higher

Table 2-6   *Southeast Asia: area and production of natural rubber, 1965*

| | AREA* | | | PRODUCTION |
| | *thousand acres* | | | *thousand tons* |
	Smallholders	Estates	Total	
Malaysia	2,840	1,990	4,830	924
West Malaysia	2,270	1,900	4,170	860
Sarawak	400	10	410	40
Sabah	170	80	250	24
Indonesia	3,220	1,250	4,470	638†
Thailand	760	80	840	213
Cambodia	10	110	120	48
South Vietnam	70	190	260	60
Burma	70	70	140	19
Philippines	—	50	50	6
Total, Southeast Asia	6,960	3,740	10,700	1,892
Percentage of world total	*88*	*80*	*84*	*83*

* Areas are estimated relating mainly to the early Sixties. The figures for Malaysia include Singapore.
† 1964
Source: International Rubber Study Group, *Rubber Statistics Bulletin*, August 1966

yield when tapping is resumed. It can withstand considerable abuse and reproduces quickly and easily; self-sown trees are a cheap substitute for replanting to the smallholder. Finally, its processing is a quick and simple operation requiring very little in the way of equipment, although it is clear that major improvements in methods of processing, packing and storing, which will inevitably involve higher capitalization, are long overdue, and in fact are being forced on the natural rubber industry by competition from synthetic rubber.

Many of these advantages arise from the fact that *Hevea* is a forest tree indigenous to the humid tropics; in planting it in Sumatran ladangs, swidden cultivators were, unknowingly, successfully reproducing its natural habitat. And although they knew little or nothing of the techniques of swidden agriculture, Malayan smallholders, in their desire both to obtain the highest return per acre through close planting and to minimise labour input by substituting periodic slashing of the undergrowth for the clean weeding of contemporary estate-practice, were adopting much sounder techniques than were the European estates. From every standpoint rubber is among the very best crops for the smallholder in the humid tropics, and that this was quickly recognized is evident from the remarkable expansion that took place in Sumatran smallholder plantings between 1908 and 1912 after the removal of restrictions on native planting of perennials. In Malaya also, planting by both Malay and Chinese smallholders grew rapidly after the rubber boom. By 1917 the area under smallholder rubber was as great as that of estate rubber in several districts of western Malaya, and the total smallholder area at this date exceeded 600,000 acres.[24] That further smallholder planting would have occurred in Malaya in the absence of interwar restriction schemes is strongly suggested by the almost explosive growth of such planting during this period in the Netherlands Indies, a development quite unsuspected by the government itself.

Estates and smallholdings   A brief summary of the respective merits and demerits of estates and smallholdings will assist understanding of the analysis of the respective fortunes of these two types of productive unit in the national surveys that follow. It has already been shown that certain crops have always been a prerogative of smallholders, and in the cultivation of these crops little extension of estate interest appears feasible or desirable. In the production of natural rubber, which began as an estate industry, there is little doubt that the view of governments and the planting communities of dependent territories was that the growth of a smallholder industry was to be deplored. In the upsurge of nationalism since World War II, and the greatly expanded interest in the problems and techniques of stimulating economic development, there has, however, been a major reassessment of the role and position of the smallholder; several economists have concluded that on economic and social grounds, smallholder production is greatly to

[24] *Jackson,* op. cit., *p. 258.*

be preferred, a conclusion politically very acceptable to the governments of all newly independent nations. The smallholder, it is claimed, has a higher degree of responsiveness to price stimuli because of his low overheads, cutting production quickly when prices fall, and expanding it when prices rise. His holding is an excellent training ground for the acquisition of managerial skills, which are in short supply in developing countries; his simple processing equipment makes very limited demands on capital, and his expenses exert a considerable multiplier effect in the economy. Moreover, an 'economy based on peasant farming gives greater economic and social stability to the country during a major depression because the farmers can always turn from growing cash crops to growing food crops.'[25] Possibly; but there is little hope either in such an economy for any sustained economic growth, for as Geertz says, such 'maximization of adaptability is a spiritless goal, elasticity perpetuated becomes flaccidity ... if smallholder rubber (or any other commercial crop) is to be a leading sector in take-off, it will have to be pursued with a fullness of commitment—and an acceptance of attendant risk—which will make its sustained development possible.'[26]

In sum, the case for the smallholder has been overstated. The estate is often inflexible, it makes large demands on capital, and in the past at least, it has relied overmuch on expensive expatriate staff. Nevertheless, if the more efficient unit is the one which can provide its workers with the higher income, the estate wins easily, a fact which the Malayan Plantation Workers Union has clearly recognized in its agitation for legislation to prevent speculators from acquiring and subdividing estates for sale as smallholdings. Moreover, problems of definition apart,[27] the distinction between smallholdings and estates from the standpoint of the local population, is sometimes not as sharp as is usually supposed. The smallholding is almost always operated as a family venture, and is only one of several lines of activity pursued by members of the family; in parts of West Malaysia, Chinese rubber smallholder families may have several members employed as estate workers, whose estate-derived income is often as large as that from the family holding. As estates increasingly prefer contract to resident labour wherever it is available, such contacts may become more common.

The vital necessity of improving the efficiency of processing and of offering a product of guaranteed technical specification to the buyer, a service which he

---

[25] *Ooi Jin Bee*, Land, People and Economy in Malaya, *Longmans, London, 1963, p. 195.*

[26] *Geertz, op. cit., p. 151.*

[27] *In Malaysia, rubber estates are defined by the Department of Statistics as 'land contiguous or non-contiguous aggregating not less than 100 acres in area, planted with rubber or on which the planting of rubber is permitted, and under a single ownership'. The International Rubber Study Group uses a similar definition in its* Rubber Statistics Bulletin, *except for South Vietnam, where the lower limit for estates is 1,200 acres. But other government departments in Malaysia follow different practices in respect of other crops, and there are ways of disguising what are effectively estates as smallholdings. See also pp. 227–8.*

expects as a matter of course from the synthetic rubber producers, strongly operates against the smallholder. It is possible to organize smallholders in ways that make possible the use of more capital-intensive methods of processing and the realization of economies of scale; cooperation is one such solution, although all too often it has greatly disappointed its advocates. But without the extended use of such new methods, the smallholder sector of the natural rubber industry may be unable in the not distant future to obtain any market for its present very unsophisticated product,[28] and the long slide in rubber prices in the Sixties (*Figure 2-4*), which looks like continuing into the next decade, poses great problems for smallholders. The diminished expectations from rubber and the greater profitability of oil palm on areas of suitable soil, have led the Malaysian government to endeavour to obtain a place for the smallholder in this currently heavily capitalized industry; the 'Pioneer' oil-mills which have achieved some success in Nigeria could, so it has been suggested, assist the development of a smallholder oil palm industry in Malaysia. But it is one thing to up-grade an indigenous traditional industry, and quite another to establish a complex agricultural industry in a country whose population is virtually ignorant of the techniques of cultivation and processing. Above all, a poor smallholder product could well prejudice the market for the high-quality product of the established estate industry, an argument that the pragmatic Malaysian government has apparently accepted.

This is the nub of the matter. The real shortcoming of the estates is not economic at all, for the large well-run enterprise has as little to fear in agriculture as in any other activity if the real test is economic efficiency—it is political. Throughout the developing world the estate is regarded as an alien importation with little basis in or connection with indigenous culture. It has introduced an alien labour force, thus increasing the difficulties of establishing national cohesion. The senior positions in the past have always been reserved for expatriates, and the estates themselves are often only part of vast economic empires whose ramifications extend throughout the economy. All these things have irritated nationalists, most of whom feel that the national resources are being used largely for the enrichment of foreigners. There is often a large irrational content in these arguments, of course, the real motivation of which is usually some kind of socialist philosophy; and they often emanate most strongly from the labour unions, whose members are among the most privileged members of the community, with real incomes far above the national level. Nevertheless such views are strongly held, and in several countries of the Third World independence has been followed by the imposition of heavy disabilities on foreign estates, or even the expropriation of their properties. By 1965 Indonesia had nationalized virtually all the foreign estates; but in Southeast Asia as in other parts of the world, such acts, and the subdivision of estates for smallholdings, have invariably been accompanied by a sharp decline in total output and in the productivity of the worker.

[28] *See p. 254.*

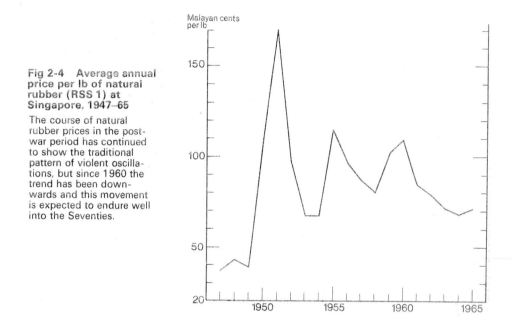

Fig 2-4 Average annual price per lb of natural rubber (RSS 1) at Singapore, 1947–65

The course of natural rubber prices in the post-war period has continued to show the traditional pattern of violent oscilla-tions, but since 1960 the trend has been down-wards and this movement is expected to endure well into the Seventies.

However, it is often overlooked that by no means all estates are owned by foreign capital; the great majority of estates in Malaysia are owned, in fact, by persons who are permanently domiciled in the country, even if they may not all be Federal citizens, although the total area of such Asian-owned estates is sub-stantially less than that of European-owned estates. The small locally-owned estate does not suffer from the political and social disadvantages of the large European estate; moreover, it has some of the economic flexibility of the small-holder, and its efficiency is suggested by the fact that between 1920 and 1960 the Asian-owned share of the estate rubber area in West Malaysia increased from about 20 per cent to a little over 40 per cent. It is partly because of the large local stake in the estate industry, which seems certain to grow in the future, that the political environment in Malaysia has been so much more favourable to large-scale estate enterprise than elsewhere in the region. Moreover, for some time the European companies have been only too anxious to recruit qualified local personnel for senior positions in their organizations.

What the countries of Southeast Asia need, of course, is an agricultural policy in which both kinds of unit can play a part in the national development programme. The large block-planting schemes of the Federal Land Develop-ment Authority in Malaysia have so far, in effect, been operated largely as estates, but they may establish a pattern of enterprise which possesses most of the advan-tages of both estates and smallholdings.

Agrarian structure

Over large parts of Southeast Asia a defective agrarian structure is an enormous
obstacle to the attainment of a higher level of agricultural efficiency, without
which no substantial increase in the general level of economic development is
possible. In large measure the responsibility for this situation rests with the
former colonial administrations, partly through their introduction of European
conceptions of land ownership, and partly through paternalist policies whose
effect was to nullify technological progress; the extra production that resulted
from the latter did not represent a permanent increase in per capita output, but
was swallowed up by population increase. But bygones are bygones, and in most
parts of Southeast Asia, the revolutions which brought national independence
provided no relief to those on the land in direst need; the greatest benefits, as in
so many revolutions, flowed to those who already had most.

Over the greater part of the region at the time of the first European contacts,
the dominant form of agrarian organization was some kind of communal tenure
in which all members of the group had usufructuary rights, and this form of
organization still survives in the areas of swidden cultivation. Claims on the produce of the land, of course, depended on social ranking, but there was no land-
owner in the European sense. Moreover, in Tonkin and the Annamite lands,
which alone in Southeast Asia had a tradition of private ownership of land inherited from China long before European penetration, the size of holdings was
limited by imperial edict, and many villages continued to possess some communal lands. In the Philippines the royal bequests, or *encomiendas*, granted by
the Spanish crown established the typical Latin pattern of large estates farmed
by tenants. Elsewhere, however, the custodians of the communal rights tended
in the new administrations established by Europeans to become *de facto* owners,
and those with usufructuary rights to be reduced to tenants. There is, of course,
nothing inherently wrong with tenancy as a form of agrarian organization, which
in some parts of the world permits a high productivity of both land and worker.
However, this requires that the rights and responsibilities of owners and tenants
are clearly defined by contract, and that the rent is, in fact, the payment made to
the landlord for the maintenance and improvement of the fixed capital of the farm,
the tenant himself enjoying the fruits of his own investment of circulating capital
and labour. Few of these conditions apply in Southeast Asia, where tenancies
are almost always determined by custom and tradition, and are based on a division
of the harvest between owner and tenant. With a rapidly increasing population
the economic position of the owner is enormously strengthened as the rural
population bids against itself for land, and the way is open for the grossest exploitation of tenants.

Landlordism and rack-renting, however, are by no means universal in
Southeast Asia. They have been extremely severe problems in Tonkin and in
parts of the Philippines, particularly Luzon; in other Vietnamese lands, the

Irrawaddy delta, the Mae Nam plain, and in parts of Java and West Malaysia, tenancy problems of varying degrees of severity existed before World War II, and in large measure remain unresolved. But over the greater part of the region, even in Java, Thailand and the Philippines, most farming families still own some land, although the size of the family holding is very small, and in the absence of a law of primogeniture tends progressively to diminish. There is some evidence, however, that this latter tendency has been encouraged by European interpretations of local customary law, and the decline may represent a comparatively recent development; in Java, the mean and modal size of holdings seems to have remained unchanged throughout the nineteenth century.[29]

The administrations of the dependent territories viewed with deep concern the diminution in the size of holdings through subdivision, the gradual growth of a landless class, and the apparently inexorable tendency for rents to rise with increased population. Their remedies included expansion of the sawah area through extended irrigation; 'colonization', in which peasants from congested parts of the country were moved to distant and lightly settled areas where they were provided with holdings large enough to ensure a satisfactory return to the cultivator; restrictions on the mortgaging and sale of land to aliens; fixing maximum levels of rents; and the provision of advice and financial assistance to cooperatives. Many of these essentially 'defensive' regulations, however, could always be circumvented, and some were never seriously enforced. Yet it is doubtful that even the most rigorous implementation could have succeeded; most of these measures, in fact, merely confirmed existing social and cultural immobility, and discouraged changes in the coefficients of production. In Malaya at least, this was clearly recognized, for the 'preservation of the Malay way of life' became a fundamental part of government policy. Large areas of land were frozen in Malay Reservations, whose inhibiting effects are clearly visible in the eastern states of West Malaysia and in the numerous lacunae of poverty in the prosperous western states, where such reservations also cover large areas.

Since 1945 communist-supported insurrections have erupted in most areas of acute social distress, although the example of Malaya shows that communism is by no means always associated with rural discontent. By themselves peasants are incapable of more than sporadic outbursts of protest, but their support is vital to the success of revolutionary movements, and the communists have moved quickly to capture any such movement of protest. Revolutions, of course, are always the product of a select group of dedicated reformers or fanatics, determined to impose their will on the largely indifferent mass of the community. In the initial stages of development, agriculture must support the emerging manufacturing and service industries, and this can scarcely avoid imposing a heavy burden on the peasantry. The problem of containing communism is greatly complicated by the fact that in the cultural environment of Southeast Asia it is

[29] *Geertz*, op. cit., *p. 97*.

impossible to expect social and economic change to come from below; it must be imposed from above, and a determined and enlightened aristocracy or intelligentsia, dedicated to the removal of all obstacles and privileges in the way of economic advancement, is conspicuously lacking in many countries.

It is largely for such reasons that cooperatives, although everywhere regarded both socially and economically as perhaps the best way of improving agricultural efficiency and freeing the farmer from the grip of the middleman, have achieved so little. Middlemen exist because of the demand for their services, and as soon as cooperatives can provide as good a service at lower cost, the middleman will disappear. It is clear that cooperatives generally in the region operate far below such a level of efficiency. Where the will to make such institutions work exists among all members, and particularly where the latter have a high level of education and a knowledge of business and accounting procedures, cooperatives can be very successful. Outside highly developed economies, however, examples of successful cooperatives are rare, and usually owe their fortune to special circumstances. Cooperatives will work in Southeast Asia so long as they are firmly controlled and supervised from above; but once the hand of government is removed —and a cooperative that cannot manage its affairs is not really a cooperative at all—interest among members speedily declines and large losses are all too easily incurred. Frequently also, in joining a cooperative the peasant exchanges exploitation by the middleman for exploitation by the cooperative's officers, and possibly by the state marketing agency with which cooperatives often work.

In some parts of the tropics, cooperatives have been successful in improving the efficiency of the smallholder by operating simple equipment producing a much superior grade of produce to that resulting from the use of traditional methods of processing. But whether crops requiring more elaborate processing can be successfully produced by cooperatives, is problematic. The smallholder cooperative organizations created by the Malaysian government for the production of high-quality palm oil are, in all but name, estates; they have central processing and accounting, and each member will ultimately become a 'shareholder' in the factory. But it has yet to be shown that a multiplicity of smallholders can maintain the discipline necessary to ensure that a continuous supply of fruit of the required degree of ripeness reaches the factory. Smallholder cane production, it is true, is well established in several parts of the world in conjunction with capital-intensive methods of milling, but all too often this lop-sided system of production leads to gross exploitation of the cultivator, who is often merely a tenant on land owned by the mill rather than an independent freeholder; this is the situation in much of the Philippine sugar industry. Indonesia's pitiful attempts to create smallholder-based cane production to supply state owned and operated mills, show all too clearly the dangers of capital-intensive unenterprise in the factory linked with capital-starved production in the fields.

There remains one other solution to the agrarian problem if the countries of Southeast Asia cannot devise an agrarian structure more in keeping with social needs—the solution adopted in North Vietnam. In theory the communist policy of sweeping away a multiplicity of individual rights in tiny parcels of land should facilitate major changes in relative factor inputs; irrigation and drainage investment should be easier if it is no longer necessary to take into account the fact that somebody's land and livelihood are likely to be destroyed. Yet history is eloquent that such a solution is no solution at all; Russian, East European, Chinese, Cuban and North Vietnamese experience all confirm that communist agrarian revolutions do not produce an increase in the productivity of the worker. Peasants will not work for a slogan, not even Chinese peasants. China's food problems were so grave after the 'great leap forward' that in 1961 the peasants received back some land for private cultivation, and through all the travail of the 'cultural revolution' they have clung on to their tiny plots; as is the case also in the USSR, the maintenance of a small private sector in agriculture is likely to be essential for some time to come. North Vietnam's precipitative collectivization resulted in such a decline in food output, and in consequent peasant uprisings, that some retrenchment was mandatory. Unless the communist countries of the Third World can secure a substantial and sustained increase in the productivity of the rural worker, their aspirations for a modern industrialized society are likely to go long unsatisfied. Increasing peasant incentives—which is exactly what Maoists repudiate—or removing the disincentives to peasant production, are likely to prove more effective agents of development in the long run.

The modern face of the great cities and the crowded indigenous quarters and squatter settlements are never far apart. Much of the new construction visible in this view of Djakarta resulted from President Sukarno's determination to provide a fitting capital for *Indonesia Raja* (Greater Indonesia).

Downtown street scene, Cebu City, Philippines.

CHAPTER THREE

Urbanization, industrialization and modernization

The hallmark of an underdeveloped economy is a labour force largely engaged in agriculture and an overwhelmingly rural population. In such a situation a low level of incomes is inevitable; the great bulk of the working population is fully absorbed in the pressing task of producing enough to eat, and the limited land and capital at the disposal of the worker ensures that his effort earns only a minute return. There are always far too many farmers in relation to other factors of production; in Indonesia it has been calculated that nearly one-third of the agricultural work-force is entirely redundant,[1] and some similar proportion probably holds for the agricultural work-force of Southeast Asia as a whole. The disparity between income per head in agriculture and that in non-agricultural occupations is particularly marked, and the transition to a modern economy with a high productivity per worker, and hence with high living standards, involves a massive transference of workers from agriculture to non-agricultural activities, and inevitably a very great increase, both absolutely and relatively, in the population living in towns. As the key to economic development is increasing specialization, the author finds the term diversification, used by many senior officials in less developed countries to describe this development, somewhat anomalous, and the joint process of urbanization and the expansion of non-agricultural activities is here referred to as modernization.

If the problem of modernization facing the countries of Southeast Asia is examined in the light of the economic history of the present highly developed economies, however, it becomes very clear that the process has to be carried out under singularly unpropitious conditions. Agriculture's share of the national labour force within the region varies from about 60 per cent for Malaysia to 85

[1] *Tjan Ping Tjwan, 'Population, unemployment and economic development'*, Ekonomi dan Kueangan Indonesia, *vol. 13, 1960, p. 455.*

per cent for Laos and Cambodia, with a mean around 70 per cent, figures which do not differ much from those of Western Europe or North America in the eighteenth century.[2] But European agriculture never possessed such a large proportion of redundant workers as its present-day Southeast Asian counterpart, partly because of the very much greater importance of animals in European farming, which require attention throughout the year and thus make possible far more effective use of rough topography than is made in Southeast Asia, and partly because rapid population growth in Europe did not really become established until the modernization process was well launched; for centuries new entrants in European agriculture for the most part merely replaced losses through normal wastage. Above all, however, the take-off, or self-sustaining economic expansion of the Industrial Revolution, was firmly based on, and was clearly conditional upon, preceding far-reaching changes in agricultural and commercial techniques, also termed 'revolutions' by an earlier generation of economic historians. The growth of trade and the expansion of towns, the development of banking, in-surance and the joint-stock company, the elimination of fallowing, the beginnings of scientific livestock-breeding and mechanized agriculture, both accelerated capital accumulation and provided profitable opportunities for investment, which were progressively expanded with the application of inanimate energy to manu-facturing and transportation. The expansion of the industrial towns in turn pro-vided large new markets for the products of agriculture, and in turn helped to raise its efficiency still more through the manufacture of mechanical equipment and fertilizers.

In Southeast Asia, on the other hand, the rapid expansion of population, brought about as in Europe by declining death rates, was largely unaccompanied by industrialization and by a more than proportionate increase in the population living in towns; the additional population had to cram itself into the agricultural sector. Moreover, through the competition of Western manufactured products, which became more severe with every improvement in transport, employment in cottage and small-scale industries which often provided a useful contribution to rural income, progressively declined. With the onset of the Great Depression, a much more traumatic experience in Southeast Asia than in either Southern or Far Eastern Asia largely because of the greater significance of world trade in Southeast Asia's economy, and the discharge of labour from Western-owned mines, factories and utilities, urban populations sank to very low levels as dis-placed workers drifted back to the villages. The population living in towns of more than 20,000 people in Java in the early Thirties was only about 8 per cent

[2] *Agriculture, of course, is often carried on in conjunction with other occupations in the Southeast Asian village, and such figures somewhat over-estimate the overall importance of agriculture in the economy. Nevertheless, although many villages contain some non-agricultural specialists, non-agricultural activities are largely part-time occupations, and agriculture always has first claim on the villager, especially at times of heavy labour input such as planting and harvesting.*

of the total population,[3] and for the Netherlands Indies as a whole, about 5 per cent. Even in Malaya, where modernization had proceeded furthest, towns exceeding 10,000 people accounted for only some 18 per cent of the total population.

Since World War II, however, urbanization has proceeded at a very rapid rate, as indeed has been the case in the whole of the underdeveloped world. Over the region as a whole, the rate of growth of the urban population has been more than twice that of total population, and in Malaya and the Philippines, and probably in Indonesia as well, more than three times as fast. Urban populations throughout the region have grown rapidly through a mass influx of in-migrants from rural areas, but probably more rapid still has been the growth resulting from natural increase and city boundary extensions. But although economic motivation has been important in the movement to the cities, it has, nevertheless, been only one factor. The rapid urbanization of Southeast Asia since 1945 is not entirely a modernizing process, for in some ways the present nature and pace of urbanization are operating to retard it.

The origin and growth of urban centres

Prior to the coming of the Europeans, the establishment of any urban centre required a favourable combination of several factors, each of which has been a powerful force promoting urban development in Europe; the indigenous town has had to serve multiple functions as a military and administrative centre, and also to carry on commercial, productive and religious activities.

The accidented, malarious and thickly forested terrain of much of Southeast Asia severely restricted overland communications, and the rivers and the sea provided the main means of cultural and commercial contact. Thus, on suitable sites at estuaries (*kualas*) along the Malacca Straits, local princelings erected fortified settlements and levied tribute on passing vessels or on produce moving downstream (particularly pepper produced by *ladang* cultivators, tin and gold), and from time to time recognized a vague suzerainty of one or other of the ephemeral sea-states that came into being in the region of the Malacca Straits and adjacent parts of archipelagic Southeast Asia. The establishment of broad and durable empires such as appeared in both Southern and Eastern Asia, which made possible and indeed necessitated at least one really large city, encountered much greater obstacles in Southeast Asia; terrain, the diversity of peoples and the resulting high degree of political instability, were all hostile to the existence of the large city, and the small size of the native state and the limited commerce it could control kept urban centres to extremely modest dimensions.

[3] *Primarily of course it is function, not size of population, that makes a town; the Javanese village tends typically to be of large size and may easily contain up to 10,000 people; even much more populous settlements in central Java are often better described as overgrown villages rather than towns.*

It was thus inevitable that the large indigenous city only appeared in the broader river valleys of the mainland and in the more open and accessible parts of Java, where extensive states came to be created with the gradual expansion of sawah irrigation and the piecemeal development of irrigation systems. Upon such an agricultural base a combination of administrative, military, religious and commercial functions of the highest order did produce urban settlements of relatively large size; nevertheless, these proved only as durable as the state that supported them. Entrepreneurial functions, whether in commerce or industry, were of minor significance in the indigenous pre-European city, whose main purpose was to act as a repository of the monuments of the cultural tradition, filling an essentially orthogenetic cultural role.[4]

With the expansion of European control, entrepreneurial forces became progressively more potent in city development, and administrative, military and religious functions became subordinated to commercial ones. New cities were created on considerations that had no validity for the indigenous population, and the form of the new cities revealed their heterogenetic culture as strikingly as did their function. For although the Europeans themselves never amounted to more than a mere handful, they encouraged and assisted the immigration in large numbers of other alien peoples, particularly Chinese, who were willing, as indigenes were not, to labour in mines, estates and utilities, and who also showed an extraordinary aptitude in acting as intermediaries between the Europeans and the local population. As well as working as skilled and unskilled labourers, the Chinese demonstrated remarkable managerial and financial ability in the different environment of Southeast Asia, where the suffocating and oppressive obstacles encountered in the homeland to what W. A. Lewis has called 'the will to economize', did not exist. Having acquired capital by thrift and hard work, the Chinese eagerly sought out speculative employments for it, eventually entering into every conceivable enterprise and often competing successfully with the Europeans themselves.

The magnitude of this immigration is substantial even against the general background of international migration in the period 1815–1914. Between the beginning of the nineteenth century and the Great Depression, some 16 million immigrants entered the small country of Malaya, and the total for the whole of Southeast Asia was probably around twice this figure. Many immigrants died in the region, but of those who survived most returned home, and probably nearly all ultimately intended to do so when the Great Depression and its political aftermath virtually caused all such international comings and goings to cease. Nevertheless, while it is true that Chinese, and indeed a variety of other aliens, had worked or traded in the region (though usually for limited periods at a time) long before the coming of the Europeans, it needs to be emphasized that the

[4] *The term used by R. Redfield and M. B. Singer in ' The cultural role of cities',* Economic Development and Cultural Change, *vol. 3, 1954, pp. 53–73.*

Chinese and the Europeans constituted a symbiosis; it was the opportunities presented by a Western-type administration, the ranks of which numbered very many Chinese employees, and access first to the European and then to the expanding world market, which enabled Chinese enterprise to establish itself and to flourish. Although deployed in a variety of rural occupations, the Chinese have always been largely urban, and are becoming increasingly so as restrictions on occupations in rural areas have been imposed on them by the new independent governments.

Oriented towards the international rather than towards the local economy, the heterogenetic city of the period of European control had a marked peripheral, and usually a coastal, location; many were established on sites where virtually no previous settlement existed. Commercial needs were the primary consideration in selecting city locations, and only later were administrative functions attached to the new centres. In the Malayan peninsula mining also became a powerful urbanizing influence, and determined a pattern of population distribution that in large part still survives. Two of the many Malayan mining towns have attained large size, Ipoh and Kuala Lumpur; both now possess important administrative functions, particularly the latter, but Kuala Lumpur's selection as the headquarters for the Departments serving the states of the Federated Malay States originally depended on its importance as the principal source of government revenue, and it is still the centre of the second most important tin-mining area in Malaya.

Apart from tin-mining, other mining activities have been incapable of producing urban centres of large size, although Palembang, an indigenous city of considerable antiquity and formerly a sea-port, has been greatly expanded by its selection as the administrative centre of the east Sumatran petroleum industry and through the construction of large refinery complexes. The indigenous city on the whole, however, has remained of small size, but two further exceptions are presented by Jogjakarta and Solo (Surakarta) in central Java, both of which have attained large size without losing their essentially orthogenetic character. This development resulted from the chance preservation of these successors to the empire of Mataram as traditional city-states, or *negara*, the *Vorstenlanden* of the Netherlands Indies. Phnom Penh, now capital of the independent state of Cambodia, is a similar example of a large indigenous city owing much to its selection as a major administrative centre by Europeans.

Of the other types of city associated with European enterprise, the railway town, a nineteenth-century creation found both in densely settled Europe and in the newly occupied lands of North America and Australia, had no opportunity to appear in Southeast Asia, where railway construction was primarily undertaken to facilitate the export of mine and estate produce. In the Netherlands Indies, Thailand, and to some extent also in Indochina, strategic considerations were, however, also of importance. Madiun, where the main workshops of the Netherlands Indies railways were located, is perhaps the closest approach to the Western railway town.

Manufacturing industry, the most powerful new factor in city development in the nineteenth century in the Western world, was an even less significant force in urbanization than was the improvement of transport, for European enterprise was virtually confined to those activities that expanded the home economy, especially the production of exportable minerals and agricultural raw materials, and to exploiting the captive colonial market for home manufactures; despite changes in colonial policy as time passed, the native economy and culture was largely left intact. Had the Europeans been real imperialists and prepared, as were some of the great empire-builders of the past, to incorporate inhabitants of new possessions into the fabric of their own industrialized society, the underdeveloped world would today be a very different place—but they were not. Moreover, Southeast Asia proved on the whole deficient of the two most important physical resources promoting the western industrial city, coal and iron ore. Official interest in manufacturing came very late and then largely through the growing menace of Japan, by which time new technologies had appeared to ensure that most new manufacturing activities would tend to be located in the primate cities. Thus until 1941 urban centres were dominated by European and alien élites and, though all cities discharged some administrative functions, the main concern was with service industries; these ministered to the needs of European or Chinese-controlled enterprise, distributed imported manufactures and foodstuffs, and in some instances procured and processed commodities produced by indigenous peasant agriculture. Apart from that based on estate produce or which was tied to its sources of raw materials, such manufacturing as existed was confined to the great port cities.

The cities in large measure continue to show the marked racial zonation of their colonial past. The central business area of large cities is typically European in appearance, but in the small town, Chinese shophouses and public buildings usually constitute the brick or stone core. In close proximity to the central business area is the Chinese quarter or 'Chinatown', generally occupying areas formerly inhabited by Europeans but with improvements in transport abandoned in favour of spacious and decoratively planted suburbs, often laid out on elevations in order to obtain the maximum benefit from air movements. In the cities but scarcely of them, occupying the valley bottoms, city margins and other unattractive locations, are the *kampongs*, *barrios* and squatter camps of the indigenous population, whose inhabitants, with only the slenderest share in the city economy, seldom entirely relinquish a connection with their ancestral villages.

The primate cities and their problems

Some countries possess a very large city which exercises a dominant influence on national life; not only does it contain a very large proportion of the total urban population, but it virtually monopolizes non-agricultural activities and plays a major role in the national culture. It has been claimed that such primate cities, to use the term of Mark Jefferson, are characteristic of newly independent countries at a low level of economic development, whereas countries with highly developed economies and a wide range of industrial activities show a ranking of city population size according to the Pareto or logarithmic normal distribution,

Table 3-1   *Southeast Asia: urbanization*

	Percentage of total population in localities of more than 20,000, 1960	*Percentage of total population in cities exceeding 100,000**	*Index of Primacy†*
Burma	*11·2*	*5·3*	*68·1*
Cambodia	*9·9*	*8·7*	*81·6*
Laos	*10·9*	*6·3*	—
Federation of Malaya	*22·4*	*10·8*	*} 60·8*
Singapore	*63·1*	*63·1*	
Sarawak	*} 16·4*		
North Borneo (Sabah) and Brunei		—	
Philippines	*17·2*	*9·9*	*82·0*
Thailand	*10·5*	*9·9*	*94·2*
North Vietnam	*} 9·4*	*7·1*	*46·7*
South Vietnam		*10·8*	*83·7*

* Figures relate to various years between 1956 and 1961 and are not strictly comparable.

† The population of the largest city expressed as a percentage of the population of the four largest cities.

Sources: United Nations, *Asian Population Conference*, New Delhi, 1963, and *Demographic Yearbook*, 1964; Norton S. Ginsburg, *Atlas of Economic Development*, University of Chicago Press, Chicago, 1961

the so-called rank-size rule.[5] For the world as a whole, it does not seem that the correlation between urban primacy on the one hand, and political status and per capita income on the other, is very marked. A high level of primacy is found in several underdeveloped countries, and appears more common among them than in countries at a higher level of economic development, but several wealthy and long-established nations also show a high degree of primacy, such as Austria, Denmark and France. Nevertheless, with the exception of Indonesia, the countries of Southeast Asia do show a very high degree of urban primacy, Thailand being one of the most extreme examples in the world (*Table 3-1*). Only North Vietnam and scantily populated Cambodia and Laos do not yet possess a 'Million City'. Rangoon attained this status in the early Sixties; Singapore will very shortly

[5] *In which $S_R = S_1/R$, where S_1 is the size of the largest city, R the rank in size of a given city, and S_R the size of a city having rank R. This by no means new observation has become the subject of a large literature in urban geography.*

join Bangkok and Manila in possessing a population of 2 millions, while Djakarta had almost certainly passed the 3 million mark by 1965 (*Figure 3-1a*). All the primate cities are continuing to grow very rapidly, for they are obtaining by far the largest share of in-migrants from the rural areas; although Djakarta's share of the combined population of the four largest cities of Indonesia in the middle Fifties was some 46 per cent, by 1962 its share had been raised to 60 per cent.

In terms of the technologies prevailing at the time, the European founders of the great cities sought control of the best natural approaches by sea and deep water close inshore, but on the shallow Sunda Shelf good natural harbours are scarce and some of the primate cities were located up-river, commanding routes into the interior. With the wider ramifications of the state in the present century, the eccentric location of the great cities produced increasing administrative strains, which became augmented by the pressures of developing nationalist movements. Even Bangkok, an indigenous foundation, shows almost as much eccentricity in independent Thailand, despite the country's southern peninsular tail, as did the capitals of dependent Burma and Indochina which were far removed from the greatest concentrations of population. Bangkok is the focus of the most populous and economically the most important part of the country, but its peripheral location is now clearly a major handicap to the government in maintaining a firm grip on the potentially productive and strategically vital northern and eastern regions, where potential separatist tendencies deriving from cultural and linguistic differences from central Thailand, and aided by an impoverished and stagnating economy, receive powerful support from Peking. Sited at the whim of an indigenous ruler, Bangkok fortuitously proved to possess all the essentials for growth of the European foundations. Though the focus of everything in Thai life and culture, Bangkok's external orientation became just as pronounced as that of any other primate city, and the fact that some 60 per cent of its population was of Chinese origin at the outbreak of World War II testifies to its equally heterogenetic character.

Just as nationalists came to regard the export of primary foodstuffs and raw materials from colonial territories as a 'drain' on the local economy, so the great cities which performed these functions and maintained their respective territories in colonial status were stigmatized as 'parasitic'. Economists since 1945 have been willing, even eager, to concede more to nationalist viewpoints than did their prewar colonial counterparts,[6] and there is something in nationalist charges. But in modern times at least, it is not possible seriously to claim that over an appreciable period any great city has been essentially parasitic. The European-created cities may initially have operated to impoverish the indigenous ruling and merchant classes and to lay heavier burdens on the peasants, but the effects of economic

---

[6] *The fact that many Western economists have obtained important consultant positions with newly independent governments in the postwar period is probably not entirely unconnected with this change of heart.*

growth within the cities themselves and their repercussions on the countryside were such that ultimately these parasitic tendencies were greatly outweighed by new productive ones that did result in an increase in incomes per head.[7] With an increasing urban population a specialized labour force came into being; the demand for food and for export crops increased, which together with improvements in transport did offer new opportunities to indigenous farmers; and the growth of processing industries at ports and the expansion of the production of inanimate energy began to lay the foundations for a higher degree of industrial activity. The charge of parasitism has tended to disappear from nationalists' vocabulary since the achievements of independence, but the indigene's deep distrust of the externally-oriented primate city is still discernible beneath the often acrimonious official relations between Kuala Lumpur (itself a potential primate city and with an alien majority) and Singapore, the largest Chinese city outside China itself.

Table 3-1 clearly shows that so far Southeast Asia has been comparatively little affected by the 'urban revolution', but since 1945 city populations, and particularly those of the primate cities, have grown very rapidly. With a very youthful population the great cities continue to experience a very high rate of natural increase, and in fact the concentration of the urban populations in the lower age-groups makes crude birth-rates very misleading as an index of the fertility of urban as opposed to rural dwellers. But it is probably only in the large cities of Malaya that natural increase has constituted the largest component of the total increase in population; elsewhere, although natural increase has been very substantial, it has been matched by rural-urban migration. The majority of the in-migrants have consisted of young males, so that the cities possess a relative deficiency of females in the younger age-groups, a situation which operates to depress the crude birth-rate of the cities; with the gradual attainment of numerical equality between the sexes in the cities it seems probable that, as in Malaya, natural increase will come to exceed the increase resulting from rural-urban migration.

The operative causes producing the tremendous postwar urban migration throughout the underdeveloped world are often classified as 'urban-pull' and 'rural-push', although the distinction is somewhat unreal; the essential fact is that the great cities offer, or appear to offer, a hope of a better life to the in-migrants and that the countryside admits no such possibility. A study of in-migrants to Djakarta revealed that the majority of the newcomers were economically better off than in the villages from which they came, but it is clear that economic motives were not always uppermost in the minds of in-migrants.[8] One of the strongest

[7] Bert F. Hoselitz, '*Generative and parasitic cities*', Economic Development and Cultural Change, *vol. 3, 1954, p. 281.*

[8] *Djakarta Institute of Social and Economic Research*, '*The urbanization of Djakarta*', Ekonomi dan Kueangan Indonesia, *vol. 8, 1955, p. 708.*

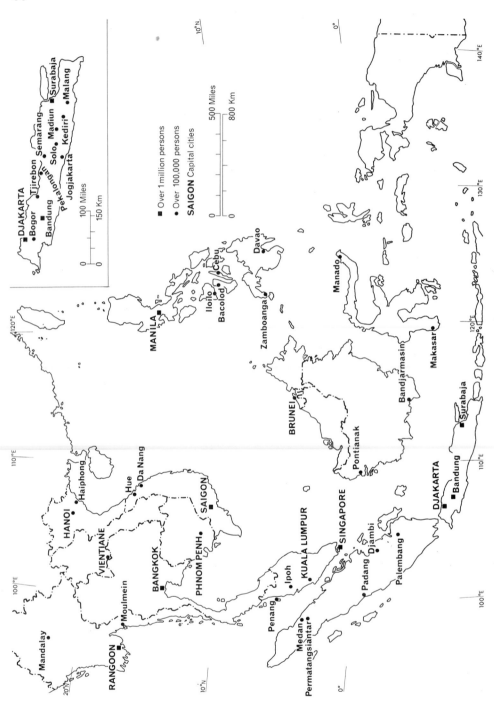

Over 1 million persons
● Over 100,000 persons
SAIGON Capital cities

Fig. 2.1(a)   Major urban centres of South-east Asia, about 1930.

87

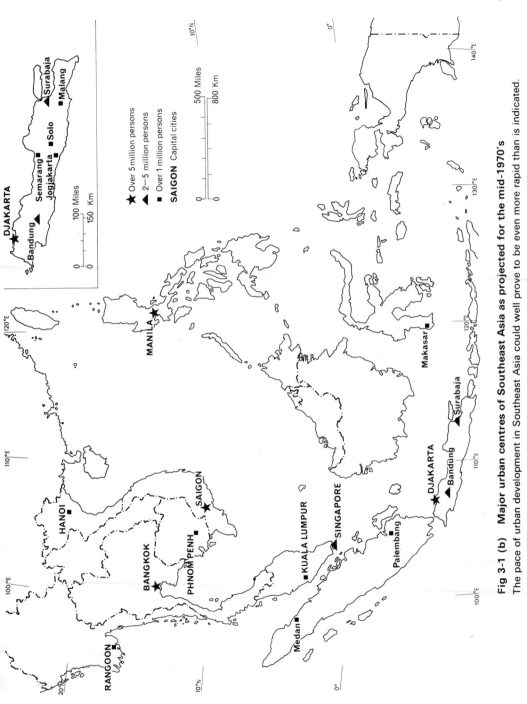

Fig 3-1 (b) Major urban centres of Southeast Asia as projected for the mid-1970's
The pace of urban development in Southeast Asia could well prove to be even more rapid than is indicated.

forces in the move to the cities has been the search for security; civil war and regional insurrections, and both large- and small-scale banditry masquerading as such, have ravaged large parts of mainland and archipelagic Southeast Asia alike since the end of World War II. Apart from relatively brief intervals, fighting has been virtually continuous in Vietnam and Burma since 1945, and the vicinities of Saigon and Rangoon have been among the areas most affected by insecurity. In Indonesia many people in West Java and in western Sulawesi have fled respectively to Djakarta and Makasar because of the depredations of the militant Muslim *Darul Islam*, while in both Malaya and the Philippines communist insurrections for many years constituted a serious threat and resulted in considerable loss of life. In Malaya the 'emergency' (1948–60) was a powerful factor in promoting urbanism, for isolated rural Chinese were consolidated into 'New Villages', two of the largest of which have since become part of the Kuala Lumpur metropolitan area. But insecurity has also been powerfully reinforced by progressive diminution in the size of holdings, increasing rural under-employment, and a growing feeling of the inadequacy of traditional village life. Rural-push factors have tended to exert their maximum effect on the misfits and least competent in the village, whereas urban-pull factors have greatest attraction for the more adventurous and enterprising, for whom the economic rewards of the city carry most weight. But sheer economic necessity is sometimes clearly the main motive in rural-urban migration. Before 1960, when the *samlor* (pedal tricycle) was abolished in Bangkok, about half the 11,000 or so registered riders in the city consisted of migrant farmers from impoverished eastern Thailand, who supplemented a farm income too low to support their families throughout the year by working in the capital, periodically returning home to help with rice cultivation, or with the harvest. Most of these temporary migrants intended to remain farmers, but they could earn more in a month in Bangkok than in a whole year working on their holdings.[9] The social attractions of city life are certainly also of significance in the rural exodus, but they are probably not as important as has sometimes been supposed.

Rapid increase of urban populations in Southeast Asia has, however, not been accompanied by, or been conditional upon, increasing industrialization; when the present highly developed economies were at comparable levels of urbanization they were considerably more industrialized, and the modernization process, measured by the proportion of total labour force engaged in non-agricultural activities, was substantially more advanced.[10] Although the primate cities of pre-industrial Western Europe and North America continued to grow during the modernization process, population growth and industrialization went hand-in-

[9] *Robert B. Textor*, From Peasant to Pedicab Driver, *Yale University, Southeast Asia Studies, New Haven, 1961, p. 28*. Betjak *(pedicab)* riding is also an occupation commonly taken up by the migrant to the cities of Java.

[10] *United Nations*, Economic Bulletin for Asia and the Far East, *vol. 10, No. 1, Bangkok, 1959, p. 19*.

hand, creating great conurbations from a 'mere village', to quote Defoe's description of eighteenth-century Manchester, and in this development the dominance of the great metropolitan centres was generally reduced. But although the ability of manufacturing industries to generate their own markets and labour supply, and thus greatly to accelerate urbanization and economic growth, receives eloquent testimony from Western Europe, North America and even from the USSR and Japan, urbanization without industrialization is another matter. By 1960 Southeast Asia had attained a degree of urbanization comparable with that of Japan in 1920, at which date Japan already possessed a considerable range of capital-intensive industries and a larger proportion of its labour force engaged in manufacturing than has Southeast Asia at present. The enlarged populations of the Southeast Asian primate cities have been compelled to seek employment in service industries or in building and construction; employment in manufacturing (with the possible exception of unskilled labouring in sawmilling and in other building-materials industries) has been largely denied them, partly through the lack of skills of most in-migrants and the strong degree of unionization among established industries,[11] and partly through the slow growth of manufacturing industry in general. As a result, service industries have become almost as over-populated as agriculture, and the cities, no less than the countryside, possess an enormous concealed unemployment; there are far too many petty retailers and hawkers, providers of personal services, or people waiting about to perform some trifling odd-job, to say nothing of professional beggars.

The cities have also amassed vast bureaucratic armies, which with the military, the intelligentsia and the unionized industrial workers, constitute the priviliged classes of newly independent countries. Despite a deteriorating economy and several 'standstill' orders on further government employment, the ranks of the Indonesian *pegawai*, or officials, have continued to augment during the lifetime of the Indonesian republic, reaching by 1960 a level of about four times the size of the old Netherlands Indies government service. The explosive potential of allowing large numbers of the relatively well-educated young persons turned out by expanded post-independence high schools and universities to remain unemployed, compels the government to provide jobs of some sort. But there is little for the new entrants in government service to do; thus they are distributed between a plethora of redundant government agencies, circulating innumerable meaningless forms, and supplementing their low incomes with other employment, thus increasing the pressure on jobs and further reducing the participation rate. Nevertheless, the support of government servants is vital to the regime, and the pegawai's loyalty is ensured by granting him privileges, such as the ability to

---

[11] *Some economists have deplored the activities of trade unions in developing countries in maintaining privileged positions for their members. By forcing up wage-rates unions reduce the 'participation rate' in employment, and often make the substitution of capital for labour financially attractive even in countries that have an abundance of the latter factor.*

purchase rice at a very much lower price than that in the 'free' market, low-rental housing, a first claim on scarce consumer goods in government shops, and priority in educational and medical services; more than half of all patients presenting at Indonesian hospitals are government servants. Students are paid large grants by the government to encourage them to remain *in statu pupillari* rather than to graduate and further swell the demand for government employment. Bandung and Jogjakarta are notable for their large numbers of 'time-serving' students, who form a very conspicuous element in the local population. While Burma has most closely resembled Indonesia in its over-inflated under-employed bureaucracy and 'professional' student class,[12] similar observations hold good in varying degrees for most Southeast Asian countries.

The service-industry oriented primate city was an inevitable consequence of colonial status, with its emphasis on commerce. Whether it serves equally well the needs of newly independent countries, which continually re-affirm their determination to cast off a thraldom to the developed world as providers of basic foodstuffs and raw materials, is another matter. Western experience notwithstanding, it is still not possible to be definitive concerning the effects of urbanization on economic growth,[13] but the economic consequences of unregulated explosive urban growth and the erosion of government authority through the invasion by squatters, of valuable urban land, often the property of the state, are very serious. There has, it is true, been some expansion of manufacturing in the cities, but the increase in industrial production has been less rapid than the increase in city populations, and the rate of increase in industrial employment has been lower still. Yet the certain appearance of super-cities with populations of some five to six millions before the end of the Seventies should *prima facie* greatly enhance the attractiveness of industrial investment (*Figure 3-1b*). But perhaps the most important function of the great cities lies in their role in accelerating the demographic transition, which may well prove to be more precipitate than was foreseen even in the later Fifties. Between 1948 and 1965 Singapore reduced its crude birth-rate from more than 50 per thousand population to 29·9 per thousand, and the government aims at a further reduction to about 25 per thousand by 1970. Singapore is in many ways unique among Southeast Asia's great cities, but it is conceivable that broadly similar trends are being established in the other primate cities, and all of them contain large Chinese populations in which the decline of fertility is likely to appear first.

[12] *Burma inherited an administrative procedure which involved thirty-nine separate steps in handling official correspondence, but little attempt at reform was made. See Louis J. Walinsky,* Economic Development in Burma 1951–1960, Twentieth Century Fund, *New York, 1962, pp. 483–5. The student population was sharply reduced after 1962 by the Revolutionary Council's closure of the non-specific and non-technical departments of the University of Rangoon.*

[13] *Eric E. Lampard, 'The history of cities in the economically advanced areas' in* Economic Development and Cultural Change, *vol. 3, 1954, p. 84.*

In some parts of Southeast Asia, and particularly in Indonesia, a policy of encouraging industrial expansion in smaller towns would have much to commend it. Such a development could accelerate improvements in agricultural efficiency by bringing large areas of the country within reach of urban markets, and it would help to relieve the tremendous strains resulting from rapid population growth on transport, utilities, housing, education and other social services in the large cities. The social and economic costs of meeting these strains involve the deployment of resources that should be employed in expanding productive facilities which would ultimately help to eliminate poverty.

Politically one of the most intractable, and certainly among the more obvious, of the problems of rapid urban growth is the infestation of large areas of the city with a scab-like crust of illegal squatter settlements, built with whatever materials come to hand. These urban sores have proliferated throughout the underdeveloped world in the postwar period, and in Southeast Asia they have often invaded the very heart of the city itself. Squatters have thus invaded the Intramuros, the old walled city of Manila, and the old quarter of Djakarta, the Benedenstadt of Batavia; they have settled on low-lying ground liable to flood, on steep hillsides, and even on city refuse dumps.[14] The high cost of urban transport compels squatters to reside as closely as possible to their places of employment, commonly the port area, the central business district, and new industrial sites in the city margins; thus they have sterilized valuable building land and greatly depressed adjacent property values. The removal of squatter camps, however, is a matter of the greatest difficulty, for politically squatters are well organized and are often the subject of considerable attention by communist or extreme left-wing groups; the longer that squatters can remain in occupation, the greater their moral claim and the probability that they will ultimately be allowed to stay. In Southeast Asia as in Latin America, the planned mass transport of in-migrants to 'pre-prepared' squatter areas is becoming a well-organized business. When squatters are eventually cleared from an area they promptly occupy the nearest vacant sites; landlords who make vigorous efforts to rid their property of squatters are liable to find themselves threatened with physical violence by militant left-wing thugs. In Malaysia the squatter problem is complicated by the fact that very many squatters are Malays, a group with special privileges under the constitution, and whose greater participation in non-agricultural activities is a declared objective of official policy; thus a government primarily dependent on the Malay rural voter is inevitably reluctant to take strong action.

Jammed together in flimsy and inflammable hutments at densities that may attain as much as 2,000 persons per acre, and without adequate light, water and sanitation, the squatter populations of the great cities are generally held to constitute a serious menace to society; crime and disease flourish and there is an

[14] D. J. Dwyer, '*The problem of in-migration and squatter settlement in Asian cities*', Asian Studies, *vol. 2, 1962, p. 151.*

ever-present risk of the latter reaching epidemic proportions. Malaria, from which the cities were generally free before World War II, has been re-introduced by the in-migrants, and the spread of such mosquito-borne diseases has been facilitated by entirely inadequate refuse-disposal in squatter camps. Fires, which are frequent, sometimes have a beneficial effect, for usually few lives are lost and when tens of thousands are rendered homeless at a time, government is usually forced to take some remedial action.[15] Nevertheless, this is seldom effective, for the place of rehoused squatters is rapidly filled by yet more newcomers; already squatters account for almost a third of the population of Djakarta, and for almost one-quarter of that of Kuala Lumpur and Manila.

Only the most rigorous action by an official body with complete authority over squatter registration, clearance and re-settlement, and with adequate financial resources, can hope to achieve any real success with the squatter problem at present, to say nothing of what may confidently be expected of the future; Metropolitan Manila (*Figure 3-2*) may have a population of more than 6 millions by 1977, and in-migrants and their subsequent city-born children in the period 1955–77 could total some 2·5 millions.[16] No such body exists in any country of Southeast Asia at the present, although the Singapore Housing and Development Board is perhaps the nearest approach, and the squatter problem, together with many other pressing issues of city growth, is bogged down in political disputes over ultimate responsibility between central and local government, or between various departments of the central government. What can be done, however, is demonstrated by the example of near-by Hong Kong, where an anachronistic but paternal colonial government has made the most determined attack on the squatter problem anywhere in the underdeveloped world. Threatened with strangulation by the vast influx of migrants, both legal and illegal from China, the Hong Kong government established a Department of Resettlement with complete authority over all aspects of the squatter problem, which in the decade after 1954 rehoused more than 600,000 squatters in multi-storey blocks. Separate industrial blocks were also erected to accommodate squatter factories and workshops removed from land required for permanent development. Singapore, which closely resembles Hong Kong in being a city-state, is the only major city to have treated the squatter problem as a matter of urgency, and has the best public rehousing in the whole region. Its 1960 Five Year Housing Development Plan envisaged the provision of some 50,000 new units, mostly two- and three-room apartments in multi-storeyed blocks, to accommodate some 200,000 people (*Figure 3-3*). This target was in fact exceeded, and a total of 60,000 new units are

---

[15] *There is some evidence from Singapore that fires have been deliberately lit in squatter encampments by left-wing groups, who have traded on the policy of the PAP government in providing immediate priority in public housing to refugee squatters in order to hold the important squatter vote. But the rehoused squatters, whose lot has been materially improved by this simple trick, often tend to thank the communists for their benefaction.*

[16] *Dwyer, op. cit., p. 155.*

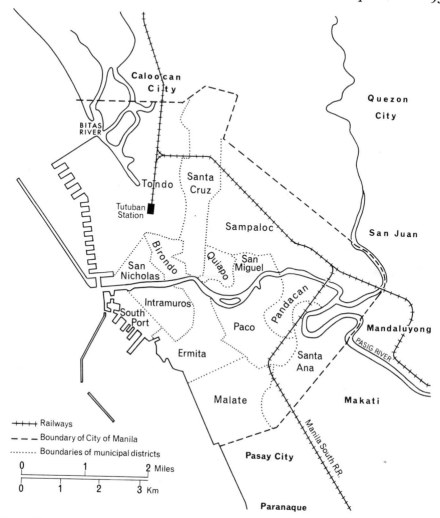

Fig 3-2 The Manila metropolitan region
Greater Manila is Southeast Asia's second largest urban agglomeration in terms of population, but is probably first in respect of geographic area. It has also the highest incidence of violent crime and some of the most intractable squatter problems of any of the region's great cities.

planned for the period to 1970. Almost one-quarter of Singapore's population resided in Housing Board units in 1966. Yet neither in Hong Kong nor in Singapore is rehousing directly subsidized by the government, and Singapore's Housing and Development Board does not even enjoy the advantage of its Hong Kong counterpart, which obtains land from the government at half the market price.

Yet to judge Southeast Asia's housing needs by the standards of highly developed countries is entirely inappropriate. Moreover, in practice the only

A million pieces of laundry hang from these blocks in Queenstown, one
of the Singapore Housing and Development Board's 'New Towns'.

House in the high-class residential area of Makati, Greater Manila.

effective way to guard against rent delinquency in resettlement and low-cost housing schemes is to restrict operations to the regularly employed and better-paid workers; applicants to the Singapore Housing Board must have a regular monthly income of not less than S$200, or about £25, so that the mass of the very poor are unaffected. Evidence from Hong Kong indicates that many squatters prefer the freedom and independence of the squatter camps to the vast pullulating resettlement blocks with their ceaseless commotion and almost complete lack of personal privacy, and indeed, some social scientists feel strongly that the squatter camp provides much greater economic and personal security, and constitutes a far healthier social environment for the raising of children. Resettlement merely releases land for other development; it does nothing to reduce the number of squatters. Nor do resettled squatters tend to move out to better housing elsewhere in the city as their income rises, for they are reluctant to devote more than a small part of their earnings to rent. The large numbers of private cars to be found in Singapore's 'New Towns' and major rehousing areas testify to many inhabitants' relative well-being, although an unknown but probably substantial proportion of such vehicles are unlicensed 'pirate' taxis.

Rather than to lock up large sums urgently needed for income-producing investment in housing for the poor, it would often make better sense to build, or to let the squatters build for themselves, low-cost huts on well-planned layouts which make adequate provision for open space and for other public amenities. The great difficulty with such schemes is that they must be located in close proximity to major centres of employment, and that the most suitable land is usually far too valuable to be so used. Where located on the margins of the cities they often fail, as the inhabitants slowly drift back to the inner areas to avoid the time and expense of travelling long distances to work. Singapore's Housing Board has even found it difficult to let all the new housing it has constructed at Jurong, some ten miles from the city centre, although this was admittedly planned in conjunction with new employment opportunities at the nearby industrial estate which have failed to materialize quickly enough as a result of the political separation of Singapore from Malaysia. But where squatters can feel they have security and are encouraged to make investment in improvement, perfectly acceptable new districts can come into being, as the experience of some Latin American cities proves. The government should encourage the new urban dwellers to help themselves and devote its own energies to combating poverty through the creation of new employment.

Just as a modernizing society requires far-reaching changes in central government, so expanding urbanization necessitates almost as revolutionary changes in local government. In powers and finance, by far the two most important aspects of city government, the primate cities, with the possible exception of Singapore and the larger cities of Malaysia, reveal a pathetic inadequacy. Only in Manila does a distinct city government responsible to the electorate now exist,

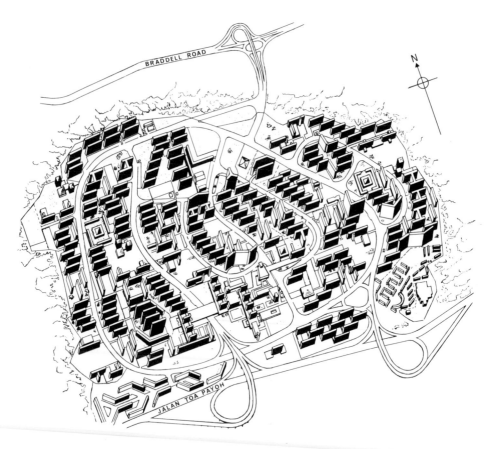

Fig 3-3   The Toa Payoh New Town, Singapore (reproduced by kind permission of the Housing and Development Board, Singapore)

With three 'new towns' and several smaller housing developments, Singapore's public housing programme is among the very best in the whole of Asia. Its low-cost housing offers facilities for privacy and the enjoyment of family life which are out of the question in Hong Kong's vast barrack-like resettlement schemes.

but, with the important exceptions noted, the branches of government that are concerned with city administration are hamstrung by inadequate powers and finance, a consequence of the ambivalent attitude of government itself to the role of the big city in a supposedly modernizing society. Thus while rural-urban migration has continued apace since independence, the latter has also produced a reassertion of traditional cultural values and an inwards reorientation in which the big city has become ambivalent; while continuing to act as the main contact with the outside world, a role that must presumably increase in importance as national development plans come to fruition, it is also increasingly called upon to act as the repository of the indigenous 'Great Tradition', to use the term of Redfield and Singer.[17] In this conflict symbols and outward forms are apt to take priority over such mundane affairs as sewage, water supply and transport. This ambivalence is most striking in Burma and Indonesia, whose respective capitals are by common consent the dirtiest of all the primate cities in the region, and the most lacking in the requirements of a metropolis of the modern world. Though Rangoon received a much-needed face-lift during the first Ne Win military government (1958–60), when large numbers of *kwetthits* (squatter settlements) and illegal roadside markets were razed by the Army and putrescent drains were cleaned out for the first time in years, the decline of the physical equipment of Rangoon continued after 1962 following the take-over by the Revolutionary Council of virtually all the city's service industries and its repudiation of the out-side world. In the opinion of one observer, the oppressive and *Nat* (spirit)-haunted Burmese jungle in the background slowly but perceptibly encroaches, threatening the city with the same fate that has befallen all the historic Burmese cities of the past.[18]

Until 1959 all but a very small part of Djakarta, by far the largest city in the region, lacked any water supply apart from that provided by the canals excavated by the Dutch in the seventeenth century, which served not only as a water supply but also as a public washing-place and sewer. Its electricity supply, telephone services and public transport would still be judged inadequate in a city one-tenth the size. Djakarta's utter incompetence to cope with any of the problems of a major urban community can be judged from a comparison of its budget with that of Singapore, admittedly the most opulent of all primate cities of the region. In 1959 Djakarta had a budget of about £2·7 millions, while Singapore with half the population had a municipal budget of some £14 millions, a rural board budget of £0·6 millions and an overlapping state budget of £25 millions;[19] and since that date the disparity has further increased. Despite this enormous inadequacy, however, very large resources acquired through foreign aid and export earnings were squandered in providing Djakarta with monuments in keeping with its role as the repository of the 'Indonesian Tradition'; these include the largest sports stadium in Asia, the world's largest mosque (still unfinished at the time of writing), and a large luxury hotel which is furnished and decorated with examples of art-forms and handicrafts from all parts of the country, but, like a similar hotel in Rangoon also built with foreign aid, remains virtually empty of the foreign visitors it was designed to attract.

In such a situation it is hardly surprising that, except in Malaysia and

---

[17] *R. Redfield and M. Singer, op. cit., p. 65.*

[18] *I. R. Sinai,* The Challenge of Modernization, *Chatto & Windus, London, 1964, pp. 165–6.*

[19] *Willard A. Hanna,* Bung Karno's Indonesia, *American Universities Field Staff, New York, 1960, No. 28, pp. 5–6.*

Singapore, urban planning has scarcely progressed beyond the most rudimentary stages. Yet despite the cost of planning and the multiplicity of claims on limited city resources, so great is the need of the primate cities of the underdeveloped world that, as Lampard has pointed out, they can scarcely afford not to plan.[20] Such urban planning as has occurred in the cities of Southeast Asia has been mainly directed towards meeting the needs of the middle classes employed in government and in other service industries—hence the 'new towns' of Kebajoran Bahru (Djakarta), Quezon City (Manila) and Petaling Jaya (Kuala Lumpur). But divorced from its economic basis, urban planning is abortive, and there are few cities in the world at present that better merit Mumford's term 'Tyrannopolis' than Djkarta. Ultimately the problems of the great cities are only soluble through rapid national economic development, in which raising rural productivity is assigned the highest priority. As it is manifestly impossible to provide sufficient employment opportunities for all the new urban dwellers, lessening the incidence of the rural-push factors is an obvious line of policy.

MINING AND MANUFACTURING INDUSTRIES

All countries of Southeast Asia use every opportunity to condemn colonial economic policies which resulted in a high degree of dependence on imports for most manufactured goods, and though they differ in their methods, all are determined substantially to raise the share of manufacturing in national product. For this reason the role of the state in industrialization has been much greater than was the case in the present highly developed economies during their modernization periods, and in some countries certain of the techniques of the centrally-planned economies have been adopted in order to accelerate the industrialization process. Varying degrees of success have attended these post-independence industrialization programmes, but in almost every country the share of manufacturing in national product increased during the Fifties (*Table 3-2*).

Nevertheless, this achievement loses much of its merit viewed against the disappointing performances of most countries in raising agricultural output and export earnings, and the industrial sector is still very small. Only in the Philippines did the share of manufacturing industry in national product between 1961 and 1963 equal that of India (16 per cent), a country that is often regarded as one of the least industrialized in Asia, and even in the Philippines the share of manufacturing industries in national product was only half that of Japan. The addition of mining and construction to manufacturing, to make up what are sometimes known as secondary industries, does not materially affect the situation, for only in West Malaysia does mining account for more than 5 per cent of national product. Few countries, however, derive a substantially larger share of their national product from mining industries, and Malaysia in this respect stands in

[20] *Lampard*, op. cit., *p. 134.*

Table 3-2 *Southeast Asia: share of manufacturing and mining in gross national product at constant prices, 1952–54 and 1961–63, and per capita industrial output 1961–63 at 1960 prices*

	Manufacturing 1952–54 percentages	1961–63	Mining 1952–54 percentages	1961–63	Per capita indus- trial output 1961–63 at 1960 prices US $
Burma	10·4	14·8	1·0	0·8	9
Indonesia	8·5	6·9	2·3	2·6	4
West Malaysia	11·2	12·6	6·5	6·1	36
Thailand	11·8	11·4	1·8	1·6	12
Philippines	11·2	16·1	1·5	1·6	30
South Vietnam	9·6	11·2	0·2	0·5	10

Source: United Nations, *Industrial Development in Asia and the Far East*, vol. 1, 1966

approximately the same position as Britain. In no country in 1960 did the share of construction in national product exceed 3 per cent, but in 1961–65, 30 per cent of Singapore's public capital investment was made in building, and in 1966 construction generated 5 per cent of the island's gross national product.

The rapid increase in city populations and the growing demand for urban employment will lead to demands for the adoption of yet more vigorous industrialization programmes, which in turn will further accelerate the drift to the cities and enlarge the numbers of those seeking employment. There is no escape from this treadmill, save in an even more rapid rate of economic development and the completion of the demographic transition. This in turn requires still more from the agricultural sector, and it is hard for those leaders of newly independent countries who believe that industrialization is the solution to all their ills, to accept that while agriculture remains stagnant the little so far achieved in the industrial sector has in some ways made matters worse. Industrialization is thus an important issue, but it is not quite so pressing as most nationalists believe.

MINING

The importance of mining as an agent of economic development is often underestimated, for in most highly developed economies the expansion of mining went hand-in-hand with increasing industrialization in a self-sustaining growth cycle. Although it is unlikely that in any part of Southeast Asia mining industries will ever come to have the importance that they at present possess in South Africa, Zambia or in the Middle East, expansion of mining industries could have a very beneficial effect in most countries. Modern Malaya, indeed, in large part owes its relative affluence to the capital and diligent labour force created by nineteenth-century tin-mining, when this industry occupied a place in the local economy broadly commensurate with that of gold in South Africa at the present.

Mining, of course, can only be carried on where mineral deposits of commercially exploitable quantity and quality occur. But the fact that Southeast Asia is probably the least important part of a continent which, with the exception of petroleum, is itself only a minor producer of most fuel and metalliferous minerals,[21] is largely a consequence of the abject failure to undertake large-scale geological survey. Even topographic surveys, which it is generally agreed should precede geological field surveying, leave much to be desired. Thus in 1952 ECAFE reported that only some 3–5 per cent of Malaya had been geologically surveyed on a scale of one inch to one mile; less than 10 per cent of the Philippines has been surveyed on a scale of 1:50,000; only 8 per cent of Java had been geologically mapped on a scale of 1:100,000 and the same percentage of Sumatra on a scale of 1:200,000; apart from generalized small-scale geological maps only a few geological sheets of Indochina on a scale of 1:100,000 had been published; and Thailand had merely a small-scale general reconnaissance geological map. Only Burma had a good cover of geological maps, about two-thirds of the country being surveyed on the one-inch or quarter-inch scales, the work of the Geological Survey of India and of the oil companies.[22] While the situation has improved since that date over large parts of the region, largely through extended use of aerial photography, the lack of security has made geological field-surveying virtually out of the question.

Geological surveying and mineral prospecting face formidable physical difficulties in the hot and humid, densely forested terrain of much of the region. Yet in some parts at least, and particularly in Indonesia, the little that has been accomplished appears very surprising; as van Bemmelen reported, upwards of five hundred foreign geologists have visited Indonesia, and a succession of eminent Dutch geologists was employed in the service of the Netherlands Indies government. But for the most part the geological talent deployed in the Netherlands Indies was preoccupied with problems of academic geology, particularly with vulcanism and orogenesis, to the neglect of economic geology.[23] Apart from the private work of the oil companies, which have built up a large body of information much of which is still unpublished, interest in economic geology in the

[21] *Following long-established United Nations usage of regarding the USSR as a distinct entity. As noted, the Chinese view of the USSR as economically and culturally a European and non-Asian power, is essentially correct.*

[22] *United Nations Economic Commission for Asia and the Far East,* Coal and Iron Ore Resources of Asia and the Far East, *Bangkok, 1952, p. 12.*

[23] *R. W. van Bemmelen's* Geology of Indonesia, *Government Printing Office, The Hague, 1949, is a clear illustration. Vol. II on economic geology is less than half the length of Vol. I which deals with stratigraphy and geological history, and* tour de force *though the work is, it is primarily a vehicle for a detailed exposition of the author's 'undation theory' of orogenesis.*

Netherlands Indies was largely confined to two periods. These were during and immediately following World War I (1917–22), and the late Thirties, when emergency conditions or the threat of attack prompted the government to undertake specific investigations of mineral deposits in order to increase local self-sufficiency.

This lack of official interest in mineral deposits was primarily a reflection of the essentially paternal colonial administrations, which never regarded the establishment of an industrialized society in which metal production and metal working occupy a prominent place, as any concern of theirs. Many indigenes have shown a small and fitful interest in mining, but on the whole it has had little attraction for the region's essentially 'vegetable civilizations', and the principal miners of Southeast Asia have long been the Chinese. With the exception of petroleum, which has remained a European speciality save in Burma where indigenes have long been engaged in small-scale production for local needs, there are few important mineral deposits that have not been long known and worked by the Chinese. For centuries Yunnanese were engaged in mining silver from Bawdwin, tin from Mawchi, and extracting rubies and jade from the Shan plateau; other Chinese peoples were mining gold in the Philippines and in the Malayan peninsula when the Europeans first arrived. Tin-mining, the region's most important mineral activity from the standpoint of the world economy, was almost entirely a Chinese activity until the present century, and despite the expanding interest of European capital since 1900, the Chinese still control a substantial share of tin production in West Malaysia and in Thailand. Moreover, they continue to provide the principal labour force for mining activities. Before World War II, Burma's mining industries also employed large numbers of Indians and Ghurkas, whose final expulsion from the country in the Sixties added a further serious obstacle to the rehabilitation of the country's mineral production.

Chinese mining is essentially labour-intensive and organized in small units, and as the metal requirements of the expanding world economy have transformed mining from small enterprises working limited high-grade deposits to the 'mass-mining' of low-grade but very extensive deposits, Chinese mining has tended to lose ground. Nevertheless, Southeast Asia appears on the whole poorly endowed with deposits suitable for modern mass-mining techniques and, present limited geological knowledge notwithstanding, it is unlikely that any substantial non-ferrous mineral deposits await discovery.

Tin

Tin-mining is by far the most important metalliferous mining industry in the regional economy, and though its scale of output is modest in relation to that of iron, this is more than offset by the high price of tin, which is by far the most expensive of all base metals. From the Yunnan plateau of southwest China a great stanniferous zone extends southwards through the Shan plateau and Tavoy coast of Burma into peninsular Thailand, Malaya and the Indonesian islands east of Sumatra; in the postwar period the Southeast Asia section of this zone has produced about 55–60 per cent of the world's supply of primary tin. In 1941, when world tin production reached its all-time peak of some 250,000 tons, Southeast Asia produced almost 70 per cent of world output, so that the past two decades have witnessed some decline in the region's contribution to the world supply of new metal (*Table 3-3*). This declining share, however, in part represents the greatly reduced contributions of Indonesia and Burma, for Indonesian

Table 3-3 *Southeast Asia: production of tin-in-concentrates, 1940, 1950, 1960 and 1966 (thousand tons)*

	1940	1950	1960	1966
Burma	5·6	1·5	0·9	0·4
Laos	1·5		0·4	0·5
West Malaysia	83·0	57·8	52·0	68·9
Indonesia	53·4	32·1	22·6	12·5
Thailand	17·1	10·4	12·1	22·5
Total, Southeast Asia	**160·6**	**101·8**	**88·0**	**104·8**
Bolivia	42·1	31·2	20·2	25·9
World total*	**239·0**	**162·3**	**136·5**	**163·1**

* Excluding China, North Vietnam, U S S R, East Germany and Czechoslovakia

Sources: International Tin Council, *Statistical Yearbook*, 1965, and Statistical Bulletin, December 1967

production has tended progressively to diminish during the lifetime of the Republic, and Burma's postwar production has never amounted to much above one-fifth of that of the later Thirties. The fall in Indonesian output is largely the result of a prolonged failure to make sufficient investment in the industry to maintain productive efficiency, and several mines heavily damaged during the Japanese occupation have not yet been reactivated. The eclipse of Burma as a significant tin-producer has arisen from disturbed political conditions, and in particular from the Karen rebellion. Many mines, including the famous tin-tungsten mine of Mawchi in the southern Shan, lie in areas outside the effective control of the central government.

Even in West Malaysia, which accounts for about one-third of world production, output has shown little tendency to grow until the mid-Sixties, but this has resulted more from a deliberate restriction of output rather than from a loss of competitive efficiency, for West Malaysia still has probably the world's lowest costs of tin production. West Malaysia's output of nearly 69,000 tons in 1966 was, however, the highest since 1941. Despite a buoyant world economy, world consumption of tin failed to grow appreciably in the postwar period, largely because of the technological changes born of World War II which have greatly economized in the use of tin in its traditional employments. Restriction of production has long been facilitated by the structure of the industry, which is dominated by a few major groups in which British capital predominates and whose interests embrace production in West Malaysia, Thailand, Burma, Congo (Kinshasa), Rwanda, Nigeria, and, before the nationalization decrees of 1957, in Bolivia also. Every group, however, contains both high- and low-cost producers, so that all have some interest in restriction. But the most fundamental fact in world tin-mining is the very high costs of production in Bolivia, a result of the disadvantages inherent in underground mining on the very elevated and isolated *altiplano*, and in part also of the difficulties in smelting its *barilla* ores. The big controlling groups in the world tin industry claim that by drawing on supplies from high-cost as well as from low-cost producers, the world's tin resources are made to last longer; moreover, concentration on low-cost Southeast Asian production would, they claim, result in an undesirable price appreciation once the region's deposits were worked out. Two further facts reinforce Bolivia's significance in the world tin industry. As tin produces such a large share of the country's export income (about 65 per cent), Bolivia has often had no choice but to offset high domestic production costs in periods of low or falling prices by devaluing its currency, thus cheapening its exports in terms of world prices; moreover, as the only tin producer of the western hemisphere, Bolivian production is strategically vital to the United States, the world's largest consumer. In practice, therefore, falling prices do not tend to drive Bolivia out of production, and paradoxically enough, low-cost producers in Southeast Asia have always been advocates of restriction.

European mining interests in the region, moreover, have received powerful support for restriction of output from Chinese mining groups, whose production costs, because of a less efficient technology, are substantially higher than those of European mines. Indonesia, which inherited a largely state-owned tin-mining industry from the Netherlands Indies government, has so far cooperated in policies of restriction, and, although initially declining to be a party to the third postwar agreement of 1965, it acceded after the fall of Sukarno. Since its output has long been well below capacity, however, as indeed has also been the case with the Bolivian industry, whose output slumped after the 1957 nationalization, this action has had little practical result.

The amplitude of the fluctuations in the price of tin exceeds that of any other metal, and arise on the one hand from short-term inflexibility of supply, and on the other from the fact that tin is largely consumed indirectly in the form of canned goods, of whose total cost tin itself forms only a very small part; thus a slight shortfall (or expectation of such) can produce a disproportionate effect on price as steel manufacturers bid against each other for the available tin supply. Violent price-fluctuations encourage manufacturers to economize in their holdings of the metal and in its use, and through the development of continuous electrolytic tinning plants, only 0·25 lb of tin are now required to produce 100 lb of tinplate. Action to limit violent fluctuations has much to recommend it, if this can be done without sacrificing the interests of the consumer. But although international commodity agreements have always stressed the desirability of reducing price fluctuations which have traumatic effects on national exchequers, in practice they have also attempted artificially to raise prices by restriction of output. The various tin agreements have been no exception, and their practical results have been, as with almost all other commodity agreements, to reduce the share of the principal producers in total world output.

The prewar agreements, which date back to the Twenties, were essentially quota agreements in which there was no representation of consumer interests except in so far as these coincided with producers, and the first postwar International Tin Agreement, concluded in 1953 but not ratified until 1956, was the first to include consuming countries as direct participants. This agreement supplemented the prewar quota system with the provision of a buffer stock, to be manipulated in such a way that prices would be kept between a floor of £640 and a ceiling of £880 per ton; when prices departed from a pre-determined middle range, the buffer-stock manager could buy or sell tin to help restore the position. Traditionally hostile to all international commodity schemes, the United States did not become a party to the agreement, but its heavy purchases of tin for its strategic stockpile in the early Fifties materially helped in keeping prices at a high level. With the cessation of stockpile purchases after 1956, the International Tin Council reimposed export quotas on producer members, as it had done before the war. But the magnitude of United States stockpile purchases earlier in the decade continued to exert a depressing effect on the market, and in 1962 it was revealed that the General Services Administration, the stockpile agency, held some 349,000 tons of metal, equivalent to two years free world output of primary tin. Subsequent releases from the stockpile, in order to ensure what the United States considered a reasonable price for the metal, reduced this figure to a little over 100,000 tons by the end of 1966, or two-thirds of one year's free world supply, and by 1971 the stockpile should be approaching exhaustion.

These releases, in effect, merely passed into the possession of the International Tin Council, through its buffer-stock manager's efforts to maintain the floor price of the second postwar agreement, concluded in 1961. This, and the third agreement negotiated on its expiry in 1966, broadly continued the provisions of the earlier agreement, and through successive upward revisions carried floor and ceiling prices to £1,100 and £1,400 per ton by mid-1966. With the devaluation of sterling in 1967 a new floor price of £1,280 was established, and the ceiling price was raised to £1,630 per ton. By this time, however, higher prices had encouraged such increased production that the agreement's Buffer

Stock manager had acquired nearly 5,000 tons of metal by the end of the year in an attempt to force the price into the agreement's middle range (£1,400 to £1,515). This price appreciation reflects the growing pressure on supplies with the expansion of the world economy and the needs of the Vietnam war; since 1963 the price of tin has never fallen below £1,000 per ton and on occasions it has been well above the agreement's ceiling price, the all-time record of £1,715 per ton being reached in October 1964. The Council's small stock was quite inadequate to exert any influence on such appreciations (no metal was ever subscribed under the buffer-stock provisions of the 1961 agreement, contributions being entirely in cash), and the gap between world consumption and production has been bridged by GSA stockpile releases. Producing countries naturally wish to see this gap translated into higher prices, which they claim will stimulate additional production, and have exerted pressure to keep stockpile releases at minimum levels. While there is some justice in producer claims for higher prices in order to stretch world tin reserves through making possible the mining of lower-grade deposits, the fact remains that very high prices can only encourage a greater use of substitute materials, particularly of aluminium, which has already firmly established itself in the important canned-goods market.

Methods of tin-mining Southeast Asia's low costs of production arise largely from the nature of its deposits. Cassiterite, or tinstone, the oxide of tin, is a very stable mineral, and the weathering of the mineralized granitic ranges of the western portion of the Malayan peninsula has produced eluvial (that is, weathered *in situ*) and alluvial deposits, eminently suitable for mining in opencast workings. Underground lode mining, as practised in Bolivia, is comparatively rare, although one such large unit exists. The heavy black tinstone is separated from the sands and gravels in which it is disseminated by physical means, such as washing with water in a sluice box, by treatment in a 'hydro-cyclone', or even by panning, the method used by numerous female 'dulang' washers who continue to make a small contribution to total output.

Indigenous mining methods, such as the Malay *lampanning* (sluicing), were limited to the shallowest and most accessible workings because of the incursion of water into the diggings, but with the expanding world economy of the latter half of the nineteenth century, supplies from such sources proved quite inadequate. By using the technologies of their homeland, immigrant Chinese were able to mine to much greater depth; the *chin-chia* (chain pump, or noria), driven by a water-wheel fed by a dam and diversion channel from a nearby stream, was employed to lift water in the workings, but where the overburden was too thick for economic removal, underground mining methods were employed similar to those known for centuries in Yunnan. Other Chinese technological innovations included improved sluice boxes (*palongs*). Nevertheless, it was their social organization which made this crude technology so economically effective, and gave the

Chinese a grip in the tin-mining industry that Europeans for long tried in vain to break. Through *kongsis* and secret societies the Chinese were able to import and deploy a very large labour force, and were capable of operating large units; some Chinese mines employed more than 1,000 workers in the latter half of the nineteenth century. Though Chinese mining was essentially labour-intensive, its capital requirements were nevertheless substantial, and here the kongsis, backed by the merchants of the Straits Settlements, provided—as in speculative Chinese export-crop agriculture—some of the attributes of the modern corporation. The steam engine and the centrifugal pump were introduced into Larut in the late Seventies, but so long as reliance had to be placed on large quantities of labour to extract the ore and convey it to the surface for treatment, the low-cost Chinese truck system which debited the *sinkheh* with the costs of his passage from China and with his food, shelter and opium, proved invincible. Most of the early European ventures into the industry ended in bankruptcies, and as a result, Chinese miners were often able to acquire steam engines and pumping equipment at a fraction of their original cost.

Gradually, however, new technologies appeared which reduced the labour requirements of the industry. Hydraulicking, in which a stream is dammed some hundreds of feet above the level of the mine and the water conveyed by pipe to the working faces which are attacked with powerful jets, or monitors, was employed in the Kinta Valley, the world's foremost tin-mining region in 1892; the gravel-pump mine, in which the washed-out material is raised for treatment by a mechanically driven pump, commenced operations in 1906; this year also saw the introduction of the dredge to Southeast Asia, a device which was finally to establish European dominance in the industry. The dredge was first used in the goldfields of Westland, New Zealand, in the Nineties, and one was acquired for gold working at Harrietville, in Victoria, Australia; this was removed and installed by the Australian-controlled Tongkah Harbour Company on the island of Phuket in southern Thailand in 1906. The first dredge in the Kinta appeared some six years later. Newer technologies have included the increased use of diesel engines and electric power, both for pumping or operating dredges and treatment plants, and the extended use of belt conveyors. In the mid-Fifties the pontoon-mounted dragline, or grab-dredge, appeared at Phuket, where offshore working has long been important, and similar methods will probably be employed in the near future off the Perak and Melaka coasts of West Malaysia. Newer technical developments in West Malaysia include the use of the bucket-wheel excavator, a German machine originally developed for brown-coal working, and improved methods of ore treatment.

Nevertheless, the bucket dredge has long been the dominant form of mining and accounts for virtually the entire Indonesian output, for some 60 per cent of that of West Malaysia and for about 40 per cent of that of Thailand. A large modern dredge involves a capital outlay of about £2 million, so that few new

Monitor in a gravel-pump mine in the Kinta valley, West Malaysia.

Palong (sluice-box) in a gravel-pump mine. Tinstone is deposited behind the transverse partitions checking the flow, and the lighter sands and gravels pass on to the tailing pond.

Large electric-powered dredge near Kuala Lumpur.

ones have been built since the end of World War II;[24] several have been rebuilt, however, and the largest have bucket ladders capable of excavating up to 150 feet below the water level of the pond or paddock in which they float, and can work deposits as lean as 0·15 lb of tin per cubic yard, although the average tenor in dredging is considerably higher. The dredge is thus very suitable for working the deep alluvials of the lowest portions of the valleys, but it needs a working area capable of providing a lengthy operating life; moving and reassembling a dredge is an operation that may cost upwards of M$500,000. Dredging and hydraulicking are entirely in the hands of European companies, but despite a multiplicity of operating units, effective control (and a substantial share of ownership) is firmly in the hands of three London-based holding companies.

Gravel-pump mines are employed wherever conditions are unsuitable for dredging, particularly in valley margins and where tin alluvials rest on pinnacles of limestone so that pockets of ore in between the pinnacles are inaccessible to the dredge. The gravel-pump mine is much less capital-intensive, requiring an outlay of upwards of M$250,000 in West Malaysia, but is more labour-intensive; it is also more destructive of the landscape than dredging, in that it produces a mass of large unsightly holes, usually half full of water, and vast areas of tailings on which little can grow. In the past it has been responsible for much flooding, silting and damage to agricultural land downstream. The disposal of tailings from all forms of mining is now strictly controlled, but the rehabilitation of mined land continues to present difficulties. The life of a gravel-pump mine is short and the palongs require frequent moving as the working face advances. Gravel-pumping largely continues to be a Chinese prerogative. Because of their relatively high costs, gravel-pump mines are very responsive to price fluctuations; with falling prices, marginal mines cease production, but when prices rise abandoned workings are successively reactivated. Such groups tend to be staunch supporters of restrictions in times of poor prices, and imposition of export control means in practice that output has to be allocated between the European and Chinese controlled sectors.

Notwithstanding the growing pressure on world liquidity and gloomy forecasts of a major recession as the means of international payment dry up, the high level of world economic activity in recent years suggests that some extension of capacity is now overdue. The chances of discovering a major new tin field in Southeast Asia do not appear very great, and it is highly likely that additional supplies will have to continue to come from fields long worked. Past estimates of the reserves of tin in the region, as is usually the case in such exercises, have proved over-conservative; but there is no reason to doubt that improved technologies and reworking of land already once mined will continue to provide all the

---

[24] *West Malaysia's first new postwar dredge commenced operations in the Kuala Langat District of Selangor in 1966; Indonesia also received a large Scottish-built dredge in that year.*

metal that the world is capable of absorbing in the near future. There is little prospect, however, that the tin industry can reverse the long decline in its labour force, and the future employment opportunities offered even by an enlarged mining industry are unlikely to be very great. Only by the adoption of progressively more capital-intensive methods can the price of tin be held low enough to discourage the use of substitute materials, and the industry's greatest contribution to the regional economy will continue to be as a source of export earnings.

Larger tin mines also recover quantities of other metalliferous minerals, even including a little gold, but the most important by-product of tin-mining is tungsten, another metal finding its principal application in the iron and steel industry. Wolfram, the principal tungsten-bearing mineral, frequently occurs in association with cassiterite but, being less stable, workable wolfram deposits are not usually found in alluvial material. Wolfram is recovered from some European treatment plants, but many regard the mineral as something of a nuisance and the only country in which production assumed major importance was prewar Burma, whose Mawchi mine was the world's largest wolfram producer. Scheelite, another tungsten-bearing mineral, occurs in several localities in West Malaysia, but production is very small.

Other metalliferous minerals

Copper minerals occur in very many districts in Southeast Asia, but the ore bodies are almost everywhere too small and too inaccessible to offer much prospect of profitable working. Even in populous Java, where the Netherlands Indies' special geological investigations earlier referred to discovered several deposits, none was large enough to justify investment in transport to connect with the island's well-developed (by Southeast Asian standards) transport systems. Only in the Philippines does a copper ore body large enough to warrant modern mass-mining techniques occur; this is the Toledo mine of central Cebu, which works ores with a metallic content of 1·15 per cent. Various methods of working the region's numerous small copper deposits have been suggested, but in view of the opportunities available for expansion of production in geologically more favoured parts of the world, particularly central Africa, any substantial increase in Southeast Asian copper production appears unlikely in the near future.

Southeast Asia contains fewer deposits of lead and zinc, whose principal ores usually occur in association; but the galena-sphalerite-chalcopyrite ore bodies of Bawdwin in the northern Shan plateau of Burma are, nevertheless, one of the great lead-zinc deposits of the world. Although proved reserves of high-grade ore appear limited, Bawdwin also possesses very extensive lower-grade ores whose magnitude has never been estimated. The Bawdwin galena has a very high silver content, a fact which long made it attractive to Chinese miners, but in addition to silver, lead and zinc, the Bawdwin workings also produced substantial quantities of copper, nickel and antimony. Before World War II, Burma was the world's fifth largest lead-producer and Bawdwin probably the world's largest silver mine. Since the establishment of the Union of Burma, however, lead output has never amounted to more than about a quarter of the prewar production level, and with the total nationalization, in 1965, of the joint enterprise that had carried on a fitful operation of the mine since 1954, complete rehabilitation of Bawdwin appears as far away as ever.

Most Southeast Asian countries possess sizeable deposits of iron ore, although Thailand and the Indochinese states appear less well endowed. Many deposits, however, including the large lateritic ore deposits of Surigao in northern Mindanao and the similar deposits in southeast Kalimantan and in central Sulawesi, cannot at present be regarded as of any great significance, as they contain proportions of nickel and chromium which render them unsuitable for treatment in the conventional blast-furnace. Deposits of high-grade ore free from such injurious impurities are not common, and best-endowed in this respect is West Malaysia, where haematite and magnetite ore bodies with an iron content of 60 per cent or more occur in Trengganu, Pahang, Perak, Kelantan and Johor. The Philippines also contains several high-grade deposits, but reserves of such ore appear much smaller than those of West Malaysia.

Iron ore production in Southeast Asia owes almost everything to the Japanese, who in the Thirties turned to the region in order to supplement the Empire's chronic shortage of ore. By 1939 Japanese-controlled mines were exporting nearly 2 million tons of ore from Malaya and about 1·25 million tons from the Philippines. Postwar rehabilitation of iron-mining was slow, but as the Japanese economy began its hectic expansion in the Fifties, ore production rose rapidly, a development that was accelerated by the Japanese iron and steel industry's steady progress away from steelworks using imported scrap and towards large integrated works based on imported ore and coking coal. Although Japan no longer has any direct interest in iron-ore production in the region, it has provided equipment and technicians to assist the expansion of the iron-mining industry of West Malaysia, where, although the largest operation is in European hands, there is also a substantial Chinese interest. In the peak year of 1963, West Malaysia exported nearly seven million tons of ore to Japan, mainly from the Bukit Besi mine in Trengganu and from the Ipoh district of Perak, and the Philippines slightly over a million tons, principally from the Larap peninsula in Camarines Norte, Luzon.

There is little prospect of any alternative market for Southeast Asian iron ore at present apart from Japan, and output reflects the level of activity in the Japanese iron and steel industry. The scarcity of local coking coals and the limited local market hinder the establishment of an iron and steel industry in the region itself; the size of units necessary for economical operation of conventional plants is far too large for the respective national economies to support. Alternative technologies, however, do offer some possibility of establishing a ferrous metallurgical industry, or some section of it, and the feasibility of such developments are examined further below. Nevertheless, it seems unlikely that any such industries can absorb a substantial proportion of Southeast Asia's ore production for some time to come.

Bauxite, the principal oxide of aluminium, resembles iron ore in that deposits, to be economically workable, have to be of high grade with a metallic content preferably exceeding 50 per cent. Bauxite is formed by the chemical weathering of clayey limestones and igneous rocks under humid tropical conditions, and it is possible that sizeable deposits could exist in several parts of the region. Commercial production at present, however, is confined to south Johor in West Malaysia, and to the nearby Riau islands of Indonesia. As with iron ore, the Japanese market is paramount; the 1966 output of about 1·7 million tons continued the general expansion of bauxite mining in the Sixties, a declining Indonesian production being more than offset by expansion in West Malaysia. Although the establishment of alumina plants in the region would appear feasible, the large power requirements and capital-intensive nature of final reduction make it unlikely that smelting plants will be set up in the future, although a metal-reduction plant has long been planned by Indonesia as part of its Asahan valley project.

Fuel minerals

The high cost of energy is a major obstacle to growth in economically backward countries, and investment in expanding energy production to achieve the economies of scale is usually of major significance in national development plans. Such investment, however, usually takes the form of expanding the output of electrical energy, which in Southeast Asia is largely produced from imported primary sources. The production of primary energy sources such as mineral fuels is still largely within the private sector, which either through changing market conditions or, more often, through increasing government interference and regulation, has tended to find opportunities for profitable production distinctly limited. In some instances the state has proceeded to outright nationalization of such mining enterprises, but the new government corporations have been generally unsuccessful in achieving significant increases in the level of output.

Though far from a major world source of supply, Southeast Asia is a larger petroleum producer than is either South or East Asia, and, given a more favourable socio-political environment, the present output of somewhat less than 30 million tons might have been doubled over the Sixties; nevertheless, although Indonesia, the largest producer, has long operated an exchange-rate system which makes international comparison difficult, petroleum is probably the region's most important mineral product by value of output. A little petroleum is produced by Sarawak and Burma, but only Brunei and Indonesia are of major importance, and the dominance of the latter is so complete that the industry's problems can only be considered against the background of the chaotic Indonesian economy. Large quantities of natural gas are also produced in connection with petroleum production in Indonesia, but for want of markets, most of this is flared.

Coals of some kind occur in almost every country of Southeast Asia, but the deposits are generally of small size and are poorly located in relation to potential markets. They are generally of a lignitic or sub-bituminous nature, occurring in rocks of Secondary or Tertiary age, and with the important exception of the anthracites of the Tonkin coalfield of North Vietnam, which also has the advantage of occurring within easy reach of the country's major port and its capital, none of them is suitable for the production of metallurgical coke. The Philippines, Burma and Thailand have planned to use their isolated coal deposits in integrated regional industrialization schemes, but the expected return on such investment appears unlikely to lead to their early implementation. Under the impact of cheap imported oil, output levels are almost everywhere trending downwards, and only in North Vietnam, which has an output of more than one million tons, has production increased in the Sixties.

MANUFACTURING INDUSTRIES

When Europeans first penetrated into Southeast Asia, the general level of technology in the region, including that of the industrial arts, does not appear to have been markedly inferior to that of contemporary Europe,[25] and in both areas the household was the dominant unit of industrial production. In succeeding centuries, however, the technological gap broadened very greatly and competition from cheap factory-made products of the colonial powers destroyed one village industry after another, forcing the rural population to depend more and more on the crowded agricultural sector. Additionally in the present century there came an inflow of Japanese manufactures, which became a flood in the Thirties when, with its low-cost labour and depreciated yen, Japan was able to push its exports, unaffected by the Great Depression. Since 1945, Hong Kong and China have taken over part of Japan's former function as a provider of cheap manufactures as that country has progressively reorientated its exports towards capital goods and 'quality' markets.

Cottage and small-scale industries

The Great Depression prompted the first positive attempts at protecting and improving the efficiency of traditional industries, and in the Netherlands Indies particularly, a considerable effort was made to provide more productive equipment for the worker in cottage industries. These achieved only modest success, but in some countries within the region resources are still being expended in supporting

[25] *Benjamin Higgins, 'Western enterprise and the economic development of Southeast Asia', Pacific Affairs, vol. 31, 1958, p. 76.*

cottage industries which, although they possess much less political influence than is the case in India, are nevertheless still attractive to the ambivalent nationalist politician who wants a modern industrial society based on the traditional cultural framework, and does not grasp that the two are incompatible. In Indonesia, where such ambivalence is widespread, cottage industries are still numerous and are particularly important in Djawa Tengah (Central Java), politically a very important part of the country.

Several names have been used to describe those manufacturing enterprises outside the scope of modern factory organization; Boeke distinguished five such types in Indonesia, which he termed *household, handicraft, cottage, workshop* and *small factory-like* businesses; of these the last-named were almost entirely in the hands of Chinese, and alone made any use of power.[26] ECAFE distinguishes between cottage industries 'carried on wholly or partly with the help of members of the family, either as a whole or part time occupation', and small-scale industries 'operated mainly with hired labour usually not exceeding fifty workers in any establishment or unit not using motive power in any operation, or twenty workers in an establishment or unit using such power.'[27] The pre-colonial Southeast Asian village had a high degree of self-sufficiency, for its unsophisticated requirements of manufactured products were largely met by cottage industries located in the village itself. The main stimulus for the establishment of small-scale industry was the needs of a princely court, and where such industries embody a vigorous artistic tradition they have usually managed to survive competition from factory-made products. Improvements in communications have occasionally made possible the specialization of whole villages in small-scale industry; in parts of Java with suitable clay deposits there are villages earning more from roofing-tile manufacture than from agriculture.

Traditional small-scale industries, however, suffer either from complex, over-long productive processes, as in the case of the *batik* industry of Java, or from a low productivity per worker resulting from the almost complete absence of power. Nevertheless, some Western economists have declaimed the virtues of cottage and small-scale industries as an agent of economic development. Low productivity per worker can be improved by such devices as the flying shuttle, a 200-year-old technical improvement which is still absent in the great majority of domestic weaving looms in the region, and, most importantly, by the use of small electric motors. Small-scale industries provide a market for locally produced raw materials; they assist in reducing imports of consumer goods, thus freeing foreign exchange earnings for the import of capital equipment; they help to mobilize local savings and provide employment opportunities operating to check the drift to the

[26] *J. H. Boeke*, Economics and Economic Policy of Dual Societies, *H. D. Tjeenk Willink, Haarlem, 1953, p. 100, and Institute of Pacific Relations, New York, 1954.*

[27] *United Nations*, Economic Survey of Asia and the Far East 1958, *Bangkok, 1959, p. 100.*

cities; and they constitute a valuable training ground for business acumen and skilled labour.[28]

As Galbraith has pointed out, however, these arguments usually emanate from experts drawn from countries where such industries have long ceased to be of any importance; all too often the products of cottage industry are of stereo-typed unimaginative design, crude workmanship and low utility.[29] In practice, traditional cottage industries tend to withdraw into areas where alternative occupations are fewest and labour is cheapest, as in the hand-loom industry of Kelantan and Trengganu in Malaya and the batik industry of Jogjakarta. The labour force in such industries is almost entirely illiterate; 95 per cent of the weavers in Trengganu are illiterate in any language. Only a small proportion of the total payments of cottage industries are made to labour. In 1936 wages amounted to only 18 per cent of the costs of the Javanese batik industry; thirty years later, and despite considerable protection and other assistance given the industry by the Indonesian government, labour's share was almost exactly the same. The whole tradition of 'homework' in the Western world is, to quote Galbraith, 'synonymous with weakness, industrial oppression and misery', and Asian experience is not one whit different. Hand-loom weavers on the east coast of Malaya earned an average wage of less than M16 cents (about 5d. or 5c. US) an hour in 1960, and the batik industry of Java appears to be relying more and more on very poorly remunerated part-time workers in order to defeat government labour regulations and the increasing militancy of the well-organized full-time workers. Industries that have to depend on an illiterate labour force, and that can only survive in areas where incomes per head are markedly below the national average, can hardly claim to be worthy of preservation.

Moreover, the output of cottage industries often includes a high import content, for it is only by using imported raw materials that anything approaching uniformity of product can be assured; local raw materials tend to be both uncertain in supply and of very varying quality. In the case of the two above-mentioned industries, imported raw materials account for about three-quarters of the payments of the Javanese batik industry and about half of those of the Malayan hand-loom industry. As a result, the greatest rewards go to the importers, who always consist of a few large firms. Attempts at overcoming this problem by restricting importing and distributing rights to producer cooperatives have achieved little or no success. Nor is there much evidence that small industries are a suitable vehicle for amassing managerial ability or for training skilled labour. Experience in the mechanization of small-scale industries in Indonesia shows conclusively that this only succeeds where the level of managerial ability is already considerable, and the only effective training of skilled workers is given in large state-

[28] *United Nations, 'Modernization of small industries in Asia',* Economic Bulletin for Asia and the Far East, *vol. II, No. 1, Bangkok, 1961, p. 25.*

[29] *J. K. Galbraith,* The Liberal Hour, *Hamish Hamilton, London, 1960, pp. 127–30.*

owned plants such as railway workshops and dockyards, and in the few large establishments of the foreign corporations still operating in the country, particularly those of the oil companies.

Fortunately, the cottage and small-scale industries of Southeast Asia are of small extent and are highly localized. The largest, the batik industry of Central Java, employs perhaps about 40,000 full-time and more than twice this number of part-time workers, and important though this is, the region clearly possesses no equivalent of the widespread hand-loom industry of India, which supports perhaps as many as fifty million people.[30] It is possible, therefore, for most countries to make a balanced assessment of the relative merits and demerits of large- as against small-scale production, and to plan for an industrial structure that contains an optimum combination of both types.

One traditional industry in the region, at least, has been transformed by the application of non-indigenous business acumen and through switching production away from traditional lines towards those of greater appeal to the world market: this is the silk industry of Thailand, which was revitalized by an American business man who was perspicacious enough to see that with appropriate reorganization the industry could produce articles highly attractive to the foreign buyer or tourist—a change which offers considerable possibilities to the Malayan hand-loom industry.[31] Another very successful cottage industry is entirely non-indigenous, and owes its fortune to its orientation *ab initio* towards the world market: this is the Chinese rubber smokehouse industry of Malaysia, which handles a substantial proportion of the country's smallholder rubber production. Such examples strongly support a conclusion that traditional industries serving traditional markets are unlikely to be made competitive through mere tinkering, and it is doubtful if the wider use of producer cooperatives, a form of industrial organization regarded with almost religious veneration in parts of the region, is any more likely to prosper. If traditional industries are to survive, they need new processes to telescope lengthy and over-elaborate production methods, or production must be reorganized to produce goods of wider appeal. Ultimately, however, the success of any industrial enterprise, large or small, rests with the complex of mental characteristics and social outlooks of those engaged in it. Although in Indonesia the policy of establishing *perusahaan induk* (literally, mother enterprises), machine-equipped producer cooperatives, has proved a miserable failure, successful new industrial enterprises have been established by groups of devout *santri* Muslims, whose religious beliefs encourage hard work, thrift and enterprise—precisely the qualities that have given the Chinese such a

[30] *The Dry zone of Burma in 1940 possessed some 200,000 handicraft workers, a large proportion of whom were children and old people, otherwise unemployable. But many of these were obviously part-time workers, and probably unemployed for lengthy periods. See J. Russell Andrus,* Burmese Economic Life, *Stanford University Press, Stanford, California, and Oxford University Press, London, 1947, p. 133.*

[31] *See p. 158.*

substantial share of the economic life of the region. To expect traditional industries to prop up established cultural values, yet at the same time play a major significant role in achieving a modern industrial society, is to ask for the impossible.

There is certainly, however, a great need for the expansion of modern small industries working in close association with large establishments, a very well-marked feature of the Japanese economy, which had special advantages for the growth of an industrial structure of this type. But such industries would have to be provided with electric power and would have to be situated in the towns. They could be located on special industrial estates, or accommodated in something like the remarkable flatted factories that have sprung up in connection with the redevelopment schemes of Hong Kong; such an aglommeration of producing units would, moreover, offer opportunities for 'external economies' through the development of linkages between individual lines of production.

Large-scale industry

Before World War II, large-scale industry was almost entirely confined to the largely European-owned processing of exportable agricultural and mineral products, and to supporting the infrastructural equipment of railways, harbours and power plants that made these activities possible. For technical reasons some of these products, such as tea, palm oil, sugar and quinine, were processed to a degree that made them fit for immediate consumption in the world economy; others such as rubber and copra received further processing overseas. Tin-mining, petroleum production and sugar-milling were, and still are, activities that also required considerable heavy engineering plants to maintain the productive equipment in working order.

The shortage of consumer goods in World War I laid the basis for the gradual growth of consumer-goods industries, and during the later interwar period a range of such industries producing commodities such as drinks and foodstuffs, which enjoyed a considerable degree of natural protection and which in part used local raw materials, were established in most of the primate cities. The distress caused by the low agricultural prices of the Great Depression prompted further state interest in manufacturing; in the Netherlands Indies, which suffered very severely, manufacturers received a measure of protection from imports, Dutch industrial concerns were invited to set up fabricating or assembly plants, sometimes in cooperation with the government, and the 'Big Six' agency and importing houses were persuaded to invest in manufacturing enterprise. Following the establishment of the Commonwealth in 1935, the Philippine government participated directly in an increasing range of industrial activities and made very substantial investments in private manufacturing concerns. The cotton textile industry, however, usually among the first to adopt a factory organization and one that has in so many instances spearheaded the advance towards industrialization, made strikingly little progress in Southeast Asia despite a high degree of protection and other forms of state assistance.

Large-scale industry received a set-back during the Japanese occupation, although the Japanese themselves improvised brilliantly with the industrial equipment at their disposal within the region in meeting the needs of their armed forces. The occupation also encouraged a proliferation of small Chinese-owned industries, some of which eventually grew to substantial size. But the postwar triumph of nationalism produced a generally unfavourable environment for European-owned enterprise. Tonkin, which possessed the largest share of the French industrial investment in Indochina, passed into the communist world in 1954; Burma and Indonesia, which had announced their intention to establish some form of state socialism at the time of independence, had completed the nationalization of all foreign-owned enterprises by 1965, although these had experienced increasing operational difficulties in both countries for many years previously.

To some extent, however, this trend was balanced by the adoption of a more liberal attitude towards private capital in industrial activity on the part of the Philippine and Thai governments. Following the inauguration of President Magsaysay in 1954, the Philippine government began to dispose of much of its industrial activities to private capital, as nepotism, corruption and inefficiency had assumed the proportions of major national scandals. After 1958 Thailand also moved to reduce the magnitude of the state interest in manufacturing, which had been encouraged by Thailand's perennial concern for its independence. Only Malaysia has been consistently opposed to large-scale state participation in industrial ventures, and with justification claims that its policy of steadily improving the infrastructure and providing inducements to private capital is the surest way to produce a high rate of industrial advance.

Even in Thailand, the Philippines and Malaya, however, a determined effort is being made to enlarge local participation in industrial activity, and, although foreign investment is invited, this is encouraged to take the form of association with local capital in joint ventures. Such undertakings may receive a variety of privileges, such as freedom from company tax for a stipulated number of years, the remission of duty on imported raw materials, protection in various forms including quantitative restrictions on imports (even Singapore, whose prosperity for over a century has been in large part dependent on its status as a free-port, has adopted this device), and allocations of foreign exchange for the repatriation of profits, although in practice most of the profits of foreign industrial enterprises are ploughed back for further expansion. For some manufacturing activities a local majority stock holding may be mandatory, but it is always possible for stock to be made available to the politically important and privileged local élite on especially favourable terms. The desire to establish a foothold in what may become an important expanding market has attracted many foreign firms to interest themselves in such joint ventures, and although American and European, principally British, capital has been mainly involved, Japan has expanded its interest very rapidly. Australia and Hong Kong also appear likely to make further industrial investment in the region in the near future. There are grounds for seriously questioning whether these concessions do in fact stimulate a more rapid rate of industrial growth, especially in view of the remarkable industrial success of Hong Kong, where manufacturing has proliferated without any kind of official inducement, but such arguments carry little weight in Southeast Asian countries, whose industrialization policies are a fundamental part of nationalism.

Where Western industrial enterprise has been deliberately restricted, however, its consequence has invariably been a steady growth of Chinese industrial power. The most striking example of this tendency is to be found in Thailand, perpetually concerned with preserving its independence against rapacious colonial powers. Shortly before World War II, Thailand nationalized a number of large Western enterprises in the region and has since refused to renew teak concessions originally granted around the turn of the century; in consequence, by 1950 more than 90 per cent of the 'foreign' investment in the country was owned in fact by the Chinese community.[32] In Indonesia also, increasingly irksome restrictions on European enterprise, in conjunction with a policy designed to divert importing and distribution from Chinese to indigenous Indonesian hands, produced a rapid increase in Chinese manufacturing. Much Chinese industry is of the small-scale type, but rice-milling, in which there are many large units, is dominated by Chinese throughout the region, and attempts by the state to displace them in favour of indigenes have in general experienced little success. The impermanence of the Chinese firm, resulting from its personal or family basis, places it at a heavy disadvantage in manufacturing *vis-à-vis* the durable and impersonal Western corporation, and this disadvantage is more marked with industries of increasing capital-to-labour ratios. Thus while every country within the region possesses, or possessed, Chinese-owned concentrations of manufacturing industries, the large Chinese industrialist typically combines manufacturing with other activities, and his manufacturing interests tend to be diversified horizontally; the vertical integration so common in Western manufacturing is seldom encountered. In Indonesia and Burma, some large Chinese industrial holdings have suffered the same fate as that of European enterprise and have been taken over by the state. One of the largest of such concentrations was that of the Kian Gwan Company, which from sugar-milling in central Java moved into many other kinds of industrial enterprise and also into construction, shipping, banking, and distribution, with ramifications throughout Southeast Asia and even beyond.

Capital-intensive industry is thus either the fruits of foreign investment,

[32] *Robert L. Pendleton*, Thailand: Aspects of Land and Life, *Duell, Sloan and Pearce, New York, 1962, p. 268.*

usually by the giant corporations of America, Europe or Japan, or, where capitalism is no longer acceptable, in the hands of the state. The most capital-intensive industries operating in the region are the refineries of the giant international oil companies. Only the Indochinese states lack a modern refinery capable of supplying the greater part of the domestic requirements of refined products. South Vietnam's first refinery was scheduled to come on stream in 1966, but construction was delayed, and the future of the project, which was supported by a consortium of the international oil companies, was still uncertain at the time of writing. Economic nationalism, however, has saddled the region with a multiplicity of small refineries, none of which is large enough to achieve the fullest economies of scale.

Conventional integrated iron and steel plants with blast-furnaces, steelworks and finishing mills still appear some way off in most countries. The only such complex at the present is the Thai Nguyen plant in North Vietnam, but inte-integrated re-rolling plants and finishing mills with electric furnaces and small blast-furnaces are in operation or under development in the Philippines, Malaysia and Singapore. Indonesia and Burma also have small, and exceedingly inefficient, steel mills already in operation. The iron and steel industry exerts a powerful attraction for the political leaders of newly independent countries, but the technological and economic problems in the way of a viable industry are numerous. The regional shortage of coking coal makes iron reduction in the conventional blast-furnace a major problem, and though such units make possible low-cost production, a modern blast-furnace of optimum size produces far more pig than any national economy in the region can absorb. So-called 'direct reduction' processes, such as the Krupp-Renn, H-iron, Wiberg-Soderfors and many other similar processes, have the advantage of using almost any kind of hydrocarbon fuel and can be operated in small units. Present experience of these is limited and none has so far been able to match the costs of conventional iron smelting; nevertheless, direct reduction could prove a better proposition for Southeast Asia than the conventional coke-fired blast-furnace, and the Japanese, who are participating in the establishment of a steel industry in Malaysia, and may also do so in the Philippines, have had considerable experience with the Krupp-Renn process on the East Asian mainland.

Other capital-intensive industries include cement manufacture, a raw-materials orientated industry now well established in almost every country although the region is still a net importer of cement, certain branches of chemical production such as fertilizers, the manufacture of rubber tyres, and motor vehicle assembly. At present no aluminium smelting takes place within the region, although there are projected schemes in both Indonesia and the Philippines. Sugar-milling and palm-oil production are also, of course, capital-intensive operations though related to the agricultural sector; tobacco and cigarette manufacture and textiles are somewhat similarly placed, but in each case there is substantial reliance on imported raw materials. Cotton textiles are very large items in the import trade of several countries, and the development of import-replacing industries of this kind is more to be recommended than attempts to break into heavily capital-intensive industries for the sake of nationalist pride. A major problem here is that the higher prices caused by tariffs have severely limited total textile consumption, and even the small existing capacity may be under-utilized. In both the Philippines and Indonesia foreign textiles can overcome tariff barriers, and to make the latter prohibitive would impose an intolerable burden on the population.

Electricity generation   Industrialization of underdeveloped countries will inevitably necessitate a substantial increase in the consumption of electric power (or more correctly, energy). Electricity generation is an industry in which the economies of scale are very substantial, and the present low level of electric power production in the region is a major factor in the high cost of electricity, which in turn is a powerful deterrent to further industrialization. The principal use of electricity in almost every country at present is for domestic lighting; consumption by manufacturing in most countries before World War II scarcely amounted to more than the line losses in transmission. West Malaysia is exceptional in the large electric power consumption of its tin-mining industry, which until very recently accounted for over half the total consumption of electrical energy in the country; tin-mining together with a substantial increase in the demand for manufacturing purposes give West Malaysia a consumption pattern which is quite unique in the region and which more closely resembles that of countries at higher levels of development (*Table 3-4*). In its per capita consumption of electricity West Malaysia again clearly indicates its superior level of economic development.

Table 3-4   *Southeast Asia: percentage distribution of energy sales of electric utilities, 1964*

	Domestic	Commercial	Industrial	Other
West Malaysia	11	16	48	25
Sabah	45	23	30	2
Sarawak	42	42	13	3
Singapore	20	32	45	3
Burma*	66	└────18────		16
Indonesia*	└────77────┘		└────23────┘	
Thailand	33	24	41	2
Philippines	30	20	39	11
South Vietnam	53	30	14	3

* 1962

Source: ECAFE, *Electric Power in Asia and the Far East,* 1964

Table 3-5 *Southeast Asia: electricity generation, 1964*

	Installed capacity (*thousand kW*)	Generation (*million kWh*)				Per capita Generation (*kWh*)	Average Plant factor
		Steam	Hydro	Diesel	Total		
West Malaysia	485	1,076	499	137	1,712	220	40
Sabah	18			35	35	69	22
Sarawak	20			40	40	49	23
Singapore	224	894		20*	914	496	46
Brunei	23			70	70	722	37
Burma	191	59	230	67	356	16	21
Cambodia	39	8		91	99	16	30
Laos	11			13	13	5	13
Indonesia	391	200	700	400	1,300	13	38
Thailand	548	626	288	193	1,107	25	25
Philippines	993	2,582	1,553	542	4,677	153	54
South Vietnam	325	241	56	277	574	37	19

* Gas turbine

Source: E C A F E, *Electric Power in Asia and the Far East*, 1964

Power supply systems are virtually confined to the respective metropolitan centres; only Luzon and West Malaysia possess even a rudimentary interconnected network. The largest power station in the region in 1966 was the 245 MW thermal plant in Makati (Manila); Singapore's Pasir Panjang station had a capacity of 177 MW, and a new extension will have an ultimate additional capacity of 250 MW. These large oil-fired thermal stations achieve a high level of efficiency, but their turbo-alternators are still well below the size of the enormous new units now coming into operation in highly developed economies. Smaller towns and most mining establishments rely mainly on diesel engines. The demand pattern inevitably results in a low plant-utilization factor, although private undertakings supplying mining activities do considerably better, as mining enterprises usually operate on a twenty-four hour schedule throughout the year, apart from brief shut-downs for maintenance.

Indonesia and Burma derive a large proportion of their production of electrical energy from hydro-electric installations (*Table 3-5*); this in itself is indicative of a failure to keep productivity rising, for in all developed countries thermal plants, which can be rapidly and cheaply erected, account for a progressively larger share of total electricity production. Hydro-electric stations are extremely expensive both in capital outlay and in time (more than a decade is usually necessary for the construction of a large project), and the relatively large share of hydro-electricity in total electricity production represents on the one hand a continued heavy dependence on prewar schemes and, on the other, the growing contribution from new multipurpose water-utilization schemes whose capital requirements have been largely met through foreign aid programmes.

The Mekong Valley Scheme

Many multipurpose water-utilization schemes have been proposed in newly independent countries since the end of World War II; the Mekong scheme differs from most of these in owing little to economic nationalism. It will affect almost all the countries of mainland Southeast Asia, and owes its origins to a study of the technical problems associated with international rivers begun in 1951 by the Bureau of Flood Control of ECAFE. The preliminary report of the Bureau elicited such favourable reaction that it was followed by a further study by the United States Bureau of Reclamation, and in 1957 by the ECAFE report, *Development of Water Resources in the Lower Mekong Basin*. The scheme involves damming the Mekong and some of its tributaries for hydro-electricity generation, extended irrigation, flood control and the improvement of navigation on the river, the freedom of which was confirmed in 1926 by an agreement between France and Thailand, and which has been honoured by the successor states to French Indochina.

The Mekong is the major river of mainland Southeast Asia and drains an area of some 310,000 square miles. For almost half of its length it occupies a series of deep narrow gorges in Tibet and western China. Deep gorges also characterize its passage across the mountains of northern Laos, and even below Vientiane the valley is still hemmed in between the margin of the Khorat plateau and the Annamite Chain. Between Luang Prabang and Kratie the river frequently flows in relatively open country, but its course is punctuated by further deep gorges and rocky constrictions in which the speed of the current makes navigation distinctly hazardous, and by falls above Savannakhet and at Khone. Below Kratie the river has created an extensive alluvial plain, and at its junction near Phnom Penh with the discharge from the Tonlé Sap, or Great Lake, the river bifurcates into two branches, the Song Hau Giang (Bassac) to the west and the Mekong to the east. The river starts to rise rapidly in the Lower Basin following the onset of the monsoon rains and attains its maximum level in September and October; its level then falls rapidly until December and thereafter more slowly, reaching its lowest point before the monsoon, although as a snow-fed river the Mekong still has an abundant discharge at its lowest level, an important consideration for power production.

Control of the Mekong and the Tonlé Sap would confer many benefits. The rapids obstructing navigation would be 'drowned'; abnormally high floods in the delta would be prevented; raising the level of the Great Lake in the dry season would improve fishing, and through its greater discharge would prevent the incursion of salt water in the delta at this time of year; additional water would enable a substantial improvement in crop yields along the lower Mekong and particularly in the poverty-stricken and relatively dry area of northeast Thailand. The unified development of six sites for electricity generation on the Mekong at Luang Prabang, Pa Mong, Thakhek, Khemmarat, Khone Falls and Sambor (the

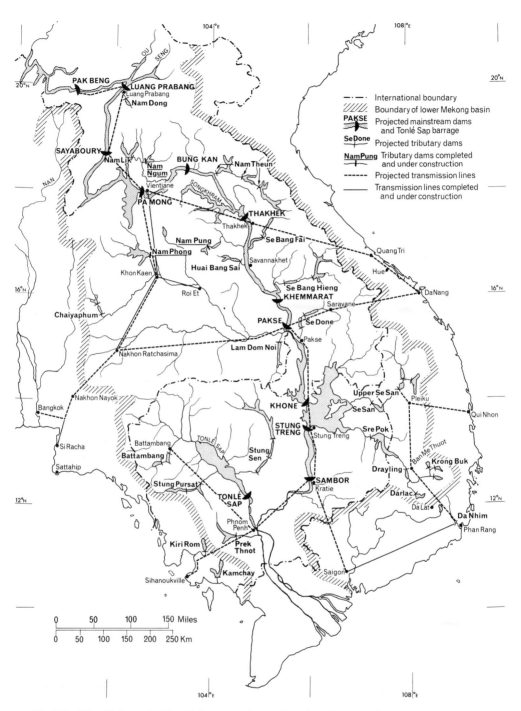

Fig 3-4   The Mekong Valley Scheme and associated national projects

The Mekong Valley Scheme is one of the most ambitious multipurpose water conservation and utilization undertakings ever envisaged, but many of the individual projects shown on this map appear unlikely to come to fruition.

Rock-blasting in the Mekong channel above Savannakhet, Laos, part of a Colombo Plan project for improving navigation.

Tonlé Sap regulation would produce no power) and one on the Nam Theun, a left-bank tributary above Thakhek, would make possible the installation of a capacity of 4·2 million kW, capable of producing a firm energy output of 37×10^9 kWh per year. Khemmarat, which would constitute the centre of an inter-connected grid, is within four hundred miles of all the important cities in the Lower Basin, a distance well within the economic limits of transmission with modern high-voltage lines.

An energy production of this magnitude is almost twenty-five times that of the total electricity output in 1962 of the countries affected by the scheme, and it is clear that such a unified development would take a very long time to eventuate, if indeed it ever comes to fruition in this form. The cost of the five 'priority' projects (Pa Mong, Khemmarat, Khone Falls, Sambor and Tonlé Sap) was estimated in 1961 at around 2,000 million US dollars, but such calculations always possess a large element of conjecture and the final cost could hardly fail to be many times as great. In absolute terms, however, this sum is not so very great —the United States provided more than six times this amount in foreign aid between 1956 and 1960—and in relation to the anticipated benefit the cost does not appear excessive. Apart from financing difficulties, formidable legal problems also present themselves. Most of the mainstream dams and their storages will be international, and the principal benefits of others will accrue to adjacent territories. Even the works on tributary streams will benefit downstream neighbours, and virtually all contries of the mainland regard each other with considerable hostility.

Against such a background, the degree of cooperation achieved by the international advisory committee of ECAFE, set up in 1957, is quite astonishing, and the evidence strongly suggests that whatever they may think of each other, the component states of the mainland all want the scheme to come to fruition. So far, constructional work has been confined to dredging and other improvements in the navigation of the main river, and on the tributary dams, which are national responsibilities; many donor-countries have contributed to funds for preliminary surveys and feasibility studies, and to the financing of the tributary dams, although by 1967, Britain alone of the major donors had declined to provide funds for the latter. Nevertheless, the Nam Phong (Ubonratana) and Nam Pung dams in northeast Thailand have been completed, work has commenced on the Nam Ngum dam in Laos, and although the Prek Thnot project near Phnom Penh in Cambodia appears bogged down in political difficulties over financing, these do not seem incapable of solution in the near future. There is even a possibility that North Vietnam can be persuaded to participate, and in April 1965 President Johnson offered large sums for the prosecution of the scheme as part of a general settlement in terminating the Vietnam war, an offer which unfortunately met with no response from Hanoi.

Whatever its final form, however, implementation of the scheme is contingent on a greatly enhanced flow of Western aid funds, for the communist powers possess neither the resources nor the desire to assist the development of the Mekong; a greater degree of regional cooperation and integration could only result in a diminution of the influence of the communist powers in Southeast Asia. Sooner or later the Vietnam war will be concluded; and if the peace agreement leads, as is quite probable, to a greater flow of resources to the Mekong Scheme, the conflict could accelerate the creation of benefits which will endure long after it has been forgotten.

II PROGRESS

CHAPTER FOUR

Thailand

As the only country within the region that has never experienced colonial rule, Thailand[1] has an especial interest. The leaders of most newly independent countries in the underdeveloped world lose no opportunity of proclaiming that the colonial period was an economic and social disaster, and almost imply that the pre-existing native society was much more humane and equitable. The world, in truth, has become increasingly weary of such harangues in the United Nations and other international fora; but the blighting effect of colonialism is still widely believed. The case of Thailand, however, strongly suggests that there may not be much in this charge after all, which may go far to explain why some demagogues of the Third World often brand Thailand as a Western puppet lacking real independence. But for over a century, in fact, Thailand practiced a neutralism far more rigorous than the present fashionable 'non-alignment', and its post-1950 attachment to the West is a sharp break with tradition. Moreover, the country strongly endeavoured to maintain an economic as well as a political independence; late nineteenth-century writers compared Thailand with Japan, the only two Asian countries to avoid loss of independence, or what was virtually the same, a division into 'spheres of influence', and many expected that 'progressive Siam' would surpass Japan in economic development.[2]

These forecasts proved erroneous, and a large share of the economy passed into the hands of alien peoples, particularly the Chinese. With a substantial share of its national product derived from the export trade, a concomitant high propensity to import, and a heavy dependence on export taxes and import duties for much of government revenue, Thailand by the beginning of this century had become almost as much a 'dual economy' as any colonial possession. It differed,

---

[1] *The spelling of Thai place-names is in accordance with the* Official Gazetteer on Thailand *of the United States Permanent Committee on Geographic Names. These spellings are normally also used in atlases published by* The Times, *Philip and Bartholomew. See also Preface.*

[2] *James C. Ingram,* Economic Change in Thailand Since 1950, *Stanford University Press, Stanford, 1964, p. 216.*

however, in one important respect. The decision to open up Thailand to the modern world and to replace the self-sufficient indigenous economy with a monetized one was, as in Japan, a decision made and imposed from above; but the limited response of the Thai people to monetary stimuli, and their strong preference for rice cultivation over all other occupations, perforce obliged the government itself to enter into all kinds of economic activity if it were not to acquiesce in allowing non-agricultural activities to pass entirely into the hands of aliens. At present the government participates in the exploitation of forest and mineral resources, engages in many kinds of agricultural processing and manufacturing enterprises, and controls a large share of transport and communications, domestic and foreign trade, and banking and finance. Nevertheless, the private sector still generates by far the largest share of national product and the essentially free economy of Thailand appears likely to endure. The bureaucratic élite, nevertheless, is generally expected to participate in private business, and its growing involvement in Chinese enterprise after 1952 was probably the decisive factor in Marshal Sarit's decision to halt the foundation of additional state enterprises.[3]

By almost every test Thailand has shown a steady economic growth since 1945; real product per capita has increased and, almost uniquely among Asian countries, rice consumption per head is now above the prewar level. A greatly enhanced domestic rice consumption has not prevented a simultaneous expansion of rice exports, in which respect Thailand is also unique among traditional Asian rice exporters, but at the same time other exports have expanded faster so that rice now produces a smaller share of export earnings than in 1939. The share of national product generated by manufacturing, about 12 per cent in 1965, is already one of the highest in the region (*Table 4-1*), and industrial output is probably underestimated in official statistics. The first Six-Year National Economic Development Plan (1961–1966), adopted in 1962, provided for an increase in industrial output of about 12 per cent per annum and an increase in gross domestic product of some 5 per cent, rising in the second stage of the plan to 6 per cent. Thailand in fact managed to do rather better than this; nevertheless, in view of a population increase of about 3·3 per cent per annum, it would still take almost two decades at the current rate of economic growth for Thailand to double its per capita product to the equivalent of that of Malaysia.

Thailand's most pressing problems arise from major regional imbalances in the distribution of income; while per capita incomes in the Central Plain are probably twice the national average, those in the Northeast are little more than half, and with falling rubber prices the peninsula has also become a region of stagnation and growing dissatisfaction. These problems are heightened by the existence of linguistic minority groups, the Lao in the east and north, and the

[3] *T. H. Silcock (ed.)*, Thailand: Social and Economic Studies in Development, *Australian National University Press, Canberra, 1967, pp. 96–8.*

Malays in the extreme south. The Lao are part of the large group of Thai-speaking peoples, but possess a different script from that of the Thais of the Mae Nam (Menam) plain, and have other linguistic and cultural differences. The political division of the Lao people by the Mekong is a potential source of danger to Bangkok, which views events in Laos itself with deep concern and has accused Peking and Hanoi of promoting communist infiltration and acts of violence in Thailand's northeastern provinces. Fortunately, the situation is not being allowed to deteriorate. Since 1962 the Community Development Administration has endeavoured to promote village self-help, to enlarge local supplies of potable water and to introduce new activities such as coconut and silkworm production; since this date also the Northeast has begun to receive considerable priority in the allocation of development expenditure, and by 1965 some two-thirds of a growing American non-military aid was also being channelled into the area. The same year witnessed the opening of an all-weather road, the so-called 'Friendship Highway', from Sara Buri to Nakhon Ratchasima (Khorat), Udon Thani and the Mekong at Nong Khai, bringing Bangkok within seven hours of the Laos frontier; though clearly of major military significance, the new road will have economic repercussions throughout the region, and a branch from Udon Thani to the Mekong at Nakhon Phanom is under construction. The establishment of regional development committees, under the personal supervision of the Prime Minister and senior ministers, for the North, Northeast and South, where the government has been slow to liquidate marauding bands of communist terrorists driven across the Malaysian frontier, is further evidence of the country's determination to remove economic grievances in politically vulnerable parts of the country.

BASIC REGIONALISMS

The heart of Thailand is the great central depression occupied by the Mae Nam Chao Phraya system, a plain with a maximum width of about 150 miles and extending some 300 miles from the northern mountains to the Gulf of Thailand. Physically the most favoured and economically the most important portion of the central depression is the triangular Bangkok plain south of Chainat, where the Chao Phraya anastomoses in several distributaries which are further interconnected by canals or *khlongs*. These channels also connect with the Mae Nam Mae Klong, draining the western hill and mountain margins of the central depression, and with the Mae Nam Prachin Buri (Mae Nam Bang Pakong) system, which drains the northern slopes of the Cardamon Mountains along the Cambodian frontier, and the Phanom Dongrak, the mountainous southern margin of the Khorat plateau. These rivers add their sediments to those of the Chao Phraya to form a compound delta which is gradually advancing on the Gulf of Thailand and which possesses the best and most easily utilized soils in the country. The

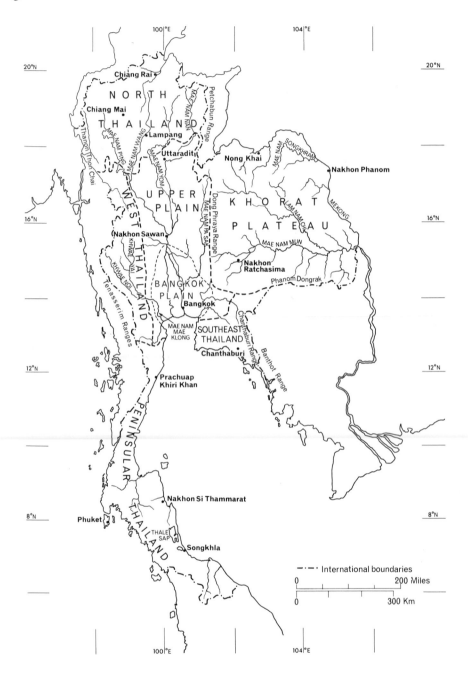

Fig 4-1   The physical regions of Thailand

The Central Plain comprises the Bangkok and Upper Plains.

flatness and extremely gentle slope of the delta (Ayutthya, some 60 miles from the coast between the Mae Nam Noi branch of the Chao Phraya and the Mae Nam Pa Sak, is only 13 feet above the level of the Gulf) is a major contributory factor in its annual inundation by the Chao Phraya. Although much of the central depression itself lies in the rain-shadow of the echelon ranges that form Thailand's western boundary and has a rainfall of less than 60 inches, too little for safe rice cultivation without supplementary water, the mountain and hill margins drained by the headstreams and tributaries of the Chao Phraya receive substantially more. Following the monsoonal rains the river starts to rise, but in its southwards passage through the plain rainfall gradually increases, and by September, the rainiest month, the whole of the delta is inundated, the flood reaching its maximum depths in October and November. The timing and depth of flooding vary according to the precipitation in the upper drainage basin and there is a substantial variation from year to year. Only in one year in three is the depth of flood at the optimum level; in other years it is either too low to ensure a good harvest except in the lowest lying districts or so high that a substantial proportion of the rice crop on the lower land is drowned. In the floods, the material deposited in the aggrading river beds during the dry season is spread over the land, providing an increment of fertility.

Northern Thailand is a mountain and plateau country transitional to Yunnan; it contains the highest elevations of the country, though summits exceeding 6,000 feet are confined to the western frontier with Burma. The region is drained by the four headstreams of the Chao Phraya, the Ping, Wang, Yom and Nan, which flow in approximately parallel courses through a series of tectonic depressions and intervening gorges. The basins have largely been cleared of their natural forest cover and, with a rice cultivation based on traditional irrigation techniques, are in many ways miniature replicas of the Central Plain. The hill and mountain slopes with their heavier precipitation are still heavily forested, and although the north produces Thailand's most valuable timber, teak or *mai sak (Tectona grandis)*, even in the richest teak areas such as the Yom and Wang basins, other species such as *deng puideng (Lagerstroemia)* and *pradu (Pterocarpus)* are cut in larger quantities. The basins are occupied by the so-called North Lao, but the uplands are occupied by hill peoples such as the Miao (Meo), Yao and Lahu, for whom maize is a more important crop than dry rice, and who also grow the temperate crops of their original homelands to the north, such as wheat, millet and buckwheat.

The north contains one of Thailand's two commercially significant coalfields, the Mae Mo lignite deposite southeast of Lampang, which with the aid of low rail freights has been consumed in the Sam Sen power station at Bangkok. Since 1960 it has also supplied a local 125 MW power station with transmission lines to Chiang Mai and is interconnected with the Yan Hee hydro-electric installation on the Ping, some 250 miles northwest of Bangkok. Yan Hee is a multipurpose project, located where the river debouches from the mountains on to the Central Plain; though it will ultimately provide electric power for some thirty-six of the country's seventy-one *changwat* (provinces), its principal benefits will accrue to central Thailand. The country's first large water-storage project, the Yan Hee (Phumiphon) dam, completed in 1963, is capable of impounding nearly 10 million acre feet of water (over 12 billion cubic metres). It will increase the flow of the Chao Phraya in the dry season by some 14 per cent, thus making possible an increase in rice double-cropping and, in conjunction with the Chainat dam on the Chao Phraya, will prevent all but the most exceptional floods in the Central Plain. In 1963 Yan Hee was equipped with a generating capacity of 140 MW, and further capacity up to the planned total of 560 MW is eventually to be installed.

The north possesses a variety of minor mineral deposits, but few appear large enough to justify the investment in improved transport facilities that would be necessary to make production economic; however, this situation may be changed as a result of the findings of the geological surveys being undertaken in the north by various foreign aid teams. The brightest prospects are perhaps in petroleum; a state enterprise has for several years produced a little oil in the Fang basin in the extreme north of the country, and major international oil companies are now prospecting in the region.

The rugged mountains of Northern Thailand are continued southwards in Western Thailand, which is drained by the Khwae Yai and Khwae Noi, invasion routes often used by the Burmese. The westernmost mountains along the frontier are drenched with rain during the southwest monsoon, but the valleys receive a lower precipitation than the Central Plain, and the whole area is a scantily populated marchland with a low living standard, removed from the mainstreams of national life.

The western echelon ranges continue southwards into the long peninsula which Thailand shares with Burma as far south as 10° N latitude. Along the coast of the Gulf of Thailand a succession of rice-growing plains reproduce the landscape of the Central Plain. Rainfall along the coast increases southwards from the Mae Nam Mae Klong, and at Prachuap Khiri Khan, where Thailand is reduced to a mere 15-mile-wide strip, the low-sun dry season typical of the Central Plain disappears. South of Victoria Point, Thailand occupies the whole peninsula to the Malaysian frontier, and the west coast ranges northwards of Phuket island probably receive the heaviest rainfall in the country and are densely forested. *Yang (Dipterocarpus alatus)* is the most important commercial timber, and the tree can also be tapped for an oily exudation still much used as an illuminant, and even more extensively used before petroleum products became widely available. The west coast receives its greatest rainfall from the so-called southwest monsoon (April–September), but this is the less rainy season on the east coast, which receives its maximum precipitation from the northeast monsoon (October–

March). Sufficient rain normally falls during the growing season to make rice cultivation independent of supplementary water, and despite variations in precipitation from year to year the east coast achieves yields above the national average.

The equatorial-like climate of the southern peninsula with its absence of a dry season confers other advantages; as in Malaysia, stanniferous alluvials resulting from rapid erosion of the mineralized cores of the mountains make for low-cost tin production and, though greatly outranked by its southern neighbour, Thailand's status as a tin producer has nevertheless increased greatly during this century. To meet the growing power demands of the tin industry, the Lignite Authority, which also operates the Mae Mo enterprise, in 1964 completed a new 40 MW power station at Krabi, based on local lignite deposits. The cultivation of typically equatorial lowland crops such as rubber and oil palm is also possible and, though the latter has yet to establish itself on a commercial basis, Thailand's output of natural rubber and its share of world natural rubber output have progressively expanded. Although coconuts are grown in almost every part of Thailand, the higher productivity in the southern peninusula is responsible for this region possessing almost two-thirds of the nation's coconut palms.

The economic similarity of the southern peninsula with Malaysia is heightened by the existence in the area of substantial numbers of non-Thai peoples. In an area bounded by Phuket, Songkhla (Singora) and the Malaysian border live some one million Malays, who resist Thai assimilation and whose main cultural contacts are with neighbouring Kedah and Kelantan; fortunately for the maintenance of good Malaysia-Thailand relations, liberation of this *Malaya irridenta* has political appeal only for the xenophobic extremists of Malaysia's Pan Malayan Islamic Party (PMIP), a regional party which so long as Malaysia enjoys prosperity appears unlikely to gain wide popular support. Of greater economic significance, however, is the existence of a large number of Chinese. Thailand's generally benign treatment of its large immigrant Chinese population is reflected by its adherence to a *jus solis*, and all persons born in Thailand irrespective of racial origin are regarded as Thai citizens. Most of the country's two million or so inhabitants of Chinese or mixed Chinese-Thai ancestry are urban dwellers, and though most numerous in Bangkok, substantial numbers in the peninsula are engaged in tin-mining and rubber production; the marketing of rubber, a commodity that constitutes the country's second most important source of foreign exchange earnings, is solidly in their hands. Tin-mining has never been an acceptable occupation to Thai people, and even rubber cultivation exerts far less appeal than rice farming, which in the vicinity of Nakhon Si Thammarat on the east coast culminates in perhaps the best cultivation practices in the country.[4]

That the peninsula is of major significance as a source of foreign exchange

[4] *Robert L. Pendleton*, Thailand: Aspects of Land and Life, *Duell, Sloan and Pearce, New York, 1962, p. 153.*

Lift nets such as these on a *khlong* near Bangkok are common throughout Southeast Asia. Floating on the water are masses of water hyacinth.

earnings, is largely the handiwork of industrious immigrant Chinese, a conclusion that is reinforced by a comparison of the southern peninsula with the physically similar region of southeastern Thailand lying between the Central Plain and the Cardamon Mountains of the Cambodian frontier. Both in annual total and in regime, precipitation in southeastern Thailand closely resembles that of the peninsular west coast, and both areas are thickly covered with rain forest. Rubber cultivation was introduced before World War I, yet despite its proximity to the capital, the Southeast remains an isolated and backward part of the country; lacking workable tin, it never attracted Chinese in large numbers as did the peninsula, and hence never acquired a smallholder rubber industry either.

The remaining physical unit and the largest of all, the low plateau of Khorat, accounts for almost a third of the total area of Thailand and for an approximately equivalent proportion of its population. In view of the Northeast's slender resource basis, its share of population must be considered over-large, and the region is an acutely depressed area. The plateau is isolated from the rest of the country by its mountainous and densely forested western and southern rims, the Dong Phraya and Dongrak, which though of no great elevation are considerable barriers to communication. The plateau slopes gently eastwards and, except along the northern margin where a few streams drain directly to the Mekong, is drained by the Mae Nam Mun and its tributary the Lam[5] Nam Chi to the

[5] Lam *indicates a stream with intermittent flow, degenerating in the dry season to a series of pools;* Nam *or* Mae Nam *indicates streams or rivers with a permanent flow.*

Transport on a Bangkok *khlong*.

Mekong. The streams of the Mae Nam Mun system have broad flat valleys which are inundated during the rainy season when the rivers rise quickly from their incised channels; flooding is assisted by the rising Mekong which blocks the discharge of the Mae Nam Mun, and by the gentle nature of the relief. The sandy soils derived from the red sandstone of the plateau are thin and poor, and during the dry season some areas become encrusted with salt by the capillary action and subsequent evaporation of ground water that has penetrated into underground salt deposits during the rainy season.

Although small parts of the plateau sheltered from the southwest monsoon by the mountainous western and southern rims receive less than 40 inches of rain, the lowest recorded in Thailand, rainfall increases northeastwards and near the Mekong exceeds 80 inches. On the whole, the Khorat plateau is not appreciably drier than the Central Plain. Its poverty arises not so much from a shortage of water but from its inability to make effective use of the substantial water resources available, for there is sufficient run-off in the Mae Nam Mun basin to irrigate the whole of the area at present under cultivation;[6] yet in any one year two-thirds to three-quarters of all padi fields in Khorat go uncultivated. The indigenous irrigation techniques employed in the basins of Northern Thailand are out of the question in the Plateau. During the rainy season the low relief and

[6] *United Nations, Economic Commission for Asia and the Far East*, Development of Water Resources in the Lower Mekong Basin, *Flood Control Series, No. 12, Bangkok, 1957, p. 48.*

slow run-off lead to waterlogging and the formation of numerous lakes, while in the valley bottoms the water rises so suddenly and stays so long that much land apparently suitable for rice cultivation cannot even be used for deep-water rice; as a result, only the valley margins, where the water depth is lower, can be utilized for rice.[7] In the cloudless, windy, five-month dry season, evaporation is intense and the land becomes parched and whitish from salt deposition; potable water is scarce and, with little or no opportunity for cropping, malnutrition often reaches serious proportions during this time of year.

Thus, although for much of the year extensive tracts suffer from an over-abundance of water, there has been relatively little attempt at water control; moreover, the terrain offers few suitable sites for the construction of modern storage dams. More importantly, however, the region's peripheral location gave it little priority with the central government in investment allocation, and such investment as was made outside the Central Plain mainly served strategic ends. Modern irrigation techniques did not appear until shortly before World War II when a number of small schemes were commenced, and it is largely to a prolifera-tion of small local projects that much of the region, and in particular the south and southwest, will have to look for an increase in agricultural productivity. Towards the north, however, the Nam Phong (Ubonratana) dam on the Nam Phong, a headstream of the Chi in Khon Kaen changwat (province), completed in 1966, is a much larger project than is generally possible; the scheme will provide water for the irrigation of some 100,000 acres and has an installed generat-ing capacity of 25,000 kW.

The greatest potentialities for additional irrigation water and for flood control lie in harnessing the Mekong itself. The proposed Pa Mong dam and reservoir a little above Vientiane would irrigate about 500,000 acres on the Laotian side of the river, and with the construction of a canal southwards through the Udon Thani water-parting to connect with the Lam Pao and the Nam Phong, head-streams of the Lam Nam Chi, would irrigate about two million acres in the Northeast. By making cropping possible during the dry season, this development would go far to alleviate seasonal food shortages in the region.

However, this lies in the future and in the meantime Thailand can do little more than press on with its own commitments on tributary projects under the Mekong scheme, and apart from the Nam Phong scheme, a 30,000-acre irrigation development on the Nam Pung in Sakhon Nakhon changwat has also been com-pleted. Nevertheless all these developments are unlikely to do more than keep pace with the rate of population increase; the plateau is virtually devoid of mineral wealth and opportunities for industrial development are likely to be con-fined to Nakhon Ratchasima (Khorat) and possibly Khon Kaen. With improve-ments in transport both seasonal and permanent emigration appear likely to increase.

[7] *Pendleton, op. cit., p. 132.*

AGRICULTURE AND ITS PROBLEMS

Thailand will probably long continue to be a largely agricultural country. Agriculture employs about three-quarters of the work-force, although progress in expanding the non-agricultural sectors of the economy is indicated by agriculture's diminishing share of gross domestic product; in 1952 this was some 44 per cent (including forestry), but by 1965 this contribution had been reduced to barely 33 per cent (*Table 4-1*). Nevertheless, agricultural products continue to provide over two-thirds of the country's export income, and although the share of rice and rubber has substantially decreased since 1950, this has been more than offset by the contributions of new agricultural exports.

Table 4-1 *Thailand: industrial origin of gross domestic product, 1952 and 1965*

	1952		1965	
	Value million baht	Per cent	Value million baht	Per cent
Agriculture	12,940	43·9	26,290	32·8
Crops	9,680	32·8	17,720	22·1
Livestock	1,250	4·2	4,150	5·2
Fishing	640	2·2	2,240	2·8
Forestry	1,380	4·7	2,180	2·7
Mining	560	1·9	1,680	2·1
Manufacturing	3,290	11·1	9,680	12·1
Construction	1,170	4·0	3,840	4·8
Transport and communications	1,170	4·0	6,000	7·5
Commerce, banking and services	10,480	35·1	32,700	40·7
Gross domestic product at market prices	**29,520**	**100**	**80,190**	**100**

Source: *Statistical Yearbook of Thailand*, 1965

Moreover, it remains true that the main impetus in expanding the national product has been an enhanced agricultural output, and this in turn has almost entirely been brought about by an expansion of the cultivated area. Over the past three decades the cultivated area appears to have grown at about 3 per cent per annum, a rate that has just kept pace with population increase and through slight improvements in productivity has resulted in slowly increasing real incomes per head. This performance is in striking contrast to the generally miserable record of Asian agriculture since the end of World War II. Though Thailand has been fortunate in possessing a relatively small population in relation to its resources of land, the main reasons for this success are to be found in an institutional environment which has made it possible for the peasant to acquire land easily by the simple process of clearing and planting a crop, and in the rational and commercial attitudes towards land which this has encouraged. Broadly similar pioneering was also possible at various times in the colonial dependencies of Southeast Asia, but Thailand alone has remained attached to a policy of free land, and technical innovation has even assisted the process of establishing a holding; the introduction of tractor ploughing into the Chiang Kham amphur (district) of Chiang Rai changwat in 1953 made it easier for young men to establish independent households with farmland of their own.[8] As a result, the proportion of the total area in farms has steadily increased and by 1960 had reached about 20 per cent of the total land area. Probably about half of the latter should be preserved under forest for erosion and run-off control, so that at the present rate of agricultural expansion Thailand has scarcely more than a further three decades of 'skimming fertility off an ever larger area of newly cultivated land' to use the words of Fisher,[9] before it begins to find itself in the position of most Asian countries, which now possess limited opportunities for expanding their cultivated area. Given political stability, however, this interval should prove sufficient for the country to carry through major technical and economic changes in enlarging the land and capital at the disposal of the farmer.

Thailand is singularly fortunate in still possessing an abundance of agricultural land in relation to its population, and in Chapter 2 it was noted that the average size of holding and the capital equipment of the farmer in Thailand are substantially larger than is usual in Southeast Asia. In 1950 the national average farm size was some 26 rai (10·4 acres), and the 1960 Census of Agriculture revealed that a population increase of more than 3 per cent per annum over the decade had caused only a slight decline in this figure (*Table 4-2*). The regions used in the Thailand Economic Farm Survey of 1953 (which relates to a 1950 sample) correspond fairly closely to the basic geographic divisions described earlier, save for the division of the peninsula and the addition to its southwest portion of part of west Thailand; applying this grouping in respect of the 1950 Agricultural Census showed that holdings were largest in the Central Plain, where the average was over 30 rai (12 acres). Only in the North did the average fall below 10 rai (4 acres), and in every other region the average size of holding was more than twice as large. Using the same grouping in respect of the 1960 Census of Agriculture reveals some diminution in the average size of holdings in all regions save the Southwest. Apart from the North, therefore, which is clearly a region of intensively farmed small holdings, in no part of the country is

[8] *Michael Moerman, 'Western culture and the Thai way of life'*, Asia, *Spring 1964, p. 37.*
[9] *Charles A. Fisher*, South-East Asia, *Methuen, London, rev. edn, 1966, p. 508.*

the relatively large average size of holding the effect of a small number of very large holdings offsetting a great majority of very small farms; on the contrary, farms of more than 15 rai (6 acres) account for more than half of all holdings (*Table 4-2*).

Table 4-2 *Thailand: distribution of holdings by size and average size of holdings, 1950 and 1960*

	1950							1960
	Total holdings	*Below 6 rai*	*6 to below 15 rai*	*15 to below 30 rai*	*30 to below 60 rai*	*Over 60 rai*	*Average size of holding*	*Average size of holding*
				percentages			*(rai)*	*(rai)*
Central Plain	*30·2*	*14·6*	*19·9*	*27·1*	*26·6*	*12·2*	*30·8*	*27·8*
Southeast	*2·7*	*12·7*	*23·0*	*29·8*	*26·9*	*7·7*	*29·1*	*28·2*
Northeast	*38·5*	*10·0*	*25·4*	*32·8*	*22·2*	*9·7*	*27·4*	*21·6*
North	*12·5*	*34·7*	*46·3*	*15·4*	*3·2*	*0·5*	*9·6*	*8·8*
Southwest	*4·5*	*15·8*	*30·4*	*29·7*	*18·9*	*5·1*	*21·0*	*23·9*
South	*11·6*	*14·2*	*32·5*	*29·6*	*19·2*	*4·5*	*27·8*	*22·6*
All regions	*100·0*	*15·0*	*26·8*	*28·4*	*21·3*	*8·5*	*25·6*	*21·7*

Sources: *Thailand Economic Farm Survey*, 1953; *Census of Agriculture 1960*, 1963

Rice cultivation and irrigation

Despite a rapid increase in the area under other crops since the middle Fifties, when Thailand's rice exports first began to feel the pressure of mounting world grain surpluses, rice still occupies some 75 per cent of the total cultivated area of the country. An almost continuous expansion throughout the present century had brought the harvested area to some 41·3 million rai, about 16·5 million acres, by 1963,[10] a figure that was some 175 per cent of the 1940 level. But over this period padi production more than doubled, thus suggesting that a fifty-year decline in the national rice yield had at last been arrested.

This long-term decline in yield was primarily the result of an expansion of cultivation on to progressively poorer land; the expectation of receiving an adequate water-supply for a good crop on the incremental land tended gradually to decrease. During the latter half of the nineteenth century expansion of rice cultivation was largely confined to the Central Plain, but although the rice area in this region continued to grow in the present century, expansion in other parts of the country, and particularly in the Khorat plateau where hydrological conditions

[10] *That for the 1964 and 1965 seasons was somewhat lower.*

are very much less favourable, proceeded much more rapidly. As a result the national average yield fell substantially, declining from more than 300 kg per rai (1,875 kg per hectare) early in the century to barely 200 kg per rai (1,250 kg per hectare) at the end of World War II; in the Central Plain, however, the decline in yields was relatively slight. Since 1955 there has been a considerable improvement in the national average yield as the country began to reap the benefits of its investment in improved irrigation, higher-yielding seeds and increased fertilizer application, and in 1963 the national average had been raised to some 255 kg per rai (1,594 kg per hectare), about the level of the late Twenties.

The dominant position of the Central Plain in rice cultivation is striking; it possesses almost 40 per cent of the total rice area and accounts for not far short of half the total rice production (*Table 4-3*). The Northeast is not greatly inferior in its rice area, but the poorer soils of the plateau and inadequate water-control result in a yield that is lowest of any major region of the country. Averages, however, conceal wide variations from district to district, and in the Isan (Northeast) these are much greater than in the Central Plain; Nong Khai and Loei changwats in the north bordering the Mekong, where hydrological conditions are more favourable, have yields which are comparable with the best recorded anywhere in the Mae Nam delta. The highest rice yields in the country are obtained in the basins of northern Thailand, where the light silty loams of the Ping valley are some of the best soils in the country. Hydrological and topographical conditions in the northern basins lend themselves to indigenous irrigation techniques, and this is the only portion of the country where rice double-cropping, or rice followed by a non-rice crop such as soya beans, groundnuts, maize or tobacco, has been a traditional practice. Rice yields in the peninsula are also above the national average, but vary greatly between the northern and southern portions and between the east and west coasts; the highest yields are achieved in the coastal plains along the Gulf of Thailand between Surat Thani and Songkhla, where the

Table 4-3   *Thailand: area, production and yield of padi by regions, 1961–63*

	Harvested area	Padi production	Yield
	thousand hectares	*thousand metric tons*	*kg/hectares*
Central Plain	2,960	4,910	1,660
Northeast	2,780	3,030	1,090
North	430	1,010	2,350
Peninsula	640	970	1,550
Southeast	100	130	1,330
Total	**6,910**	**10,050**	**1,450**

Source: Calculated from *Statistical Yearbook of Thailand*, 1964

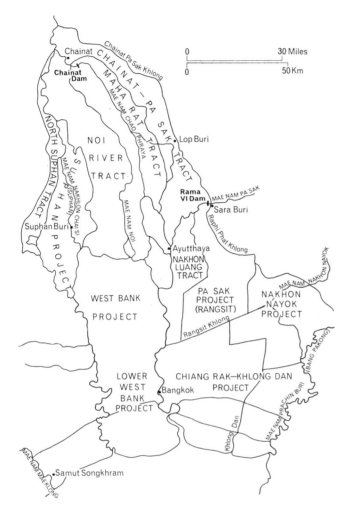

Fig 4-2 Irrigation projects in the Mae Nam Chao Phraya Plain, Thailand

First proposed more than half a century ago, an integrated irrigation system serving the whole of the lower Chao Phraya is gradually approaching completion.

cycle of cultivation is some six months out of phase with that of the west coast, the northern peninsula and the Central Plain.

The many varieties of rice grown in Thailand are usually grouped into glutinous and non-glutinous kinds, of which the latter only are significant in international commerce. Glutinous rices have long been the preferred food of the North and Northeast, but the strong demand for non-glutinous varieties in the world market and their higher price have resulted in a steady decline in the proportion of rice-land devoted to glutinous varieties. About 80 per cent of the lowland rice area is set out with rice transplanted from specially prepared seed-beds, but regular transplanting in rows, an operation that facilitates weeding with the push-hoe, is still little practised. Transplanting results in a higher yield than broad-

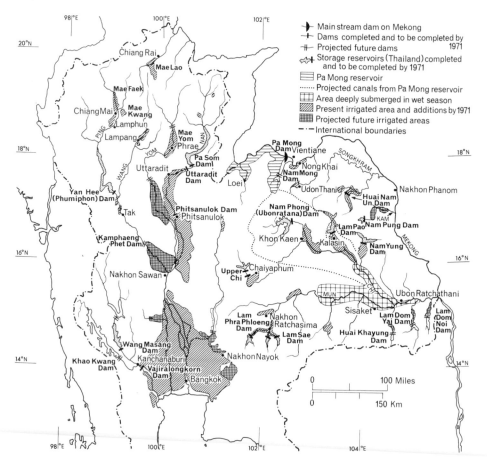

Fig 4-3 **Developmental projects in north and northeast Thailand** (source: Thailand National Plan 1967–71)

Flood control and irrigation projects, and road construction, spearhead the government attack on the poverty of the Isan (northeast).

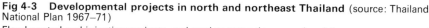

casting, and is thus the preferred method of cultivation wherever possible, despite its heavier labour requirements; broadcasting, however, is the only way of planting areas subject to deep and rapid inundation, where it is sometimes necessary to sow in more than two feet of standing water. For such operations the seed is first sprouted and great care is taken to see that the water in the field is free of suspended material at the time of sowing; otherwise mud settles on the shoots and prevents them from emerging above the water level. Deep-water, or 'floating', rice varieties cannot be transplanted because of the brittleness of their stems; they may grow to a length of up to 18 feet and require harvesting from boats. Broadcasting, however, is also resorted to as an emergency measure if for some reason a transplanted crop fails.

As improved water-control is usually the easiest way of increasing rice output, in most parts of Thailand traditional methods of irrigation reflecting the Chinese origin of Thai material culture are widely employed. These include brushwood and earth dams, and for lifting water onto the fields, pitch-covered baskets, wooden scoops, foot-operated wooden chain-pumps, and, in northern Thailand, large bamboo water-wheels equipped with scoops. In the Central Plain many canals, some of considerable antiquity, have been dug to facilitate the distribution of the rising Chao Phraya over the land, but it was not until towards the close of the nineteenth century that modern irrigation works first appeared with the construction of the Rangsit scheme northeast of Bangkok, between the Chao Phraya and the Mae Nam Nakhon Nayok, a tributary of the Mae Nam Bang Pakong. Begun by private capital the work was taken over by the state, and Thailand appeared to be following the example of neighbouring dependent territories with the establishment of a Department of Irrigation.

The proposals of its first consultant, van der Heide, an irrigation engineer from the Netherlands Indies, for a comprehensive irrigation and protection system covering the whole of the delta were rejected as too costly; and after the construction of canals across the southern portion of the plain between the Mae Nam Bang Pakong and the Mae Nam Mae Klong, official interest in irrigation expired until shortly before World War I, when a run of years of low water and resulting crop failures compelled some ameliorating action. A British consultant, Sir Thomas Ward, produced a long-range plan for a number of projects that could ultimately form part of an overall plan for all the rivers of the delta and of the northern portion of the peninsula, yet although work had begun on several of the recommended projects, relatively little had been completed by 1939. The initial selection of the South Pa Sak area and the comparatively early date of completion of this scheme (1924) primarily reflected the power of the large landowners of the adjacent Rangsit district to the south, who had most to gain from the project, and in 1931 this strength was again demonstrated in the completion of the Chiang Rak-Khlong Dan scheme to the south of Rangsit. But other projects commenced between the wars, such as the Suphan (Mae Nam Nakhon Chai. Si) in the western portion of the delta, the Nakhon Nayok in the east and the Chao Phraya West Bank, had to wait until the Fifties, when the high rice prices of the postwar period provided the stimulus to bring long protracted works to completion.

All of these projects, however, total only a small portion of the potential irrigable area, which the United States Operations Mission (USOM) has estimated at over seven million acres, and although they improved local hydrological conditions over parts of the plain, there was still no adequate safeguard against an overall shortage or over-abundance of water in the delta. This need, however, was in part met in 1956 by the completion of the Chainat barrage across the head of the Chao Phraya delta at virtually the same location suggested in van der Heide's plan of a half century earlier. Chainat is mainly intended to regulate the distribution of water over the whole of the lower plain and its effectiveness is greatly augmented by the storage of the Yan Hee (Phumiphon) reservoir. Distribution canals from Chainat serve fourteen new irrigation projects in the central portion of the plain, many being areas previously subjected to deep flooding and capable of growing only relatively low-yielding deep-water rice. These areas can now be converted to medium-term transplanted rice production and most can be double-cropped. A substantial part of the cost of these new schemes has been met by loans from the International Bank for Reconstruction and Development (World Bank).

The resources devoted to modern irrigation works in other parts of the country have been substantially fewer. Prior to World War II the only project in North Thailand was that of Mae Faek on the Mae Ping in the Chiang Mai-Lamphun district, completed in 1933 and irrigating some 70,000 acres, and new projects since completed on the Ping, Wang and Yom only raise the total area served by state works to barely 200,000 acres. The Nan river is still entirely uncontrolled, and so long as this situation continues the danger of serious flooding in the Chao Phraya valley will not be entirely eliminated.[11] By 1970, however, the Pa Som dam on the Nan will be completed, and with diversionary dams at Uttaradit and Phitsanulok will assist irrigation in the upper plain. In the Northeast, where the need might be judged the greatest, irrigation has been largely a post-1950 development. In 1963 only some 250,000 acres were served by modern works, about half of this area within three schemes on the upper and middle Mun in the southwest portion of the Khorat plateau. The difficulty of constructing dams in the low terrain has led to a greater reliance on tank irrigation than in other parts of the country, and the International Bank Mission regarded this as the most promising line of development;[12] nevertheless the area served by the 133 tanks operative in 1963 amounted to only about half that affected by river-based state works, and only about one-fifth of the entire rice area of the Northeast has the benefit of any irrigation facilities.

Problems of the rice industry and agricultural diversification

The land and the capital at the disposal of the average Thai farmer, some 10 acres with two buffaloes and 1·6 oxen to work it, according to the Farm Survey of 1953, are available only to the wealthier farmers in most other parts of Southeast Asia. Moreover, almost 90 per cent of farmers are owners, fragmentation is modest (the national average in 1953 was some 2·7 plots per farm), and farm debt is relatively slight. Only one-fifth of all farmers had incurred any indebtedness over the pre-

[11] *International Bank for Reconstruction and Development,* A Public Development Program for Thailand, *Johns Hopkins University Press, Baltimore, 1959, p. 42.*
[12] ibid., *p. 44.*

ceding five years according to the 1953 Survey, while the average farm debt amounted to only 1·8 per cent of average farm assets and to but 18·3 per cent of net farm income. These figures go far to explain the relatively high level of material welfare in Thailand and the considerable political and social stability of the country.

National averages, however, conceal regional and sectional disparities, and it is clear that the situation of many farmers in certain parts of the country leaves much to be desired. More than a third of the farms in the Central Plain are operated by tenants, and in parts of the plain nearest to Bangkok, and particularly in the Rangsit area, ownership is concentrated in large units and the incidence of tenancy is extremely high. Most owners are absentees and members of the nobility with important positions in the administration; tenancies are usually granted for a year only, and lacking all inducement to improve his efficiency the tenant's only concern is to take as much out of the land as he can in the shortest time. The landlord has no interest in improvement either, for he is able to take advantage of the increasing competition for land due to population increase and to push up the level of rents with every change of tenancy. Moreover, while average farm indebtedness appears too low by the standards of economically more advanced countries and farmers should be able to increase their productive efficiency by greater borrowing for productive purposes, in the Central Plain it is clearly far too high, for in the 1953 Survey more than a third of farmers in this region were indebted and the average farm debt amounted to almost two-thirds of average net farm income. These facts in large part reflect the higher incidence of tenancy in the plain and the limited facilities for obtaining credit, a situation which obliges many farmers to seek credit from the landlord or middleman. This is by far the most unsatisfactory of all forms of credit; under the *tog khao* system, that is, the disposal of padi for cash in advance of harvesting, effective interest rates may amount to as much as 50 per cent per month.

Apart from suffering from a dearth of credit facilities, it has long been believed that the producer receives only a small share of the proceeds from the sale of rice in the market, and that a much larger share accrues to the complex chain of distribution which includes rice-assembling middlemen, local storekeepers, warehousemen, millers, and the government officials (in the form of graft). Most middlemen are Chinese and, in Thailand as in other parts of Southeast Asia, the alien middleman is customarily regarded as a parasite on the producer. There is little evidence that the Chinese middleman in Thailand, or anywhere else for that matter, is any more rapacious than the indigenous moneylender or landlord; indeed, such evidence as exists rather suggests the contrary.[13] The middleman renders an essential service, but his costs are high because he has to assemble commercially marketable quantities of all grades from a multiplicity

[13] *J. M. Andrews*, Siam: Second Rural Economic Survey, *The Bangkok Times, 1935*, p. 314.

of small producers, many of whom retain a large part of their total output for their own consumption. Some recent evidence, however, suggests that the Thai rice trade is surprisingly efficient. Only 20 to 30 per cent of the domestic retail price appears to be absorbed in distribution costs, and farmers in the Central Plain may generally receive some 79 per cent of the final price.[14] Moreover, strong competition between dealers limits fraud and graft. It is worth remarking that the widespread use of transistor radios in Southeast Asia has gone far to remove one of the major sources of peasant weakness, market ignorance, for growers can now keep themselves informed of the latest quotations in the capital for rubber, rice, copra or other cash crops.

The Thai government also exploits its peasants. Between 1946 and 1955 it possessed a monopoly of rice procurement for export, acquiring rice from the millers at a stipulated price and making it available to exporters at a price that reflected the high price of rice on the world market. The justification for the insulation of the domestic from the world rice situation was primarily to break the grip of the Chinese on the rice trade and to encourage greater Thai participation, but it also preserved a low and stable internal rice price, keeping the cost of living low. Nevertheless, as peasants generally consume much of their own rice, they were paying a substantial subsidy to the privileged urban population. Mounting corruption and the growing pressure of world grain surpluses caused the government to return the export trade to private hands in 1955, and thereafter it confined its interest to an export tax, or 'premium'; from the peasants' viewpoint, however, the effect was the same.

The rice premium has been the subject of much contention. Some economists feel that to prevent the peasant from realizing the full world market price for his output greatly discourages peasant initiative and produces distortions in the economy, and certainly the baleful effects of such policies are only too obvious in Indonesia and Burma. The export tax is heavy, amounting to nearly 100 per cent of the farm price,[15] yet the peasant indifference and stagnating levels of output of Burma and Indonesia do not appear in Thailand. There are several reasons for this. Rice growing is still a preferred occupation for most Thais, and although opportunities for transfer have certainly increased in recent years, movement out of the traditional village rice economy is not easy. More to the point perhaps, the low cost of living made possible by the premium has enabled Thailand to maintain a free open economy with few restrictions on imports, so that the Thai peasant has been able to acquire as a matter of course valued consumer goods that his Burmese or Indonesian counterpart can only obtain, if at all, at very high prices on the black market. Moreover, the traditional Thai respect for authority is enhanced by the solid evidence of economic growth in the form of new infrastructural investment such as roads, irrigation and water supply, schools and clinics.

[14] *Silcock (ed.)*, op. cit., *p. 222.*
[15] ibid., *p. 222.*

The premium has certainly encouraged peasants to consume more of their own rice output, and in common with all export taxes, it has promoted a shift out of rice production into that of alternative untaxed crops such as maize, jute, kenaf and sugar. This has been one of the main reasons for its retention, for, whatever its original purpose, the premium has become a key instrument in government development strategy. But while it has, in effect, acted as a subsidy to almost all other economic activities and assisted agricultural diversification, it has detracted from another objective of policy, namely, a shift away from a continually expanding rice area of generally low productivity towards more efficient production with higher yields on the existing area. Large resources have been used to up-grade the efficiency of the rice industry, but because of the undervaluation of the output it is not easy to determine if the best allocation of investment resources has been made.

In a situation in which the average farmer has less than three tons of padi a year to market and can only obtain credit at usurious interest rates, the development of cooperative marketing and credit facilities appears extremely attractive. Thailand possesses three forms of cooperative organizations: credit cooperatives, land cooperatives (dealing with the acquisition of land, farm improvements, equipment and technical assistance), and marketing cooperatives. Credit cooperatives date from 1916, and marketing cooperatives from 1938; all are closely controlled by the state, which over three decades has invested substantial resources in promoting and expanding cooperative organizations. There is relatively little to show for these efforts; credit cooperatives, the most important, had less than 200,000 members in 1962 and probably accounted for less than 20 per cent of total farm credit, while marketing cooperatives handled less than 5 per cent of the padi trade. The strong government control and the fact that the state has provided some 95 per cent or so of the capital of cooperatives, is the major reason for the limited degree of success; with so little of their own resources at stake, members of cooperatives feel no sense of obligation to their societies. Moreover, many farmers pledge their crop to middlemen against a cash advance and hence have little for disposal to marketing cooperatives. Nor, in general, do these offer an attractive service to farmers; as a Thai economist has remarked, 'the cooperative renders little advertising service to the members and assumes no risk bearing ... it does not provide a service for the assembling of padi any better than that provided by the middleman ... members are sometimes corrupted by the cooperative agent, both by receiving a lower price for padi and incorrect measurement.'[16] Despite their support by the state, cooperatives are hopelessly undercapitalized; they cannot offer their members the advantage of low prices through the bulk buying of equipment, fertilizers and other farm necessities, nor have they adequate storage facilities. They are perpetually short of managerial personnel, and the

[16] *Chaiyong Chuchart*, Rice Marketing in Thailand, *University Microfilms Inc., Ann Arbor and London, 1961, pp. 179–80.*

underpaid cooperative official is often tempted to use his position to exploit members. Silcock, however, asserts that the main purpose of the cooperative was to serve nationalist and welfare goals in preventing Thai farmers from becoming heavily indebted to Chinese middlemen and losing their land, and that only since 1950, with the creation of large cooperatives in both the Central Plain and the Khorat plateau, have cooperatives been seriously regarded as agents of development.[17] The new societies have been provided with adequately trained personnel, and through pursuing realistic loan policies have achieved much success. How far this movement can spread is conjectural; but only when members have a substantial financial stake in their societies and feel some personal commitment to them will widespread success become possible. Thailand's experience, as with that of many other countries, underlines the necessity of an intelligent and educated farm population in creating viable cooperatives.

The large sums spent on irrigation, and particularly in extending double cropping, are also contentious. Between 1959 and 1963 Thailand allocated some 4,500 million *baht* (approximately \$212·5 million) in implementing World Bank recommendations concerning irrigation, and the total irrigated area in 1964 was some 10·5 million rai (4·2 million acres). Thailand's various Ministries, which, by virtue of the large patronage they dispense, often resemble a collection of warring empires, have contended whether funds used for making water available to promote off-season cropping might not have been better employed in raising the low yields of the main crop; but the slow rate of improvement in the rice farmer's living standards seems a poor return on irrigation investment, although the effect of the rice premium has to be taken into consideration. Moreover, there is a great deal to suggest that irrigation, as in many other parts of Southeast Asia, has over the long term generally made things worse for the farmer; it can hardly be accidental that the greatest incidence of tenancy and indebtedness in Thailand, as in Indonesia and the Indochinese states, is precisely where irrigation is most intense. All but a small fraction of irrigation expenses have been incurred in the Central Plain, but in the present century the most rapid increase in rice output has come from the neglected Khorat plateau, where farmers responded to the improved transport facilities offered by the railway to enlarge their incomes by growing more rice. In the absence of major agrarian reorganization, the extension of irrigation has tended to rivet on Southeast Asian countries an agriculture with relatively inflexible factor coefficients of production, and has delayed or thwarted changes in those coefficients capable of ensuring greater productivity of the land and the worker.

Crop diversification also has been retarded, and here, too, the experience of the Northeast is significant. Since the later Fifties, the most important change in the pattern of Thailand's export trade has been the growing contribution of new products, particularly maize, but kenaf, of which Thailand has become the

[17] *Silcock (ed.)*, op. cit., *p. 246.*

world's largest exporter, and jute have also been of growing importance. None of these crops is in any sense new, maize having been grown for centuries in all parts of the country, but since 1950 the area under maize has witnessed a six-fold expansion to reach a harvested area exceeding 0·5 million acres and, despite a rapid appreciation of tin prices since 1961, maize has displaced tin as the third most important export by value. This increase in maize production has been made possible by the introduction of hybrid high-yielding varieties under a joint USOM-Rockefeller Foundation project, and by higher prices in foreign markets, particularly Japan. While it is true, as Silcock points out, that more than half the maize is now grown in the Central Plain,[18] the fact remains that the new crop was first widely taken up in the Khorat plateau, where the experimental work with hybrid varieties was begun, and only after the Northeast had demonstrated the profitability of production did cultivation spread into the Mae Nam plain. The Northeast also took the lead in the expanded cultivation of kenaf, whose production leapt with the difficulties of expanding world jute production and Thailand's own mounting needs for sacking; though only a small producer in comparison with either India or China, Thailand's kenaf output was estimated at some 200,000 tons in 1966, of which some 70 per cent was exported. Despite the threat of competition from synthetics such as polypropylene, it is quite possible that if manufacturers could be assured of a continuity of supply in what is a new and relatively untried fibre in world markets, the demand for kenaf would increase rapidly.[19] The peasants of the Khorat plateau have been able to respond to the price stimuli offered by changing conditions in the world market largely because their agriculture was not confined within the strait-jacket of elaborate irrigation systems. In view of the Northeast's low rice yields further agricultural diversification makes very good sense, and major irrigation projects seem inadvisable except where, as with the Mekong scheme, this constitutes a relatively inexpensive part of multipurpose developments. Such diversification is in fact being promoted by the National Development Plan, which will require an enhanced industrial crop production; Khorat has long been the principal supplier of Thailand's small output of such crops as cotton and tobacco, and it is well placed to enlarge its production as import-replacing industries based on these crops gather momentum.

Unfortunately the most desirable varieties of cotton, the medium-stable American types, do not do well in the country, and native Thai cottons have a staple length of barely $\frac{3}{4}$ inches. The Cambodian No. 13, with a staple length of $\frac{7}{8}$ inches, has been used for mixing with local cottons, but as Thai ginneries practise no seed selection it is in short supply. British technical assistance teams with experience of cotton cultivation in similar environmental conditions in Africa have introduced improved varieties, and have shown that with a rigorous spraying-

[18] ibid., *p. 252.*

[19] F A O Monthly Bulletin of Economics and Statistics, *vol. 13, September 1964, p. 18.*

schedule cotton can be a profitable crop. The fact that cotton is an off-season crop makes it particularly suitable for areas such as the Northeast, with a long period of enforced idleness. Virginia tobaccos, which are increasingly in demand in Thailand with the growing preference for American-style cigarettes, also require soils that occur only exceptionally, but sugar cane succeeds in most parts of the country, and in view of the fact that a flourishing sugar industry, largely under Chinese control, existed in the eighteenth century, the country's heavy dependence on sugar imports right up to 1940 is striking. The sugar industry succumbed to competition from rice, a more profitable and less labour-demanding crop, but since 1946 the area under sugar cane has grown rapidly and the country is now virtually self-sufficient, although its per capita consumption of centrifugal sugar of less than 5 kg per annum is very low even by Asian standards.[20] The competitive position of the sugar industry is weak because of low productivity in both field and factory. There are numerous primitive animal-powered presses and cottage processing units, but only two mills of any size, both with obsolete equipment. The fact that centrifugal sugar production is largely in the hands of the state may go far to explain this situation.

An increase in the technical efficiency of industrial crop production in the peripheral parts of the country could have been secured with the investment of but a fraction of the resources that have gone to expand irrigation facilities in the Central Plain. It is true that the government now feels itself obliged to devote part of the proceeds of the rice premium to improving the efficiency of the rice industry, but in the past the larger landowners have had a powerful voice in the scheduling of irrigation projects, and it is difficult to believe that their influence is now any less. Thailand makes no charge for irrigation water, the costs of which are recovered from the land tax. The latter, however, contains no development component reflecting the potential higher productivity of land provided with improved water-control, and the recommendation of an International Bank Mission for the imposition of an irrigation tax has gone unheeded.[21] It is, of course, imperative that farmers should make the fullest use of the opportunities offered by irrigation, but in practice the use of water facilities and maintenance of distribution channels leaves something to be desired.[22]

Other agricultural activities and forestry
Natural rubber Natural rubber can account for almost one-third of the country's export earnings, as during the Korean crisis, but its share has since slowly declined to about half that figure (*Tables 4-4* and *4-6*). Rubber planting

---

[20] *There is, of course, as in other Southeast Asian countries, a substantial rural consumption of non-centrifugal sugars produced not only from sugar cane but also from other crops such as the coconut and palmyra palms.*

[21] *International Bank for Reconstruction and Development*, op. cit., *p. 52.*

[22] *Silcock (ed.)*, op. cit., *p. 251.*

moved into Thailand from Malaya following the 'rubber boom' of 1908, and with an enormous area physically suitable for *Hevea* cultivation, Thailand could have become a producer of the first importance. But it rejected the opportunity of acquiring a foreign-owned estate industry, and that a sizeable smallholder one developed was largely through the enterprise of the non-Thai peoples of the southern peninsula—the Chinese who, as in Malaya, moved into rubber production from tin-mining, and the Malays, who found in rubber smallholdings a profitable supplement to rice production.

Table 4-4 *Thailand: percentage value of exports by commodities, 1920–64*

	Rice	Rubber	Tin	Teak	Maize
1920–24	68·2	0·8	8·6	4·5	—
1935–39	53·5	12·9	18·6	4·2	—
1948	50·5	13·4	5·9	3·4	—
1951	48·0	30·1	5·1	3·3	—
1955	43·5	25·1	5·9	3·7	—
1960	29·9	29·7	6·2	4·1	—
1962	34·6	22·2	7·6	1·8	1·5
1964	35·8	16·5	8·0	2·1	13·3

Sources: J. C. Ingram, *Economic Change in Thailand since 1950; Statistical Yearbook of Thailand, 1964; Bangkok Bank, Monthly Review*

Growth, however, was initially very slow, and the planted area at the height of the post World War I boom probably did not exceed 150,000 acres, by which time Malaya had nearly a million acres in smallholdings. The collapse of the boom and the long period of planting restrictions, enforced first by the Stevenson scheme (1922–1928) and then by the International Rubber Agreement (1934–1941) concluded between Malaya, Ceylon and finally the Netherlands Indies, gave Thailand its chance; by refusing to be a party to restriction and remaining outside the agreements, Thailand profited by the 'price umbrella' and the planted area grew steadily, reaching 400,000 acres by the outbreak of World War II. The ebullience of the world economy after 1945, when for several years natural rubber stood at a premium above synthetic, encouraged further substantial growth; by 1963 the planted area had attained some 1·3 million acres,[23] of which about 18 per cent was immature, and Thailand's output of nearly 200,000 tons was then not far short of 10 per cent of world natural rubber production.

[23] *This is the official figure of the Ministry of Agriculture; that quoted by the International Rubber Study Group* (Table 2-6) *is considerably lower. Silcock records a figure of 2·7 million rai (1·08 million acres) for 1962. op. cit., p. 254.*

The southern peninsula has continued to retain a strong grip on natural rubber production, the four southernmost changwats, Narathiwat, Yala, Songkhla and Pattani accounting for over 60 per cent of total output. Rubber cultivation virtually ceases north of 9° N latitude in the peninsula, but about 5 per cent of national rubber output is produced in Southeast Thailand, the Chanthaburi district possessing the largest estate in the country. About 70 per cent of the planted area is believed to consist of holdings of less than seven acres; estates (i.e. holdings exceeding 100 acres) account for less than 10 per cent of the planted area. These larger properties are almost entirely in Chinese hands, as is also the situation with the medium holdings of between 25 and 100 acres. One obstacle to the development of an estate industry has been the law limiting individual land holdings to not more than 40 rai (10 acres), although in practice evasion has been common and a number of large Chinese properties have been confiscated by the state on the grounds that they were illegally acquired. The absence of an estate sector, however, has made Thailand much less able to meet the challenge of synthetic rubber than Malaysia, for it has never been able to support a rigorous programme of research into new and improved ways of producing and consuming rubber, and alone of the major natural rubber producers it has made no technological contribution to the industry. A high proportion of trees are of unselected materials and more than thirty years old. The national average yield per tapped acre in 1963 was thus only about 400 lb per annum as compared with over 600 lb in Malaysia (nearly 800 lb in 1967), and the disparity will widen in the future as Malaysia's large new plantings of high-yielding material come into bearing. The greater part of Thailand's rubber output consists of the lower grades R S S[24] 3, 4 and 5, and there is little production of concentrated latices or of other sophisticated rubbers for which special processing and packaging equipment is necessary.

Since 1960 Thailand has launched a replanting and new-planting scheme modelled closely on that of Malaysia, financed by a cess on exports (0·4 baht per kg in 1965). Subsidies paid over four years as work proceeds are available to smallholders with not less than 2 rai (0·8 acres) under rubber, but the total sum payable (the equivalent of some $180 US per acre) is less than that paid to smallholders under Malaysia's scheme, and there is a chronic shortage of suitable planting material. A further difficulty is that many smallholders do not possess legal title, and are thus ineligible for replanting grants; in some southern provinces three-quarters of all holdings are of the *Sor Kor Nung* type, a declaration by the occupant that he is the 'owner', but this is not necessarily accepted by the government. As in Malaysia, government estates for the propagation of high-yielding clonal seed and budwood for supply to smallholders have had to be established. Ultimately it is hoped to replant some 400,000 acres, and by 1970 an output of some 250,000 tons is forecast.

[24] *Ribbed smoked sheet. The traditional method of grading sheet, however, bears little relationship to suitability for most manufacturing purposes.*

Some low-grade rubber such as cup-lump (the air-congealed coagulum remaining in the tapping cup) slab and inferior sheet is exported for re-milling in Penang, but the greater part of the latex output is processed on or near the holding with very simple equipment and smoked at a nearby Chinese-owned smokehouse. A number of larger processing centres, some with equipment for producing crêpes and latices, have been established by the government in an effort to improve quality and exploit new markets; some of these new plants are intended for operation by cooperatives. Malaysian experience both with state-owned central processing stations and with small cooperative centres for processing latex from Malay smallholders, does not suggest any strong possibility of success. Though two research units have been established, at Kor Hong near Hadyaai and at Thanto in Yala changwat in the centre of the rubber-producing area, they possess nothing like the status and facilities of Malaysia's superb Rubber Research Institute with its regular and close connections with all sections of the industry; moreover, nothing has been done to implement the recommendation of the World Bank that the Rubber Division of the Ministry of Agriculture should be removed from Bangkok to the rubber-growing areas.

Almost certainly, the best way of assisting Thailand's rubber industry to improve its efficiency at what is now clearly the eleventh hour, would be the creation of an estate sector, not of large foreign-owned units, but of small estates of upwards of 100 acres, owned by Thai nationals. In Thailand, as in all countries of Southeast Asia, there is a strong preference for investment in land and real estate over productive enterprise, a choice that also reflects the relatively backward capital market. Thus much saving remains unmobilized which would probably be tapped if it were possible to acquire land on relatively easy terms for rubber or other tree crops, particularly in view of the fact that many hoarders are reasonably well informed on agricultural matters. This would almost certainly enlarge the land holdings of the Thai Chinese, but only through such a policy, or through direct state participation, is Thailand likely to obtain a footing in the profitable but capital-intensive oil palm industry, now booming in Malaysia. Malaysia is to provide technical assistance to Thailand in establishing oil palm plantations, but it appears unlikely that private capital will be allowed any significant role in the new industry.

Other crops and livestock   Thailand produces a multiplicity of other crops, but despite this it makes substantial imports both of foodstuffs and agricultural raw materials. Much of these imports could be replaced by domestic production, and this is being encouraged by the National Development Plan; however, any major change in land use appears unlikely in view of the general poverty of Thailand's soils, the strong preference for valley bottom land and rice cultivation, and the lack of experience in alternative production. Nevertheless, the output of several minor crops shows a marked upward trend; in addition to maize, kenaf, cotton and jute, tapioca and oilseeds also show appreciable increases in output. Tapioca is largely restricted to the peninsula, where it is mainly grown by Chinese; it is consumed as a food only by the poorest classes, but large quantities are processed into starch or fed to hogs. The present small production of oilseeds contrasts markedly with the large output of neighbouring Burma and, in view of the limited role of oils and fats in Thai diet and the large area physically suitable for their production, this deficiency should be rectified. Soya beans, dietetically the most valuable of all and a crop whose production has expanded very greatly in Indonesia over the past two decades, are still of very minor significance, though there has been some increase in the production of castor beans, an industrial oil crop.

Thailand has a large livestock population which amounts to no less than some 40 per cent of Southeast Asia's buffaloes and some 25 per cent of its cattle and pigs. Almost half of Thailand's seven million water buffaloes and a somewhat lower proportion of its cattle and pigs, both of which number around five million, are kept in the Northeast; this region makes a substantial export of animals to the Central Plain, where local livestock production is insufficient. But the low productivity of livestock means that prices are relatively high and the per capita consumption of both meat and milk is very low; there is some evidence that there are too many animals, and a smaller livestock population of higher productivity would appear advantageous. Most of the buffaloes and a substantial proportion of the cattle population are used for work purposes; greater mechanization of rice cultivation, as in northeast Malaya, would make much of the buffalo population redundant. The buffalo, however, can be an acceptable dairy animal, and further research in this direction is desirable. Similarly, improved transport should lead to a reduction in the number of oxen kept for draft purposes, and enhanced opportunities for the production of livestock products of higher quality. Unfortunately, the natural pastures admit of little possibility of improvement, but in some areas production of fodders could be integrated with that of food crops.

Forest industries   Forests cover about 70 per cent of Thailand, and although the productivity of forests is generally very low, forest products have nevertheless made a considerable contribution to Thailand's export earnings for more than three-quarters of a century. Virtually all of this has been derived from the teak trade, for although Thailand has a substantial production of other timbers this is entirely consumed within the country. A large proportion of the teak output, in fact, is also consumed domestically, and in this respect teak is more akin to rice, rather than to rubber and tin, among the country's traditional exports.

As earlier noted, though commercially the most important component of the forests of North Thailand, teak is ecologically speaking of minor importance. Its distribution is highly uneven, numbers and rate of growth being largely dependent on soil conditions; teak can reach a good commercial size in 85 years on rich well-drained soils, but on poor metamorphic rocks over 150 years may be required. This slow rate of growth makes the conservation of the capital stock a matter of importance, and there is evidence to suggest that illicit felling since 1945 has caused a sharp reduction. A lengthy growth-cycle is compounded with an extended production period; teak has to be girdled at least two years before felling to render the logs light enough to float, and even when placed in the head-streams of the Ping, Wang and Yom, a further five years is often necessary to carry the logs to the Bangkok sawmills. It is therefore many years before changes in the rate of felling are communicated to the volume of sawn timber production.

Following European entry into the teak industry after the Eighties of the last century, production grew rapidly; since 1910, however, when teak attained its greatest relative importance in the Thai economy, output has fluctuated considerably but with no clear tendency for overall growth. The half-dozen European companies that dominated the industry leased about 40,000 square kilometres when their concessions expired in 1955, and worked closely with the Forestry Department which specified the rate of cut. Since 1955, operation of the teak forests has in theory been shared by the state and a joint venture of state and private capital, though in practice the European companies continued operations as the agents of the government. However, the efficiency of the industry has suffered through illegal fellings and log thefts; every year between 1957 and 1962 witnessed a decline in output, but there was an improvement in 1963 and it is difficult to read much into the official figures of the volume of teak production. Almost certainly, the Chinese, who were never entirely displaced from the industry, have increased their share of sawn timber production, for the greater part of the large log losses through thefts at the junction of the northern valleys and the Central Plain must ultimately have passed into their hands.

Much of the capital invested in teak extraction is in the form of elephants, of which perhaps as many as 10,000 are employed in the northern forests. Tractors have not replaced elephants in hauling logs to streams because they cannot perform the animals' other essential function, which is to keep the logs moving at critical points in the stream bed during the very brief 'floating rises' when sudden heavy spates enable headstreams to carry the logs downstream. A number of light logging-railways, however, were constructed by the European companies to supplement the limited transport capacity of the headstreams, and temporary dams are also occasionally built to enlarge the volume of water available for log transport. Below the lowest falls, logs are assembled into rafts at the stations of the former concessionaires for the final two hundred or so miles via the government checking station at Pak Nam Pho (Nakhon Sawan), at the junction of the Ping and Yom, to the sawmills of Bangkok.

Teak now accounts for scarcely 10 per cent of the total volume of timber production. Nearly one-third of the timber volume consists of *yang (Diptero-*

carpus alatus) which is cut in large quantities in Southeastern Thailand, principally by Chinese. A second major area of *yang* production is the Surat Thani area
in the east of the peninsula.

MINING AND MANUFACTURING

Thailand's status as a tin producer steadily increases; though its output is still
only about one-third of that of Malaysia, mismanagement of the tin-mining
industry in both Bolivia and Indonesia has so reduced the output of these traditionally major producers that Thailand could well establish itself as the free
world's second largest producer in the near future.

The methods of occurrence of Thailand's tin deposits and the organization
of the industry are very similar to those of Malaysia. Over three-quarters of
Thailand's tin output is produced from stanniferous alluvium derived from the
westernmost of the peninsula's granite-cored ranges, which extends southwards
from Ranong to the island of Phuket where desultory tin-mining has been
carried on for many centuries both by Thais and immigrant Chinese. Phuket
accounts for about one-quarter of total production and the Takua Pa valley in
Phangnga changwat to the north for about one-fifth. To the southeast a further
four stanniferous ranges extend towards the Malaysian border, and these produce
the balance of Thailand's output; these tinfields, lying mainly in Nakhon Si
Thammarat, Trong, Songkhla and Yala changwats, contain most of the country's
lode mines.

In contrast to the rubber industry, Thailand's tin industry has made major
technical innovations, both the bucket-ladder dredge and the grab-dredge for
offshore working being first employed in the country. Apart from a Thai half-
interest in one dredging company, dredging is exclusively a European and
Australian activity, but Japanese participation appears a likely future development. The dredging sector of the industry is closely controlled by the London
holding companies; five dredging companies form part of Malaysia's largest tin
group, Anglo-Oriental (Malaya) Limited. European capital-intensive mining
methods, however, appear to have been less successful in Thailand than in
adjacent Malaysia; dredging generally accounts for 35–40 per cent of Thailand's
output as against nearly 45 per cent in Malaysia, but Thailand lacks the *large*
hydraulicking and underground lode mines of Malaysia, which bring the European
share of the Malaysian industry up to some 60 per cent. The principal reason for
this disparity between the two countries has been the much more favourable
political and economic climate of both dependent and independent Malaya, but
isolation and transport facilities greatly inferior to those enjoyed by the Malaysian
industry have also impeded Thailand's dredging industry. Following World
War II there was a marked reduction in the number of dredges operating in the
country, but since the middle Fifties the number has been stabilized at between

twenty and twenty-five; in Malaysia, very cheap firewood resulting from the extensive rubber replanting programme has maintained the profitability of many old steam-powered dredges, but in Thailand such obsolete equipment has largely been retired from service.

Some 44 per cent of Thailand's output in 1964 was produced by gravel-pump mines and some 14 per cent from small mines; both types being largely owned and operated by Thai Chinese. The many high-cost small producers and the international connections of the European companies have given Thailand a considerable interest in restriction, and the country has been a party to every International Tin Agreement. Nevertheless, the government has long endeavoured to enlarge the local stake in the industry; future mining concessions north of the Kra isthmus are to be reserved for local capital, which is slowly entering the dredging section through participation in joint ventures.

In 1965, however, Thailand achieved a long-sought goal when the Phuket smelter, a joint venture between the American Union Carbide Corporation and local capital, with an annual capacity of 20,000 tons of concentrates, came into operation. Since the primitive Chinese smelters ceased to be economic in the face of competition from large mechanized smelters in the late nineteenth century, Thailand's concentrates have been sent to Malaya for treatment, or occasionally to smelters in other countries. There are considerable economies of scale in tin smelting and in the past the scale of output has never been enough to justify domestic smelting, which has only been carried on in times of emergency such as during and immediately following World War II. Production is now large enough to support a smelter of economic size, however, and exports of concentrates are no longer permitted. The new smelter experienced severe technical difficulties after coming into operation, but further extensions of capacity are envisaged.

Manufacturing industries

Although manufacturing has made great strides in Thailand since the end of World War II, in terms of output and employment the manufacturing sector is still very small. The 1960 census revealed that of an economically active population aged eleven years or more totalling almost 13·8 millions, only 471,000 or some 3·4 per cent, were engaged in manufacturing; but even this figure included some 70,000 unpaid family workers and very many thousands of workers in seasonal activities such as rice- and sugar-milling. According to an estimate made for the International Bank there were approximately 16,000 industrial establishments (excluding Government factories) in 1957, but only a little over 300 of these, or some 2 per cent of the total, employed over 50 workers.[25] What proportion of the total industrial work-force was employed by the larger establishments is not known, but it is clear that Thailand has not yet attained the stage of industrial

[25] *International Bank for Reconstruction and Development*, op. cit., p. 89.

A Bangkok hand-loom weaver.

evolution of Malaysia and Singapore, where large units already account for a substantial proportion of the industrial work-force. This is suggested by the fact that some 146,000 workers in manufacturing in 1960 were engaged on their own account; most of these, together with the unpaid family workers, were in all probability engaged in cottage industries.

In many parts of Thailand, and particularly in the Khorat plateau where incomes are low and transport facilities poor, the village meets much of its requirements of manufactured products through domestic industries. Prominent among cottage industries is the spinning and weaving of both cotton and silk from locally produced raw materials, and though the future of domestic cotton weaving appears doubtful in view of the growth of a modern mill industry in Bangkok, the survival of the handicraft silk industry is assured, thanks to the work of the American, J. Thompson, who first appreciated that the special lustre found only in hand-woven Thai silk could exert a strong attraction to the foreign buyer. Thai silk, in fact, cannot become a factory industry, although Bangkok and towns such as Nakhon Ratchasima (Khorat) and Chiang Mai have large workshops where an effort is made to ensure some uniformity of quality, and the organization of the industry resembles that of the Domestic System of the eighteenth-century British woollen industry, in which middlemen provide weavers with raw materials and advance cash and equipment. The larger workshops reel and dye their own silk yarn, but the middlemen get their yarn dyed by specialists, so that there is a considerable degree of variability in the colour of each consignment to the home workers—a fact which adds to the special appeal of the finished product, for each piece is often unique. Production is probably about half a million square yards annually, most of which is exported, and the steady increase in output has long made Thailand's own raw silk production inadequate; substantial quantities of yarn are imported from Japan, but further expansion of silkworm rearing is being vigorously encouraged in the north and east. Despite a high labour content, however, the value of Thailand's silk exports is still less than one-tenth that of Japan.

Although the Thai government participates in almost every kind of industrial activity in the factory sector, there is little doubt that it is an inefficient producer, and it is generally agreed that save for defence production, utilities and communications, industrial activity should continue to rest largely in private hands. The record of the National Economic Development Corporation, a government-sponsored body which engaged in the sugar, sacking and paper industries and which made large losses in the Fifties, has discredited direct state participation in manufacturing, but the many Ministries that have a stake in industrial production are reluctant to see a diminution in their industrial interests, as this would adversely affect the patronage at their disposal, on which their standing with the élite depends. Although various measures have been taken to promote private industry, such as exemptions from profits tax for a number of years, remission of taxes on exports, foreign exchange allocations for the repatriation of profits and the provision of special financial assistance for the establishment or modernization of certain industries, none of these incentives has so far proved really effective. Nor could it be otherwise while the government is so suspicious of its Chinese population and of the large foreign enterprise that it is unwilling to see their respective shares of industrial activity expand greatly; thus, in the absence of any marked inclination of indigenes to engage in manufacturing, it is driven to participate itself. In practice, of course, the difficulty is resolved by allowing members of government and key government servants to become directors or shareholders in Chinese or foreign enterprises, but with a capital contribution more nominal than real.

Factory industry is mainly concerned with the processing of primary products and with the production of consumer non-durables for the domestic markets. Among the former are the milling of rice, sugar and timber, and the manufacture of tobacco, jute sacking, and cement; prominent among the latter are cotton textiles, clothing, furniture and footwear. All of these industries consists mainly of locally-owned units, but the more capital intensive, such as sugar and cement, are largely in the hands of the state, which also possesses lucrative monopolies in tobacco and distilling. But for higher manufactures requiring assembly as well as processing, and for those involving a very large capital investment per worker, such as petroleum refining and iron and steel, heavy reliance must continue to be made on foreign enterprise. Thailand's largest industrial establishment is the Thai Oil Corporation refinery at Si Racha, some 80 miles southeast of Bangkok, with a capacity of 35,000 barrels a day (1·75 metric tons per annum) and able to accommodate tankers of up to 53,000 d.w. tons; the refinery was constructed by private capital with heavy support from several of the international major oil companies, and will revert to the state in 1977. There is also a state-owned refinery at Bang Chak in Bangkok, which with only one-seventh of the capacity of Si Racha will find competition severe, and a very small field refinery in the Fang basin in the extreme north of the country, where Thailand's present miniscule petroleum output originates. This may, however, be augmented as a result of new prospecting by foreign oil companies both in the Fang basin itself and offshore in the Gulf of Thailand. An iron and steel industry is also a future possibility, and feasibility studies have been undertaken by Krupp, but the dismal record of Burma's steel venture should caution against over-rapid involvement.

Japanese capital is increasingly active in manufacturing, and is largely responsible for the rapid growth of the cotton textile industry, which by 1965 possessed nearly 200,000 spindles and was beginning to show signs of over-capacity. Despite protective tariffs, mills find competition from Hong Kong severe. The foundations of a motor vehicle industry have been laid, with plans by Toyota and Honda for local assembly of automobiles, motorcycles and agricultural machinery; here Japanese manufacturers are especially favoured, having already acquired a large share of the vehicle market through extremely aggressive selling allied with very generous credit facilities. A Firestone plant opened in 1965 is capable of supplying the whole of the country's requirements of automobile tyres with a surplus for export, and as a result tyre imports have been rigorously limited; but as both Malaysia and Singapore have followed precisely the same policy with large new tyre plants of rival manufacturers, the prospects for any substantial export sales in other parts of Southeast Asia do not appear bright.

Apart from such industries as sugar-milling, cement and paper manufacture which for technical reasons are raw-material oriented, factory industry is overwhelmingly concentrated in the Bangkok area. The large market, with a much higher income per head than the country as a whole and with the opportunities of maintaining close contacts with officials in key ministries, financial institutions and the great import-export houses, makes Bangkok an irresistible magnet for new industrial investment. Speculation in industrial land, a consequence of the shortage of supply, has become a matter of some concern, and it is hoped that the development of factory estates in the provinces will ease the pressure on the capital and provide a much-needed increase in local employment. Such major regional centres as Chiang Mai and Nakhon Ratchasima would appear the obvious choices for such development, but if they are to become effective 'growth points' they will have to be provided with low-cost services and, possibly, with subsidized transport; the high cost of electric power outside the metropolitan area alone is a major obstacle to any industrial decentralization and appears unlikely to be remedied before the completion of the Mekong scheme. An interesting development is the Mae Mo industrial 'complex' northeast of Lampang. Exploitation of this lignite field began in 1959 to provide electric power for the construction of the Yan Hee (Phumiphon) dam, and in addition to feeding the power station, lignite is also used in a urea and ammonium sulphate plant supplied through aid from West Germany.

TRANSPORT AND TRADE

Although strategic considerations provided the main motivation for the adoption of modern methods of transport in Thailand, to some extent this is also true of additions and improvements effected since 1945. Areas that present the greatest problems to national security have tended to receive the greatest investment, although the metropolitan area has inevitably attracted a substantial share of expenditure on new transport facilities. The metre-gauge national railway system, to some extent supplemented by the development of internal air services, tied the various regions to Bangkok, but within the regions themselves largely traditional forms of transport prevailed. Timber and rice reached the mills of Bangkok via the waterways, and in the wet season the only transport available over much of the delta was by means of boats, the capital itself being threaded by many khlongs, or canals. In Khorat, where the rivers are unnavigable, ox-carts constituted the principal means of transportation, while in the peninsula, coastal shipping has always been a powerful competitor with the railway.

Despite its strategic motivation the railway system markedly stimulated economic development in many parts of the country, facilitating an expansion of rice cultivation in the Khorat plateau and making possible exploitation of the lignite of the north. Utilization of the system, however, shows a pattern typical of underdeveloped economies with freight ton-miles substantially below passenger miles; indeed, only Malaysia among the countries of Southeast Asia has a utilization pattern approximating to that of countries at a high level of development, in which freight ton-miles are by far the greater. Despite the acquisition of considerable new equipment, freight traffic has grown only slowly since the middle Fifties, and the gradual extension of the road system, whose new links often paralleled the railway, has provided a new element of competition. One of the railway's major difficulties is that the carriage of goods to and from stations is a monopoly of the state-owned Express Transport Organization (ETO), whose high charges and general inefficiency have forced many former rail users to acquire their own motor vehicles. Rice is still the most important freight item, providing about one-sixth of freight revenue, but is closely followed by petroleum products; building materials and cement constitute a third important source of freight income.

The motor vehicle came relatively late to Thailand; even by 1937 there were scarcely 10,000 vehicles in the country, substantially less than existed at that time in Singapore alone and only one-fifth of those in the Philippines. By 1965 the number had grown to nearly 150,000 (excluding military vehicles), but this still compared very unfavourably with the situation in either West Malaysia or the Philippines (*Table 4-5*). One of the principal reasons for the limited use of motor vehicles in the past has been the desire of the government to protect the railway system from competition, so that road construction obtained only the barest minimum of investment; moreover, in the delta, and even within the metropolitan area itself, water transport provided a cheaper and often more convenient alternative to overland transport. In the postwar period the relative prosperity of the country has led to a large increase in the number of vehicles in Bangkok, and many of the old khlongs have been filled in, greatly changing the appearance of the city. Half the vehicle fleet is located in the metropolitan area, but new road construction in the provinces after the mid-Fifties, led to a great expansion in vehicle numbers outside Bangkok, and the provinces have a steadily increasing share of commercial vehicles. Between 1965 and 1972 the Highways Department plans to construct some 7,000 miles of provincial roads, of which about one-third will be in the Northeast; the Central Plain, however, will also benefit. For new trunk roads Thailand will probably continue to rely heavily on foreign aid; connections between the capital and northern Thailand, and southwards via the peninsula to the Malaysian border, are long overdue. Apart from new road con-

Table 4-5   *Southeast Asia: motor vehicles in use, 1965*
(thousands)

	Passenger cars	Commercial vehicles	Vehicles per 1,000 population
Burma	25·2	24·8	2·0
Cambodia*	16·4	9·3	2·4
Laos	6·0	1·9	3·9
West Malaysia	159·6	45·6	25·6
Sarawak	8·2	1·7	12·4
Sabah*	8·0	3·3	22·6
Singapore	108·4	23·0	69·0
Philippines	168·7	103·8	8·4
Thailand	66·8	87·0	5·1
South Vietnam	34·3	33·2	4·2
Indonesia*	151·0	108·4	2·6

* 1964

Source: United Nations, *Statistical Yearbook*, 1966

struction, Thailand also faces a heavy burden in road maintenance; the climate takes particularly severe toll, to say nothing of the damage caused by greatly overloaded buses and trucks, and unless initial construction is sound and maintenance is rigorous, roads can quickly fall to pieces. Fortunately, since 1960 there has been much improvement in road maintenance as Thailand received new equipment and technical assistance through foreign aid programmes. As is the case in most countries of Southeast Asia, road transport is an activity in which Chinese predominate, and increasingly rigorous restrictions have been placed on the operations of Chinese hauliers and on the employment of Chinese in an effort to increase the share of Thai participation in the industry. Two state companies, one to provide passenger and one to provide freight services, have been set up and given a monopoly of certain services. Lacking sufficient vehicles, however, both organizations have had to license private operators. The inefficiency of the E T O, which has a monopoly of transporting freight to and from the port of Bangkok, is a major cause of port congestion, and its rates appear excessive.

Bangkok dominates the foreign trade of Thailand, handling nearly three-quarters of the country's export trade and some 95 per cent of its imports. Bangkok only became accessible to ocean-going vessels in 1955 with the dredging of a channel through a bar at the mouth of the Chao Phraya; before that time ships anchored off the Ko (island) Si Chang in the Gulf of Thailand and discharged into lighters; though there were repeated proposals for the dredging of a channel, the lightering interests were politically strong enough to thwart them. Nevertheless, the port is still accessible only to vessels of up to 10,000 g.r.t., and is in danger of being by-passed by the 'container revolution' in world shipping. The International Bank Mission of 1959 considered that neither the construction of a deep-water port in the Gulf itself, nor any major improvements in other penin-

Table 4-6 *Thailand: composition of foreign trade, 1966 (million baht)*

EXPORTS f.o.b.		IMPORTS c.i.f.	
Rice	4,001·7	Manufactures	8,584·3
Rubber	1,855·5	Machinery and transport	
Kenaf	1,652·6	equipment	6,007·0
Maize	1,529·4	Petroleum products	2,295·3
Tin	1,290·7	Foodstuffs	2,093·3
Tapioca	686·5	Tobacco and beverages	885·0
Teak	243·0		
Total	**14,419·1**	**Total**	**24,481·4**
(including others)		(including others)	

Source: *Bank of Thailand Annual Economic Report,* 1966

sular ports, would be economically justifiable,[26] but these conclusions now appear to require review. The difficulty and expense of maintaining the dredged channel in the Chao Phraya, the development of the oil-refining complex at Si Racha with its own deep-water facilities and good road connection with Bangkok, and the desirability of attracting the new container vessels will make the construction of a general cargo deep-water port on the Gulf ultimately inevitable. The site for such a port is still the subject of much contention. Laem Krabang south of Si Racha has been suggested by IBRD consultants, but the Americans already have built a deep-water naval base at Sattahip further south, which might also be used in part for commercial services. Although it remains true that Penang is the logical outlet for much of the southern peninsula, Thailand has taken steps to eliminate the dispatch of tin concentrates and rubber to Penang for processing and re-export, and port improvements at Phuket have already been effected in connection with the new tin smelter. There would, however, appear to be a need for at least one major new port in the peninsula, but whether this should be Phuket or Songkhla is still undecided at the time of writing.

The most striking development in the direction of Thailand's overseas trade is the large and growing importance of Japan as a trading partner; Japan now accounts for about half of Thailand's total trade turnover (imports plus exports), but it is much more important as a supplier of Thailand's imports than as a market for Thailand's exports; nevertheless, only Pan-Malaya (that is, West Malaysia and Singapore) outranks Japan in the latter respect and a considerable proportion of Pan-Malaya's imports from Thailand are later re-exported. The growing adverse balance of trade with Japan has markedly assisted the penetration of Japanese capital into the Thai economy.

[26] *International Bank for Reconstruction and Development*, op. cit., *pp. 140–2.*

CHAPTER FIVE

The Philippines

If Latin America is judged as possessing the greatest immediate development potential of the three great deposits of human misery that constitute the so-called Third World, then the Philippines, and for broadly similar reasons, stand in the same relation to Southeast Asia. The first dependent territory to develop a coherent sense of nationality free from the complications of appeals to past glories which in the Philippines simply did not exist; a largely homogeneous and literate population which in four centuries of contact with the West has developed a culture which owes as much to the Occident as to the Orient; a broad resource basis with a modest mineral wealth; a heavy involvement in the world economy with special relations with the world's largest and most affluent single market, that of the United States—all of these appear special advantages in comparison with the developmental prospects in most Southeast Asian countries. But as in Latin America, consolidation of these assets in rapid and self-sustaining economic growth is being long delayed.

In some ways, the postwar economic growth of the Philippine economy has been impressive enough; in the Fifties real national product increased by about 7 per cent annually, and since 1960 the rate has been around 6 per cent.[1] But with a rate of population increase of more than 3 per cent per annum, this performance is pulling back little on Malaya's commanding lead in economic well-being within the region, and there is clearly much that is very wrong, both with the Philippine economy and with the socio-political framework within which it operates.

Perhaps the most glaring shortcoming is the low productivity of almost every branch of agricultural production and that of food production in particular, a situation that in large part reflects an agrarian organization hopelessly out of touch with social needs and one of the worst tenancy problems within Southeast

[1] *Gerardo P. Sicat (ed.)*, The Philippine Economy in the 1960's, *Institute of Economic Development and Research, University of the Philippines, Quezon City, 1964, pp. 5-6. These figures, however, appear over-optimistic to some Western economists.*

Table 5-1 *Philippines: industrial origin of net domestic product, 1965*

	Pesos millions	Per cent
Agriculture, forestry and fishing	5,778	33·5
Mining	375	2·2
Manufacturing	3,072	17·8
Construction	638	3·6
Transport, communications and utilities	478	2·8
Wholesale and retail trade	2,066	12·0
Ownership of dwellings	1,313	7·7
Public administration and defence	1,707	9·9
Other services	1,803	10·5
Total	**17,230**	**100·0**

Source: United Nations, *Economic Survey of Asia and the Far East*, 1966

Asia. The country also experiences chronic balance-of-payments difficulties which only large American economic aid and military expenditure have prevented from becoming very much worse. This situation has in large part arisen through the failure of the traditional exports to expand, for on a per capita basis the area devoted to the traditional export crops is in fact lower than before the war, and only in a year of very high prices for Philippine products, such as 1963 when the price of sugar in the world 'free market' reached £100 per ton, does the country show an export surplus, whereas this was achieved in most years before 1941. And not surprisingly in a largely Catholic country, virtually nothing has been done to grapple with the problem of a very high rate of population increase save through resettlement in less congested islands; but by 1975, at the present rate of population growth, there will be no more land available for new agricultural settlement on relatively thinly populated Mindanao, Mindoro, Samar and Palawan, which have so far provided some relief from the growing pressure on land in Luzon and in certain of the Visayan islands.[2]

The economic gains made since 1950 have in all probability enlarged still further the pre-existing gross disparities in the distribution of income between classes. The rural worker in particular seems to be little better off; hence the continued drift of the landless and others who have abandoned the struggle to make ends meet on the farm to the slums of Tondo and the squatter settlements of other parts of Greater Manila. These early gains, moreover, were achieved cheaply with relatively little capital investment, through postwar rehabilitation

[2] *Robert E. Huke*, Shadows on the Land, *The Bookmark, Inc., Manila, 1963, p. 152.*

schemes which produced an immediate and appreciable increase in output; when the time comes to replace this capital, costs are going to be very much higher.[3] This consideration probably goes far to explain the marked deterioration in the physical equipment and operating efficiency of every kind of transportation medium since 1960, a situation that results in recurrent shortages and high prices of consumer goods on the one hand, and on losses and delays to the export trade on the other.

Most of these pressing problems originate in the structure of Philippine society, and in particular, the concentration of land and political power in the hands of a few extremely wealthy families, a legacy of four centuries of Spanish rule. Such maldistribution could theoretically result in a high rate of saving, its principal economic justification, but in the Philippines this is not the case; the rate of saving is low, and as the wealthy are generally unwilling to invest in other enterprises than real estate, these are starved of capital. Inevitably, therefore, much non-agricultural activity represents the fruits of either Chinese or foreign, principally American, capital and enterprise, and the role to be accorded the foreigner, including the local Chinese, in the development of national resources is a major and acrimonious political issue.

Nevertheless, the Philippines to a large extent retains the advantages and flexibility of a free and open society. A rigorous reform programme dedicated primarily to the improvement of the lot of the poorest members of society could still be successfully mounted, and the country has certainly never lacked dedicated and reforming leadership. In the past, however, programmes such as that envisaged in the 1963 Agricultural Land Reform Code have invariably bogged down through Congressional opposition, but it appears unlikely that the country will be permitted time for more than one further effort before widespread rural discontent explodes in new paroxysms of violence.[4]

THE PHYSICAL BASIS

Physically, as well as in other ways, the Philippines presents several similarities with Indonesia to the south. There is a comparable dissemination of the national territory over a multitude of islands; the same four-fold pattern of landforms, comprising active volcanoes, non-volcanic mountains, hill-lands and plains; and despite the greater latitudinal range of the Philippine archipelago, a broadly

---

[3] *Benjamin Higgins*, Economic Development, *Norton and Company, New York, 1959, p. 63.*

[4] *Crime, including armed robbery, reached alarming proportions in the Sixties, not only in Manila where it had become virtually a feature of daily life, but also in the provinces. Criminal elements were being regularly let out of jails to continue their depredations, and there was widespread corruption in the police force, in the customs and excise, and in Congress itself. The communist* Hukbalahap *movement has continued to ravage parts of central Luzon.* Far Eastern Economic Review Year Book, *Hong Kong, 1965, p. 251.*

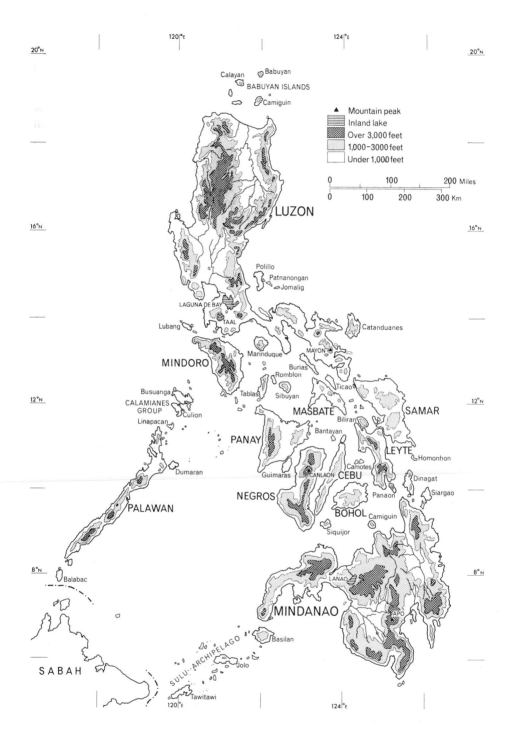

Fig 5-1 The Philippine Islands and their relief

similar east-west rather than north-south arrangement of climatic types. The two largest islands, Luzon and Mindanao, account for two-thirds of the Philippine national territory, and the addition of eight other large islands (Mindoro, Panay, Negros, Cebu, Bohol, Leyte, Samar and Masbate) grouped around the Sibuyan and Visayan seas, and the eccentric Palawan raises this proportion to nearly 95 per cent. The two largest Indonesian islands, with the addition of the next largest nine, account for very similar proportions, but the Philippine archipelago is much more compact than its Indonesian counterpart, and despite a greater linguistic diversity has clearly the greater national cohesion.

All the major islands possess great physical variety, which reaches its maximum in the large island of Mindanao with its high, rugged and densely forested mountains, huge volcanic peaks ascending to nearly 9,000 feet, elevated rolling plateaus and broad marshy lowlands. As throughout Southeast Asia, the most significant distinction in terms of human activity is between lowlands capable of producing padi (or *palay* in Tagalog, the adopted national language) and all other land, which from the Filipino farmer's viewpoint is dry land. Unlike mainland Southeast Asia and Indonesia, the Philippine islands possess no extensive river systems whose broad alluvial plains lend themselves to conversion into major rice-bowls, and even the most extensive lowland, the Central Plain of Luzon, measures only some 120 miles by 60 miles. Although apparently a major physical unit on the topographic map, the Cagayan valley of northern Luzon is nothing like as level and contains much rolling topography, and is therefore much less important as a producer of *palay*. The only other area of smooth level topography in Luzon is the Bicol lowland of the southeastern peninsula, the long and narrow coastal plains of Ilocos in the northwest and Zambales in the west, both being dissected by numerous westward-flowing streams.

The Agusan and Cotabato valleys of Mindanao are the next most extensive lowlands after the Central Plain of Luzon, but possess a large area of swamp-land as well as more undulating topography; forested and unpopulated wildernesses at the turn of the century, they have filled up rapidly through state colonization schemes and private immigration. The remaining plains are small in comparison, though very significant in the economy of their respective islands. Among the more important are the plain of east-central Panay, a major palay area; the plain of northwest Negros, the country's principal sugar-producing region; and the plains of both the eastern and western coasts of Mindoro, much of which still remain little used.

Although the Philippine archipelago cannot approach the intense vulcanism of Java, it has, nevertheless, several exceedingly active volcanoes which have given rise to the most imposing landforms and have profoundly affected the lives of the peoples of their vicinity. Active vulcanism occurs in the Batan and Babuyan islands to the north of Luzon, while southern Luzon contains six active volcanoes whose extensive deposits have weathered into what are by Philippine standards very fertile soils. Batangas province south of Manila, an important area for dry rice and citrus production, contains one of the most active volcanoes in the country, Taal. The present crater is situated on a small island in the middle of Lake Taal, which itself occupies a vast caldera produced by a paroxysmal prehistoric explosion. After the 1911 eruption which killed some 1,200 people the island was proscribed to settlement; nevertheless, about 2,000 persons were estimated to be living on the volcano when on September 28th 1965 it blew up in another violent eruption, and most were believed killed. Mayon, a few miles northwest of the town of Legaspi in Albay province, is equally active and its smooth symmetrical cone rising to nearly 9,000 feet is possibly the most perfect in the world.

Canlaon, in northern Negros, is the only active volcano in the Visayas, though most islands contain recently extinct, or more probably dormant, volcanic peaks. Mindanao, however, demonstrates a more active vulcanism: a broad belt of volcanic mountains south of Lake Lanao has active peaks reaching over 9,000 feet, whose volcanic deposits of ash and tuff interbedded with basalt lava flows have built up extensive high plateaus in Lanao del Sur and Bukidnon provinces. The island of Camiguin off the coast of Misamis Oriental in northern Mindanao has been created by the dangerous Hibok-Hibok, whose last eruption in 1951 killed over 1,000 persons. Vulcanism also occurs in southern Mindanao, where Mount Apo west of Davao (nearly 9,700 feet) is the highest point in the Philippines. In general, however, it is only in restricted parts of central and southern Luzon that volcanically derived soils of above average fertility occur, and these do support a high population density. But the relationship is only a pale replica of that of Java, for the Philippines possesses no broad plains enriched by volcanic ejectamenta such as those of north or central Java, and most soils of more ancient volcanic origin are very deficient in plant nutrients.

The remaining physical division, the non-volcanic mountains and hilllands, occupies perhaps some 60 per cent of the surface area of the country. Included within this large area are the extensive rolling plateaus of Bukidnon and Lanao in Mindanao and a number of smaller tectonic basins such as those in the cordilleras of Luzon; the utilization of all these for agricultural purposes presents no great difficulties. However, about one-fifth of the total land area has slopes of more than 20° and should be withheld completely from agriculture, and a rather larger proportion has slopes of 10–20° on which the only form of agriculture that can be safely practised without producing greatly accelerated soil erosion is a careful tree-crop cultivation. But the cupidity of the logging interests with their powerful connections in Congress, has resulted in many steep slopes being denuded of their forest cover without provision for regeneration, and population pressure has forced innumerable peasants to practice clean, row-crop cultivation on slopes far too steep for such practices. The result is a problem of soil erosion which is as severe as anywhere in Southeast Asia, and could already be fairly described as of disastrous proportions. Rugged eroded hills, and great

The smooth cone of Mayon in southeast Luzon forms a backdrop for a scene of rural domesticity.

expanses of man-made *cogon* (*Imperata* species) grasslands constitute the most conspicuous physical elements in very many islands; almost two-thirds of the cultivated land of the densely populated, hilly limestone island of Cebu has lost more than 75 per cent of its top-soil and broad stretches have been laid to waste.[5] Soil erosion is, however, not only a problem affecting steep slopes, for it has also reached serious proportions in many areas of mild relief.

Although it has been customary to distinguish four major climatic regimes, the Philippines present many variations on a basic humid tropical theme. Throughout the archipelago temperature ranges are not of real consequence, although that of the Cagayan valley is unusually large by Southeast Asian standards, and climatic variation largely consists in the presence or absence of a dry season, its duration and the time of year at which it occurs; on such considerations the cropping pattern and the seasonal rhythm of agriculture largely depend. Unlike Indonesia, the Philippines possesses only a small area with a long and fierce dry season, and a precipitation of less than 60 inches is confined to a few restricted rain-shadows such as a small part of the Cagayan valley, southeast Palawan, the southeastern extremities of Negros and Cebu, and the Zamboanga district and the head of Sarangani Bay in southern Mindanao, the lattermost area being the only place in the Philippines where the precipitation is not much more than 40 inches.

Most of the lowlands receive from 60 to 80 inches and most uplands over 100

[5] *Huke*, op. cit., *p. 64.*

inches. Precipitation is particularly torrential even for Southeast Asia, as from one-quarter to one-third is derived from typhoons, or *baguios*. These tropical revolving storms are generated over Micronesia to the east, and on the average some twenty-five a year pass over the Philippines, usually between July and November. Most typhoon tracks lie north of a line passing through the northern Visayan Islands, so that the east coasts of Samar and southern Luzon are particularly buffeted; southwards the incidence of typhoons becomes progressively less, and southern Mindanao is almost entirely free of typhoon damage. The violence of the Filipino *baguio* is notorious, the most severe ever recorded having deposited more than 40 inches of rainfall in twenty-four hours. But around one-tenth of all typhoons reach disastrous proportions, with winds exceeding 100 miles an hour and a rainfall of from 20 to 30 inches in twenty-four hours, and they cause tremendous damage. Coconut, abacá, sugar and banana plantations are particularly susceptible to typhoon damage, and in coastal districts mountainous seas and tidal waves can cause considerable loss of life.

Virtually the entire eastern margin of the Philippines experiences a heavy, year-round precipitation, with particularly heavy precipitation during the season of the so-called east monsoon, November to January; such conditions are most suitable for the cultivation of perennials. The west coasts of Luzon, Mindoro and Palawan have a marked high-sun rainy season from May to October and a dry season of around four months, though in places this extends to almost six months; aridity is greatest in the early months of the year, and in Ilocos and Abra provinces particularly, serious water shortages can occur. This monsoonal regime is eminently suitable for rice or sugar cultivation. Between these two coastal margins a number of intermediate types can be detected, including areas with a short dry season of one to three months, occurring either in the low-sun season, as in much of Panay and western Negros (a major sugar-producing area), or even in the middle months of the year as in the Cagayan valley, the Sibuyan Sea coast of Luzon, and in the central Visayas. Both intermediate types occur in small areas of northwestern Mindanao, but over the greater part of the island rainfall is copious at all times in the year, and in practice, therefore, essentially equatorial crops succeed virtually everywhere.

Under such climatic conditions virtually all of the Philippines with the exceptions of the highest summits must have supported a forest of some kind before the spread of agriculture, and even at present forests constitute the most extensive vegetational association in the islands, although the proportion of the total land area occupied by forests has been very variously estimated, reflecting the different definitions adopted by each authority. The official estimate of the forest cover in 1962 records a figure of 31 per cent of the total surface as under commercial forest and a further 13 per cent as non-commercial forest, but other authorities rate this proportion far too high. *Cogonales* and similar open park-land were estimated at only some 18 per cent of the total land area, a decidedly conservative figure, and some 35 per cent as being cultivated land, the balance consisting of swamp-land.

As throughout Southeast Asia, the dipterocarps constitute the most important forest species in areas with a heavy year-round rainfall; commercially the most important are the various *Shoreas*, source of the 'Philippine mahogany', or *lauan*. Some dipterocarps also occur in areas where the dry season is of relatively short duration so that the soil never dries out to any depth, and these tend to produce more durable timbers; but in those parts where the dry season is pronounced, dipterocarp forests are replaced by a more open forest of shrub with occasional tall trees which drop their leaves in the dry season, and many bamboos and woody scramblers. This forest is sometimes called *molave* after the molave tree *(Vitex parvifolia)*, but this species does not occur in all dry forests. The productivity of the *molave* forest is low, but it produces some of the most valuable timbers in the country; *ipil (Intsia bijuga)* and *tindalo (Pahudia rhomboidia)*, both arborescent legumes, are noted for their durability and strength. Above 3,000 feet in the central cordillera of Mountain province, Luzon, mixed forests of oak, *Pinus insularis* and *Pinus merkusii* occur, whose timber is of considerable local significance, while tidal flats support a *Rhizophora* mangrove forest, whose value as a source of charcoal, the principal means of cooking in much of rural Southeast Asia, has resulted in much over-cutting.

Probably less than one-third of the total forest area now consists of primary forest, and this is confined to the remoter and more inaccessible parts of the country, above all on the various cordilleran slopes. Reduction of the primary forest has proceeded apace throughout the present century, largely through the extension of the agricultural area but also through the growth of a commercial lumber industry, which has expanded its production of timber more than sixty fold. Primary forests still cover parts of the Central Cordillera and the Sierra Madre in northern Luzon, and also areas of central Mindoro, Negros and Palawan, but the only really extensive areas now lie in the Agusan, Davao and Cotabato provinces of Mindanao. As the logging companies follow the receding virgin forest into the mountainous parts of the country increasingly distant from the main markets, costs of production must trend upwards.

Some two-thirds of the total forest area thus consists of secondary forest. Lumber companies are obliged by law to spare sufficient trees to ensure regeneration, but even where this is done squatters all too often move on to the land and destroy the remaining trees in *caiñgin* cultivation. Such practices, and periodic cutting and burning, produce either an open woodland and grassland locally known as *parang*, in which *cogon* and other pernicious grasses such as *talahib* *(Saccharum spontaneum)* are prominent, or broad *cogonales*. The extension of the latter has been most rapid in the western portion of the country where the dry season aids firing, but extensive areas of the wetter east have also been allowed to degenerate into grassy wastes.

Forestry, of course, is only one method of using land, and in the Philippines, as in all newly independent countries of the inter-tropical world, the only form of land use that really matters to a largely rural population is agriculture. Much, but not all, of the shortcomings of forest policy and practice can be traced to the highly unsatisfactory agricultural situation. Most regulations which attempt to utilize the forest experience of the United States are consistently flouted, often with the connivance of the highest officials, and designated Forest Reserves and National Parks have been repeatedly invaded; these institutions, imported from abroad and incorporated into the 'positive law' enforced by the machinery of the state, are at variance with the local 'living law' by which the population regulates its day-to-day life.[6] Administrative and financial shortcomings, moreover, have led to interminable delays in implementing reafforestation projects, and some schemes dating back before 1920 had not even been commenced more than three decades later.[7] For its failure to protect its large original natural forest wealth, the Philippines is ultimately going to have to pay a very heavy price.

THE AGRICULTURAL SCENE

About 60 per cent of the Filipino work-force is engaged in agricultural pursuits, yet these generate only a little more than 30 per cent of national product (*Table 5-1*). Low productivity is a characteristic feature of Filipino agriculture, and this applies to food crop, industrial crop and livestock production alike. Moreover, productivity is low even by Asian standards, and only India, which has a relatively large area with a rainfall of less than 40 inches, records lower national average yields. No such climatic excuse can be offered for the poor agricultural performance of the Philippines, and the causes of its inefficiency are primarily to be sought in the institutional environment.

Three crops dominate Philippine agriculture, rice, corn (maize) and coconuts (*Table 5-2*). As throughout Southeast Asia, rice is in general the preferred crop and its cultivation has been pushed into all those parts of the country where production is possible, including some where conditions are far from optimum. Although the three major crops are broadly non-competitive for land, the addition of the next three most important, sugar, abacá and tobacco, which collectively make up the so-called 'big six' crops and occupy nearly 90 per cent of the total harvested area, does introduce some element of competition. Sugar competes with rice, and tobacco with corn; but corn is from the economic standpoint an extremely flexible crop, being cultivated either on its own or in conjunction with other of the 'big six' crops, or even with minor crops such as roots,

[6] *Karl J. Pelzer, 'Agriculture, vegetation and rational land utilization in the humid tropics', Paper H-13, Ninth Pacific Science Congress, Bangkok, 1957, pp. 28-30.*

[7] *Joseph E. Spencer, Land and People in the Philippines, University of California Press, Berkeley and Los Angeles, 1952, p. 211.*

Table 5-2 *Philippines: area and production of major crops, 1965–66*

	AREA	PRODUCTION
	thousand hectares	*thousand metric tons*
FOOD CROPS	8,300	
Rice (rough)	3,110	4,070
Corn (shelled)	2,110	1,380
Roots	260	1,470
Legumes and vegetables	110	250
Coffee	50	40
EXPORT CROPS	2,235	
Abacá	200	135
Tobacco	90	60
Sugar cane	230	1,400 (centrifugal sugar) 60 (muscovado)
Coconuts	1,050	1,490 (copra) 455 (coconut oil) 260 (copra cake) 80 (desiccated coconut)
Rubber	3	6
Kapok	3	2

Source: *Central Bank of the Philippines, Eighteenth Annual Report,* 1966

tubers and legumes. Thus only in the case of rice and sugar does competition for land occasionally assume acute proportions. The higher profitability of sugar in the early Sixties led to some transfer of land from rice to sugar cultivation in the Central Plain of Luzon, the Philippines' principal rice-bowl; but unlike the practice in Java, where rice and sugar production were closely interlocked, in the Philippines the two crops are mainly produced in separate areas and under distinctive organizations. Filipinos, however, have seldom had enough of either; after many years of struggle and a progressive increase in the rice area, national self-sufficiency in rice in the early Sixties still seemed far off. Imports of rice between 1946 and 1962 averaged nearly 70,000 tons annually, and in 1963 the rice import bill amounted to some $27 million. For many years the rice situation has been an exceedingly acrimonious political issue, and although per capita consumption has been slowly increasing and has done so much more rapidly since the introduction of 'miracle' rice, that of sugar continues to be restricted by a high internal price designed to free output for the export market.

Rice and food crops

A little more than 40 per cent of the total cultivated area of the Philippines is normally under rice, a rather low proportion for a Southeast Asian country, a

Fig 5-2   Administrative divisions of the Philippine Republic, 1966

Owing to a continued increase in population some of the provinces have since been subdivided. Samar is divided into Northern, Western and Eastern Samar; Cotabato into Cotabato del Norte and Cotabato del Sur; Davao into Davao Oriental, Davao del Norte and Davao del Sur; and Mountain Province into Kalinga-Apayao, Mountain Province, Ifugao and Benguet.

fact that in part reflects physical conditions for rice (*palay*) cultivation considerably less favourable than are found in the countries of mainland Southeast Asia. Lacking broad alluvial deltas on the scale of those produced by the mainland rivers whose regimes assist rice cultivation through annual flooding, the palay area of the Philippines is disseminated in numerous and for the most part closely circumscribed areas; even the most extensive, the Central Plain of Luzon, now possesses only a little more than 20 per cent of the total harvested area. Sixty years ago this region accounted for no less than 42 per cent of the harvested area, and its relative decline in importance reflects the expansion of new palay areas in the Cagayan valley and in the Bicol lowlands of Luzon, in the eastern Visayas and in Mindanao; collectively, these newer areas have expanded their share of the rice area from 10 per cent to 40 per cent, while over the same period the total rice area increased more than six-fold.[8] Expansion of the palay area is still continuing at about 2 per cent per annum, but opportunities for further increases in the lowland palay area are distinctly limited and the greater part of the increase consists of upland, or dry palay; thus between 1953 and 1959 the lowland palay area increased by some 225,000 acres, but upland palay by nearly 700,000 acres.[9]

Dry palay now accounts for about 20 per cent of the harvested area, but as the yield of dry palay is at best little more than half that of lowland palay, the share of total output is very much less. The greater part of upland rice production is grown by shifting cultivators, but very many *caiñgineros* are not true swidden cultivators; they are lowland Filipinos who have resorted to this method of cultivation in response to mounting pressure on land. *Caiñgins* have been illegal for many years; but most go undetected and even where reported seldom lead to eviction, and each year perhaps as much as 120,000 acres of forest land are newly cleared for additional ones. In some parts of the country dry rice is grown on permanent fields in the manner of the *tegalan* or dry fields of Java, but the careful embanking, erosion control and manuring practised on many Javanese *tegalans* is seldom encountered in the Philippines.

Lowland palay is grown on flooded fields, and almost always with the transplanting method. Preparation of the land and the seed-bed is undertaken from May to July, transplanting from June to August and harvesting from October to December in the Central Plain of Luzon and in other western rice-growing districts such as the plains of the Ilocos and Batangas, and the Central Plain of Panay. Transplanting of late or long-term varieties which need early transplanting is facilitated by a technique known as *dapog*. A prepared seed-bed is covered with banana leaves which are lightly pressed into the mud, on top of which an inch-thick layer of rice hulls, chopped straw or sawdust is placed; the seed-bed is

[8] *Huke*, op. cit., *pp. 219–20*.

[9] *United States Department of Agriculture*, The Philippines: Long Term Projection of Supply of and Demand for Selected Agricultural Products, *quoted in Gerardo P. Sicat (ed.)*, op. cit., *p. 102*.

soaked with water and sown with seed, and from seven to ten days after sowing the seedlings can be rolled up like a rug in the banana leaves and taken to the fields for transplanting. About 24 man-days and 5 *carabao* (buffalo) days on the average are needed to cultivate an acre of rice-land. Though virtually unemployed for long periods, most Filipino rice farmers nevertheless make much use of hired labour at harvests, a practice that substantially cuts into their own return.

Discontinuity in the use of both land and labour throughout the year is a marked feature of the Philippine rice economy. As only about 12 per cent of the cultivated area is irrigated, double-cropping is very restricted, and during the dry season from November to May the greater part of the Central Plain of Luzon produces little but poor grazing for the work animals. The wet-season rice crop depends almost entirely on flooding resulting from the slow run-off in the flat and low-lying plain; but neither in reliability nor amount does the rainfall of the Central Plain of Luzon match that of the Irrawaddy delta of Burma, where irrigation is also of little consequence, nor are there major river systems whose natural flooding can be relied on to ensure a good crop. Only in the terraced fields of the Ifugao and Bontoc peoples of the Mountain province of Luzon, constructed for the most part thousands of years ago, are water systems and water control effectively integrated into the agricultural landscape.[10] Elsewhere irrigation facilities are restricted to the few schemes serving Church and Friar lands built in the Spanish period, and the limited works constructed by the American and Philippine administrations in the present century.

The total area served by the diversion schemes constructed in the early nineteenth century by the religious orders never exceeded 60,000 acres and was divided between provinces immediately adjacent to Manila. An Irrigation Division was established by the American administration in 1908, but progress was slow until the Twenties, and by the onset of the Great Depression about 200,000 acres, lying mainly in the Central Plain and on the northwest coast, had been provided with irrigation facilities in about a dozen separate schemes. Further development was delayed until after World War II, but by 1964 the total area served by government deviation-distribution works of so-called National Irrigation Systems had been raised to nearly 800,000 acres. A further 375,000 acres were served by pump irrigation from streams under communal or Irrigation Service Unit schemes, small-scale works undertaken by private landowners or by cooperatives with some government financial assistance. The larger schemes are concentrated on the Central Plain of Luzon, the main sources of supply being the Pampanga, Agno, Tarlac and Angat rivers. Apart from one scheme in Iloilo province, Panay, one in Cotabato province, Mindanao, and one in Negros Occidental, irrigation in the Visayas and in Mindanao is limited to a few small-scale communal and Irrigation Service Unit projects.

Not only is the proportion of the cultivated area that is irrigated very small,

[10] *Spencer*, op. cit., *p. 151.*

but even the major schemes provide little assistance to dry-season cropping as they lack storage facilities. The policy of guaranteeing only the wet-season crops allows tremendous quantities of water to go to waste in the Central Plain; moreover, large resources of underground water, including artesian supplies, remain untapped.

As over two-thirds of lowland palay is dependent on natural rainfall alone, there are considerable variations in yields from year to year and from district to district. Before World War II the national average was some 25 *cavans* per hectare (one cavan equals approximately 44 kg or 2·1 Imperial bushels); in 1958 it was still only 27 cavans and in 1967, 29 cavans per hectare. Yields from irrigated lands, however, average approximately double those from unirrigated lands. Extension of the irrigated area by itself appears to offer the possibility of transforming the Philippines from a rice-deficiency to a rice-surplus area, but given the agrarian organization of the Philippines, with its high incidence of tenancy and the enormous political power of the landowning class, there has so far been an inexorable tendency for virtually the entire benefits of irrigation to pass to the landlords; indeed, cases are known of tenant farmers practising double-cropping with the aid of irrigation being materially worse off than neighbours working unirrigated land producing a single crop.[11] Similar considerations have operated to restrict the introduction of other techniques known to be capable of producing a higher productivity, such as selected seeds, fertilizers and insecticides; the tenant cannot obtain credit to make possible their utilization except on the most usurious terms, and the fact that the landlord appropriates a disproportionate share of the enhanced productivity effectively throttles all initiative.

The Agricultural Census of 1960 revealed that over the country as a whole there was little difference between the proportion of palay farms operated by full-owners (44 per cent) and by tenants of various kinds (40 per cent). Nevertheless, the incidence of tenancy increased over the intercensal period from 1948, and continued to grow even in those provinces that in 1948 already had the highest proportion of the total farm area operated by tenants. These were the provinces of Bulacan, Manila, Cavite, Nueva Ecija, Tarlac, Pampanga and Negros Occidental, all save the last within the rice-growing Central Plain of Luzon. In all of these provinces two-thirds or more of all farms were operated by tenants. The extreme condition was demonstrated by the province of Pampanga, where over 85 per cent of all farms and a little over 81 per cent of the farm area were operated by tenants. While rice farms operated by full-owners average 3·5 hectares, those operated by tenants are rather less than 2·2 hectares; in general, the average size of rice farms increases from north to south of the country, being lowest in the congested Ilocos Norte province of Luzon (1·2 hectares), and highest in Cotabato province in Mindanao (4·6 hectares). Yields on tenant-operated farms, how-

[11] D. J. Dwyer, '*Irrigation and land use problems in the Central Plain of Luzon*', Geography, *vol. 45, 1964, pp. 241–3.*

ever, tend to be a little higher than on owner-operated farms, for many tenants are forced by social and economic pressures to use labour beyond the point where the return to incremental labour in cultivation is equal to the prevailing wage rate, or opportunity cost. Yields tend also to be higher in the newer rice areas of the east and southern portions of the country, where soil erosion and depletion have not yet reached the proportions of the longer-cultivated west and north, but there is little doubt that over large parts of the country yields are declining; despite an increase in the harvested area from 1960 to 1965 rice production remained virtually stationary.

It is against this unpropitious background that the recent introduction of genetically superior rice strains has to be considered. In 1962 the International Rice Research Institute, jointly financed by the Ford and Rockefeller foundations, was established at Los Banos, south of Manila, and in what must be judged an extremely short time assessed by the results achieved in other Asian rice research stations, developed a number of new varieties with greatly improved performance. One of these new strains, IR-8, demonstrated under trial yields so vastly superior to those of traditional varieties (although they were not significantly better than those of at least two other new varieties) that it was immediately dubbed by the Philippine press and public 'miracle rice'. The use of this name proved to have powerful consequences, for it greatly assisted the adoption of the new variety by the Filipino farmer, who whether Christian or Muslim, as with all people of Malay stock is fundamentally an animist, and a strong believer in miracles, fate and the spirit world.

The performance of IR-8 is certainly impressive. Its average yield has been some 150 cavans per hectare as against only 28 cavans for traditional varieties, and the best recorded so far is 279 cavans per hectare. These figures and the variety's surprisingly ready acceptance by Filipino farmers have led very many Filipino politicians, and even some agronomists and rural sociologists, to conclude that the country's long struggle for rice self-sufficiency is all but over; they claimed that by 1969 rice imports would be abolished for ever, and thereafter the country would steadily become a major rice exporter. Yet sober analysis suggests that the more extravagant forecasts at least are unlikely to prove true, and that Filipinos can hardly expect a single technical achievement to set to rights so grossly defective an agrarian organization. An FAO Study Group does not believe that there will be any significant change in the Philippine's rice-producing ability before 1975.[12] The government also has some doubts apparently, for although its rice imports in 1966/67 were subsequently re-exported, it continued to make arrangements for rice imports in the 1967/68 season.

It is, of course, quite impossible to realize the yields achieved under rigorously controlled conditions in experimental stations over millions of hectares in the

---

[12] *Bernardino Ronquillo, ' Self sufficient ', Far Eastern Economic Review, vol. 58, 1967, p. 530.*

Winnowing rice, Laguna, southwest Luzon.

country at large, and even though IR-8 has so far performed well in the field, to multiply the current average by the total palay area to obtain a potential total production is quite illusory. As IR-8 matures in about four months and theoretically, therefore, three crops could be taken in a year, further to multiply this figure by three as some Filipinos have done, is to depart from all contact with reality. 'Miracle rice' requires exacting and expensive fertilizer and irrigation inputs, and there is virtually no possibility that these can be made available over the greater part of the palay area for some considerable time to come. Even if they were, it would still be necessary for farmers to desire to make these inputs, and as indicated, the principal reason so far for the adoption of the variety has been not its properties but its name.[13] In fact, the work of the International Rice Institute so far has benefited others far more than the Filipino farmer, for landlords and others continue to appropriate the largest share of any increased productivity. Despite the spread of IR-8, new transplanting systems such as the Masagana and Margate, named after their originators, and the launching in 1964 of a Rice Production Crash Program to increase production of dry-season rice (*palayad*), Filipinos still find it difficult to purchase all the rice they would like at a price they can afford; in 1967 the price of rice averaged double that of the previous year. It would seem that fearing to face either the enormous difficulties of implementing major and long overdue agrarian reforms or the potentially explosive consequences of failing

[13] *The heavy 1968/69 crop produced such a price drop that government was obliged to support IR-8 prices as farmers began switching production to higher-priced traditional varieties. There is some fear that high IR-8 yields may also prove fugitive, i.e. diminishing with time.*

to meet this challenge, the Filipino élite is clutching at anything that offers the prospect of making such a painful decision unnecessary. If such indeed is the case, the high hopes raised by IR-8 are likely to go unrealized. Most landowners, moreover, are exceedingly apprehensive that a greatly enlarged productivity would result in a large fall in rice prices, and hence in their incomes. In fact, the desire of the élite to maintain a high level of rice prices is of fundamental importance to an understanding of the problems of the rice industry, and goes far to explain the limited success of the government in solving them.

Rice shortages deriving from inefficient techniques in the field have been compounded by poor methods of preparation. Some three-quarters of all Philippine rice-mills are of the small and inefficient *kiskisan* type, which not infrequently give a recovery rate of only 45 per cent of the original palay volume. The anticipated greater productivity of the palay area will thus make new investment in milling mandatory, and under the Four Year Economic Development Program 1967–70, it is proposed to replace some 4,000 small mills by large modern units.

Other food crops   Of the remaining food crops, corn is by far the most important, and accounts for nearly one-third of the total harvested food-crop area; for many peoples it is a more important cereal than rice, and for the Cebuanos of the central Visayas it is virtually the only cereal consumed in large quantities. Corn has a greater climatic tolerance than rice and is suited to a wider variety of topographic and soil conditions; it also requires a much lower labour input. It can be combined with either upland or lowland palay cultivation, with the production of other food crops, or with industrial crop production such as tobacco, sugar or coconuts; moreover, it is possible to take two crops a year in many parts of the country, and in some areas even triple-cropping may be practised. But while it is true that for many Filipinos corn is a very acceptable food, the great increase in corn production since 1941 and the enhanced share of corn in the food consumption pattern of Filipinos generally since before World War II, must in considerable measure be ascribed to the difficulties encountered in expanding rice production; *carabao* numbers were cut by half during the war, and not until the middle Fifties was the prewar national herd regained. Properly prepared, corn is dietetically a better food than polished rice, but from a Southeast Asian viewpoint the increasing substitution of corn for rice can only be regarded as evidence of social and economic decline.

This decline is clearly observable in the landscape in many parts of the country, the extreme example being Cebu, where corn cultivation has been pushed to make use of every patch of land where it is physically possible. Cebu's original forest has been entirely removed except for patches on the highest central portions of the island, and widespread corn monoculture on the bare limestone slopes has resulted in an enormously accelerated soil erosion; according to the

Soil Survey of Cebu, some 38 per cent of the land surface of Cebu had lost *all* its top-soil and some of its sub-soil, and a further 25 per cent had lost from 75 to 100 per cent of its top-soil.[14] It is scarcely surprising that Cebu corn yields are virtually the lowest in the country and that despite its large output, the island is a substantial deficit area.

The dominance of corn in Cebuano agriculture is primarily a result of an increasing population pressure since the early nineteenth century. Although rice was raised wherever water resources made it possible during the early Spanish period, the limited number of permanent streams, their small basins and short and direct flow from the mountains to the sea, ruled out extensive rice cultivation, and until the late eighteenth century the principal food crop of this relatively dry and largely limestone island was millet. A rapid increase in population appears to have occurred in Cebu earlier than in the Philippine archipelago generally, and as corn yielded a much higher production of food per acre than millet, the latter was slowly pushed out. By the American occupation in 1898, corn was being grown on most of the land under cultivation.[15] Thus for more than half a century the Cebuano farmer has been trapped; a treadmill of rising population has forced him to push cultivation higher and higher up the slopes, to eliminate crop rotations and to practise a corn monoculture whose yields progressively diminish. Cebu has long been an island of heavy emigration, but unless the circle can be broken and much land retired from cultivation, disaster is certain.

In newer areas of corn cultivation, such as the Davao and Cotabato provinces of Mindanao and the Cagayan valley of Luzon, yields are substantially higher than in Cebu. Davao is now by far the largest corn-producing province, and Cotabato, despite a smaller harvested area, also has a larger output than Cebu, for long the leading producer. Rapid expansion of corn production in the Cagayan valley also had raised its production above that of Cebu by the early Sixties. Nevertheless, the fact remains that overall yields are deplorably low by world standards, and corn production, as with that of palay, largely expands through an extension of the cultivated area.

The cultivation of other food crops such as roots, tubers, legumes and vegetables appears relatively much less important in the Philippines than in Indonesia; sweet potatoes (*camote*) are very widely grown and occupy an important part in the diet of many Filipinos, but the limited consumption of tapioca is evidence of a higher living standard than in those parts of Indonesia closest to the Philippines, and the small tapioca area is largely confined to southern Mindanao and the Sulu archipelago. On the other hand, such valuable crops in diet as soya-

[14] *Bureau of Soils, Department of Agriculture and National Resources,* Technical Bulletin No. 17, *Manila, 1954, quoted by Huke, op. cit., p. 64.*

[15] *Canute Vandermeer, 'Corn cultivation on Cebu: an example of an advanced stage of migratory farming',* Journal of Tropical Geography, *vol. 17, 1963, p. 174.*

beans and groundnuts, though of increasing importance, are nothing like as extensively cultivated as they should be, nor do Filipino farmers make much use of legumes as green manure, a common practice in Java. A wide variety of tree crops could be grown in the Philippines, but except in the case of those that can effectively be considered as indigenous, the institutional environment appears to have operated against any market expansion of cultivation. Coffee and cocoa production have expanded with protection from imports, but output of both is still small.

Industrial crop production

In contrast to the faltering growth of food production, the output of industrial crops has grown rapidly during the present century and has continued to outstrip food production since independence. Industrial crops, which include coconut products, sugar, abacá and tobacco, account for only some 18 per cent of the cultivated area but produce some two-thirds of export earnings (*Tables 5-2* and *5-4*). All find a large market in domestic consumption and both coconut products and sugar could be considered food crops. However, they receive a rather more elaborate processing than do rice or corn, and all other economic considerations compel their grouping with other export-oriented crops.

Of the four crops, the only large earners of foreign exchange earnings are coconut products and sugar. Yet in neither can the Philippines be regarded as an efficient producer, and to a large extent the present prosperity of coconut and sugar producers depends on the one hand on their access to the highly privileged and protected market of the United States, and on the other, to windfalls arising from the shortcomings or misfortunes of competitors, such as Indonesia in the case of coconut products, and Cuba with sugar. These present advantages will not long endure; coconut products compete in a highly competitive world market for fats and oils, and other vegetable oils, particularly palm oil, appear certain to strengthen their competitive position. Sugar prices are notoriously unstable; after reaching record levels in 1963, the price of sugar in real terms by mid-1965 had reached a lower level than during the Great Depression. Abacá, once a mainstay of the Philippine economy, is now of only minor importance, but it also faces increasing competition from cordage produced from man-made fibres such as nylon and polypropylene. Tobacco exports have ceased to be of any real significance since the onset of World War II, and indeed in many postwar years the country was a substantial net importer. Most importantly, however, under the terms of the United States Revised Trade Agreement of 1955 (usually called the Laurel-Langley agreement), which regulated the volumes of privileged Philippine exports to the United States, the preferences accorded to Philippine products are gradually to be phased out and by 1974 Philippine imports into the United States will meet the full rate of duty. Some success has attended efforts to find alternative markets, but for any major reorientation an increase in productive efficiency appears imperative.

Coconuts Since 1945 the Philippines has become the world's largest producer of coconut products, a role previously held by the Netherlands Indies. The Philippines has produced from 60 to 70 per cent of world copra production in most postwar years, and its copra quality is in general superior to that of Indonesia, the second largest producer. Nevertheless, through lax harvesting of unripe as well as ripe nuts and through the widespread use of poor drying facilities, the quality of Philippine copra leaves much to be desired, and does not command as high a price as that of either Malaysia or Ceylon.

The expanding world economy of the second half of the nineteenth century and the more liberal attitude of Spain towards Philippine trade with the rest of the world laid the foundations for the transformation of coconut cultivation from a purely subsistence to a highly commercialized activity, but by the turn of the century coconut products accounted for scarcely 5 per cent of the value of exports. With access to the enormous and rapidly growing United States market following the establishment of the American administration, the planted area commenced an expansion interrupted only by the Great Depression and World War II. During the latter about one-fifth of the coconut area was lost through damage and neglect, but this was made good by the early Sixties, when the planted area of some 1·05 million hectares (some 2·6 million acres) reached a level nearly eight times that of half a century previously. Coconut products in the Sixties produced some 30 per cent of export earnings, displacing sugar, the leading prewar export by value, from the premier position.

The greater part of this enormous expansion was the product of peasant initiative, a further example of the responsiveness of the Southeast Asian smallholder to price stimuli. As noted in Chapter 2, the American administration discouraged corporate investment in agriculture, and limited corporative landholdings to 1,204 hectares (nearly 3,000 acres). Although it was always possible to circumvent the restrictions on land ownership, coconut cultivation never encouraged much corporative participation because the return was higher in other lines of investment. The Philippines thus does not possess large coconut estates on the scale of those found in Ceylon, Indonesia, or Malaysia (though in these countries also, smallholdings are the more important units of production), and the typical coconut estate is relatively small and privately owned. Estates of more than 50 hectares (124 acres) accounted for only about 15 per cent of the coconut area in the 1948 Agricultural Census, but such estates produced a considerably larger proportion of copra output and were responsible for all but a very small proportion of the best grades. It is highly likely that estates have enlarged their share of copra output since 1948, for they have enjoyed more of the fruits of official and private research than have smallholders, and have suffered less loss

through the operations of corrupt and inefficient government marketing organizations.[16]

The productivity of the coconut is highest in those areas where the precipitation regime ensures a continuously moist soil throughout the year; where a dry
season is marked, as in the Central Plain and northwest coastlands of Luzon,
coconuts are a minor crop. A coastal location is often considered desirable and the
plant in fact will tolerate a certain amount of brackish water, but it also does
quite well in inland locations up to an elevation of 2,000 feet. Southwest Luzon,
particularly Laguna and southern Quezon province, was long the leading coconut area; but the importance of Laguna, the Bicol lowlands and Sorsogon has
declined with rapid expansion of the planted area in the eastern Visayas and in
the coastlands of Mindanao. The newer southern plantings have a higher productivity than the older areas of the north, partly because plantings have a more
favourable age-composition with fewer elderly trees, and partly because there is
less susceptibility to typhoon damage. The coast of Zamboanga del Sur is noteworthy as the only part of the country where large coconut estates are the dominant productive unit.

By the standards of Ceylon, the Philippine coconut industry is extremely
inefficient. Despite new postwar plantings, far too many trees are more than
thirty years old and beyond maximum productivity. Most smallholders plant
unselected nuts and reduce the vigour of the young palms by inter-planting soil-
depleting catch-crops; only larger estates plant selected seedlings and use leguminous cover crops such as *Calapagonium* or *Pueraria*, which check the incursion
of *cogon*. But low productivity is also in part the result of the widespread neglect
and abandonment of plantings during World War II, when the ravages of the
rhinoceros beetle, a major coconut pest, largely went unchecked; postwar new
plantings provided ample opportunities for a rapid expansion of this pest. The
rhinoceros beetle lays its eggs in rotting vegetation on the ground, the adult
beetle climbing the palm to feed by boring a hole near the crown and sucking the
sap; the holes are used as breeding places by another serious pest, the red-striped
weevil, which eats out the centre of the tree. Spraying with insecticides appears
to have little effect and also eliminates natural predators, so that biological
methods of control are likely to prove the most efficient means of reducing the
ravages of these pests, and in Ceylon and Malaysia some success has been achieved
by the use of predatory wasps of the *Zooliid* species. But regular harvesting and the
prompt removal of all material likely to provide breeding places are also essential,
operations which smallholders often fail to carry out. Since the end of World War
II, *kadang-kadang*, or yellow-mottle, a virus disease causing a gradual decline in nut
production and eventual death, has also assumed serious proportions. No effective remedy has yet been discovered for this disease, and some fifteen years' work
at the Legaspi research station has produced no results, largely in consequence of

[16] *Spencer, op. cit., p. 203.*

a high turnover of staff. The only means of preventing the spread is by prompt cutting out of infected palms as soon as detected, an operation that smallholders are loath to perform so long as the tree continues to produce some fruit. Meanwhile, the cutting of a 'disease free zone' across Luzon will, it is hoped, prevent further extension of the disease.

A well-managed estate with selected trees in Ceylon and Malaysia is capable of producing more than 3,000 lb of high-grade copra per acre per year. Few Philippine estates approach this figure and the average copra yield for smallholders is probably not much more than 500 lb per acre. Only some 20 per cent of the complete fruit is effectively utilized in the Philippine industry; some charcoal is produced from husks, which are also used for copra-drying, but many parts of the fruit at present wasted are potentially usable. The best copra is produced from ripe but not over-ripe nuts, dried in a hot-air blast in a machine kiln; this produces clean, unscorched copra with a uniform moisture and low free fatty acid content, which on crushing yields a 'soft' oil eminently suitable for use in margarine or shortening manufacture. Hot-air driers are very largely an estate prerogative; smallholder copra is either sun-dried, or, more usually, smoked over a fire of burning husks. Such copra is charred and dirty, and produces 'hard' oil with a high free fatty acid content, less suitable for use in food industries. In Malaysia and Ceylon many smallholder cooperatives have successfully up-graded their copra through the use of small hot-air driers designed for local conditions; the Philippines Coconut Administration (PHILCOA) has endeavoured to introduce similar driers for Filipino cooperatives, but progress so far has been meagre.

Before 1939 about half of Philippine copra output was crushed in mills within the country, but considerable capacity was lost during the war and the peak pre-war level of coconut oil exports, some 180,000 tons, has never been regained. Only about one-third of the present copra output is now locally crushed; more oil is consumed domestically than in 1939, and the United States, the traditional export market, has itself become the world's largest exporter of vegetable oils. The Laurel-Langley agreement of 1955 fixed the quota of Philippine coconut oil that could be imported into the United States free of duty at 160,000 tons annually; this quota was not in fact filled until 1963, but in 1965 it was reduced to 120,000 tons. On the other hand, the volume of copra exports in the early Sixties had been carried to twice prewar levels, and Western Europe had displaced the United States as the chief buyer. But in future the European Economic Community will satisfy a larger share of its vegetable oil needs from privileged African 'associated states', and the Philippines may well face a problem of unmarketable surpluses of coconut products.

Following an ECAFE coconut conference in 1962, the Philippines and Indonesia, the two leading coconut producers, agreed to establish a joint coconut commission, but as political relations between the two countries subsequently cooled, little was done to implement this decision. An International Coconut Agreement is a possibility, but similar commodity agreements have so far achieved little success in stabilizing either prices or production. Industrial uses could provide a further outlet for coconut products, and a coconut-chemical plant, a joint venture between Mitsui and PHILCOA to produce glycerine, alcohols and plasticizers from coconut oil, is to be erected in southern Quezon.

Sugar   The Philippine sugar industry has followed a similar course of evolution to that of coconuts. A long period as a primitive subsistence activity was succeeded by a gradual increase in more capital-intensive methods and the beginnings of an export trade in the latter half of the nineteenth century, which in turn laid the foundations for very rapid growth following the establishment of the American administration—a growth, moreover, that took place despite the opposition of powerful United States domestic sugar producers and competition from other privileged suppliers to the American market. By the outbreak of World War II sugar had become the leading Philippine export, and though outranked by coconut products in the postwar period, it temporarily regained the premier position with the high sugar prices of 1963.

Sugar is a herbaceous perennial and although in the Philippines it is usually harvested after twelve months for both plant and ratoon canes, occasionally cane may be in the ground for as long as eighteen months. A dry period is necessary for harvesting and to maximise the sucrose content of the cane, so that areas with no clear dry period are therefore unsuitable. However, the dry season must not be prolonged unless supplementary water is available. Sugar cane is also very demanding of soil conditions, and is the only major Philippine crop that regularly receives heavy applications of nitrogenous and phosphatic fertilizers.

These requirements effectively restrict sugar cultivation to areas of suitable soils in the western Visayas and western Luzon. The Central Plain of Luzon, the earliest centre of production, Batangas and northwest Negros, areas with relatively fertile volcanically-enriched soils, account for almost 90 per cent of cane production, the balance being shared by Panay, Cebu and Leyte. Only in Pampanga province in the Central Plain of Luzon is irrigation water used for sugar cultivation, and in contrast to the sugar industry of Java where replanting is necessary after every harvest, Philippine practice allows each plant cane crop one ratoon. In many sugar districts planting and harvesting are carried out simultaneously, usually from October to December in Luzon, and from November to March in Negros. At such times large numbers of contract workers move into the sugar districts from other parts of the country, Ilocanos from the congested northwest supplying most of the additional labour for the Central Plain of Luzon, and Panayanos and Cebuanos for the plain of northwest Negros. For nearly seven months of the year, however, the sugar industry cannot provide regular employment for the resident labour force.

The transformation of the sugar industry from a producer of crude, non-centrifugal *muscovado* to one based on the export of crystalline sugar largely followed on the tariff agreements of 1909 (Payne-Aldrich) and 1913 (Underwood-Simons), by which limitations on duty-free Philippine imports into the United States were removed. American interests were quick to appreciate the profit potential of a modern sugar industry based on low-cost Filipino labour, and the number of modern *centrales* with vacuum boilers and centrifuges steadily increased. Filipino capital also participated in the expansion of the industry, several mills being erected with the assistance of the government-controlled Philippine National Bank. Despite restriction on the ownership of land by aliens and corporations, American companies had acquired more than 260,000 acres by the outbreak of World War II, of which the greater part was sugar land, and Filipino corporations owned even more.[17] Until 1934, when the United States initiated its present sugar policy of allotting quotas to privileged suppliers, the sugar industry expanded continuously, and to handle the record production of almost 1·5 million tons in that year some forty-five mills were in operation. Thereafter restriction and the physical destruction caused by World War II caused a sharp downturn. Many mills did not resume operations after the war and some cane-growing areas such as eastern Mindoro, where the modern industry may be said to have commenced with the erection of the country's first vacuum-boiler in 1910,[18] reverted to the production of non-centrifugal *muscovado*. Not until 1962 was the prewar peak output regained, but the number of mills at present in production is only half that of 1940. Thus, despite a greater average capacity per mill, severe pressure was experienced during the boom of the early Sixties, and further extensions to capacity are in hand. There are considerable economies of scale in sugar-milling, but so far the average size of mills in the Philippine industry has been lower than that of Cuba, Hawaii, or interwar Java. Government assistance has been made available for extensions to plant and for acquiring *centrales* from alien interest, and by 1960 only two mills, both quite small, remained under alien ownership.

But while major changes have occurred in the mill section, field operations still leave much to be desired. The introduction of modern high-yielding varieties was long delayed and many growers still plant old traditional varieties; for a major producer and exporter of cane sugar, Philippine expenditure on cane breeding and on sugar research must be judged quite inadequate. Despite some improvement since the mid-Fifties, yields of sugar per acre are substantially below those of Australia, South Africa or Taiwan, all of which likewise make limited use of irrigation water for cane cultivation.

As in rice production, the primary responsibility lies in an unsatisfactory

[17] *Karl J. Pelzer*, Pioneer Settlement in the Asiatic Tropics, *American Geographic Society, New York, 1945, p. 91.*

[18] *Huke*, op. cit., *p. 313.*

agrarian organization. Even before World War II a large proportion of the land-holdings once owned by foreign sugar corporations had returned to indigenous ownership, and this process has continued since 1945; but this has brought little improvement to the lot of the individual cultivator. The dominant unit of production remains the estate, and in Negros Occidental, the principal sugar province, these are exceptionally large by Philippine standards. But unlike the rubber estates of Indonesia or Malaya, the Philippine sugar estate is typically a collection of tenancies, although large estates also cultivate some land directly. Tenants are remunerated according to the sugar content of the cane they deliver to the mill, and the fact that landlords almost invariably have interests in milling gives them abundant opportunities for exploiting tenants, who thus carry by far the largest share of the real costs of the highly discontinuous labour cycle. The incidence of tenancy is on the whole higher for sugar farms than for rice farms, and agrarian unrest is acute, especially during the slack season. Mechanization has so far been largely confined to ploughing and field preparation on the larger directly-farmed holdings; weeding, cutting and loading are entirely manual, although narrow-gauge tramways are used for cane transport to the mills. The sugar industry, in fact, is entirely dependent on, and in turn perpetuates, an under-employed and impoverished peasantry.

It is, of course, the privileged position of the Philippines in the United States market that has made it possible for such a relatively inefficient producer to become a major exporter, for the United States pays to its privileged suppliers for their quotas under the Sugar Act a price which on the average has been some two to three times the going world price. Philippine domestic consumption has long been restricted in order to meet the American quota. Increasing population, however, has obliged the Philippine Quota Board to make larger allocations to the home market, and the level of domestic consumption in the Sixties has been more than double that of prewar years. In 1956 the Philippines obtained an annual United States quota of 950,000 short tons, but following the embargo on Cuban sugar imports the quota was raised to 1·05 million short tons. The Philippines had further windfalls in the form of additional non-quota allocations when other privileged American suppliers such as Puerto Rico proved unable to meet their respective quotas. Since 1962, however, the United States has begun to move towards a more flexible sugar policy, and will gradually scale down the present large premium price it pays to privileged suppliers; the rigid quota machinery operated since 1934 appears likely to be modified in favour of some system of contracting from a wider range of suppliers than in the past, and countries such as India and Australia, as well as several Latin American countries, have obtained their first foothold in the American sugar market.

Despite the strength of the Philippine sugar lobby in the United States Congress whenever the Sugar Act is debated, it seems fairly clear that the sugar industry will sooner or later have to strengthen its competitive position in the world market if it is to survive as a major support of the Philippine economy. In 1974 when the Laurel-Langley agreement expires, exports to the United States will meet the full rate of duty, and though at present it appears unlikely that the Philippines will lose all its present privileges in the American market at that date, the problem of surpluses is already menacing. Under the stimulus of the astronomic prices of 1963, the 1964/65 season output of 1·86 million tons of sugar was an all-time record, and greater than the combined American and domestic quotas could absorb. So far, Philippine success in finding additional markets in the world at large has been minimal, for many other sugar producers are also seeking additional markets for expanded outputs.

Other industrial crops The two remaining industrial crops, abacá and tobacco, are very much less significant in national economic life. In the past, however, their importance has been very much greater than is the case at present and, within the restricted areas in which they are cultivated, both assume a major role in the local economy.

Abacá (*Musa textilis*), source of the fibre commercially known as manila and regarded in the cordage trade as a 'hard hemp', is a member of the banana genus, though of smaller stature and more demanding both in climatic and soil requirements than edible bananas. It is indigenous to the Philippines, and although numerous attempts have been made to cultivate it elsewhere, none has really succeeded. The reason for this lack of success lies largely in the exacting and skilled labour necessary for stripping the fibre from the leaf-sheaths in which it is embedded, and since 1961, when American plantations in Central America were wound up, the only commercial producer outside the Philippines has been the neighbouring territory of Sabah (North Borneo).

Abacá needs a rich soil and when grown in estates is regularly treated with nitrogenous fertilizers. It needs a high humidity and plentiful soil moisture throughout the year to ensure maximum productivity, so that areas with a dry season are avoided. Coastal location to facilitate transport of the bulky fibre is also desirable, but along the eastern coast of the archipelago, typhoons constitute a major hazard, as the plant is very susceptible to damage by high winds; it is therefore grown in naturally sheltered spots, or protected by windbreaks of coconuts or other trees. As a herbaceous perennial, abacá is ready for harvesting some eighteen months after planting, and thereafter can be cut twice a year, but as there is no seasonal check to growth it is possible for large plantations to arrange year-round harvesting. This consists of severing the leaves and chopping the trunk close to the ground; the petioles are then peeled off and conveyed to a processing shed or factory in which the fibre is stripped from the pulp. Smallholders use manual stripping, pulling the strips, or 'tuxies', between a serrated knife blade and a hardwood block; by varying the serrations on the knife blade and the pressure with which it is applied to the block, many grades of fibre from fine to coarse can be produced. The finer the grade, the greater the waste and the lower the yield, and smallholders have developed great skill in assessing from reports of price movements in the Manila market which grade will earn them the maximum return for a given labour input. On the larger holdings semi-mechanical stripping is commonly employed, and a few of the largest estates operate expensive decorticaters similar to those employed on sisal estates.

The location and structure of the abacá industry have experienced profound changes during the present century. The Bicol area of southwest Luzon, once the principal focus of production, now produces less than a quarter of the total output; more than one-half of current production now originates in Davao, other Mindanao provinces together with Leyte and Samar making up the balance. In contrast to sugar and coconut production whose rapid growth was triggered by the American occupation, abacá was already of major significance in the economy of later Spanish times, and around the turn of the century produced nearly two-thirds of the country's export earnings. Thereafter, although the planted area and output continued to grow slowly until 1929, abacá steadily declined in relative importance, and its share of export earnings plummeted to merely 6 per cent in the depths of the Great Depression, a figure that has since fluctuated between a high of almost 10 per cent in the early postwar years and a low of scarcely 4 per cent in 1965. World War II and its aftermath did enormous damage to the industry, and not until 1962 was the prewar planted area regained. But in view of the abacá industry's low efficiency and the strong competition from synthetic cordage fibres, prospects of exceeding the prewar peak output of 160,000 tons in the foreseeable future appear slight.

These fluctuating fortunes were accompanied by, and in large measure were contingent upon, major changes in the organization of production. In Bicol and in the Visayas, abacá has always been a smallholder activity, but the rise of Davao as the premier area was largely the result of a remarkable development of estate production on the part of Japanese immigrants. In 1904, Japanese workers originally brought in to assist with road construction moved to the Davao area and began to purchase land for abacá cultivation, and from such fortuitous beginnings an enormous estate industry was created over the next thirty years. Through the use of Filipino 'dummies', Japanese corporations eventually controlled over 120,000 acres of land, and as production expanded more workers were recruited both from Japan and from the Philippines themselves. With more than 20,000 Japanese residents, Davao by the outbreak of World War II had become virtually an exclave of Japan, and the country's largest investment in Southeast Asia. Japanese skill and technical ability had by then created an estate enterprise that could stand comparison with any, and the corporations had managed to achieve an integration between estate and smallholder production that is still rare in the production of tropical crops. Experienced Japanese and Filipino estate workers were established on holdings of their own and provided with selected planting material, fertilizers, irrigation facilities and technical assistance, in return for an undertaking to sell their output to the sponsoring corporation. These well-managed enterprises, plus the area's freedom from typhoon damage, gave to Davao a strong competitive advantage in abacá production, and smallholders in other parts of the country gradually moved to the production of other crops such as coconuts.

After World War II the Davao plantations were invaded by squatters and adventurers, and the disposal of the Japanese holdings became a free-for-all in the worst Philippine 'land-grab' tradition. Enormous damage was done both to the land and to the growing stock by ignorant and inexperienced operators and production slumped drastically. Additionally, in Bicol disease and neglect greatly reduced productivity. Abacá has always been largely exported in raw unprocessed form, and the absence of a factory cordage industry is surprising in view of the many domestic uses made of abacá fibre. As a cordage fibre abacá's principal competitor has long been sisal, which has the advantage of lower cost, but since World War II first nylon then polyester cordage has provided strong competition, and in the near future polypropylene could give the industry the *coup de grâce*. Even in the middle Fifties, the United States Department of Commerce doubted the ability of the abacá industry to survive for very long.

The postwar fortunes of the Philippine tobacco industry resemble more closely those of sugar than of abacá, for the demise of the Cuban cigar industry has provided welcome additional markets for the Philippine product; by 1962 nearly 60 per cent of United States cigar imports were derived from the Philippines, as against less than 20 per cent a decade earlier.

Though small quantities of tobacco are grown in most major islands, commercial production is almost entirely confined to Luzon, where the Spaniards introduced the plant to the Manila area at an early date. Cultivation later spread into the Cagayan valley and the Ilocos plain, where climatic and soil conditions proved most suitable. Until the late nineteenth century, tobacco cultivation and manufacture constituted a profitable state monopoly, but in the Eighties much of the government tobacco assets passed to a large Spanish company, usually known as the Tabacalera, which still dominates the cigar section of the tobacco industry. This organization owns large areas in the Cagayan valley, the principal area for the production of so-called native tobaccos suitable for the production of cigar fillers and wrappers, but as so often in Philippine agriculture, most of the work of cultivation is performed by tenants.

Following World War II, the rapidly growing popularity of American cigarettes made from flue-cured Virginia tobaccos converted the Philippines from a large tobacco exporter to a substantial net importer. To counter this situation high tariff barriers were erected to protect a domestic Virginia tobacco industry, which is based on the Ilocos plain where soils have proved particularly suitable for the cultivation of tobaccos of this type. Rapid expansion in the number of leaf-curing sheds greatly expanded the demand for firewood, and vast areas of the northwestern provinces have since been deforested to the accompaniment of accelerated erosion. Curing of Virginia tobacco is an exacting operation, and imperfect curing and manufacture has made the Virginia section of the industry extremely vulnerable to American competition. Despite the imposition of progressively more severe penalties and improved controls, the volume of cigarette smuggling is enormous. Marketing arrangements also have long been unsatisfactory. In 1954 a government body, the Philippine Tobacco Administration, was established to prevent speculation, to provide farmers with fair and stable prices, and to assist the development of tobacco cooperatives, but as has proved too often the case in Southeast Asia, government-sponsored marketing created almost as many abuses as it removed. Production of Virginia tobacco increased rapidly with the payment of high guaranteed prices, the planted area increasing almost tenfold between 1954 and 1962; but no premium was paid for quality and the government quickly found itself in possession of a growing surplus of low-quality leaf which could not be marketed at any price. It was hoped to reduce the surplus by blending with high-quality imported tobacco, but the surplus stock acts as a drug on the market and all attempts to up-grade production through differential prices have been defeated.

Despite an expansion since 1945, almost wholly accounted for by the Virginia section, the tobacco industry demonstrates most of the problems that plague Philippine agriculture. Low productivity of the soil and the worker, an inadequate attention to research, imperfect processing and marketing, all contribute towards the industry's low competitive standing.

Agrarian organization and agrarian reform

Fundamental to improving the low level of efficiency of Philippine agriculture is the question of land reform, and it is not too much to say that it has been clearly recognized as such for over sixty years. Golay argues that raising the productivity of Philippine agricultural resources and achieving a socially more equitable distribution of the agricultural product are separate problems,[19] and it is true that many attempts at achieving such a distribution through the break-up of large holdings have usually led to a decline in output, and not infrequently to the ultimate resuscitation of the original estates. Nevertheless, this dismal history merely confirms the folly of transforming the tenant into an owner while doing nothing to alleviate the very unfavourable ratio of land and capital at his disposal. Without adequate credit and marketing facilities, such policies are foredoomed to failure.

The largely feudal nature of much of Philippine agricultural organization

[19] *Frank H. Golay,* The Philippines: Public Policy and National Economic Development, *Cornell University Press, Ithaca, 1961, p. 271.*

A Moro fishing village near Zamboanga, Mindanao.

even today traces its origins to the social organization of the early Malay immigrants, but the Spanish occupation immeasurably strengthened *caciquismo*, the power of the landlord class. Some present holdings have descended from the royal bequests, or *encomiendas*, of the sixteenth century, while others were created during the nineteenth century under royal decrees making possible registration of titles; prominent among the latter were the holdings of the religious orders, the so-called Friar lands. Other large holdings were created by foreign corporations, which by the outbreak of World War II had managed to acquire more land than the Church and Friars ever possessed.[20] Nevertheless, the great majority of estates are owned by individuals and nearly 90 per cent of the total are of between 125 and 450 acres. A few estates are worked by their proprietors, but the great majority are farmed by tenants; these are usually cash tenants, or *inquilinos*, in the case of land owned by corporations or devoted to the production of export crops, but overwhelmingly *kasamas*, or share tenants, in the case of rice-land. As noted, the incidence of tenancy is very high in all of the most favoured agricultural areas, but even where tenancy is not extreme, as in the densely populated Ilocos lowlands, it is frequently found that the proportion of part-owners is relatively high. Only in remote and little productive parts of the country such as Mountain province of Luzon, Sulu, Palawan, and Samar does the proportion of full-owners reach a very high figure. As more than half of all farms worked by owners are less

[20] *Pelzer*, op. cit., *p. 91*.

than five acres, and are less than half this size in Ilocos and in Cebu, the economic situation of the owner is often little superior to that of the tenant.

American, Commonwealth[21] and Republic administrations have repeatedly wrestled with the issues of land reform through the acquisition and break-up of large estates, the imposition of maximum rents, and through agricultural colonization in undeveloped parts of the country. Only with the last has any enduring success been achieved; all attempts at solving the tenancy problem have foundered on the rock of landlord-dominated Congressional opposition. Little is achieved by detailing the provisions of prewar attempts at reform, from the purchase of the Friar lands in 1904 through the Rice Share Tenancy Act of 1933 to the Rural Progress Administration of 1939. After 1945, however, land reform took on a new urgency in the face of the communist-led *Hukbalahap* insurrection, which from being a guerilla movement directed against the Japanese rapidly became a movement of agrarian protest widely supported by the oppressed peasantry of the the Luzon plain. On becoming President in 1954, Ramon Magsaysay, who had played a leading part in quelling the Hukbalahap rebellion, pushed through the Agrarian Relations Act which limited the landlord's share to 30 per cent of the net harvest on the best rice-land where the tenant provided all implements and animals as well as labour. This enactment proved as ineffective as all previous attempts at rent control, and was supplemented in 1955 by a Land Reform Act, which aimed at the purchase and division of estates in areas of agrarian conflict. But by restraining the operation of the act to contiguous land, and by requiring acquisition proceedings to be initiated by a majority of tenants, Congress succeeded in greatly reducing the scope of the act; moreover, through its control over the purse strings, Congress can always bring the operation of any land-reform measure to an effective halt by failing to vote appropriations. In 1963 the Macapagal administration introduced a new consolidating law, the Agricultural Land Reform Code, a far-reaching measure aimed at abolishing share tenancy and replacing it by a system of leaseholds with farms of large enough size to give the occupant a socially acceptable standard of living. Once again, the Bill was only approved by Congress after emasculation; land in share tenancy under fishponds, tree crops and sugar was exempted, and tenants' rights to initiate expropriation proceedings against estate owners were very circumscribed. Complex machinery to provide credit and technical assistance to the new lease-holders is also envisaged under the Code, but its only practical significance so far has been to disrupt rice production by encouraging landowners to shift to sugar cultivation wherever possible.

Under the Four Year Economic Development Program 1967–70, a further attempt is to be made to grapple with the land problem. A new Land Authority is to convert 75 per cent of all share tenancies (which number some 500,000) into

---

[21] *That is, the period from 1935 to World War II, intended as a preparation for full independence.*

leaseholds by 1970, and over 190,000 hectares are to be acquired by the Land Bank for eventual redistribution to some 64,000 leaseholders, of which 90,000 hectares are to be redistributed in the first four years of operation. But unless the administration can persuade Congress to provide adequate financial underpinnings for the operation, it is unlikely to be any more successful than the schemes of the past.

Attempts by the administration to improve the lot of the peasant through cooperatives, state marketing schemes and credit organizations have likewise accomplished little, and moreover, have provided numerous additional opportunities for politically influential Filipinos to enrich themselves or their relations at the public expense. Cooperatives have expanded rapidly in the postwar period, but as in Thailand, the limited personal stake of the farmer in his cooperative is a major handicap to the establishment of effective and viable associations. The activities of the Farmers Cooperative Marketing Associations (FACOMAS) have always had a large political content; loans have been made for unauthorized purposes and to poor credit risks, management has often been incompetent and dishonest, and it was scarcely surprising that in 1959 over four-fifths of the FACOMAS were reported as operating at a loss.[22]

Rather more success appears to have accompanied government land colonization schemes, in which landless Filipinos from congested parts of the country have been established on new settlements created in the public domain. Planned colonization dates as far back as 1913, and by 1935 some 35,000 people had been settled in Mindanao through various government agencies. During the period of the Commonwealth three sizeable settlements were made by the National Land Settlement Administration (NLSA), two in Southeastern Cotabato, Mindanao, and one in the Cagayan valley of Luzon. The NLSA was reorganized after 1945, but when wound up in 1950 it was heavily in debt and the capital expenditure per settler had risen to prohibitive levels. Further agencies were created to continue the work of planned settlement, including the politically oriented Economic Development Corps of the Army, which undertook four schemes in the Cagayan valley for the rehabilitation of Huk rebels. These attracted great publicity as the 'Philippines' answer to communism', but the number of settlers involved was quite trivial and the whole operation was quite irrelevant to the pressing problem of tenancy in rice-growing areas. Since 1954 land colonization has been under the control of the National Resettlement and Rehabilitation Administration (NARRA); in 1963 only five projects were still active and eleven were in process of being wound up. NARRA appears to have been no more successful than its predecessors. Only some 6,000 families per year or only one-tenth of the annual rural increase have been settled on the land, and at huge expense by any criteria.

Private colonization on public land has been more rapid, although this too has produced many abuses. Large areas of public land have been acquired by

[22] *Golay*, op. cit., p. 289.

those with political influence in the hope that unsuspecting settlers will start developing them; only after the settler has put in considerable labour does the 'land-grabber' appear, who then demands an extortionate sale price or compels the unfortunate settler to pay rent. Philippine land-law, which recognizes not effective occupancy but priority in filing a claim as evidence of ownership, and the regressive tax structure with its low taxes on land, encourage speculation of this kind. The release of land from the public domain for settlement has proceeded only very slowly, an operation that the Land Reform Act of 1955 was also intended to accelerate. Though improvement in the machinery for the registration of titles has since been greatly improved, lack of a complete cadastral survey and delays in the issue of titles continue to expose the settler to the operations of the politician and speculator.

In view of this long and dismal record it must be concluded that legislative action to relieve rural poverty is unlikely to succeed, and if the present democratic political processes cannot achieve a solution to the problem without widespread violence, the future for the country is dark indeed.[23]

MINING, MANUFACTURING AND SERVICE INDUSTRIES

Non-agricultural activities generate some two-thirds of Philippine national product, a large proportion for a country at a comparatively low level of economic development. They are, however, closely confined to Greater Manila and a few

[23] *Golay*, op. cit., *p. 291.*

Salt-pans at Paranaque, Manila Bay, Luzon.

other major urban centres, and it is all too easy to gain an over-optimistic impression of the economic well-being and prospects of the country from the comparative opulence of the metropolis, whose fearsome slums tend to be discounted in the face of burgeoning new factories and sizeable tracts of perhaps the most luxurious residential development in Southeast Asia.

Mining employs only 0·3 per cent of an estimated national work-force of around eleven millions, but it produces some 2 per cent of national product. Even on the most optimistic assessment, the country's mineral resources appear only modest, and reserves of mineral fuels are particularly slender. Despite major exploratory activity since 1945, petroleum has not been discovered in commercial quantities, and the numerous coal deposits are of small size, do not produce coke suitable for employment in conventional blast-furnaces, and are poorly located in relation to markets. The present small coal output is derived from Cebu and from Malangas, Zamboanga, and is largely consumed in the manufacture of cement.

The paucity of mineral fuels has stimulated hydro-electricity generation, and several large installations have been completed or are under construction. Manila originally derived much of its electric power from a small prewar station in Laguna, and has since shared in the output from two large new plants on the Agno river in Mountain province, north Luzon, Ambuklao and Binga, with a total capacity of 175 MW. Completion of the Angat river scheme in Bulacan, a multipurpose project, will add a further 200 MW of hydro-electric capacity to help with the growing needs of the Manila area. The only hydro-electric plant outside Luzon is at Iligan in Mindanao. Although the Philippines has a relatively large potential hydro-electric capacity, it is quite certain that little of this will ever be harnessed, as the best power sites lie far removed from the main load centres and are located in extremely difficult terrain. As noted, more than half the country's output of electrical energy is derived from thermal plants, and the pressing need for more capacity in the shortest time makes it certain that the share of thermal plants in total energy production will increase in the future.

The endowment of ferrous and non-ferrous metalliferous minerals is rather more substantial. Iron-mining has been noted as an important activity, but its prosperity at present depends on the strength of the Japanese market. The wealth of iron ore and the country's substantial imports of steel products have long suggested the establishment of a domestic iron and steel industry, although, as in most newly independent countries, the main motivation for the industry is political. In the early Sixties a small steel furnace and rolling mill was established at Iligan in Lanao del Norte, to use power from a newly completed 50,000 kW capacity generating station on the Maria Christina falls of the Agus river. Despite the unfavourable location of the plant both in relation to sources of raw materials, such as scrap and usable iron ore from southern Luzon, and in relation to markets, the National Steel Corporation, a government undertaking, in 1968 completed the addition of two L-D converters and a further electric furnace, which with fabricating plants gave an annual capacity of 256,000 tons of finished steel. The prospects of attaining a competitive iron and steel industry thus do not appear bright; nevertheless, pig iron production, based on Surigao ores in a modern 'direct reduction' process is a possibility in the future. Unfortunately the plant is poorly located in relation to markets and to present and potential sources of raw materials, so that its prospects of achieving competitive efficiency cannot be rated very highly.

Copper production in the past has looked mainly to the home market; though a minor and rather high-cost producer, under the stimulus of strong economic nationalism the Philippines has become self-supporting in its copper requirements. High prices resulting from the demands of the Vietnam war and from fortuitous series of strikes and other troubles in major producers such as the United States and Chile, have however provided a major stimulus to production in minor producers such as the Philippines, and in 1966 copper concentrates occupied the fourth position in the list of exports for the first time. In the inter-war period gold-mining was also an activity of some significance, and the country has been numbered among the first dozen producers. But as the price of gold has remained unchanged since 1934, rising cost levels have made much mining unprofitable, and the present small production which comes from a handful of mines in the Baguio area is only maintained with the aid of a subsidy (*Table 5-3*).

Table 5-3   *Philippines: production of minerals and lumber, 1966*

Gold (*thousand fine ounces*)	451
Silver „ „ „	1,092
Copper (*metal content, thousand metric tons*)	71
Chromite ore (*thousand metric tons*)	560
Iron ore „ „ „	1,485
Coal „ „ „	69
Lumber (*million board feet*)	397
Logs „ „ „	3,412

Source: *Central Bank of the Philippines, Eighteenth Annual Report*, 1966

The price appreciation of silver resulting from the growing world demand for the metal for industrial purposes has, however, caused a marked upsurge in Philippine production.

Philippine manufacturing has followed a similar course of evolution to that of most other countries of Southeast Asia, and despite a professed adherence to the principles of free enterprise and capitalism, government has involved itself in as wide a range of manufacturing and service industries as has any Southeast Asian government whose economic policy is an alleged socialism. This involvement, moreover, goes back long before independence, for the National Development Corporation, the state's principal agent for participation in manufacturing and service industries, dates from 1919. Although expansion of the industrial sector is universally accepted in the Philippines, a more pressing social and political consideration has been to increase Filipino participation in industrial activity, and it could be argued that this pressure has been severe enough to reduce the overall rate of industrial growth. Economic nationalism involves not only reducing the sphere of operations of foreign-owned enterprises, but also those of the local Chinese, a powerful reason for the adoption by the Philippines in the Constitutional Convention of 1934 of a *jus sanguinis* in place of a *jus soli* in determining citizenship. Apart from direct participation in manufacturing and service industries, the state has endeavoured to enlarge the Filipino share by various fiscal and monetary devices such as tax remission, import duties and quotas, and allocations of foreign exchange. All of these amount to a substantial degree of subsidization of Philippine manufacturing by the state, but the Philippines at least has few illusions that its infant industries are ultimately going to grow up and to acquire internationally competitive levels of efficiency. Production is overwhelmingly directed at the heavily protected home market, and there is little disposition to contest exports with powerful industrial adversaries such as Japan or Hong Kong.

About 250,000 workers, some 10 per cent of the adult labour force, are engaged in manufacturing, and of these about half are employed in the Greater Manila area as defined by the Philippines Central Bank. A further 20 per cent of the industrial work-force is, however, employed in provinces adjacent to the metropolitan area, and in centres entirely tributary to the capital. In more distant provinces, manufacturing is confined to the processing of agricultural products for export markets, such as sugar-milling, the production of coconut oil and dessicated coconut, sawmilling and pineapple canning (the latter an activity restricted to Misamis Oriental, where a subsidary of the American Dole organization operates a cannery serving its large pineapple estate in Bukidnon), and to raw material oriented industries such as cement. It has already been remarked that in many lines of production, Philippine processing stops far short of what is achieved in other countries. Thus abacá is largely exported raw instead of being manufactured into cordage, and much timber leaves the country in the form of logs instead of plywood veneer, sawn wood or board products. Sugar, moreover, is largely exported raw as the American quota includes only 50,000 tons of refined sugar, and there are only two sugar refineries, both in the Greater Manila area.

Consumer goods industries are overwhelmingly situated in the Greater

Manila area, with a few establishments located in other major urban centres such as Cebu City. Textiles, clothing, furniture, footwear, and food, drink and tobacco industries are the most important manufacturing activities, but engineering and more capital-intensive industries such as vehicle assembly, glass-making, pharmaceutics and chemicals are already well established. The larger establishments tend to be concentrated along the Pasig river, although four oil refineries, among the country's largest industrial establishments, are situated on the shores of Manila and Batangas Bays.

Large establishments tend to be mainly foreign-owned, but even these have a substantial Filipino-held equity, and the fact that a local majority holding is mandatory for new joint ventures probably discourages many potential new foreign enterprises. The average Filipino or Chinese-owned industrial establishment is of very small size, and much of this small-scale industry is located in the densely populated inner urban areas such as Binondo and Tondo, where it is scattered among slum housing. The outer urban areas, however, contain some large locally-owned establishments, of which the new integrated textile mills are the most conspicuous. Though its roots go back before 1940, the present Philippine textile industry is largely a post-World War II development. With substantial state assistance in the form of tariff protectives, import quotas, dollar allocations and in other ways, the industry has grown extremely rapidly, and in all probability far too rapidly for its long-term health. There is already evidence of overcapacity and several manufacturers have declared their inability to survive without further heavy subsidies from the state.[24] Despite P L 480 supplies from the United States, the country's balance-of-payments situation has caused difficulties over supplies of raw cotton, and some manufacturers have attempted to cultivate cotton in Mindanao. More importantly, the productivity of labour in the industry is very low, and many of the 40,000 or so workers now employed are probably redundant.

TRANSPORT AND TRADE

In transportation and in distribution also, Filipinization has been vigorously pursued, and this objective has apparently carried more weight than improvements in facilities and in efficiency. For a country whose national territory is as comminuted as the Philippines, improved transport is a *sine qua non* for a higher level of economic development. Existing facilities are heavily concentrated in Luzon, but resources for their maintenance, to say nothing of the provision of better transport services in other parts of the country, appear quite inadequate.

As the Philippines never possessed an inter-island shipping service as efficient as that provided by the Dutch shipping line K P M for the Netherlands Indies (and until 1957, for Indonesia also), it has not suffered as has its southern

[24] Asian Textile Annual, *Far Eastern Economic Review, Hong Kong, 1962, p. 124.*

neighbour from the economic dislocations resulting from the sudden termination of the services of an efficient carrier and its replacement by a multiplicity of sub-sidized local firms with totally inadequate equipment, whose only effective competition has been to make the largest losses in the shortest time. The greater part of the inter-island transport was locally owned even before World War II, although much was in reality owned by Philippine Chinese, and most of the vessels at present operating between the islands are war-surplus vessels acquired from the United States. Operating costs are high, terminal facilities are poor and, in the case of minor ports of call, often virtually non-existent. Losses through damage and pilfering even at major ports, and particularly in Manila itself, are severe, while vessels operating in the Sulu archipelago are armed to repel piratical attacks, which still continue to levy some toll. Largely in consequence of its central position, Cebu City handles a slightly larger volume of inter-island shipping annually than the national capital, but in international trade Manila has no rival for the value of its foreign trade turnover exceeds that of all other Philippine ports combined.

As a nation of islands in which most bulk commodities can usually be moved easily by coasting vessel, the Philippines has less need of a railway network than most other Southeast Asian countries. Apart from a short length of line in central Panay and the light 2 ft. 6 in.-gauge tramways of the sugar-producing areas of western Negros, railways are synonymous with the state-owned Manila Railroad of 3 ft. 6 in.-gauge, serving the Central Plain and the Legaspi peninsula of Luzon. Heavily damaged during World War II, the system has since been modernized and equipped with diesel haulage, but freight traffic has been virtually stationary since the middle Fifties and passenger traffic has declined under the fierce com-petition of bus lines. An extension into the Cagayan valley has been approved, but possibilities of any substantial increase in revenue-earning capacity appear slight. But subsidized though the railway may be, it is highly likely that road transport is even more heavily subsidized through the use of social capital by road hauliers, for which they pay only a fraction of the real maintenance cost. The number of motor vehicles per 1,000 people (8·4 in 1965) is high by Southeast Asian standards, and there are few settlements of any size without bus services. But while it may be true that the Philippines has the best road net in Southeast Asia,[25] only a very small proportion of this is hard-surfaced, and the general con-dition of the road system is far inferior to that of Malaysia. Only Luzon, in fact, has an adequate road network, and though it is possible to travel from one end of the island to the other on paved surfaces, even in this island all but a very small proportion of the road surface is unpaved, and in other islands hard-surface roads are confined to the main urban centres.

Both passenger and freight traffic handled by Philippine internal airlines is

[25] *Alden Cutshall*, The Philippines: Nation of Islands, *Van Nostrand, Princeton, 1964, p. 89.*

Table 5-4   *Philippines: composition of foreign trade, 1966 (million US $)*

EXPORTS		IMPORTS	
Logs and lumber	208·4	Machinery (non-electric)	151·3
Copra	169·9	Transport equipment	109·9
Centrifugal sugar	115·9	Mineral fuels	84·1
Copper concentrates	83·1	Base metals	84·0
Coconut oil	75·5	Cereals	52·8
Abacá	18·7	Electrical machinery	36·0
Plywood	18·2	Textile fibres	34·9
Desiccated coconut	17·7	Chemicals	30·7
Copra meal and cake	17·2	Textiles, manufactured	30·6
Canned pineapple	8·9	Dairy produce	28·6
Total, 10 leading exports	**733·5**	**Total, 10 leading imports**	**642·9**
Total exports	**836·8**	**Total imports**	**852·8**

Source: *Central Bank of the Philippines, Eighteenth Annual Report*, 1966

Table 5-5   *Philippines: direction of foreign trade, 1966 (million US $)*

	Imports from	Exports to
United States	284·5	322·6
Northwest Europe	135·0	156·0
West Germany	42·2	57·1
Britain	37·9	7·1
Middle East	37·3	1·0
Japan	243·9	278·3
Indonesia	22·3	0·2
Other Asian countries	44·9	43·9
Total, all countries	**852·8**	**836·8**

Source: *Central Bank of the Philippines, Eighteenth Annual Report*, 1966

increasing very rapidly, but although of importance in maintaining national cohesion and facilitating the task of administration, air transport offers little relief to the pressing transport problems of most islands.

Before World War II more than two-thirds of the trade of the Philippines was conducted with the United States; this proportion has fallen steadily since 1945, and in 1966 only some 39 per cent of Philippine exports went to the United States, which provided in the same year only 33 per cent of the Philippines' imports (*Table 5-5*). But through its foreign aid, payments for military installations in the country and PL 480 shipments, the United States occupies a position of considerably greater significance in the Philippines balance of payments than would appear from trade statistics. Shortage of dollars has been mainly responsible for the reduction in the share of the United States in Philippine imports, a development that has been favourable to Japan. The EEC, and West Germany in particular, have also been of increasing importance as trade partners; but no important alternative market for Philippine exports is yet in sight, and the prognosis for most export industries is poor. In the past much of the country's overseas trade and a substantial part of its internal trade were in the hands of Philippine Chinese or foreign, mainly American, companies. The diversion of the greater part of commerce into the hands of Filipinos has proved comparatively easy, and the government is now endeavouring to make the whole of the distributive trades a Filipino preserve through the Retail Trade Nationalisation Act of 1964. This has proved difficult to enforce. The scope of the Act is not clear, and it could be construed as applying also to all forms of intermediate sale as well as final sale to the ultimate consumer. Thus it has been strongly resisted by American firms, which claim that the Laurel-Langley agreement, which gives Americans parity with Filipinos in the development of national resources, exempts them from the provisions of the Act.

CONCLUSION

The dominant feature of Philippine economic life since 1945 has been an intense nationalism. In some sectors of the economy there have been conspicuous advances and there is much that encourages hope for further economic growth. But the fact remains that the great mass of the population remains largely untouched by these developments. While it may be true, as Golay claims, that the landowning mestizo élite has been defeated on a number of important economic issues, these have mostly concerned government control over foreign exchange earnings and assistance to other sectors of the economy.[26] In fact, the Nacionalista party, which is supported by a majority of landowners, is an even more ardent supporter of economic nationalism that the Liberal party, and the economic policy of President Marcos has been to provide further state aid to the expansion of the non-agricultural sectors. Getting new industrial activities established behind high tariff barriers is not all that difficult, as several countries at a low level of development have proved; revitalizing a worn-out agriculture is another thing entirely. Export prospects of most Philippine products are poor, and after a run of years in the Fifties in which the rice deficit was almost eliminated, from 1960 to 1965 it grew year by year, making the Philippines second only to Indonesia among Southeast Asian countries as a rice importer. Perhaps this problem has now been

[26] *Golay,* op. cit., *p. 415.*

solved. But in the early Fifties one of the best qualified experts on the Philippines remarked that 'The primary problems of the Philippines today are problems of rural economy, just as the primary problems of China during the 1930's were problems of rural economy. . . . A group of Chinese leaders gambled on trade and industrialization alone, without agrarian reform, but beset with increasing corruption and the Sino-Japanese war, they finally lost everything.'[27] This remark appears as true at the present as when it was written. The very large United States aid received by the Philippines since 1945 has, paradoxically, enabled the country to postpone grappling with the basic agrarian problem. In the Five Year Development Plan 1963–67, only 7 per cent of the budgeted investment was allocated to the agricultural sector. The Philippines may not be able to defer its reckoning for very much longer.

[27] *Spencer*, op. cit., *p. 235.*

CHAPTER SIX

Malaysia and Singapore

Whether Malaysia or Thailand should be awarded the premier honours for the best economic performance in Southeast Asia since 1945 is largely a matter of personal preference. Since 1960 the Malaysian economy has had the lower growth rate; but as Malaysia's per capita product is nearly three times that of Thailand and the rate of population growth is lower, the average Malaysian has probably enjoyed a larger improvement in living standards than has his Thai counterpart. Malaya,[1] it is true, already enjoyed by far the highest living standards in Southeast Asia even in 1939, and its productive equipment was not very seriously affected by the Japanese occupation; nevertheless, real product per head has increased by more than 2 per cent per annum in most years, despite the diversion of resources, much needed for internal development, to combating the communist rebellion during the periods of the Emergency (1948–60) and the Indonesian confrontation (1963–66). Malaysian exports have not shown the periods of almost explosive growth that have characterized those of Thailand, but export income has augmented steadily, and the effort made to maintain the competitive efficiency of Malaysia's principal product, natural rubber, against synthetic substitutes finds no parallel in any other country at a low level of development. Moreover, even despite the slower growth of export earnings since 1961, consequent on gradually declining natural rubber prices, the economy has continued to expand rapidly through the allocation of more resources towards the domestic market.

This performance has been an impressive one, and the general well-being of the country and the efficiency of its administration is obvious even to the most casual visitor; roads, utilities, public housing and social services, in particular, set standards unmatched elsewhere in Southeast Asia. The Malayan dollar has been one of the hardest of currencies, and both Malaysia's and Singapore's foreign exchange reserves in 1967 amounted to the equivalent of more than six months'

[1] *The reader should bear in mind the distinction between Malaya and Malaysia made in the footnote on page 4.*

imports, a proportion only matched in Southeast Asia by that of Thailand. A scarcity of foreign exchange, which acts as a major constraint to the economic development of many Asian countries, appears unlikely in the near future, despite the decline of export prices. Few parts of the underdeveloped world are more thoroughly aligned towards the West, and the most conservative banker could find little to complain of in Malaysia's economic and financial policies, which are the essence of orthodoxy. Whether capitalism and private enterprise are suitable vehicles for the rapid achievement of higher living standards in the Third World are questions that even in Malaysia, and still more so in Singapore, give rise to impassioned argument, but there is little doubt that in Malaysia itself such policies have worked.[2] Moreover, the government and at least a substantial proportion of the population, if not a majority, feel that no major change is required from a policy of continuing to allow maximum freedom to the private sector and restricting government activity in economic affairs largely to improvements in the infrastructure. Thus the First Malaysia Development Plan 1966–70 postulated a private sector investment of M\$ 6,160 million as against a public investment (including defence) of M\$ 4,550 million.

The most fundamental of the many unique features of Malaysia received comment in Chapter 1; the country has been carved out of the wilderness over the past century by immigrant peoples, in response to the economic opportunities offered them by export industries directed to a rapidly expanding world economy. Thus Malaysia is not bogged down by an overpopulated outworn food-producing agriculture; indeed Malaya, in all probability, has not had a majority of its workforce engaged in food production since about 1850, and the expansion of food output has been directed at meeting an increasing demand from the growing numbers engaged in export and non-agricultural industries. The rice areas of Malaysia, it is true, now demonstrate most of the pernicious features of defective agrarian organization common to many parts of Southeast Asia, and so far Malaysia has achieved little more success in grappling with this problem than have its neighbours. But in Malaysia at least, an unwillingness to take decisive action has not primarily arisen from the political power of the landlords, but from the nature of its plural society. For the basic cause of Malaysia's economic strength is at the same time the principal source of its internal weakness: an acquisitive alien population has been allowed to undertake economic ventures that, initially at least, were unattractive to indigenes, and to grow to such proportions that it has threatened to become a majority. Although the formation of Malaysia in September 1963 was designed to overcome this weakness, subsequent events

---

[2] *An eloquent and informative contrary view is that of J. J. Puthucheary, in* Ownership and Control in the Malayan Economy, *Eastern Universities Press, Singapore, 1960, whose opinions are closely mirrored by E. L. Wheelwright in* Industrialization in Malaya, *Melbourne University Press, 1964. However, the two countries that have most closely followed policies of the kind these authors advocate, Indonesia and Burma, are precisely those whose living standards have shown the least tendency to improve.*

merely underlined the fragility of the political units that have succeeded the former British possessions and protectorates of equatorial Southeast Asia.

The architect of the new state and its dominant unit was the Federation of Malaya, subsequently known as West Malaysia. This itself was a union of all the prewar political units on the Malayan peninsula, and its creation in 1948 meant that a delay of some three decades had been allowed to elapse since the peninsula had attained economic and *de facto* political unity; as Fisher points out, that an attempt was not made to secure a common Malayan sense of nationhood at this earlier date when communal feelings were much less intense, can now only be regarded as a major error.[3] Moreover, such was the antagonism of the peninsular Malays to the overwhelmingly Chinese-populated island, that the Federation of Malaya did not include Singapore, and long before the two units achieved independence Singapore and Kuala Lumpur were tending to drift away from each other.[4] Since independence the Federation has had throughout a government of the right, but successive Singapore governments have moved progressively to the left. Nevertheless, the bonds of a common economy, reinforced by a common currency and banking system and a widespread feeling that the two territories were essentially complementary, continued to restrain forces making for antagonism, and the concept of Malaysia, in which the addition of the large Chinese population of Singapore to that of the Federation would be counterbalanced by the simultaneous accretion of the larger non-Chinese populations of the British Borneo territories, had much to commend it. In practice, however, the effect of the enlarged Federation was further to reduce the Malay proportion of the total population. Moreover, the tendency for Singapore's Prime Minister, Lee Kuan Yew, to regard himself as the spokesman for all the Malaysian Chinese, and in particular his campaign for a 'Malaysian Malaysia', was regarded as an intolerable interference with West Malaysia's internal affairs and an attack upon the special privileges awarded to Malays in the federal constitution.

Yet in a genuine federation such an interest would surely have been legitimate, and in the light of subsequent events it would appear that the Singapore leader had offended some understanding reached with the Federal Government at the time of the merger over the extent of his involvement in federal politics. Whether Singapore was expelled from Malaysia in August 1965 cannot be debated here, but, in the event, the separation proved no solution to the problems

[3] *Charles A. Fisher*, South-East Asia, *Methuen, London, rev. edn, 1966, p. 602.*
[4] *The Federation of Malaya achieved independence in 1957 and Singapore in 1959, although the latter had attained a high degree of self-government as early as 1955. Singapore's peculiar position, however, found expression in Britain's continued responsibility for foreign relations and defence, and internal security was entrusted to a triumvirate consisting of representatives of Britain, Singapore and the Federation. Whether Singapore was legally independent on its accession to Malaysia in November 1963 is a matter for specialists in international law, but full independence, with membership of the United Nations and the I B R D and I M F, came after its separation from Malaysia in August 1965.*

faced by either. As with India and Pakistan, they appeared unable to co-exist without friction either together or apart, and despite professions of an intention to cooperate, the likelihood of each taking positive action to damage the economy of the other began to appear a serious menace. Little progress has been made at the time of writing with a trade treaty to replace the proposed 'Common Market' which lapsed with separation, and the announcement that the two countries could not even agree over the continued operation of the common currency after June 1967, plunged their business communities into deep gloom.[5]

The situation in the Borneo territories, or East Malaysia, also gives rise to much concern, even though Indonesian confrontation ceased in mid-1966. Though many of the indigenous peoples are basically of Malay stock, few regard themselves as Malays, and most are in fact non-Muslim; moreover, memories of past misrule by the once large and powerful Malay sultanate of Brunei, whose truncated modern descendant elected to remain outside Malaysia, has left among many peoples a deep mistrust of the Malays and resentment at what they regard as interference in their affairs from Kuala Lumpur. The Borneo peoples, in fact, have no wish to exchange a British colonialism for a Malay one, but the principal advantage of the union is that it will give them development funds far greater than are likely to be forthcoming from any other source. Though proportionally much less important than in West Malaysia, the Chinese nevertheless constitute the largest ethnic group in East Malaysia, and their support will ultimately be vital for the continued adhesion of Sarawak and Sabah to Malaysia. The maintenance of pro-Alliance[6] governments in the two territories has proved a difficult exercise, and the younger Chinese of Sarawak in particular have been infiltrated by the so-called Clandestine Communist Organization, whose members, often in concert with Indonesian regular troops and 'volunteers', carried out terrorist attacks during the confrontation on the pattern of those common in Malaya during the Emergency. The sudden separation of Singapore from Malaysia without any prior consultation with the Borneo territories was deeply resented by the local

[5] *In August 1966 Malaysia announced that the new Malaysian dollar would be defined in terms of gold instead of in sterling as in the past, and that Commonwealth preferences on a wide range of imports would be cancelled. These measures may have been designed as retaliation for Britain's failure to provide sufficient finances for the defence component of Malaysia's First Five Year Plan and, as Kuala Lumpur believed, Britain's more accommodating attitude towards Singapore. Nevertheless, the first measure was strictly speaking an obligation resulting from Malaysia's membership of the IMF, and the abolition of preferences could be regarded as a justifiable means of increasing revenue needed for the implementation of the First Malaysia Plan. Brunei, which has also used the Malayan dollar since 1946, also introduced its own monetary unit, the Brunei dollar, in mid-1967.*

[6] *The union of the Malayan Chinese Association, the United Malay Nationalist Organi- zation and the Malayan Indian Congress, which though created specifically to fight the 1955 election in the Federation of Malaya, has proved surprisingly durable, winning every subsequent election in West Malaysia. However, in the elections of May 1969 it lost the two-thirds majority necessary to amend the constitution, which previously it had changed at will.*

Chinese, and attempts by Singapore to create goodwill, such as the offer of University scholarships to Sarawak and Sabah students, have been viewed with the deepest suspicion in Kuala Lumpur.

Although religious and cultural differences among Malaysia's leading communities are large enough to constitute major sources of friction, there is no doubt that it is the great inequality in the distribution of income between the main ethnic groups that polarizes these differences and precipitates them so forcibly into the political arena. Moreover, this inequality has persisted despite many years of government effort to achieve a reallocation of income more in keeping with the distribution of political power, which still rests very largely with the predominantly rural Malays. In 1957, as in 1947, Chinese incomes were about three-fifths and Malay incomes a little over one-fifth of the Malayan total income.[7] There is little reason for believing that any appreciable change has occurred since that date, despite heavy expenditure on rural development, irrigation and other investments which benefit mainly Malays. Though no ethnic group in fact has a monopoly of poverty and most of Malaysia's Chinese are people of very humble circumstances, without a greater equality in the distribution of income between the main ethnic groups it is difficult to see any prospect of long-term stability for Malaysia.

THE LAND AND THE PEOPLE

The term Malaysia has often been used by Western writers to indicate the Malay peninsula and the archipelagos to the south and east (though usually the Philippines have been excluded) and despite the division of the Malay world between two colonial empires, use of the term survived right up to the outbreak of World War II.[8] In the changed political and economic circumstances of the postwar world there has been little attempt to resuscitate the former use of the term Malaysia, and the present Malaysia is a state put together to achieve fairly circumscribed political objectives. Of its two major units, East Malaysia is much the larger, being some 77,000 square miles in extent, as against only 51,000 square miles for West Malaysia. Some 400 miles of sea separate the two components at their closest points in the extreme south, but northwards the distance increases; Kota Bharu is almost a thousand miles distant from Kota Kinabalu (Jesselton),

---

[7] *T. H. Silcock and E. K. Fisk (eds.),* The Political Economy of Independent Malaya, *Australian National University Press, Canberra, and University of California Press, Berkeley and Los Angeles, 1963, p. 3.*

[8] *As for example, in Rupert Emerson,* Malaysia: A Study in Direct and Indirect Rule, *Macmillan, New York, 1937. Charles Robequain, however, included the Philippines in his* Le Monde Malais, *Payot, Paris, 1946, and regarded this title as synonymous with* Malaisie, *a term which he reluctantly rejected only because of possible confusion with the then British-administered Malay peninsula (op. cit., p. 9). Robequain's work was trans-. lated and first revised by E. D. Laborde as* Malaya, Indonesia, Borneo and the Philippines, *Longmans, London, 1954.*

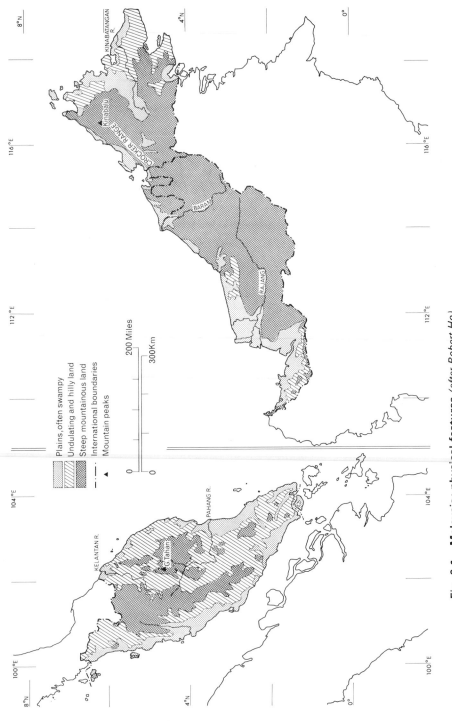

Fig. 6-1 Malaysia: physical features *(after Robert Ho)*

Plains, often swampy
Undulating and hilly land
Steep mountainous land
International boundaries
Mountain peaks

200 Miles
300 Km

KINABATANGAN R.
Kinabalu
CROCKER RANGE
BARAM
RAJANG
KELANTAN R.
G. Tahan
PAHANG R.

and all of Sabah is closer to Manila than to Kuala Lumpur. Despite Fisher's assertion that in Southeast Asia the land divides but the sea unites, this geographic separation, compounded by difficulties of navigation on account of both the nature of the opposing coasts, with their general absence of good harbours, and the strong winds and high seas of the northeast monsoon season from November to April, presents a major obstacle to the maintenance of national cohesion, and recalls the somewhat similar situation of Pakistan.[9] Moreover, contact between the two units has always been via Singapore, and on the foundation day of the new state there was no direct sea or air link between them.

Singapore's geographic location has been much emphasised in the past as the major reason for its economic and strategic importance. The latter at least has been greatly overstated, and Singapore's commercial significance is very largely the result of its history as a free port, which it is now in part to abandon, and the closely interconnected network of commercial interests between the Chinese merchants of Singapore and their counterparts in other Southeast Asian cities, much of which ultimately derive from ties of family and clan. Singapore's survival as a regional entrepot depends mainly, as Ho points out, on whether Southeast Asian countries find its use more convenient or cheaper than duplicating its facilities.[10] In practice this largely turns on the speed with which the nationalist movement in each country will endeavour further to restrict the economic activities of the local Chinese population, and from Singapore's viewpoint the outlook is discouraging.

Undulating hill-lands and highly accidented mountains together occupy a large part of Malaysia. The dominant relief forms of the Malayan peninsula are a series of roughly N–S aligned granite-cored ranges. The longest is the Main Range, which extends continuously from the Thai frontier almost to Melaka (Malacca) and contains most of the peaks in the peninsula exceeding 5,000 feet. Its alignment is assymetrical, being much closer to the west coast than to the east, and it is paralleled to the east and west by similar complex ranges, which are however more discontinuous and generally lower and shorter, although the Tahan range of southern Kelantan and Pahang contains Malaya's highest point, Gunong Tahan (7,186 feet). In several parts of central and north Malaya steep-sided limestone hills are very prominent features of the landscape, and other karst-like features such as solution cavities occur on the low limestone ridge separating Perlis from Thailand. South of Melaka the mountains are restricted to isolated peaks such as Mount Ophir, and much of southern Malaya consists of an undulating low upland, parts of which, however, by virtue of soil quality, have proved specially advantageous for large estate enterprises.

Economically, the plains and the adjacent foothills are of overwhelming

[9] *R. Ho, in Wang Gungwu (ed.)*, Malaysia: A Survey, *Frederick Praeger, London and New York, 1964, p. 26.*

[10] ibid., *p. 27.*

significance. Along the west coast from Perlis to southern Johor extends an almost continuous plain, broken only between Port Dickson and Melaka, which reaches its maximum width of some 40 miles in the lower Perak valley. This plain has played an important role in the economic development of the country, and except where occupied by swamp or mangrove much has been planted to a varied succession of crops; indeed, in several places changes in land utilization can still be observed in progress. By contrast, the plains of the east coast are narrower and less continuous; the most extensive areas of low level land are the deltas of the Kelantan and of the Pahang-Rompin river systems. There is a profound difference between the use made of these two areas: the Kelantan delta is relatively well-populated and is one of Malaysia's principal rice areas, but the lower Pahang is relatively empty and undeveloped. Apart from small Malay or immigrant Indonesian settlements at each *kuala* (estuary or stream junction), occupation of the west coast plain did not precede, but followed, that of the low but accidented foothill country lying between the Main Range and the heavily forested and often swampy plain. This narrow belt has been of fundamental economic significance, as along the break of slope deposits of tin-bearing gravels occurred in several valleys in Perak, Selangor, and Sungei Ujong (now part of Negri Sembilan). Under the stimulus of the expanding world market of the nineteenth century, immigrant Chinese swarmed into the tinfields, and their crude camps were often the first settlements in this part of the country. Although streams and rivers continued to be the main arteries of communication, primitive tracks were soon cut linking the mining centres on various rivers. Thus the outline of the road system came into being, and although some of the early mining camps were later abandoned, others grew to form sizeable cities. Towards the end of the century, the alignment of the main longitudinal railway closely followed that of the old roads,[11] and the new communication pattern, which had largely been created to further development of the tin industry, made possible the success of large-scale agricultural enterprise and inevitably greatly influenced its location pattern, although it was no more than a fortunate accident that *Hevea* rubber proved so well adapted to the environment of the foothill zone.[12]

Lacking tin, no such sequence is observable in the Borneo territories, although in Sarawak the occurrence of gold deposits did produce a paler replica of the Chinese tin-rushes of the peninsula. Though larger than West Malaysia the resources, both present and potential, of East Malaysia appear much smaller and there is also a great disparity in the resource endowments of its two units; Sarawak is much the poorer of the two and is unlikely to be able to contribute

[11] *The first railways in Malaya were to link major mining areas with the coast, such as that between Taiping and Port Weld (1884), and Klang to Kuala Lumpur and Telok Anson to Batu Gajah.*

[12] *Large-scale agricultural enterprise in Malaya did not begin with the Europeans; but the Chinese enterprises that preceded them were largely ephemeral speculative ventures, whose occupation of the land was purely temporary. See pp. 61–63.*

anything to the overall economic development of Malaysia for some time to come. This disparity between the two halves of Malaysia was heightened by the unexpected refusal of the small but oil-rich state of Brunei to accede to the new Federation, a decision which was confirmed by the establishment of Brunei's own monetary unit.

The Borneo territories largely turn their backs on Indonesian Kalimantan by virtue of the NW–SE mountainous divide that forms the main water-parting of the great island, although the mountains by no means form a continuous range. Sarawak shows a threefold division of a flat low-lying plain, an intermediate foothill country and rugged mountains with summits occasionally rising above 7,000 feet. Large areas of the coastal plain are regularly flooded, and the low mangrove-fringed coast and extensive swamps make much of the area very repellent. The limestone hills and the gold, silver and cinnabar (mercury) lodes of the Bau district in the foothill zone of western Sarawak do, however, suggest a similarity with the tin-bearing areas of western Malaya. Sabah is distinctly more mountainous than Sarawak, but though the proportion of flat level land is considerably lower, the plains are much more accessible and, in general, possess soils superior to those of Sarawak. North of Brunei Bay the west coast plain becomes narrower and more discontinuous, and is cut off from the interior by the high and rugged Crocker Range, which contains Mount Kinabalu (13,455 feet), the highest point of Southeast Asia. Eastwards lie generally lower, but still highly accidented, upland masses, but along the eastern coast lie a number of discontinuous plains, some of which have considerable agricultural potential, such as the Kinabatangan lowland near Sandakan.

Few parts of Malaysia have a rainfall of less than 100 inches per year, and much of Sarawak and Sabah receive almost half as much again. Only in the north-east and northwest extremities of Malaya is there an approach to a dry season, but dry spells of up to a month are not uncommon and can cause 'wintering', or defoliation, of rubber trees. This usually occurs in March or April, and at such periods latex flows may be so reduced that many smallholders may not find it worthwhile to tap their trees.

The vegetational response to this regime of constant high temperature and humidity, with soils that never dry out, is a forest of extraordinary richness. Despite the growing demands for agricultural land, forests still cover some 70 per cent of the surface area of Malaya, 73 per cent of that of Sarawak and 80 per cent of that of Sabah, constituting one of Malaysia's major sources of export earnings and indeed the largest in both Borneo territories. More than half of the total forest area of nearly 90,000 square miles consists of official Designated Forest Reserves, but not all of these are commercially productive; forest reserves lying at over 1,500 feet or so in elevation are largely so designated in order to protect headwaters from erosion. The commercial forests under the control of the Forest Department are protected by regulations governing timber exploita-

Chinese charcoal kilns at Trong, coastal Perak. The fuel consists of *Rhizophora (bakau)* poles. As the commonest method of cooking in Southeast Asia is over a charcoal brazier, similar plants are found in all areas of extensive mangrove forests; demand, however, tends to outrun supply.

tion and regeneration, but outside the Forest Reserves there has been much 'timber-mining'. Although Malaysia accounts for about one-quarter of all world exports of hardwood timbers, mounting domestic demand gives rise to concern over the continued availability of large exportable surpluses, and improved forest management, with greater attention to up-grading the proportion of commercially valuable species in the extraordinarily rich lowland forest, is mandatory if the importance of forestry in the national economy is to be maintained. The most valuable species are *chengal (Balanocarpus heimii)*, *keruing (Dipterocarpus* species*)*, *kapur (Dryobalanops aromatica)*, and various types of *meranti (Shorea* species*)*, but even the most numerous, the *meranti*, do not usually produce more than five or so trees of commercial size per acre, even under favourable conditions, and heavier hardwoods, such as *keruing*, produce fewer. The productivity of the forest, some 200–500 cubic feet of timber per acre, is thus very low,[13] but this is in part a consequence of the backwardness of the sawmilling industry, which consists of a large number of small, poorly located, under-capitalized units which demand top-quality full-size logs and refuse those of a size that would be more than welcome to European or North American mills. Sawmilling is almost exclusively a Chinese industry, although in Sabah some mills

[13] *Ooi Jin Bee*, Land, People and Economy in Malaya, *Longmans, London, 1963, p. 289.*

are operated by large European timber concessionaires such as the Bombay Burma Corporation. In West Malaysia most mills are located in the towns, in part because of security considerations arising from the Emergency, so that costs of transport are considerable and there is virtually no utilization of waste or by-products. Both West Malaysia and Sarawak prohibit the export of logs in order to encourage further domestic processing,[14] but Sabah has no such restriction and, together with the Philippines, has been the principal source of log supply for the booming forest-products industries of Japan, Taiwan and South Korea.

Timber extraction is closely governed by considerations of accessibility, though in West Malaysia logs may be moved by road over a hundred miles to the mills; Singapore, the most important sawmilling centre in the peninsula, obtains most of its supplies from northeast Johor (Johore), and this state and Perak lead in the production of forest products in West Malaysia. In Sabah, timber exploitation is most active in the vicinity of the northeast coast, where numerous parallel-flowing rivers and a much-embayed coast have facilitated exploitation of the magnificent dipterocarp forests; in contrast, the forests of the west coast are poorer, and because of the steeply rising Crocker Range the problem of accessibility is much more severe. Forestry accounts for no less than one-third of the gross domestic product of Sabah, and the value of output of forest products is half as much again as that of West Malaysia. Exploitation of the undoubtedly great forest resources of Sarawak presents greater physical difficulties and the value of its forest-products output is little more than one-quarter that of Sabah; nevertheless, it is still by far the largest source of export earnings.

Population

The salient features of the racial composition of the population of Singapore and Malaysia are indicated in Table 6-1. The dominant position of West Malaysia in the new federation is obvious, but Singapore's population is also substantially greater than that of East Malaysia, a situation that gave special significance to the allocation of additional seats in the Federal House of Representatives during the brief period of Singapore's adhesion.[15] In West Malaysia, Malays constitute 50 per cent of the population, and following the practice of the former British administration, regard themselves as the indigenous inhabitants or the 'sons of the soil' or *Bumiputera*. There is something in this view, but by no means as much as most Malay leaders claim; much of Malaya was quite unpopulated a century and a half ago, and a very large proportion of the present Malay population is descended from comparatively recent immigrants from Indonesia. Much

[14] *However, the export of second-quality logs is permitted, as are exports to Singapore, on payment of a duty.*

[15] *The Federation of Malaya Lower House contained 104 seats; this was enlarged in the new Federation of Malaysia by the addition of 16 seats for Sabah, 24 for Sarawak, and 15 for Singapore.*

Table 6-1 *Malaysia and Singapore: ethnic composition of population, 1963 (thousands)*

	Singapore	West Malaysia	Sarawak	Sabah	Malaysia	*Percentage Malaysia*
Malays*	249	3,837	142	32	**4,011**	*44·7*
Chinese	1,335	2,841	255	117	**3,213**	*35·8*
Indians and Pakistanis	146	843			**847**	*9·4*
Ibans (Sea Dyak)			254		**254**	*2·8*
Kadazan				160	**160**	*1·8*
Other indigenous		4	150	177	**331**	*3·7*
Other non-indigenous	45	135	9†	13†	**157**	*1·8*
Total (all races)	**1,775**	**7,660**	**810**	**499**	**8,969**	***100·0***

* Including some Indonesians in Singapore and West Malaysia, and mainly Indonesians in Sabah
† Includes Indians and Pakistanis
Source: Projections based on latest census in each state

of the Malay population of Perak, Selangor, Negri Sembilan and Johor, in particular, is descended from Indonesian immigrants over the past century, attracted to Malaya by the prosperity resulting from the rubber and tin industries. The Chinese are certainly aliens, but there are records that they have been economically active in the peninsula for many centuries, and though it is true that for many years a small proportion of the Chinese and Indians settled permanently, they adapted themselves to the economic and social life of the country as they found it.[16] Unlike the Malay immigrants who were seeking settlement on the land, non-Malay immigrants moved into the monetized, capitalist sector of the economy, and this movement was either encouraged or tacitly supported by the British administration, at least until the Great Depression. Singapore is overwhelmingly a Chinese city, but within West Malaysia the Chinese form nearly 40 per cent of the total population, and in Sarawak they constitute the largest ethnic group although their share of the population is only a little over 30 per cent.

The geographic distribution of the population varies considerably between the main racial groups, the Malays and indigenous peoples being the least urbanized and the Chinese by far the most, with Indians and Pakistanis, as in other demographic characteristics, occupying a median position. In 1957, some 73 per cent of the Chinese population of the Federation of Malaya lived in urban areas, as against only 19 per cent of the Malays.[17] The high degree of urbanization in the Chinese community is primarily responsible for its disproportionate share on a population basis of the national income; nevertheless, the Chinese have long been the most powerful urbanizing forces in the peninsula. Economic opportunity was the principal inducement to Chinese immigration into Malaya, and

[16] *Silcock and Fisk (eds.), op. cit., p. 7.*
[17] *Hamzah Sendut, in Wang Gungwu (ed.), op. cit., p. 90.*

Chinese market gardens for temperate vegetables and strawberries, Cameron Highlands, West Malaysia.

the greatest rewards were for long offered by tin-mining, which until well into the present century was a highly labour-intensive industry. Though the greatest concentrations of Chinese have long been in the two island entrepots of Singapore and Penang, whence came much of the finance for Chinese tin-mining and speculative large-scale agricultural enterprises, the distribution of the Chinese population on the mainland still shows a close relationship with areas of past and present tin-mining. After the rubber boom of 1909–12 many Chinese families in mining settlements found that operating a rubber smallholding could be easily and profitably combined with other activities, and over much of West Malaysia the typical Chinese smallholder is now, in fact, a town-dweller.

Chinese rural settlement was in large part a consequence of the Great Depression, when many unemployed Chinese urban workers squatted on unoccupied land, and this drift was confirmed and accelerated during the Japanese occupation when many more Chinese fled the towns to escape persecution and semi-starvation. Under the resettlement policy carried out during the Emergency, most of these Chinese squatters were relocated in 'New Villages', some of which were of large size; thus the earlier pattern of Chinese avoidance of isolated rural settlement was re-established. Though originally brought into the country to work on

large European estate enterprises, 34 per cent of the Indian and Pakistani community lived in towns in 1957, so that Indians and Pakistanis are relatively almost
twice as urbanized as are the Malays.

Postwar Malay migration to the towns has been very marked, and on a racial
basis the Malays have recorded the largest proportionate increase in the urban
population; but this has so far done little to modify the essentially Chinese
character of most of Malaysia's cities, and the Malay population remains at
present as it always was, overwhelmingly rural.[18]

Peoples of Malay stock came as immigrants to the peninsula in order to
establish rural settlements; and the preservation, so far as possible, of the way of
life of these 'sons of the soil' became a tacitly accepted part of British policy,
which found practical expression after 1913 in the establishment of 'Malay
Reservations', in which the sale of land to non-indigenes was forbidden. Under
the British administration the petty riverine territories of the Malay sultans became enlarged into substantial land areas bounded by the major watersheds, and
the rulers themselves accumulated great personal wealth—particularly where, as
in Johor, they followed a liberal policy of granting favours, especially access to
land, to non-indigenes. The immobile mass of the peasantry, or *raàyat*, however,
remained largely devoted to the traditional life of fishing, padi planting and coconut growing. While it may be true that Malays are not particularly conservative
in their way of life, as is evidenced by the rapidity with which they took up the
planting of rubber smallholdings, many of which eventually passed into the hands
of the early European rubber companies, Malay society is certainly not achieve-
ment-motivated, and the Malay farmer's contact with the monetary economy is
all too likely to be through the agency of the Chinese shopkeeper or middleman.[19]
The old paternalist colonial attitude, however, has been continued with little
modification by the post-independence government, and the Deputy Prime
Minister has never ceased to reiterate that the aim of the Rural Development Plan
is to provide the rural areas with social services and economic opportunities the
equal of those in the towns, a manifestly impossible goal on which the First
Malaysia Plan maintains a discreet silence. It can scarcely be denied that despite
a village tradition of *gotong-rojong* (self-help), the Malay community looks mainly
to the government for an improvement in its social and economic well-being, an
improvement which so far the government has largely been unable to effect. The
vital necessity of placating the rural Malay voter, the ultimate source of power
under the constitution, means that government is committed to spending large
sums on services and facilities in rural areas on which the return is, at best, only

[18] *This situation, however, will not endure, and within some two decades about half the
Malay population will be urban.*

[19] *Restrictions on the sale of land, the one large asset possessed by the Malay community,
may however have operated against the accumulation of capital, as was certainly the case
with the Javanese peasantry under the more rigorous land policy of the Netherlands
Indies government.*

modest and where economic improvements, such as greater productivity in padi farming, have been obstinately long delayed in coming about. Malays enjoy special privileges in the allocation of scholarships for higher education and in appointment to senior posts in government service, but so far there is little evidence that this very understandable attempt to reduce the disparity in opportunities open to the two main racial groups, which Malays in large measure attribute to the former colonial rule, has produced a much-needed greater social mobility in the Malay community. Its main effect has been to maintain Malay control of the executive to buttress that exercised over the legislature. The evidence strongly suggests that the best-off Malays are those in areas where the Malay share of the total population is lowest; as the proportion of the Malay population decreases, so its living standards improve.

In Sarawak and Sabah, which lacked deposits of tin, the incentives for Chinese immigration were much less, and a smaller proportion of the Chinese population is urban than in West Malaysia; nevertheless, the urban centres of East Malaysia are, if anything, even more Chinese. The small Malay population is confined to the coasts and is mostly engaged in traditional occupations, but in Sabah many Indonesian immigrants are employed in estates and in other enterprises in the capitalist sector. The indigenous non-Malay peoples of Sabah and Sarawak who are still a majority, though a declining one, form a very mixed group indeed with at least forty distinct languages.[20] Some have become lowland padi planters and have taken up the cultivation of cash crops such as rubber, but very many remain devoted to the practice of shifting agriculture, which in West Malaysia is confined to a few thousand aboriginal groups such as the Senoi. The multiplicity of groups regarding themselves as possessing a distinct identity poses many serious questions for the future adhesion of Sarawak and Sabah to the Federation of Malaysia, and any attempt to maintain for the Malays a position of privilege such as they hold in West Malaysia is unlikely to be accepted. Both Borneo territories are concerned to maintain the control over immigration granted to them under the Malaysian constitution, a matter of particular importance to Sabah, whose recent rapid economic growth has produced an acute labour shortage. Singapore, which urgently needs additional employment opportunities, is especially anxious to secure a larger share in the Sabah labour market, but entry permits for Chinese are only granted for limited periods.

The virtual end since the Great Depression of a pioneer demographic structure in Malaya with a high proportion of adult males in the total population, and its replacement by a more settled structure in which immigration and emigration have been largely reduced to minor significance and in which a greater degree of equality in the sex ratios among non-Malays has been established, will inevitably have far-reaching political and economic repercussions. These do not appear likely to involve any marked change in the relative numerical strength of

[20] *T. Harrison, in Wang Gungwu (ed.) op. cit., p. 170.*

the three major racial groups at least for the next generation, although the evidence is conflicting and complex. Birth rates for all three communities since 1950 have amounted to between 40–50 per thousand, being highest for the Malays and lowest for the Chinese, a reflection of differing degrees of urbanization. On the other hand the Chinese have the lowest death rate, and very much the lowest infant mortality rate, although all communities have shown significant decreases in mortality. Since the middle Fifties, however, all appear to have experienced some decline in fertility, but it has been most marked in the urban Chinese; between 1948 and 1966 Singapore's live birth rate fell from over 50 to less than 30 per thousand, and with the adoption of the government's plan for extending techniques of family planning, mainly through the use of the intra-uterine device, it is hoped that by the early Seventies the birth rate should be reduced to around 20 per thousand. Because of its very high infant mortality the Malay community's potential for further growth is large, but further reductions in fertility cannot be ruled out. Even if the proportion of Malays in the total population of West Malaysia does increase somewhat, because this will involve an increase in the proportion of children in the Malay community, its share of the population over twenty-one years of age will decline—a movement that could adversely affect its electoral representation, for by the early Eighties the so-called immigrant communities will have a majority in this age group.[21]

More important, however, are the consequences for economic development and planning. The favourable conditions of the past, when the labour force grew much more slowly than the total population, are about to disappear, and by the end of the Sixties total population and the population of working age will be expanding at about the same rate of 3 to 3·5 per cent per annum.[22]

So far the pressures created by these demographic changes have been mainly confined to the educational field, but because they have coincided with the government decision to provide universal education, their economic consequences have already been severe in that greatly increased resources have had to be allocated to accelerated school-building and teacher-training programmes. These have had to be planned and executed as matters of extreme urgency, and inevitably a substantial cost penalty has been incurred; moreover, there is no prospect of any relief from the heavy educational charge on the budget for some time to come. The full impact on the employment position will not be felt for another decade, but already school leavers are finding it increasingly difficult to obtain jobs and many face periods of protracted unemployment.[23] Singapore,

---

[21] *Silcock and Fisk (eds.), op. cit., p. 81.*

[22] *Between 1931 and 1957 population growth in Malaya averaged 2·2 per cent per annum, but the increase in the male labour force only 0·4 per cent per annum.* ibid., *p. 77.*

[23] *In the major towns the unemployment rate among males aged 15 to 19 was believed to be 27 per cent in 1965, but this high figure probably reflected some movement of youths from rural areas.* First Malaysia Plan, *p. 79.*

which has continued to experience a net immigration from the mainland since the end of the war, felt itself obliged in 1965 to place restrictions on the employment of unskilled workers who were not Singapore citizens. But so long as free movement is permitted across the causeway connecting it with Johor,[24] Singapore can be regarded merely as the major urban centre of the peninsula, and all urban centres have been heavily affected by rural in-migration. This movement to the towns has fundamental consequences for economic planning, for jobs in urban areas will have to be made available at a rate to match the increasing urban population if serious unrest is to be avoided. With a Malaysian urban population growth of around 4·5 per cent per annum, the contrast between government application to rural development and the abandonment of industrial and commercial activities, the main providers of urban employment opportunities, to the private sector, is therefore somewhat striking. The latter may possibly be able to provide the additional jobs, but if it cannot, pressure for further government intervention in manufacturing is likely to augment, particularly as the Malay share of the urban population grows. In an urban economy dominated by Chinese and European employers, the hiring of Malays is largely motivated by political considerations. Nevertheless, any serious intervention in the free and open economy, to which undoubtedly Malaysia owes much of its present relative prosperity, is likely to tear the ruling Alliance asunder. Although the rural-urban movement may ultimately produce greater communal harmony, its more immediate consequences are difficult to foresee.

THE AGRICULTURAL BASE

Agriculture supports about 55 per cent of Malaysia's work-force and generates nearly 35 per cent of its national product, figures which suggest that the disparity between incomes per head in agricultural and non-agricultural occupations is markedly less in Malaysia than in any other country of Southeast Asia. In fact, nearly 60 per cent of Malaysia's total agricultural work-force of about 1·2 million workers is engaged in the production of agricultural products requiring substantial processing, and about half, or some 27 per cent of the total labour force, in the production of natural rubber, an activity that normally accounts for about 25 per cent of the gross domestic product (*Table 6-3*). Malaysian agriculture thus consists of a dominant industrial crop sector (*Tables 6-4 and 6-5*), much of which is

[24] *This may no longer obtain in the future, as one of the consequences of separation may be the erection of full control over the movement of peoples between Malaysia and Singapore similar to that usually maintained at international frontiers. In 1966 Malaysia, ostensibly to counteract Communist infiltration, erected a large building on the Johor side to control the flow from Singapore. As about a million crossings of the causeway are made every month the delay and disorganization caused by a full control system would be enormous. Motor vehicles, which formerly made the crossing with a minimum of bureaucratic red-tape, now require temporary import permits, and there have been growing complaints over delays at the crossing.*

Table 6-2 *Malaysia and Singapore: gross national product, 1965*

	TOTAL *million M $*	PER CAPITA *M $*
MALAYSIA	8,729	928
West Malaysia	7,663	952
Sarawak	618	737
Sabah	448	862
SINGAPORE*	3,023	1,600

* Gross Domestic Product

Source: *First Malaysia Plan*; Statement by Singapore Finance Minister to Parliament, August 26th, 1966

Table 6-3 *West Malaysia: industrial origin of gross domestic product, 1960 and 1965*

	1960		1965*	
	million M $	*percentage of total*	*million M $*	*percentage of total*
Agriculture, forestry and fishing	1,976	*38*	2,406	*34*
Rubber	1,233	*24*	1,504	*21*
Agriculture and livestock	568	*11*	647	*9*
Forestry	85	*2*	125	*2*
Fishing	90	*2*	130	*2*
Mining and quarrying	306	*6*	382	*5*
Manufacturing	453	*9*	766	*11*
Construction	158	*3*	360	*5*
Electricity, water and sanitary services	70	*1*	123	*2*
Transport, storage and communications	189	*4*	247	*3*
Wholesale and retail trade	817	*16*	1,100	*16*
Banking, insurance and real estate	71	*1*	116	*2*
Ownership of dwellings	245	*5*	305	*4*
Public administration and defence	339	*6*	425	*6*
Other services	596	*11*	853	*12*
Gross domestic product at factor cost	**5,220**	*100*	**7,083**	*100*

* Preliminary

Source: *First Malaysia Plan*

highly capitalized, producing for its employees income-levels only marginally inferior to those of workers in non-agricultural activities, and a smaller and very much poorer food-crop producing sector whose workers would be even worse off than they are at present were it not for the large transfers made to them from industrial crop production and from other sectors of the economy, in the form of guaranteed rice prices, irrigation schemes and other expenditure on rural development.

This preoccupation with export-oriented industrial crop production has clearly served Malaya well in the past, notwithstanding the experience of the Great Depression and the Japanese occupation; what is not so clear is how well it will serve in the future. Much is heard of the need for diversification in view of natural rubber's past violent oscillations in price and its present slow price depreciation in the face of competition from synthetic rubbers. But no alternative to rubber capable of earning anything like the same income per unit area has been proven. The oil palm, it is true, does appear under certain soil conditions to be more lucrative at present prices, but palm oil production involves yet more capital-intensive methods and is as equally subject as rubber to extreme short-term supply elasticity, which makes for price instability. Moreover, the crops which Malaysian agricultural diversification could involve are precisely those which their present producers have been urged by the International Bank and others to diversify out of; it does not make very much sense for Malaysia to move into cocoa or sugar while Ghanaians and Filipinos are being urged to forgo further expansion of these crops. Diversification towards a greater degree of self-sufficiency in food production finds its main justification in the political rather than the economic field. So far, the very large sums invested in expanding rice production have produced a disappointing return, although it is just possible that Malaysia may be on the verge of a major breakthrough which would greatly improve the present economic position of the rice cultivators, and substantially reduce the burden on the country's balance of payments of a large volume of food imports.

The estate industries

Estates are by no means so important in the Malaysian economy as is popularly supposed, and large European-owned estates even less so; 40 per cent of the planted area of rubber estates is on properties owned by Asians, the great majority of whom, if not 'Federal citizens', certainly regard Malaysia as their permanent domicile. Nevertheless, estates are significant enough. In West Malaysia, where all but a handful of Malaysia's estates are located, they provide employment for about 300,000 workers (about as many as are engaged in the operation of cash-crop smallholdings) and can occasionally generate more than 40 per cent of total export earnings; they also account for about 60 per cent of the total foreign investment in the country. The popular association of Malaysia with estate cultivation probably reflects the political influence of estate industries with the former

Table 6-4   *West Malaysia: area and production*
            of principal crops, 1966

	thousand acres	thousand tons
Rubber	4,042	925
Estates	1,813	514
Smallholdings	2,229	412
Oil Palm	304	
Palm Oil	—	183
Palm kernels	—	43
Coconuts	506	
Estates	63	28 (copra)
Smallholdings	443	—
Tea	8	7,660 *(thousand lb)*
Rice	898	
Padi	—	899
Milled equivalent	—	585
Fruits	214	
Canned pineapples	—	57
Food Crops*	214	—
Spices	33	—
Miscellaneous	67	—

* Tapioca, sweet potatoes, sago, sugar cane

Source: *Monthly Statistical Bulletin of West Malaysia,* October 1968

Table 6-5   *East Malaysia: area and production of*
            principal crops, 1964 (thousand acres)

	Sabah	Sarawak
Wet padi	64·3	109·6
Dry padi	27·4	170·5
Rubber	243·5	308·1
Coconuts	102·0	65·4
Oil Palm	17·5	—
Abacá	5·1	—
Pepper	—	5·7
Sago	—	34·0

colonial administration, and the fact that the accessibility and statistical records of estates make their study so very much easier than that of smallholders. Even today it is only for estates that up-to-date and reliable statistics of planted area, production, yield and employment are regularly available.

Nevertheless, in no other newly independent country in the humid tropics are foreign-owned estate enterprises so important in the national economy, and they continue to be accepted as having a major part to play in future economic development. The disabilities which have been imposed on estate operations in Ceylon and Indonesia since these two countries achieved independence thus find no parallel in Malaysia, and although some vociferous minority groups clamour for nationalization, their present appeal is very small. The break-up of estates and their transfer from European to Asian ownership is strongly resisted by the National Union of Plantation Workers, the only really large and influential organized labour group in the country, whose experience has shown that this invariably leads to reduction in employment opportunities and a deterioration in workers' living standards.

It is by no means easy to provide a satisfactory explanation of why Malaysia's estate industries have been able to escape the irrational manifestations of nationalism that have struck down their Indonesian counterparts. Some factors can be detected, however; influential though they were, the Malayan planters never possessed the political power of their counterparts in Deli who, in practice, themselves decided what was legal and what was not. The much earlier adoption of a liberal labour policy on estates, such as the abolition of indenture and penal sanctions on breaches of contract, left the Malayan estate industries in much better shape than those of Indonesia to adapt to the challenge of nationalism, whose origins and course of development were very different in the two countries. Since 1957 the government has made it clear that smallholder cash-crop production is to count for very much more than it has in the past, and that crops such as the oil-palm that did not readily lend themselves to such smallholder production could expect no assistance. But as competition from synthetic rubber steadily grew, even this policy was modified, and in 1964, after many years of refusal to permit such alienations, the government announced its intention of permitting the acquisition of land for new planting by estates. Unfortunately, the change has been too long in coming, for by this time most European estates at least were well launched on a policy of reducing their planted area.

To regard Malaysia's estate sector as a homogeneous entity is as indefensible as to fail to differentiate between the many classes of smallholders. There is no uniformity, moreover, in the definition of estates either among crops or among the various Malaysian territories, or even between the Departments of Agriculture and Statistics of West Malaysia, each of which has adopted its own definition. Historically, any holding planted with rubber exceeding 100 acres and managed as a single unit has been regarded as an estate in Malaya, but in Sabah the term is reserved to properties exceeding 250 acres and in Sarawak to those exceeding 1,000 acres.[25] Geographically, estate production is dominated by West Malaysia, which had 96 per cent of the total planted estate area of about 2·2 million acres in 1960, and commercially by rubber, which occupied some 88 per

---

[25] *Strictly, these are 'large estates'; Sarawak also recognises a category of 'holdings in the range 100–1,000 acres', implying that everything else is a smallholding. D. W. Fryer, in Wang Gungwu (ed.), op. cit., pp. 228–9.*

cent of the estate-planted area in the same year. Malaysian estates are essentially monocultural, some 90 per cent of all rubber estates (defined by the Department of Agriculture as those with three-quarters or more of their cultivated land planted to rubber) possessing no other cultivated land at all, but there is a small group of about a dozen large estates located on the lower Perak, Bernam, Selangor and Langat rivers that practise multiple cropping. These estates all date from the pre-rubber era, and were established around the turn of the century for the production of coconuts, coffee or lowland tea; though much of their land has since been converted to more profitable crops such as rubber and oil palm, some of the old lines of production are still maintained.

Estate managements, nevertheless, are very alive to the possibility of switching to more profitable lines of production, and along many parts of the Selangor and Perak coastlands coconuts and rubber are being replaced by oil palm, a crop which in the Sixties experienced a minor boom following the availability of replanting grants (described below) for the conversion of old rubber-land to the production of other crops. Nor has the old speculative basis of large-scale agricultural enterprise entirely vanished, for some Chinese estate owners in the Klang area have cut down rubber and replanted with oil palm, not because they have any real evidence that oil palm cultivation is more profitable, but simply because having noted that European estates in the neighbourhood are actively pursuing such a policy, they have concluded that they had better get into the new industry also.[26] A remarkable relic of the speculative past of large-scale enterprise is the Chinese illegal cultivation of tapioca, which has become a serious problem in parts of Perak and Kedah. This activity, which is made possible by the plant's short maturation period, is now the work of large operators using bulldozers, tractors and other heavy equipment to clear virgin forest or forest reserves, and is highly organized to prevent detection. The operators work deep in the forest, covering the tracks left by their vehicles after they have moved in; after a few days the land is cleared and prepared for planting and the equipment is then moved out.[27]

The basic division in estate industries is between the Asian estates, which are largely owned by private individuals or by groups and *kongsis*, which usually also exercise managerial functions, and the European-owned estates which are the property of public companies. The latter, in turn, are largely in the hands of some fourteen agency houses, which between them control over one million acres of rubber-land, equivalent to about 85 per cent of the total area planted with rubber on European estates. Four of the houses control more than 100,000 acres under cultivation, and the largest, Harrisons and Crosfield Limited, over 230,000 acres. The agency houses dominate the Malaysian economy; their large agricul-

[26] *Personal communication from Miss Tan Koon Lin.*

[27] *The Sungei Siput area had become notorious for this activity, according to a statement of the Mentri Besar (Chief Minister) of Perak.* The Straits Times, *November 22nd, 1965.*

tural enterprises are buttressed by their strong grip on much of the export-import trade and their substantial shipping interests, and some have also ventured into tin-mining and manufacturing. Through interlocking directorates they have connections with virtually every kind of European enterprise in the country.

The agency houses have been much criticized as saddling estate production with an inflated cost structure, but there are advantages of scale in agriculture as in other lines of production. The houses' centralized scientific and technical services could not be supported by individual estates, and it is extremely doubtful that a rubber industry with a competitive structure would have accumulated the enormous fund of technical and scientific knowledge that is the industry's main defence against competition from substitute materials. There is indeed considerable scope for further concentration in estate industries, for the agencies operate through control rather than ownership; though the houses were largely responsible for the flotation of most estate public companies at the time of the 1909–1912 boom, nominating themselves as the managing agency, it is somewhat surprising that this apparently loose structure has been able to survive so long and to fend off several take-over attempts.

Apart from their structure and ownership patterns, European estates differ from Asian estates in being of larger average size, in having a higher proportion of high-yielding material in their planted stock, and in possessing a labour force whose racial composition and conditions of employment are in marked contrast to those of the work-force on Asian estates. European-owned rubber estates averaged nearly 2,500 acres in 1965, as against only 450 acres for Asian estates, and although only 8 per cent of European estates were less than 500 acres in size, nearly 80 per cent of the Asian estates fell into this size category; in the case of crops other than rubber, the disparity in size is even more marked. The greater proportion of high-yielding material found on European rubber estates gives them a correspondingly higher output per tapped acre (976 lb in 1965 as against 654 lb for Asian-owned estates), but this disparity should be reduced as the immature area of high-yielding material on Asian-owned estates comes into bearing. Nevertheless, only 68 per cent of the planted area on Asian rubber estates consisted of high-yielding material in 1965, as against 85 per cent on European-owned estates (*Table 6-6*).

But even this situation represents a dramatic improvement on that of a decade earlier, and is largely the result of the Rubber Industry Replanting Board, Fund A, which was specifically intended to improve the planted material on the smaller, that is, Asian-owned estates. Under the scheme a replanting grant of M$ 400 per acre financed by a cess of $4\frac{1}{2}$ cents per pound on all rubber exported, is available to estates to replant or new-plant up to 21 per cent of their planted area with high-yielding material. This figure is that suggested by the Mudie Mission[28]

---

[28] Report on the Mission of Enquiry into the Rubber Industry of Malaya (Mudie Report), *Government Printer, Kuala Lumpur, 1954.*

of 1953, and is based on the assumption that the economic life of a rubber tree is some 30 years, after which there is a marked falling off in latex output. To maintain such a cycle of production a 3 per cent per annum replanting rate is desirable, and with a gestation period of seven years, an estate should, therefore, have at any one time some 21 per cent of its planted area as immature. The assumption of a 30-year economic life can be questioned, and in view of the fact that European estates now start tapping after only five years, the estimate for the optimum immature area appears somewhat excessive. But the Mission was impressed by the unfavourable age-composition of Malaya's rubber trees (in 1953, 48 per cent of all trees on rubber estates were over 28 years old and 35 per cent were over 33 years old), and felt that only an accelerated rate of replanting with high-yielding material could maintain the competitive position of Malaya's natural rubber industry *vis-à-vis* synthetic rubber.

Table 6-6   *West Malaysia and Singapore: area, production and yield per tapped acre of natural rubber, 1965*

	European estates	Asian estates	Smallholders
Planted area *(thousand acres)*	1,068	791	2,470
Immature area *(thousand acres)*	264	250	n.a.
High-yielding material *(thousand acres)*	913	536	n.a.
Tapped area *(thousand acres)*	787	507	n.a.
Production *(thousand tons)*	343	148	379
Yield per tapped acre *(lb)*	976	654	n.a.

Source: *Rubber Statistics Handbook, 1965,* Department of Statistics, Kuala Lumpur

This unfavourable age-composition was largely the result of the war and of prewar restriction schemes which prevented new planting, but it was most un-favourable on the smallest, that is, on Asian-owned estates. Large estates could more easily retire land from current production for replanting, and it was very much easier for them to obtain clonal[29] planting material through their parent

---

[29] *A clone is a race of plants with a common genetic inheritance, so that each individual has identical characteristics; they may be propagated by bud grafting (clonal stumps) or through sowing clonal seeds. Clones are identified through an abbreviation of their origi-nating stations, e.g. Tjir (Tjirandji), PB (Prang Besar), RRIM (Rubber Research Institute of Malaya). Prewar clones such as Tjir 1 yield 800–1,200 lb per acre per annum as against 400–450 lb for unselected material, but modern ones such as the RRIM 600 series yield over 2,000 lb, and the 700 series are reported as having produced over 4,000 lb under trial conditions. High yield, however, is not the only criterion; estates have to weigh maximum yield against resistance to disease, good bark characteristics, resistance to trunk snap, and longevity. Labour has also to be considered, as modern clones are tapped less frequently than unselected material.*

agency houses, which maintain estates specializing in research, such as the famous Prang Besar and Chemara estates; further stock derived from such material can be propagated in an estate's own nursery.

European estates are dominant in Perak, Selangor and Negri Sembilan; here the early acceptance of British Residents and large areas of unoccupied land, made accessible through new overland communications created to serve the tin-mining industry, were the foundations for the rubber boom of 1909–12. Asian estates, on the other hand, are most numerous in Johor and Melaka. Development in Johor came much later than in the three western states of the old F M S (Federated Malay States), but once begun growth was very rapid indeed, largely in consequence of a generous land alienation policy and the relatively limited areas that were sterilized in Malay Reserves. The average size of estate in both the European and Asian sectors in Johor is well above the national average; some of the European properties are of very large size, the two largest estates in the country, both planted to oil palm, being located in the state. Nevertheless, even Malaysia's largest rubber estate of nearly 18,000 acres, the Tanah Merah near Port Dickson, and its largest oil palm estate of some 20,000 acres, the Ulu Remis estate near Layang Layang in south Johor, both part of the Guthrie group, are small in comparison with the giants of East Sumatra, where land was available on much more generous terms. There are, however, some large concentrations of Chinese estates, some of which were Japanese-owned before the war. In Johor, Lee Plantations Limited, part of the Lee Kong Chian complex of holdings with ramifications in sawmilling, pineapple canning, tin smelting, banking, insurance, commerce and manufacturing and almost certainly the largest concentration of Chinese capital in the country, controls over 18,000 acres, and Melaka, which has a long tradition of large-scale Chinese agricultural enterprise, possesses a Chinese equivalent of an agency house.

It is well known that European estates employ mainly resident Indian workers, and the necessity of providing housing and other services to stipulated legal standards for such resident workers is a major contributant to the high operating costs of such estates. Asian estates, on the other hand, are largely Chinese-owned; in 1953, the last year for which a racial distribution of the ownership of Asian estates is available, Chinese owned 23 per cent of the total estate area as against only 7 per cent which was Indian-owned. The labour force on Chinese estates consists overwhelmingly of non-resident Chinese, for such contract labour is generally more productive and requires fewer fringe benefits, greatly reducing overheads. For the same reason it is increasingly preferred by European estates wherever it is available; thus in areas of active tin-mining or at no great distance from urban centres, Chinese contract labour may amount to half or more of the total labour force on European estates, and occasionally the entire tapping force. In practice the lower overhead costs of the small Chinese estate go a long way towards overcoming their lower output per tapped acre, and in terms of return

Applying 2-4-D yield stimulant below the tapping cut on the Rubber
Research Institute of Malaya's estate near Kuala Lumpur, West Malaysia.

on investment the small Chinese estate may occasionally be more efficient than the large European one. This, however, merely reflects the fact that Chinese enterprise in general disregards many items necessarily included in European cost analysis. The labour of the manager-owner or of his family may well not be reckoned in monetary terms, and occasionally the estate factory may also be used by smallholders, or the estate output supplemented by purchase from small-holders.

The steadily increasing costs of tapping labour, which the Mudie Mission estimated could amount to 40 per cent of operating costs, and the growing com-petition from synthetic rubber, have forced on estates improvements in both their operating efficiency and the nature of their product which in several respects must be judged long overdue. As the Mudie Mission remarked, 'Malaya can do nothing about the price of synthetic rubber; it can only conform to it', and since 1960, when the so-called stereoregular synthetics (polyisoprenes and polybut-adienes) appeared, natural rubber has been confronted with a chemically identical substitute. About 40 per cent of total world rubber consumption (about 5·4 million tons in 1965) is appropriated by synthetic rubber in uses such as treads and sidewalls of automobile tyres in which superior technical properties confer on synthetic a decided advantage, and only about 15 per cent of the total market, mainly in cements and speciality tyres, is reserved on technical grounds to natural rubber. Thus, over some 45 to 50 per cent of the total market synthetic and natural rubber compete, largely on price considerations.

As tapping and fixed costs are so large a proportion of total operating expenses, costs per unit are sharply reduced through pushing up the yield per tapped acre. The average yield per acre for all tapped high-yielding material on European estates was nearly 1,100 lb in 1965, and the trend is sharply upwards; yields of a ton or more have been attained on many estates, and it appears that the RRIM 700 clonal series in conjunction with high ladder tapping can produce yields of more than double this figure under field conditions. Estate policy, therefore, is to expand output on a declining area; properties which for one reason or another do not readily lend themselves to replanting, or whose operations through geo-graphical remoteness cannot easily be integrated with those of the present group's other properties, have been sold off and effort has been concentrated on replant-ing and re-equipping the best properties. Thus by 1968 estate-planted area had declined by some 250,000 acres from the 2·03 million acres of 1953, and the downward trend will continue; but over this period estate output rose by some 40 per cent, and despite the rapid increase in the smallholder-planted area, the ratio of estate to smallholder output (about 58:42) remained virtually constant.[30]

Properties sold by European companies have largely been purchased by

[30] *Unselected seedlings' contribution to total estate output declined from 54 per cent in 1955 to 18·5 per cent in 1964. As a result of the replanting policy, the First Malaysia Plan estimates that estate output will rise by 6·5 per cent annually over the Plan period.*

speculators, some of whom have reaped fortunes through satisfying the strong desire of many Malaysian peoples to have a stake in the land, by cutting up such properties into smallholdings and selling them off on fancy terms. The fact that since 1960 replanting grants for smallholdings under 10 acres have enjoyed a premium of $350 per acre over replanting grants for estates, has increased the attraction of estate subdivision to speculators. Where possible estate companies have preferred to divert rubber-land to oil palms, but this transfer requires special topographical and soil conditions.[31]

Replanting, however, has not been the only contributor to improved efficiency; areas scheduled for future replanting can achieve a significant increase in yield through the use of stimulants such as 2–4–D, which is painted on the bark beneath the tapping cut; high tapping with ladders has proved very productive particularly with some modern clones, despite the extra labour costs involved; and on large estates improved methods of latex collection and mechanical handling of latex churns at the factory have also contributed to cost reduction. The latter improvements will of course become necessary on many more estates as the large area of immature and young high-yielding rubber gradually comes into full production; and with the necessity of having in any case to replace existing factory equipment to cope with the larger outputs, more sophisticated methods of processing and packaging are certain to be adopted in order to meet the growing requirements of manufacturers for rubber of precise and consistent vulcanizing

[31] *Some estates have been sold for urban development and much estate land in the Klang valley, where many of the early estates were created, appears ultimately destined for this end.*

Table 6-7 *West Malaysia and Singapore: rubber area new-planted and replanted, 1960–65 (thousand acres)*

	NEW-PLANTED		REPLANTED		TOTAL		TOTAL
	Estates	Smallholders	Estates	Smallholders	Estates	Smallholders	
Average 1955–59	16·2	16·2	72·6	58·9	88·8	75·1	**163·9**
1960	21·7	15·1	75·2	69·5	96·9	84·6	**181·5**
1961	17·7	67·4	70·5	57·3	88·2	124·7	**212·9**
1962	10·0	82·5	63·1	69·1	73·1	151·6	**224·7**
1963	8·7	100·3	58·7	83·4	67·4	183·7	**251·1**
1964	6·1	57·5	59·0	79·7	65·1	137·2	**202·3**
1965	4·9	39·8	53·2	91·4	58·1	131·2	**189·3**

Source: *Rubber Statistics Handbook, 1965,* Department of Statistics, Kuala Lumpur

qualities. It appears highly likely that these new methods of processing and semi-manufacture will be concentrated on the larger and most accessible estates within each major house.

Rather more than half of all estate output is in the form of ribbed smoke sheet (RSS). It is graded according to a traditional system which placed a premium on lightness of colour with no regard to technical characteristics. RSS production is a simple process which involves coagulating the latex with dilute formic acid, rolling the coagulum into sheets and stabilizing them in a smokehouse; the sheets are then pressed into bales of about 250 lb for export. In processing and in the transport of the bale to its final destination, contamination by dirt and deterioration through oxidation can result in variations in vulcanizing characteristics which are a major nuisance to the manufacturer, and the need for an improved system of grading has long been obvious. For some years the leading European agency houses have been producing special rubbers of the crumb or flocculated type, such as the Dynat of the Guthrie group, and Harub of Harrisons and Crosfield, while the similar Heveacrumb process has been developed by the Rubber Research Institute of Malaya. In these new processes the latex is subject to mechanical and chemical treatment, the resulting crumb is vigorously washed and dried, and the final product is baled in polythene wrappings to prevent contamination with foreign material. These new processes not only make possible the treatment of all types of produce such as cup lump, tree lace and scrap as well as latex in integrated operations, but also offer substantial economies in both capital and operating costs. In 1963 the Malaysian government introduced its own scheme for the introduction of technical grading for general-purpose natural rubber, Esemar (Standard Malaysian Rubber). SMR rubbers are graded according to the dirt and ash content, and the proportions of copper, manganese, nitrogen and volatile constituents present; the sheet, crepe, or crumb from which it is produced is then compressed by heavy-duty presses into bales of 70–100 lb, and these are wrapped in polythene for shipment to avoid contamination. The scheme, in which all the major European agency houses participate, is intended to reassure manufacturers of constant quality, and by 1966 involved nearly forty estates and ten re-milling factories with a capacity of nearly 100,000 tons of SMR annually. Another product which is peculiar to estates and for which demand is expanding rapidly is concentrated latex, which in 1965 accounted for nearly 20 per cent of estate output; this is produced in centrifuges, treated with ammonia to prevent coagulation, and needs specialized equipment for transport and storage.

These technical advances would appear to throw the balance of advantage strongly towards estate production, for clearly the adoption of such sophisticated methods is quite out of the question for most smallholders, and particularly Malay smallholders. They are also for the present at least, beyond the capacity of most Asian-owned estates. It is accepted, therefore, that in the struggle against

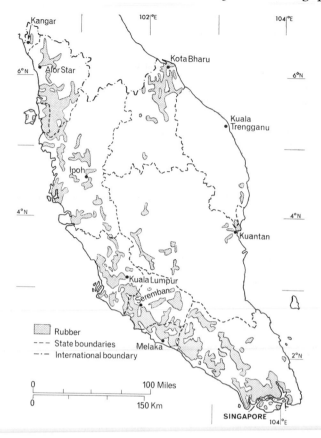

Fig. 6-2   Land utilization in West Malaysia—rubber

This diagram, together with Figures 6-3 and 6-4, is based on land utilization maps of the Survey Department of the Federation of Malaya, which show land alienated for particular classes of use. In practice, however, any particular piece of land may or may not be used for the purpose originally stipulated, but because rubber has generally proved by far the most profitable crop until very recently, little rubber-land has been diverted to alternative uses.

synthetic rubber the large estate has a very important role, and the 1966–70 Malaysian Plan postulates that part of the anticipated capital inflow and investment originating in the private sector will involve an extension of the estate area by some 200,000 acres or more. It is very many years since land alienations for estate development were permitted,[32] and the change of policy is evidence of the

---

[32] *Strictly speaking, estates do not possess freehold title but have a lease in perpetuity, for which they pay an initial survey premium and an annual rent depending on the crop planted.*

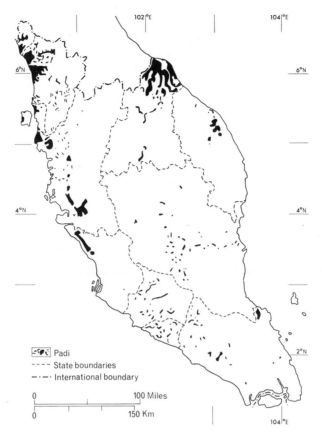

Fig. 6-3   Land utilization in West Malaysia—padi
The distribution of padi-lands corresponds closely with that of the rural Malay population, and most of the land in Malay Reservations carries a stipulation that cultivation is restricted to padi and other food crops. Nevertheless, some such land has been illegally planted to rubber in every state of West Malaysia.

pragmatism with which Malaysia approaches its developmental problems. But whether European estate companies will respond to the offer is doubtful; it is unlikely that they will wish to acquire additional rubber-land, but land suitable for oil palms would probably be attractive. Many local investors, however, would almost certainly prefer to put their savings into estate development, which is well known and understood in the country, rather than into non-agricultural activities, and an extension of the Asian-owned estate sector would appear to be sound policy.

However, by early 1968, the long slide in rubber prices which had carried the level to below M 50 cents per lb, roughly that of 1949, had cast a deep gloom over the industry (*Figure 2-4*). This low level was not so much the direct result of competition from synthetic rubbers, but reflected contributory fortuitous events such as a long strike in the American tyre industry, the increasing sales of dirty rubber at very low prices from Indonesia, which was desperate for every scrap of foreign exchange, and sales from the United States GSA stockpile. Apart from bringing pressure on Washington to halt such sales, the Malaysian government invited other natural rubber producers to discuss common problems at Kuala Lumpur, and itself took the extraordinary step of entering the Singapore market in order to shore up prices. As experience has shown that few attempts by the governments of primary-producing countries to influence commodity prices have achieved any great measure of success, Malaysia appeared to be in danger of throwing good money after bad. But the extreme vulnerability of the smallholder, and particularly the Malay smallholder, should prices fail to improve, or if the traditional smoked sheet should fail to find a market against more sophisticated competition, is fraught with the gravest consequences for the ruling Alliance.

The oil palm industry   The oil palm is intermediate between the major crops of Malaysia, rubber, padi and coconuts, and minor ones such as pineapples and tea. The industry is at present almost entirely an estate prerogative, and though a pygmy in comparison with rubber production it is the second largest estate industry in Malaysia, and growing very rapidly. In 1966 the planted area in West Malaysia exceeded 300,000 acres and, at the rate of expansion of the previous three years, it will attain half a million acres before 1975. Over this period it appears probable that the share of oil palm products in total export earnings will rise from about 3 per cent to 10 per cent or more.

The oil palm is unique among major vegetable oil crops in that the oil extraction takes place at, or in close proximity to, the actual site of fruit production, and not at the market; this is because the ripe fruit bunch is heavy and bulky to transport, and must be processed within twenty-four hours of harvesting. The processing operation is more complex than that of rubber and there are economies of scale, so that the production of oil palm products tends to be a much more concentrated industry, each agency house having only one or two companies engaged in production. In the early years of the industry, units of 2,000 acres were considered the minimum for profitable exploitation, but the drive to exploit economies arising from technological progress led to the creation of some very large units, two of which exceed 20,000 acres. At present, units of 5,000–8,000 acres are probably closer to the optimum, but smaller estates can operate profitably if they are close enough to share common processing facilities. The capital-intensive nature of the industry limited its appeal to an independent government dedicated to improving the lot of the rural cultivator; but demonstrated profitability and the cloudy future of natural rubber soon produced a quickening of interest, and since

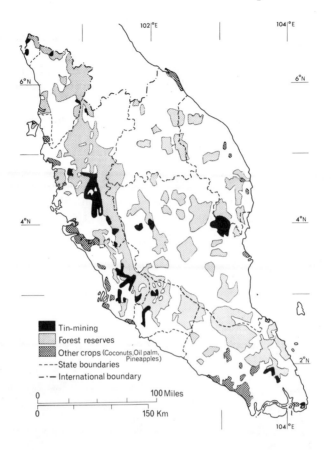

Fig. 6-4 Land utilization in West Malaysia—other crops, tin-mining and forest reserves

Although over 80 per cent of the estimated coconut area is disseminated between a multiplicity of smallholdings scattered along both west and east coasts, large estate plantings occur in coastal Perak and Selangor. Much of these estate plantings, together with much estate rubber-land where soils and terrain permit, are being converted to oil palm, so that together with the large new plantings scheduled for the eastern states, the area under oil palm in the early Seventies will be much more extensive than at present. Pineapples are a minor crop, largely confined to the peat-lands of west Johor.

The area affected by active tin-mining, on the other hand, is much smaller than appears in this map. About one-third of the total Forest Reserve area is highland forest, intended primarily to protect against accelerated run-off and erosion.

1960 government has endeavoured to create a place for smallholder production through official land-development schemes.

Although the African oil palm (*Elaeis guineensis*) was introduced into South-east Asia almost three decades before *Hevea* rubber, the first commercial plantings in Malaya were not made until 1917, by which time the natural rubber industry was well established. The discovery in 1901 of the hydrogenation process for hardening vegetable oils into fats had led to a greatly increased demand for such oils, but the oil palm was only one such raw material; moreover, the African territories of the powers were the principal sources of supply, for in parts of West Africa and the Congo basin semi-wild palmeries had long constituted an important part of the native economy and were able to meet a growing export trade. It was the Lever plantations in the Belgian Congo that first demonstrated the profitability of estate production of a high-quality palm oil with a low free fatty acid content (F F A), a development that was followed in 1911 by the first commercial plantings in East Sumatra. In providing the experience and planting material for the establishment of a Malayan oil palm industry, East Sumatra helped repay its debt to Malaya for *Hevea* rubber, but the Malayan oil palm industry lagged far behind that of Sumatra right up until World War II. In large part, this late

Rubber being replaced by oil palm, Selangor coast, West Malaysia.

development and slow growth reflected the great profitability of rubber and the fact that areas with the most suitable soils for oil palm cultivation were much more limited in Malaya. By the late Twenties the industry, if still small, was well launched and the foundations were laid for future expansion; while rubber production had become subject to restriction schemes, in Johor large areas of suitable soil were then alienated for oil palm cultivation on very generous terms. The oil palm industry, moreover, recovered from the Great Depression quicker than did rubber, and by 1941 the planted area had attained nearly 80,000 acres, more than double that of 1929.

The severe damage and deterioration of estates and factories as a result of Japanese occupation, the Emergency and, until 1953, the prices paid by the British Ministry of Food for palm oil which were generally well below those obtaining on the free market, were substantial handicaps to the postwar rehabilitation of the industry. But the planted area grew steadily during the Fifties and after 1960 the industry entered the most rapid period of growth in its history, as other agency houses followed the example of the prewar pioneers and began converting rubber and coconut land to oil palm.[33] By 1968 Malaysian palm oil production had surpassed that of Indonesia, and by 1975 it appears probable that it will also exceed that of the Congo (Kinshasa) and be closely challenging Nigeria's for the premier position, unless these African countries demonstrate greater resolution in grappling with their enormous socio-political difficulties. By 1966 the planted area of 304,000 acres had exceeded that of Indonesia, and the disparity will widen rapidly in the future.

The Malaysian industry, like that of Indonesia, is primarily a producer of high-quality palm oil with a low free fatty acid (FFA) content; such oils are eminently suitable for use in food industries such as margarine, shortening and confectionery fats. The joint product of the oil palm fruit, palm-kernel oil, is much closer in chemical composition to coconut oil; for some purposes palm-kernel can be interchanged or mixed with palm oil, but it is especially in demand for soap-making and for pharmaceutical and toilet preparations. Although the principal product of the Nigerian industry, palm kernels are merely a profitable by-product in Southeast Asia; kernels are exported for crushing, but the shells are used for estate boiler fuel and road metal. The principal variety planted before the war was the *Deli dura*, a derivant of an African form developed in East Sumatra for its high oil content, with a pericarp constituting 50–70 per cent by weight of the fruit, but for most new plantings the *tenera* is preferred. This is a hybrid of the *dura* and another African variety the *pisifera*, which, though it has a pericarp amounting to some 99 per cent of fruit weight and no shell, is generally sterile and therefore has no commercial value. *Tenera* fruits and bunches are smaller than

---

[33] *The four houses primarily responsible for the establishment of the oil palm industry in Malaya were Socfin (Franco-Belgian), Guthrie, United Plantations (Danish) and Harrisons and Crosfield.*

those of the *dura*, but this is offset by the production of more bunches per palm, and by their richer oil content.

The oil palm starts to bear fruit in its third year, an advantage over both rubber and coconuts, and attains its peak yields in the eighth to fifteenth years. The limit of economic life is generally set by the increasing cost of harvesting tall palms, but it is generally about 30 years; a short-trunked dumpy variety has been bred, but the high proportion of female inflorescences that go unpollinated in this variety has made it commercially disappointing. On well-drained coastal clays of Perak and Selangor, oil palms now produce some six tons of fruit bunches to the acre, yielding more than two tons of palm oil; no other crop has given such a high yield or been so remunerative. As more than 2 million acres of such soils on Malaya's west coast are planted with rubber, padi and coconuts, the scope for replacement is large. On the volcanic soils of Sabah, oil yields of 2·4 tons to the acre have been recorded; though similar soils are very limited in extent in West Malaysia, they are now being reserved for oil palm cultivation. Harvesting the fruit bunches is usually performed weekly, but dry periods and the age-composition of the planting affect harvesting frequency and the interval may vary from four to twelve days. Harvesting accounts for at least 20 per cent of total costs so that in this respect the oil palm is not markedly a better proposition to estates than rubber, and the cost of labour, moreover, trends steadily upwards.

Fruit bunches from mature palms weigh upwards of 50 lb, so that an efficient transport system is mandatory and a level topography a great advantage. The intensity of roads and light railways on oil palm estates is thus very high, for every effort is made to keep the distance over which fruit has to be manhandled (the more handling the higher the FFA) to a minimum. Large estates prefer railway systems; though initially more expensive than roads these have lower operating and maintenance costs and can be moved to suit any change in estate layout. Moreover, there is less physical damage to fruit bunches in transport, and if bogey-mounted fruit cages which can be run straight into horizontal sterilizers at the factory are employed, all further fruit handling can be avoided. All large estates use the hydraulic press method of pressing, the older centrifugal type now being regarded as much less efficient; the latter, however, is quite suitable for small estates and some Chinese estates have managed to acquire such equipment.

Geographically, oil palm estates at present are located in two main areas: in a discontinuous belt some twenty miles inland from the west coast extending from Telok Anson to Sepang, and along the main road and railway line to Singapore in Johor. Although the oil palm industry began in Selangor, both Johor and Perak surpassed it in planted area by 1930. Since 1956, however, as a result of new plantings Selangor has regained second position, and in the future it could well overhaul Johor; in 1964, 40 per cent of the immature oil palm area in Malaya was in Selangor, the highest proportion of any state, and 79 per cent of this represented new plantings. The new plantings in Selangor largely represent the transfer of land from rubber and coconut production; largely because this state was the first to experience the impact of the European planting boom in the early part of the century, the average size of oil palm estates is low. Though Johor has far fewer estates, their average size is very much larger; two are virtually of 20,000 acres in extent and another exceeds 10,000 acres, and together these three estates account for some 27 per cent of Johor's planted oil palm area. Perak occupies a median position, having fewer estates than Selangor, but of larger average size.

The growth of the oil palm industry well illustrates the tendency for population and economic activity in West Malaysia to become more concentrated in the western states. The existence in this part of the country of a concentration of factories which can process fruit from immature estates until it becomes economic to provide them with factories of their own, and the location of the bulk terminals at Butterworth, Port Swettenham and Singapore, make locations outside this region much less attractive. There is, however, a possibility that the large new plantings contemplated by the FLDA (Federal Land Development Authority) could create another focus of the industry in Pahang and possibly extending into Trengganu, that is, in predominantly Malay-populated areas.

The Federal Land Development Authority was established in 1956, largely to take over responsibility from the state governments for settling landless rural workers on smallholdings; the states, however, can still undertake their own schemes, and because they have complete control over the allocation of land, remain a very important element in rural development. Since its inception the FLDA has cleared large areas of virgin forest and established many schemes, mostly involving the planting of rubber, which are further considered below. The FLDA intends to restrict its interests to rubber and oil palm as these are the only two crops so far proved capable of yielding a sufficiently high return to make such schemes financially sound. The first oil palm scheme was commenced in 1960 near Kulai, Johor, and by 1964 eight further schemes totalling 18,000 acres had been launched, amounting to 14 per cent of the area then developed by the Authority. The Authority has been actively seeking areas suitable for oil palm cultivation in the eastern states, which have by far the greatest land resources, and some 30,000 acres near Jerangan, Trengganu, have been declared suitable. The greatest effort, however, is to be made in the 'Jengka triangle' between Jerantut, Maran and Temerloh, where 150,000 acres of volcanic soils are to be reserved for oil palms. Here the FLDA will be able to launch several contiguous schemes, which should achieve substantial economies in the provision of roads and services in comparison with past policy of distributing effort among widely separated schemes in several states. Processing and marketing should also be more easily accomplished, and it is hoped that on the basis of the oil palm industry an industrial complex, sustained by enhanced local food crop and livestock production, will eventually be created.

Nevertheless, the problems of integrating smallholders into palm oil production on block new-planting schemes are extremely formidable, for the authority possesses no specialist staff with deep experience of cultivation and processing, and few if any settlers initially know anything about the crop. In its rubber schemes the FLDA has allocated settlers to their holdings once the land has been planted, but this will clearly not be possible in oil palm schemes, for which a different organization remains to be developed. The place of the Malaysian oil palm industry in the world vegetable-oil economy has been gained through concentration on a quality product, and any compromise in quality in the interests of smallholders would be likely to have very serious consequences. To produce high-quality oil implies meticulous harvesting, efficient transport and centralized processing in modern, well-equipped factories. Thus the settler could not even harvest his own land, though he might be responsible for its maintenance; initially at least, the degree of direction and supervision of the settler would have to be rigorous, and it is doubtful if this surveillance could ever be entirely relaxed. To be economically viable each scheme will need to have central processing, and inevitably, central accounting and central management; thus, by definition, it would not be a collection of smallholdings but an estate. Nevertheless, it would be very different from either a European-owned one with overseas shareholders, or a privately-owned Asian estate; it would perhaps be best described as an intermediate organization in which, while the settler was in one sense an estate labourer, he was also a shareholder with a stake in the land and the factory. Such an organization would probably fall short of estate-standards of efficiency, but in offering the prospect of genuine partnership between local and overseas interests the search for a solution to the problems posed appears abundantly worth while.

The Kulai scheme, the first to come into production, avoided most of the difficulties by being attached to an existing estate and factory, which processes fruit bunches for smallholders, markets the proceeds and distributes the profits between the parent estate and the smallholders on the basis of their respective fruit output. The estate has also provided planting material, instruction in cultivation and supervision. An alternative organization proposed by the FLDA involves a 'nucleus' estate and factory, in which a European company constructs a factory in return for the alienation of a tract of land for company oil palm cultivation. The factory would also process smallholder fruit from the associated scheme, but would ultimately pass into the ownership of a 'settler-shareholder' cooperative once the settlers had redeemed their loans to the authority. Companies approached, however, feel that the land area so far offered is inadequate, and claim they would need security of tenure for at least three cycles of production (90–99 years) to make investment justifiable. In its oil palm schemes for East Malaysia, the FLDA has sought the cooperation of the Commonwealth Development Corporation, which has considerable experience in oil palm cultivation and in Kenya operates several factories for processing smallholder tea on behalf of the

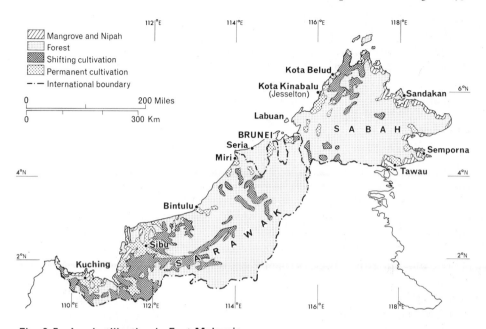

Fig. 6-5   Land utilization in East Malaysia
In comparison with well-documented West Malaysia, knowledge of land use in East Malaysia is rudimentary.

Kenya Tea Board, but for the Jenka triangle development contemplates erecting its own factories. However, this would necessitate the recruitment of a corps of experts and specialists, personnel who scarcely exist outside the European estate sector; it could also result in the FLDA becoming something not unlike a European agency house, a function very far removed from that for which the authority was established. Moreover, if it is intended that the FLDA shall develop its oil palm operations as a competitor to the European houses, the failure of government to provide adequate research facilities appears unlikely to promote this end.

The importance of research can scarcely be over-estimated. In the early days of the industry, the Department of Agriculture played a major role in the development of improved planting material and in promoting better techniques of cultivation and processing, but since 1960 the Department has been virtually unable to spare any resources for oil palm research, and its valuable collection of material has been dispersed to the large estates that participated in its breeding programme. Research is thus now entirely a private matter, and though there are three private research stations each supported by a major agency house, there is inevitably some waste and duplication of effort. Inevitably, companies are chary of passing on information to their rivals; moreover, contact with oil palm research organizations in other parts of the world is slowly declining. The industry

urgently needs a central research establishment similar to Malaysia's famous
Rubber Research Institute, but the government argument has been that the
planted area is too small to justify this at present, and that as the industry is
entirely an estate matter, it should finance its own research. This official niggard-
liness towards a rapidly expanding industry contrasts markedly with the allocation of M $75 million for coconut research and rehabilitation, a crop of markedly
lower profitability. In thus misallocating resources by fostering less remunerative
forms of production in order to appease its Malay electorate, the government has
departed far from its usual pragmatism in economic affairs and confirms the
suspicions of the non–Malay peoples.

Other crops: estates in East Malaysia   The remaining estate crops together
occupy less than 100,000 acres, of which coconuts account for about three-
quarters. About half of the estate coconut area is owned by European companies,
and is shared by about a dozen large estates in the Bagan Datoh peninsula of
Perak and along the lower Bernam river in Selangor. Most of these began as
subsidiaries of Ceylon companies, but many former coconut estates have been replanted with rubber and oil palms. Tea occupies a little over 8,000 acres, about
half of which is located on three estates in the Cameron Highlands of Pahang,
but a little lowland tea is produced on a few mixed estates in coastal Selangor;
Malaysia, in fact, produces some excellent teas, but its relatively high labour
costs clearly debar it from ever becoming a major producer. Pineapples as an
estate crop are a Chinese prerogative, and nearly all of the 20,000 acres of pineapple estates are located on the peat-lands of west Johor.

    In East Malaysia estate enterprise is poorly developed, and in Sarawak it is
virtually non–existent. Largely through the policy of the former British North
Borneo (Chartered) Company administration and because of its substantial areas
of fertile volcanic soils, Sabah has constituted a more congenial environment for
estate enterprise. Tobacco was formerly a crop of some significance to European
planters but its cultivation has long been abandoned to smallholders, and as in
West Malaysia, rubber is now of major significance. Postwar commodity shortages
and the interest of the Commonwealth Development Corporation were largely
responsible for introducing two new crops to Sabah, cocoa and abacá. Neither now
seems likely to realize the prospects originally entertained, but the oil palm may
well repeat the success it has achieved in West Malaysia; Unilever is developing
a 10,000-acre estate in the Labuk valley near Sandakan, and other estates in the
Tawau and Mostyn areas have plans for expansion. Three CDC nucleus oil
palm schemes are planned for Sabah, and one for Sarawak.

Smallholding cash crops: rubber

Malaysian farmers are unique among the peasants of Southeast Asia in that a
far higher proportion of them are mainly dependent for their livelihoods on the

production of crops for ultimate sale in export markets and in competition with estates, from which, indeed, smallholders originally derived much of their knowledge of production. The expansion of smallholder cash-crop production in Malaysia in the present century has been no less remarkable than that of estate enterprise; but largely because of the inaccessibility of many smallholdings, the formidable linguistic barriers in communicating with smallholders and their frequent deep suspicions of government, knowledge of smallholder production is still very limited. It is thus doubly unfortunate that the 1960 Census of Agriculture in the Federation of Malaya threw so little light on smallholder activities, but through the work of the Smallholders Advisory Service of the Rubber Research Institute, and the State Rubber Replanting Boards, a clearer picture of smallholder production is gradually being acquired.

Smallholder cash-crop production is in effect virtually synonymous with smallholder rubber, and as with Indonesia, the area under rubber smallholdings has long been under-estimated; in 1960 rubber smallholdings were estimated at some 1·5 million acres or about 45 per cent of the total area under crops, when the actual area planted to smallholder rubber was almost 1·9 million acres.[34] In 1961, probably about 90 per cent of the estimated 300,000 acres planted with rubber in Sarawak was on smallholdings, and 55–60 per cent of the estimated 173,000 acres under rubber in Sabah. Since that time the smallholder rubber area in Malaysia has grown steadily by about 3 per cent per annum through the sub-division of estates, through 'fringe alienation' and state group settlement schemes, but primarily through the large new block settlement schemes of the FLDA, and by 1966 it appeared likely to reach an area of 2·5 million acres in West Malaysia. This increase more than offset the reduction in the estate acreage, so that between 1960 and 1965 the total area planted to rubber increased from 3·9 million acres to 4·3 million (*Table 6-6*). There is little doubt that were it not for the restrictionist land-alienation policies of the States the smallholder area would have grown even faster.

In its marked lack of seasonal labour inputs, an ability to grow on a wide variety of soils, tolerance of abuse and neglect, simple processing requirements and production of a year-round income, rubber comes close to being the ideal smallholder crop. Smallholdings, however, are far from homogeneous, and the tendency of many writers to generalize on the basis of experience of one class of smallholding has been extremely misleading.[35] Though historically all holdings

---

[34] *Ooi Jin Bee*, op. cit., *p. 189;* Rubber Statistics Handbook, 1964, *Department of Statistics, Kuala Lumpur.*

[35] *See, for example, the description of a rubber smallholding in Ooi Jin Bee, op. cit., p. 218, which is entirely inapplicable to Chinese smallholdings. P. T. Bauer in* The Rubber Industry: A Study in Monopoly and Competition, *Longmans, London, 1948, also fails to distinguish between types of smallholders; though the work is largely a declamation of the virtues of the smallholder, the author's ignorance of many aspects of smallholder production greatly detracts from his conclusions.*

planted with rubber of less than 100 acres have been regarded as smallholdings, a much clearer picture of the complex pattern of production is obtained by regarding all holdings of less than 25 acres as 'peasant' holdings, and those between 25 and 100 acres as 'medium holdings'. According to Jackson, in 1952 (the last year for which figures of a racial break-down of the smallholder area are available) over 80 per cent of the total smallholding acreage consisted of holdings of less than 25 acres of rubber, and the average size of holdings in this category was only 3·4 acres. Of the rubber acreage on peasant holdings 56 per cent was owned by Malays, whose holdings had the smallest average size of any racial group (3·13 acres), and 36 per cent was Chinese-owned, the average size of Chinese peasant holdings being 5·2 acres. The situation with medium-sized holdings was very different; though less than 10 per cent of the total rubber smallholding acreage, almost 60 per cent of these holdings were Chinese-owned, with an average size of 42 acres. Indians owned 15 per cent of the medium-holding acreage and Malays a mere 5 per cent; the average Malay medium holding was only 28 acres. Jackson concludes that figures of the racial distribution of smallholders are therefore not likely to be very significant; using the more practical test of the proportion of the total smallholding rubber acreage owned by each ethnic group, 47 per cent was Malay-owned, 41 per cent was Chinese-owned and nearly 8 per cent was Indian-owned.[36]

These figures clearly indicate that the Chinese share of the smallholder rubber area is far larger than has been supposed, and strongly suggests that in terms of output the Chinese contribution is the largest of the three main ethnic groups, probably by a substantial margin. For not only are Chinese smallholdings in general worked more intensively than Malay ones, but they are of larger average size and therefore tend to have a larger proportion of replanted high-yielding material. This disparity in productivity must inevitably increase with the passage of time, and the fact that replanting schemes have most benefited Chinese smallholders is not yet widely appreciated.

On the basis of operation and geographical distribution, at least four major classes of rubber smallholdings are distinguishable:

(a) *Malay smallholdings*, in which rubber production is an integrated part of a peasant economy involving padi, fruit and coconut cultivation and fishing. Such smallholdings are very numerous in areas of traditional Malay settlement such as the valleys of Negri Sembilan, the Kelantan delta, the Batu Pahat district of Johor and much of Kedah and Pahang, but they also occur in Perak, Selangor and Melaka, particularly in Malay Reservations. Such holdings tend to be of low productivity with a large proportion of over-aged trees; there is often a high incidence of divided and multiple ownership, absentee ownership, and of owners who let out

[36] *J. C. Jackson, in Wang Gungwu (ed.), op. cit., pp. 247–52.*

Settlers' houses and newly cleared land at the FLDA Kampong New
Zealand scheme, Pahang, West Malaysia.

their holdings to tenants.[37] Output is almost entirely disposed of in the
form of unsmoked sheet.

(b) *Chinese smallholdings* in areas of past or present tin-mining, or in the
vicinity of major urban centres; holdings of this type are common in
Penang and Province Wellesley (now part of Penang state), in many
parts of Perak and Selangor, in Melaka and in south Johor, all areas of
long-standing Chinese settlement. Most of these smallholdings are far
from forming part of a peasant economy;[38] they are operated as part of a
complex system of family activities involving many aspects of national

[37] *In a Malay Reservation in Selangor, Fisk found that only 5 per cent of the holdings
were operated by the registered owner, but nearly 80 per cent were worked on a tenancy
or share-cropping basis; only 37 per cent of the Malay-owned farms were operated by
Malays as against over 50 per cent which were rented to Chinese. 'Tenancy' was thus a
major factor in poverty, but why owners should prefer to rent out their holdings rather
than work them themselves is not explained. In fact, very few Malay owners will work
a neglected and over-aged lot, or replant it, so long as there is a tenant prepared to pay
rent. See E. K. Fisk,* Studies in the Rural Economy of South-East Asia, *University of
London Press, Singapore, 1964, pp. 50–63.*

[38] *See D. W. Fryer and James C. Jackson, 'Peasant producers or urban planters?', Pacific
Viewpoint, vol. 7, 1966, pp. 198–228, for an analysis of some Chinese smallholdings in
Selangor and the Group Processing Centres serving them.*

economic life, a situation that is rendered possible by the fact that most smallholding families live in towns or cities, or in the large New Villages created during the Emergency. The return from the holding may account for a surprisingly low proportion of total family income, which is often augmented by the contributions from male members engaged in tin-mining or urban occupations, and from unmarried females employed as contract workers on neighbouring estates. The multiplicity of sources of income facilitates replanting, and the holding is tapped on every day that it is possible; moreover, so long as there is no other more profitable employment for some unoccupied member of the family, it is tapped regardless of the going rubber price. A much higher proportion of the output of Chinese smallholders is marketed as smoked sheet, particu-larly in Selangor, where group processing centres handle much of Chinese smallholder production.

(c) *Smallholdings on subdivided estates* Between 1951 and 1960 nearly 200,000 acres of former estate rubber-land was divided up for small-holdings, almost invariably into operating units of less than 10 acres in size in order to qualify for the maximum replanting grant. While sub-division has been widespread in the western states of West Malaysia, attaining its greatest magnitudes in Perak and Johor, it is not easy to discern any particular geographic pattern. The estates involved have been those in the smaller size categories, and often consisted of those neglected or damaged during the occupation and the Emergency, or which for one reason or another were too difficult or too expensive to replant. Operating units on subdivided estates have been mostly sold on credit to town dwellers, and speculators or rubber dealers, and seldom to the members of the former estate tapping force, some of whom have continued in employment as hired tappers, under generally much poorer working conditions. Whether the break-up of estates has resulted in economic or social loss is not entirely clear, but in contrast to the ex-perience of estate subdivision in most other parts of the inter-tropical world, in Malaysia no serious decline of output seems so far to have followed.

(d) *Smallholders of block planting schemes*, such as those of the FLDA or of individual states. Since its establishment in 1956 the FLDA has be-come the principal organization engaged in block planting, and by 1968 had initiated some seventy-four schemes, about one-third of which had been completed, and which involved a total area of some 244,000 acres. A marked feature of later schemes has been an increased attention to oil palm cultivation in units of progressively greater size. Land for FLDA schemes is provided by the States, and in theory, applicants of any race or from any part of the country are eligible for selection providing they meet the authority's requirements regarding landlessness, agricultural experience and number of dependants. Once a scheme is approved, the land is cleared and planted to rubber in a series of phased operations usually undertaken by contractors. Settlers are then moved in and are allocated a holding of 10 to 12 acres, comprising six to eight acres planted to rubber, which they then have to maintain, two acres of *dusun* (orchard) and a quarter-acre house plot which the settlers have to plant themselves.

These smallholdings are designed to be large enough to provide sufficient employment for the settler's family and to yield an income from which he can repay to the authority over fifteen years the developmental costs of establishing his holding.[39] The schemes have proved very expensive, largely because of high overheads, the heavy charges made by contractors, and the maintenance grants which are paid to settlers over the first two years until their crops start to produce an income; indeed, at about M\$ 3,000 per acre, the capital costs easily exceed those of establishing estates. In practice FLDA schemes have been managed exactly as estates, and it is possible that when the rubber-land comes into bearing some kind of central processing may be undertaken, as is also intended for some State schemes. Though located in every state of West Malaysia and in Sarawak and Sabah, FLDA schemes are most numerous in Johor and Negri Sembilan, though in future Pahang will be the major focus of attention.

Between 1961 and 1965 the FLDA hoped to initiate twelve new schemes a year, involving 48,000 acres annually; but shortage of staff and the high prices charged by contractors for clearing and planting, to say nothing of the mutual jealousies and suspicions of the States that supplied the land, prevented this target from being reached, and the authority was able to do no better than an annual average of about 25,000 acres. The First Malaysia Plan anticipates a total of 141,000 acres of new development during the period 1966–70, of which 103,000 will be opened to rubber and 38,000 to oil palm; these schemes, together with the completion of those outstanding, should involve the settlement of over 21,000 families to bring the total settled by the authority since its inception to nearly 34,500 families, involving some 207,000 people. In view of the rapid population increase and the impossibility of providing sufficient new employment opportunities in the non-agricultural sector, it is highly desirable that the FLDA target should be raised substantially in subsequent plans.

Replanting and processing As a result of the restrictions imposed on rubber planting by the interwar Stevenson Scheme (1922–28) and the International

---

[39] *The average value of a planting is estimated at some M\$ 2,000 per acre, and repayment to amount from M\$ 50 to M\$ 150 per month.*

Rubber Agreement (1934–41), the age composition of trees was very unfavourable at the end of the Japanese occupation. The yield per tapped acre on smallholdings was only 300 lb, as against 450 lb on estates when the first government-
assisted smallholder replanting scheme was launched in 1952.[40] Since this date a
determined attack has been made to replace the large stock of elderly unselected
trees on smallholdings by modern high-yielding material, through the payment
of subsidies which cover a large part of the costs of replanting, though the smallholder is expected to make some contribution himself. Smallholder replanting has
been largely financed through the allocations to Fund B from the cess levied on
all rubber exported; but unlike estates, which can claim that all replanting has
been self-financed by the industry, smallholder replanting has received additional
resources from the government through a number of channels. Initially M$ 400
per acre, replanting grants were progressively raised to M$ 750, and M$ 800
per acre for holdings of 5 acres or less by 1962, a sum which is calculated to cover
some two-thirds of the costs of replanting. Grants are paid in seven instalments,
the first being paid only when the smallholder has cleared and prepared his land
to the satisfaction of the State Replanting Board; a high standard of maintenance
is required throughout, and in particular the eradication of *lalang* (*Imperata*
species). Planting material and fertilizers are debited against the grant; the former
is now largely in the form of budwood, which eases the pressure on scarce supplies
of high-yielding material and is supplied from the Replanting Board's own
nurseries.

The initial replanting target in 1952 was to replace about one-third of the
existing smallholder area by 1959, but in the event only some 315,000 acres, or
two-thirds of the target, was actually replanted. Since 1960 performance has
improved, and in 1963 the area replanted rose to 53,400 acres, the highest recorded
in any year since assisted replanting began. However, after more than a dozen years
of intense effort, and including the contribution from new planting, only about
55 per cent of the total smallholder area in West Malaysia was estimated to be
under high-yielding material at the end of 1965, though this figure should be
raised to 65 per cent by 1970.[41] In Sarawak only 30 per cent of the smallholder
rubber area is believed to be planted with high-yielding material.

Several factors have operated strongly against the achievement of a high
rate of replanting. Targets were arbitrary; but ignorance and suspicion on the
part of smallholders, administrative delays and difficulties over the supply of
fertilizers and planting material, multiple ownership and lack of a clear title, and
the existence of holdings on slopes too steep to come within the scope of official
schemes, have all contributed. But the major disincentive to replanting has clearly

---

[40] *Wang Gungwu (ed.), op. cit., p. 254. The ban on new planting of rubber was not lifted
    until 1947.*
[41] First Malaysia Plan, *pp. 99, 111. As a result of the replanting quota introduced in 1967,
    however, this target may not be achieved.*

Chinese group processing centre in Selangor, West Malaysia. This centre is designed so that finished sheet from the smokehouse (at the rear) can be moved straight into an adjacent storeroom to await transport to Kuala Lumpur. Old rubber-wood fires the smokehouse furnace.

Smallholders processing rubber at a group processing centre. The coagulum is turned out on a steel plate, flattened roughly with the feet, and after passing through the smooth and ribbed mangles the resulting sheet is ready for smoking. The smallholder is late in getting back from his holding; at the busiest period (mid-day) his bicycle would not be permitted to clutter the floor. Note the acid bottle and measuring spoon.

been the loss of income over the period in which the replanted holding takes to come to maturity. Those with very small holdings cannot afford to forgo income over the five- to seven-year gestation period, particularly where the holding makes a very large contribution to the total family income. In practice, regional performance in replanting has largely been an index of the Chinese-owned share of the total area of all smallholdings; between 1953 and 1961 Chinese smallholders replanted nearly two-thirds of the total area replanted by smallholders.[42] For not only is the average size of Chinese smallholdings much larger than their Malay counterparts, thus making it easier to replant without serious loss of income, but many Chinese smallholder families have additional sources of income not generally enjoyed by Malays. Melaka, where (as noted earlier) the Chinese have long held important agricultural interests, has been the only State consistently to have exceeded its annual replanting quota, and has been especially successful in organizing block replanting of contiguous holdings, an operation offering substantial economies. In 1967, however, the government announced its intention of establishing a replanting quota of some 45,000 acres annually, a decision that would delay the complete replacement of the smallholder area by modern material by a decade, and began to advise smallholders wherever possible to consider diversification into other crops.

Nevertheless, despite the fact that replanting grants do nothing to compensate for the loss of income from an established holding, the age and material composition of rubber even on 'peasant'-sized holdings has materially improved. To some extent the problem of the very small-sized holding has been eased by so-called 'fringe alienation' schemes administered by the States; these provide new land near existing villages to permit farmers to enlarge their holdings, and some 116,000 acres was so distributed between 1961 and 1963. Such schemes have involved Malay farmers almost exclusively and have proved very disappointing in relation to the use actually made of the additional land. The difficulties experienced by Chinese in obtaining land has encouraged much illegal squatting, and in West Malaysia alone the total area so affected is undoubtedly very large, perhaps not greatly inferior to that involved in official block planting schemes.

Some three-quarters of all smallholder rubber is disposed of as unsmoked sheet to local dealers, and virtually all of that produced by Malay smallholders apart from the very small contribution made by the latter to new government central processing centres. The processing of latex into unsmoked sheet is a very simple operation in Malay kampongs, usually performed in a shed or shelter near the smallholder's house. Selling unsmoked sheet always involves smallholders in some loss, as the dealer has to estimate the dry rubber content and thus inevitably makes an allowance in his favour. By arranging for his rubber to be smoked the smallholder avoids this loss and also gets a better price; Chinese smallholders thus endeavour to market their rubber as smoked sheet wherever

[42] *Wang Gungwu (ed.)*, op. cit., *p. 260*.

possible. In Selangor particularly, Chinese smallholder rubber is processed in Group Processing Centres, in which a smokehouse operator provides a 'factory shed' and simple equipment for smallholders to process their rubber, leaving it with him for smoking. The smallholders retain ownership of their sheet, though in practice many sell through the smokehouse operator who, if not a dealer himself, almost invariably possesses a relative or close acquaintance who is, and they pay a smoking charge to the operator. Group processing centres of this kind involve a relatively small capital investment which is speedily recouped. They have very low overheads and are ideally suited to Chinese social structure; with their aid, smallholders can easily produce RSS 2, or even RSS 1 if they are prepared to put in the extra time in processing. The centres are usually located either in towns, or in New Villages, so that they are close to the smallholder's place of residence.

The obvious advantages of such centres have led to attempts to popularize their use among Malay smallholders, sometimes as cooperative ventures, but Malay participation has so far been very meagre and operation of a Group Processing Centre is much less suited to Malay social and family life. To avoid losses of income among Malay producers through the sale of unsmoked sheet, and to assist smallholder participation in the new methods of processing and packing being currently pursued on estates, the government has established a number of large central processing centres, some capable of producing upwards of a ton of RSS 1 a day. The centres so far established, mainly in Johor, Negri Sembilan and Selangor, have incurred heavy losses, largely because their overheads are very high. Such stations offer smallholders a chance to participate in the new processing technology, but so far the stations operate far below capacity as the prices they offer for latex are lower than those paid by dealers. Thus they have exercised minimal appeal to Chinese smallholders interested in maximizing income, who in any case tend to regard them as yet another subsidy by the government to the Malays.

Other smallholder cash crops Other cash crops produced by smallholders include coconuts, coffee, pineapples and pepper, but only coconuts, which are a traditional crop of Malay agriculture, are of more than minor significance. Around the turn of the century, the demand for coconut oil from the expanding margarine industry resulted in the establishment of many European estates along the west coast of Malaya, but the greater profitability of rubber led to an abandonment of European interest, except on the heavy clays and peaty soils to which rubber was not well suited. The way was thus left open for smallholders to profit from the growing demand for vegetable oils, and by 1940 the planted area exceeded 600,000 acres. Since then there has been some decline, largely through failure to replace losses through damage and neglect during the occupation; and mainly because of the increasingly unfavourable age-composition of trees, copra production between 1960 and 1965 fell by nearly 25 per cent. In contrast to the estates, which are virtually restricted to the Bagan Datoh peninsula of Perak and to the adjacent Selangor coast south of the Bernam river, coconut smallholdings are widespread along the west coast, being particularly important along the west coast of Johor; they are also of major importance along the coasts of Trengganu and Kelantan, where rubber smallholdings are relatively uncommon.

The Malaysian smallholder coconut industry shares most of the short-comings found in that of Indonesia or of the Philippines. Though accounting for less than one-sixth of the total planted area, estates produce some 20–25 per cent of copra output (*Table 6-4*). In part this reflects the greater interest of small-holders in fresh nuts, but there is no question that the productivity of the average Malay smallholder is very low; few smallholders produce as much as 1,000 lb of copra per acre each year, whereas European estates now have to do better than 3,000 lb to avoid being replaced by oil palm. The smallholder combines coconut production with other activities, and labour input on mature holdings is largely limited to harvesting nuts; but over-frequent harvesting, often of unripe nuts, and the use of sun or smoke drying combine to make smallholder copra of poor quality. Smallholders have a large proportion of very elderly trees, but as tall coconuts do not reach maximum productivity until they are some 30 years old the incentive to replant is small, despite a replanting subsidy of M$ 500 an acre. The importance of the coconut industry to the Malay rural voter, however, is evidenced by the introduction in 1963 of a coconut rehabilitation and replanting scheme, with substantial financial resources. As improved varietal material is in very short supply, operations so far have been largely confined to drainage improvements and replanting with whatever material is locally at hand. It is unlikely that the present decline in smallholder output can be arrested for at least another decade, and in the absence of a large and flourishing estate sector able to finance research, major improvement in the efficiency of the industry appears likely to be even more protracted. Most of Malaysia's copra output is crushed in the country to supply the soap and cooking oil industries, and in some years Malaysia is a net importer of copra. With rising population and declining production this tendency appears likely to be confirmed in the future.

Food-producing agriculture

Malaya has been a food importer almost since it began to be incorporated in the world economy, and the question how far it should endeavour to be self-sufficient in its food requirements has been a contentious issue for many decades. The Great Depression first illustrated the dangers of an economy dependent on industrial crops proceeds for its food requirements, and these were underlined during the Japanese occupation when many urban dwellers experienced serious food shortages. In view of the pressure on world rice supplies and the uncertainty of future export earnings, Malaysia does well to insure itself against any future emergency. But the real purpose of the prewar efforts of the British administration and, *a fortiori*, those of independent Malaysia to achieve a greater degree of self-sufficiency, was to transfer income to the poorest section of the community, the rural Malays. But to non-Malays well aware that the costs of rice production in Malaysia have remained more than twice those of Thailand or Burma, the traditional rice suppliers, the large subsidy paid to the padi growers represents a significant addition to their costs of living. Moreover, the high domestic price of rice resulting from the government support programme inevitably encourages the smuggling of rice from Thailand, which on the east coast particularly has been difficult to check.

On the whole, the vigorous post-1957 policy of greater self-sufficiency in rice has not succeeded, nor has it achieved any marked redistribution of income in favour of the padi grower. It is true that rice production has increased at a creditable rate in comparison with Asia's generally miserable agricultural performance over the past decade, but in relation to the large additional resources deployed in improved drainage, irrigation, high-yielding seeds and fertilizers, to which must also be added the large expenditure in rural development, the results by 1966 could only be regarded as disappointing. Padi output in West Malaysia, which accounts

Table 6-8 *West Malaysia: area, production and yield of padi, 1965–66*

	Thousand acres		Yield
	Wet padi	Dry padi	Gantangs per acre*
Perlis	48	1	520
Kedah	279	5	532
Penang and Province Wellesley	36		432
Perak	106	7	342
Kelantan	117	14	229
Trengganu	44	12	237
Pahang	33	4	283
Selangor	47		538
Melaka	20		374
Johor	9	1	413
West Malaysia	**853**	**45**	**403**

* One gantang = 17 lb approx.

Source: *Monthly Statistical Bulletin of West Malaysia*

for more than 80 per cent of Malaysia's total output, increased from 830,000 tons in 1960–61 to 899,000 tons in 1965–66 (*Table 6-4*), an average increase of some 2·3 per cent per annum, but of this nearly 2 per cent represented the increase in the harvested area, which in the 1965–66 season amounted to some 850,000 acres.[43] But both the area harvested and the yields have fluctuated in a capricious manner, and in the 1963–64 season rice production actually declined. With increasing population there has been no significant decline in the volume of rice imports, which in 1966 amounted to over 200,000 tons, but in 1964 imports exceeded 400,000 tons, the highest recorded since the early postwar years. While some fluctuations in output can be attributed to weather conditions, the basic inability of government to get to grips with the defective agrarian organization in the padi areas was patently obvious.

While padi is grown in all states of West Malaysia some 70 per cent of the total production originates in the coastal plain of the northeast extending from the Krian district of Perak to Perlis, and in the Kelantan delta (*Table 6-8* and *Figure 6-3*). The greater seasonality of the northeast and northwest offers climatic conditions which, though far from optimum, are better suited to padi than is the more uniform regime of the rest of the peninsula, and the increase in the padi area has been largely achieved through expansion in these northern areas, which has more than offset the decline in the planted area in the south. This decline would have been even more marked were it not for the large irrigation and colonization schemes of Sungei Manik in Lower Perak near Telok Anson, and Tanjong Karang on the Selangor coast south of the Bernam river, which commenced in the early Thirties and continued fitfully over the succeeding three decades and can be regarded as the precursors of the modern F L D A schemes.

These were not the first planned development schemes in Malaya as the Krian irrigation scheme was constructed between 1901 and 1906, but more than 70 per cent of the Krian rice area had in fact already been settled by private initiative before the scheme began. The Krian works provided greater security for the ricelands already occupied and enabled rice cultivation to be further extended; but part of the increased planted area could have been more profitably employed producing other crops, and even by 1910 there was evidence of large indebtedness among pioneer farmers to Chettyar moneylenders. Settlers continued to drift off to better-paid occupations in nearby rubber estates and in the towns, just as they did in the later Sungei Manik and Tanjong Karang schemes undertaken by the Department of Irrigation and Drainage, created in 1932; in both these schemes the laborious task of forest clearing fell, initially at least, on the settlers. Development schemes based on major drainage and irrigation works have all proved extremely expensive (even Krian ultimately cost seven times its original estimate), but the work has been pressed on since 1945 and the large area of west coast swamp forest awaiting reclamation suggested the possibility of self-sufficiency in padi in the not-distant future. But over half the 750,000 acres regarded as potential padi-land subsequently proved to consist of unsuitable acid peat encumbered

[43] *Additionally some 50,000 acres of low-yielding* padi bukit, *or dry rice, is planted annually, mostly in Kelantan and Trengganu.*

with stumps and submerged trunks, and in 1954 the International Bank Mission to Malaya considered that any approach to a high degree of self-sufficiency was impracticable. Just over a decade later the Bank came to revise its opinion, for in granting large loans for the prosecution of the Muda and Kemubu river schemes it made such a goal realizable for the first time.

This change in outlook arose through the postwar success of double-cropping in Province Wellesley, the best-farmed major padi area in Malaya, which suggested that if sufficient water could be made available double-cropping could eventually be extended over much of the Kedah plain. Increased double-cropping in conjunction with seeds of proved high fertilizer response offered a quicker and easier means to self-sufficiency than the slow and laborious clearing and drainage of virgin swamp to extend single-cropping. With the final completion of the Tanjong Karang scheme in 1965 only the Trans-Perak scheme in the Bruas-Sitiawan area of Perak, of the projects originally conceived before independence, remains uncompleted.

Malayan padi is typically long-term, occupying the land for six to seven months, and is of the *indica* strain. Though yields are greatly influenced by water availability, fertilizer application produces only a limited response, and in 1965 it was doubtful that as much as 15 per cent of the area sown to single-crop padi received any fertilizer or organic manure at all. Prewar attempts to cultivate off-season padi were a failure, but the introduction of *japonica* varieties from Taiwan during the Japanese occupation laid the foundations for success. The danger that the cultivation of an off-season crop could lead to reduced yields from the main season crop, the severe pest damage arising from indiscriminate japonica cropping, and the special water requirements necessary for successful double-cropping, constituted problems that have been resolved only slowly since 1945. Moreover, farmers had to be desirous of planting two crops, and not hindered from so doing by an inappropriate agrarian organization.

Province Wellesley, with its lighter soils, well-distributed rainfall and availability of water first from the Sungei Kulim and later from the Muda river pumping scheme to the north, has proved eminently suitable for double-cropping; some of its Chinese rice farmers, indeed, had long practised vegetable cropping during the off season. Through the development of shorter-term main crop varieties and the reduction of time spent in preparation through mechanization, a two-crop cultivation cycle was eventually brought within the compass of twelve months. Mechanization removed another major objection to double-cropping, the reduction of animal grazing; most fields are now prepared by contractors using tractors equipped with rotary-tiller equipment instead of ploughs, and the buffalo has become an uncommon sight in the Province. In 1962, Province Wellesley possessed some 51 per cent of the 21,000 acres of double-cropped rice in West Malaysia, though this proportion has since fallen as the practice has spread to other States; in the 1965–66 season a total of 89,500 acres were planted

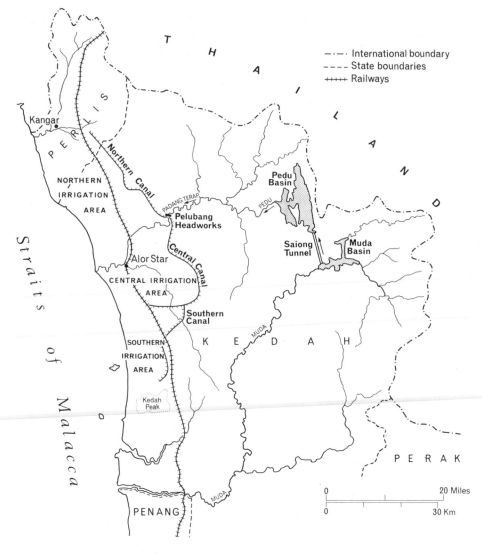

Fig. 6-6 The Muda river project, West Malaysia
Harnessing the water resources of the Muda and Padang Terap will permit the extension of double-cropping over a large part of the Kedah-Perlis plain.

to two rice crops, or about 10 per cent of West Malaysia's total padi area. On the east coast nearly 2,000 acres served by the Salor pumping scheme are double-cropped, and there is also a small double-cropped area near Kuala Trengganu. In this part of the country the yield from off-season padi is usually appreciably higher than that of the main season crop, whose flowering occurs during the cloudy east monsoon season.

While the works on the Bernam river completed in 1965 will make possible the extension of double-cropping to 50,000 acres in Tanjong Karang, the main impetus to extended double-cropping will come from the Muda river project, which will enable some 130,000 acres of rice-land in the Kedah-Perlis plain to be converted to double-cropping and add a further 131,000 acres of new land to the double-cropped area (*Figure 6-6*). The Muda scheme is expected to add some 270,000 tons a year to Malaysia's total padi production. The smaller Kemubu scheme will enable some 55,000 acres in the Kelantan delta to be converted from single- to double-cropping; both these northern schemes are intended to result in a trebling of the net cash income of the farmers affected, although this would still be substantially below what they could earn from rubber holdings of equivalent size planted to high-yielding material at 1966 prices. These benefits, however, will not be fully realized until after 1970, and in the meantime the use of new main crop varieties bred from *indica* and *japonica* crosses such as Malinja, Mahsuri and Ria should make a substantial contribution to production if the institutional obstacles to change can be overcome.

There is no doubt that these difficulties lie at the heart of the rice problem; the incentive to double-crop is non-existent if the farmer is no better off as a result of his enhanced output, and in 1966 not all the land capable of being double-cropped was sown to a second crop. When double-cropping first came to north-west Malaya landlords charged no rent for the second crop, but at present the rule is to lease such land for the whole year at just under twice the usual rent for a single crop; in Kelantan also, the usual practice is for the landlord to claim half a share of each crop. Similar difficulties retard the wider use of fertilizers, for the landlord appropriates an over-large share of the enhanced output. The realization that Malaya with its efficient export-orientated agriculture had a tenancy problem in its rice industry which in essence differed little from that of the more notorious areas of tenancy in Southeast Asia, came slowly; but, as in the latter, the knowledge appeared to have little effect on government ability to act. Although only about half of the 130,000 or so padi farms in West Malaysia are operated wholly or partly by tenants, the incidence of tenancy is far higher in the two major rice-bowls, the Kelantan delta and the Kedah plain; in the latter it has been estimated that some 80,000 rice farms are in the hands of only 2,000 families.[44] In the southern states, Melaka, Negri Sembilan and Selangor, on the other hand, some two-thirds of all padi farmers are owner-operators. Although rents are increasingly demanded in cash (and before cultivation occurs, thus increasing the burden on the tenant who is usually obliged to borrow), the great majority of all rentals are paid in rice, the national average rental being slightly under one-half of the crop.

[44] R. Ho (ed.), Guide to Tours, *Regional Conference of Southeast Asian Geographers, Kuala Lumpur, 1962 (mimeo.), p. 103.*

The problem of tenancy is compounded with an excessive fragmentation of holdings, a problem common in all agricultural areas affected by Islamic law. In the Krian district and in Kedah, the peasant (as in Thailand) was originally allowed to claim title to all the land he could bring into cultivation, and holdings averaged about seven acres, more than could be conveniently cultivated by one family. Holdings in Krian now average only 2·5 acres and those of Kedah a little more than 3·5 acres; but in Kelantan the average size of padi holding is only 2 acres and in Trengganu it is even less. As there is equal division among all heirs under Malay customary law, within a few generations large holdings are reduced to scattered fragments. Although physical fragmentation is usually avoided, the number of claims on a plot can reach staggering proportions; Gosling has reported a $\frac{1}{240}$th share of a plot measuring 0·075 acre in Trengganu, by no means a unique case.[45] With a multiplicity of claims on tiny holdings producing a crop that offers the poorest return of any major crop grown in the country, it is scarcely surprising that probably around three-quarters of all padi growers have chronic debt problems. While the fundamental cause of debt is low productivity, it is exacerbated by the common practice of contracting loans for non-agricultural purposes, and the principal motive for saving is to effect the *haj*, or Mecca pilgrimage. Perpetually short of cash, the farmer is often obliged to mortgage his share of the harvest in advance, and in Kedah and Perlis this has usually been effected through the credit system known as *padi kuncha*, which takes its name from the local standard unit of rice measurement.[46] This credit chain embraces banks, millers, dealers, middlemen, shopkeepers and padi farmers in descending order, and finances the cultivator while he waits for his crop to come to maturity; the earlier he pledges his kunchas of padi the lower the proportion of the final retail price he receives. Although the kuncha system has been declining since the end of the war with the growth of alternative sources of credit, it will certainly survive for many years to come.

In grappling with the problem of low productivity and rural indebtedness, the government, as with that of the colonial period, has hesitated at any major interference with the Malay way of life, which would be the inevitable price of effective reform; but if the Malays are powerless to change their social environment themselves, as appears to be the case, there is little choice. Nevertheless, government has connived at the circumvention of enacted reforms such as the recording in writing of all tenancy agreements, and has not seriously tried to prevent further co-ownership and subdivision. The National Land Code now prohibits subdivision of holdings smaller than one acre, and Kelantan has itself legislated against subdivision in the case of plots of less than one-quarter of an acre, but even this is not rigorously applied and in any case is rather like bolting the stable door after the horse has fled. The First Malaysia Plan 1966–70 promises action

[45] R. Ho (ed.), op. cit., p. 103.
[46] One kuncha *is approximately 840 lb, and in 1967 was worth about M$ 150.*

Limestone cliffs and sawahs, Kuala Kangsar, West Malaysia.

Cultivating ricefields in the traditional manner, Melaka, West Malaysia.

Preparing double-cropped rice-land by means of a tractor with attached rotary cultivator, Province Wellesley (Penang), West Malaysia.

to raise existing holdings to economic size through the Federal Land Consolidation and Rehabilitation Authority; but what constitutes an economic holding? Even if through better seeds, more fertilizer and improved water-control the present West Malaysian average padi yield can be raised from about 2,500 lb per acre to the 5,000 lb achieved in Tanjong Karang, what sort of livelihood does this offer to a farmer with five acres, a holding about twice the average size of those in major padi areas? In practice, the government plans are little more than an extension of methods already proved ineffective. The farmer will receive security of tenure and his weak financial position will be improved; the new Bank Bumiputra in conjunction with Apex cooperative banks will provide credit at reasonable interest rates, and cooperatives in conjunction with the new Federal Agricultural Marketing Agency will market the padi farmers' output and distribute fertilizers and tools. Nevertheless, the basic problems of rapid population growth and unsatisfactory agrarian structure in the padi areas are unlikely to be affected. Though the government must make some show of reform to satisfy its non-Malay supporters, in return for the transfers made to padi growers through a high internal price for rice (which necessarily involves government control of the rice import trade), nominal charges for irrigation water and large expenditure on community development, major changes in the complex of socio-economic institutions in the Malay community are very unlikely. Such a policy would give the militant Muslim opposition Pan Malayan Islamic Party (PMIP), which has controlled the Kelantan lower house since 1959, the opportunity to do the ruling

Alliance severe damage by appealing to the strong communal feelings of the Malay electorate of the padi areas. But the creation of more cooperatives to combat the monopolistic position of the local middleman is a policy that, though attractive in theory, is all too likely to be ineffective in practice. There is little evidence so far that cooperatives in Malaysia have been able to offer their members any better services than the middleman, and easier credit to farmers, fishermen, etc., could swiftly lead to a large increase in bad debts.

Padi production in East Malaysia has stagnated for some years at a level of about 120,000 tons, and the two territories are regularly large rice importers. Yields in Sabah, about 1,300 lb per acre, are not much more than half those of West Malaysia, and in Sarawak they fall below 1,000 lb per acre. This low productivity reflects the primitive methods of cultivation, particularly in Sarawak, where less than 40 per cent of the padi area consists of wet padi (*Table 6-5*), of which only about 2 per cent is irrigated. Some 70 per cent of Sabah's padi area consists of wet padi, but both territories face major problems in transforming the shifting hill-cultivators of dry rice and other swidden crops into sedentary commercialized cultivators.

One possibility of expanding the income of the rice cultivator appears worthy of further examination; this is the cultivation of sugar on rice-land. Malaysia is in fact the second largest sugar importer in Asia after Japan, and by virtue of its high per capita income has an unusually large sugar consumption. There is no real reason why more of the 220,000 tons or so of sugar imported annually should not be locally grown, and indeed it is often overlooked that in the former Province Wellesley a flourishing sugar industry grew up in the latter half of the nineteenth century, and was still profitable when its proprietors sold out to take advantage of the appreciation in land values created by the rubber boom. The prospects of establishing a sugar industry have been investigated by Australian experts provided under the Colombo Plan, but combining rice production with sugar cultivation in northern Malaya in the manner of the sugar industry of Java would appear to make good sense, for there was nothing technically inefficient about the Java sugar industry, even if the division of the proceeds between peasant and planter remained grossly inequitable. It should not be beyond the bounds of possibility under Malaysian conditions to devise an industrial organization with a greater degree of social justice, and this would seem to make better sense than committing large capital sums in opening up virgin areas for extensive sugar cultivation.

MINING AND MANUFACTURING

In its contribution to national product, manufacturing in Malaysia has lagged behind Thailand and the Philippines. But this is more than offset by a relatively much greater contribution from mining in Malaysia, and the share of secondary industry (mining, manufacturing and construction) in the respective national products of the three countries is not significantly different.

The importance of tin-mining in the creation of modern Malaya can scarcely be overstated. Technological change in the mining industry and the rapid growth of natural rubber production have greatly reduced the share of tin-mining in total employment, government revenue and in export earnings since the early years of this century; but the high tin prices realized after 1963, when it became clear that growing world demand was outstripping production, led to a sharp up-turn in the role of tin in the economy, a development that was all the more welcome as it coincided with a fall in rubber prices. Since 1965 tin exports have generated nearly a quarter of Malaysia's net export earnings, double the share of that achieved in the early postwar years. Under the stimulus of higher prices and the new floor and ceiling prices (£1,280 and £1,630 per ton) of the Third International Agree-ment, Malaysia's tin-mining industry in the late Sixties was ebullient; many marginal gravel-pump mines had been reactivated, the first completely new dredge since the end of the war was about to go into operation, the first Chinese pene-tration had been made into the dredging sector and there was every prospect of an early Japanese entry into the Malaysian smelting industry.

With more than 1,100 mines in operation, including sixty-five dredges, Malaysia's production of tin-in-concentrates in 1967 of over 72,000 tons represen-ted a record level for postwar production, and an early attainment of the all-time peak output of 1940–41 appeared very probable. Nevertheless, the more discern-ing leaders of the tin industry are well aware of the dangers of continued high prices in encouraging the use of substitute materials such as aluminium and plastics in tin's principal field of employment as a packaging material, to say nothing of the possibility of promoting larger releases from the United States strategic stockpile. The fact, moreover, that tin could easily be won from so many parts of Malaya has inevitably tended to discourage attention to other minerals, although iron and even gold are not infrequently found in association with tin-stone deposits. This shortcoming is now well on the way to being rectified, but the growth of manufacturing will necessitate, and in part also will be contingent upon, an increase in output of the less valuable non-metallic minerals such as moulding sands and materials for the glass, ceramics and allied chemical process industries, which so far have been almost entirely neglected.

The occurrence of tinstone deposits, methods of mining and the organization of the tin-mining industry were discussed in Chapter 3, and here attention will be confined to aspects of the industry that are particularly pertinent to Malaysia. Despite cyclical fluctuations reflecting the general world economic situation, Malaysia's tin output has remained remarkably constant over half a century, but as world output has trended steadily upwards, Malaysia's share has declined from about 50 per cent at the turn of the century to only 30 per cent on the eve of World War II; since 1955, however, the fall in production of both Indonesia and Bolivia has helped to raise Malaysia's share of world output to some 42 per cent in 1966. The rising price of tin metal after 1962 resulted in the re-opening of over 400 small gravel-pump mines whose working had previously been uneconomic, and the Chinese section of the industry, which usually accounts for about a third of Malaysia's output, has always been in the forefront of demands for higher prices.

The great majority of Malaya's 1,100 mines are, in fact, very small producers using a comparatively simple technology. The total area actually affected by mining leases is extremely small, only a little more than 400,000 acres (*Figure 6-4*), no more than a patchwork of pieces even in each major tinfield; although it is unlikely that any important new fields await discovery on land, existing fields probably contain many unworked tin-bearing areas.[47] Parts of the extensive areas of Malay Reservations, particularly those in the Kinta valley, are almost certainly stanniferous, and the government hopes that prospecting in these areas will promote Malay participation in the industry. The long neglect of offshore working, though carried on for decades off Phuket and Bangka, can only be explained by the ease and profitability of mining on land, but in the near future this deficiency should be remedied as leases granted off the Perak and Melaka coasts begin to be worked. Although the large electric dredge is gradually supplanting the old steam dredges[48] and the diesel engine has taken over operation of the gravel pump, technologies have changed little since the Twenties. But in the Sixties a new machine appeared, the small bucket-wheel excavator, and this was found very suitable for opencast mining in the Kuala Lumpur area.

So long as wet mining is permitted the dredge has a clear cost advantage, and the employment of the enormous bucket-wheel excavators used in some European brown-coal fields does not yet appear to be a practical proposition. But it may prove necessary at some future date to place further limitations on the despoliation inevitably caused by wet methods of tin-mining, which have been particularly severe with gravel-pumping; the discharge of tailings into streams (forbidden since 1925) and accelerated erosion resulting from forest removals for mining purposes have menaced downstream agriculture with expanding deposits of sand and silt, and have seriously increased liability to flooding. Land worked by gravel-pumping leaves a series of deep pits generally filled with water, whose restoration to agriculture is normally too costly; most dredging however takes place on uncultivated swamp-lands, and usually produces little apparent change in the landscape. Dredges are now compelled to discharge the finer particles and slimes above the coarser sandy tailings, but in the past the burying of the finer particles most conducive to regeneration of the vegetation under coarse sandy deposits has laid large areas to waste. The man-made deserts resulting from indiscriminate

[47] *The discovery of tin on a hillside near Ipoh, in September 1964, provoked a wild 'tin-rush' until the authorities moved in to determine ownership.*

[48] *The rubber replanting programme has produced large quantities of cheap fuel wood so that these are still very profitable; a wood-fired dredge originally built in 1914 was still operating at Rasa, Selangor, in 1966.*

past mining are virtually useless for agriculture, although with heavy manuring some limited areas of tailings have been converted into vegetable plots by Chinese market gardeners.

It has long been accepted policy that land containing workable minerals should not be pre-empted for other purposes, and in most mining areas, and particularly in the Kinta valley which accounts for some 55–60 per cent of Malaya's tin output, there is a steady loss of agricultural land to mining. New methods of treatment have made it possible to rework abandoned mining areas, and any forecast of the extent of Malaysia's tin reserves is an extremely hazardous exercise. But if the future of tin-mining in Malaya is to turn largely on the ability of improved separation techniques to make profitable the working of progressively lower grade *karang* (tin-bearing ground), some modifications of the traditional gravel-pump techniques, which allow much potentially recoverable tin to be lost in the tailings, seem necessary; certainly the Chinese *palong*, or sluice box, erected by rule of thumb without drawings of any kind, appears long overdue for replacement by the hydrocyclonic jig, but it is also essential that the system of taxation should encourage the highest rate of extraction possible, and this is not the case at present.[49]

For many years Malaysian production of primary tin metal exceeded domestic production of tin-in-concentrates, as its smelters also processed concentrates imported from Burma, Thailand and Indonesia. The export of concentrates from Thailand has been forbidden since the opening of the Phuket smelter in 1964, and those of Indonesia which were cut off during confrontation will again disappear when that country's new Bangka smelter comes into operation. Smelting is concentrated in Penang state, where the Georgetown plant of the Eastern Smelting Company, an organization largely owned by London holding companies, handles the output of mines controlled by the three large European managerial and secretarial agencies in the industry, and the smelter of the Straits Trading Company at Butterworth, a Chinese organization, serves most of the Chinese mines. In 1964 the Ishihara Sangyo Company, a pioneer of iron-mining in the peninsula, commenced work on a new smelter at Klang which should provide a stimulus to Chinese mining in the Kuala Lumpur area, where normally about a quarter of Malaysia's output originates.

Iron and bauxite Malaya has long been known to possess large deposits of high-grade haematite ores, but problems of accessibility and distance from markets precluded development until the interwar years, when through Japanese enterprise Malaya began to assume an increasing importance to Japan's iron and steel industry. Since 1950 the booming Japanese industry has provided a great stimulus to iron-mining, and output rose from 1·5 million tons in 1955 to a peak

---

[49] *This could be achieved by replacing the present excise, based on the weight of concentrate, by one based on tin content.*

of 7·3 million in 1963. The greater part of iron ore output originates from a handful of large mines in the eastern states, the largest of which is the Bukit Besi mine of Eastern Mining and Metals Limited in Trengganu, which produced over 3 million tons in the peak year. Another very large mine is being developed at Bukit Ibam in the Rompin District of Pahang, but the reported discoveries of extensive new ore bodies in the state have since proved disappointing.

In the eastern states iron-mining is exclusively a European enterprise, but the boom of the later Fifties led to a rapid growth of Chinese iron-mining in Kedah and Perak, and in particular in the Ipoh district. Chinese iron-mining is more capital-intensive than Chinese tin-mining, and the ore is extracted by open-cast methods using shovels or dragline excavators. Japanese capital has assisted the development of the largest Chinese mines, and some senior technical personnel for these enterprises has also been recruited from Japan. The future of Chinese iron-mining, however, does not look promising; the entire industry is virtually dependent on the Japanese market, and the development of the enormous ore resources of Western Australia, in which Japanese producers have a very large stake, will permit the survival of only the largest and most efficient of Malaysia's iron mines.

Bauxite deposits are widely distributed in both West and East Malaysia, but commercial exploitation is restricted to Johor, where four mines are in operation, and to Sarawak. Bauxite production began shortly before World War II, also through Japanese enterprise, and is still directed at the Japanese market although production is now entirely in Chinese hands. With the opening of two new mines in Johor in 1965, Malaysia's production in that year exceeded one million tons for the first time.

Manufacturing industries

Malaysia's preoccupation with export-oriented agricultural and commercial activities has tended to discourage the growth of manufacturing. The Federation of Malaya Census of Manufacturing of 1963 enumerated an industrial employment of some 160,000, or about 6 per cent of the work-force, but the total number engaged in manufacturing of some kind, including handicrafts and estate processing, was certainly very much larger—probably around 250,000. The First Malaysia Plan distinguished three categories of industrial activity: the processing of agricultural products in factories off estates, such as rubber-milling and latex preparations; industries producing consumer and intermediate goods from local or imported raw materials, most of which use relatively simple productive processes; and capital goods industries and consumer and intermediate goods industries requiring more capital-intensive production methods. Of these three categories, the second, which accounted for some 68 per cent of the total value added in manufacturing, was by far the most important, while processing off estates contributed 21 per cent, and capital-intensive industries 11 per cent.

Apart from processing off estates, the only major industrial groups to employ more than 5,000 full-time workers were food preparations, timber, rubber, metal working and mineral products, and printing and publishing. More than 80 per cent of all industrial establishments employed less than ten workers, but such establishments contributed only 14 per cent of the new manufacturing output, and Malaysia's industrial structure is relatively mature. A small number of large firms (that is, with more than 50 workers) accounted for over 40 per cent of the total employment in manufacturing, and in Singapore, where firms employing more than 100 workers accounted for a similar proportion of the manufacturing employment even before 1960, and for more than 60 per cent if the establishments of the Armed Forces and the Public Services were included,[49] this maturity is even more marked. The typical industrial unit is the small Chinese-owned family firm, but the larger the unit the more likely it is to be European-owned. The capital-intensive industries, which inevitably consist of large units, are solidly in European hands, although the post-1960 influx of Japanese capital in joint ventures with local interests has begun to modify this situation. But some large units, either Chinese or European-owned, exist in processing off estates and in consumer-goods industries; the latter, however, are mainly characterized by small units of low capitalization, so that entry is easy and the mortality rate high.

Despite this comparative maturity, the Rueff (IBRD) Mission of 1963 commented that manufacturing generated a smaller share of gross national product in Malaysia than it did in Thailand or the Philippines, where per capita product was only half as high. The First Malaysia Plan, however, estimated the contribution of manufacturing to GNP in 1965 as 11 per cent (*Table 6-3*), a significant increase on the 6 per cent of the Rueff Mission, and it postulated an increase in industrial output of 10 per cent annually, an expansion that was expected to generate some 36,000 new jobs. This, however, is only a small proportion of the total employment opportunities that must be created if the present unemployment rate is not to rise in the face of the anticipated increase in the number of new entrants on the labour market by 1970. Malaysia's high wage structure, which reflects the comparative affluence of the tin and rubber industries, discourages foreign industrial investment, and new foreign enterprises tend to be capital-intensive and economize in labour as far as possible.

Nevertheless, the political and economic stability of the country and the prospect of a Malaysian 'Common Market' of over ten million people of high purchasing power by Asian standards, have led several foreign manufacturers previously exporting finished products to Malaysia to settle behind its tariff barriers. These manufacturers have little alternative if they wish to retain their customary share of the market and to participate in its future growth, and issues for such companies floated on the Kuala Lumpur market have been heavily

[49] *J. J. Puthucheary*, Ownership and Control in the Malayan Economy, *Eastern Universities Press, Singapore, 1960, p. 101.*

over-subscribed. Such support, however, has not been extended to local concerns, most of which have tended to rely on the traditional Chinese sources of capital.

Malaya's industrial basis consists of its processing industries and a small heavy industrial base to support them, such as the railway workshops of Sentul (Kuala Lumpur), the dry docks and ship-repair facilities of Singapore, and the forges, foundries and machine shops of Ipoh and Kuala Lumpur which service the heavy equipment of the tin-mining industry. Since independence, the greatest industrial growth has been in import-substituting industries which have suffered from nearly all of the disadvantages common in developing countries. The small size of the market means limited production runs and high costs, problems that have been compounded by the separation of Malaysia and Singapore in 1965. At that date, firms with 'pioneer status' enjoying tax holidays and other concessions accounted for only 17 per cent of the total value of industrial output of Malaysia, and for only 8 per cent of the employment in manufacturing;[50] though growing rapidly, their overall impact had clearly not been very great. But the potential loss of the 40 per cent of the peninsula's purchasing power represented by Singapore gave pause to those foreign companies contemplating entry into local manufacture, and presented those that had already launched such enterprises with very great problems.

Fortunately, the physical quotas imposed on each other's manufacturers by Singapore and Malaysia immediately following separation were soon removed, but neither has been prepared to grant any tariff concession to the other, and even some old established concerns such as Ford, which began assembling vehicles at its Bukit Timah plant at Singapore in the Thirties, have encountered serious difficulties. Indeed, the motor vehicle industry appears likely to emerge as the major industrial casualty of separation; both governments are determined that as many vehicles as possible are locally assembled, but the divided market is too small to support all the manufacturers who had expressed interest in assembly to maintain a permanent footing in both countries, and Mercedes-Benz is in the unfortunate position of having begun a bus and truck plant in Singapore and an automobile plant in Malaysia. Yet both states realize that the additional employment opportunities likely to be created by local assembly are very small, and could well be off-set by the decline in employment in the distribution and repair of imported vehicles; their main hope is that local assembly will encourage the growth of component and accessory manufacture. The duplication of plants in Singapore and in Malaysia, neither of which appears likely to reap the fullest economies of scale, could well be further encouraged by national development plans.

Indeed, this trend has become apparent not only in vehicle assembly, and tyre and battery manufacture, but also in the location of oil refineries, flour mills,

[50] First Malaysia Plan, *p. 126.*

Malayawata Steel Mills, Prai, West Malaysia.

sugar refineries, cement works, electrical appliance and cable manufacturing plants, breweries, and tobacco and monosodium glutamate factories, all of which are considerably more capital-intensive than the simple consumer industries of the past; it has also been followed in the development of an iron and steel industry. This duplication of facilities can to some extent be justified, although it would have been better to supply southern Malaya from plants in Singapore, and northern Malaya from plants in the Klang valley, the Kinta valley or the Butterworth area. But there appears no justification whatsoever for two independent attempts to launch integrated iron and steel works. One such plant could in all probability eventually be supported in the peninsula; two certainly cannot be. On balance, the most logical site for a plant serving the whole peninsula would appear to be Singapore, which was the first to undertake such a development in its Jurong industrial estate. After separation Malaysia, with the assistance of Yawata of Japan, pressed on with its own plans for a steelworks at Prai, which it has equipped with a small charcoal-fired blast-furnace whose fuel supply consists of old rubber wood. Both the Jurong and Prai works are essentially finishing mills, producing simple steel products such as structural rods and bars, Jurong largely from scrap produced by shipbreaking, and Prai from Perak iron ore; both use the electric furnace method of steel-making, but in neither does a conventional blast-furnace appear likely in the foreseeable future, as this would produce far more pig than either economy is able to consume.

Malaysia's largest new industrial plants owe their location in large part to physical factors such as the existence of suitable raw materials, or to deep-water facilities in close proximity to major urban centres; this is the case with the sugar refinery and Malayawata steel plant at Prai, the Shell and Esso refineries at Port Dickson, the Lumut flour mill and the Tasek (Ipoh) cement works. But the great majority of new import-substituting industries are inevitably market-oriented. There was little room for new factories in the old industrial areas of Kuala Lumpur along the roads to Ipoh and Sungei Besi, which contained a multiplicity of Chinese-owned building material and engineering establishments, and most of the larger new plants have sought accommodation in the industrial estate of Petaling Jaya, Kuala Lumpur's satellite town. This estate has been Malaysia's most conspicuous industrial success, and to provide for the overflow a further estate is being created at nearby Batu Tiga, so that in the near future the whole of the Klang valley between Kuala Lumpur and Port Swettenham can scarcely avoid constituting one urban-industrial complex. Similar success has also attended the Tasek estate north of Ipoh, but whether the remaining industrial estates planned or under construction at Johor Bahru, Seremban, Kuantan, Taiping and Butterworth will be sought after is another matter; the first Johor Bahru estate, which began promisingly, could well find its prospects blighted by the separation.

The development of industrial estates, however, is an individual State responsibility, and there has been no overall control or clear policy on the part of the federal government. Without some more positive direction it appears all too likely that many estates will largely go untenanted. This lack of direction is in large part a reflection of Malaysia's belief that industrialization is largely a matter for the private sector, with some assistance from the state in the form of tariff and tax concessions through the granting of 'pioneer status'. Thus Malaysia still lacks the Industrial Development Authority recommended by the Rueff Mission and there is no organization responsible for overall long-term industrial planning. The Ministry of Commerce does possess an Industrial Development Division, and the Malaysian Industrial Development Finance Corporation provides financial assistance to manufacturers through loans or by participating in the equity; but both these bodies are fully occupied with individual factory projects and the work so ably performed by Singapore's Economic Development Board is neglected.

TRANSPORT

Malaysia's excellent transport and communications network goes far to explain the country's high level of development. Although the railway system and the earliest roads were largely created to serve the needs of the tin-mining industry, the motor vehicle fortuitously came to Malaysia just in time to profit by and greatly to facilitate the rubber boom, and many estates have depended entirely on road transport from their first beginnings. In the number of motor vehicles per 1,000 of population and in the great preponderance of automobiles over commercial vehicles in the total vehicle stock, Malaysia and Singapore show an economic maturity found nowhere else in Southeast Asia (*Table 4-5*, p. 162).

As in most countries at a high level of development, Malaysia's railway system has been stagnating for some time, and the 1,300 miles of metre-gauge track operative in 1966 represented a decline on the prewar figure. Although total rail traffic has increased since 1950, there has been a fall in the number of passenger-miles and freight ton-miles over the Malayan Railway since 1961, and at a time when total national traffic was increasing rapidly. The declining freight traffic was for a time concealed by increasing rail shipments of iron ore, and it is clear that the railway faces increasing competition even in bulk traffic; oil palm estates that had made extensive use of rail tank-cars suffered severely during the long 1962 rail strike, and have since greatly reduced their dependency on the system. Though long-distance passenger traffic has held up well, the railway has also lost heavily on short-haul passenger traffic, a decline which the newly acquired diesel railcars have appeared unable to arrest.

Many of the railway's difficulties can be ascribed to an indifferent management and poor labour relations, and this malaise has also affected other enterprises under the control of the Malayan Railway (a state body), notably the harbour of Port Swettenham. Delays and derailments have been frequent, and operating costs are kept high through over-staffing. But as railway employment is almost exclusively an Indian prerogative and the Railwaymen's Union of Malaya is second in importance in the organized labour movement to the National Union of Plantation Workers (also overwhelmingly Indian), retrenchment has been difficult. The political vociferousness of the Indian community endears it neither to Malays nor Chinese, and although the administration had to concede in 1965 that railway workers were government servants and thus entitled to all the privileges entailed by that status, it has been reluctant to meet all the railwaymen's demands and relations have remained poor. It appears obvious that the only real future for the railway system lies in its being operated as an independent corporation on strictly commercial lines; union resistance to this development is in effect another example of the tendency for organized labour in developing countries to perpetuate privilege. The 116-mile Sabah railway between Beaufort and Tenom clearly has no future, but it is to be retained in operation for the time being.

Road transport, on the other hand, has greatly benefited from the heavy outlay on road construction, which under the Second Federation of Malaya Five Year Plan, 1961–65, amounted to some 15 per cent of developmental expenditure. The distribution of roads is very uneven, both between East and West Malaysia, and between the west coast and east coast states of the latter. East Malaysia has only some 1,000 miles of road outside urban areas, but West Malaysia has some 2,800 miles of federal trunk highways, about 6,400 miles of State roads and

The old port along the Melaka river, West Malaysia.

The bridge at Marang, Trengganu, one of many built to replace former ferries on the east coast trunk road of West Malaysia.

10,500 miles of private estate roads. The system of federal financing for road construction enforces high standards of construction and maintenance; over 80 per cent of the roads outside urban areas are paved, and the excellence of the system strikes even a casual visitor. This 'over-construction' has not been to the liking of the International Bank, which rigorously insists that roads should only be built to standards adequate for the anticipated traffic.[51] But under Malaysian climatic conditions, roads have to be well built and well maintained to last, and the fate of recent Indonesian roads that have fallen to pieces within a few years of construction, is not lost in Malaysia.

Before World War II the major urban centres of Malaya's east coast were most easily reached by sea, but by 1966 through road communication was possible from the left bank of the Kelantan river opposite Kota Bharu to Kuantan and Kuala Lumpur, without the interruption of a single ferry, and by the early Seventies it will be possible to travel all the way along the east coast to Singapore. Access to the east coast has been improved through the Temerloh–Maran road constructed during the emergency, and by a link between Gemas and Temerloh. The lack of a road connection across the northern portion of the country will eventually be made good by the East-West Highway from Grik to Batu Melintang, which will give through—though still somewhat circuitous—connection between Butterworth and Kota Bharu; however, construction will not begin before 1975, and preliminary work was long held up by proposals for a more southerly route which would open much of interior Trengganu. East Malaysia has a major trunk road project paralleling the coast, the economic wisdom of which appears debatable, although strategic considerations are also undoubtedly involved. This will extend the Kuching-Simanggang road (completed in 1962) to Sibu by 1970, and will connect Miri with Bintulu; the 100-mile gap between the latter and Sibu will, however, remain.

Over the road system Chinese bus and truck operators provide services to every community of any size, and repeated attempts have been made by government to enlarge Malay participation in the profitable and rapidly expanding road-transport industry. Licences for taxi operation in rural areas are in theory reserved for Malay applicants; a share of the capital of urban bus companies has been reserved for Malays; and bus services to new FLDA schemes, or to communities provided with road access for the first time through the Rural Development Plan, are wherever possible allocated to Malay cooperatives. All of these measures, together with the zonal restrictions placed on the long-distance carriage of goods by road, have been largely abortive. Nearly three-quarters of all commercial vehicle licences are for the carriage of operators' own goods, but as these are freely granted, many operators of such licensed vehicles have illegally acted as

---

[51] *But one can never be sure what the magnitude of this will be. It has been aptly remarked that those uncompromising road builders of the past, the Romans, would never have obtained an International Bank loan for highway construction—they built far too well.*

common carriers. Despite increased vehicle taxes and duties on petroleum products, it is fairly clear that road services in Malaysia are underpriced, and that the charges made do not cover the full economic costs of road construction and maintenance.

Malaysia's growing international trade has made port improvements mandatory, and further port investment is contemplated in the First Malaysia Plan. Port Swettenham, however, the major project with four new ocean berths on the North Klang Straits, has proved a disappointment, particularly in respect of cargo discharged, which has remained obstinately at about the 1·5 million ton level of the early Sixties, and much cargo has been repeatedly over-carried to Singapore. A persistent shortage of lighters, used mainly for the loading of export cargoes, and recurrent labour troubles have also blighted the operation of the port, and on past experience, Singapore has little to fear from its new rival. Despite this poor showing, however, further ocean berths are to be provided in the First Malaysia Plan by 1970, a development that appears premature. Malaysia's principal port, Penang, was severely hit by the Indonesian confrontation, cargo loaded falling by half between 1961 and 1964, and there had been little recovery by 1968. Penang is eventually to lose its traditional free-port status, but local agitation for its retention is strong, and the central government has shown its suspicion of the island's dominantly Chinese population and Georgetown's left-leaning City Council by selecting Butterworth on the mainland as the site for major port improvements to serve the northern peninsula.

Singapore's suspicions that several of Malaysia's transport projects were ultimately intended to damage the economy of the island state have also been augmented by the completion of the new Subang international airport in the Klang valley some fifteen miles from Kuala Lumpur; two major airports within 250 miles of each other makes little sense to international air carriers operating modern jet aircraft. Singapore's view is an extreme one, for ultimately all of Malaysia's new transport facilities will be fully utilized by expanding locally-originating traffic. Nevertheless, it cannot be denied that the timing of some projects has been unwise, given present political relations between the two states.

SINGAPORE

Despite the separation agreement and the currency split, the diamond-shaped island of Singapore which comprises all but an infinitesimal fraction of the Republic's 225 square miles is still an integral part of an economy embracing the whole of the Malayan peninsula, and with its bustling population of nearly two millions is by far its principal urban focus. During the brief union from 1963 to 1965 Singapore was often fancifully called 'The New York of Malaysia', an epithet that recognises the role of the city's merchants and financiers in promoting many of the peninsula's agricultural, mining and commercial activities. It is

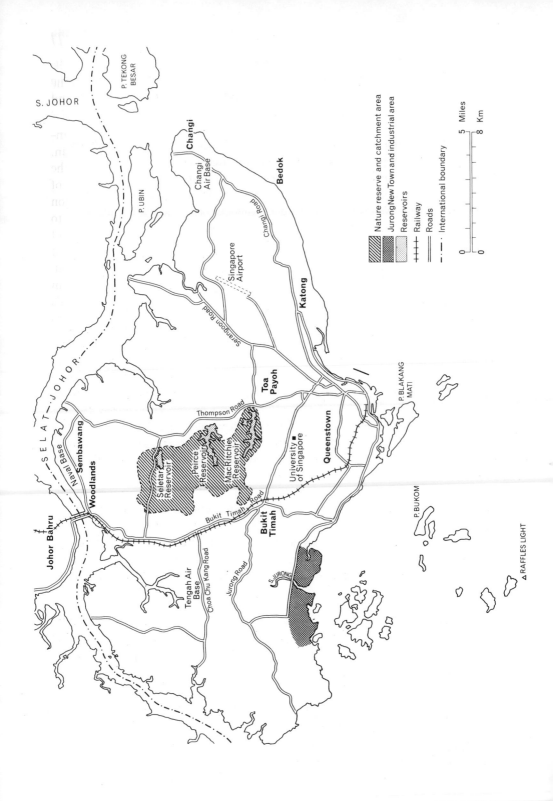

S. JOHOR

P. TEKONG BESAR

Changi

Bedok

Changi Air Base

P. UBIN

Changi Road

Katong

Singapore Airport

Serangoon Road

S E L A T   J O H O R

Toa Payoh

P. BLAKANG MATI

Thompson Road

Sembawang

Naval Base

Queenstown

Seletar Reservoir

Peirce Reservoir

MacRitchie Reservoir

University of Singapore

Woodlands

Bukit Timah

Bukit Timah Road

Johor Bahru

Tengah Air Base

Choa Chu Kang Road

Jurong Road

S. JURONG

P. BUKOM

△ RAFFLES LIGHT

Nature reserve and catchment area
Jurong New Town and industrial area
Reservoirs
Railway
Roads
International boundary

Miles
Km

5
8
0
0

not only the peninsula's largest port, handling about one-third of Malaysia's exports, but also the biggest in Southeast Asia and normally fifth largest in the world in terms of registered tonnage entering and clearing. Its entrepot trade still accounts for perhaps as much as 15 per cent of the island's GNP, and underlines Singapore's role as the major focus of the Nanyang Chinese, for much of this trade originates from the close family, clan and secret society connections binding the Singapore Chinese with their compatriots in neighbouring countries of Southeast Asia. The latter, it is true, are endeavouring as far as possible to reduce their dependence on Singapore by trading directly with the outside world, but Singapore is still confident that it can continue to use its connections to good advantage through virtuous fiscal and financial policies, which, it is anticipated, will make the new Singapore dollar a most desirable currency for the Nanyang Chinese and others to hold. It scarcely needs saying that Singapore is also the major focus for the Chinese of Malaysia, and as noted, has steadily gained population through net immigration from the mainland.

Singapore's two most urgent requirements are more land and more jobs; of these the latter is by far the more urgent, for new land can in fact be created at a price that gives a handsome return to the government, but to create an additional job at present requires an investment estimated at around S$ 20,000. Nevertheless, land use presents many problems in a congested and densely populated island. Under the pressure of a rapidly mounting population, all of Singapore island has become effectively urbanized. By 1965 land under rubber and coconuts, the dominant forms of agricultural land use in the past, had shrunk to a mere 20,000 acres, and the speedy disappearance of even this small area could confidently be foreseen. In the highly urbanized environment only specialized forms of agriculture such as intensive vegetable or poultry and pig production can survive; indeed, at the time of separation Singapore had built up a large export trade in eggs and poultry across the causeway. The release of land at present occupied by the British bases will provide some relief from the land shortage, but the economic consequences of an early evacuation of these facilities, the largest employers on the island, will be extremely serious. Further land, however, can be won through reclamation, as with the east coast project, and in connection with the Jurong Industrial Estate.

The most striking land use changes have resulted from the public housing programme, which is probably the best in Asia and, though involving fewer people than the Hong Kong settlements, is vastly better conceived in that in

---

opposite:

Fig. 6-7 Singapore island

Additionally to its large Jurong development, the government of Singapore plans further industrial facilities in the Naval base, whose conversion to commercial use will be assisted by using part of the £50 million aid pledged by Britain as compensation for the withdrawal of all British forces.

Singapore's low-cost housing, personal and family privacy is preserved. Singapore is justly proud of the accomplishments of its Housing and Development Board, which between 1960 and 1966 erected more than 50,000 housing units, and in the latter year provided accommodation for almost a quarter of the island's population. This development has involved the construction of complete 'new towns' such as Queenstown, Jurong and Toa Payoh, and the reconstruction of large parts of the old 'Chinatown' west of the Singapore river (*Figure 3-3*). Mounting population and the government's industrial programme also require a massive expansion of utilities. For many years Singapore has depended for its water supply on the storage facilities in the Pontian hills of south Johor, and the island's own reservoirs are for distribution purposes only. Supply is now proving inadequate, and in some years droughts have compelled periodic rationing through restricting the use of public standpipes, which are widespread throughout the island. Singapore has commenced a long-term water project on the Johor river which would provide an adequate supply for the next twenty years, but separation has made the dangers of relying on a possibly hostile source of supply area increasingly clear, and it is likely that some alternative will be considered, possibly a desalination plant, which could be made economic in connection with a large nuclear power station. Singapore already has the highest per capita consumption of electrical energy in Southeast Asia, and further large extensions to capacity have been planned for Pasir Panjang, Singapore's main generating station, and in a new 240,000 kW plant at Jurong, to bring total capacity to 704,000 kW by 1970.

The mainstays of Singapore's economy are the British bases and the entrepot trade, which together probably account for some 35 per cent of GNP. By 1971 the British will have withdrawn completely, and though additional economic aid from Britain and a defence agreement will soften the blow, a large net addition to unemployment is inevitable. Singapore's major entrepot trading partners are Malaysia and Indonesia. Malaysia can confidently be expected to continue to make use of Singapore as a major outlet for the produce of south Malaya. Indeed, Malaysia's ability to divert traffic, should it wish to do so, will be circumscribed through the decision of the major shipping lines serving the region to make Singapore the container port of the peninsula. The use of containers is revolutionizing world shipping, and once the handling equipment and terminal facilities are installed at Singapore there will be no room for a competitor. To take maximum advantage of this development, Singapore's efficient harbour authority has a major improvement and modernization project in hand, the East Lagoon scheme involving eight new ocean berths, for which the International Bank has provided a major loan.

The future of the Indonesian trade is more uncertain; this was severely reduced by the confrontation, but the termination of the conflict had brought no appreciable increase in the import of Indonesian rubber, copra and other 'Straits produce' by mid-1967, despite the offer of a loan by Singapore merchants to finance the import of essential consumer goods to Indonesia from Singapore. But it appears doubtful that with a difficult financial stabilization problem and an acute shortage of consumer and intermediate goods of all kinds, Indonesia can afford to by-pass the efficient emporium on its very doorstep. In all probability the entrepot trade will continue to grow slowly, but it must inevitably account for a diminishing share of national product.

The grain terminal, Jurong, Singapore.

It is thus largely to manufacturing industry that Singapore must look for economic salvation, and the outlook has become distinctly less favourable since separation. The new 15,000-acre urban-industrial complex of Jurong is particularly at hazard, for this was constructed to provide a location for new capital-intensive industries looking to the Malaysian market, which because of their large floor-space requirements could not be accommodated in Singapore's older industrial areas, or which needed special facilities, as was the case with the shipbreaking and iron and steel industries. It is difficult to see much future for consumer-goods industries having to pay high wage rates and serving only a tiny home market; exports are essential, and the government accordingly has offered very substantial tax concessions and other privileges to manufacturers exporting a high proportion of their output; Singapore feels that Africa, Latin America and

Eastern Europe are particularly promising markets for its manufactures. On the whole, industrial performance has been impressive; in 1965 industrial employment amounted to some 47,000 workers and value added in manufacturing to nearly S$ 320 million. The increase in manufacturing activities in fact offset the decline in employment resulting from confrontation with Indonesia, and in Singapore's first year of full independence was largely responsible for a resumption of an upward-trending per capita income, for in the last year of union the latter had in fact declined. Nevertheless, the rate of creation of new employment did not match the demand for jobs, and although the government admitted to an unemployment rate of some 10 per cent of the work-force, the real rate was almost certainly much higher. Singapore's best hopes of industrial success may well lie in its ability to hold a stable wage level while labour costs in Hong Kong, Japan, Taiwan and other Asian competitors trend slowly but inexorably upwards, and there is plenty of evidence that the government intends to administer this stern policy despite its professed socialist intentions. But only real cooperation with Malaysia can remove the shadows over Singapore's future.

Fig. 6-8   Jurong Industrial Estate: distribution of factories and numbers of employees, 1967

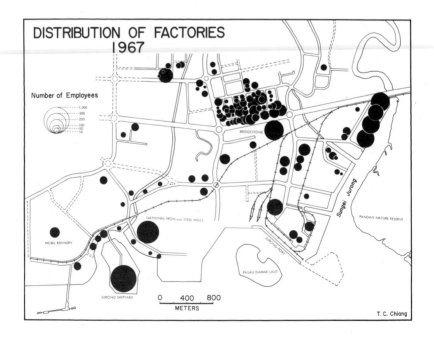

TRADE

The trade of Malaysia and Singapore is a particularly complex matter to unravel, and separation adds new political overtones to trade statistics. The two states are now each other's principal trading partner, but it has been the usual practice in the past to regard trade between West Malaysia and Singapore as internal trade, thus avoiding much double counting, and to use 'Pan-Malayan' figures in relations with the outside world. In addition to such statistics there are trade figures for West Malaysia and for Singapore which exclude trade between them, figures which include such trade, and finally there are separate statistics for Sabah and Sarawak.

Pan-Malaya has long had a very high per capita foreign trade even by world standards, and in most years the balance of trade has been very favourable. Since 1960, however, the declining price of rubber and increasing imports resulting from national development plans have produced a run of unfavourable years; nevertheless, both states have built up very impressive foreign reserves (estimated in 1966 at about £300 million for Malaysia and £100 million for Singapore), and unfavourable trade balances are unlikely to jeopardize their development plans for some time to come. Although Britain is Pan-Malaya's principal trading partner in total turnover, the United States is normally the most important export market, and the peninsula has long been a major dollar-earner for the sterling area. Japan, however, which takes virtually the entire Malaysian output of iron ore and bauxite, has become a close rival to the United States, and its accession to the premier position in the near future appears virtually assured. The peninsula is also unique in Southeast Asia in regularly having a large export trade to the EEC, though on a national basis Britain is usually the third best customer. Britain is still the largest supplier of Pan-Malaya's imports, although here also it is losing ground to the United States and Japan (*Table 6-10*).

Rubber has often accounted for 60 per cent or more of Malaysia's export earnings, but the decline in rubber prices in the Sixties, together with a sharp appreciation in the price of tin, which fortunately went far to maintain stability in Malaysia's export earnings, resulted in this proportion falling below 40 per cent in 1965. Traditionally, Malaya has exported more rubber than it produces, the balance being made up of Indonesian rubber sent to the peninsula for processing. These imports of Indonesian rubber were greatly reduced by the confrontation and appear unlikely to regain their former magnitude. Rubber and tin together, however, still produced more than 63 per cent of export income in 1965, but this is a substantially lower figure than that of a decade earlier, and is indicative of some success in broadening the export base. Iron ore and other minerals appear unlikely to account for a much larger proportion of export earnings in the future (unless petroleum should be discovered offshore in Sarawak), but the growing significance of oil palm products and timber has been noted.

Table 6-9   *Malaysia: composition of foreign trade, 1966 (million M $)*

	West Malaysia	East Malaysia	Total
GROSS EXPORTS			
Rubber	1,396	78	1,474
Tin metal and concentrates	792		792
Timber	99	368	467
Iron ore	136		136
Palm oil and kernels	127	2	129
Canned pineapple	44		44
Copra and coconut oil	27	11	38
Pepper			22
Bauxite	17		17
Total (including others)	**3,120**	**725**	**3,845**
IMPORTS			
Food, drink, tobacco	667	188	855
Inedible crude materials	129	2	131
Mineral fuels and lubricants	195	250*	445
Chemicals	225	25	250
Manufactures	671	134	805
Machinery and transport equipment	644	146	790
Total (including others)	**2,633**	**746**	**3,379**

* Includes imports from Brunei for Sarawak refinery

Source: *West Malaysia Quarterly Statistics of External Trade,* December 1966

Table 6-10   *Malaysia: direction of foreign trade, 1966 (million M $)*

	Exports to	Imports from
Singapore	948	390
United Kingdom	274	634
Other Commonwealth countries	311	712
USA	483	208
Japan	698	407
European Economic Community	396	307
USSR	248	5
Eastern Europe	75	8
Thailand	39	314
China	4	240
Total	**3,845**	**3,379**

Source: *West Malaysia Quarterly Statistics of External Trade,* December 1966

Table 6-11 *Singapore: direction of foreign trade, 1966 (million Singapore $)*

Exports to, f.o.b.		Imports from, c.i.f.	
West Malaysia	907·6	West Malaysia	943·5
Overseas countries	2,466·0	Overseas countries	3,122·1
Total	**3,373·6**	**Total**	**4,065·6**

Source: *Singapore Trade and Industry,* August 1967

BRUNEI

The Sultanate of Brunei, two enclaves in East Malaysia totalling some 2,200 square miles, is like the oil-sodden petty sheikdoms of the Middle East, an anachronism. Though the major focus of Islam in the former British Borneo Territories, it has refused to enter the Federation of Malaysia, an act that was a distinct setback to the new state. It has been an odd quirk of fate that has resulted in the shrunken remnant of a once great state becoming the fourth largest producer of petroleum in the British Commonwealth after Canada, Nigeria and Trinidad, and royalties and taxes from the 3·5 million tons of petroleum produced from the Seria fields in 1965 produced a revenue for the Brunei government of some M$130 million, equivalent to US $430 per head of Brunei's population of close on 100,000. Enjoying the doubtful luxury of no income tax, and indeed a very low level of taxation in general, the reluctance of Brunei to share this stream of wealth with the pragmatists of Kuala Lumpur is scarcely surprising.

Oil accounts for some 95 per cent of the value of Brunei's exports; its only other resource of any significance is some 27,000 acres of rubber. Oil was first discovered in British Borneo at Miri, Sarawak, in 1910, and this field still produces some 50,000 tons of crude annually; however, this is a trickle compared with the flow from the Seria field across the Brunei border, where after a prolonged search oil was discovered in 1929. At its peak in the Fifties, Seria produced more than six million tons annually, but output has since declined and the economic life of the field may not last to the end of the century. No major new terrestrial discoveries have been made, and the Shell companies are now concentrating exploratory drilling in offshore waters at the mouth of the Baram river, which forms the southern boundary of Brunei with Sarawak.[52] Crude from Seria is conveyed by pipeline to Lutong in Sarawak for export, where there is a small refinery which also handles Miri crude.

Since 1962, when a revolt by the left-oriented Party Ra'ayat was crushed only by the intervention of large British forces, Brunei has taken some further

[52] *New offshore production had in fact raised Brunei's total production to some six million tons by 1968.*

steps to adapt itself to the modern world, and expenditure on economic development and on social services has greatly increased. The regime, however, is still
authoritarian, and is ultimately dependent on foreign troops, for whose costs in
1966 it was still paying nothing. The postwar history of Southeast Asia scarcely
suggests any stability for such a state, and the future of Brunei clearly lies in
closer association with Malaysia, or with the units that at present make up its
eastern wing.

WHITHER MALAYA?

At the end of 1967 the Malayan peninsula, already suffering from the effects of a
sharp decline in its export prices, received a further blow through the devaluation
of sterling, which speedily led to events underlining the fragility of its apparent
social and political stability. Malaysia and Singapore both suffered losses in their
reserves through Britain's action, but these were in part recouped through the
shabby trick of devaluing the old Currency Commission notes and coins still
circulating in both countries alongside their new monetary units. Little of the
latter had in fact reached the hands of the public, and the devaluation of the old
units in the face of tacit promises by both governments to redeem such money at
par, sparked off a bloody riot in Penang which for a time threatened to degenerate
into open Chinese-Malay conflict. Scarcely had the situation been restored when
the British decision to accelerate the run-down of its defence installations in the
peninsula and to withdraw completely by 1971 produced profound dismay,
particularly in Singapore, where apart from the vital part they played in the local
economy, the British forces were Singapore's best guarantee against possible take-
over by either Indonesia or Malaysia. While the Singapore Prime Minister had
fancifully likened his country to the 'Israel of the East' in a potentially hostile
Malay world, the prospect of large defence expenditure in the immediate future
was not lightly to be contemplated.[53] However, Britain's willingness to train both
Singapore and Malaysian personnel in the operation of the equipment it will leave
behind (which will necessarily involve cooperation between the two states) and
pledges of additional development aid went some way to allay hostility at this
further let-down, and, somewhat unexpectedly, a defence agreement between the
two states began to appear, for the first time, a distinct possibility. As defence and
economic cooperation have been closely linked in both states' bargaining position
since separation, it is to be hoped that the new accord can be broadened into one
that will preserve the peninsula's economic unity and restrain polarization of
communal issues.

With dramatic suddenness, however, all that Malaysia had achieved in more
than a decade of independence appeared likely to disappear in the aftermath of

[53] *Singapore's determination to defend its independence, however, was demonstrated by
the introduction of compulsory military service for all young able-bodied males.*

five days of bloody communal rioting following the federal elections of May 1969, and although the disturbances were virtually confined to Kuala Lumpur, the alarming polarization of communal feeling in the country and the depths of mutual Malay and Chinese suspicion and mistrust cast a dark shadow over the future. The destruction of much Chinese property and the heavy toll of Chinese lives inevitably had repercussions in Singapore, where there were attacks on the Malay quarter of Geylang Serai, and further deterioration in the relations between the two states appears only too probable.

III STAGNATION

CHAPTER SEVEN

Indonesia

Indonesia is not only the largest and most populous of the states of Southeast Asia, but it also occupies a vital strategic position between the Indian and Pacific Oceans. These facts, and the steadily increasing expenditure on its armed forces, gave particular significance to the growing power of the Indonesian Communist Party (PKI), which, completely discredited after its abortive *coup* at Madiun in 1948, had become by 1960 the world's largest communist party outside the Eastern bloc itself. Since the second destruction of the PKI following the *Gestapu* plot of October 1965 and Indonesia's admission of its utter bankruptcy, the country's new leaders have endeavoured to suggest that strategic considerations should reinforce economic ones in prompting the West to provide aid on a scale sufficient to deter a second resurrection of the communist menace. The collapse of the Indonesian economy is not lightly to be contemplated apart from its domestic effects; until 1958 Indonesia was the world's largest producer of natural rubber and traditionally has been the second largest producer of tin; it is the second largest producer of copra after the Philippines and before World War II occupied the premier position. It is the only large Asian producer of petroleum east of the Persian Gulf, and was once, and could be again, a leading producer of palm oil, sugar, tea, coffee, kapok, quinine, pepper and spices. So wide is its range of products that during the Sukarno regime many prominent Indonesians declared that their country's endowment of natural resources was exceeded only by those of the United States and the USSR; but such exuberance revealed all too clearly a lack of understanding of the true nature of resources, and was largely a demonstration of allegiance to President Sukarno's doctrine of the 'continuing revolution' and all its symbolic and ideological trappings.

In reality, Indonesia's resources even on the most optimistic assessment appear only modest in relation to its large and rapidly expanding population. They are also very maldistributed, a factor which operates strongly against the maintenance of national cohesion. Given an efficient and dedicated administration, it would not be too difficult even in a relatively short period considerably to enlarge the stock of resources, but this Indonesia has never had. Whatever its potential, Indonesia is still a very poor country. Per capita product is probably a little above that of India, but in real terms product per head in 1960 was less than in 1939; it was possibly even less than in 1919. Throughout the lifetime of the Republic the economy has shown great instability, the rate of growth at times falling well below that of a population increase of about 2·7 per cent per annum; exports have stagnated and there have been frequent acute shortages of essential consumer goods through the disruption and at times the complete cessation of the import trade, and through the failure of domestic food production to expand rapidly enough. The fabric of Indonesian life has been rotted through continuous and, finally, runaway inflation. Between 1948 and the end of 1959 there was an eightfold increase in total money supply, but between 1959 and the end of 1966 money supply expanded more than 600 times and the value of the rupiah fell to less than that of the paper on which it was printed.[1] All efforts at eradicating the growing volume of corruption have proved abortive, partly because of the very low salaries paid to government officials, and partly through the complicity of Ministers and high officers in the armed forces.

Indonesia's economic ills have been patently obvious for so long that some Western observers have debated why the economy did not collapse long ago. Indonesians have shown a high degree of fortitude in coping with life under increasingly difficult conditions, but the country kept going through living off its fat in consuming capital, thus retreating more and more into a subsistence economy, and through foreign aid. After 1958 Indonesia began to receive very large external assistance from both the Western and communist worlds, and though far too much of this was for military purposes, it did provide a few more years of grace. But retribution for a decade of prodigality could not be indefinitely postponed, and the *Gestapu* revolt of September 30th, 1965, in which the PKI was deeply implicated, brought Indonesia to a supreme crisis. By 1966 reserves of foreign exchange were exhausted and, as anticipated export earnings were less than the service on a foreign debt estimated at almost US $3,000 million, Indonesia began to default on its commercial debt to foreign suppliers.

The immediate reasons for Indonesia's economic crisis were clear enough. The doctrine of the 'continuing revolution' had led to the allocation of almost half of the total budget expenditure to the grossly swollen armed forces, which, on paper at least, made Indonesia the most formidable military power in Southeast Asia. Repayments on the loans from Eastern bloc countries for the supply of

---

[1] *In August 1959, 500 and 1,000 rupiah notes were suddenly reduced to ten per cent of their face value, and the exchange rate for official transactions was lowered from 11·40 rupiah to the United States dollar to 45 rupiah. In December 1965 the new rupiah, equivalent to 1,000 old rupiah, was introduced, but by May of the same year the black market rate had fallen to 50 new rupiah to the United States dollar. Inflation reached its peak in 1966 when the increase in money supply amounted to 714 per cent, but the attempt to restrain the monetary increase in 1967 to some 10 per cent of that of 1966 was defeated by a year-end rice shortage.*

military equipment would constitute a heavy drain on future export earnings, and threatened Indonesia's negotiations for a rescheduling of its commercial debt and for further economic aid from the West, as the latter could make no concessions if these merely freed resources for meeting indebtedness to the communist world.[2] Yet despite the mortgaging of future exports, inflationary pressure was steadily pricing Indonesian exports out of the world market. The regional insurrections of 1957–58, the long struggle for *Irian Barat* (West New Guinea) and the confrontation of Malaysia all accelerated the depletion of foreign exchange reserves, while vast sums were committed to the construction of unproductive monuments in Djakarta, such as the Asian Games Stadium, the Sukarno Tower, the world's largest mosque and a great complex of buildings to accommodate *Conefos*, the conference of 'new emerging forces', intended by President Sukarno to rival the United Nations and establish his claim as the principal spokesman of the Third World.

But ultimately, Indonesia's economic chaos reflects deep-seated economic and cultural differences among the various peoples of the national territory, which have never possessed any real unity save that forged through opposition to Dutch rule. This division goes far to explain the government's long preoccupation with Irian Barat, which was virtually the only issue on which most Indonesians thought alike, and when that 'Indonesia irredenta' was effectively restored to the nation in 1963,[3] the creation of Malaysia fortuitously provided a new channel for diverting domestic discontent against a foreign enemy.

The most fundamental division in Indonesia is between Java, historically always the most populous island of Indonesia, and the Outer Islands, or Outer Provinces (*Table 7-1*). Java (including Madura) possesses some 65 per cent of

[2] *In a series of complicated negotiations between 1966 and 1968, Indonesia managed to reach accommodation with its creditors; the first payments under the rescheduled programme will be made to the West (including Japan) in 1972. The USSR and its satellites have agreed to a broadly similar arrangement, but there is scant prospect of any reimbursement to China in the foreseeable future.*

[3] *On the transfer of sovereignty to Indonesia in 1949 the Dutch retained control of West New Guinea, a decision that Indonesia was never prepared to accept. In many ways the territory proved an embarrassment to the Dutch, and preparations for eventual self rule were well advanced when after much sabre-rattling a half-baked Indonesian airborne invasion took place. The Netherlands, however, were persuaded by the Western powers to accept a transfer of the territory to Indonesia, after a brief interregnum under UN administration. Indonesia agreed that a plebiscite should be held in 1969, by which the indigenous inhabitants would decide their own future, but on assuming control of the administration in 1964 promptly declared that any such plebiscite would be quite unwarranted. The Suharto government, however, reaffirmed Indonesia's intention of honouring its obligations, and arrangements were made for conducting a plebiscite in mid-1969. Indonesia, however, refused to allow a 'one man—one vote' ballot, pleading that the primitive state of the population made such sophistication impossible, but in reality because it feared that a free and open vote would result in an embarrassing rejection of its occupancy, a fear that the open revolts in many parts of the country indicated was well grounded. Indonesian rule will be ensured by the approbation of a small and carefully selected council of headmen and regional representatives, and there is no question that this decision will be greeted with relief by the United Nations.*

Indonesia's population and, although earning only some 6 per cent of the country's export income, absorbs a very large share of total imports and development expenditure. To many peoples of the Outer Islands Java is a parasite, and the national revolution has appeared little more than the replacement of a Dutch exploitation by a Javanese one. In the early years of the Republic the Outer Islands, it is true, provided many key members in several administrations, but the political instability which has existed since the birth of the Republic meant

Table 7-1   *Population of Indonesia, Census 1961*

	millions
Greater Djakarta	2·91
West Java	17·61
Central Java	18·41
East Java	21·82
Jogjakarta	2·24
Java and Madura	**62·99**
Atjeh	1·63
North Sumatra	4·96
West Sumatra	2·32
Riau	1·23
Djambi	0·74
South Sumatra	4·85
Sumatra	**15·73**
West Kalimantan	1·58
Central Kalimantan	0·50
South Kalimantan	1·47
East Kalimantan	0·55
Kalimantan	**4·10**
North and Central Sulawesi	2·00
South Sulawesi	5·08
Sulawesi	**7·08**
Bali	1·78
West Nusa Tenggara	1·81
East Nusa Tenggara	1·97
Bali and Nusa Tenggara	**5·56**
Maluku	0·79
West Irian	0·76
Total	**97·01**

Source: Nugroho, *Indonesia in Facts and Figures,* Djakarta, 1967

that in practice much power rested with the senior officials of the public service, a large proportion of whom were drawn from the Javanese nobility of the old *Vorstenlanden* (Principalities). With the passage of time, the balance of power swung sharply to those politicians with the greatest appeal to the masses of over-crowded Java. Concerted opposition to Java in the *Daerah* (Outer Provinces) is, however, effectively limited by the latter's own deep-seated differences; both the Christian Minahasans of northern Sulawesi (Celebes) and the militantly Muslim Atjehnese of north Sumatra dislike the Javanese, but they have few other political or economic interests in common. Each major island, even Java itself, is divided by strong sectional or regional interests; thus central Sumatra received no support from the northern or southern portions of the island during its revolt against the central government in 1957–58.

In practice, however, disposal in the Provinces since the mid-Fifties has largely rested in the hands of the local military commanders, and the adoption of a policy in Djakarta is no guarantee that it will be implemented in the *Daerah*. Several peoples of the Outer Islands have an 'achievement society' in which personal initiative and the acquisitive spirit are much stronger than is the case with the peoples of Java, and perhaps the most commercially minded of the indigenous peoples of Indonesia are the Minangkabau, originally resident in the highlands around Lake Singkarak but now widely spread in central Sumatra. Moreover, as the armed forces offer by far the best openings for merit in Indonesia, the peoples of the Outer Islands have been heavily represented in the higher commands, and some regional army commanders have used regional export earnings for local developmental purposes, remitting only a small part to the Ministry of Finance in Djakarta; more, unfortunately, have diverted such pro-ceeds largely to their own pockets. In Java, the devout *Santri* Muslim groups have shown a much greater degree of economic initiative than have the *Abangan* Javanese, whose adherence to Islam is but a thin veneer on an animist and Hindu-influenced base.

The most economically active section of the population, however, is the three million or so Indonesian Chinese, the bane of many nationalists, who fear the *Orang Tiong Hoa* much more than the Europeans. Many restrictions have been placed on the economic activities of the Chinese, but so far all have proved unavailing. Since the *Gestapu* revolt, the attack on the Chinese has been intensi-fied; their shops and stores have been attacked and looted, and many Chinese have been injured or killed in riots, or in general massacres such as that per-petrated by the Dayaks in Kalimantan (Indonesian Borneo) early in 1968. In north Sumatra large numbers of Chinese were incarcerated in special camps for transportation back to China. The justification for these attacks has been the alleged support given by the Chinese community (and the Peking Embassy) to the P K I, and there is something in this charge; but the *Ampera* (*Amanah Perasaan Rakjat*, or 'message of the people's suffering') cabinet, formed in 1966 by General

Suharto, and its reshuffled successor, the 'development' cabinet of 1968, well knew that the difficult problem of economic recovery from the excesses of the Sukarno regime would be immensely more complicated if the country were to be denied the use of the business acumen and capital of its Chinese population, and though the cabinet certainly cannot openly protect the Chinese, it has done what it can to temper excesses of anti-Chinese sentiment.

THE LAND

The force of van Bemmelen's contention that the East Indian archipelago is the most intricate part of the earth's surface is evident even from a small-scale atlas map, for Indonesia's national territory of some 576,000 square miles[4] is distributed between more than 13,000 islands, spread over three million square miles of sea. Such a fragmentation of the national territory is only equalled by the neighbouring but more compact Philippine Republic, with which Indonesia has many close physical, cultural and economic similarities. However, the greater part of the land area is accounted for by a very few large islands; Kalimantan, Sumatra, Sulawesi and Java together make up almost 85 per cent of the national territory, and the addition of the next five largest islands, Halmahera, Seram (Ceram), Indonesian Timor, Flores and Sumbawa, raises this figure to 90 per cent.

The multiplicity of islands arranged in single or double festoons or arcs, indicates great structural complexity, which is also apparent from a number of other phenomena. Foremost among these is vulcanism, which is well developed along the inner arcs of the double festoons; Indonesia is the most strongly active volcanic region in the world, Java alone having 53 active volcanic centres, and the total for the whole country being almost 150.[5] Vulcanism, intense seismic activity and the pronounced negative gravity anomalies discovered south of the main Sunda arc extending from Sumatra to Tanimbar and recurving through the Ceram Sea and Molucca Passage, strongly suggested to the geologists of the Netherlands Indies a mountain system in process of formation. Their preoccupation with academic problems of orogenesis and continental growth had unfortunate economic consequences, as noted earlier.[6]

Indonesia is composed of parts of all four major structural units of Southeast Asia and the Southwest Pacific, the Sunda Shelf, the circum-Sunda Mountain System, the Sahul Shelf and the circum-Australia Mountain System. The Sunda Shelf, on which stands the great island of Borneo, extends east to the Straits of Macassar and south to the coasts of Sumatra and Java, and is the partially sub-

---

[4] *Excluding West New Guinea (estimated at 161,000 square miles), of the 13,667 islands of Indonesia, 7,623 are unnamed and 12,675 are uninhabited; Nugroho, Indonesia in Facts and Figures, Djakarta, 1967, (mimeo.) p. 4.*

[5] *R. W. van Bemmelen, The Geology of Indonesia, Government Printing Office, The Hague, 1949, vol. 1, p. 190.*

[6] *See pp. 100–101.*

merged extension of the Asian continent; the Riau (Rhio) and Lingga groups, Bangka, Belitung (Billiton) and the Karimundjawa islands indicate a former land connection between the Malayan peninsula and Java, parts of which may well have existed into the Christian era. In the east of the archipelago the similar Sahul Shelf, which includes the enormous island of New Guinea and the Aru islands, is an extension of the Australian continent. Wrapped around the southern margin of the Sunda Shelf is a young mountain system, traceable through Sumatra, Java and Nusa Tenggara (literally, southeast islands, and sometimes called Sunda Ketjil), and on the northern margins of the Sahul Shelf the mountainous backbone of New Guinea and the Solomon Islands form part of an analagous circum-Australia system. The two mountain systems intersect in the northern Maluku (Moluccas), where the tectonic complexity of the archipelago attains its maximum.

Although Mount Kinabalu (13,680 feet) in Sabah forms the highest point in Southeast Asia proper, the Sunda platform is distinguished by a relative absence of strong relief, and elevations exceeding 5,000 feet in Borneo are confined to restricted areas. By far the greater part of the island lies below 600 feet, and along the western, southern and eastern coasts there are very extensive alluvial swamps. Extreme geological youth and vigorous relief are, however, very characteristic of the Sunda Mountain System, and in contrast to the Sunda platform where there are no currently active volcanoes, vulcanism is often intense; it is the incidence of vulcanism, and particularly vulcanism derived from basic magmas, that largely determines the density of population and the intensity of land use in Java and Sumatra. In the easternmost islands of Sunda Ketjil vulcanism disappears, but even east of Lombok the close relationship between vulcanism and population density becomes less marked, for volcanic areas in Sumbawa and Flores carry much less dense populations than those in the islands to the west. In part the reason is climatic and there are fewer opportunities for irrigation, but cultural factors are probably more significant. Halmahera in northern Maluku also has a very light population density despite the presence of several active volcanoes, but across the Molucca Passage the large and mountainous island of Sulawesi reflects in somewhat paler fashion the patterns of Java and Sumatra. Active vulcanism on this island is confined to the Minahasa peninsula of the northeast, an area of markedly higher population density than the rest of the island and the home of the Minahasans, one of the most distinctive and colourful groups in Indonesia. However, in the southern portion of the southwest peninsula, active vulcanism ceased so recently that the agents of erosion have not yet had sufficient time to remove all the plant nutrients derived from volcanic ejactamenta, and this part of the island also has a higher than average population density.

The structural complexity of the larger Sunda islands is very great, but in essence both Java and Sumatra comprise three major divisions parallel to their

Fig. 7-1 Administrative divisions of Indonesia

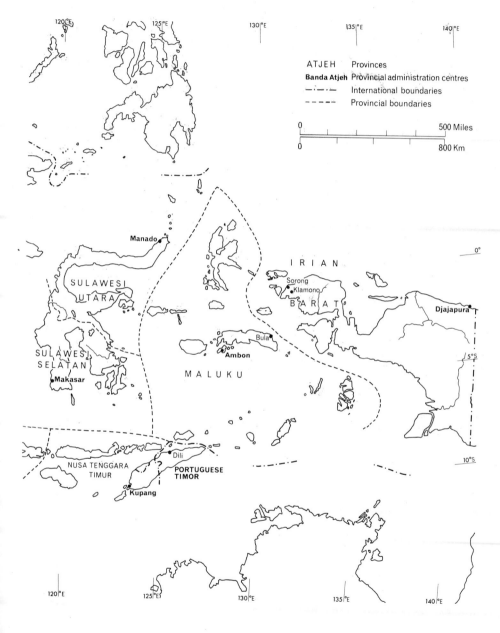

ATJEH   Provinces
Banda Atjeh Provincial administration centres
—·—·—   International boundaries
– – – –   Provincial boundaries

0 _____ 500 Miles
0 _____ 800 Km

long axes. The western portion of Sumatra consists of a high but narrow complex mountain system, the Barisan, rising in Kerintji to 12,470 feet, the highest point in Indonesia proper. The Barisan presents a steep slope to the Indian Ocean but a more gentle one inland; there is little coastal plain except in Atjeh, and rivers flowing to the Indian Ocean are short and torrential. The Barisan is a zone of great crustal instability, and along its entire length stretches a remarkable rift, the Semangko zone, sections of which are blocked by young volcanoes and the out-pourings of fissure eruptions; this zone is also distinguished by the frequency and violence of its earthquakes, which probably exceed those of any other part of the earth. Within the Barisan, which broadens into an extensive highland mass around Lake Toba, there are several tectonic basins supporting dense popula-tions, although these nowhere approach the densities attained on the plains of Java. Eastwards of the Barisan extends a sub-montane hill country, the source of Indonesia's most valuable resource, petroleum; this in turn gives way to a broad alluvial lowland where the land has gained on the sea, a process that has continued apace even in historic times.

This threefold arrangement of structural elements is not so evident in Java, whose major physical units lack the continuity of those of Sumatra. The major relief elements are often fragmented into blocks, and are separated by broad intervening plains which not only afford easy communication throughout the length and breadth of the island, but by virtue of the fertility of their soils have long constituted a major attraction to settlement. However, the southern portion of the island consists of a series of plateaus largely composed of Tertiary lime-stones, which weather to a thin and poor soil whose cultivation presents pro-gressively greater difficulties eastwards as aridity increases. In some areas a barren karst landscape has developed, such as that southwest of Jogjakarta, where on the Gunong Kidoel, or Gunong Sawu, the most poverty-stricken population in the whole island scratches a miserable living, periodically suffering acute shortages of both food and potable water and combating recurrent attack by plague-in-fested rats who find permanent sanctuary in this desolate landscape. In Djawa Tengah (Central Java), however, the Southern Mountains are breached and a broad fertile plain, enriched by volcanic ejactamenta carried out to sea by the Seraju river and then thrown back along the shore by current action, carries an extremely dense population. Other though less extensive breaches also occur in Djawa Timur (East Java), where the sawahs of Lumadjang once supported the largest sugar enterprise in the island.

North of the Southern Mountains lies a volcanic belt, broadening in Djawa Barat (West Java) into an upland mass created from the products of several complex cones, and containing the former lake basins of Bandung and Garut. The magmas of the west Java volcanoes are more acidic than those of the great vol-canic massifs to the east, and their ejactamenta is less beneficial to the soil, so that West Java has the lowest population density of the island's three provinces.

From the Slamet eastwards, however, the volcanoes assume the form of great conical masses separated by broad fertile plains, structures that continue eastwards in Bali and Lombok. North of the volcanic belt is a zone of Tertiary plateaus and hill-lands which in the limestone areas of Rembang and Madura resemble parts of the Southern Mountains, but the zone is punctuated by isolated volcanoes such as the Karang, in the island's western extremity, and the Murjo on the north coast. Towards the Java Sea, however, the plateaus give way to plains built up from the erosion of the volcanic masses to the south. In West Java this north coast plain is broad and continuous, but east of Tjirebon it is fragmented into a series of small plains separated by hill or plateau masses. The coastal plains are very intensively cultivated, and in Central Java possess population densities probably higher than those found in any other agricultural region of the world.

Nevertheless, the divisions of major significance to human activity do not conform to the major physical units but in general are arranged athwart them: North, Central and South Sumatra, and West, Central and East Java are the major cultural and economic divisions of the two islands, and essentially similar patterns of land use have been imposed on very differing types of country. The distribution of peoples and their material culture is thus of greater significance in the use made of resources and the efficiency of that use than considerations of topography and climate, an observation that in large measure holds good for the whole of Southeast Asia.

Though larger than Java, Sulawesi lacks that island's extensive plains and is distinctly more mountainous; active vulcanism is also much less intense. Overland communication is nowhere easy, and the coasts for their length are remarkably devoid of good natural harbours. Sulawesi is certainly not a potential extension of Java in terms of its capacity to absorb part of the population pressure from the more populous island, but because of its wealth in metalliferous minerals it could make a greater contribution to the Indonesian economy in the future than at present. The rugged non-volcanic islands of Nusa Tenggara and Maluku, even allowing for their small populations, appear to possess too limited a resource base to offer any real prospects of a higher level of development, and Irian Barat (usually, Irian), despite its small petroleum output, is likely—for Indonesians as it was for the Dutch—to consume more resources than it generates. Structurally and ethnographically New Guinea is quite distinct from Southeast Asia, its closest affinities being with the Australian continent. It contains some of the most inaccessible mountains, the most forbidding swamps and perhaps the most primitive people in the world; unlike eastern New Guinea, at present administered by Australia but moving at a respectable pace towards self-government, Irian has no active volcanoes to offset the impoverishment of the soil inevitable in a humid tropical climate. Indonesia already had a surfeit of mountain and swamp before acquiring Irian and the value of the territory lay entirely in its usefulness as a device for maintaining national cohesion during a period of increasing political and economic strain. Over-large resources have already been devoted to isolating the territory from Indonesia's debased rupiah, and in any rational national development or recovery programme investment in Irian cannot be expected to receive any priority.

Uniformity is the dominant characteristic of the climate of Indonesia, a consequence of its position athwart the equator and the fragmentation of the national territory between broad intervening seas. The only interruptions in a temperature regime of continuous heat occur at elevations, but for the most part these are of very limited extent; only in the Snow mountain system in Irian is there an extensive area of mountains rising above the tree-line, Carstenz Top (16,500 feet), renamed Gunung Sukarno in 1964, and a few other peaks rising above the snow-line.

It is in the amount and distribution of rainfall that the various parts of Indonesia show the most significant climatic differences. The greater part of Indonesia receives a heavy and generally well-distributed rainfall, but from central Java eastwards a well-marked dry season occurs, which as the Australian continent is approached becomes increasingly severe; the north coast of Sumba receives only about one inch of rain from July to October, and the north coast of Timor is almost equally rainless. But even in areas of marked wet and dry seasons, rainfall is largely the result of intermittent frontal activity, and orographic control is very strong. Many islands show striking differences both in the amount and distribution of rainfall between their northern and southern, or eastern and western coasts.

The changes in atmospheric circulation have long been known in the country as monsoons. From November to April over much of Indonesia the winds are from the west or northwest; this is the period of the West monsoon, synonymous with the rainy season in central and east Java and Sunda Ketjil, but from April to October, the period of the East monsoon, these areas experience dry conditions. Thus winds may be onshore at one time of the year and offshore at another, and islands such as Sulawesi with extensive coasts facing all quarters have extremely complex rainfall patterns. The practical effect of such complexity is to produce very varied agricultural rhythms so that a rice harvest of some magnitude is taken in every month, not only in the country as a whole but also in most of the major islands. Those parts of Indonesia with continuously humid climatic conditions, Sumatra, West Java, Kalimantan, the greater portion of Sulawesi and Maluku, also show considerable differences in their respective rainfall regimes, but the differences are of no real agricultural significance.

The natural vegetation of much of Indonesia is an evergreen forest of one sort or another, but over very large areas it has been replaced by a man-made grassland of *alang-alang* (*Imperata* species) through repeated cutting and burning. This debasement of the forest has had most severe consequences in the eastern islands where the dry season is most severe, and the barren eroded hills of Timor with their wild cattle recall more the landscapes and way of life of northern Australia than those of the larger islands to the west. The magnitude of the forest loss in Indonesia is enormous; indeed it seems possible that Indonesia may account for as much as half of total world forest removals within the humid tropics. Despite the severity of the attack on the forests, however, Indonesia until very recently never had a timber export trade of any significance, though the forests of Sumatra, Kalimantan and Sulawesi have long supported the collecting of *damar* (obtained by tapping the conifer *Agathis*, a common forest tree at elevations) and rattan; these items, together with other so-called 'Straits produce', eventually find their way to the entrepots of Singapore and Penang. To the Dutch the most valuable forests were the teak forests of the limestone hills and plateaus of Rembang and other parts of north Java; these were carefully upgraded by the Forestry Department, but Java's teak forests have suffered severely since independence and much valuable timber has been wasted as fuel wood. Since 1961, however, Japanese capital has combined with the state to operate timber concessions in Kalimantan, and in marked contrast to the experience of similar joint ventures in exploiting other Indonesian resources, these operations have proved quite successful.

THE AGRICULTURAL BASE

Agriculture generates more than half of Indonesia's national product (*Table 7-2*). The country's agricultural problems are not unique in Southeast Asia, but the scale on which they occur suggests comparison with densely populated India and Pakistan rather than with the remainder of Southeast Asia. Only in North Vietnam is the problem of maintaining basic subsistence so severe, but overcrowded Java is more than twice as populous as Tonkin. Yet Indonesian agriculture in its capacity to generate a large export income differs appreciably from that of Southern Asia, and with no problem of aridity to combat, its difficulties should prove considerably more tractable. To resolve them, however, will require a greater degree of economic realism than Indonesian leaders have so far been prepared to adopt.

It is in Indonesia that the contrasts between sawah and ladang agriculture outlined in Chapter 2 are most striking, for the two systems exist side by side in several parts of the country. The distinction largely corresponds to that between *Pertanian Rakjat*, indigenous peasant agriculture devoted mainly to the production of food crops, and *Pertanian Perkebunan*, or estate agriculture engaged in the cultivation of cash crops largely for an export market; nevertheless in the Outer Islands many indigenous farmers are engaged in export-oriented cash crop production, and in parts of Java sawah agriculture has also been involved in

Table 7-2 *Indonesia: industrial origin of net national product, 1958 and 1965*

1960 prices, in billion rupiahs

	1958 Value	1958 Percentage	1965* Value	1965* Percentage
Agriculture	194·9	50·4	227·1	52·8
Farm food crops	124·3		153·9	
Farm non-food crops	26·6		28·0	
Estate crops	12·9		10·8	
Livestock products	17·3		18·0	
Fisheries	5·7		8·1	
Mining	9·7	2·5	13·6	3·2
Industry	51·3	13·3	51·1	11·9
Large and medium	21·5		21·1	
Small-scale	29·8		30·0	
Construction	6·8	1·8	7·8	1·8
Electricity, gas	0·8		1·4	
Transport and communications	11·5	3·0	15·2	3·5
Wholesale and retail trade	57·8	15·0	73·1	17·0
Banking, cooperatives	2·8		3·3	
Rent of dwellings	7·2	1·9	7·9	1·8
Government and defence	25·6	6·7	8·9	2·1
Services	21·2	5·5	22·8	5·3
Foreign net investment	3·1		4·5	
Net national product	**386·5**	*100·0*	**429·5**	*100·0*

* Estimated

Source: *Bank Negara Indonesia*

Batak houses in the Toba highlands of north Sumatra.

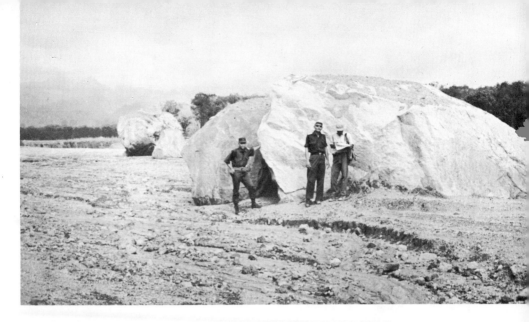

Cultivated land destroyed by a *lahar* (mudflow) in the disastrous Kelut eruption of 1966 in East Java.

commercialized cash crop production, a development that had far-reaching consequences.

Indonesian agriculture thus presents a high degree of complexity and for convenience the division adopted here is between food-producing agriculture and export-orientated agriculture. This distinction is far from complete as several crops grown for export purposes are also consumed on the home market, and indeed in increasing quantities, but it assists identification of Indonesia's most pressing agricultural problems. Perhaps the most important is that Indonesia, formerly self-sufficient in food when it was the Netherlands Indies, is now increasingly in deficit as the rate of population growth outstrips the rate of increase in food production. But scarcely less important is that Indonesia's export trade, which is largely made up of agricultural products, has stagnated for many years. The country has thus been progressively less able to finance the import of raw materials and capital goods for a higher level of economic development after it has met a mounting bill for food imports. In 1961 rice imports alone were absorbing around 15 per cent of total foreign exchange earnings, but by 1965 this proportion had risen to nearly 25 per cent.

Food-producing agriculture

Under the pressure of a rapidly increasing population, the Netherlands Indies ceased to be a major food exporter during the latter half of the nineteenth century. Throughout most of the present century it was in food deficit, although net food imports, principally rice, fluctuated greatly. In some years, such as 1927 when

The landak ('porcupine'), a push hoe for weeding sawahs, introduced into the Netherlands Indies from Japan in the Thirties: south Java plain.

net rice imports totalled nearly half a million tons, they reached an extreme level, but in favourable years the country could just break even. Against this background the achievement of the Republic in raising rice production by some 40 per cent between 1950 and 1964 appears respectable, particularly in view of the fact that government itself discouraged production by frequently making forced purchases from peasants at less than market prices. As in India the extra inputs have somehow been made to feed the flood of new mouths, but it has, nevertheless, been a losing battle; while total food production has increased throughout the life of the Republic, per capita food consumption has declined. Moreover, diet has become progressively more debased; the share of rice has diminished and that of rice substitutes and starchy staples such as maize and tapioca has increased. This trend is also of long standing, for per capita rice consumption appears to have begun its long decline shortly after 1850. Rice production grew at an annual rate of about 3 per cent during the Fifties, but between 1961 and 1967 the rate of increase dropped to about half this figure, and if Indonesia is to have any hope of achieving self-sufficiency in the near future it must aim at an increase of about 6 per cent per annum. Expansion of non-rice food crop production has, it is true, proceeded more rapidly, but this is little comfort in view of the marked preference for rice in local food consumption patterns. In 1965 President Sukarno advised his countrymen to eat more maize to combat the rice shortage; but the inability of his government to meet the subsidized rice ration to the Army, the Civil Service and to the professional élite on which it depended for support was a material factor in the political upheavals at the end of the year.

Three major types of land use participate in food crop production: *sawah* or embanked, and usually irrigated, rice-land; *tegalan*, dry unirrigated land; and *pekerangan*, orchard or garden land of the house compound. Though present in all the larger islands, this threefold division is most striking in Java, where only in estate areas of the Priangan uplands of West Java and in parts of Besuki in the extreme east, does agriculture assume any very different organization. The strong preference for rice has made sawahs the most desirable form of agricultural land in Java, and the sawah area has trended steadily upwards through improved irrigation. But Java has no master river systems of the scale of those in mainland Southeast Asia, where vast areas of flood plain of low productivity still await modern storage and regulatory works; opportunities for large new irrigation schemes are few, and their cost-to-benefit ratio is unlikely to be very favourable. The increase in the irrigated area, nevertheless, was not entirely the result of pressure on food supplies, for among the most powerful agents making for expansion in the present century were the sugar companies, which under the Land Rents Ordinance of 1870 were permitted to hire village sawahs for sugar cultivation. Since independence the sugar industry has almost completely collapsed, and although it may be going too far to assign to it the major responsibility for Java's present crushing demographic and agricultural problems, the influence of the sugar industry was profound. At its height, before the onset of the Great Depression, the industry involved all the best sawahs in Central and East Java, and the reservoirs, or *waduk*, constructed by the sugar companies made possible a great expansion of *padi gadu*, or off-season padi grown during the East monsoon.

Tegalan, or dry-field agriculture, shows greater variations in cultivation practices, and under the most favourable conditions, as in the densely populated limestone island of Madura, it is highly developed. Slopes are carefully terraced and the embankments protected from erosion by hedges or cover crops; crop rotations are regularly practised and the fields themselves are either heavily manured with buffalo or ox dung, or green manuring with legumes is incorporated in the rotation. But in Java itself such elaboration is less common and the poorest types of dry field are almost indistinguishable from ladang; population pressure in Central and East Java has encouraged a substantial increase in illegal squatting on formerly uncultivated waste and forest on mountain sides, which in the days of the Netherlands Indies were reserved for the protection of the drainage and irrigation system. Before 1939 it was regarded as essential to maintain a forest cover of not less than 30 per cent of the total surface area for this purpose, but by 1960 Java's forests amounted to only a little over 20 per cent. More rapid run-off, accelerated erosion, the silting of irrigation channels, and ultimately an even more depressed peasantry, have been the inevitable consequences of this largely un-controlled and unrecorded attack on Java's few remaining forests.

The rice situation   From the very imperfect statistical evidence available, Indonesia in the early Sixties appeared to possess some 12·5 million acres of wet-rice fields, of which Java and Madura accounted for about 8·75 million, the balance being located mainly in Sumatra, Sulawesi, Bali and Lombok. Of the unknown but much larger area of dry fields some 4·25 million acres are annually devoted to dry rice production, of which about three-quarters are located in the Outer Islands. However, not all of the wet-rice area consists of sawahs with full irrigation control, for it includes areas without irrigation facilities and others where the onset of the West monsoon brings insufficient rain to flood the fields for planting (*Table 7-3*). Under these conditions rice is grown for some weeks on dry fields, which, as the rains increase or as irrigation water becomes available, gradually become flooded and are then managed as sawahs. This type of cultivation closely resembles methods of rice cultivation found in northeast and north Thailand, and in Java, where it occurs throughout the island though always in small patches, it is known as *padi gogorantjah*. Other specialized regional methods of cultivation included in the wet-rice area, include the deep-water rice of the lower Tjimanuk and Solo valleys in Java and in parts of south Kalimantan, identical to the 'floating' rice grown in parts of the Mae Nam plain of Thailand and in the Mekong delta, and various methods of planting swamp margins under conditions of either rising or falling water-levels, practised in east Sumatra. But

Table 7-3   *Indonesia: distribution of irrigated and non-irrigated sawah, 1957*

	Rain-fed	Technically irrigated	Semi-technically irrigated*	Total sawah	*Percentage irrigated sawah to total sawah*
		thousand hectares			
Sumatra	160	90	100	**350**	*54·3*
Java	1,220	1,500	710	**3,430**	*64·4*
Kalimantan	140		280	**420**	*66·7*
Sulawesi	75	5	40	**120**	*37·5*
Nusa Tenggara	20		160	**180**	*88·9*
Total	**1,615**	**1,595**	**1,290**	**4,500**	***64·1***

* Indigenous works not in control of Irrigation Department

Source: ECAFE, *Water Resources Development in British Borneo, Federation of Malaya, Indonesia and Thailand,* 1959

in Java, probably some 95 per cent of the harvested wet-rice crop is taken from sawahs, and the island's dry rice, or *padi gogo*, is produced on permanently culti-vated tegalan with regular crop rotations and usually involves some kind of manur-ing. In the Outer Islands, however, dry rice is *padi ladang* grown as part of the swidden cycle, and never receives any manure.

The harvested rice area has steadily increased with growing population and by 1964 the 17 million or so acres harvested represented virtually twice the 1937 level. This increase has been achieved through the extension of the sawah area, by diverting sawah land formerly used for the periodic production of crops such as sugar and tobacco to rice, and by increased multiple cropping; wherever possible also, tegalan and areas of *padi gogorantjah* have been converted to sawahs. The possibilities of further extensions to the sawah area differ very greatly between the Outer Islands and Java. In the former, although it would be technically possible to achieve enormous increases, the cost-to-benefit ratio appears unlikely to be very favourable, and the more grandiose schemes that have been suggested, such as draining the swamps of East Sumatra or of South Kalimantan, would necessitate a prodigious capital investment. These projects involve the con-struction of main drainage canals extending from Bandjarmasin to Pontianak in Kalimantan (480 miles), and from Palembang to Tandjongbalai in Sumatra (550 miles), and many miles of subsidiary canals to connect the reclaimed land with tidal rivers. Given Indonesia's parlous economic situation, it is unlikely that any resources will be devoted to such schemes, on which indeed the country wasted many millions of rupiahs in the Fifties, for decades to come.

Table 7-4   *Indonesia: harvested area of principal food crops, 1964* (thousand hectares)

	Padi sawah and gogorantjah	Dry-field padi	Total padi	Maize	Tapioca	Sweet potatoes	Peanuts	Soybeans
West Java*	1,260	225	1,485	230	300	140	90	40
Central Java	1,000	50	1,050	950	410	130	70	130
Jogjakarta	70	30	100	30	50	5	10	20
East Java	970	60	1,030	1,560	480	140	120	290
Total, Java and Madura	3,300	365	3,665	2,770	1,240	415	290	480
Total, Indonesia	5,310	1,670	6,980	3,450	1,530	590	370	570

* Including Greater Djakarta

Source: Nugroho, *Indonesia in Facts and Figures,* Djakarta, 1967

In Java, where the need is greatest, opportunities for further expansion of the sawah area are closely circumscribed, but only two-thirds of Java's sawahs benefit from irrigation facilities, which for the most part consist of run of the river gravity-deviationary schemes incapable of providing much water for the dry-season cropping. In West Java, where for climatic reasons the sugar industry was absent, greater reliance is made on rain-fed sawahs than elsewhere, but in 1967 the country's largest irrigation project was finally brought to completion in the province. This is the Djatiluhur multipurpose scheme, located where the Tjitarum river debouches from the mountains above Purwakarta, a project constructed by a French consortium and in large part financed by French aid. The scheme's origin dates back to the Walahar weir of 1925, which provided water for some 90,000 hectares of wet-season rice but served only 10,000 hectares in the dry season; the water impounded by the present dam, however, will guarantee *padi gadu* (dry season rice) on some 80,000 hectares, and with the associated Tjurung works downstream will provide 240,000 hectares of wet-season rice with full water control. The Djatiluhur power station will be provided with a generating capacity of some 150,000 kW, which will help to relieve Djakarta's depressing semi-permanent black-out, but every major developmental project in Indonesia has lagged far behind schedule, and Djatiluhur's frustrating delays do not augur well for similar future schemes. Preliminary surveys were begun by the Dutch in 1945, and when construction eventually began in 1953 completion was planned for 1961; nevertheless, the transmission line to Djakarta was still unfinished at the end of 1967 and in 1969 the power station was not operating at full capacity. Several small irrigation schemes have also been undertaken in

Central and East Java, some of which have been carried to completion, but every-where work has proceeded slowly and fitfully.

Large areas have been released for rice cultivation through the collapse of Java's sugar and tobacco industries, which has greatly facilitated increased multiple cropping. Sugar not only occupies sawahs for fourteen to sixteen months, but also uses very large quantities of irrigation water; and on the grounds that the investment in sugar cultivation was very much larger than that in rice, the sugar interests always claimed priority in the use of available water supplies. The slow but continuous increase in the index of double-cropping is another long-established feature of Java's agriculture, but it is likely that over-investment in expanding the harvested area has operated to delay the attainment of the vastly greater productivity of land and labour mandatory for any permanent solution to Java's rural problems; the island should instead be looking towards the retirement of much of the poorest sawahs where yields fall well below those of the national average.

But while many of the *kebupaten* (smaller units of local government) of the three provinces of Java take a rice harvest in every month, the general availability of rice throughout the year varies very greatly. The most important harvest by far is that taken in April at the end of the rainy season (or rainier season in West Java), and the critical period in the rice supply situation is in the early months of the year preceding this harvest. Rice harvests at other times of the year are purely of local significance, and in some areas, as in parts of the *Daerah Istemewa* (Special District) of Jogjakarta, three rice crops a year may be taken. The off- or dry-season crop demands a high labour input, and because of the necessity to plant quickly maturing varieties, the yield is low. But where sawahs receive insufficient irrigation water for a second rice crop, as is the case with most of those not served by technical irrigation works (that is permanent works operated by the state), other food crops such as maize, sweet potatoes, groundnuts, soybeans and other legumes, collectively known as *polowidjo*, are grown. These, together with tapioca and taro, are the principal crops grown on *tegalan*, many of which also have multiple cropping patterns (*Table 7-4*).

In the Netherlands Indies a distinction was made between rice-surplus and rice-deficient areas, and normally nearly all of Central and East Java fell into the latter category. West Java, which had the smallest population of the three provinces and the largest sawah area, was usually a surplus area; indeed, on the north coast plain in the vicinity of Indramaju there was once a flourishing 'rice plantation' industry in which European companies produced high-quality rice for export on leased village sawahs. This activity has long disappeared and with the hectic postwar growth of Djakarta as the largest metropolitan centre in Southeast Asia, West Java's former surplus has been replaced by a heavy deficit. As noted, in a bad year the Netherlands Indies could import up to almost half a million tons of rice, but normally the deficit was very much smaller. However, the aftermath of occupation and civil war caused the new Indonesian Republic initially to make large rice imports, which fortunately it was able to finance through the higher prices earned by its export products during the Korean war. Slowly the deficit was reduced as agricultural rehabilitation proceeded, and by the middle Fifties rice imports had been brought below a level of 100,000 tons annually. However, this relatively good performance appears to have been largely the result of favourable weather; from 1955 onwards the rice deficit steadily mounted and in 1963 Indonesian rice imports rose above one million tons a year. But with the enormous cost of the Irian campaign and the confrontation of Malaysia, the charge on foreign exchange became intolerable, and for a time in 1964 and 1965 rice imports were banned completely. Nevertheless, the maintenance of the ban proved politically impossible as the government's domestic rice procurement programme fell further and further behind schedule, and one of the first acts of the new government of 1966 was to endeavour to beg or borrow the vital 60,000 or so tons of rice necessary to meet the ration of the privileged armed forces and the bureaucracy, whose support was vital to the continuance of the new regime. Meanwhile rice prices in the cities sky-rocketed and were the cause of renewed demonstrations by the student organizations, which had played a leading role in encompassing the downfall of Sukarno.

Agrarian structure and the problems of raising food production The basic cause of the chronic rice shortage is the low productivity of both land and worker. Low productivity is in part a consequence of the physical environment; whatever the original richness of the volcanic soils of Java, centuries of rice monoculture have greatly reduced their content of soluble minerals and potash deficiencies are particularly widespread. Inadequate water-control also makes for low productivity; this particularly concerns sawahs located in mountain valleys and foothill areas served by indigenous irrigation systems fabricated from local materials. One million hectares planted to high-yielding varieties on sawahs with full water-control, and provided with the necessary fertilizers and pesticides, would not only abolish the need for rice imports but would also permit the retirement of many marginal rice terraces, such as those scarcely a metre in width, where the real costs of production are extremely high. The number of work animals has not yet regained prewar levels, nor has this deficiency been alleviated by the use of mechanized equipment. But low productivity is much more a consequence of shortcomings in the institutional system governing the use of land. According to Geertz, the absence of any opening for the exercise of peasant initiative produced a progressively more intricate or involuted peasant agriculture in which the basic structural imbalance remained unchanged.[7] Whether or not Geertz is correct in attributing primary responsibility for this agricultural suffoca-

---

[7] *Clifford Geertz,* Agricultural Involution: The Process of Ecological Change in Indonesia, *University of California Press, Berkeley and Los Angeles, 1963.*

tion to the Culture System (1830–70) and the growth of the sugar industry, the Indonesian government has exploited its farmers in ways that have proved just as effective deterrents to enhanced productivity as those arising from the impact of European capitalism on peasant agriculture.

By the outbreak of World War II, rapid population growth in Java and pressure on land had produced a class of landless peasants which, despite all the efforts of the Dutch administration, had shown clear evidence of growing for nearly half a century. Nevertheless, the problem had probably not then reached the proportions attained in other congested parts of Southeast Asia, and tenancy was far from the burning issue that it had become in Lower Burma or in the Luzon plain. Most families, in fact, owned some land; but what they owned was usually insufficient to provide continuous employment throughout the year, and all too

Table 7-5 *Indonesia: estimated production of selected crops, 1966*

	thousand metric tons		thousand metric tons
Rice, milled	9,990	Sugar	1,050
Maize	2,870	Estate (centrifugal)	580
Tapioca	10,850	Smallholder (non-centrifugal)	470
Sweet potatoes	2,310	Tea	40
Rubber	720	Estate	30
Estate	220	Smallholder	10
Smallholder	500	Coffee	120
Oil palm products	200	Estate	10
Tobacco	120	Smallholder	110

Source: Nugroho, *Indonesia in Facts and Figures,* Djakarta, 1967

often yielded but the minimum of subsistence. Since 1945 it would appear that the situation of Java's peasantry has become considerably worse; sample surveys of villages in varying rice-growing areas have shown an incidence of landlessness among heads of households exceeding 40 per cent, and that of those with insufficient land to support a family throughout the year can attain a similar proportion. No doubt these are extremes, but the evidence of an increasing dependence on wage labour and a widening gap between rich and poor farmers is unmistakable; in 1957, 90 per cent of all sawah owners in Java possessed less than one hectare (approximately 2·5 acres) and no less than 78 per cent owned less than half a hectare.[8] The national revolution, as so often the case in Asia, passed over those most in need, and the wealthier landowners with contacts in the parties

[8] United States Joint Publications Research Service, *No. 5249, p. 7, quoted by Karl J. Pelzer in Ruth McVey (ed.),* Indonesia, *HRAF Press, New Haven, 1963, p. 126.*

and in the administration found many new opportunities for enriching themselves and enlarging their holdings.

As Pelzer remarks, although there are no official records to indicate the size of the problem, it is clear that moneylender landlords exercise *de facto* control over a large portion of the land in Java, and that a great many apparently independent farmers are in effect share-croppers.[9] The collapse of the sugar and tobacco companies, formerly the principal source of cash employment in much of Central and East Java, has increased applications made to moneylenders, and all too often cooperatives, which receive special mention in the constitution as the best means of assisting the peasant to overcome his economic weakness, have constituted a new source of exploitation. Many cooperative managers have allied themselves with the larger farmers and with senior officials to divert supplies such as fertilizers and tools purchased at fixed government prices into the profitable private market, to finance such operations from cooperatives' funds, and to dispose of members' produce through black market channels. The 'padi centres' created under the Three Year Rice Production Programme of 1959 also proved subject to much fraudulent practice. Five hundred centres were to be established under the programme, which was designed to make Indonesia self-sufficient in rice by 1962, and were intended to assist peasants in the acquisition of improved seeds, fertilizers and tools, and to provide farm credit; repayment was to be made in kind at government fixed padi prices, or in cash at a 25 per cent interest rate. But by 1961 the price paid by the government was considerably less than that on the free market, and the padi centres in effect became collection agencies for the government's rice ration scheme to the armed forces, the bureaucracy and other privileged classes. It is doubtful that there is any greater disincentive to production than forced deliveries at less than market prices. The attempt at rice self-sufficiency was abandoned, and inevitably, increased utilization had to be made of tapioca, which in President Sukarno's fatuous 1965 'Go to Hell' speech on American aid was claimed as the equivalent of imported dried milk.

Indonesia's shortage of foreign exchange, a direct consequence of the demise of its export industries, has compounded the difficulties of grappling with the rice problem. After 1963 Indonesia ceased to import modern pesticides, one result of which was a sharp increase in the incidence of malaria and other mosquito-born infections in rural areas, and even the small output of the only modern fertilizer plant, the urea plant at Palembang, was earmarked for export (and to Japan of all countries) in order to help finance essential imports. Indonesian farmers are now very conscious of the value of fertilizers, which change hands at fancy prices on the black market, but the country lacks the transport facilities to get the fertilizer to the fields where it is needed, and above all, it lacks a competent administrative machine capable of implementing a fertilizer distribution scheme even if supplies could be made available. The general response of the Sukarno

[9] *Karl J. Pelzer, in Ruth McVey (ed.), op. cit., p. 126.*

regime to an increasingly severe rural problem was the production of grandiose plans departing progressively further from reality, and of yet more slogans for public incantation, as meaningless as their predecessors.

This attitude was well exemplified in the programmes for transmigration and agrarian reform. Transmigration has a history dating back to 1905; its intention was to remove peasants from overcrowded parts of Java to new settlements in the Outer Islands, where holdings would be large enough to provide a socially acceptable living standard. Although the Dutch steadily improved their transmigration machinery the operation remained exceedingly expensive, largely because of the necessity to provide irrigation works for the new settlements carved out of the forest. The Dutch, however, never managed to move more than 60,000 persons in a year, and the total number affected up to the outbreak of World War II was less than a quarter of a million. Since the revolution, the Indonesian Department of Transmigration has continued the previous Dutch policy and by 1959 had sponsored a total of over 220,000 migrants. Numerically this was as good a performance as the Dutch had accomplished over forty years, but the annual rate never approached the level attained in the later years of the Dutch administration. In the newest settlements, which were located mainly in South Sumatra (as with the Netherlands Indies programme) but with some schemes in Kalimantan, Sulawesi and even in Bali, where 22,000 people were resettled after 1961, there was a significant reduction in the size of holding provided for the new colonist. Whereas the Dutch had provided holdings of some 2·5 hectares, the average of the most recent colonies has been only some 1·2 hectares. Another menacing development was for control of the transmigration programme to pass to the P K I. Moreover, it is highly likely that in the decade after 1955 in-migration to the cities of Java, and particularly to Djakarta, from the Outer Islands, exceeded the flow of transmigrants from overcrowded Java.

There is much that can be questioned in the transmigration programme, and especially its tendency to produce innumerable 'little Javas', thus spreading the problem of overpopulation still wider and delaying the agricultural breakthrough which must accompany self-sustaining economic growth. It locks up large capital sums on which the return is at best only modest and, in any case, is long in coming. It cannot provide for more than a minute fraction of Java's annual population increase. Nevertheless, it continues to exercise a major influence in national life, and on the transmigration issue as on most others, the government has taken a decidedly Javanese view. Progressively grander transmigration targets were set despite the failure of previous schemes to reach their goals, and in May 1965 a gigantic new transmigration scheme was launched by Presidential decree in which 100,000 families involving nearly half a million persons were to be resettled during the following year. Probably less than one-tenth of this number were in fact affected, and for many years spontaneous unassisted migration is believed to have exceeded that sponsored by the government and other semi-official bodies such as the armed forces veterans' organizations.

The preoccupation of the Netherlands Indies government with trans-migration and irrigation left few resources over for a direct attack on the rural problem through agrarian reform. But the steady growth of landlessness and tenancy which continued into the lifetime of the Republic, and, in particular, a formidable increase in the strength of the P K I in those parts of Java where these problems were most acute, had by 1960 made agrarian reform a matter of urgency, and in that year the Sharecropping Law and the Basic Agrarian Law were promulgated. These new measures should have initiated changes as decisive as those of the Agrarian Law and the Land Rents Ordinance of 1870, which set the whole pattern of agricultural development in the Netherlands Indies. In practice they were little more than empty gestures. The Basic Agrarian Law, in contrast to the old Agrarian Law which had vested ultimate ownership of all land in the state and claimed all uncultivated land as 'waste' and the property of the state[10], re-cognized private ownership in land, although this right was to be confined to Indonesian citizens. But to encourage a wide distribution of land ownership a maximum size of holding was stipulated. This was to be fixed according to the population density of the regency, a unit of administration in the Dutch era; where the population density fell below 50 persons per square kilometre, as in the Outer Islands, the maximum family holding was to be 15 hectares (37 acres) of sawah or 20 hectares (55·4 acres) of dry land, or *tanah kering*; but where the population density exceeded 400 persons per square kilometre, as in much of Java and Madura, the limits were set at 5 hectares (12·4 acres) of sawah or 6 hectares (14·8 acres) of unirrigated land. Land in excess of these amounts was to be confiscated and redistributed to those without land or with insufficient land, and with monumental legerdemain the minimum holding was fixed at two hectares, just about sufficient to support a family. Three years were to be allowed for completing redistribution in Java, and five for the Outer Islands. The Share-cropping Law attempted to fix the level of rents for tenant farmers and to have all tenancy agreements registered with the authorities. The tenant was to be left with not less than half the crop on sawahs and two-thirds on tegalan; to provide security of tenure, agreements were to be valid for not less than three years for sawah and five for tegalan, and a maximum limit of three hectares was set per tenant for land held under such agreements.

Unlike the corresponding Burmese legislation, that of Indonesia did pro-vide for financial compensation for dispossessed owners, mainly in low interest-bearing bonds, and peasants receiving land through redistribution were to make repayments to the state over a fifteen-year period. But although land reform and share-cropping committees were established throughout the country, the new

---

[10] *In reality there was very much less than appeared; much of the so-called 'Woeste-gronden' was in fact periodically used by swidden cultivators, and to deny access to such land was to place them under a heavy disability.*

acts were merely counters in the endless game of political manoeuvering between the President, the Army, the PKI and the PNI (Nationalist Party), and were as far removed from reality as most of the other measures and slogans of the period. There was just not enough land available in Java to implement the legislation even if the will to do so had been present, as the government well knew. According to a survey of 1957, some 32,000 among the 9·2 million owners of sawah in Java possessed more than 5 hectares, and of these only about 6,000 owned more than 10 hectares; the 18 million hectares that would be necessary to provide all owners with the legal minimum amounted in fact to more than twice the estimated total cultivated area of Java and Madura.

This double talk had extremely serious repercussions. Land reform made little progress against the entrenched opposition of the larger landowners and of the custodians of *adat* (customary law) which still regulated much village land in Central and East Java, but in any case the technical problems of survey and registration exceeded the capacity of resources available to deal with them. The PKI threatened to take action if the land reform measures were not implemented within the original time schedule, and in 1964 a series of sporadic peasant revolts led by the communists broke out in Central Java, in which several larger land-owners were murdered. Though the revolts were brought under control by the Army, the President could not afford to be outbid by the PKI in the matter of land reform and was obliged to come to its support. A communist demand for arming the peasants was resisted, but with the increasingly close association of the President with the PKI, events moved swiftly to the abortive *coup* of September 30th–October 1st 1965, and the massacre of communists and their supporters throughout Java.[11] As a result, the cause of land reform in Indonesia has probably been set back by a decade.

The belief that land reform was not indispensable to improvement in agricultural productivity was one of the bases of the BIMAS (*Bimbingan Massal*, or Mass Guidance) programme, developed at the Bogor Institute of Agriculture in West Java in the early Sixties. Trial investigations showed that by actually living with rice farmers even agriculture students without extension experience could achieve marked increases in yields, by demonstrating the use of modern high-yielding varieties in conjunction with fertilizers and pesticides. After 1963 the programme expanded rapidly, and in 1966 affected almost 500,000 hectares of rice-land. But the student resources were clearly over-extended, and with the political upheavals of that year, results proved disappointing. Nevertheless, the programme attracted the support of the World Bank, and the Suharto administration still has high hopes for the scheme, which has been resuscitated for inclusion in Indonesia's new Five Year Plan, announced in 1969.

[11] *Estimates of the number of communists and their sympathizers murdered as a result of the rising range from 50,000 to over one million. Even on a conservative basis, however, it appears that the casualties produced in a few brief weeks of the massacres exceeded those of the Vietnam war since 1960.*

In the Outer Islands, population pressure and agrarian reform nowhere constitute issues of the magnitude encountered in Java, for much agriculture consists of export-orientated cultivation of perennials. There are, however, some areas of predominantly sawah agriculture where population pressure is beginning to give cause for concern, such as the Padang Highlands and parts of Tapanuli in Sumatra, and in Bali, Lombok and the Makasar area of Sulawesi. All of these are likely to become mirrors of Java within the next two or three decades unless modernization of the Indonesian economy speedily gets under way. In the meantime, the debasement of Indonesian diet and landscape continues apace.[12]

Export-orientated agriculture

Agricultural products account for some 60 per cent of Indonesia's export earnings, a figure that has fallen since the early Fifties when the proportion was nearly 80 per cent; the decline largely reflects the growing contribution to foreign exchange earnings of the expanding petroleum industry. Yet the stagnation in the agricultural export industries is striking enough. With the single exception of natural rubber, volume exports of every major agricultural product were lower in the early Sixties than they were in 1939, but even rubber exports were lower than they were a decade earlier. Production and export levels of formerly important commodities such as sugar, tobacco, cinchona (the source of quinine), pepper, tea, kapok, and sisal seem unlikely to regain 1939 levels of output in any period one can foresee; indeed, some of these industries such as cinchona and sisal appear to have gone for ever (*Tables 7-5* and *7-10*). Although allowance has to be made for the under-assessment of exports resulting from smuggling (estimated to cause a loss to the nation of at least $200 million annually), and in the case of some products for a greatly enlarged domestic consumption, there is no doubt that even the best managed agricultural export industries have marked time for over two decades. After 1960 the situation of the export industries deteriorated sharply; exports (excluding petroleum) which in 1951 were valued at nearly $900 million had fallen to $435 million in 1965, and the target for 1966 was set at only $360 million.[13] But even now, given appropriate injections of additional capital and managerial and technical skills, the export industries could be very greatly expanded. This is an important consideration, for the modernization of the Indonesian economy should not be held back by chronic balance-of-payments constraints and foreign exchange shortages of the kind that have plagued India; if it really wanted to, the country could increase very substantially its export earnings, even despite the deteriorating terms-of-trade position which has affected primary producing

---

[12] *See p. 50.*

[13] *Indonesia later claimed exports of more than $500 million for 1966, although even this was scarcely adequate to meet the country's basic import requirements; however, part of the export decline represented a drop in the unit value of exports. Indonesia's crisis could hardly have come at a worse time in view of the prevailing world political and economic situation; see p. 438.*

countries in the Sixties. The removal of many of the past deterrents to export production has been given high priority by the Suharto administration, and in 1968 agreement was finally reached with the foreign estate companies for the return of properties nationalized during the Sukarno regime.

Nearly all of Indonesia's export crops are perennials, produced in the essentially ladang agriculture of the Outer Islands. Export crop production, though reaching its apogee in the large European-owned estates, has nevertheless long been a major activity of several indigenous peoples; it was the cloves, nutmeg and mace of the Moluccas that first brought Europeans into the Indonesian seas, and the pepper of Sumatra and Borneo were important exports long before these islands passed under European control. Indigenous farmers have also proved adept at cultivating cash crops introduced by Europeans, such as tobacco and rubber, and in the latter at least proved formidable competitors to estate production. In the Netherlands Indies peasant and planter were able to compete according to their respective efficiency, although in indirectly governed areas such as the Principalities (*Vorstenlanden*) of Java and the Sultanates of East Sumatra, the planters were able to obtain exceptionally favourable terms for the use of land which gave them a decided advantage. The balance of production between smallholder and estate in the Thirties provides strong support for those who argue that the peasant is the more efficient producer of many tropical products. In copra, spices, pepper and kapok, production was overwhelmingly in smallholder hands, and it was only in crops that require complex and expensive processing such as the oil palm, sisal, sugar, tea and *kina* (cinchona) that the smallholder was really unable to compete, although by having his output processed at an estate factory smallholders were sometimes able to make a small contribution to production. Since that time the balance of advantage has swung sharply in favour of the smallholder, largely for political reasons (*Tables 7-6* and *7-7*.) In the early Fifties, estates accounted for about 30 per cent of foreign exchange earnings, a proportion that declined to a little less than 25 per cent a decade later.

Such a development was inevitable in view of the determination of Indonesians to have 'economic' as well as political independence, though what a truly 'national economy' consisted of was never clearly defined except that in practice it meant that all the 'plums' in the economy were to be reserved to indigenous Indonesians, which by definition excluded all Chinese. While the high prices of export commodities during the Korean war constituted an incentive to higher output, estates faced mounting difficulties over acquiring visas for key foreign personnel and import licences for essential processing equipment and spare parts; they also had to contend with an increasingly militant labour force over which communist-dominated unions exercised strong control, continuous pilfering of their produce, restrictions on the repatriation of profits and dividends, invasion of their property by squatters, and uncertainty over the renewal of their

Table 7-6   *Indonesia: planted area and production
of estates, 1965*

	Rubber	Oil palm	Sugar	Coco-nuts	Tea	Tobacco	Cinchona	Cocoa
Number of estates	671	42	55	118	127	35	23	23
Planted area (thousand hectares)	505	108	94	21	70	11	2	6
Harvested area (thousand hectares)	394	88	94	18	63	11	2	5
Production (thousand metric tons)	228	157*	777	7	47	9	2	1

Coconuts and Tobacco relate to 1962

* Palm oil

Source: Nugroho, *Indonesia in Facts and Figures,* Djakarta, 1967

Table 7-7   *Indonesia: area and production of smallholder
commercial crops, 1965*

	Planted area *thousand hectares*	Production *thousand metric tons*
Coconuts	1,870	1,250 (dry copra)
Coffee	260	90
Tea	60	40
Rubber	—	470
Sugar cane	65	410
Tobacco	160	80
Pepper	40	50
Cloves	70	10
Kapok	140	25

Source: Nugroho, *Indonesia in Facts and Figures,* Djakarta, 1967

land leases. These difficulties were compounded by periodic attacks by militant Muslim fanatics opposed to the government, such as the *Darul Islam* in West Java, an important estate area, and, more seriously, by the regional revolts of 1957–58, which caused heavy damage to the processing equipment of several estates in the country's most important estate area, northeast Sumatra.

The squatter problem was a particular concern of the Deli area of Sumatra, the old *Cultuurgebied* of the Netherlands Indies (*Figure 7-2*). Here the unusually favourable terms obtained by estate companies from the local Sultans and the richness of the soils derived from the volcanic tuffs of the eruptions of the Lake Toba area, led to rapid development of estate agriculture after 1863, when Jacob

Nienhuys obtained a concession that laid the foundations of the Deli tobacco industry. The tobacco companies required access to large areas of land, for by experience they found that the quality of their unique cigar-wrapper leaf could only be preserved through a method of cultivation that was in essence a modification of the local swidden system; tobacco was grown only once every six to nine years, after which the land was allowed to revert to secondary forest. In theory the indigeneous inhabitants were allowed to use land between cycles of tobacco cultivation for food production, but in practice these rights were suppressed.[14] During World War II inhabitants of the Batak highlands were encouraged by the Japanese to settle on unoccupied land in East Sumatra, and the movement continued apace after 1950. The production schedules of the tobacco companies were thus disrupted, but all attempts at preventing further influx, to say nothing of removing the existing squatters, proved abortive. Squatters also moved into rubber areas, impeding replanting and new planting, and brought sisal cultivation, the latest and most capital-intensive of all East Sumatra's estate industries, to a complete end by cutting irrigation channels for rice cultivation through the plantings.

Although the loss of foreign earnings through the disruption of tobacco production was serious enough, the question of lease renewals threatened to pose an even greater threat to the national economy in the long run. Estates in Indonesia occupied land under varying conditions and only in West Java, where in the early nineteenth century land was sold by the Daendals and Raffles administrations to private buyers, did they possess freeholds. The greater part of these privately-owned lands continued to be worked by tenant subsistence farmers, but some holdings, of which the P & T Lands (*Pamanoekan en Tjiasemlanden*) was the largest and most famous, took up perennial cash-crop cultivation in the latter half of the nineteenth century and these eventually passed into the hands of Anglo-Indonesian Plantations Limited, which continued to hold title to the P & T Lands until 1958 when all estate freeholds were abolished. Such freehold estates, however, only accounted for some 9 per cent of the total estate area in 1958; all other estates operated with varying kinds of leasehold, of which the most important were the 'agricultural concessions' granted by local rulers in the indirectly governed parts of the Netherlands Indies, and in particular, by the Sultans of Deli, Langkat and Serdang in East Sumatra. These concessions were for periods of seventy-five years and were very favourable to the planters in that the rights of the local population to the use of land were not clearly defined; indeed, the concessionaires usually took over the feudal rights of the ruler in the land, traditionally half the produce of the cultivators. This of course was useless to the planter, and in practice he obtained something of much greater value,

---

[14] *On the system of cultivation used by the tobacco companies and the origins of the squatter problem, see Karl J. Pelzer, 'The agrarian conflict in East Sumatra', Pacific Affairs, vol. 30, 1957, pp. 151–9.*

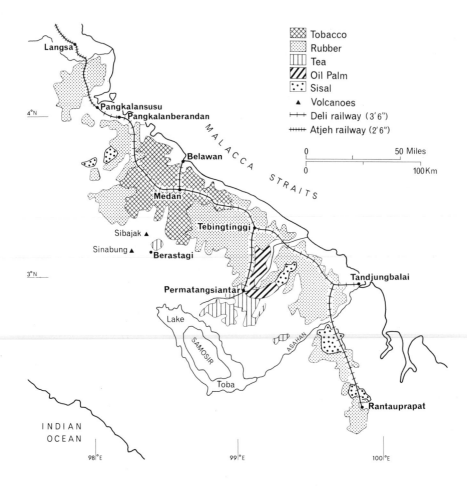

Fig. 7-2 The plantation industries of northeast Sumatra
This map merely indicates in a general way the areas within which designated crops might be
cultivated, and is not an indication of the planted area. Much of the area shown as devoted to
tobacco is either uncultivated or has been invaded by squatters.

namely the peasants' labour, although this was a much greater asset to the sugar planters of the densely populated Principalities of central Java than it was to the Sumatran planters. Exploitation of peasants by the planters provoked government intervention; in 1919 it was decided that no new concessions should be granted, and that on expiry existing concessions would be replaced by leases of the *erfpacht* type. These were granted under the provisions of the Agrarian Law of 1870, which empowered the Netherlands Indies government to lease land unencumbered by native rights to non-indigenes for up to seventy-five years; first made in West Java and in East Java, erfpacht leases were gradually extended to directly governed parts of Sumatra and though never as important as in Java, they became of major significance in North Sumatra. Additionally, in Central and East Java, sugar and tobacco companies rented village sawah land under the terms of the Land Rents Ordinance, which because of the specific provisions to safeguard the rights of peasant cultivators, made perennial crop cultivation impossible.

By the early Fifties many of the erfpacht leases had already fallen in and the balance would do so by 1965. Replanting was urgently necessary on many estates, not only to make good the damage and neglect resulting from the Japanese occupation and the revolution, but also to strengthen their competitive position against synthetic substitutes. A thirty-year lease extension proposed by the government was unacceptable to the planting companies as it would permit no more than one cycle of planting for most tree crops, which did not justify the investment necessary. With little or no inducement to replant, estates made no effort to expand their output of improved high-yielding planting material, and estate research and that of specialized institutions such as AVROS, the organization of the East Sumatra planters, virtually ceased. Thus when the foreign-owned estates finally passed into the hands of the state through the nationalizations of 1958 and 1964,[15] there was a dearth of material for replanting and new planting and little prospect of a speedy re-establishment of competitive efficiency.

Following on Indonesia's failure to obtain support for its claim to Irian at the United Nations in 1958, all Dutch-owned estates passed into the control of the PPN (*Pusat Perkebunan Negara*), a body originally set up to operate former Netherlands Indies government estates acquired on the transfer of sovereignty. Labour discipline and productivity on government estates was always markedly poorer than on the private estates, and the organization's limited resources of managerial and technical ability were further extended by the new take-overs.

---

[15] *Legally they were not nationalized but 'taken-over' or sequestrated to prevent any interruption of production. The typical Indonesian nationalization formula for foreign-owned enterprise was for the workers, usually in one of the militant unions under PKI control, to occupy a plant, thus forcing the government's hand. In 1964, however, the Army, anxious to forestall the communists, took over British and other foreign-owned estates itself.*

However, the banning of strikes following the regional revolts of 1957–58 some-what eased the labour problems. Other foreign-owned estates and 'mixed' enterprises (that is, those involving Dutch and other foreign capital) were allowed to continue operations, but under the Basic Agrarian Law of 1960 all private estates were obliged to surrender part of their land to the government. Most estates in fact held large areas unplanted; but whatever their original rights, estates could hold further occupancy for no more than twenty years. How-ever, land newly leased under the Basic Agrarian Law could be held for up to twenty-five years, with the possibility of further extension. After many years of government indecision, the new legislation and an improvement in United States–Indonesian relations prompted the American-owned estates to step up their replanting activities, but few British companies followed their example. In-deed, several British estates had been earlier sold off for a fraction of their real worth and most of the remainder had been let on contract to Indonesian nationals. In 1964, as a result of Britain's support to Malaysia in resisting Indonesia's con-frontation policy, not only all British-owned estates but those belonging to American, Belgian, Italian and even Chinese interests were also taken over.

The provision of the Basic Agrarian Law thus proved as much a dead letter in cash-crop production as it did in subsistence agriculture. The government estates never demonstrated that they could perform as well as the private estates they superseded, nor did expansion of their activities involve any improvement in living standards of estate workers. The decline of estate production led to a large increase in the share of the smallholder contribution to total output, but this resulted more from operation of the laws of mathematics than from any improve-ment in the smallholder's economic position, for the smallholder cash-crop producer, as with the Javanese *tani*, was also heavily exploited by the govern-ment. Nevertheless, the statistical record is far from the whole story, as it is well known that a substantial share of government estate output is unrecorded and the proceeds from its disposal pass into the pockets of estate managers, senior Army officers and local officials.[16]

In 1966 the Ampera government announced its intention of returning sequestrated properties to their former owners, an operation which it hoped would improve its prospects of acquiring large Western aid as well as further its economic stabilization programme, and a lengthy and inconclusive dialogue between the government and foreign interests ensued. The government con-templated joint ventures of the state and private capital, but appeared willing to grant to the companies the entire proceeds of production for some years as com-pensation for the take-overs; nevertheless, the companies were inevitably reluc-tant to make the large investment that would be necessary to rehabilitate their

---

[16] *Part of the smallholder output unquestionably represented pilfering from estates; more-over, some estate output was also deliberately concealed as smallholder produce, as this was easier to smuggle and thus produced a higher return.*

run-down properties, especially as the government appeared unwilling to release the estates' residential accommodation and the question of tenure remained undecided. In 1968, however, London Sumatra, one of the larger units in the Harrisons & Crosfield agency house, reached agreement over the terms of its return to Indonesian operations, which were reported as involving a tenure renewal of thirty years.

Natural rubber   Natural rubber is Indonesia's most important agricultural export and until 1963, when it was supplanted by petroleum, her largest net source of foreign exchange. The Netherlands Indies profited from the interwar rubber-restriction schemes which severely limited new planting in British rubber-producing territories, and through rapid new planting became by 1938 the world's largest natural rubber producer. Indonesia regained the premier position from Malaya in 1953 but lost it once more in 1957, and now appears to have little prospect of ever overtaking its rival. Total rubber production has to be inferred from figures of rubber exports, and these substantially understate the true position as even during confrontation much rubber continued to be smuggled out in the barter trade across the Straits of Malacca; but Malaysia's rigorous replanting and new planting programmes and new methods of preparing, grading and packaging natural rubber have set standards that Indonesia appears incapable of matching. Given the planting material and the administrative and financial machinery to make use of it, only a truly heroic programme of replanting will ensure Indonesia's survival as a major producer in an increasingly competitive total rubber market.

Yet the Netherlands Indies contribution to the natural rubber industry was profound. It was in East Sumatra during World War I that the selection of high-yielding clonal rubbers began, and the large Sumatran estates later pioneered in producing concentrated latex for export in bulk.[17] Many estates were of extremely large size, and those of the American rubber companies, such as that of HAPM, a United States Rubber Company subsidiary which sprawled over 76,000 acres near Kitan, or the 40,000-acre Wingfoot estate of Goodyear at Dolok Merangir, were the largest rubber estates ever created. Such enormous units were in large part the consequence of the favourable terms of the agricultural concessions, and the East Sumatran estates not only set records for size but also for speed of clearing and planting. This, however, was achieved at a heavy social cost that the great estate companies and the local rulers later had cause to regret; much of the post-independence policy towards the foreign estates in Indonesia can only be understood in the light of their history of forced and indentured labour, the use of penal sanctions against workers breaking contracts with employers long after these practices had disappeared in Malaya, and the estate's suppression of native rights in land.

[17] *Another major scientific contribution from East Sumatra was the discovery of the role of vitamins in diet, a study that arose from investigations into the nutrition of estate labour.*

Rubber cultivation was first introduced into East Sumatra from Malaya, and although estates were also later established in parts of adjacent Atjeh and Tapanuli, in the Priangan area of West Java and in Besuki in East Java, East Sumatra has remained the principal estate rubber area, with around 70 per cent of the estate-planted area of about 1·2 million acres. According to the International Rubber Study Group, Indonesian estate production amounted in 1964 to 220,000 tons, a figure that is in all probability a considerable under-assessment, but taking these figures at face value would give an overall output per acre of some 410 lb per annum. But assuming about 10 per cent of the planted area was immature as against a desideratum of 21 per cent,[18] this would raise the output per mature acre to some 450 lb per annum. However these figures are regarded, it is clear that Indonesia's estates are a very long way from attaining the levels of efficiency of their Malaysian counterparts.

The growth of smallholder rubber production in the Netherlands Indies was a striking illustration of the response of indigenous peasants to market stimuli. As in Malaya the simple techniques of cultivation and processing were very quickly learned, and *Hevea* rubber proved ideally suited to the ladangs of many Sumatran peoples. Long accustomed to planting pepper and coffee on their clearings, *Hevea*, a forest tree, needed even less attention, and in seven years a planting had become a valuable asset created at very little cost to the cultivator. The interwar restriction schemes, however, provided a major stimulus to 'native production', for the Netherlands Indies government for long refused to be a party to international restriction in order to protect the interests of the indigenous cultivator. When it finally became a participant in the International Rubber Agreement (1934–41), the physical difficulty of locating and enumerating the extent of peasant holdings proved enormous, and in fact the expansion of peasant production continued quite unsuspected by the government.

As with its predecessor, the Indonesian government has never possessed more than very imprecise estimates of the total smallholder-planted area and its output. Official figures of smallholder rubber exports are heavily underestimated, as a very large volume of smallholder rubber has always moved in an illegal barter trade with Malaya, and these exports were used by rebellious Sumatran Army commanders in 1957–58 to finance the costs of the war. For what it is worth, the smallholder rubber area in 1951 was estimated at 3·2 million acres, although this figure was the same as that quoted by the Dutch a decade previously. Smallholder production in 1964 was estimated at some 419,000 tons, giving an overall natural rubber production of some 639,000 tons. But in view of the low prices paid by the central government for exports through official channels and the limited availability of consumer goods in exchange for the steadily depreciating rupiah, smallholders and dealers have had every incentive to under-declare.

Though overwhelmingly located in the Outer Islands, the distribution of

[18] See p. 230

Estate smokehouse, Deli, east Sumatra.

Smallholder making slab rubber, Palembang district, south Sumatra.

smallholder rubber production differs significantly from that of estates, being greatest in those parts of Sumatra that were directly administered in the Netherlands Indies; Palembang, Djambi and Lampung are thus much more important than East Sumatra and Tapanuli, the major estate areas. But other very important areas of smallholder production exist in West Kalimantan, and in South and East Kalimantan; here many smallholdings are owned by Chinese, who do not practise a ladang system of agriculture but manage their holdings very much in the manner of the Chinese rubber smallholders of the adjacent portions of East Malaysia. Kalimantan smallholders probably produce about 30 per cent of Indonesia's smallholder rubber as against some 50–60 per cent from Sumatra, but the Chinese smallholders produce a superior product, processing their output in the form of ribbed smoked sheets as in Malaysia. Most Sumatran smallholders, faced with formidable transport problems and often living at some distance from their ladangs, have tended to reduce processing to the simplest form possible; the collected latex is merely poured into a wooden box and allowed to coagulate from exposure to the air, thus producing so-called slab rubber. This eventually finds its way into the hands of Chinese merchants with connections with the dealers of Singapore and Penang, where large remilling plants have long existed to process Sumatran slab.

But even before confrontation the Indonesian government had endeavoured to check the export of smallholder rubber in this crude form, and to encourage a greater degree of domestic processing. Though the production of ribbed smoked sheet is a very simple operation, a greater domestic participation in processing would involve substantial investment. It would require, above all, greatly improved transport in south-central and south Sumatra, where such few roads as there are have suffered heavy damage since 1941, and many have disappeared altogether. Without such investment it is difficult to see how smallholders can up-grade their product.

The most unsatisfactory aspect of the smallholder rubber industry, however, is the very unfavourable age-composition of trees, and the fact that much of the limited new planting that is going on is largely of unselected material. In much of Sumatra and Kalimantan where there is no shortage of land, new planting makes better sense than replanting, and avoids loss of income during the gestation period. But the official replanting schemes, such as that of 1961, which planned to replant one-third of the estate area and one-sixth of the smallholder area, exist largely on paper; and without adequate supplies of high-yielding material, which is in short supply in every natural rubber producing country, there is little prospect of implementing them. Indonesia has also fallen far behind in the production of new forms of rubber such as concentrated latices, and rubbers of guaranteed technical specifications.

In 1963 an American economic mission, after some pungent comments on the state of the Indonesian economy, recommended a $45 million World Bank

Loan for rubber replanting, of which $39 million was to compensate for export losses during the maturation period. Indonesian intransigence over the formation of Malaysia and its withdrawal from the World Bank and the International Monetary Fund prevented any action being taken to implement this recommendation.

Sugar and tobacco   The sugar industry is no longer of any major significance in the Indonesian economy. The Netherlands Indies once had an annual production of some three million tons of refined sugar, and as an exporter was exceeded only by Cuba. Indonesia's centrifugal sugar production in 1966 was less than 600,000 tons and crystalline sugar was virtually a semi-luxury, exchanging hands at fancy prices in the black market (*Table 7-5*). But the sugar industry had such a profound effect on the development of Java's agriculture and on population structure and rural psychology that it merits more than a brief dismissal.

The sugar industry is confined to Central and East Java and its most distinctive feature is that virtually all the cane for modern mills is planted on rented village sawahs; cane occupies the land for some 14–16 months and the land then reverts to the production of rice and other food crops. Only one-third of the village sawah land can be occupied by cane in any one wet season, and sugar cultivation thus moves in great blocks over the sawah land according to a rigid production schedule (*Table 7-8*). This pattern of cultivation was determined by the Agrarian Law and Land Ordinance of 1870, which although preventing the

Table 7-8   *The cycle of sugar cultivation in Java*

VILLAGE SAWAH LAND

	First area	Second area	Third area
Dry season—1966	Planting of cane (May–July)	Harvest of old cane (June–November)	Polowidjo*
Wet season—1966/67	Cane	Rice	Rice
Dry season—1967	Harvest of old cane (June–November)	Polowidjo	Planting of cane (May–July)
Wet season—1967/68	Rice	Rice	Cane
Dry season—1968	Polowidjo	Planting of cane (May–July)	Harvest of old cane (June–November)
Wet season—1968/69	Rice	Cane	Rice
Dry season—1969	*As for Dry Season—1966*		

* Food crops such as maize, sweet potatoes, groundnuts, soybeans and other legumes are collectively known as polowidjo.

Source: After van Hall and van de Koppel (eds.), *De Landbouw in den Indischen Archipel,* 1946

ownership of land by non-indigenes, endeavoured to make land available for
enterprises that needed much capital investment, while at the same time protecting the rights of indigenous cultivators. Thus the peasant was allowed use
of the land for food crop production through two successive wet seasons, a stipulation that made perennial crop cultivation, or even the usual practice of one crop
of plant cane and two ratoon crops, impossible. Cane thus had to be planted
afresh each season. Through a system of leasing, the planters were confirmed in
their use of land for long enough to justify heavy investment in cultivation,
transport and processing. Leases of up to a maximum of $21\frac{1}{2}$ years were permitted,
through which the companies were able to exploit the tani's perpetual shortage
of cash—the further the lease ran, the lower the rent. In effect the *tani*, the legal
owner or the holder of usufructory right, became a labourer on his own land, and
the rent was a form of credit.

The laws of 1870, however, merely confirmed a system that had grown up
long before, for as early as the eighteenth century Javanese sultans had been trans-
ferring their feudal rights to aliens for the production of cash crops for distant
markets. Under the *apannage* system the holder of feudal rights, the nobleman or
patuh, was entitled to but half the rice crop; but what the planters wanted was the
land and the labour to work it. Forced labour thus predated the Culture System,
and it continued after 1870 in the Principalities of Jogjakarta and Solo, except
that it was operated on behalf of private interests instead of the state. In these
indirectly-ruled areas the planters not only occupied half the land instead of one-
third as in the government territories, but also enjoyed the use of compulsory unpaid labour until as late as 1918.[19] With such advantages the Vorstenlanden
ranked as the leading sugar-producing areas of the country until the Twenties,
when they were surpassed by the Surabaja, Malang and Kediri districts, but
their sugar industry continued to be of major importance right down to the outbreak of World War II.

At its height before the onset of the Great Depression, cane cultivation
occupied nearly 500,000 acres rotated over some 1·5 million acres of the best
sawahs of Central and East Java, and exercised a profound effect on rural life.
It was by far the largest source of wage employment in rural areas, and the heavy
applications of nitrogenous fertilizer used for cane production greatly benefited
the succeeding food crops. Save in the most important test of all, man-hours per
ton of sugar, the industry was remarkably efficient; through meticulous irrigation
and the development of high-yielding canes, sugar output per acre was raised to
the highest levels in the world; the famous variety POJ 2878 developed at the
Pasuruan research station in the early Twenties effected a major revolution in
tropical agriculture and has been widely used in breeding more modern varieties.
In sugar, as in tea, the Netherlands Indies of the Twenties had probably the

[19] D. W. Fryer, '*Jogjakarta: economic development in an Indonesian city state*', Economic
Development and Cultural Change, *vol. 7, 1959, p. 457.*

world's lowest costs of production, but this was achieved at high social cost. The rent received from the companies together with the wages for working on sugar-land never fully compensated the peasant for the loss of his food crops, and in Geertz's view, the sugar industry was the decisive factor in stifling peasant initiative and confining indigenous agriculture in a rigid mould. The tani could never rise higher than a field hand or factory labourer, since all positions involving the slightest responsibility were the prerogative of aliens or Eurasians; nor could the smallholder obtain a share in the industry as mills were forbidden to accept his cane. The expansion of the sugar industry with its intensive irrigation made a high rate of population increase inevitable, but yet denied it any chance of an agricultural revolution which could have offset an increasingly unfavourable man-land ration.[20]

There is some truth in Geertz's thesis, though not as much as is claimed, and the Javanese tani was certainly not the most oppressed peasant in Southeast Asia. That the sugar industry was detested by the majority of villagers is not open to doubt, for during the Revolutionary War about half of all the mills in Java were destroyed. Some were rebuilt in the Fifties with financial assistance from *Bank Industri Negara*, a new state development bank, and the Chinese-owned share of the industry certainly increased; in 1958, however, the entire industry passed into the hands of the state, although the largest Chinese concerns such as Kian Gwan, which operated four large mills in the Semarang area, were taken over in earlier outbursts of anti-Chinese feeling. Restrictions on processing small-holder cane were removed, for smallholder cane was now eagerly sought after by the mills as their own production was inadequate.[21]

Shortage of seed cane and fertilizers, a deficiency of managerial and technical ability, an inefficient and intractable labour force, and, above all, prices for cane that did not reflect the price of sugar on the internal market, all combined to keep productivity much lower than before the war; yields of crystalline sugar in the Sixties were around 1,000 kg per hectare (about 4 tons per acre) compared with the prewar average of 1,600 kg per hectare (about 6·4 tons per acre). As a result, many of the fifty-five or so mills in operation found it difficult to keep their plant fully employed during the harvest season, and since 1961 peasants in sugar dis-tricts have been compelled to devote part of their land to cane, for delivery to the mills at quite unrealistic prices. Thus the wheel has come full circle; as Pelzer remarks, this policy differed little from that of the forced deliveries of the colonial period.[22] Subsequent government pronouncements indicated that a solution to the problem of raising sugar production is expected to be found in dry-field

[20] *Geertz, op. cit., pp. 72–80.*

[21] *Some smallholder cane was grown under contract to mills even before World War II. But as most smallholder cane was grown on dry fields, the yield of sucrose per ton was much lower than that of cane grown on sawahs, which made for difficulties in mill opera-tions.*

[22] *Karl J. Pelzer, in Ruth McVey (ed.), op. cit., p. 145.*

mechanized cane cultivation in the Outer Islands. Until then, it appears that most Indonesians will have to depend largely on traditional non-crystalline *gula* for their sugar requirements, and for sugar exports prospects remain bleak.

Before 1939 tobacco also was grown on rented sawahs in the Principalities, but in the important estate area of Besuki in East Java, where much land was held under *erfpacht*, production by tenants under contract to the European curing houses was as important as that by estates themselves. It was, however, on the agricultural concessions of the Deli area that tobacco production reached its apogee, where enormous areas were reserved for the cultivation of probably the world's most exacting, and certainly its most highly priced, agricultural product —the celebrated Deli wrapper leaf. Java, however, also specialized in cigar tobaccos, principally fillers and binders, and the increasing preference for Virginia cigarettes even in Indonesia itself has inevitably affected the tobacco industry. Attempts have been made to grow Virginia tobaccos in the Jogjakarta and Solo areas, but in a smallholder industry it is difficult to maintain the meticulous cultivation and harvesting practices necessary for a product of high uniform quality, and most growers find production of the *krosok* tobaccos used in indigenous-type cigarettes an easier task. Moreover, the smallholders have been as much exploited by the officials of the Virginia tobacco cooperatives as they were by the old estate companies. Apart from the problems caused by squatter infiltration, the Deli area has also suffered severely from declining standards of cultivation and harvesting; wrapper tobacco must be rigorously inspected for holes and protected from insect damage. Unlike other Indonesian tobaccos, Deli wrapper leaf is a unique product, and the decline in exports primarily reflects Indonesia's own internal disorders. Even before 1958 the Deli Maatschappij, the most famous of the Sumatra planting companies, had threatened to withdraw from production, and on the nationalization of their properties in that year the Dutch companies began a long and confused legal battle over the ownership of leaf from their former estates delivered to foreign markets. But whatever the past history of the Sumatran estates, it seems doubtful that the wrapper tobacco industry can survive without the skill and knowledge of the companies.

The decline of the sugar and tobacco industries has a special significance in that it has sharply reduced Java's contribution to total export earnings, and has made that island appear more of a parasite on the Outer Islands than ever before. It also suggests that the diminution of capitalist enterprise in Javan agriculture, far from acting as a stimulus to peasant initiative, has resulted in a recrudescence of economic and social relationships little different from the traditional feudalism.

Other export crops All other crops may be conveniently grouped together. Some, such as the oil palm, coconuts and tobacco are lowland crops; tea and *kina* (cinchona) are restricted to the uplands; and coffee may be grown in either environment, although it is largely a lowland crop. Copra, coffee and pepper are almost exclusively produced by smallholders, whereas the oil palm, tea and kina are virtually restricted to estates. But all have levels of output well below those of 1938, and for some output is even below that of 1928.

In terms of export earnings and in general significance to everyday life, the coconut is the most important of these secondary export crops. Coconuts are widely grown for local consumption throughout Indonesia, and are planted at surprisingly high elevations in Java. Export production, however, is more restricted and is largely a prerogative of the northern peninsula of Sulawesi, particularly the Minahasa area, and the Sangihe and Talaud islands to the north. Large-scale planting commenced here around the turn of the century and was greatly encouraged by the growth of the margarine and hydrogenated fats industries, in which Dutch companies played a pioneer role. In the interwar period Indonesia was by far the world's largest copra producer, but since 1945 it has been surpassed by the Philippines.

All of the difficulties that confront the Philippine industry occur on an even larger scale in Indonesia. Prolonged neglect and the ravages of the rhinoceros beetle have greatly reduced productivity, and probably more than half of all plantings are more than fifty years old. Processing methods are crude and, in general, Indonesian copra is of low grade. Domestic consumption of coconut products has grown very rapidly, thus reducing the surplus available for export, and for many years producers were exploited by the Copra Fund, a state body which made compulsory purchases at unrealistically low prices. A profitable barter and smuggling trade thus developed between northern Sulawesi, Maluku and the southern Philippine ports, very similar to that conducted between Sumatra and Malaya; in eastern Indonesia also, local Army commanders used part of the proceeds of the barter trade to finance developmental projects within their areas.

The oil palm industry in the Netherlands Indies began almost a decade after the first commercial plantings of *Hevea* rubber, although the African oil palm had in fact been introduced into the country as long ago as 1845. Once established, however, development was very rapid, as it became apparent that in equatorial Southeast Asia the oil palm did even better than in its native African environment, and that it could produce more than twice as much oil per acre as coconuts. The industry has been entirely confined to East Sumatra and, in order to exploit economies of scale, estates are of very large size. The oil palm needs more rigorous care and attention than rubber, and although estate processing plants were rehabilitated after the war, poor maintenance in the field and consequent infestation by insect pests such as the rhinoceros beetle and red-stripe weevil, and damage by rats, have kept productivity low. Estate operations were severely affected by the 1957–58 Sumatran revolt, and guerilla attacks on estate factories continued even after the end of the revolt; as a result further productive capacity was put out of action and even a decade later had still not been restored. The expanding world market for vegetable oils has thus largely been to the benefit of Indonesia's competitors, particularly Malaysia, where a rapid expansion of the oil palm area threatens to leave Indonesia's palm oil production far behind by 1970. Moreover, Indonesia's chances of obtaining a stake for the smallholder in the industry now appear slim.

Broadly similar misfortunes have befallen tea, once another major export industry. Before 1939 Netherlands Indies tea enjoyed a high reputation for quality and, with perhaps the world's lowest cost of production, was strongly competitive in world markets. This situation was partly the result of very favourable natural conditions; there was no poorer-quality lowland tea production as in India, for the tea-gardens were planted on deep volcanic soils at elevations of 4,500 to 6,000 feet. The principal producing areas were the Puntjak district between Bogor and Sukabumi and the Pengalengan-Santosa district of West Java, where climatic conditions made possible pluckings at intervals of about twelve days throughout the year. A number of minor tea-producing areas were located at similar elevations on the volcanic massifs of Central and East Java, but another important area was the Permatangsiantar (usually, Siantar) district of East Sumatra, where some very large estates were planted shortly before World War I. By 1950, all the gardens in the major producing areas of West Java were overdue for replanting, but in view of their vigorous pruning and spraying policies most estates could probably have succeeded in maintaining output per bush had sufficient labour been available. The Sundanese labour force of the West Java tea districts was somewhat less militant than the Javanese labour of the Sumatran rubber estates, but it was hardly cooperative, and on most tea-gardens, labourers endeavoured as soon as possible to get back to the private plots provided by the estate, on which they grew cabbages, leeks and other profitable temperate-climate vegetables for sale. The labour shortage compelled many estates to purchase 'wet' leaf from smallholder producers, and some large estates in the Siantar district were forbidden to produce leaf themselves and forced to purchase it from local farmers, who in fact became tenants on the estates' land. Tea, however, is far from an ideal smallholder crop, for even where centralized processing can be made available, tea bushes need regular treatment with fertilizer and meticulous spraying to control fungoid diseases such as blister blight and red rust, as well as insect pests; thus, the increased share of production originating from smallholders has been accompanied by a marked decline in quality. Although a substantial part of the Indonesian tea industry was British-owned before the take-overs of 1964, the industry was unable to match the greatly enhanced productivity achieved by its Indian and Ceylonese competitors. Nevertheless, the tea industry has shown surprising resiliency; the leaf cannot be disposed of except through an estate factory, so the problem of pilfering is not severe, and the planted material, though elderly, is still healthy. Given new processing equipment and better labour discipline, the industry might still recover, but rapid expansion of tea production in African countries such as Kenya and Malawi, which have much lower costs than even the most efficient Asian producers, has cast a deep gloom throughout the industry.

The Pengalengan district was once also famous for its *kina* (cinchona) estates, whose bark output was processed into quinine in a state-owned plant in Bandung. The development of synthetic anti-malarials during World War II was a major blow to the cinchona industry and during the early Fifties kina gardens were replanted to tea wherever possible.[23] Bark output in 1964 was scarcely 2,000 tons, less than one-sixth that of 1939.

A brief reference may be made to spices, the oldest exports of what is now Indonesia. Pepper, the most important, is still grown on Sumatran ladangs, but the more important producers are the Chinese smallholders of Bangka and other islands east of Sumatra, and of Kalimantan. Pepper is not only a very soil-depleting crop, but it is very prone to violent price oscillations; pepper cultivation is thus well suited to the Chinese temperament, which is notorious for its partiality for speculative ventures. The supply situation is further complicated by the manipulations of the Chinese merchants of Singapore, who have long controlled the pepper trade of Indonesia and Malaysia, and who endeavour from time to time to rig the market. The more famous spices, such as the nutmeg and mace of Banda and the cloves of Ternate and Tidore, are still grown on their original islands, but Java,

[23] *It is worth pointing out, however, that continued production of quinine is highly desirable, for some plasmodia are occasionally resistant to synthetic anti-malarials.*

Tea estate near Santosa, Priangan highlands, West Java. Wattle trees provide light shade and supply fuel for the factory.

Sumatra and Sulawesi all produce a little. Cloves are in great demand for the production of *kretek*, or local cigarettes, but production was quite inadequate long before 1939, and large imports were made from Zanzibar. Little success has attended postwar efforts to stimulate domestic production.

MINING AND MANUFACTURING INDUSTRIES

Despite its direct interest in many kinds of mineral production, the Netherlands Indies government paid insufficient attention to mining industries as an agent of economic development. Since independence the role of minerals in the national economy has grown considerably; from generating only 15 per cent of export earnings in 1925 the contribution of minerals had grown to over 30 per cent by 1954 and to over 37 per cent a decade later. In large part this statistical increase has reflected the large fall in the volume of most agricultural exports, but, in both quantitative and monetary terms, mineral exports continued to grow throughout the life of the Republic. In comparison with the overall stagnation of economic activity in the country, the recent history of the mineral industry has been highly anomalous, largely in consequence of the extraordinary economic strength of the petroleum companies. But petroleum apart, production levels of every other mineral have tended to decline, even in the face of rising prices.

Petroleum

Petroleum production and refining is Indonesia's largest and most capital-intensive enterprise. Since 1963 it has displaced rubber as the largest source of gross foreign exchange earnings, although the large imports necessary to undertake oil production reduce the industry's net earnings below those of rubber. Yet, remarkable though it has been against the local background of economic stagnation, Indonesia's oil industry does not rank very highly in a world industry doubling its output every decade, and the country's output of some 24 million metric tons in 1965 represented a smaller proportion of world output than did the 1955 output of 14 million metric tons. In 1965 complete nationalization of the petroleum industry was close at hand and a repetition of the dreary consequences of similar action in Mexico, Argentina and Iran appeared the most likely fate of the Indonesian industry. Fortunately, unforeseen political changes enabled this fate to be avoided.

About 90 per cent of Indonesia's petroleum output is produced by three foreign companies that until 1960 represented five of the seven 'majors' in the world oil industry. The oldest and until the middle Fifties always the largest producer was the Bataafsche Petroleum Maatschappij (BPM), later renamed Shell Indonesia, whose interests in the country date as far back as 1885. BPM was created by a merger in 1907 of the Royal Dutch Company's interests in North Sumatra and East Java with those of the British-owned Shell Company in East

Borneo, and from such humble origins has grown the world's second largest oil company. Jersey Standard's interests date from 1912 with the formation of the Nederlandsche Koloniale Petroleum Maatschappij (NKPM), with concessions mainly in South Sumatra; this company, in which Socony-Mobil also had an interest, became the Standard Vacuum Oil Company (Stanvac) after World War II.[24]

The two other 'majors', California Standard and Texaco, effected entry in the interwar period through their subsidiary Nederlandsche Pacific Petroleum Mij (now known as Caltex Pacific). Operations began in north-central Sumatra in 1935 and the company has since maintained an aggressive expansionist policy. The balance of output is derived from three state-owned entities, which operate BPM concessions that the government refused to hand back after 1950, and those worked by BPM on behalf of a joint venture with the former Netherlands Indies government (the Nederlandsche-Indische Aardolie Maatschappij, or NIAM) which was taken over completely by the government in 1957. Thus the new state has had a small share in petroleum production from its inception, which it has continuously endeavoured to enlarge. Although the demands of the PKI and the oil workers' unions for outright nationalization were resisted, after 1960 ultimate state ownership of the entire industry became accepted policy. Despite this threat, however, petroleum production continued to rise, almost entirely through expansion in Caltex's Minas field.

In West New Guinea the three major oil companies combined in the Nederlandsche Nieuw Guinee Petroleum Mij, which in the peak year of 1955 produced almost half a million tons from fields in the Klamono area of the Vogelkop (Bird's Head) peninsula. An eight-inch diameter pipeline connected the fields with the port of Sorong, but despite heavy investment in new exploration, the company failed to locate any new fields of commercial significance and production fell steadily in the later Fifties to about half peak level. The company was on the point of withdrawing from production when in 1964 the area passed to Indonesian control. Thereupon the company sold out to the government, and was renamed Sorong Petroleum.

From the earliest days of the industry Sumatra has always been the important producing island, oil having been discovered in many anticlinal formations to the east of the Barisan in parts of north, central and south Sumatra (*Figure 7-3*). East and southeast Kalimantan produce the balance of about 15 per cent of total output, apart from a mere 0·2 per cent derived from the old fields of Java at Tjepu in Rembang and in the Surabaja district. Most of Indonesia's oil production before 1960 came from so-called '5a contract' concessions, granted, under a 1918 amendment to the 1899 Mining Law, for a duration of forty years. By the later

[24] *The Standard Vacuum Oil Company was dissolved in 1960 under American anti-trust laws, and the company's properties were divided between its two parents. The Indonesian operations passed to a new concern, Esso Eastern Limited.*

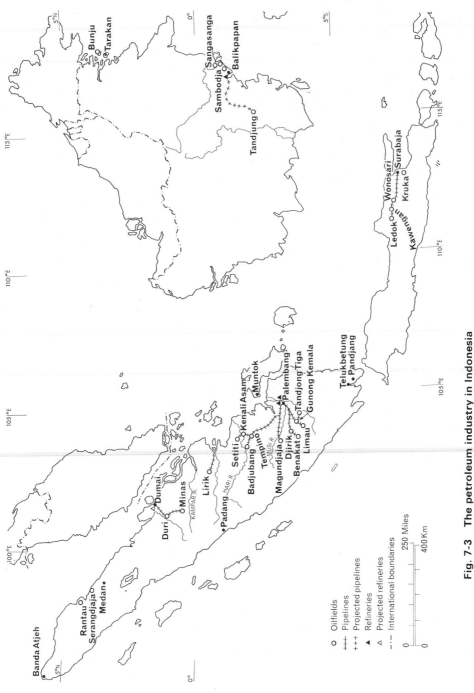

Fig. 7-3 The petroleum industry in Indonesia
Not shown on this map are the offshore operations of Japanese and American companies in the waters of Atjeh and the Malacca Straits.

Banda Atjeh
Rantau
Serangdjaja
Medan
Duri
Dumai
Minas
Padang
Lirik
Setiti
Badjubang
Tempino
Magundjaja
Djirik
Benakat
Limau
Gunong Kemala
Kenali Asam
Muntok
Palembang
Tandjong Tiga
Telukbetung
Pandjang
HARI R.
MUSI R.
KAMPAR R.

Bunju
Tarakan
Sangasanga
Sambodja
Balikpapan
Tandjung

Ledok
Wonosari
Kawengan
Kruka
Surabaja

○ Oilfields
+++ Pipelines
+++ Projected pipelines
▲ Refineries
△ Projected refineries
-·- International boundaries

0   250 Miles
0   400 Km

100°E   105°E   110°E   115°E   5°N   0°   5°S

Fifties, therefore, most of these concessions had a short life expectancy, and the companies were increasingly concerned about their renewal; no new concessions had been granted for over twenty years and exploratory work had come to a complete standstill. Indonesia's production was entirely derived from existing prewar concessions, and particularly from fields discovered immediately before the war and which could not then be developed, such as the Minas, Bekasap and Duri fields of Caltex, and the Lirik field of Stanvac. The companies continually represented that even the maintenance of production necessitated a continued proving of new reserves, and that in the absence of new concessions, their planned investment in new drilling, pipelines, refineries and terminal facilities could not be implemented.

Although the oil companies, and BPM in particular, suffered from the disabilities general to foreign enterprise in Indonesia, they were initially protected by their 'let-alone agreements', under which in return for the payment of a fixed sum in dollars the companies were allowed to retain the balance of their foreign earnings, from which they were to rehabilitate their refineries and other equipment. The agreements, which also provided for a maximum of 'Indonesianization', that is, the recruitment and training of Indonesians for skilled jobs in oilfields and refineries, lasted until 1954, when they were replaced by a 50:50 sharing of the profits of local production between the government and the companies, on the model of similar agreements in Venezuela and the Middle East. In this way Shell's Pladju and Stanvac's Sungei Gerong refineries, both situated on the Musi river near Palembang, were rebuilt and enlarged after their destruction during the war. The companies' profits were, however, entirely derived from the export of crude oil, and the necessity of supplying the growing domestic market with refined products involved them in increasingly large losses; under the pressure of inflation, product prices fixed by government became increasingly

Table 7-9 *Indonesia: mineral production, 1965*

	thousand metric tons
Petroleum	23,910
Pertamin	560
Permina	1,040
Permigan	90
Caltex	15,950
Shell	3,440
Esso	2,830
Tin concentrates	14·9
Bauxite	688
Coal	272
Nickel	130

Source: Nugroho, *Indonesia in Facts and Figures,* Djakarta, 1967

out of line with those of the free market. Fortunately Caltex possessed no prewar refinery, though it came under increasingly severe pressure to construct one.

In their dealings with the government, however, the companies held a trump card; they could always threaten to withdraw from production in what was for them a relatively small theatre of operations. Costs of production in Indonesia, moreover, were much higher than in Venezuela, the Middle East or North Africa. Indonesia's numerous oil structures are small and widely scattered, and although wells are generally shallow, climate and terrain combine to make exploratory and developmental costs high. Output per well is little more than half that of Venezuela, and almost one-twentieth of that of the Middle East. Indonesia's heavy paraffinic crudes are often waxy and sulphurous, thus presenting special problems in transport and refining. As the majors were under increasing pressure to raise production in several host countries whose shut-in surpluses were large enough to exceed Indonesia's output without the drilling of another well, Indonesia's increasing hostility towards the oil companies after 1960 was thus inviting disaster. Unburdened by refinery and product problems, and anxious to exploit the booming Japanese market for crude with its new fields, Caltex, however, could afford to adopt a more ambitious policy than its rivals, and constructed a 30-inch pipeline across the swamps of east Sumatra, linking its Minas, Bekasap and Duri fields with a new harbour at Dumai and the Malacca Straits, capable of accommodating tankers of up to 80,000 d.w.t. Both Stanvac and Shell also had plans for new pipeline construction, the former from its Lirik fields to a terminal on the Siak river and the latter to link its Tandjung field in southeast Kalimantan to the coast, but neither felt the situation justified their implementation.

In 1957 the joint venture with Shell in the Djambi area of central Sumatra was taken over completely by the state, but the new organization, now known as Pertamin (*Perusahaan Tambang Minjak*), has never attained the 1·5 million tons production level of its predecessor, although it is the largest of the three state oil entities. That three such organizations were deemed necessary reflects perhaps not only Indonesian preference for duplication and administrative complexity, but also regional pressures and the demands of the PKI-dominated oil workers' unions. The prewar Atjeh concessions of BPM which were not returned to the company, produced more than one million tons of crude in 1938, and were operated by a variety of agencies before 1960 when their operation was entrusted to Permina (*Perusahaan Minjak Nasional*). These north Sumatra fields had long been the subject of abuse by officials and workers for their own private profit, and their operation at times had reached the proportion of major scandals. Similarly, BPM's concessions in Java, taken over by local workers in 1949, were organized as Permigan (*Perusahaan Minjak dan Gas Bumi Nasional*), which will probably assume responsibility for all future operations in Java and in eastern islands, including Seram, where in the past some oil was produced by BPM from the Bula district.

The role of the state organizations was defined in the long-awaited new Mining Law of 1960, which declared that eventually all Indonesia's oil would be exploited by the state corporations; if, however, they were not in a position to do so, foreign firms could contract to assist, payment for such services being made as a percentage of production. Such contracts were to be of twenty years' duration and on a 60:40 production share basis, but the foreign companies could expect no additions to any old concessions they might hold. These provisions were broadly similar to those made between the international oil companies and Argentina in 1959 (hence the term 'Argentine agreement'), but in fact they were not so very different from those already embodied in the old 1918 Law, which also made provision for state ownership and joint ventures as well as for normal commercial concessions. But given the tax structure and other levies, to say nothing of the price control system over internally distributed products, the companies found the new conditions unattractive and output stagnated. Nevertheless, growing pressure in the world oil business from aggressive 'independents' produced some takers; the Pan American Indonesia Oil Company, a subsidiary of Indiana Standard, entered into an agreement with Pertamin as exclusive contractor, and was granted a ten-year exploration and twenty-year exploitation contract for a large area of central Sumatra close to Caltex's Minas field, for which that company and Stanvac had long been pressing. Other independents followed as contractors to one or other of the state entities—Union Oil in north Sumatra, Amoco (American Oil Company) in central Sumatra, and Mitsui and other Japanese interests in both land and offshore production in Shell's old Atjeh concessions. In conformity with its new obligations to OPEC (Organization of Petroleum Exporting Countries), the government also attempted to step up its share of the profits of existing production by the three major companies by insisting on a 60:40 division.

The Indonesian offer was too little and too late. Promising new fields did not materialize and other oil-producing countries found that under the mounting world shut-in surplus, an expanding production was bringing a static return. Newer entrants to the industry such as Libya and Nigeria were, moreover, prepared to allow sales at a substantial discount in order to establish their market position. The revenue from the petroleum industry, which was to provide a very large share of the foreign exchange for the Category A projects in the Eight Year Development Plan, failed to materialize, and increasing political and economic instability provided no climate for a greatly enhanced foreign investment. Indonesian oil exports declined by almost one-third between 1961 and 1964, and with rapidly declining reserves of foreign exchange the government was obliged to reach some accommodation with the companies. The Tokyo agreement of November 1963 appeared to mark a turning point in the industry. Although eventual state ownership of the entire industry was confirmed, this would be programmed according to the performance of the state entities, and with the offer of new concessions in areas they had long sought, the three major companies were prepared to accept a 40:60 production share.

As so often in Indonesia's brief and tragic economic history, this reappearance of rationality was short-lived. The confrontation of Malaysia led swiftly to the sequestration of all British assets, and as evidence of American support for Malaysia grew, the American companies also came under attack. All foreign oil companies were placed under the supervision of the state in 1965, and to prepare the way for the final take-over of all refining activities, local sales were also absorbed by the government at mid-year.

As domestic sales of products resulted in huge losses, this was a purely prestige venture. For many years the price of petroleum products had been kept at artificially low levels by the government, with the inevitable result that supplies disappeared into the black market. Much of the pressure on the government for unrealistically low product prices came from the P K I, which wished to maintain the very low fares charged for public transport, and on taking over the internal distribution of products the state was obliged to pay a huge subsidy to cover the losses of the distributing agencies. At the end of 1965, however, all Shell's assets were taken over, for which the company was to receive $110 million in compensation over a five-year period. With the political changes following the suppression of the P K I *coup* and the elevation of economic development to a position of high priority among the goals of the Suharto administration, the outlook for the petroleum industry brightened considerably. The Sultan of Jogjakarta, Deputy Prime Minister for Economic Affairs in the Ampera cabinet, declared that the Shell take-over was a waste of public money, but it is improbable that the company will be allowed to continue to operate. As with all host governments in the world petroleum industry, Indonesia will undoubtedly continue to press strongly for an increasing share in the exploitation of its petroleum wealth, but after an almost disastrous 1966, when precipitate increases in gasoline prices caused public transport to disappear from the streets of Djakarta and for a time petroleum exports virtually ceased, output commenced to grow, and by 1968 attained a level of 28 million tons. Indeed, at the end of the year, Indonesia suddenly became one of the most eagerly contested areas in the world for exploratory rights as the government began to receive bids for the potentially rich offshore areas in the Java and South China Seas. Whether the mood of optimism can be sustained remains to be seen, but for the first time in almost two decades the petroleum industry faced the future with confidence.

Tin

Throughout most of the century Indonesia has vied with Bolivia for the position of the world's second largest tin producer. By an odd quirk of fate, however, tin-mining in both countries since the middle Fifties has operated under distinctly uncongenial political and social conditions and production has sharply declined.

This loss of production from two major producers has been an important factor in the sharp appreciation of tin prices, which by 1966 had reached a level almost double that of a decade earlier. Nevertheless, there were other powerful influences helping to push up prices, and the inability of the Indonesian industry to respond was symptomatic of the general stagnation of the economy.

Rehabilitation of the tin industry was speedily accomplished after the end of the Japanese occupation; by 1948 the production level of the immediate pre-war years was regained, and in 1954, with some eight new dredges in operation, the pre-Great Depression maximum of nearly 36,000 tons was equalled.[25] From then on, however, production fell almost continuously to a little less than 13,000 tons in 1963, and though there was a recovery in 1964 this was not maintained. The primary reasons for the decline of the industry were the failure to make the investment necessary to maintain capital equipment in working order, and the growing shortage of managerial and technical ability.

Indonesia's tin deposits occur in a chain of islands off the east coast of Sumatra, and geologically are a continuation of those of the Main Range of Malaya. Normally about two-thirds of Indonesia's tin output is derived from the large island of Bangka, the balance coming largely from Belitung (Billiton) with a small contribution of around 10 per cent from Singkep. Small unworked deposits also exist in some of the islands of the Riau group. Although the modes of occurrence of the deposits and their working are very similar to those of the West Malaysian and Thai industries, the organization of the industry in Indonesia has long been quite different from that of the mainland, and the impact of tin-mining on economic life has been much less marked. In place of the multiplicity of producers of the mainland, the tin-mining industry had been largely in the hands of the state for over a century before Indonesian independence. Thus the new Republic acquired from the Netherlands Indies complete control of the mines on Bangka, and a 62·5 per cent share of a joint enterprise with private capital in the exploitation of the Belitung deposits; a subsidiary of this latter company worked the Singkep mines. The Belitung agreement was renewed for a further five years in 1953, but following the diplomatic break with the Netherlands in 1958 the joint venture was finally liquidated. With the departure of its Dutch personnel the industry went into a swift decline.

Situated on a series of islands removed from the mainstreams of national life, it is hardly surprising that the tin industry has not exerted the strongly developmental influence in Indonesia that it did in both Malaya and Thailand. The Dutch did allow old mined areas to be reworked by Chinese contractors, but the fact that entry was virtually impossible in the face of a government monopoly denied the opportunities for private capital accumulation from the profits of tin-mining that existed on the mainland. Few Indonesians had any contact with the industry, which was heavily dependent on an alien labour force,

---

[25] *The all-time peak was 1941, when 53,400 tons of tin concentrates were produced.*

and hence it could exert little pressure in Djakarta for a claim on investment allocation in national development plans. This was to prove a costly oversight.

Limitations on Chinese participation are largely responsible for the fact the proportion of total output originating from gravel-pump mines is much lower than in the West Malaysian and Thai industries. Less than one-third of Indonesia's tin is produced from gravel-pump mines, and as this method of mining speedily adjusts to changes in price, the Indonesian industry thus tends to demonstrate a lower supply elasticity than that of mainland producers. Many of the larger mines make use of suction dredges to remove the barren overburden before bringing the bucket dredge over the tin-bearing ground, and in Bangka 'sea tin' is won by bucket dredges operating offshore. As in West Malaysia a small production is derived from underground lode mines, but the largest of these, the Klappa Kampit mine on Belitung, has not been rehabilitated since its flooding during the Japanese occupation.

Three small and obsolescent smelters on Bangka were not reactivated after World War II, and Indonesia's concentrates have been sent to the Netherlands, Malaysia and the USA, according to the varying state of political relations with these countries; thus shipments to the Netherlands were suspended between 1959 and 1962, and those to Malaysia after 1963. To avoid dependence on foreign smelters, a new plant with an annual capacity of some 25,000 tons is under construction at Muntok on the west coast of Bangka, on the site of an old prewar plant. In 1966 a large new British-built dredge was delivered to Bangka, and an accelerated investment programme was planned for the industry by the Suharto government, which set an output target of 25,000 tons for 1969.

Other minerals

Apart from minor products of local importance such as limestone, sand and clay, the remaining minerals of Indonesia can be divided between those of current economic significance such as coal and bauxite, and those that have been fitfully worked in the past or have never been worked at all, but might become of greater significance in the future. This latter group includes iron, manganese, base metals and precious metals.

Indonesia possesses several coalfields, and before World War II the Netherlands Indies exported over 100,000 tons annually. In 1941, the peak year, almost two million tons were raised, and even in the mid-Sixties the industry could probably have extracted well over one million tons with its existing equipment. Output, however, remained less than half of capacity. This low output reflects the decline in the productivity of the labour force and the inadequate maintenance of equipment, common to most Indonesian enterprises, but poor transport facilities also strongly operate against the coal-mining industry.

Indonesia's coals are all of Tertiary age and vary widely in quality from lignites to anthracites. The best are of the bituminous and sub-bituminous types, but all kinds can occur within a single coalfield, as is the case in the Bukit Asem field of South Sumatra. Although suitable for heating and gas making, no coals have so far proved capable of making metallurgical coke, a major obstacle to the establishment of an iron and steel industry based on conventional technologies; nevertheless, an iron and steel industry based on 'direct-reduction' remains a possibility. Indonesian coals are, therefore, mainly of types that have experienced the heaviest competition from alternative fuels, but there is little doubt that more coal would be consumed were it available.

As with tin-mining, the industry is entirely in the hands of the state. Coal-mining in the Netherlands Indies was never very profitable except in times of emergency, and it was largely to safeguard supplies at such times that the state felt obliged to continue production. A handful of private collieries, all situated in east Kalimantan, existed up to the outbreak of World War II, but the only one to continue production after 1945 was the Parapatan mine near Balikpapan, owned by the KPM, the Dutch inter-island shipping line. All the private mines passed into the hands of the state with the take-over of Dutch property in 1958.

Coalfields occur in several localities in Java, Sumatra and Kalimantan, but commercial production is confined to Sumatra. The east Kalimantan fields have the advantage that they are situated on or near the coast, and so avoid the for-midable transport problems encountered by the Sumatran industry. Unfor-tunately, they occur in an area where petroleum production is well established, and do not possess the specialized markets available to the Sumatran collieries; it thus seems unlikely that they can ever again account for about a third of total coal production as they did before 1939. The two major producing fields are those of the Umbilin valley in the Padang highlands near Sawahlunto, and Bukit Asem, near the town of Muaraenim in South Sumatra. Production in the Bukit Asem field began only in 1919, and this field has the best quality coals. It is the only field in which shaft mining has been employed, but opencast working is now standard.

As with most mining industries, the coal industry suffered very severe damage during the Japanese occupation, and rehabilitation was longer delayed than in tin or petroleum production. At the Umbilin field the damage was particularly severe, and the destruction of the rack sections on the difficult gradients of the West Sumatra railway system were a further major obstacle. In the more acces-sible Bukit Asem field served by the South Sumatra railway, reconstruction pro-ceeded more rapidly, but despite the introduction of modern earth-moving machinery and conveyors, the productivity of the mainly Javanese labour force failed to improve and output per man-day is still markedly lower than in 1939. The main markets for Indonesian coal were always in the railway systems and for bunkering. While the latter has been greatly affected by the virtual disappearance of the coal-fired vessel, accelerated dieselization of the railways was in large measure enforced by the difficulties of raising coal production. Umbilin coal is also employed in the state-owned cement plant at Padang. The development of an iron and steel industry might assist the industry, but many 'direct-reduction' iron smelting processes can also make use of fuel oil or other hydrocarbon fuels.

Bauxite-mining is a very modern industry, beginning only in 1935. It is confined to the island of Bintan in the Riau group of south of Singapore, and under the stimulus of the booming Japanese market, output has been carried to nearly twice the prewar level. But its technical requirements are modest; extraction is easily accomplished with modern excavating machinery and the only additional treatment necessary is washing and drying. The industry's labour force is almost entirely Chinese, and close proximity to Singapore helps confer an element of dynamism rare in Indonesia. The Riau bauxite deposits occupy an important place in the proposals to establish a modern electro-chemical and electro-metallurgical complex in the Asahan valley of North Sumatra.

Copper, lead, zinc, nickel, manganese, gold, silver and diamonds have all been produced in small quantities in the past, but the small size of the deposits, their remoteness from major centres of population and inadequate means of transportation have proved major obstacles to exploitation. Perhaps the greatest potentialities are in iron ore, which has never been mined commercially in Indonesia. Known iron reserves amount to more than 500 million tons, but this figure includes the large lateritic deposits of Larona in southeast Sulawesi. These deposits amount to some 370 million tons with a 49 per cent iron content, but as the ores also contain chromium and nickel they are unsuitable for treatment in the conventional blast-furnace. Prewar experiments to smelt these ores were unsuccessful, but new technologies now offer greater possibilities of success; early utilization of Sulawesi ores is unlikely, however, as the more accessible titaniferous ores of West Java and the Kanggal area of South Sumatra have been selected as the basis of a national iron and steel industry. The abandoned First Five Year Plan (1956–60) envisaged an output of 350,000 tons of pig iron by 1963, but no action to establish the industry was envisaged during the plan period. Proposals for the industry were embodied in the Eight Year Development Plan of 1960, and a steelmill, to operate on scrap or imported pig and financed through Russian aid, was originally scheduled to come into operation in 1967, but following the upheavals of 1965–66, work came to an abrupt halt. The Suharto administration, however, succeeded in enlisting the help of a private West German group, and the project is to be completed by 1970. There is little question that the appeal of the industry is mainly one of emotional nationalism, and it is regarded by the Suharto administration as differing little from the prestige projects of the Sukarno era.

Manufacturing industries

In 1958 manufacturing industries accounted for some 13 per cent of Indonesia's national product,[26] a proportion that tended to decline with the passage of time

[26] D. S. Paauw in *Ruth McVey (ed.)*, op. cit., *p. 176.*

(*Table 7-2*). Manufacturing is thus not appreciably less significant in Indonesia than in Southeast Asia as a whole, but the dualism which characterizes Indonesian agriculture also extends to the manufacturing sector, and the large employment in cottage and small-scale industries suggests that India provides a more appropriate comparison. Before World War II only 300,000 workers of an estimated total industrial employment of 2·8 millions were engaged in factory industry, and more than 100,000 workers are still employed by the *batik* industry of Java.[27] Manufacturing is thus probably rather more important in the national economy than is suggested from its share of national product in view of the difficulties in recording the output of cottage industries. Nevertheless, because of the chronic shortage of raw materials and spare parts resulting from Indonesia's shortage of foreign exchange, since 1963 most Indonesian factory industries have seldom worked at more than 30 per cent of their capacity, and in 1966 the factory sector accounted for no more than 5 per cent of national product. The deplorable condition of manufacturing received emphasis in the President's *Dekon* speech of 1964 dealing with the economic situation, and over the following two years the situation continued to deteriorate.

Yet in the range of its activities at least, the Indonesian industrial heritage from the Netherlands Indies might be deemed to have been more generous than that of most other Southeast Asian countries on gaining independence. Most large-scale industry was, it is true, mainly concerned with processing locally produced raw materials for export, but the foundations for domestically oriented production were laid during World War I and after the Great Depression, when government concern over excessive dependence on overseas suppliers in times of emergency prompted a quickening in the pace of industrial growth. During the former period the government entered directly into manufacturing, with plants for the production of cement, paper and railway rolling-stock, but a more determined effort to promote industrial development came after 1931 when the devaluation of the yen resulted in a flood of cheap Japanese imports. To encourage local industry and to alleviate unemployment a policy of protection for Netherlands Indies industries was instituted; the large Dutch trading companies were persuaded to enter into manufacturing either directly or in joint ventures with the government, and in the later Thirties several large Dutch and foreign firms with international manufacturing operations set up plants in the country. Japan's growing imperial ambitions stimulated plans for further extension of manufacturing, which were aborted by the invasion. Also participating in this industrial growth were enterprises founded by Chinese, who may perhaps be regarded as the real pioneers of manufacturing; Chinese were engaged in sugar production in the early eighteenth century and in this, as in other lines, they were never entirely displaced by European enterprise.

While small Chinese industrial enterprise proliferated during the occupation,

[27] ibid., *p. 179; see also above, pp. 114–5.*

the Japanese showed considerable ingenuity in utilizing existing heavy industrial equipment to meet their war needs. The Revolutionary War, however, caused greater damage than the occupation, and involved the loss of around 60 per cent of the total capital investment in industry, although the greater part of this was accounted for by the destruction of the sugar mills. But since 1950, manufacturing has offered little attraction to indigenous Indonesians in comparison with the huge profits to be obtained in commerce. The limited supply of indigenous capital and entrepreneurial skills has meant that the state alone has the resources to launch new capital-intensive industries; moreover, a majority of Indonesians have continued to accept the desirability of a socialist society of some kind, in which a large part of the industrial sector was in the hands of the state. Only in this way could Indonesia obtain a truly national economy, that is, one in which as much as possible of all economic activities were to be controlled by indigenous Indonesians, and in which the role of foreign and Chinese enterprise would be closely circumscribed.

From its beginnings, Indonesia has had a profusion of industrialization programmes and development plans, and it has created a plethora of banks and financial institutions to assist their implementation. The Emergency Industrialization Programme of 1951, the Five Year Plan of 1956–60 and the Eight Year Development Plan of 1960 each witnessed an increase in government participation in the industrial sector; each in turn has had to be abandoned. A succession of co-ordinating bodies for all the many programmes devised by Indonesia's vast and corrupt bureaucracy has only added to the confusion, but the private sector, which on several occasions has shown signs of injecting life into the stagnating industrial body, has been repeatedly checked. With the creation in 1965 of the Consultative Body for Private Capital (*Bamunas*), to canalize all private capital, and the Private Development Bank to which all private business was compelled to subscribe, the prospects for private industry appeared grim in the extreme.

At the outset, however, it was the intention that the role of the state should be largely that of an initiator. Once it had got projects under way their operation would be handed over to private enterprise or to cooperative organizations; nor was foreign capital to be excluded from investing in new enterprises, save in certain industries of strategic importance such as power production, transport and defence equipment. Such was the rationale of the Emergency Industrialization Programme of 1951, which enlisted considerable foreign aid for the construction of a variety of large-scale projects involving cement, rubber milling, heavy chemicals, cotton spinning, glass making and coconut products. However, one of the largest schemes, a cement plant at Gresik near Surabaja, was not completed until 1957 and similar delays attended every other project; even when completed, many lay idle or operated only at a fraction of capacity because managerial ability was lacking. Almost by default, therefore, the government was obliged to assume production itself. Meanwhile the programme for assisting cottage and small-scale industries through the *perusahaan induk*, a central processing station for producer cooperatives and able to undertake difficult stages of manufacture, failed through administrative incompetence, and in some cases, as with a West Java ceramics *induk* at Plered which found itself compelled to draw its clay from pits some 200 miles away in East Java, through inexcusably bad geographic locations.

The failure of the Programme led to deep disillusionment with private capital, and later plans witnessed an extension of direct government participation in industry. With the concept of a 'Guided Economy' came a growing preoccupation with prestige and heavy industries, such as power, chemicals, iron and steel and other metalliferous industries. The First Five Year Plan thus set a target for 1960 of 900,000 tons of cement, 100,000 tons of fertilizers, and an additional 130,000 kW of generating capacity; yet the targets for cotton textiles involved only 160,000 spindles and 120 million metres of cloth, and even these very modest goals were not attained. Work on the special projects left over from the 1951 programme, the Djatiluhur and Asahan schemes, proceeded at snail's pace, and these were eventually incorporated into the still more grandiose Eight Year Development Plan of 1960, compiled by a committee bereft of any professional economic advice and headed by a former Minister of Justice who was better known in the country as a poet and mystic. When the six generators of Djatiluhur are installed, Indonesia will add another much-needed 150,000 kW to its inadequate electric power capacity, but the first two units did not start functioning until well into 1965, four years after the original target date for completion of the whole project.

Implementation of the still larger Asahan scheme appeared even in 1968 to lie in the more distant future, even though its origins, as with Djatiluhur, date back to Dutch investigations carried out before the war. The Asahan river of north Sumatra drains the great Lake Toba to the Malacca Straits, and in falling over the lake's mountainous eastern margin possesses a potential capacity of one million kilowatts. The Japanese made further investigations during their occupation of the country, and in the 1951 industrialization programme an electro-chemical and electro-metallurgical complex was to be created, using Asahan power not only for aluminium smelting based on Riau bauxite as envisaged before the war, but also for the production of fertilizers, pulp and paper and steel. But despite further work by Swedish engineers the project never got started, and construction of the first dam and powerhouse was entrusted to the Russians under an aid agreement of 1959. By 1970 it was intended that Asahan would be capable of supplying 320,000 kWh of electric energy, but although work was to commence in 1965 the preliminary surveying had still not been completed by that date. Given the changed political circumstances of Indonesia, it is not surprising that the country did not continue the agreement in 1966.

The Eight Year Development Plan of 1960 is noted for the three hundred and thirty-five so-called Category A projects, whose foreign exchange requirements were to be derived from supporting Category B projects, joint ventures of the state and foreign capital in exploiting Indonesia's natural resources. Almost one-third of the planned investment was for industrial development, in which the largest allocation was for the cotton textile industry whose spinning capacity would be increased from some 130,000 to two million spindles. In the event, none of the joint ventures arranged operated satisfactorily, and the underlying assumption of the plan, that the main burden of development could be passed on to the foreigner, was of course entirely fallacious.

In terms of employment, and probably in contribution to national product also, textiles and apparel constitute Indonesia's most important manufacturing industry. About one-quarter of the industrial work-force of some half a million workers in establishments with more than ten employees are so engaged, and there is a very large unrecorded employment of part-time workers in domestic and cottage industries; there are probably more than one million traditional handlooms in the country and about 200,000 of the improved type introduced in 1929 by the Bandung Technical Institute. However, less than one-quarter of Indonesia's annual cloth consumption is woven in the country, and even this necessitates large imports of yarn. The scope for further growth of the textile industries is therefore very great; nevertheless, Indonesia cannot even make efficient use of the equipment it already has. A chronic shortage of raw materials keeps plants operating at only a fraction of capacity, a difficulty that is compounded by lack of spare parts and an irregular and capricious electric power supply. Mill equipment is old and of low productivity; as only the Tjilatjap mill is air-conditioned, it is not possible to produce higher-count yarns and thus better-quality fabrics, and the finishing section is particularly poorly equipped. It would be possible to enlarge output through multiple shift-working, but even if raw materials and power supplies were available, a proportionately higher consumption of domestically produced cotton cloth would impose a heavy burden on the population, as home-produced cloth cannot compete with imports.

Even before World War II the Netherlands Indies government had a substantial interest in the cotton textile industry through joint ventures, and the Republic inherited an industry with a complex production structure. While private capital still exists in spinning, this is increasingly a state responsibility, mainly because it is so unprofitable. Spinning is one of the basic industries subject to price control; thus with mounting inflation these industries have been unable to obtain adequate supplies of raw materials or spare parts, and their output has slumped. Another consequence of such unrealistic pricing, of course, has been that supplies of price-controlled goods have disappeared into the black market. Weaving and knitting, on the other hand, are largely left to private enterprise, but costs are high as these sectors have to compete for a share of imported yarn, whose

allocation has been the subject of repeated scandals. The larger integrated spinning and weaving establishments mostly originate from prewar ventures of
European business houses, such as those at Bandung, Garut, Tegal, Semarang
and Pasuruan, but small weaving and knitting sheds owned mainly by Chinese
occur throughout Java, although these are most numerous in the west. Indonesia's
largest spinning mill is the government-owned plant at Tjilatjap, one of the long-
delayed projects of the 1951 Emergency Industrialization Scheme.

The Eight Year Development Plan proposed a considerably enlarged and a
geographically more dispersed spinning industry; this, it was hoped, would encourage private capital to invest in new weaving mills in the vicinity of the new
plants, thus spreading employment opportunities more widely through the
country. Of the dozen new mills envisaged, Sumatra was to get two (Medan and
Padang), and Kalimantan, Sulawesi and Bali one each at Bandjarmasin, Makasar
and Denpasar respectively; the remaining mills were to be located at or near
existing centres of textile production in Java; some of the new plants were also
to be equipped with modern automatic power looms. While existing capacity is
so under-utilized, further expansion into new areas does not appear very justifiable; moreover, as the new mills have been financed and equipped from a
variety of sources but mostly from the proceeds of a Chinese loan and Japanese
war reparations, smooth and integrated operations are likely to present many
problems.

After textiles, the food, drink and tobacco industries rank next in importance
in factory industry. Several of the larger European firms in these industries, such
as Unilever and British-American Tobacco, had already withdrawn from production before the take-overs of 1964. Chinese capital moved into these industries
on an increasing scale as the government attempted to squeeze Chinese enterprise out of commerce through 'Indonesianization' policies. With the exception
of the oil refineries, whose fate is still uncertain, virtually all heavy industry is in
the hands of the state; this includes the railway workshops of Manggarai (Djakarta)
and Madiun, the shipyards of Djakarta and Surabaja, cement, heavy chemicals
and petrochemicals, rubber tyres, some heavy engineering establishments mainly
devoted to the servicing of sugar mill equipment, and an embryonic iron and steel
industry. Though mainly concentrated in the two great port cities of Djakarta
and Surabaja, some industries in this group are raw-material oriented, but except for the Palembang petrochemical plant and the long-established cement plant
near Padang, these are also largely confined to Java. Indeed, it seems possible that
manufacturing industries are now more heavily concentrated in Java than they
were in the Netherlands Indies.[28]

[28] *D. S. Paauw in Ruth McVey (ed.)*, op. cit., *p. 179.*

TRANSPORT AND TRADE

Indonesia inherited what was in many ways a remarkable transportation system for a country lying athwart the equator, but facilities were unevenly distributed throughout the country and had suffered many years of damage and neglect through the occupation and revolutionary war. But the backlog of maintenance and repair has grown steadily throughout the life of the Republic; transport has been starved of investment, and even when made it has been in ways which have not produced the greatest stimulus to production. Many of the minor ports have received virtually no attention at all since 1940, while conditions at major ones have become progressively more chaotic. In many parts of Java and Sumatra existing roads are fast falling to pieces and in some cases have disappeared completely, while vast sums have been allocated to prestige projects such as the Trans-Sumatra and Trans-Kalimantan highways which are unlikely ever to be completed as planned. New locomotives and rolling-stock have been acquired for a railway system whose track and supporting works are in such poor condition that the new equipment cannot achieve its potential productivity. The newly created national shipping fleet spends much of its time in harbour because vessels are repeatedly rendered inoperative through lack of maintenance and a shortage of operating personnel. The national airline, Garuda, continues to lose large sums despite the fact that it operates with one of the highest load factors in the world. Without rapid improvements in the transportation system Indonesia's prospects of economic recovery, or even of remaining a unitary state, will be greatly jeopardized, and it is scarcely surprising that the World Bank mission, established in Djakarta in 1968 to assist the Indonesian government in its recovery programme, has made the rehabilitation of transport its first priority.

Shipping

Indonesia's geography should confer the maximum priority on an efficient coastal and inter-island shipping service, for few major centres of population and economic activity are far removed from the sea. The development of regional specialization is clearly contingent upon parallel and co-ordinated improvements in both overland and marine transport, but the continued decline of shipping services has thrust many of the islands more distant from Java into a progressively greater self-sufficiency. Soap, matches, kerosene and many other basic essentials had virtually disappeared from the markets of Timor and other eastern islands by 1966, although areas fortunate enough to have exportable commodities capable of being smuggled to Malaysia or the Philippines managed to maintain continuity of supplies.

The backbone of the coastal and inter-island service was the Dutch-owned shipping line KPM (*Koninklijke Paketvaart Maatschappij*), which when taken over by the state in 1958 operated more than 120 vessels totalling over 200,000 registered tons; it handled more than 90 per cent of all cargoes on inter-island shipping services and an even higher proportion of the passenger traffic. The company was much disliked by nationalists who resented the continued dependence on Dutch capital and enterprise for an essential service, and plans for the line's complete replacement by nationally-owned shipping lines were made early in the life of the Republic. KPM's main traffic consisted of bulk cargoes such as copra, rubber, salt, sugar, oil palm products and rice, and the carriage of animals such as horses and cattle was an important feature of the services from Nusa Tenggara. KPM was frequently charged with exploiting its near-monopoly position through levying exorbitant rates, an accusation that was partly merited, for its rate structure continued to reflect the restrictionist attitudes of the Thirties. Nevertheless, KPM provided a regular and reliable service, and possessed the appropriate equipment for its various routes. Freighters of between 3,000 and 6,000 tons moved between the major ports of Java, Sumatra and Malaya, and on the more important services in the east such as that between Surabaja and Makasar, while numerous smaller vessels of 1,500 to 3,000 tons operated services to minor ports of the main islands and served the scattered primitive ports of the eastern archipelago, where facilities seldom amounted to more than an open roadstead in which vessels could anchor while discharging into *prahus* (indigenous craft).

By 1958 more than a hundred national shipping lines had been created, of which the state-owned *Pelni* (*Pelajaran Nasional Indonesia*) was the largest. None had the right equipment, and services tended to be erratic in the extreme; all, moreover, lost enormous sums which had to be made good from public funds. Most of Pelni's vessels were too large for coastal traffic and too small for inter-island services, but a substantial proportion of the fleet has always been idle. When the KPM fleet was seized it proved impossible to operate because of a shortage of trained personnel, and essential services were only maintained by chartering foreign vessels, mainly from east European countries. When established in 1952 it was intended that Pelni would control 80 per cent of all inter-island traffic by 1960, but this figure had still not been attained by 1966, when the company had some eighty-six ships totalling nearly 150,000 tons; some 60 per cent was quite inoperative as a result of poor maintenance, lack of spares and shortages of officers and crews.

Failure to conduct an efficient inter-island service did not deter Indonesia from venturing into the much more exacting field of trans-oceanic shipping, and from piling up equally staggering losses. As in inter-island shipping, a multiplicity of operating companies were created, but all were ultimately supported by the state; in 1964 these were reorganized into a handful of companies, of which Djakarta-Lloyd is the largest. By 1966 this line had acquired nearly forty vessels, mainly on charter, and operated services to Europe and Japan; but of the nine vessels owned, four were later handed over to foreign creditors as the company was unable to meet its debts. Indonesia also established a state-owned freight and stevedore agency to ensure that as large as possible a share of Indonesia's trade is handled by the national shipping lines.

Since mid-1966 the Suharto administration has endeavoured to reduce the enormous overheads of the national shipping lines and to up-grade their efficiency, but progress to 1969 was slow. Exporters have again been allowed to choose the shipping lines they find most convenient, instead of being bound to use the expensive and heavily protected state lines, but about one-quarter of the shipping component of Indonesia's total trade turnover is in the hands of the national lines.

While the situation in the shipping industry continues to be unsatisfactory in the extreme, the condition of the ports has long been a major national scandal. The First Five Year Plan provided for improvements at Tandjungpriok (Djakarta), Semarang, Bandjarmasin, Balikpapan and Belawan (Medan), but little of the funds allocated were ever applied to construction. Congestion and delays at Indonesia's main port, Tandjungpriok, have steadily augmented, and at times losses through damage and pilfering have assumed enormous proportions; attempts to improve the chaotic conditions at the port nevertheless resulted in the downfall of one Cabinet in the early Fifties, following which no serious attack on the problem was made. Despite the fact that the port handles almost two-thirds of Indonesia's total trade turnover, it possesses a quite inadequate proportion of the total customs and port personnel in the country, and improvements in port administration must clearly precede any plans to up-grade its physical facilities.

Overland transport

Progressive deterioration has also been the fate of Indonesia's rail and road system; even the new roads that have been built have fallen to pieces within a few years because of faulty construction resulting from the corruption of contractors and officials.[29] The only exceptions to this miserable record have been the roads built by the oil companies in conjunction with their exploratory and development activities.

As with so much else in Indonesia, overland transportation facilities are grossly maldistributed, Java having too much and the important export-producing areas of the Outer Islands too little, but in part this is the legacy of the Netherlands Indies' greater concern for strategic rather than economic considerations in the alignment of roads and railways. Over 40 per cent of the 50,000 miles of road and over 60 per cent of hard-surfaced roads are in Java, and nearly 70 per cent of the 4,600 miles of railway.

The road system of Java has its main axis in the Great Post Road built in the early nineteenth century by Governor-General Daendals, which extends from one end of the island to the other paralleling the north coast, and during the present century a second main east-west route roughly aligned through the centre

[29] *The fate of the road between Djakarta and its satellite town of Kebajoran Bahru is but one of many such examples.*

Suburban train service, Djakarta. One reason for the large losses made by the railway is obvious.

of the island was added. Apart from in densely populated Central Java, there are few connections between north and south coasts. The road system has always primarily served the movement of people rather than goods, and so far the motor vehicle has not made the economic impact it has had in other parts of the region, for the ratio of vehicles to population is among the lowest of any Southeast Asian country (*Table 4–5, page 162*).

Before the advent of the railway, the principal method of moving goods was by river and sea, but the only railways whose construction was primarily motivated by commercial considerations were the privately-owned undertakings serving the sugar area of Java, and the fragmented railways system of Sumatra. The only other island to possess a railway was Sulawesi, where a short stretch of line in the Makasar area was closed in 1930. Even in Sumatra the narrow 2-ft. gauge line from Banda Atjeh (formerly Kotaradja) connecting with the Deli system at Pangkalansusu was constructed in the last decade of the nineteenth century to assist the pacification of Atjeh after a long and strenuous military campaign had finally established Dutch rule.

Before World War II the Netherlands Indies railways were among the best 3 ft. 6 in. gauge systems in the world. The roadbed and engineering works survived the occupation and the revolutionary war surprisingly well, and fortunately all of the major viaducts and bridges escaped destruction. But much track was in urgent need of relaying, and the vital rack sections of the West Sumatra system serving the densely populated Padang highlands and the Umbilin coalfield were destroyed during the occupation, a loss that, as noted earlier, greatly impeded the rehabilitation of the coalmining industry. Administration of the railways was entrusted to a new state corporation, the DKA (later, PNKA), although the important and very profitable privately-owned Deli railway, which served the estate area of East Sumatra and in which the Deli company had a large interest, was not taken over until 1958. Large sums have been allocated to railway improvements in successive development plans, but graft and corruption in contracts for track improvement led to much unsatisfactory work, and in the Sixties a succession of serious accidents involving heavy loss of life underlined the extent of the deterioration in operational efficiency. As new diesel-electric locomotives and rolling-stock were delivered for service on the main routes of Java, existing obsolete equipment was transferred to the Sumatran system, to the intense irritation of many Sumatrans, who felt that as the new equipment had been acquired from the proceeds of their exports, they had a prior claim. The deterioration in transport facilities, allied with the steady drift in the terms of trade between the Outer Islands and Java in the latter's favour, were important factors in provoking the 1957–58 regional revolts.

In common with the railways of many underdeveloped countries, the Indonesian railways have a very high passenger-utilization factor, the number of passenger miles per mile of line being surprisingly high; in 1961 this figure amounted to 1,350 compared with 1,160 for Britain. This high utilization factor reflects the political expediency of keeping rail fares low in poor countries, where the state usually controls the railway system, and in Indonesia's case the real utilization factor is certainly very much higher than it appears, as a large proportion of fares paid go straight into the pockets of the PNKA's employees, and a very large number of passengers manages to avoid paying fares at all. But while passenger traffic has roughly quadrupled compared with prewar years, freight traffic, always the most important source of revenue to the Netherlands Indies railways, has declined, a situation that in large measure reflects the demise of Java' sugar industry, the most important source of railway revenue before the war. Because of the coal traffic in the South and West Sumatra systems and the movement of estate produce on the Deli railway, the Sumatran railways have always had a higher freight utilization than that of the Javan railway system.

The poor condition of the road system, and balance-of-payments difficulties which have strictly limited the import of motor vehicles, have protected the railways from much competition. Motor vehicle imports have always shown a great preponderance of private cars over commercial vehicles, and much of the existing stock of buses and trucks is fit only for the scrap heap. Probably about one-third of the entire motor vehicle fleet was inoperative in 1966 for want of tyres or essential spare parts. Diesel-engined commercial vehicles are still a rarity, as the skilled personnel capable of maintaining these vehicles is very limited, and although diesel buses were provided under Colombo Plan aid their operation has not been a success. Bus services, operated mainly by Chinese, link all the main cities of Java, but they are relatively much more important in Sumatra, where the rail system is not continuous. Since 1938, through road communication has been possible from Banda Atjeh in the north to Pandjang in the extreme south, but many sections are frequently impassable in bad weather. Work on improving this Trans-Sumatra highway is to be undertaken with aid from West Germany, but the section that most merits attention and on which investment should be concentrated, is that between Medan and Padang, Sumatra's main trunk road. The USSR agreed to provide aid for the construction of a Trans-Kalimantan road from Bandjarmasin in the south to Balikpapan and Samarinda on the east coast; short stretches of this road already exist, but implementation of the project does not now look likely for very many years.

Thus despite its favourable endowment from the Netherlands Indies government, Indonesia's transport situation by 1966 had reached a stage of acute crisis. Operation of the railway system was breaking down, the accident rate had greatly reduced public confidence, while perhaps as much as three-quarters of the entire road mileage could only be saved from final disintegration by immediate repairs, for which resources were simply non-existent. Harbours and godowns (warehouses) were choked, inviting mass pilfering, while some islands remained unvisited and short of supplies for weeks on end. In his emergency recovery programme the Sultan of Jogjakarta, Deputy Prime Minister for Economic Affairs, attached major importance to resuscitation of the transport system, but only massive Western aid can now save the situation. Fortunately, the World Bank, from which Indonesia withdrew in 1965 but rejoined after the establishment of the Suharto administration, has taken a lead in harnessing such aid, which has as its first priority the resuscitation of much of Indonesia's run-down and cannibalized road transport fleet.

Trade

The salient features of Indonesia's trade pattern have already been indicated. Far from succeeding in broadening its export base, Indonesia has experienced great difficulty in maintaining exports of its traditional lines; the only exception to the pattern of stagnation has been the petroleum industry, but even petroleum exports fell in the Sixties, and export earnings from petroleum fell still more as a result of the world-wide pressure on petroleum prices through mounting shut-in surpluses. Java's share of exports, moreover, has tended continually to decline; though it once provided nearly a quarter of the export earnings of the Netherlands Indies, sugar exports fell to virtually nothing after the middle Fifties.

As the pressure of inflation mounted after 1960 and political stability appeared more distant than ever, exports suffered a sharp decline and by mid-1966 had fallen to about half the country's potential capacity. To boost sagging exports the Ampera government attempted a progressive liberalization of the financial restrictions governing the export trade, and, by means of the so-called BE (export bonus) system, allowed the exporter a small proportion of the foreign exchange proceeds of his overseas sales, which could then be disposed of in a legal free market and applied to the import of consumer goods. A variety of similar schemes were tried in the Fifties without conspicuous success, but the Suharto administration

Table 7-10 *Indonesia: direction and composition of foreign trade, 1963*

million US $

EXPORTS		IMPORTS	
U.S.A	98	U.S.A.	174
Japan	52	Japan	55
Malaysia and Singapore	75	Western European countries	131
Netherlands	2	Hong Kong	31
Britain	154	Mainland China	36
Mainland China	36	Other Eastern bloc countries	35
Other Eastern bloc countries	35		
Total Exports, f.o.b.	**696**	**Total Imports, c.i.f.**	**562**

million rupiah

EXPORTS*		IMPORTS	
Rubber		Rice	3,155
Smallholder	6,094	Other consumption goods	3,783
Estate	4,382	Cotton textiles	422
Petroleum and petroleum products	12,195	Petroleum products	1,421
Tin concentrates	1,295	Other raw materials and intermediate goods	7,524
Coffee	1,178	Machinery	2,645
Palm oil	1,168	Other capital goods	3,656
Copra	999		
Tobacco	991		
Tea	756		
Others	4,426		
Total	**33,484**	**Total**	**22,606**

* F.o.b. prices, 1964

Note—Trade figures for 1963 are close to the targets set in the recovery programme for 1970, and reflect a more normal export pattern than in later years.

Source: *Bank Negara Indonesia*

has been able to raise the exporter's share of his foreign exchange earnings, and ultimately it hopes to permit him the full value of his earnings. Since 1966 the share of capital goods in the import trade has at last begun to rise, but so long as the government feels that it has to continue a policy of strict control over the allocation of foreign exchange for imports, the opportunities for profitable evasion of the regulations will remain. Moreover, large imports of rice, which is considered an essential import, and of other foodstuffs continue to exercise a depressing effect on imports of raw materials and consumer goods, and since the administration, to survive, has to show that it can achieve an increase in the living standards of the average Indonesian, the political consequences could be important. By 1968, however, Indonesia claimed that exports had regained the level of the early Sixties, and some foreign observers and international agencies began to feel that the most difficult period of the recovery programme had been passed.

The direction of trade has always been heavily influenced by political considerations. Indonesia was quicker to move away from a heavy trade dependence on the former colonial power than most other newly independent countries in Southeast Asia, but this applied more particularly to imports, and the United States had become the largest supplier by the early Fifties. Largely because of the many Dutch concerns still operating in the country, the Netherlands continued to be the main destination of Indonesian exports until the diplomatic break of 1958. After that date, however, Indonesia sought to divert trade from Holland to other Western European countries, for Indonesian produce was normally re-exported from the Netherlands. But as Indonesia became steadily more anti-Western and the policies of Guided Democracy and Guided Economy got under way, what the President termed socialist countries (that is the Eastern bloc) and Nefo (New Emerging Forces, or the underdeveloped Third World) were destined to receive a greater share of Indonesia's export trade. Malaya and Singapore, too, were to receive less produce from Indonesia, for the entrepot functions of Singapore were particularly detested by nationalists as depriving the nation of part of its foreign exchange earnings; as much produce as possible, therefore, was to be shipped direct. However, neither the Eastern bloc nor Nefo proved capable of absorbing a significantly larger proportion of exports, nor in fact could the services of the Malayan entrepots be entirely dispensed with, as they provided an essential processing service without which much Indonesian smallholder produce could not be marketed. But after 1963, while relations with the Netherlands markedly improved and under the stimulus of $100 million of Dutch credits, trade again began to flow to Amsterdam, trade with Malaysia and Singapore was banned during the confrontation; nevertheless, much illicit trade continued to take place across the Malacca Straits.

From the later Fifties onwards, however, the growing importance of Japan both as an export market and as a source of imports was the most fundamental change in Indonesia's trade pattern, and if the many joint ventures concluded

Slab rubber loaded for transport to Singapore.

between the Indonesian government and Japanese private capital had succeeded, the volume of trade would have increased still faster. Nevertheless, the United States continued to occupy a vital role as a major supplier of foodstuffs and agricultural raw materials such as cotton under the P.L. 480 programme, and as in the case of Egypt, this dependence set some limitations to anti-Western feeling. The end of confrontation was expected to see a quick renewal of trade with Malaysia and Singapore, but this has been long in coming, and if, as seems probable, Indonesia receives greatly enhanced Western aid, the experiment of importing much capital equipment from Eastern bloc countries is likely to be discontinued.

CONCLUSION

Indonesia's brief economic history has been tragic. The country came into existence at a period of very high prices for its exports, and its productive equipment had on the whole survived the troubled period since 1939 reasonably intact; few new countries in the postwar period, in fact, enjoyed a more auspicious start. But in an atmosphere of growing political instability, sensible economic policies, the essential prerequisites for the fulfilment of any development plan, had little chance of prevailing. After a decade and a half of 'continuing revolution', the country was merely offered a policy of *Berdikari*, or 'self-reliance', in which the average citizen could expect no more than a barely adequate ration of food, clothing and shelter. Indonesia has manifestly failed to use its large foreign exchange earning capacity to further its economic development. Despite the growing economic chaos, nevertheless, it was claimed that the Indonesian nation was forged. But the fact that schoolchildren in Banda Atjeh at one end of the country and Djajapura (Sukarnapura) at the other end could be taught to chant *Gandjang Malaysia* (Crush Malaysia) is no proof of nationhood; informed Indonesians had long before expressed a contrary opinion: 'More than ever it is obvious that as long as political instability reigns in Indonesia, no economic policy directed towards the development of the country will and can be feasible . . . neither can those authorities concerned plan a financial and monetary policy in relation to this development . . . the central government has paid too little attention to the desires and needs of regions outside Djakarta, especially the regions outside Djawa. Thus Parliament fell short of its duty and by implication the government also, because it simply gave itself too little opportunity to consider the whole territory of Indonesia, with its manifold interests, needs, wants and desires.'[30]

That Parliament itself disappeared, to be replaced by Guided Democracy, made little difference; and with the passage of time the extraordinary behaviour of the President resembled more and more that of the Sunans of Mataram, the feudal monarchs of the pre-Dutch empire of Central Java. By mid-1966 the share of the Indonesian government of gross national product had been reduced to a mere 2 per cent, a share scarcely adequate even to maintain the facade of a modern state. Central budgetary control had disappeared and the government had no way of making good the enormous shortfall between revenue and expenditure except through the use of the printing press. Despite its past prodigality, therefore, the government was spending nothing like enough to get the economy off the ground; the government of nearby Malaysia's share of gross national product was more than ten times that of its confronter. But the prospect of mobilizing domestic resources of comparable magnitude was negligible, and in its travail Indonesia could only turn to nations for whom its complete economic collapse would be a tragedy to be prevented at all costs, that is, the industrialized nations of the West, the despised Oldefo (Old Established Forces) of President Sukarno.

Indonesia's economic problems would still yield to rational and pragmatic policies, but in examining the domestic scene in early 1966 informed Indonesians could only conclude that 'What we see is neo-feudalism to an extent unknown even in the feudal centres of our past history'.[31] That primary responsibility for setting the tottering economy aright should fall to the Sultan of Jogjakarta, a hereditary prince who embodies all Java's feudal traditions, is both ironic and

[30] Report of Bank Indonesia, *1956–57, Kolff, Djakarta, 1957, p. 16. Dr Prawiranegara, Governor of Bank Indonesia (now Bank Negara Indonesia), joined the Sumatran rebels, but later returned to the service of the central government.*

[31] Indonesian Herald, *April 9th, 1966.*

prophetic. The targets of the new administration, such as the final arrest of the inflationary process and the restoration of the 1960 export income by 1970 are realistic, but by mid-1968 the average Indonesian could see little improvement in his lot. Disappointment with the economic performance of the new regime reinforced fears for a renewal of civil war with supporters of the old President and with the communist underground organizations, and in Java there was an increasing tendency for peasants to seek escape in new religious cults. Even the distinguished economist and former Governor of Bank Indonesia, Dr Prawiranegara, declared that Indonesia's economic problems were primarily the result of a decline in moral values.[32] Unpalatable though it may be, however, there is no connection between a high level of morality and a rapid rate of economic growth; indeed, the experience of many developed and developing countries alike is that the contrary has often proved the case.

Yet despite the fact that structural change in the Indonesian economy had been minute since the establishment of President Suharto's 'New Order', there was an almost euphoric air in the writings of Western commentators on Indonesian economic affairs by mid-1969. Some modest gains, it is true, had been achieved; inflation had slowed, exports were expanding (although still well below the country's capacity even with its existing equipment), petroleum output attained a record level and prospects for offshore production appeared dazzling. It is, of course, possible that the worst is over for Indonesia, and that the wishful thinking of Western journalists proves to be justified. But if Indonesia's new Five Year Plan turns out to be as dusty a document as its predecessors and the country's massive rural problems remain unsolved, the future can only be further paroxysms of violence.

[32] *Husein Rofe, 'Insja'allah—God willing'*, Far Eastern Economic Review, *vol. 59,* 1968, p. 27.

CHAPTER EIGHT

The Union of Burma

Burma is the largest of the states of mainland Southeast Asia, and its resource endowment is clearly capable of supporting its not overlarge population at a high level of welfare by Asian standards. Yet despite the bounty of nature, Burma shares with Indonesia the unhappy distinction of a per capita product that in real terms is lower than that of 1939, and not until 1961 was the prewar volume of agricultural production regained. Burma's history since independence has been scarcely less turbulent than it was during World War II, but between 1962, when government by a military Revolutionary Council was instituted and the factious and corrupt politicians were once more reduced to impotence, and the diplomatic break with China in 1967,[1] Burma to most purposes contracted out of the modern world. No country outside the communist bloc has been more difficult to enter, and throughout this period it was far easier for the Westerner to travel in China. To some extent Burma's withdrawal represented a desire to return to a life dominated by traditional Burmese values;[2] but it is more likely that the embargo on visitors is primarily intended to disguise from the outside world the 'appalling mess', to use the words of General Ne Win himself,[3] into which the Burmese economy has deteriorated following the wave of nationalizations decreed by the Revolutionary Council. Since 1962 Burma has rapidly moved towards a centrally-planned type of economy, but so far its ruling junta has refrained from any policy of agricultural collectivization.

Many of Burma's difficulties arise from the fact that the independence agreement of 1947 gave a virtual monopoly of political power to the Burmans, a

---

[1] *General Ne Win, Chairman of the Revolutionary Council, first took over the government in 1958, but after a frenzied burst of reformist activity the Army surprisingly returned power to the politicians in 1960.*

[2] *In this chapter the term 'Burman' relates to the dominant Burman peoples, resident mainly in the Dry Zone and in the Irrawaddy delta. 'Burmese' refers to the peoples and culture of the whole Union of Burma.*

[3] *Speech to Seminar of the Burma Socialist Programme (Lanzin) Party, Rangoon, December 13th, 1965.*

situation that has been quite unacceptable to the non-Burman peoples of the Union, many of whom have been in more or less continuous revolt against the central government ever since. But it has a more deep-seated origin. Burma is torn between the ancient and the modern, between the pull of its Buddhist traditions and the historic kingdoms of the past, and the excitements and dangers of the modern world; it wants the products of a modern, industrialized and commercialized society but recoils from the social strains and adjustments that are the inevitable concomitants and precursors of such an economy. This is the real dilemma of Burma, and one looks in vain for any promise of its speedy resolution.[4]

THE RESOURCE BASIS

By the standards of Southeast Asia, Burma's physical geography would appear to be unusually favourable for the development of a high degree of national cohesion and economic welfare. The heart of the country is a broad central depression occupied by the Irrawaddy-Chindwin system, a much more extensive lowland than the Central Plain of Thailand. Moreover, in contrast to the Mae Nam, the Irrawaddy is navigable for steamboats for nearly 800 miles from its mouth, or was in prewar days, when specialized vessels up to 300 feet in length regularly ascended as far as Bhamo. Small craft could ascend a further 150 miles to Myitkyina, and on the Chindwin steamers could reach Homalin, some 400 miles from the junction with the Irrawaddy near Pakkoku. North-south trending ridges limit the maximum width of the Irrawaddy valley lowland north of the delta to some forty to fifty miles, but only the low Pegu Yoma, whose maximum elevations seldom exceed 2,000 feet, separates the lower valley from the equally broad valley of the Sittang.

Nevertheless, this great natural highway only acquired importance as a major commercial artery with the establishment of the British administration, and significantly, its role has drastically diminished since independence. Such unity as Burma ever possessed came not through the positive influence of its master river, but from the constraints of its formidable mountain and plateau ramparts. These effectively limited contacts with India and China, and forced on Burma an introspection that it still finds exceedingly difficult to throw off; in all its long history, Burma never possessed an ocean-going ship.[5] Before World War II no railway or road suitable for wheeled traffic penetrated the highly malarious valleys leading to the gaps across the Patkai Range, where summit heights exceed 12,000 feet, or across the lower Naga and Chin Hills to India, and though the principal mining camps of the deeply dissected Shan plateau in the east which

---

[4] *For a trenchant discussion of the nature and origins of the 'Burmese dilemma' and of its stifling influence on economic development, see I. R. Sinai,* The Challenge of Modernization, *Chatto & Windus, London, and Norton & Co., New York, 1964, pp. 108–79.*

[5] *ibid., p. 108. Ocean-going vessels were, however, being built at Rangoon from Burmese teak in the eighteenth century, but the shipwrights and crews were European.*

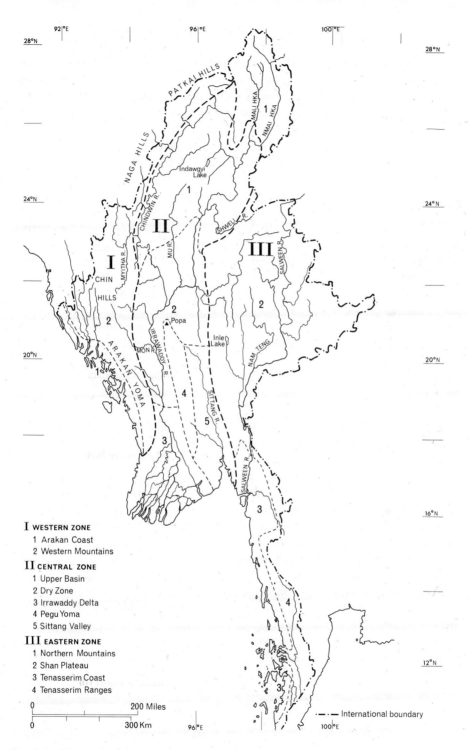

I WESTERN ZONE
  1 Arakan Coast
  2 Western Mountains

II CENTRAL ZONE
  1 Upper Basin
  2 Dry Zone
  3 Irrawaddy Delta
  4 Pegu Yoma
  5 Sittang Valley

III EASTERN ZONE
  1 Northern Mountains
  2 Shan Plateau
  3 Tenasserim Coast
  4 Tenasserim Ranges

0   200 Miles

0   300 Km

—·—· International boundary

Fig. 8-1 The physical regions of Burma

covers virtually a quarter of the country had been provided with rail or road connections, the only access to the Yunnan plateau of China was by porterage and pack animal. Less severe obstacles such as the Arakan Yoma, where heights range from 3,000 to 6,000 feet, and the ranges of Tavoy and Tenasserim, were also devoid of effective communications, and the Arakanese and Tavoyese, though essentially of Burman stock, possess their own dialects and a pattern of interests not always in conformity with those of the Burmans of the central depression.

Under the stimulus of the war emergency, the logistic problems of the Allies in the Burmese and Chinese theatres were met through the construction of the Ledo Road leading from Assam to Mogaung and Chungking, and the Burma Road from Lashio to Kunming; but without massive assistance from air transport even these links would have proved ineffective. The Japanese were likewise obliged to improve road communications from central Burma to the Arakan coast, and by means of the infamous Burma-Thailand railway linked Lower Burma with Thailand via the Three Pagodas pass. Since independence each of these three major wartime contributions to Burma's transport system have been allowed to lapse into disrepair; the track and many of the constructional works on the Thailand railway have disappeared, and over long sections the wartime roads are no longer passable even to jeep traffic. Many works, it is true, were hastily and lightly built and could scarcely be expected to stand the ravages of time and a tropical climate; but it is clear that the government has had no interest in them, or indeed, in any alternative improved connections with the outside world. Not only does Burma constitute the only really large gap in the proposed Pan-Asia Highway from Istanbul to Singapore and Saigon, but it has maintained a sublime indifference, and since 1962, an open hostility to the project, which has had the active support of ECAFE and of every other Asian country through which it passes.[6] If its formidable natural barriers will no longer suffice to shut out the outside world, Burma appears determined to reinforce them with man-made ones. It is precisely for this reason that shabby, dirty Rangoon is now avoided by all major international airlines; the government has made it plain that it no longer wants them to come.

The hill and mountain peripheries of the Irrawaddy lowland form the homelands of the many non-Burman peoples, who probably amount to almost 40 per cent of the total population. Their distribution is exceedingly complex, for population migrations are still actively going on. Following the establishment of the British administration, the Karens, the largest and most sophisticated of the non-Burman groups and numbering around 2 millions, spread from the southern Shan states into which they had been pushed by the Burmans and established themselves in considerable numbers in the Irrawaddy delta and in the Moulmein

[6] *Long sections of this road, motorable at all seasons, already exist, but Burma refuses to allow motor vehicles to cross its frontiers.*

area. Many hill peoples, such as the Chins, and more primitive groups such as the Palaungs and Nagas, practise *taungya*, or shifting cultivation, while others such as the Shans and Kachins combine this with valley-bottom padi cultivation.

The mountains' principal contribution to the national economy has been through mining and forest industries, which in 1939 accounted for almost 40 per cent of export earnings, although this figure also includes the contribution from the petroleum industry of the Irrawaddy valley. Save for a trifling indigenous petroleum production from hand-dug wells, mining and forest industries were solidly in the hands of aliens before 1940, but all have now passed into the control of nationalized corporations and output has greatly declined. Even before nationalization, however, the depredations of rebel Karens and other dissident factions had reduced mineral output to a mere token, and unsettled conditions still hamper the half-hearted attempts of state organizations to resuscitate production. Nevertheless, even a consolidation of the government's present tenuous hold on the marginal hill and mountain regions seems unlikely to stimulate mining and forest output, in the face of the government's continued indifference to market forces and a xenophobia that obliges it to overlook a pathetically obvious shortage of indigenous expertise in the management and operation of large-scale enterprise. It is not certain which is the greater economic indictment of independent Burma—its failure to raise agricultural output or its apparent indifference to its magnificent forest and mineral endowment. Thailand, with what must be judged the poorer natural heritage, in greatly expanding both rice production and rice exports while simultaneously increasing other exports still faster, shows what could have been possible.

The geographical heart of Burma, the repository of Burmese culture since the Middle Ages and until the late nineteenth century probably the most populous part of the country, is the so-called Dry Zone focussing on Mandalay, in which, unusually for Southeast Asia, precipitation falls below 40 inches. Although irrigation in the Dry Zone does not present any outstanding technical problems, its development has been long in coming, and a mixed agriculture in which rice takes its place along with maize, millets and a variety of legumes, oilseeds and industrial crops, has become firmly established. After the British occupation the Dry Zone lost its dominant position and was supplanted by the delta, where from 1870 onwards an export-oriented rice economy focussed on Rangoon grew rapidly. Physically the Irrawaddy delta presents conditions which approximate to the optimum for rice cultivation in Southeast Asia; a regular and reliable precipitation of over 80 inches falling in the high-sun season assures a satisfactory crop every year without the expense of irrigation, and water control is largely a matter of drainage and flood prevention. The vast deltaic swamp-lands proved readily convertible into sawahs, giving rise to an unusually high man-land ratio, and the average size of holdings is, in fact, the largest of any mainly food-producing agricultural region of Southeast Asia. This favourable combination of human and physical conditions gave to Burma the lowest costs of rice production in the whole of Southeast Asia.

The creation of the delta rice-bowl is one of the most striking examples in Southeast Asia of the autonomous creation of a large capital asset by peasant farmers through response to the price incentives of the world market; in comparison, the postwar attempts to provide an alternative 'socialist' stimulus can only be regarded as a resounding failure. And ironically enough, although Rangoon is the most obvious product of the economic metamorphosis wrought by colonialism, independent Burma is more sharply focussed on Rangoon than the country ever was in the past; nearly 90 per cent of all postwar development expenditure has been appropriated by the metropolitan area, which with the other main towns is virtually all of the country solidly in the control of the central government. Economically speaking, Burma has degenerated into a series of islands, whose only effective links for many years were provided by the worn-out Dakotas of Burma Airways. 'Burma cannot hope for many years to become one economic unit', wrote Tinker in 1960,[7] an eventuality that seems as far off as when it was written.

AGRICULTURE AND ITS PROBLEMS

Long before the outbreak of World War II, Burma's agriculture presented a dichotomy which, if not as complete as that in the Netherlands Indies or in Malaya, was nevertheless striking enough. Burma never developed a very significant plantation crop agriculture, for which investment opportunities were

[7] *H. Tinker*, The Union of Burma, *Oxford University Press, 3rd edn, London, 1960,* p. 296.

Table 8-1 *Burma: industrial origin of gross national product, 1964–65*

	million kyats	Percentage
Agriculture and fisheries	3,120	21·4
Forestry	510	3·5
Mining	120	0·8
Industry, Construction	4,620	31·7
Transport, Communications and utilities	1,010	6·9
Government services	1,450	10·0
Ownership of dwellings and personal services	670	4·6
Trade	3,070	21·1
Total	**14,570**	**100·0**

Source: *Budget Report,* 1965/66

much richer in the more equatorial parts of Southeast Asia; the fundamental division was between the diversified subsistence agriculture practised in Upper Burma,[8] and particularly in the Dry Zone where from time to time rice was—and indeed still is—in short supply, and the export-oriented commercialized rice agriculture of the delta and other parts of Lower Burma. Largely because so many Burmans are subsistence farmers, whose unwillingness to dispose of their surplus through the legal, but unprofitable, channels steadily augmented during the Sixties, agriculture's share of GNP is grossly understated in official statistics (*Table 8-1*).

The rice industry

Burma's large prewar export trade included no contribution from 'rice plantations' such as existed in prewar Java or Cochinchina, but originated from a large number of peasant producers. Before the Great Depression most of these were owners, who had inherited their holdings from relatively recent immigrants from Upper Burma. The organization of the rice industry closely resembled that of the Mae Nam plain of Thailand, but in Burma the stimulus of the enormous and assured Indian market had pushed commercialization much further. By 1939 Burma's exports had risen to over 3 million tons, nearly three times as large as those of Thailand, and about two-thirds were consigned to India. Not only were the rice merchants and millers overwhelmingly alien, as was also the situation in contemporary Thailand, but so were many landowners as well. By the outbreak of World War II it was officially recorded that more than a quarter of the agricultural land of Lower Burma, nearly all of the first quality by Burmese standards, had passed into the hands of Chettyars, a small immigrant group of south Indian moneylenders.

Throughout much of Lower Burma rice cultivation is virtually synonymous with agriculture. Not only do soil and climatic conditions make cultivation of any other crop difficult, but the return on land and labour under rice is far higher than that of any other of Burma's traditional crops. Jute production, a possible alternative, is hamstrung by the firm grip of India and Pakistan with their lower labour costs on the world market, and despite all independent Burma's attempts to achieve self-sufficiency in sacking requirements, only 70,000 acres were planted to jute in 1966. The extreme reliability of rainfall ensures a successful crop in every year, and makes the insurance conferred by the multiple-crop pattern of Upper Burma unnecessary; moreover, the assured market has long made rice the virtual equivalent of cash, and cultivators could easily raise money against the security of rice-land. In 1964, the best year for Burma's economy since the take-over by the Revolutionary Council, production, milling and marketing of

[8] *Upper Burma comprised all those parts of the country apart from the Arakan coast, the Irrawaddy delta, the lower Sittang and Salween valleys and the peninsula, which collectively formed Lower Burma. The Shan states formed a third unit.*

rice accounted for no less than 50 per cent of gross domestic product and for about 90 per cent of export earnings.

As in the Mae Nam plain, there has traditionally been little rice double-cropping in the Irrawaddy delta, and until comparatively recently there was little difference in the yields achieved in these two major rice surplus regions of continental Southeast Asia. Burma also shows evidence of a long decline in rice yields during most of this century, but in contrast to the experience of Thailand, there is nothing to suggest that this decline has at last been arrested. Moreover, whereas Thailand's production of padi has increased steadily since 1945, Burma's remains obstinately static. Not until 1960 was the prewar level of padi production regained, and even in 1964 output stood at only 110 per cent of that of 1939; thereafter it fell disastrously, that for 1966–67 being the lowest for a decade and only 90 per cent of the prewar figure. A rapidly increasing population, stationary yields and an inability to expand the sown area have been responsible for a sharp decline in the volume of rice exports compared with the 1939 peak, and although Burma regained from Thailand its traditional role as the world's leading rice exporter in 1953, it lost it again in 1964. Every year between 1963 and 1968 witnessed a further decline in the volume of rice exports, on which the foreign exchange earning capacity of the country largely depends, and in 1968 exports fell to barely 340,000 tons, virtually eliminating the country as a major exporter. This fall largely reflected the decline in the sown area, and in 1967 acute rice shortages were experienced in several parts of Burma itself.

Burma's postwar agricultural performance has thus been unusually poor even by Asian standards, and although allowance must be made for the depredations caused by the war, which resulted in the abandonment of about a third of the cultivated area of the Irrawaddy delta and the reduction of national buffalo numbers by an even greater proportion, and by postwar rebellions and civil disturbances, the principal reason has been the government's agricultural policy. Ironically enough, one of the government's chief concerns has been to strengthen the cultivator against the landlord, but in practice its intervention has proved disastrous. The now-departed alien landowners were at least able to ensure that the land was cultivated by somebody, but much formerly cultivated land now lies idle. Agricultural policy, however, has been influenced not only by the tenancy problem but by the country's inability to reduce its dependence on rice exports for foreign exchange earnings.

The tenancy problem   Though prewar Burma's tenancy problem was as acute as that of any part of Southeast Asia, it was not, as was the situation in Luzon or Tonkin, the product of shortcomings in the social structure operating over a lengthy period of time. It burst on the country with great swiftness; still of modest proportions by 1930, in the ensuing decade it was to become a flaming issue and a powerful stimulant to militant nationalism. It was, moreover, peculiarly a problem of the Irrawaddy delta and of other rice areas in Lower Burma: in the Dry Zone, by contrast, its significance was minimal.

The primary cause of the growth of tenancy was the impact on the unsophisticated Burman cultivator of an expanding world demand for rice, and the need for credit while bringing rice-land into cultivation. With the high rice prices obtaining until the end of the first decade of the present century, the opening up of new rice-land was financially very attractive. In this process the Chettyars played a key role, lending money against the security of rice-land. Erratic price movements over the next two decades got many farmers into difficulties, but with the onset of the Great Depression rice prices fell very heavily. Nevertheless, having become accustomed to relatively high living standards with a substantial import consumption, cultivators were seldom willing or able to make downward readjustments; the burden of debt mounted steeply, and with the fall in land values consequent on prolonged low rice prices, the market value of the pledged land frequently came to be less than that of the outstanding debt, so that peasants had little or no incentive to make repayment. Thus many Chettyars were driven to foreclose, but it is clear that they did so with great reluctance. They had no desire whatever to cultivate the land themselves, and foreclosure meant finding a suitable tenant, thus diverting time from the much more profitable occupation of moneylending. Chettyar holdings appear to have amounted ultimately to between two and three million acres, and by 1939 this small group of scarcely 20,000, and the British administration which had stood by and allowed the situation to develop, were under hot attack from Burman nationalists.

Whether Burma would have benefited from a legal sanction against the sale of land to non-indigenes, such as was provided in Java by the Netherlands Indies Agrarian Law, is debatable. With the advantage of hindsight, however, it is difficult to resist the conclusion that the Chettyars were more sinned against than sinning. The way was always open for more business-minded Burmans and Karens to acquire large holdings in similar fashion, and some in fact did so.[9] The Chettyars made the great expansion of Burma's rice export trade in this century possible, and brought a fund of managerial ability into a country whose stock of that commodity was singularly deficient. Their honesty and integrity was never in question. Poorly paid Chettyar clerks and agents handled large sums of money in isolated districts and were clearly subject to considerable temptation; but there is no evidence that they ever misappropriated any of their company's funds, in marked contrast to the behaviour of the indigenous officials of Burma's credit and cooperative societies, whose record both before and after independence shows a depressingly high incidence of default and malpractice. Since 1947 the Chettyar investment, estimated at $180 million in 1930, has been completely lost and the community driven out. But it is entirely possible that with only a

[9] *J. Russell Andrus*, Burmese Economic Life, *Stanford University Press, Stanford, California, and Oxford University Press, London, 1947, p. 67.*

little encouragement, Chettyar capital and enterprise might have been diverted into non-agricultural channels.

Nevertheless, the demise of the Chettyars did little or nothing to improve the lot of most of the delta's rice cultivators; after independence the Chettyars' titles were worthless and those who could sold out to indigenes for what they could get. The problem of cultivators without land or with uneconomically small holdings remained, and in 1948 came the first of a series of acts concerning tenancy and land reform, all of which have been little more than pieces of paper. Under the Land Nationalization Act all holdings in excess of 50 acres were appropriated by the state, but orchards, rubber and religious lands were exempt; however, no vesting date was ever set and in the only district in which the Act was applied it proved a complete failure.[10] The Tenancy Act of 1950 fixed maximum rents, and an act of 1953 raised the lower limit of the 1948 nationalization provisions and conceded the principle of compensation to ex-landlords, for which the government of India had been pressing. But little or no redistribution to the landless or to those most in need ever took place, a scarcely surprising situation in view of the complete absence of new surveys. In practice, those who had been working the land became *de facto* owners; nor were they obliged to contribute towards compensatory payments to former legal owners. The latter, in fact, got nothing, as pleading inability to pay, the government made no provision for compensation either.

Moreover, the agricultural changes did nothing to raise the low level of efficiency of the rice farmers; as Tinker remarked, 'now that foreclosure and dispossession no longer operate, the Burmese cultivator has little incentive to learn the basic lessons of the mechanism of credit.'[11] Even the question of rents was left unsettled; there was little that even indigenous landlords could do to enforce payment, and the government could take no action while Burma's belligerent communist parties and other extremist groups were continually bidding over its head for peasant support. That the new socialist Burma should tolerate such an anomaly as rent eventually became quite unacceptable. Under the Tenancy Law of 1963 the Revolutionary Council abolished all rents and vested the disposal of land in the state; on declaring the act effective in April 1965, General Ne Win expressed his horror that Burma still contained some 350,000 landlords, whose exploitations, he asserted, constituted an affront to the national socialist programme. But all reforms, in fact, were largely on paper, and other aspects of agricultural policy continued to impede the expansion of output.

Other agricultural problems   Widespread rural lawlessness notwithstanding, Burma's extreme tardiness in regaining its 1939 rice-harvested area also reflected the postwar sellers' market. Despite the dislocations resulting from the Karen

[10] *Tinker*, op. cit., *p. 229.*
[11] ibid., *p. 232.*

and communist revolts, Burma in the early Fifties could still produce not only enough rice to satisfy an enhanced domestic demand but also a surplus of over a million tons; with a world price level some six times that of 1939 as against a general price appreciation of about three times, even such a level of exports ensured for Burma an opulence that confirmed the nationalist claim that Burma was inordinately rich, and that only the activities of aliens prevented the country from enjoying the full bounty of nature. As Burma's subsidiary export industries, minerals and timber, had collapsed with the war, government endeavoured to exploit the rice situation by establishing for itself a monopoly of rice procurement for export, and by paying its peasants very much less than it received in the world market. This policy was also pursued by Thailand, but in Burma the exploitation of the peasants was much more severe; in the early Fifties peasants received the equivalent of a mere £10 a ton for rice which the government then disposed of at from £50 to £60 a ton.[12] Under such circumstances it was scarcely surprising that a subsidy for the reclamation of abandoned rice-land originally introduced by the British Military Administration proved ineffective, and was eventually abandoned in 1954.

Burma's development plan, launched in 1952 and intended to create a socialist welfare state by 1960,[13] envisaged an 80 per cent increase in general agricultural production by the latter date. This target would involve an increase of the padi area by three million acres, groundnuts by 700,000 acres, long-stapled cotton by 200,000 acres and jute by 150,000 acres. These increases were to be achieved by reclamation of abandoned land and by enlarging the irrigated area, and were to be undertaken *pari passu* with the extension of credit, consumer and marketing cooperatives. None of these objectives proved possible of attainment.

At the outbreak of World War II about 1·6 million acres, nearly all situated within the Dry Zone, were irrigated, but there were few large modern works and a substantial proportion of the irrigated area was watered by indigenous methods such as tanks and wells. Irrigation suffered greatly through the Japanese occupation, but despite a shortage of staff and equipment in the Irrigation Department several substantial schemes were included in the Eight Year Development Plan, of which the largest was the Mu River project (*Figure 8-2*). This scheme, whose origins date from long before the war, was intended ultimately to irrigate over 1·1 million acres, and to permit dry-season cropping of maize, groundnuts, sesame and other non-rice crops. Another large scheme was planned to irrigate 2·4 million acres in the Yamethin, Toungoo, Pegu and Hanthawaddy Districts in the Sittang valley. But even if the resources for the construction of such schemes had been available, it is highly unlikely that they could have been brought to

[12] Tinker, op. cit., p. 238.

[13] Pyidawtha—The New Burma. Report on long-term programme for Economic and Social Development, *Economic and Social Development Board, Rangoon, 1954.* Pyidawtha *is strictly untranslatable, but implies a happy prosperous condition arising from the full realization of mutual help and cooperation.*

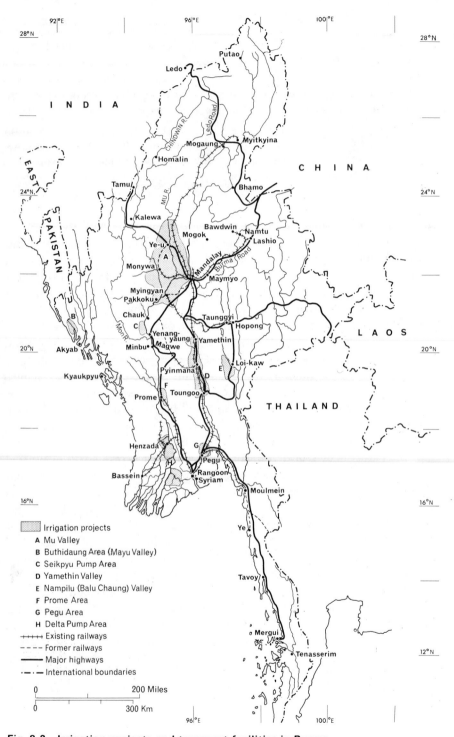

Fig. 8-2 Irrigation projects and transport facilities in Burma
Most of the irrigation projects of the *Pyidawtha* plan shown here exist only on paper.

completion, given the anarchy that prevailed over much of central Burma. In 1965–66 the total irrigated area in Burma was only 1·86 million acres, a mere 8·6 per cent of the total cultivated area, although for the Dry Zone itself the percentage of the cultivated area under irrigation was rather more than double. Work on the Mu River scheme did not begin, in fact, until 1963, when the project received backing from the United Nations Special Fund. With so much land still uncultivated in the delta, and some 5·6 million acres throughout the country estimated to be lying fallow each year, the implementation of these large irrigation schemes appears highly questionable, although it must be conceded that chaotic transport conditions have aggravated the tendency of the Dry Zone to be in rice deficit.

Implementation of the Development Plan was also hampered by the difficulties experienced after 1954 in marketing rice surpluses. With the decline in the price of rice consequent on the recovery of Asian agriculture from the effects of the war and the availability of cheap food grains under American Public Law 480 aid schemes, Burma did not follow Thailand's example of restoring the rice trade to the private sector. It chose instead to barter increasing quantities of rice in government-to-government deals with Eastern bloc countries, on terms which were to prove greatly to its disadvantage. It acquired considerable quantities of inferior Russian and eastern European manufactures, which not infrequently differed considerably from the items agreed upon, and on one occasion at least, when a large consignment of poor Czech cement arrived in Rangoon at the end of the dry season and after filling all available storage space had to be stacked on the wharf, proved a positive embarrassment. Moreover, substantial quantities of Burmese rice held in store by Eastern bloc countries were eventually put on the world market in competition with Burma's own supplies.

Since 1964, on the other hand, Burma has been unable to benefit from steadily appreciating rice prices on the world market because of its own shortages, and in 1966 it had to default on 70,000 out of 200,000 tons of rice it had contracted to Ceylon.[14] With the poorest harvest for a decade in 1966–67, the official rice procurement machinery broke down, and after sporadic rioting in several cities the government permitted a temporary restoration of private trading in rice, and allowed peasants to sell directly to members of the public. Shortages immediately disappeared; but unable to profit by its experience and with the better weather of the 1967–68 season and prospects of a more normal crop, government control of the rice trade was re-established. Despite annual increases in the official price paid to peasants for rice, this is still too low to encourage a greater use of fertilizers or to prevent a flourishing black market. Shortages of

[14] *This decision had important political repercussions in Ceylon, which found it necessary to cut its subsidized rice ration. According to the Ceylonese Food Minister, Mr M. D. Banda, who visited Rangoon in December 1966 to plead Ceylon's case, the rice shortage was due to the large areas remaining uncultivated, and the destruction of rice-mills by the insurgents.*

The Union of Burma

fodder impede expansion of the animal work-force, a situation that has led the government to make large imports of Eastern European tractors, but on whose operations it continues to make very large losses. In 1968 restoration of the Irrawaddy delta's prewar rice-harvested area still seemed as far away as ever.

Other crops

Output of the principal subsidiary food crops, maize, groundnuts, pulses and sesame, has expanded greatly since 1945, the increases in respect of maize and groundnuts, as in most other countries of Southeast Asia, being particularly striking (*Table 8-2*). Burma, however, has yet to appreciate the dietetic advantages of the soya bean, which remains a very minor crop despite the fact that it appears to be well suited to conditions over much of the country. This situation probably arises from the preference for sesame and groundnut oils in the national oilseed consumption pattern, but as Burma was never self-sufficient in its vegetable oil requirements before the war the neglect nevertheless appears surprising. Expanding vegetable oil production, moreover, has scarcely kept pace with population increase, and the per capita consumption is now below the prewar level, although the latter was admittedly high by Southeast Asian standards.

Table 8-2 *Burma: area and production of major crops, 1965–66*

	thousand acres	*thousand metric tons*
Padi	12,390	7,930
Millets	380	50
Maize	210	260
Wheat	410	90
Sesame	2,000	60
Groundnuts	1,300	280
Pulses	1,710	310
Cotton	570	40
Tobacco, Burmese	100	20
Tobacco, Virginia	20	30
Sugar cane	140	1,430
Jute	70	13
Rubber	215	12

Source: *Budget Report,* 1967/68

The cultivation of these subsidiary food crops is very largely a prerogative of the Dry Zone where they are grown principally as wet-season crops, although there is a little double-cropping where irrigation facilities are available. In Lower Burma, where cultivated land is pre-empted by rice, the scope for extension of subsidiary cropping in the dry season is immense; but this would require the provision of expensive irrigation works, for which it is difficult to see justification in the light of a 1940 estimate that there were then more than 19 million acres of uncultivated waste, much of it within the Irrawaddy delta, suitable for conversion into rice-land.[15] However optimistic this estimate may be, it would nevertheless appear that an enhanced production would be more quickly and cheaply achieved by reclaiming swamp and waste than by extensive large-scale irrigation works. A less expensive solution to the problem of seasonal unemployment in the delta would appear to lie in a much greater attention to livestock production.

Burma has a substantial industrial crop production; cotton, sugar cane, tobacco, rubber and jute collectively occupied more than one million acres in 1966, but much of the output of these crops was for immediate consumption in local industries using primitive indigenous techniques. Targets set for the production of cotton, sugar and jute in the Eight Year Development Plan proved impossible of attainment because of attendant difficulties in the industrialization programme, although since 1960 some of the originally planned production levels for that year, such as for cotton, have been surpassed. But even before the war Burma's cotton acreage averaged almost 500,000 acres and, despite some improvement in yields, the virtually equivalent area planted in 1965–66 does not represent much of an advance if Burma aims at a large increase in the proportion of cotton textiles produced from domestic raw materials.

Cotton, as with sesame and millet, is a crop of poor soils and is grown exclusively in the Dry Zone. The commonest native Burmese cottons, such as *wagale*, have a staple length of less than $\frac{5}{8}$ inches and cannot be spun into counts above 16; hence they produce very inferior cloth. The financial return on cotton is low in comparison with that of other crops, and cultivation is thus largely confined to marginal areas. Attempts to establish improved longer-stapled varieties have achieved only modest success, and strains with a staple length of up to $\frac{7}{8}$ inches, such as *Mahlaing 5* and Cambodian varieties, still occupy only a very small proportion of the total cotton area.

Tobacco and sugar cane are widely grown for local consumption, but the cultivation of cane destined for centrifugal mills is confined to the Delta. Despite a very low per capita sugar consumption, Burma was nevertheless obliged to make substantial sugar imports before the war, and is still some way from attaining self-sufficiency in centrifugal sugar. Tobacco is yet another crop of greatest significance in the Dry Zone, but production is largely restricted to dark native tobaccos, though some success has been achieved with the cultivation of the more profitable Virginia types on suitable soils. Since 1962 the import of sugar, tobacco, coffee and other food products has been greatly restricted, partly because of the country's foreign exchange position, but also in order to encourage greater domestic production.

Hevea rubber was planted in Burma as long ago as 1896, but the factors

---

[15] *Andrus*, op. cit., *p. 44.*

making possible the rapid growth of the natural rubber industry in Malaya and the Netherlands Indies never existed in Burma. The physical environment itself proved much less favourable, for although rubber has been grown as far north as Myitkyina in Upper Burma and there is still a small area planted to rubber on the southernmost margins of the Pegu Yoma north of Rangoon, the lengthy wintering during the dry season makes production relatively unprofitable except in periods of very high prices. Moreover, while it took seven years to bring rubber into bearing in Malaya, nine or more years were necessary in Burma. The most favourable conditions for *Hevea* were found to be in Tenasserim, where the soil remains moist throughout the year, but here the large number of rain-days during the southwest monsoon from April to September results in many tapping days being lost, for tapping cannot take place in heavy rain. Tenasserim, however, possessed all but a small proportion of the 215,000 acres under rubber in 1965, the greatest concentration being in the Mergui district with about a third of the total planted area.

Opium is the principal cash crop of the hill-tribes of Burma's eastern margins, but both cultivation and processing are laborious operations. The woman is scoring the poppy seedcases with a three-pronged blade; and the white exudate is allowed to coagulate for twenty-four hours before collection.

Most of Burma's rubber estates of over 100 acres were owned by the British trading companies operating within the country, and before the war three-quarters of their labour force consisted of Indian workers. Burmans find employment as estate workers or even as rubber smallholders unattractive, and since 1945, with the progressive diminution of the Indian community, estates have faced a chronic labour problem. Moreover, despite protestations of good intentions by government, estate owners never felt secure from the threat of nationalization and thus had little incentive to replant; most in fact had sold out to local interests long before 1960. It is thus difficult to foresee any future for Burma's small natural rubber industry; its trees are old and of unselected material, and there is in any case virtually no stock of high-yielding material with which to replant. Although production was stationary for many postwar years, since 1962 it has declined, and the estimated 1966 production of about 12,000 tons was less than the prewar average.

Any review of Burma's agricultural situation must emphasize that any improvement either in production or productivity must await major improvements in the transportation system, which in turn presupposes a much higher degree of government authority throughout the country than exists at present. But, assuming that they can get their produce to market, it is also useless to expect peasants to produce unless they can obtain something useful in exchange for their output. The post-1962 wave of nationalizations resulted in the complete disruption of the distribution system and made desirable consumer goods such as cotton cloth, soap, matches, condensed milk, cooking oil, kerosene, etc., unobtainable by very many peasants; consequently, they have little incentive to sell any surplus produce. In 1966 offices and factories in the major cities experienced a high rate of absenteeism, as workers took time off from their jobs to join in the search for rice. However, while resisting major changes in its procurement machinery, the government improved the availability of more desirable consumer goods such as transistor radios in subsequent seasons, so that peasants were willing to dispose of more of their surplus to the state. Nevertheless, the enhanced domestic consumption that this permitted further reduced the exportable surplus.

Forest products

Before World War II forest products accounted for about 6 per cent of Burma's export income; virtually all of this contribution originated from exports of teak, Burma accounting for about 75 per cent of the world total. The peak years of the teak trade were, as in Thailand, the Twenties, but production maintained a level of little less than half a million cubic tons right up to the outbreak of the war. Production of other hardwoods such as *pyinkado (Xylia dolabriformis), in-kanyin (Dipterocarpus* species*)* and *padauk (Pterocarpus* species*)* totalled an almost equivalent figure, but these timbers were little known outside the country itself. Three British companies, of which the Bombay Burmah Corporation was the largest, operated concessions in the Pegu Yoma, northern Tenasserim and the adjacent southern portions of the Shan plateau, and in the hill-lands of Upper Burma.

Despite a level of exports only about half the prewar peak, teak now generates a larger share of export earnings than it did before the war, and in 1965 it accounted for about 10 per cent of the total. The prospects of Burma's teak industry, however, appear bleaker than that of Thailand. Burma inherited a forest stock which had been protected by a scientific forestry service extending over half a century, and growing teak was declared state property as early as 1855. But most Burmese peoples resented forestry regulations that denied them access to forest materials, and so strong was this feeling that the constitution of 1947 guaranteed to the population the right to cut wood in the forests. The results of this decision, inevitably, were an abasement of the forest composition and major damage to the growing stock.

In 1945 all teak concessions were cancelled and the operation of the teak industry was entrusted to a public corporation. But illegal felling and theft of logs in transit to the mills of Rangoon and Moulmein has continued to take place, and much of this material eventually found its way into the sawmills of the private sector. With the post-1962 nationalizations and the elimination of private sawmills, teak production fell heavily.

MINING AND MANUFACTURING

As a planned socialist state, Burma might have been expected to press on rapidly with the expansion of non-agricultural activities. Yet its success in promoting industrialization has been distinctly meagre; within Southeast Asia only Indonesia presents such an equally striking contrast between industrial aspiration and realization, and even Indonesia has managed to raise the contribution of mineral production to national product. Burma's industrial plans have been characterized by hastily prepared grandiose schemes in which new projects depended on scarcely completed or incomplete preceding ones, and sometimes even on projects that had not been implemented. If 'by 1958 the shortcomings of hasty over-ambitious development had been realized by thoughtful Burmans,'[16] the latter proved powerless to influence the course of events; industrial production continued to follow an erratic course, and even successfully launched state undertakings were offset by dislocations resulting from the progressive nationalization of the private industrial sector.

Mineral industries

Burma's mineral endowment has been noted as perhaps the richest of any country of continental Southeast Asia. In 1939 minerals collectively accounted for some 40 per cent of exports by value, of which petroleum products alone made up some

[16] *Tinker, op. cit., p. 128.*

27 per cent, the balance of the mineral contribution being provided by base metals and silver bullion. In 1965 all minerals generated scarcely 6 per cent of export earnings, and on balance Burma was a petroleum importer. It is difficult to visualize any development that would give such a stimulus to the industrialization of Burma as a speedy resuscitation of its once important mineral industries. Though much of the responsibility for their demise can be attributed to the operations of insurgents, the government cannot escape heavy censure for policies which have discouraged production whether organized on a private, mixed, or public basis.

Burma has produced more than a million tons of crude petroleum per annum, and though of minor significance, even by the standards of world production at the time, prewar Burma was the largest producer within the British Empire. Except for a miniscule production from Kyaukpyu island off the Arakan coast, Burma's petroleum output has originated entirely from anticlinal structures located on either side of the Irrawaddy valley, between Pakkoku near the centre of the Dry Zone and Thayetmyo at its southern margin. Burmans have produced petroleum from hand-dug wells for many centuries, and there is still a small illegal local production both from indigenous hand-dug and from abandoned drilled wells.

Modern exploitation dates from 1886 with the foundation of the Burmah Oil Company, so that, as with Indonesia, Burma is no upstart newcomer to the industry. The Yenangyaung field was for long the principal producer, but in 1940 its output was overtaken by that of the new Chauk field some 50 miles to the north. The oilfield equipment and associated plants, together with the three Syriam refineries near Rangoon, the largest of which had a 20,000 barrels per day throughput, were thoroughly demolished in 1942, and were later subject to repeated Allied bombing. However, the biggest obstacles to resuscitation of production were the acute differences of opinion between the British oil companies and the Burmese government over the question of compensation, and assurances of profitability to justify the large new investment necessary for rehabilitating the industry.[17] These issues were unresolved, but by pooling resources of the three companies involved and with some participation from other international oil companies, considerable progress was made in renewing production. But the Yenangyaung field was occupied by insurgents during the Karen rebellion of 1949, the pipeline to Syriam was cut and barge traffic on the Irrawaddy brought to a halt. Thereafter this field was abandoned, and Lower Burma and Rangoon had to depend on imports for their petroleum needs, while attention

---

[17] *The Burmah Oil Company fought a long legal battle over compensation for the destruction of its properties at the request of the British government, but after the House of Lords had decided in its favour a retroactive bill of 1965 absolved the British government from any liability for payment. It is only fair to point out, however, that though the act was passed by a Labour government, it had been prepared by the preceding Conservative administration.*

was directed to supplying central Burma from the more northerly fields at Chauk and Lanywa, which remained in the control of the government. In 1954 a joint enterprise, the Burma Oil Company, was formed in which the state held a one-third share; this went some way towards meeting nationalist pressure for a complete take-over but the company operated under many irritating restrictions, such as an inability to discharge redundant workers, and rehabilitation was slow. A new small refinery was opened on the Chauk field in 1954, and in 1957 the first stage of a new refinery to replace that existing before the war was opened at Syriam. In the decade after 1955 petroleum output climbed from about 25 per cent to 55 per cent of the prewar level, and Burma once again became self-sufficient in many petroleum products, although at a very low per capita consumption.

Had Burma been willing to allow the continued participation of foreign capital in the petroleum industry as Indonesia did, production might have expanded more rapidly. But after 1962 it was clear that despite the Investment Act of 1959, passed to encourage foreign investment in the country, there was no place for the foreigner in mining or heavy industries. Petroleum production together with that of other minerals was taken over completely by the state in 1964; a desultory search for new oilfields in the Irrawaddy valley and in the Delta did prove the existence of a number of new oil and gas fields, but the new Petroleum and Minerals Development Corporation lacked both the human and physical resources to bring them into production. Burma has thus joined the select group of countries that have been willing to sacrifice a prosperous petroleum industry to political dogma, and the 1965 production of some 550,000 tons was only a fraction of what might have been possible given pragmatic economic policies.

Burma's once important metalliferous mining industries have fared little better. The lead-zinc-silver Bawdwin mine recommenced operations in 1952 as the Burma Corporation, jointly owned by Burma Mines (the prewar operating company) and the government, but the chaos of Burma's transport system and difficulties in obtaining equipment and staff restricted the output of lead and zinc concentrates to less than 50,000 tons in most years. The complex of tin and wolfram mines at Mawchi in the troubled Kayah (formerly Karenni) state in the southern Shan plateau have never been able to resume regular operations since the end of the war, as the area has seldom been controlled by the central government. Low world prices for most base metals in the early Sixties, and the threat of nationalization, had produced a sharp decline in production even before the final takeover. But subsequent higher prices, particularly for tin, have failed to stimulate production, as 'socialist' Burma has largely isolated itself from market influences. In 1964 the country produced only 770 tons of tin concentrates despite the highest price ever recorded on the world market. This small output came largely from small Chinese producers, the former European dredges in the Tavoy area having long ceased to be operative.

Commercial production of rubies at the famous Mogok mine in the
northern Shan plateau of Burma ceased during the Great Depression, but a
desultory indigenous mining activity continues.

Despite an inability to promote the speedy rehabilitation of its important
prewar mining industries, Burma has nevertheless continued to show interest in
the development of further mining activities, at least on paper. In 1951 Burma
acquired the services of a group of American engineering consultants, Knappen-
Tippetts-Abbett (KTA), whose report issued in 1953 proposed a grandiose
collection of mutually-supporting mining and manufacturing projects, which
were incorporated into the *Pyidawtha*, or Eight Year Development Plan. Implementation of these projects would have constituted a considerable challenge to a
government with far greater managerial and administrative resources at its disposal than those of Burma. Major prominence was given to the development of

the Kalewa brown coal deposits, located in the valley of the Chindwin almost 600 miles from Rangoon; these deposits had long been known before the war, but their exploitation had never been economic as imported Indian or South African coal was much cheaper. The Kalewa deposits, nevertheless, were to form the basis of a proposed complex of heavy industries at Myingyan in the Dry Zone, which after the Rangoon and Akyab areas was to constitute the third such industrial concentration.

Determined to have that favourite status symbol of many underdeveloped countries, an iron and steel industry, Burma commissioned the German concerns Krupp and Demag to discover domestic iron ore deposits and to assist with the foundations for such an industry. Substantial deposits of iron ore were discovered in the Taunggyi-Maymyo area of the Shan plateau, but production both of coal and iron ore has never exceeded 10,000 tons a year and neither mining activity can yet be regarded as economic. Burma's iron and steel industry is confined to an electric furnace and rolling plant at Insein (Rangoon), whose raw material requirements are proving difficult to meet and whose finished products are very far from competitive either in price or quality.

Manufacturing industries

Rice-mills and sawmills accounted for some 70 per cent of Burma's prewar thousand or so factories, but total factory employment was only some 90,000 workers, an infinitesimal proportion of the total labour force. Only one-fifth of these were employed in establishments with more than 100 workers. There were, in addition, perhaps as many as half a million largely part-time handicraft workers, of whom about half were engaged in cotton spinning and weaving. To Burmese nationalists this modest industrial development created under foreign rule was almost an insult, but it was not inconsiderable in the light of the general economic situation of the country, and a few large establishments, such as the oil refineries at Syriam, the smelters and ore-dressing plants at Namtu serving the Bawdwin mines, the dockyard and foundry of the Irrawaddy Flotilla Company in Rangoon, the railway workshops at Insein, and the large cement works at Thayetmyo in the Irrawaddy valley, which used natural gas from nearby oilfields as fuel, provided the basis for a further expansion of heavy industry. Nationalists were also incensed that only about a third of all factory employees consisted of Burmese workers, the balance consisting almost entirely of Indian immigrants.

Most of newly independent Burma's factious political parties concurred in a determination to have a socialist economy modified in some vague way by the tenets of Buddhism, and nationalization of all water-transport facilities occurred as early as 1949. That other sectors of the economy would also pass into public ownership at some future date was never really in doubt, but ravaged by war and rebellion, Burma could not immediately dispense with foreign capital and managerial skill.

In adopting an industrialization policy which reserved key and heavy industries to the state and light industries to Burmese nationals, leaving only a very narrow field to foreign capital, Burma's experience has closely resembled that of Indonesia. The *Pyidawtha*, or Eight Year Development Plan, proposed to achieve self-sufficiency in salt, cement, jute sacking, and certain branches of chemical and low-grade finished steel products, and to expand production of a wide range of consumer goods. The main instrument of the industrialization programme was a state corporation, intended to work closely with similar corporations administering agriculture and rural development, and mining. The decline in rice prices after 1955 led to the dropping of some projects, but even those completed ran into severe difficulties and, in the event, the nationalized corporations merely expanded opportunities for the corruption and chicanery which had been characteristic of Dynastic, British and Republican Burma alike.[18] The scrap supply derived from war-damaged plant which was to supply the steel mill at Insein was soon exhausted, local supplies of medium-staple cotton for the new spinning and weaving mills proved quite inadequate, and a pharmaceutical plant could not market its output of vitamins and drugs. Burma's deteriorating balance-of-payments position obliged it to seek aid from Eastern bloc countries, and there were considerable delays in the supply of plant and equipment. All the state-owned plants made heavy losses, inevitable in view of the fact that they were grossly overstaffed and seldom operated at even 50 per cent of their planned capacity.

During the first regime of General Ne Win (1958–60) the Army itself became directly interested in industrial production through the Defence Service Institute. This organization was initially concerned with the supply of provisions and equipment to military personnel, but through acquisitions from the private sector and by direct investment the Army's manufacturing interests rapidly expanded into many lines of consumer goods and eventually into distribution, banking and even shipping. When the civil government resumed office in 1960 the Burma Economic Development Corporation, in whose management the Army also participated, took over much of the Army's manufacturing interests, and plants such as the Thamaing (Rangoon) spinning and weaving mill, whose output had been largely earmarked by the defence services, were gradually allowed to accept orders from the private sector. This state-owned plant, the largest cotton mill in the country, was erected in 1951 with the help of American aid, but in 1958 its capacity was greatly extended through Chinese economic assistance. In 1960 the Lawpita hydro-electric plant on the Balu Chaung, a tributary of the Salween, with an initial capacity of 84,000 kW (to be doubled when its secondary stage is implemented) and constructed with Japanese war-

---

[18] *Sinai*, op. cit., *pp. 129–30.*

reparations aid, commenced operations and considerably relieved the power shortage in the Rangoon area.

Nevertheless, Burma's slow industrial progress prompted the government to re-examine the question of the role of foreign capital, even though pressure for complete nationalization remained strong; production of most consumer goods continued to be dominated by a few large joint-venture organizations of the state and foreign companies, such as ICI and Unilever, which operated on normal business lines. The Investment Act of 1959 endeavoured to encourage further joint ventures by offering freedom from complete nationalization for ten years and, in the case of certain industries, for up to twenty years. Agreements with Japanese manufacturers for the assembly of motor vehicles and the manufacture of electrical apparatus were concluded, but there was little interest from Western manufacturers; in the event, it proved that the Burmese were not really interested in joint ventures as such, but wished to have foreign firms provide plant, raw material and technical personnel for the production of their products by the Burma Economic Development Corporation.

After the second military take-over in 1962, nationalization of the whole industrial field proceeded rapidly. Previous experience of nationalization in Burma had already made clear what the result of such action would be; production declined sharply and the construction of new plants came to a standstill. In addition the Revolutionary Council proceeded with the nationalization of all banking and insurance, the import and export trade, and retail distribution. By 1963 virtually all foreign-owned business ceased functioning, and by 1965 the private sector outside agriculture had virtually ceased to exist.

Thus fifteen years of faltering industrial planning had given to Burma a range of new prestigious but high-cost industries, whose future is obscure. The overwhelming bulk of the new industrial investment was in the Rangoon area. Elsewhere, large industrial establishments were confined to the three cement plants at Thayetmyo in the Irrawaddy valley, the textile plants at Myingyan and Mandalay, and the sugar-mills at Bilin and Pyinmana, neither of which were operating at capacity in 1966.

TRANSPORT AND TRADE

Inadequate transport is the greatest single obstacle to the achievement of a higher level of economic development in Burma; but so long as considerable sections of the population are opposed not so much to the present government as to any government at all, major improvements in the transport system are out of the question. Before World War II the railways and water transport shared almost all freight and passenger traffic. Roads in Burma were few and poorly maintained, even by the standards of India (*Figure 8-2*). The motor vehicle was scarcely known in Burma until after 1920, and even in 1965 the country possessed only some 50,000 motor vehicles and had the lowest ratio of vehicles to population of any country in Southeast Asia.

In 1965 Burma claimed some 2,405 miles of railway line, a figure which slightly exceeds that of 1940, but the war and the postwar rebellions had done tremendous damage to the system. During the war the Japanese removed the second track between Rangoon and Toungoo, the busiest portion of the whole railway system, and it has never been replaced; during the troubled early Fifties the main line to Mandalay virtually ceased to exist, and every station save that of Pegu was burned down.[19] By the middle of the decade, however, rehabilitation was able to proceed more easily. In 1961 the great Irrawaddy bridge at Ava, blown up in the British retreat in 1942, was finally repaired, and work began on the Mokpalin bridge over the Sittang. As a result of the purchase of new diesel locomotives and rolling-stock, operating efficiency was much improved, and in 1964–65 the railways carried some 54 million passengers, mostly within the Rangoon area, more than two and a half times the prewar figure; freight traffic, however, remained at only a little less than half the prewar level of four million tons. Although agricultural produce provided more than three-quarters of the prewar freight revenue, the most profitable item was always the long-distance haul of metals from the Namtu smelters to Rangoon, a traffic that at present is very greatly reduced.

Passenger traffic on prewar Burma's waterways was very substantially less than that handled by the railways, but the volume of freight moved by the two systems was in all probability very similar. Much of the freight traffic on waterways consisted of the movement of rice within the Irrawaddy delta, where the many small streams and distributaries, tidal within sixty or so miles of the sea, provided cheap transport in almost every direction. The Twante Canal, originally cut in 1883 and progressively widened, connected the eastern branch of the Irrawaddy with the rice-mills and warehouses of Rangoon. The canal was also used by the vessels of the Irrawaddy Flotilla Company, which in linking Rangoon with Bassein and Mandalay, employed what were probably the largest shallow-draft vessels operating on inland waters anywhere in the world. Nationalization, the systematic destruction of all navigation aids, and the abandonment of regular recording of shoals and other obstructions brought long-distance water traffic to an almost complete standstill, and recovery has proceeded very slowly. Nevertheless, the delta rice traffic, which has always been largely handled by a multiplicity of small craft, remains; in 1965 the volume of freight handled by the nationalized Inland Water Transport Corporation was about 0·5 million tons, but this was in all probability only a small part of the total water-borne freight traffic. Burma entered into the ocean-going shipping industry in 1952, but the state shipping corporation has had an operational history not very different from

---

[19] *Tinker*, op. cit., p. *287*.

that of other state-owned corporations. Two vessels of its fleet of seven sank, and in 1961 the remainder became the nucleus of the Burma Five Star Line, a subsidiary of the Army's Defence Services Institute.

With the dislocation of so much of its prewar transport facilities, Burma inevitably has had to make greater use of road transport. The acquisition of vehicles and spares, however, became progressively more difficult as Burma proceeded with its policy of nationalization with little or no compensation, and by the early Sixties, such supplies from Western sources had completely dried up; only the timely arrival of new Japanese equipment through war-reparations aid enabled public road transport services to be maintained. After 1962 Burma's brusque rejection of American aid led to the abandonment of work on a new 430–mile highway connecting Rangoon and Mandalay, a project which the contemporary Chinese invasion of Assam suggested might be abandoned with advantage to the West. But after this date the overworked Burma Airways Dakota fleet, which somewhat surprisingly had proved equal to all the demands made on it, began to receive new Fokker Friendship aircraft, and despite the disruptive activities of the Karen People's Liberation Army, the Kachin Independence Army, the Chin State Party, the New Mon State Party, the Shan Underground Brigade, not to mention those of the 'White Flag' Communists and the rival, so-called Trotskyite, 'Red Flag' Communists composed largely of ethnic Burmans, the government was succeeding in maintaining its links with the main economic foci of the country.

Trade

Unlike Thailand, Burma has become more dependent on rice than it ever was before the war. The share of export income generated by rice increased from

Table 8-3 *Burma: principal exports, 1962–63 and 1966–67*

	million kyats	
	1962–63	1966–67
Rice	784·1	291·6
Other agricultural products	245·6	98·7
Teak	157·3	81·6
Hardwood	7·1	0·9
Metals and ores	48·4	22·1
Others	20·2	5·9
Total	**1,262·7**	**500·8**

Source: Central Statistical Department, Rangoon

some 50 per cent in 1939 to nearly 70 per cent in the Sixties (*Table 8-3*), and if one of the main objectives of Burma's socialist programme was to speed the country's transition from an export-oriented one-crop economy, the policy can only be judged a disastrous failure. Despite Burma's flirtations with the Eastern bloc, the pattern of rice exports is not greatly different from that before World War II, except that Southeast Asia now absorbs almost as much as the Indian region, and in some years Indonesia has been by far the largest individual purchaser. Singapore, Malaysia and the Philippines are also large buyers of Burmese rice in most years, but Ceylon over several years has been a better customer than either India or Pakistan. For most of the Sixties, the Indian region and Southeast Asia have absorbed some 80 per cent of Burma's rice exports, but after 1964 China also became an important market, a fact reflecting China's considerable grain-foods deficit and its growing political interest in Burma. With the diplomatic breach with Peking, resulting from the anti-Chinese riots of 1966, trade with China fell heavily, and in view of Burma's economic difficulties an early restoration of trade with China to its former level appears unlikely.

If independent Burma has been unsuccessful in its attempts to diversity the pattern of exports, it has been equally unsuccessful in its policy of import substitution. Burma is still far from self-sufficient in cotton textiles, and the low efficiency of domestic mills means that even high import duties give little protection. Among consumer goods, cotton fabrics and cotton yarns are the largest items in the import trade, and others of major significance are condensed milk, paper, pharmaceutics and petroleum products, most of which have been the subject of major domestic industrial effort. Britain, however, has not only been displaced from its prewar position as Burma's chief supplier of imports by Japan, but after 1964 was relegated to third position by China, largely as a result of that country's greatly enhanced economic aid; indeed, in 1965 about 40 per cent of all foreign loans committed or disbursed in Burma originated in Peking, but after the diplomatic breach Chinese aid ceased abruptly, and all Chinese technical assistance personnel were withdrawn.

Foreign trade passed completely into the hands of the government after 1964, although separate agencies were established to handle individual commodities and to deal with private foreign buyers, and for government-to-government sales. Many thousands of commercial businesses were absorbed, and the take-overs fell with particular severity on Burma's small remaining Indian community, as they were meant to do. Indians were further hit by the demonetization of large-denomination Kyat currency notes and by the nationalization of retail distribution, which in effect deprived most of them of any means of making a livelihood. Some 50,000 Indians left the country in 1964, the last of a community once numbering more than one million; many were in great penury as they were forbidden to take any property or items of value with them. Burma denied that any expulsions had taken place and pointed out that the new regulations applied to Burmese and aliens alike; nevertheless, relations with India became very strained.

CONCLUSION

Burma is still a comparatively unimportant part of Southeast Asia, and to the world economy it is unquestionably of much less significance than it was in 1939. Burma's new leaders have shown enthusiasm, but little else; the ordinary Burman at present is little if at all better off than his prewar counterpart. The traditional Burmese society has continued to constitute an almost insuperable obstacle to economic development and, as always in the past, Buddhism continues to provide a cloak of respectability for widespread corruption and violence; it is at least a credit to the generals who have run the country since 1962 that they perceive that Buddhism *per se* cannot constitute an institutional framework for a modern industrialized society. But in adopting yet more of the economic characteristics of the communist powers, Burma is clearly running contrary to a well-established trend in underdeveloped countries, which in general have been moving away from grandiose and over-ambitious forced-draft industrialization programmes on Eastern bloc lines, and lavish expenditure on largely unproductive symbols and monuments to national prestige or to the vanity of the ruler.

Unlike Indonesia, Burma so far has fortunately avoided both the 'personality cult' and foreign adventure, being apparently content to remain uniquely 'Burman'; but the anti-Chinese riots of 1967 were clear notice to the government that serious trouble could be expected from the urban areas if a marked improvement in living standards was further delayed. Though Burma was in fact expelled from the sterling area in 1967 for persisting in its endeavours to convert sterling into other assets, there is some evidence that the country is about to reconsider its economic policies, and although no departure from a strict official neutralism is likely, some softening in political relations with the West is quite possible. Implementation of Peking's threatened assistance to the Kachins and other dissident groups would present Burma with a very grave situation, and would certainly imperil the Four Year Plan introduced in 1966, which has as its target the raising of per capita income to some $78, an increase of $15 over the plan period. It is abundantly clear, moreover, that with a primitive agriculture and declining rice exports, Burma cannot finance an import programme capable of launching an effective modernization process.

The greatest Western scholar of Burma, J. S. Furnivall, believed in the Fifties that the survival of Burma at all was little short of miraculous; its continued survival may be no less of a wonder. However, another well-known observer of Southeast Asia has remarked that 'the pessimists have been proved wrong. Burmese recovery is no miracle and is based on an honest implementation of well-conceived legislation.'[20] This image of Burma as a pragmatic and progressive country, trying to find a middle-road between capitalism and communism, with a welfare society and yet reconciled with its traditional beliefs, was probably the most successful postwar political confidence trick in the whole of Asia.

[20] *Erich H. Jacoby*, Agrarian Unrest in Southeast Asia, *Asia Publishing House, London and New York, 1961, p. 108.*

CHAPTER NINE

Vietnam, Laos and Cambodia

Fate has reserved its hardest blows in postwar Southeast Asia for the lands that, until the Geneva agreement of 1954, still constituted for all practical purposes the Union of Indochina. Large parts of Burma have known no real peace since 1945, and the blood bath produced by the abortive communist *coup* in Indonesia in 1965 probably produced more casualties in a few brief weeks than those resulting from a decade of war in Vietnam. Yet despite their strong centrifugal tendencies, both Burma and Indonesia have managed to preserve their territorial integrity, and though it may be true that the cultural divisions of the Union of French Indochina were deeper, the greatest tragedy attending its break-up has undoubtedly been the severance of the essential unity of the Vietnamese people themselves. Differences between Hanoi and Saigon are certainly of long standing, but the present hostility between North and South Vietnam has little to do with the squabbles of the past; it is the bitter fruit of an essentially homogeneous population divided over the fundamental organization of their society.

It is Vietnam's greater misfortune that the larger issues have become involved in this conflict. Feeling itself cheated of the full fruits of victory through the obduracy of the late President Ngo Dinh Diem of South Vietnam in refusing to hold the elections provided for in the Geneva agreement, which would almost certainly have delivered the country south of the 17th parallel to the Vietminh,[1] and faced with mounting economic difficulties to which it saw no solution save through the annexation of the South,[2] the Politburo of North Vietnam reactivated

---

[1] *Short for* Viet Nam Doc Lap Dong Minh Hoi, *originally the Vietnam Independence League, a multi-party organization, but later captured by the communist (Lao Dong) party. The name has also been used to designate North Vietnam itself. With a population of some 14 millions as against 12 millions for South Vietnam in 1956 when the elections should have been held, the North was confident that it could win any overall national election; the delay, in effect, was intended as little more than a face-saving device for the French. The term* Vietcong, *or National Liberation Front, is a contraction of 'Vietnamese Communist'.*

[2] *P. J. Honey, in Guy Wint (ed.),* Asia: A Handbook, *Frederick Praeger, New York, 1966, p. 250.*

its liberation movement in the South, the Vietcong, and plunged the country into a war which has become absorbed in the containment of the Chinese revolution. Vietnam has become a testing ground for Mao Tse Tung's theory of world revolution—that men are superior to materials and the forces of nature, and that through ideological dedication all obstacles must inevitably be overcome. Thus the lightly equipped but highly mobile peasant forces must prevail, however sophisticated the modern armies arranged against them—although the increasingly complex weapons acquired by North Vietnam from Russia from 1965 onwards suggests that there is perhaps no substitute for modern military hardware after all. By 1967 American military assistance to South Vietnam had made it plain to the outside world that North Vietnam could not succeed in its take-over programme; but perhaps because it is the only way in which excessive dependence on China can be avoided, for the facts of geography do not permit North Vietnam the opportunities enjoyed by North Korea in profiting from Sino-Soviet differences, and because it feels that the Vietnam war is increasingly unpopular in the United States itself, North Vietnam ferociously continued the struggle. At the end of January 1968, the commencement of the *Tet* or Vietnamese lunar New Year, North Vietnam launched its major offensive of the war, a simultaneous attack against virtually all the cities of the South. In the fighting some three-quarters of the old imperial city of Hue was destroyed, but although winning much publicity for the North, the attacks were all beaten back. There was no popular rising against the government of the South as Hanoi had hoped, South Vietnam's own army performed unexpectedly well, and the savagery of the communists in the cities they had temporarily occupied produced a renewed wave of support for the Saigon government.

As a result of the war large areas of the Mekong delta, the world's third largest rice-exporting region before 1939 and with a potential rice production greater than that of either the Irrawaddy delta or the Mae Nam Chao Phraya plain, have been abandoned to cultivation and South Vietnam has become a major rice importer. After mid-1965 the French-owned rubber estates, which up to that time had been largely unaffected by the fighting, came under attack by the Vietcong, and in subsequent military operations, which included the defoliation of almost half the rubber area by aerial spraying, production declined drastically, augmenting still further the growing trade deficit. This was largely made good by United States economic aid, and by 1966 nearly three-quarters of South Vietnam's total import requirements were financed under the Commodity Import Program of the Agency for International Development (AID); by 1968, however, this share had fallen to about one half, as American aid funds were progressively shifted towards greater emphasis on project aid and on para-military security and pacification programmes. But despite the magnitude of American assistance, the government's own mounting defence expenditure continued to produce enormous and expanding budget deficits, whose inflationary pressure was further intensified by the local currency demands of some 500,000 American defence personnel. Chronic inflation and the widespread corruption produced by the enormous and loosely administered aid programme have greatly added to the strains caused by the political ambitions of rival military leaders and have gravely handicapped the national war effort.[3]

Nevertheless, despite the possession of perhaps the best physical resource basis for heavy industry of any part of Southeast Asia, North Vietnam's economic situation is also parlous. The balance of food production and consumption has always been delicately poised, and increases in output have probably done no more than keep pace with population growth. To meet its indebtedness to other communist countries for capital goods and essential imports, North Vietnam has had little to offer save its coal and other minerals, and these products have not found markets easy to come by. After 1965 the escalation of the war and American air attacks made agricultural operations increasingly difficult, and the newly completed factories, mills, power stations, and transport facilities were only able to operate at a fraction of their capacity, even if the bombing was unsuccessful in bringing their operations to a complete halt. There is little doubt that despite its cries of outrage at alleged attacks on civilian targets by American bombers, it was the gradual destruction of much of its physical infrastructure that was the major factor in North Vietnam's appeal to the court of world public opinion for a stop to the bombing.

Nor are the Vietnamese alone in their division. Across the Annamite Chain, some two-thirds of Laos and perhaps half its population are controlled by the *Pathet Lao*, a communist body initiated and supported by Hanoi, but much of this occupied territory is held by North Vietnamese regular forces in guarding the so-called Ho Chi Minh Trail, in reality a complex of tracks and jungle paths, by which North Vietnam infiltrates men and supplies into the South. The economic position of Laos is tragically ludicrous; before 1939 the Kingdom was a small rice exporter, but at present it is in heavy food deficit, and with its enormous armed forces for its size of population, which account for virtually three-quarters of budget expenditure, Laos is virtually the pensioner of the West. Apart from the produce of one small tin mine, the country has only trifling exports to set against its large and growing import bills, and its colossal trade deficit is met through enormous foreign aid. The Royal Laotian Government has received for many years the world's highest per capita aid,[4] but this has been

---

[3] *The gross inefficiency and corruption in the American aid programme have been revealed in several Congressional Committees of Enquiry, but have throughout been condoned on the grounds that the necessity of preventing economic collapse as the war effort mounted, justified departures from the customary procedural safeguards. Precisely similar arguments have been advanced to explain away the equally deplorable irregularities in American aid to Laos.*

[4] *Between 1954 and 1960 Laos received an average of $156 per capita aid per annum from the United States. The total extent of American commitments to Laos since is classified, but economic aid, excluding contributions to the Foreign Exchange Operations Fund and*

expended in ways that have mainly benefited the bureaucrats in Vientiane, and has had minimal impact on the rural population. It is thus scarcely surprising that this massive assistance has promoted neither national cohesion nor economic development. Laos has enormous economic potential, particularly if the Mekong scheme is fully implemented, but it is difficult to see any real future for the country except in the context of a general political settlement in the Indochinese lands between the great powers.

The only relief from the gloomy picture of war and stagnation is presented by Cambodia, largely because of the extraordinary capacity of its Chief of State and former King, Norodom Sihanouk, whose obduracy in insisting on complete independence for Cambodia at the Geneva agreement of 1954 finally wore down the Vietminh and their Russian supporters. In securing international acceptance of Cambodia's refusal to grant to the communists any special privileges such as they obtained in Laos, where the *Pathet Lao* was allowed to 'regroup' in the two northern provinces of Sam Neua and Phong Saly, Cambodia won for itself more than a decade of peace in which national integration and economic development could proceed free from outside interference. This Cambodia was perspicacious enough to reinsure by following a rigid neutralist policy, which in 1963 led it to refuse further United States economic aid and to accept such assistance from Peking.

Cambodia is not a small country, an appellation that invariably earns a stinging rebuke from its Chief of State, and its present population could well be considered meagre in relation to its large resources of unused and little-used land. It has always been a food surplus area, and there is great scope for further expansion of food exports. Cambodia's per capita GNP has increased by some 6 per cent per annum since 1960, and though the claimed per capita product of $122 in 1965 may owe much to the political necessity of demonstrating that economically the Khmers are doing just as well as the Thais, the country's economic performance merits higher commendation than it has generally received in the West. Nevertheless, should the Vietnam war continue, Cambodia's privileged immunity from the Indochinese turmoil may not endure; though hotly denied by the government, Cambodia has purchased the freedom to deal with its own dissidents by turning a blind eye to incursions across its frontiers by the Vietcong, and by following a policy of friendship with China that in the opinion of many Western observers departed far from its professed neutralism. But in 1967 a series of incidents in Battambang province perpetrated by the *Khmers Rouges*, a Cambodian communist body which had formed part of Ho Chi Minh's anti-French forces, suggested that the country's immunity from communist subversion and

---

the Commodity Import Program, amounted to nearly $60 million in 1966–67. Laos also receives assistance from Britain, France, Japan and Australia. The Royal Laotian Army is the only defence force in the world, apart from the United States Armed Forces themselves, entirely paid for by the American taxpayer.

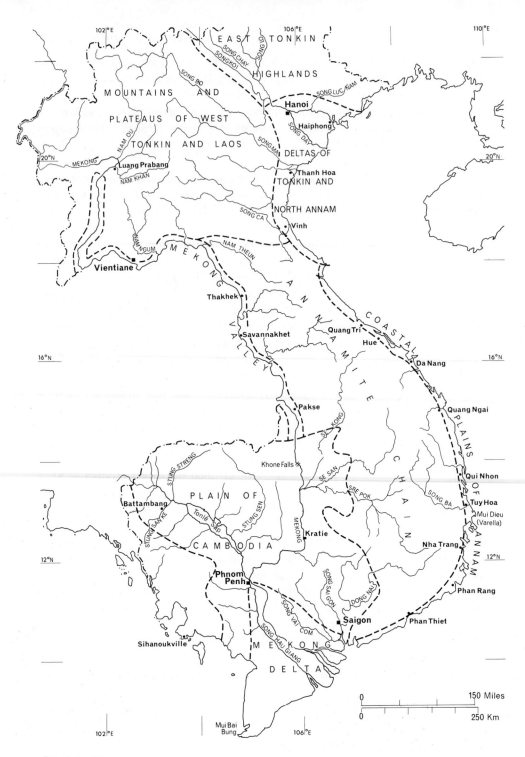

Fig. 9-1 The physical regions of Indochina

terrorism could no longer be guaranteed. In an outburst against the *Khmers Rouges*, Sihanouk in May 1966 had already virtually admitted that Cambodia had provided sanctuary for the Vietcong, and petulantly asked if he deserved this treatment 'at the hands of his friends'.

Hanoi's attempted take-over of the South, its effective occupation of much of Laos, and terrorist activities in both Cambodia and Northeast Thailand by bands of guerillas deriving their inspiration and material support from North Vietnam, are alarming the Lao, Khmer and Thai peoples alike. For over a thousand years, the Vietnamese, or Annamites, have been pressing southwards, dispossessing other peoples of their land and imposing their Sinicized culture on the conquered territories. Thus the once great Champa empire was overthrown and the Chams reduced in numbers to a few ignominious thousands; the Mekong delta of Cochinchina was seized from the Khmers and, but for fortuitous French intervention, the Vietnamese might have advanced to the borders of the Tonlé Sap. Since 1956 many thousands of the hill peoples of the basaltic plateaus of the central Annamite chain have been ejected from their traditional homelands by the government of South Vietnam, in order to make room for Vietnamese settlements. Whether from the North or the South, the Vietnamese are objects of fear and suspicion to the other peoples of the Indochinese peninsula; why should the process of Vietnamese expansion not continue until the whole of the peninsula is engulfed? The present pattern of events may well suggest to the non-Vietnamese peoples that there are no limits to Vietnamese ambition.

The physical background: ethnic groups and factors in land use

The Indochinese lands epitomize the physical characteristics of the massive larger peninsula of which they form part; nowhere is the contrast between mountain and plain, wet and dry season, or sawah and swidden more clearly demarcated. Though somewhat fanciful, the French geographers' description of Indochina as two bags of rice slung from a coolie yoke emphasized the essential features of the human and economic geography of the old French Indochina with its two major rice bowls, the Songkoi or Red river delta of Tonkin and the Mekong delta of Cochinchina, connected by a string of small fragmented plains along the coast of Annam; by implication it also underlined the essentially negative character of the extensive mountain and plateau systems, and suggested the very secondary role in the former Union held by Cambodia and Laos, both of which in fact possess large areas of plain. Only the Vietnamese possess a material culture capable of converting plains into areas of high population density, through elaborate multicropping practices of Chinese origin.

The Mekong is one of Asia's major rivers, yet its human significance has always been far less than that of the Songkoi, whose length and discharge are greatly inferior; however, implementation of the Mekong Valley scheme could finally reverse this historical pattern. The subordinate position of the Mekong derives in part from the extensive areas of infertile old alluvium in the Lower Basin and the formidable obstacles to navigation, which have prevented the river from becoming a major artery of communication; but it owes more to the material cultures of the Lao and Khmer peoples, whose use of the land has always been light in comparison with that of the Vietnamese. Though nominally under Cambodian control, large areas of the delta were virtually unoccupied when the first Vietnamese settlements were made in the seventeenth century; indeed, much of the best rice-land, situated in the western delta, was settled only after the turn of the present century.

The Mekong is unbridged throughout its entire length in Southeast Asia. Much of the Lower Basin appears from a small-scale map to be a continuous plain, but it is in fact a series of plains, some extensive such as that of Vientiane, others closely confined, particularly where the river approaches the Annamite Chain. Nevertheless, even the largest plains of Laos and east Cambodia consist mainly of infertile sandstones, and extensive areas of new alluvium suitable for *na* (rice-fields) are sparsely distributed. Only the Tonlé Sap basin was able to provide the basis for a major state, and to the east political fragmentation was confirmed by the obstacles to navigation on the Mekong.

The delta, which may be said to commence at Phnom Penh and to include the Song Vai Com (Vaico) and Song Sai Gon (Saigon) lowlands, presents altogether kinder conditions, particularly in its central portion, which is densely populated; the western portion, however, where under the influence of strong off-shore currents the land is advancing rapidly to the southwest, required large capital investment in drainage channels excavated in the thick subsurface peat to bring into cultivation. This was the prewar Trans-Bassac, an area of large properties farmed by tenants and owned by absentee French, Chinese and occasionally Vietnamese, landlords in Saigon; these 'rice plantations' were a unique feature of the prewar economy of Cochinchina, and only found a parallel elsewhere in Southeast Asia in the contemporary Dutch 'rice estates' of the Indramaju area of West Java, although the Dutch companies cultivated the land themselves. Long an area of acute agricultural unrest, much of the land west of the Song Hau Giang (Bassac) was abandoned after 1945, and many of its inhabitants fled to the safety of Saigon. With the choking of the canals much land has reverted to the wilderness, and the area is a major stronghold of the Vietcong.

The hydrological conditions for rice cultivation in the Mekong delta are among the most favourable in the whole of mainland Southeast Asia, for a series of natural regulatory features ensures that only exceptionally does excessive flooding affect the rice crop; serious flooding did occur in 1966 and in 1961, but before the latter date there were only seven instances of disastrous flooding in fifty-six years. The most important of these regulatory agencies is the Tonlé Sap, a former arm of the sea cut off by sediments from the Mekong and jointly drained by the Mekong and Song Hau Giang. From June to October the rise in the lower

Mekong forces water to flow backwards into the lake, which expands to more than three times its extent in the dry season and in places attains a depth of over forty feet. Additionally, parallel to the lower Mekong there are a number of depressions, or *beng*, connected to the river by natural and sometimes man-made or enlarged channels known in Cambodia as *prek*, which gradually fill as the river rises. At its maximum, however, neither the Tonlé Sap nor the *beng* can cope with the Mekong discharge, and a large volume of water overflows between Chau Doc and Long Xuyen to make its way westwards to the Gulf of Thailand, relieving the pressure on the flood to the southeast which forms the basis of the delta's rice industry.

A thousand miles of generally rocky and inhospitable coasts, battered by strong northeast winds for part of the year and frequently devasted by typhoons, separate the Mekong delta from that of North Annam and Tonkin; though punctuated by scattered small plains, these are much encumbered with sand dunes, marshes and expanses of brackish water, and seldom contain more than very restricted areas of new alluvium. Historically important as stepping stones in the Vietnamese southward advance, communication between the two major deltas via the plains of Annam was never easy, and it is scarcely surprising that the maintenance of political unity in the Vietnamese lands has presented repeated difficulties. Not until 1936 was the difficult central section of the *Transindochinois* railway between Tourane (now Da Nang) and Nha Trang completed, thus providing through rail communication between Saigon and Hanoi after nearly forty years of effort; and the mountainous spurs of the Annamite Chain, such as the Deo Hai Van (Col des Nuages) between Hue and Da Nang, are today the haunts of the Vietcong, just as they provided refuge for outlaws in the days of the Mandarin Post Road.

The delta of North Annam and Tonkin is the heartland of the Vietnamese, but it presents physical conditions which make far greater demands on human effort, ingenuity and social organization for its utilization than does the delta of the Mekong, and the return for this effort, as noted in Chapter 2, is distinctly meagre. Closely confined by steep and often heavily deforested mountain and hill-lands, the greater part of the delta is below ten feet and much even below three feet in elevation. Above the delta, the Songkoi, whose rectilinear alignment is one of the most striking features of the physical geography of continental Southeast Asia, is deeply entrenched, and at the Chinese frontier it is only some 250 feet above sea level. Its major tributaries, the Song Lo (Rivière Claire) and Song Bo (Rivière Noire) are similarly incised, so that—unusually for a major river—the variations in the discharge of the Songkoi as it debouches on to the delta are enormous; the highest floods, which can occur at almost any time between June and October, can have more than forty times the flow of the dry season minimum. The impermeable shales and schists which cover much of the catchment give rapid run-off following heavy rains, but that from the limestones, which are widespread in the mountains of north Tonkin, is delayed, so that not only can major floods continue unabated for several weeks but they can also reoccur in unpredictable fashion. Much of the delta is thus seriously at hazard, and only centuries of labour in flood-protection works, an activity that has almost completely obliterated the original physical features of the delta, has made possible its intensive agricultural utilization; without regulation, in one year in every two on the average, the very important rice harvest of the Vietnamese fifth lunar month (June) would be lost.[5] Thus flood control and drainage was always a primary concern of the Annamite state, whereas irrigation was essentially a private or village responsibility.

But despite the high degree of administrative competence in mobilizing the population for the construction and maintenance of flood-control works, the Annamite dynasties were never able to ensure protection from major disaster, and repeated famines occurred through the periodic destruction of the rice crop; not only were the dykes often poorly aligned and constructed, but efforts at control were repeatedly negated through the gradual rise in the bed of the Songkoi resulting from continuous deposition. Straightening, strengthening and heightening of the dykes continued throughout the period of the French administration, but not until the Hanoi dykes were raised to a height of nearly 45 feet following the disastrous floods of 1926, when almost one-third of the delta was inundated, was complete protection from major disaster finally achieved. Since 1965 there have been several unconfirmed reports of attacks by American aircraft on the dykes, but so far the destruction of the main protective works against the Songkoi, which would certainly be a major blow to the economy of North Vietnam and would probably precipitate a major food crisis, does not appear to have been seriously considered by the United States, which has repeatedly denied any intention to destroy the North Vietnamese state. Meanwhile, despite the regime's draconian discipline and labour service, there is much evidence that work on the dykes is performed more tardily and less efficiently by the rural population than in the past.

Apart from the fact that because they flow above the level of the land, the Songkoi and its principal distributaries can take no part in the drainage of the delta itself, the problem of water control is complicated by the incursion of saline water along the coast, a severe problem in the dry season when brackish water can penetrate far inland, particularly in the eastern portion of the delta. Nevertheless, through a system of *casiers*, basins enclosed by dykes and equipped with gates to control the inflow and outflow of water, it has often proved possible to combine irrigation, drainage and prevention of the incursion of saline water,

[5] *Pierre Gourou*, L'Utilisation du Sol en Indochine Française, *Centre d'Études de Politique Étrangère, Presses Universitaires de France, Paris, 1940, p. 219. English edition:* Land Utilization in French Indochina, *Institute of Pacific Relations, New York, 1945.*

in integrated operations. While a few parts of the delta have modern large-scale irrigation facilities with a pumped water supply, the greater part still depends on laborious indigenous irrigation techniques, nor have major irrigation projects received any high priority in North Vietnam's investment programmes.

Climatically the northern delta also appears less favoured than that of the Mekong. True, the dry season is less severe, but in neither area is it of long duration, a situation that is only encountered on the coasts of central Annam, but winter temperatures can occasionally fall below 45° Fahrenheit and the cultivation of most low-latitude perennials is economically impossible. The winter drizzles of Tonkin, called by the French *crachin*, while beneficial to the fifth-month rice crop, bring much discomfort to the population. At such times the delta, with its villages closely encircled by thick hedges of thorn and bamboo, presents a depressing landscape.

Mountains occupy more than 60 per cent of the Indochinese states, but only exceptionally do they exceed elevations greater than 6,000 feet and they seldom constitute any real barrier to communication; the Annamite Chain is easily crossed in several places. Yet so far the significance of the mountains has been largely confined to their climatic effects, and their contribution to national economic life has been small, a situation that is largely attributable to the steepness of their slopes, the general poverty of their soils, and their highly malarious character. South of the Ai Lao, a pass which provides an easy route across the Annamite Chain between Hue and Savannakhet, there are extensive areas of basalt, such as the plateaus of the Bolovens, Dac Lac (Darlac), and parts of the Mnong and Di Linh (Djiring), whose agricultural possibilities have been little exploited. There is evidence, however, that in both Vietnams the mountains will play a more positive role than in the past, partly through the settlement of Vietnamese in the highland areas, but more importantly, through a reassessment of the place in national life of the indigenous inhabitants. These are the *montagnards*, a term seldom used by the French but adopted by the Americans as a collective for the hill people, for whom the insulting Vietnamese term *moi* (savage) or the Lao *kha* (slave), are indignities no longer to be borne.

The montagnards are of complex origin, those of the south being generally of Malayo-Polynesian or 'Indonesian' extraction and those of the north often showing affinities with the Mon-Khmer peoples, but there are at least fifty major tribes with many sub-groups; ethnic complexity reaches its maximum in northern Laos, where the Thai (sharing only a common language with the lowland Thais), Man (Yao), Miao (Meo) and Muong show scant regard for national frontiers. In the early Sixties the montagnards were estimated to number about 600,000 in South Vietnam, perhaps 6 per cent of the total population, but in North Vietnam they were considerably more numerous, some estimates being as high as two million, or 14 per cent of the country's population. None of the hill people has ever achieved overall tribal cohesion and the highest unit or organization has always been either the clan or the village; all are essentially *rai* (swidden) culti-vators, but some groups such as the important Rhadé tribe of Darlac province also have a few sawahs in hydrologically favoured spots. While the Rhadé have maintained frequent contact with the lowland Vietnamese via the valley of the Song Ba (Song Da Rang), the only river to breach the Annamite Chain, most mountain people traditionally regard the Vietnamese as enemies. On the whole, however, they have demonstrated little anti-white feeling.[6]

As in Malaya where the military significance of the aboriginal hill people in a guerilla war was clearly appreciated by the communist insurgents at the outset, so the Vietminh moved quickly to enlist the support of the hill people against the French by promises of autonomy and freedom of cultural expression. North Vietnam has thus followed the Soviet pattern in granting nominal self-govern-ment to ethnic minorities, the Thai-Miao autonomous region west of the Songkoi being established in 1955, and the Viet Bac region north of the Songkoi, the most populous highland region in Indochina, in 1956. In addition to possessing their own regional administrators, in 1964 the hill people were reported to have some 60 representatives out of a total of some 450 in the admittedly impotent National Assembly at Hanoi, compared with only four montagnard seats in the scarcely more effective 120-member Assembly in Saigon. In contrast, South Vietnam has followed a policy of assimilation, enforcing the use of the Vietnamese language and law in the highlands, policies which have also been applied to other minorities such as the Cham, the Khmer and the Chinese. The removal of montagnards from their traditional territories, either in order to establish Vietnamese settlements or to protect the tribesmen from contact with the Vietcong, and in particular, the abolition in 1958 of the montagnards traditional rights of tenure, had near-disastrous consequences, for it almost certainly encouraged Vietcong infiltration and in 1964 culminated in a Rhadé revolt in Darlac province. Since that time the United States has endeavoured to assist the economic and social life of the hill people, and to persuade the government of South Vietnam both to recognize their aspirations and to assure them of a place in the new state. Only through some such accord can the agricultural and water resources of the highlands be effec-tively mobilized for South Vietnam's economic development.

VIETNAM

Following the Geneva agreement, the unitary economy of the Indochinese Union was fragmented into four separate national economies. Laos and Cam-bodia had always been backwaters and their separation gave rise to little concern, but the division of the Vietnamese lands along the Song Ben Hai, close to the 17th

[6] *Vietnamese were prevented from entering montagnard territory by the French adminis-tration. At the end of last century a French adventurer, Mayrena, endeavoured to establish an independent kingdom among the Sedang of the Kontum-Pleiku region.*

parallel, appeared economically disastrous. The North, with its deposits of coal and metalliferous minerals, contained not only all the very limited development of heavy industry in Indochina but also a very large share of its consumer-goods industries. But with a precarious food balance, it needed the food surpluses of the South, which was almost entirely devoid of mineral deposits and possessed very little industry apart from the processing of its agricultural products. A substantial proportion of the North's production of coal and cement had long been exported, but it was always the South, with its rice and rubber, that constituted the principal export-generating region of Indochina. What is now North Vietnam earned only 18 per cent of the Union's exports in 1939, but consumed 42 per cent of its imports,[7] and the regime's chronic trade deficit and its inability to earn any substantial sums in hard currencies have constituted major constraints to economic growth. The population exchanges arranged after 1954, however, left North Vietnam with a culturally more homogeneous population. The traditional Buddhist-Catholic rivalry was heightened in the South by the influx of some 900,000 Catholic refugees, and the task of establishing national cohesion was further complicated by the existence of militant religious sects, the Cao Dai and the Hoa Hao, to say nothing of the local Vietminh whose organizations temporarily went underground.

Since separation the two Vietnams have endeavoured to make good the ravages of war and the economic deficiencies they inherited at birth; but even before such progress as was achieved was jeopardized by renewed hostilities, each had received enormous aid from their respective supporting blocs, and, with the rising tempo of the war, aid-flows from both the West and the Sino-Soviet countries increased sharply. Between 1955 and 1960 the United States provided $1,145 million of economic aid and a further $442 million of military aid to South Vietnam.[8] Thereafter, United States economic aid increased year by year to a maximum of $706 million in the 1966 financial year, and although there was some decline in this figure in later years, it was more than offset by mounting military aid, which became a charge on the United States' own military budget. In total, American economic aid to South Vietnam from the Geneva agreement to 1968 amounted to more than $4,000 million; but this figure was dwarfed by the United States' expenditure in its own military effort in the country, which by the end of 1968 was estimated at running at some $3,000 million a month, a substantial part of which eventually found its way into the South Vietnamese economy by channels both legal and illegal.

In relation to the resources available to them, Sino-Soviet countries have also provided lavish assistance to North Vietnam. Between 1955 and 1961 China provided 1,830 million old, or pre-1961, roubles (nominally equivalent to $457·5

[7] *Theodore Shabad, 'Economic developments in North Vietnam', Pacific Affairs, vol. 31, 1958, p. 51.*

[8] *U S Army,* Handbook on Vietnam, *Government Printer, Washington, 1962, p. 447.*

million) and the USSR 1,330 million old roubles ($332·5 million) in grants and credits, and aid is reported to have accounted for 70 per cent of Hanoi's total revenue in 1955 and for 42 per cent in 1957.[9] The magnitude of Sino-Soviet aid since 1961 is unknown and information on North Vietnamese budgets is scanty, but deliveries under China's aid programme were subject to repeated delays, and in all probability Moscow has displaced Peking as the North's principal source of aid; China lacks the more sophisticated weapons such as missiles, which the North has required for defence against air attack, and its ability to assist has been compromised not only by mounting economic problems but also by the administrative chaos resulting from the Cultural Revolution. Peking can scarcely view with equanimity increasing Soviet influence in a neighbour of China's without a common frontier with the USSR, and is known to have placed restrictions on the use of China's railways for the carriage of Russian supplies destined for Hanoi.

The return on these respective aid-flows, however, has differed considerably in the two Vietnams, and there is little doubt that in terms of economic growth, Sino-Soviet aid has been by far the more effective. More than 80 per cent of American economic aid to the South before 1965 was absorbed by the Commodity Import Program, which is intended to provide the essential commodities and equipment to keep the country operating. Since that date South Vietnam has financed a larger share of its imports from its own financial resources, but it is difficult to resist the conclusion that so long as the United States directly or indirectly underwrites all the country's import bills, the 'will to economize' and to expand the country's own resources is gravely reduced. Moreover, large quantities of luxury and semi-luxury goods regularly found their way into the programme, and there have been repeated scandals involving large-scale pilfering at the port of Saigon and the appearance of scarce consumer goods and even military stores on the black market. The multiple exchange rate system, designed to reduce the black market in dollars, has itself been the subject of much abuse, and by keeping the prices of imports at artificially low levels has promoted the diversion of goods into the black market where their true scarcity value has been reflected; to discourage this tendency, in mid-1966 the Vietnamese piastre was, in effect, devalued by about half.[10] Some United States funds, it is true, and those from other donors such as France, Japan, West Germany and Australia, have been devoted to project aid, but much American so-called project aid has in

[9] Yoshinori Nakano, 'Economic conditions in North Vietnam', The Developing Economies, vol. 1, No. 2, 1963, p. 225.

[10] The official rate, formerly 60 Vietnamese piastres to the US $, was raised to 80, and the financial transfer rate, the rate for US Military Currency, was raised from 73·5 to 118. Since September 1965, United States forces in Vietnam have been paid in Military Payment Certificates in order to contain the growing black market in dollars, which was estimated at some $20 million per month before the introduction of the new system of payment.

fact concerned counter-insurgency schemes rather than income-earning projects. The fact remains that South Vietnam, a sovereign state, offends many Asian nationalists by its manifest lack of economic independence; indeed, every escalation of the war has increased its economic dependency on the United States. It is not easy to suggest a way out of this dilemma while the war rages, but only if a much larger proportion of the aid to Vietnam is devoted to purposes of production, rather than consumption, will it ever become possible for the South to rid itself of the incubus of appearing in many Asian eyes an American puppet.

Sino-Soviet aid, on the other hand, has been almost entirely devoted to providing complete installations, equipment, raw materials or personnel for the expansion of North Vietnam's industrial capacity, and in particular for the development of fuel and power and associated heavy industries, which in conformity with economic policy in centrally-planned economies, have received maximum investment priority. Some funds have been made available for the expansion of certain essential consumer industries such as cotton textiles and medicinal preparations, and for enhancing agricultural production. But as in all communist countries, supplies of consumer goods are severely rationed, either directly or through state pricing policies, and the import of capital goods, which amounted to 70 per cent of total imports in 1958, rose to over 90 per cent of the total in 1960.[11] The results have been impressive. North Vietnam has acquired the only fully integrated iron and steel plant in the whole of Southeast Asia, and alone has made sufficient advances in metallurgical and heavy engineering industries to undertake the complete manufacture, as opposed to assembly from imported parts, of capital goods such as machine tools, locomotives and rolling-stock, and rice and sugar mills. On the agricultural front, however, North Vietnam appears to have been no more successful than any other communist country in raising food production per capita, and the general standard of living remains, as it was before World War II, among the lowest in Southeast Asia. With the intensification of the war have come reports of severe food rationing and serious shortages in parts of the country. It was clear also that industrial production was falling well below the targets of the First Five Year Plan (1961–65), and while the South has added greatly to its transport facilities through the new harbours and roads constructed by the United States, facilities which ultimately can be expected to make a major contribution to economic development, the aerial bombardment of the North was forcing it to rely more and more on unsophisticated forms of transport such as the bicycle and sampan.

The economic situation in South Vietnam

Whether the communist capture of the Vietnamese nationalist movement at the end of World War II could have been averted, is an issue for the political scientists. But it is undeniable that although the substantial support given to the Vietcong

[11] *Nakano*, op. cit., *p. 94.*

by the peasants of the South has in part been extracted by threats and atrocities of extreme brutality, agrarian unrest has been a powerful factor in the communist appeal. Unfortunately, events in South Vietnam have enabled the communists to compound this appeal with nationalism, by claiming that the foreigner has a powerful interest in preserving landlordism, and in a population with a high degree of illiteracy and whose knowledge of the world is confined to the village, to make such a claim is often to have it accepted. With their experience in Japan, Taiwan and Korea, where agricultural reform enhanced political stability and accelerated economic development, the American advisers to the government of South Vietnam have been constant advocates of agrarian reorganization. But even the most equitable system of land redistribution, and no such description could be applied to the reforms so far effected in the South, is unavailing without simultaneous expansion of the non-agricultural sectors of the economy; here South Vietnam's experience has been at variance with that of Taiwan or South Korea. Only some 2·4 million hectares (6 million acres) were under cultivation in South Vietnam in 1966 (*Table 9–1*), less than 14 per cent of the country's total area. About one million hectares of land went out of cultivation in the Mekong delta during the war of independence, but after the Geneva agreement some of the abandoned land was used for the resettlement of many of the 900,000 mainly Catholic refugees who moved from north of the demarcation line; some 500,000 refugees are claimed to have been settled on such projects as the Cai San scheme, where 50,000 families were established on 3-hectare plots. But by 1962 scarcely half of the abandoned land had been reclaimed, and with increasing insecurity in the delta, the cultivated area trended steadily downwards. In addition to the abandoned land, several million hectares of potential rice-land still await re-clamation in the far west of the delta, to say nothing of the possibility at some future date of draining and bringing into cultivation part of the half a million hectares of the *Plaine des Joncs*, a vast reed-covered natural *casier* below the level of the Mekong. Ineffective drainage by the Song Vai Com has led to such an accumulation of toxic active alumina in the soil that agriculture is largely impossible, and the area constitutes another major refuge of the Vietcong. Anomalously in Asia, therefore, South Vietnam's agrarian problems in no sense originate in a shortage of land, and possession of the delta, with its vast agricultural potential in an Asian world likely to go increasingly hungry, would constitute a glittering prize for the communists.

Rice occupies over 90 per cent of the cultivated land of South Vietnam, and although the diversification of agricultural production towards an enhanced output of other foodstuffs and industrial raw materials has been part of government policy since 1960, little has been accomplished. The tiny fragmented holdings and communal lands typical of prewar North Annam and Tonkin become less common south of Binh Dinh, and in old-settled parts of the delta such as My Tho province, the average size of properties before 1939 was around 5 hectares, more than four times that of the Tonkin delta. But whereas in the latter area almost every farming family owned some land, two of every three farmers in Cochinchina were landless tenants, or *ta dien*, paying a share rental which could amount to 50 per cent of the harvest and even more when the tenant was indebted to the landlord. Except on the higher sandy ridges, which were largely inhabited by a relict Cambodian population, small properties scarcely existed at all in the western delta; in the province of Bac Lieu (now An Xuyen)[12] in the early Thirties, properties in excess of 50 hectares accounted for 65 per cent of the area of all holdings. Altogether in the Mekong delta, some 300,000 hectares passed into the hands of French citizens or companies; the largest of the latter, the *Domaine Agricole de l'Ouest*, eventually possessed over 20,000 hectares.

Although the high incidence of large properties in the Trans-Bassac reflected government policy of promoting large-scale European agricultural enterprise, it was facilitated by the heavy cost of bringing the area into cultivation. Enormous quantities of peat and silt encumbered with the buried remains of swamp forest were removed in the drainage operations carried out by the Department of Public Works, and by 1930 the amount of material removed equalled that excavated in the construction of the Suez Canal.[13] The government recouped the heavy costs of canal construction by selling land in large blocks, so that only those with access to large quantities of capital could become landowners; moreover, subsidiary canals and a potable water supply had to be provided by the purchaser. Some colonization schemes for the resettlement of landless peasants from Tonkin and Annam were considered by the government along the lines of contemporaneous schemes being undertaken in the Philippines and in the Netherlands Indies, but in the financial stringency of the Depression little was done, and most of the tenants on the new lands were drawn from central and eastern Cochinchina.

Generalizations regarding tenancy in the developing world are often overdrawn, for many social conventions may mitigate apparent inequities. This has certainly been the case in Vietnam; where land is in the hands of a few large owners many tenants are able to rent sizeable areas also, and can consequently earn relatively high incomes; many tenants often have a relative for a landlord; and non-resident landlords are likely to be ignorant of the true production of the land and hence charge lower rents than those on the spot.[14] Moreover, where a tenant is heavily indebted to a landlord, the latter has a powerful financial interest in continuing the tenancy. But on the enormous ramifications of a traditional credit system which embraced virtually every rural family either as a lender or borrower, the Great Depression with its catastrophic fall in rice prices fell with traumatic impact. Many tenants in the new western lands with virtually no hope

[12] *The names and boundaries of the provinces of South Vietnam have changed several times according to the exigencies of the military situation.*

[13] *Charles Robequain*, L'Indochine, *Armand Colin, Paris, 1952, p. 131.*

[14] *James B. Hendry*, Study of a Vietnamese Rural Community Economic Activity, *Michigan State University, 1959, p. 31.*

of ever meeting their obligations had no recourse but to flee, while small proprietors ejected for debt saw their holdings swell the growing area held in large properties. A situation thus arose not unlike that of the Irrawaddy delta of Lower Burma, and its consequences were broadly the same; at the end of World War II many of the landlords fled, and the Vietminh acquired effective control of large areas of the delta. In such areas the Vietminh levied taxes in kind quite as burdensome as the rents charged by the former owners, but it was able to convince the peasants that with the final defeat of the French, the landlords, many of whom had abandoned their land, would be dispossessed, whereupon ownership would pass to the cultivators. A similar policy was followed by the fiercely anti-communist para-military religious sects, the Cao Dai and the Hoa Hao, in the areas under their control, so that for many years peasants over large parts of the delta paid no rent as such, a situation that was fraught with consequences for the land reform eventually introduced by the Diem regime in 1956.

Progress in land reform was fitful and slow. An ordinance of 1955 required all tenants to have written contracts valid for five years, and the level of rents to be fixed between 15 and 25 per cent of the harvest, dependent on the fertility of the land in question; but many landlords, having received no rents for years, regarded the measure as a government guarantee of their incomes, and in areas under firm government control the legal maximum rent often became the minimum. An ordinance for the redistribution of rice-land followed in 1956; this limited the area that could be retained in individual ownership to 100 hectares, plus an additional 15 hectares, where appropriate, to defray the costs of ancestor-worship practices. Any land in excess of the maximum was to be acquired by the state for resale, existing tenants to have priority in redistribution. Landowners were to be compensated according to a schedule of prices based on the productivity of land, 10 per cent of the compensation being payable in cash and the balance in government bonds. Those granted land under the redistribution were to pay in six annual instalments, each approximately equal to a year's rent.

After many initial difficulties had been overcome with American aid, some 400,000 hectares of rice-land had been redistributed by 1960 and a further 600,000 hectares awaited acquisition. The measure had obvious shortcomings; landlords could easily transfer part of their holdings to relatives, and having the right to select which portion of their holdings they wished to retain, inevitably preserved for themselves the best land in the safest areas where the demand for land was greatest, leaving for the state the poorest and most inaccessible land, or that with the greatest security hazard. In practice redistribution was effected on the basis of administrative convenience rather than on that of need; many of those most in want were even unable to obtain the official forms on which application for land had to be made, or to complete them correctly. Thus those tenants who were fortunate enough to acquire land were regarded with hostility by the landless who were often more deserving, but as in general recipients seldom received more

Table 9-1 *South Vietnam, Laos and Cambodia: area and production of selected crops, 1966*

	AREA *thousand hectares*	PRODUCTION *thousand metric tons*
SOUTH VIETNAM		
Padi	2,400	4,400
Rubber	42*	46
Maize	36	44
Tapioca	43	236
Coconuts and copra	42	23
Sugar cane	30	935
LAOS†		
Padi‡	920	740
Maize	40	20
CAMBODIA		
Padi	2,180	2,380
Maize	134	136
Rubber	49	51
Cotton	6	4

* Tapped area
† 1965
‡ Including upland rice

Source: ECAFE, *Economic Survey of Asia and the Far East,* 1966

than 2 hectares, the overall effect on the pattern of land ownership was small. While the upper limit of 100 hectares might be considered over-large, its reduction would not have greatly altered the rural picture in those areas under government control; in the village of Long An province studied by Hendry, even if all the land had been divided equally between all families, each would have received only 1·6 hectares. In short, redistribution merely substituted one set of inequalities for another. Land reform is necessary for political reasons, but it requires many supporting services to be economically effective, as there is never enough land to meet all claimants; in Hendry's words, it 'tends to perpetuate the marginal holder, delays adjustment to more productive industrial activities, and offers the promise of a substantial improvement that it cannot keep'.[15] But after 1960 renewed hostilities negated much of what had been accomplished and made further redistribution increasingly difficult.

In the fields of rural credit and marketing, government activity was also ineffective. Credit and cooperative organizations largely originated with the interwar French administration, but failed to achieve any real popularity with the

[15] op. cit., *p. 31.*

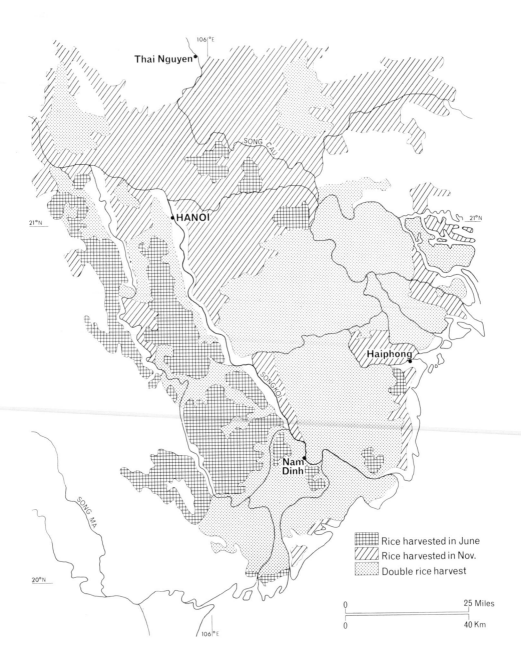

Fig. 9-2(a)   Rice cultivation in the Songkoi delta *(after Gourou)*

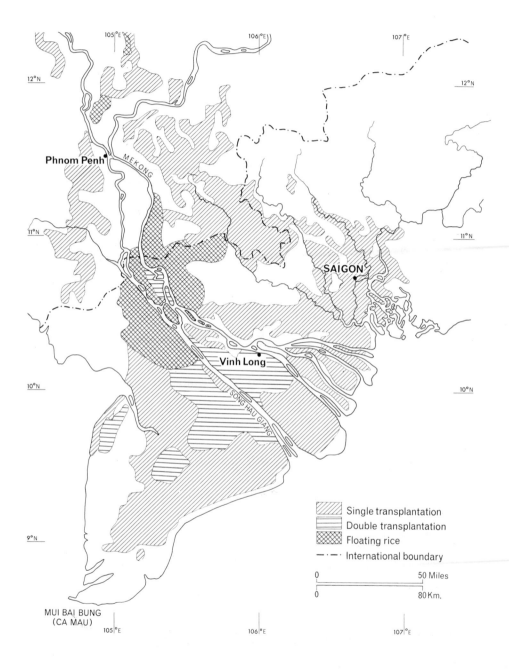

Fig. 9-2(b) **Rice cultivation in the Mekong delta** *(after Robequain)*

Vietnamese, who like the Chinese prefer their traditional social organizations, based on family and clan, to govern economic relations. A programme to eliminate the practice of selling rice futures to merchants and moneylenders was instituted to 1956, and the following year saw the establishment of the National Agricultural Office to consolidate all pre-existing state farm credit agencies. This was financed largely by American aid funds, and offered small short-term loans in cash, kind or services, to farmers at an interest rate of one per cent per month; medium-term loans of up to five years were also available, and in the case of large farmers, long-term loans of up to fifteen years for irrigation or other major improvements. But as farmers judged to have insufficient capital were ineligible for loans, the greatest benefits accrued to the large farmers, for whom normal commercial credit was usually available. Few of the cooperatives or the Farmers' Associations that followed them proved viable, and most small farmers continued to use traditional credit sources to cover their yearly expenses. The level of indebtedness as measured by the share of household gross annual income was, admittedly, generally low; but in view of the low level of the latter and the minimal margin for saving, the real burden imposed by interest rates which could amount to 30 per cent was undoubtedly extremely heavy.

Meanwhile, the agriculture economy in the delta was further dislocated by the agroville and strategic hamlet policies, aimed at regrouping the rural population in large villages which could be sealed off from contact with the communists, and which would provide some urban amenities in the countryside. Their inspiration was the successful resettlement policy carried out during the Malayan Emergency, but the very different conditions obtaining in the two countries were clearly insufficiently appreciated. From its inception the policy aroused much criticism and failed to achieve the results expected; after more than twenty agrovilles had been created, in 1962 further work was abandoned.

Land reform having failed to make any significant improvement in the productivity of either the land or the worker, the decreasing rice area, or more precisely the harvested rice whose output was available to the Saigon government, has presented the country with a growing imbalance between food imports and exports. Before World War II Cochinchina conducted a rice export trade of almost one million tons annually, and although in most years after 1954 South Vietnam found it difficult to exceed 200,000 tons, nearly 300,000 tons of rice were exported in 1963. Thereafter, decline was rapid; less than 50,000 tons were exported in 1964, and in the following year the country became for the first time a net importer. With the rapid deterioration in security in the delta, imports of rice, at first from Thailand and later from the United States to feed Saigon and the rice-deficit areas of coastal South Vietnam, became a flood; in 1965–66 over 400,000 tons of rice were imported and in 1967 imports reached the enormous level of 950,000 tons. Much of the rice shortage arose from the fact that the transport of rice from surplus areas in the Mekong delta to Saigon was being prevented by the Vietcong,[16] whose own requirements were also sharply expanding; but these unexpectedly large import requirements were an important contributory factor in the rapid appreciation of rice prices in 1966–67, and augmented the heavy pressure on world cereal stocks arising from the successive failures of the Indian monsoon in 1965 and 1966. Additionally, South Vietnam was also obliged to make increasingly large imports of other foodstuffs such as milk products, flour, pork and fish (*Table 9-2*).

These mounting food imports were only possible through enhanced foreign foreign aid, and represented an abnormal situation; nevertheless, the country's low agricultural productivity must be judged serious in view of the fact that the demographic situation throughout the rural areas probably does not differ substantially from that of the village described by Hendry, in which for every death there were more than five births.[17] Even before 1939 the average padi yield in Cochinchina was only some 1,300 kg per hectare, lower than that of contemporary Burma or Thailand, and by the Sixties the average of some 1,250 kg per hectare represented a further decline in the relative standing of the Mekong delta. In the older settled parts of the delta such as Long An province, nitrogenous and phosphatic fertilizers have been used since the Thirties, and are recognized as essential for the production of the higher-priced better grades of rice. In general, however, manurial and irrigation techniques in the Mekong delta are less well developed than in North Annam and Tonkin, and are reflected in significantly lower yields. These, it is true, are gained with a lower labour input than is necessary in the north, but substantially more than half the sawahs of the Tonkin delta produce two rice crops a year. In the Mekong delta, however, a dry-season rice crop can be taken only in especially favoured low-lying areas or in those where underground water supplies can be reached with relatively shallow wells; even so, it is a risky venture.

Opportunities for expanding the double-cropped area, however, could ultimately be very great. In the northwest of the delta along the Song Hau Giang in the provinces of Chau Doc, Kien Phong (formerly Sadec) and An Giang (formerly Long Xuyen), the great depth of the flood necessitates the cultivation of low-yielding floating rice, and even further south in Vinh Long the depth of flood water is still too great for normal stem varieties to succeed (*Figure 9-2b*). The long-stemmed varieties grown in this area have to be held back from early vegetative growth which might cause lodging, by a system of double transplanting unique to South Vietnam; this practice also gives time to clear the land of the excessive growth of weeds during the dry season, during which the soil never dries out. In all of these districts, improved irrigation and drainage would make possible the taking of two crops of higher-yielding normal-stemmed varieties, a change which,

---

[16] *Although large areas in the delta have been under communist control for almost two decades, the Vietcong has generally allowed the sale of any surplus after its own needs were met.*

[17] *Hendry, op. cit., p. 61.*

as noted in Chapter 4, is being effected in the similar low-lying areas of the Mae Nam Chao Phraya plain in Thailand, where in the past only the cultivation of floating rice has been possible. The Mekong Valley scheme, and in particular the Tonlé Sap barrage, would greatly facilitate the extension of double-cropping in the delta, and would also prevent the penetration inland of brackish water during the dry season, which at present prevents double-cropping in coastal areas where conditions are otherwise suitable.

Nevertheless, while waiting for these international projects to come to fruition, South Vietnam could do considerably more than at present to up-grade agricultural techniques and, of course, the central coastlands are entirely its responsibility. The coastal plains have less than a third of the rice area of the Mekong delta, but yields are appreciably higher, despite the general poverty of the soils south of Mui Dieu (Cap Varella) and poor irrigation facilities which make the use of broadcast sowing far from uncommon. The higher rice yields of central Vietnam are produced by the larger and more fertile plains north of Mui Dieu, whose wet season comes with the Northeast monsoon, but as with the Mekong delta these areas have also been subject to increasing Vietcong attacks.

In company with many new Asian nations, South Vietnam, believing that its traditional large food surplus made agricultural improvement economically of minor importance, paid too great attention to industrialization, and its approach to agricultural issues has been almost entirely motivated by political considerations. However, in mid-1967 the growing agricultural crisis prompted a new Minister of Economics to announce a new economic policy with greater emphasis on agriculture and the use of an expanded range of agricultural products as the basis for industrial development; the proposals included a new Agricultural Development Bank and an enhanced domestic fertilizer production. Whether the new policy will have greater success than those pursued in the past remains to be seen, but the survival of an independent government in South Vietnam could well turn on its ability to convince the peasantry that it has their economic well-being at heart. So far it would not be too much to say that its attitude to this vital question has been largely one of indifference.

South Vietnam's second largest agricultural resource, and leading export by value, is natural rubber. The first planting of *Hevea* rubber in Indochina is believed to have occurred as long ago as 1897, but, as in Thailand, initial growth of the industry was slow, and it was not until the Stevenson Restriction scheme of the Twenties that rubber planting began to expand rapidly. But unlike Thailand, Indochina's rubber industry owes little to smallholder activity and was created by a handful of large French companies, each controlling several estates located on the red and grey basaltic soils of eastern Cochinchina and the adjacent portion of Cambodia; the largest of the groups is the *Société Financière de Caout- chouc* (Socfin), which is also active in Malaysia and formerly in Indonesia also. Although the peak tapped area of over 90,000 hectares was attained in 1940, the planted area continued to expand right up to 1945. But many estates suffered heavy damage during the war of independence, and by 1966 communist molestation had reduced the tapped area to but 47,000 hectares. Yet despite each estate having to maintain its own private army, and a chronic labour shortage resulting from recruitment difficulties and the continued loss of workers to better-paid jobs in Saigon, production after 1945 rose in almost every year to some 78,000 tons in 1960. Part of this increase represented the improved techniques of tapping and fertilizing, but the contribution from replanted high-yielding clones has probably been much greater than previously supposed. As with the communist insurgents in Malaya during the Emergency, the Vietcong saw no point in bringing estate operations to a complete standstill, for as long as estates operated, the communists could continue their depredations on supplies of food, equipment and cash moving over the roads. But after 1962 the increased tempo of Vietcong military activities constituted a growing menace, and with frequent interdiction of the roads to Saigon, several estates had periodically to stockpile rubber. Late in 1966 American forces re-opened the Saigon-Loc Ninh road, the estates' main artery of communication, but output for the year was only 46,000 tons, and the trend was steadily downwards. Successive defoliations carried out by aerial spraying in order to reduce cover for the Vietcong resulted in the suspension of tapping for months at a time, and output for 1968 from a tapped area of only 34,000 hectares was scarcely 30,000 tons.

As the rubber estates in South Vietnam have on the whole been well maintained, given reasonable security conditions the expansion of output could be speedily resumed. However, to justify the heavy investment in the new methods of rubber production and processing necessary if the country is to remain a competitive producer, estates must have adequate assurance of continued use of the land, and the political outlook at present appears likely to discourage the companies from undertaking further capital investment save that aimed at 'holding' operations; Cambodia represents a much better risk. Extreme insecurity and labour problems have also adversely affected South Vietnam's small coffee and tea industries on the basaltic highlands, and have negated any possibility in the near future of establishing an oil palm industry or of expanding the present small output of centrifugal sugar.

The problem of rural insecurity is unquestionably the greatest issue facing the government and its foreign allies. It is unlikely that any purely military solution can be found, but all past efforts in support of military operations, including the agrovilles and more than 3,000 strategic hamlets, have been of little avail. Since 1965 specially trained pacification teams have been assigned to selected villages to promote the spread of better agricultural techniques, to encourage self-help, and to stiffen anti-Vietcong resistance through military training and by appeals to Vietnamese cultural traditions which emphasise the essentially alien character of communism. But so far this curious mixture of nationalism, economic betterment and semi-religious indoctrination has been little more successful than earlier attempts at winning the cooperation of the peasants. Unfortunately, the Americans' own rural pacification programme has been greatly impeded by disputes between the military authorities and civilian agencies over ultimate control, and positive results have been very slow in coming.

Manufacturing industries   South Vietnam inherited very little modern industry and its resources of fuels and metalliferous minerals are distinctly meagre; moreover, the cottage industries so important in North Annam and Tonkin were much less numerous in the south. Industrial policy has thus been directed at developing local capacity to replace those manufactures previously imported from the north; at making fuller use of domestic sources of power and raw materials; at increasing the supply of Vietnamese skilled labour and managerial and entrepreneurial ability through financial assistance to new industries; and by government participation in industry, either directly or in joint ventures with private domestic or foreign capital. While foreign investors have been assured against war-risk and nationalization, the government has insisted on a majority or even a total interest in branches of industrial production deemed of vital national importance. However, the transfer of much French-owned industry after 1954 to the hands of the Saigon Chinese, as a result of the imposition of exchange controls and restrictions on the remission of profits, did little to encourage other potential foreign investors, and was scarcely a victory for the policy of enlarging Vietnamese participation in manufacturing.

For many years South Vietnam's principal activity was rice-milling, an activity which was heavily concentrated in the Saigon-Cholon area, and under Chinese or French control. Capacity at present is much lower than in 1940 as a result of the destruction of many mills in the long years of war and civil disturbance, and the industry has long been in need of new construction and rehabilitation; however, relatively little has been done, perhaps partly because the Chinese might be judged able to look after their own interests, and partly because of the declining level of rice production. Most other industries established during the French administration, such as distilleries, breweries and soft drink plants, match factories, sawmills, rubber mills and other plants processing agricultural products, were also located in the Saigon-Cholon area. Outside this area the only large establishments were the cement works at Lang Tho near Hue, inoperative in 1968 because of Vietcong attacks, and a sugar mill and refinery at Tuy Hoa on the Annam coast.

Economic considerations have inevitably compelled the location of most of the new industrial establishments created since 1954 in the metropolitan area, but even where attempts have been made to locate industry in other parts of the country, the lack of security has often rendered them abortive. Among such projects are the development of the country's only coalfield at Nong Son, some twenty miles southwest of Da Nang, an oil refinery capable of supplying virtually all of Vietnam's needs and an associated petrochemicals plant originally planned for Nha Trang, and cotton and sugar mills at various points on the Annam coast such as Da Nang and Quang Ngai. Mining at Nong Son was resumed in 1957 after a shut-down that had endured since the Great Depression, and by 1961 production reached some 80,000 tons. Through United States AID assistance it was planned to raise this figure to some 250,000 tons by 1964, using the output in a 25,000 kW generating station and in a complex of coal chemical plants at nearby An Hoa producing coal-gas, liquid air and synthesized ammonia for the production of nitrogenous fertilizers; the foreign exchange costs of the complex were to be met by an aid agreement with France and West Germany. However, from 1965 onwards, by cutting the road from An Hoa to Da Nang, the Vietcong brought operations at the site to a virtual standstill and prevented the installation of equipment that had already arrived in the country. With the construction of

Table 9-2 *South Vietnam: composition and direction of foreign trade, 1965*

US $ million

IMPORTS		EXPORTS	
Iron and steel products, metal manufactures	56·1	Rubber	26·0
		Tea	2·1
Machinery and electrical equipment	48·0	Others	7·4
Yarns and textiles	33·4	**Total**	**35·5**
Textile fibres	13·4		
Chemicals, fertilizers	24·9		
Petroleum products	22·5		
Rice	22·5		
Milk products	18·5		
Cement	10·1		
Wheat flour	8·9		
Total, including others	**377·3**		

	Imports from	Exports to
United States	181·9	1·4
Taiwan	47·1	—
Japan	32·9	3·9
South Korea	18·2	—
Malaysia and Singapore	13·1	2·4
France	12·0	11·9
West Germany	8·1	5·6
United Kingdom	6·0	4·4
Total, including others	**377·3**	**35·5**

Source: *Viet-Nam Statistical Yearbook*, 1966–67

alternative road access it was hoped to recommence work in 1967, but even this proved impossible, and completion of the project appears unlikely before the end of hostilities. A similar fate has befallen the Japanese-built hydro-electricity project on the Da Nhim river near Da Lat, part of a Japanese reparations agreement. The first phase of the 160,000 kW scheme was completed in 1965, but destruction of the 230 kV transmission line to Saigon has deprived the capital of much-needed additional power supplies, and restoration of the line appears out of the question until a political settlement is reached; meanwhile, Saigon has been equipped with a large oil-fired thermal plant. Hopes for the establishment of a petroleum refinery have also been dashed. Plans for a refinery at Nha Trang supported by a consortium of international oil companies envisaged that the plant would come on stream in 1966, but work never began, and although an alternative location at Cam Ranh bay, site of a large American base, was suggested, the interest of the companies perceptibly declined as the war continued unabated. Better fortune has attended the Ha Tien cement plant on the Gulf of Thailand coast, which when in full production should meet about half of the country's cement requirements.

But even the new plants in the Saigon area have not been immune from attack. Early in 1966 a large new cotton mill in suburban Thu Doc, originally intended for Da Nang, was heavily damaged by the Vietcong, and much damage was done to the industries of Cholon during the Vietcong *Tet* offensive of early 1968. The destruction of much of the textile industry was particularly serious, as rapid expansion through joint ventures of domestic and foreign capital had endowed South Vietnam with some 150,000 modern spindles and over 3,000 automatic looms, enough to bring the country within striking distance of self-sufficiency in cotton textiles. A year after the offensive several mills had not been rebuilt, and those in operation were working at far below capacity. Other new ventures in the Saigon area have included plants for the assembly of motor scooters and bicycles, and for the production of a wide range of chemicals and pharmaceutics, paper products, jute bags, bicycle tyres, and for many consumer goods, but these also had failed to regain pre-*Tet* offensive levels of output by mid-1969.

Encouraging though this may seem, the proliferating and indiscriminate aid-supported import programme appeared to constitute almost as great a menace as the Vietcong, by threatening to throttle some of the new infant industries at birth. The textile industry in particular was severely affected, for after 1965 such a flood of imports poured into the country that in 1967 textile stocks were estimated at about the equivalent of three to five years' normal consumption, and with the market completely glutted, work at several plants came to a standstill.[18] A ban on the import of the types of textiles that could be produced in the country was hastily imposed, and further protection for Vietnamese industries appeared likely.

[18] Far Eastern Economic Review, *vol. 55, 1967, p. 460.*

With its agricultural production declining, manufacturing in a critical condition, its transport facilities continually interrupted by Vietcong attacks and crippled by bureaucratic inefficiency and corruption, its export trade scarcely amounting to one-tenth of the value of imports and trending steadily downwards, an import trade which appeared to be getting out of hand with an ominously large proportion of luxury and semi-luxury items, and heavy inflationary pressure, South Vietnam in 1967 appeared a nation *in extremis*. Nevertheless, the new administration of General Van Thieu not only survived the *Tet* offensive, which in retrospect may prove to have been the turning point of the war, but gradually began to acquire a stability unknown since the overthrow of the regime of Ngo Dinh Diem. The government won further respect for its independent attitude over the Paris peace talks with North Vietnam, and notwithstanding its authoritarian nature, the prospects of achieving a greater degree of political cohesion in South Vietnam appeared better than at any time in the Republic's short and tragic history. If this goal can be achieved in the near future, South Vietnam may well duplicate the success of South Korea, not only in resisting communist aggression but also in achieving a high rate of economic advance.

The economy of North Vietnam

After a brief period of reconstruction and rehabilitation designed to restore production levels to those of 1939, North Vietnam in 1958 launched a Three Year Plan to eliminate private enterprise and to lay the foundations for a socialized industrial state. The First Five Year Plan (1961–65) which followed continued the policy of allocating maximum priority to the expansion of basic industries such as iron and steel, fuel and power, engineering and metallurgical industries and chemicals, while providing for a more limited growth of certain consumer-goods industries such as cotton textiles, and for increased agricultural production to support the industrial advance. Sweeping successes in both the industrial and agricultural fields were claimed by the government for the interim plan and for the first years of the Five Year Plan. After 1964, however, official references to the Plan became increasingly rare, strongly suggesting that its production targets were not going to be reached, and with increasing American attacks on industrial and transport installations it appeared likely that the Plan had been dropped.

Evaluation of North Vietnam's economic progress is exceedingly difficult in view of a Hanoi reticence concerning physical outputs and budget allocations that is extreme even by the Eastern bloc standards, but there is little doubt that until 1965 at least, industrial expansion had been rapid. As with other communist powers, however, agriculture has proved the weakest sector; complete socialization has been impossible to effect, and there is little evidence of any significant permanent increase in the productivity of the rural worker. Such a course of events is perhaps scarcely surprising, for resources of raw materials were both numerous and favourably located in relation to major centres of population; moreover, the French left behind in full working order an unusually broad industrial base by Southeast Asian standards, and Tonkin and North Annam contained in their village handicraft industries a reservoir of skilled labour suitable for redeployment in modern industry. Any government dedicated to economic growth should have been capable of harnessing these resources for a substantial industrial advance, and in addition, the economic aid received from other Eastern bloc countries, while not attaining the lavishness of that bestowed on some Asian countries by the West, has consisted almost entirely of industrial equipment or training in its operation. In contrast, North Vietnam's overcrowded and poverty-stricken agriculture presented problems for which no possibility of an early breakthrough existed, and the methods by which the claimed increases in output have been realized would almost certainly have been more productive had they been effected through the exercise of peasant initiative.

Unlike the situation in the Mekong delta, the agricultural structure of the deltas of Tonkin and North Annam before World War II contained no large properties owned by absentee landlords exercising quasi-feudal rights over their tenants, but was largely made up of a mass of tiny intensively fragmented properties[19] and occasional communal lands; these may have amounted to perhaps a fifth of the cultivated land of the Songkoi delta, and about a quarter of that of North Annam. Some two-thirds of all rural families owned some land, but for the great majority this amounted to less than 0·5 hectares. Gourou considered, however, that his own estimates of the size distribution of holdings in the delta of the Songkoi understated the true extent of largish properties.[20] All too often, the small proprietor was an owner in name only; for all practical purposes the real owner was the moneylender, usually a Vietnamese landlord but occasionally a Chinese trader or Chettyar Indian, and in the lower delta particularly, the creation of large holdings had proceeded apace. The Tonkinese peasant thus occupied a position not unlike that of the *tani* of Central Java, who had also in effect become a tenant on his own land, paying interest on unsecured loans (in the face of the government ban on the pledging of land against advances there was in fact nothing that the peasant could offer as security) of between 30 and 50 per cent of the harvest, and thus, on double-cropped land, effective interest rates of 60 to 100 per cent per annum. Even the communal lands, which were let out to the landless, carried rents that amounted to 40 per cent or more of the harvest. From such

[19] *When on one occasion the Forestry Department wished to lease a block of 2·5 hectares of rice-land in Bac Giang province (now Ho Bac) for the establishment of a nursery, it had to negotiate with seventy-six different owners. Robequain, op. cit., p. 109.*

[20] *Figures of the number of proprietors by size of holdings indicated that some 37 per cent of the cultivated land in the delta was held in properties of less than 5 mau (1·8 hectares) and that 27 per cent was held in properties of from 5 to 10 mau (3·6 hectares). No allowance was made for communal lands. See Gourou, op. cit., pp. 229–30.*

crushing burdens the only escape was to the almost equally miserable life of the *ta dien* in the Trans-Bassac or to the rubber plantations of the south.

The Vietminh's advocacy of land reform thus found a large measure of support, and in distinguishing between landless and poor peasants, medium peasants, and rich landowners, it followed the early course of the Chinese agricultural revolution; with the promise of free land, the poor were invited to denounce wealthy neighbours, whose land together with that of 'colonialists' and the communal lands were to be made available for redistribution. Eventually, between one and two million acres of land in North Vietnam out of a total of perhaps nearly five million acres under cultivation were redistributed; but as in South Vietnam, the amount made available to each recipient was far too small to effect any significant change in the general pattern of tiny farms. Redistribution was carried out with harshness and occasional brutality, and in 1956 local resentment at the way in which the agrarian changes were being affected boiled over in sporadic outbreaks of open hostility; in the Song Ca delta of Nghé An province a miniature 'peasants' revolt' was suppressed only after considerable bloodshed. But although no other communist government has possessed the candour of President Castro of Cuba, who has openly declared that the optimum size of peasant holdings is nil, as however much land the peasant has, he will always ask for more, each is of the same opinion. North Vietnam has had to limit the socialization of agriculture to 'work-exchange' teams and to relatively simple cooperatives under the control of local party cadres; production targets in such cooperatives are laid down in accordance with the overall national plan, but individual ownership of land and animals is retained and the output is shared between the member and the cooperative. The resistance to the formation of higher cooperatives in which land, animals and equipment are all pooled, has been so formidable that the government has been compelled to proceed with caution, and full collectivization has been applied only in certain limited areas of the delta where masses of small tenants were already effectively aggregated in latifundia.

Thus the pattern of a multiplicity of small family farms generally less than two hectares in extent remains, and although cooperatives may have been able to effect some increase in productivity through improved drainage and irrigation or through better agricultural techniques, the limited land and capital at the disposal of the farmer means that the fundamental problem of low productivity in the face of rapid population increase, the principal cause of the enormous prewar rural indebtedness, remains. Nevertheless, up to 1960 agricultural progress appeared satisfactory; a padi production of some 5·4 million tons, twice that of 1939, was claimed for 1959. But this was the high-water mark of the agricultural effort; only in 1964, perhaps North Vietnam's best-ever crop year, was this figure exceeded and in most years of the Sixties production hovered below the 5 million ton level, although the Five Year Plan envisaged a target of 7 million tons. With population growing at a rate around 3 per cent per annum, North

Vietnam was making little progress in the struggle for greater agricultural self-sufficiency.

The agricultural advances of the early years were almost certainly the result of an extension of the cultivated area. In the deltas this took the form of land reclamation along the south coast of the Songkoi delta, and increased multiple cropping, some areas even experimenting with triple-cropping, a practice virtually unknown outside very limited districts in south China. But the greatest contribution probably came from increased dry-field cultivation outside the coastal deltas, a development which is likely to have been of greatest significance in the better-favoured hill and valley country of the Songkoi's 'Middle Region'. The scope for further increases in the cultivated area is distinctly limited. Even before World War II over half the cultivated area was double-cropped, and to raise this proportion significantly involves the provision of additional water to the high lands in the northern and eastern portions of the delta so that farmers can take a crop in June as well as in November, and adequate drainage to the low-lying western portions where the depth of the flood and problems of water control make the usual November harvest impossible; both objectives involve major works of construction (*Figure 9-2a*). Land reclamation has gone on in coastal Tonkin for more than two centuries, but it is a laborious and hazardous undertaking, and cannot on the average add more than around 1,000 hectares annually to the cultivated area. Opportunities for expanding dry-field agriculture are much better, but to maintain the productivity of dry fields is exceedingly difficult, and such a system of agriculture is much better suited to the cultivation of maize and other food crops less acceptable to the Vietnamese than is rice. True, the large disparity between rice yields in south China and those in Tonkin suggests that a substantial improvement in the latter should not prove too difficult. Nevertheless, the difference is in a very real sense indicative of the greater productivity of a warm temperate than of a tropical environment; there is no Chinese technique of cultivation unknown to the farmers of Tonkin, who alone of all the indigenous peoples of Southeast Asia make extensive use of human manures. North Vietnam has in all probability intensified still further its employment of organic manures of all kinds, but large increases in yields are only likely to come with widespread use of improved seeds and greatly enhanced consumption of chemical fertilizers; in these developments, every communist country including the USSR lags far behind the standards of the West or of Japan.

Even more necessary is the improvement of the low productivity of the rural worker; the extra output derived from extended multiple cropping, green manuring, etc., all too often involves a disproportionate increase in labour input. The increased productivities of soil and worker that could be inferred from the 1959 level of production were presumably the result of favourable weather conditions, for they have not been sustained. Improved techniques including the use of tractor-drawn equipment have been employed on the new state farms created in upland areas and in parts of the lower delta; but these new units which may amount in total to perhaps as much as 300,000 acres, are largely engaged in the cultivation of more valuable industrial crops such as sugar cane, cotton and other vegetable fibres, and coffee and tea, in which large-scale methods are economically sound. In wiping out the medium and large proprietors, the regime destroyed the most enterprising and efficient section of the rice-farming community which still accounts for at least two-thirds of the total population, and the present pattern of small farms linked in cooperatives appears unlikely to be able to effect the increase in production necessary to support a continued high rate of economic growth.

With the intensification of the war, agricultural problems have mounted; the drafting of virtually the entire young male population into the armed forces has increased the susceptibility of the rice crop to natural hazard, although the army is regularly called in to assist with the harvest. In 1966 there were reports of serious food shortages in many parts of the country following poor harvests resulting from inclement weather, and with the disruption of transport through air attacks it was becoming apparent that government policy was to let traditional rice-deficit areas fend for themselves by encouraging the increased use of maize and other rice substitutes.

In general the industrialization programme has experienced similar fortunes to those of agriculture. Between 1956 and 1961 industrial output grew by perhaps as much as 150 per cent, but thereafter obstacles to further expansion proved steadily more intractable, exacerbating the economic strains created by North Vietnam's mounting indebtedness to its aid donors. Until 1961 the principal aim was to restore the levels of mining and manufacturing output of the years before World War II, a task that presented no very great difficulties despite the closure of some mines since the Great Depression, the damage and neglect suffered by others in the war of independence, and the removal by the departing French of much modern machinery; these difficulties were gradually overcome through the provision of trained personnel and equipment by China and the USSR. Tonkin produced over 80 per cent of the total mineral output of old Indochina, but in view of the limited domestic demand, the French had worked its deposits of coal, iron ore, tin, zinc, chromite and gold only when the possibility existed of a profit-able export trade. Coal-mining was anomalous, however, in that the railways, power generation and the cement industry made up a substantial local market, but half of Tonkin's low-cost output was regularly exported, as was also a similar proportion of its cement production. Suitable local raw materials and the low cost of fuel, a major item in total costs, had promoted the establishment of cement production in Haiphong around the turn of the century, and successive expansions had made the plant one of the largest industrial establishments in Southeast Asia, with an output of almost 300,000 tons on the eve of World War II. Further plant expansion raised the level of output in 1965 to around twice that of the prewar peak.

In Hanoi, as in many cities of Southeast Asia, the bicycle and pedal trishaw
fill an important role in the carriage of both people and goods.

In the event, North Vietnam was obliged to continue the French policy of
pushing the export of minerals, particularly coal, in order to contain its growing
trade deficit and to amortize its indebtedness to its aid donors. But part of the
expanded mineral output was intended to find its major markets in the new
power plants, metallurgical establishments and the complexes of heavy industry
to be created during the Five Year Plan; some of these were completely new, but
others such as the machine-tool plant at Haiphong or the Gia Lam locomotive
works at Hanoi were essentially expansions of prewar undertakings. This stage of
the industrialization programme inevitably encountered greater obstacles than
did the period before 1961, for it involved the co-ordination of several raw material
supplies, whose further assembly was repeatedly delayed by shortages of labour
and the failure of donors, particularly China, to deliver equipment in good time.
The most important new industrial complex is at Thai Nguyen in the Viet Bac
Autonomous Area, where large deposits of good-quality ore existed which had
been fitfully worked by the French. The project involved an integrated iron and
steel plant complete with coke ovens and by-product plants for the production of
fertilizers and other chemicals; a second blast-furnace was completed in 1965

when the plant was believed to have a capacity of some 250,000 tons of iron and steel products. The soft coal of the nearby small Phan Me and Tuyen Quang fields is unsuitable for coking, and the principal source of fuel is the Quang Yen field north of Haiphong. This is Southeast Asia's leading coalfield, not only by virtue of output but also because its anthracitic coals, though not entirely satisfactory for the conventional blast-furnace, are more suitable than the soft Tertiary coals of other Southeast Asian fields; moreover its coastal location less than fifty miles from a major port has greatly facilitated exploitation and the development of an export trade. By 1964 production was raised to some 3·2 million tons, not perhaps a great advance in view of the new mechanical equipment which had been installed after 1961 to replace the old hand methods in the more productive eastern portion of the field near Hon Gay, where underground shaft mining is the principal practice.

Other minerals such as zinc, also found in the Thai Nguyen area, and tin, a product of Pia Ouac massif south of Cao Bang, are raised in increasing quantities, although it is likely that the greater part of this production also is exported. Low prices for zinc have long depressed output, despite the fact that Tonkin is very favourably endowed with zinc blende deposits, but price considerations have less significance for centrally planned economies; on the other hand, the rising price of tin on the world market almost certainly acted as a fillip to North Vietnam's production, which may have amounted to around 3,000 tons in 1965. Antimony, nickel, lead and cobalt are all mined in small quantities, and of non-metallic minerals the apatite (phosphate) deposits of Lao Cai which supply a Soviet-built fertilizer plant in Hanoi, have perhaps received the greatest emphasis.

Investment in consumer-goods industries, in contrast, has been much more limited, although much of the expansion that has taken place also represents the fruits of foreign aid. Prominent in this group has been the cotton textile industry, which produces, of course, intermediate as well as essential consumer goods; here also the regime was fortunate in having a sound prewar basis on which to build, with large plants in Nam Dinh and Haiphong. These were originally established in order to produce yarn to supply Tonkin's numerous handloom weavers, and the domestic sector of the industry, now reorganized in cooperatives, is still of considerable significance. However, the mill sector with its productive new Chinese machinery is now of major importance, and to the large prewar plants have been added an integrated mill in Hanoi, said to have 50,000 spindles and large weaving and finishing sections, and several small knitting and apparel-making plants. As is usual in communist countries, output largely consists of the coarsest cloths, and consumption is restricted through high prices to the domestic market.[21]

[21] *A cotton jacket, the standard apparel for all workers, cost about half the monthly salary of an unskilled factory worker in 1961; no appreciable increase in real incomes seems likely since that date. See Michael Field,* The Prevailing Wind: Witness in Indo-China, *Methuen, London, 1965, p. 343.*

Food processing is the only other branch of consumer industry to experience rapid expansion, new rice-mills, sugar refineries, fish-processing plants, tea factories, and plants for the processing of tapioca and soya beans having been established either in the major cities or in appropriate locations in relation to raw material supplies. In view of the major role played by the bicycle both in the economy and the war effort of North Vietnam, plants for the assembly of bicycles and for the manufacture of bicycle tyres might almost be regarded as capital-goods establishments.

After 1964, however, the increasingly severe constraints to growth imposed by the failure of exports to grow, and particularly exports to countries outside the Eastern bloc, severe shortages of skilled labour and delays in the supply of aid-financed equipment, were compounded by the growing demands of the war effort and the steady attrition of transport facilities under American air attack. The new power stations that had raised North Vietnam's generating capacity to perhaps nearly 200,000 kW by the middle Sixties were repeatedly put out of action, and damage to the large new Uong Bi station on the Quang Yen coalfield, and to the Thac Ba dam and hydro-electricity station in Thanh Hoa province has been particularly severe. Attacks were also made on the Haiphong cement plant and the Thai Nguyen complex; in mid-1967 North Vietnam, realizing its extreme danger should the Americans unleash an all-out air attack, intensified its propaganda campaign that the destruction of the Songkoi dykes would be a war-crime without parallel. War factories were decentralized and many smaller plants literally went underground, but such measures were clearly out of the question for the major raw-material oriented, capital-intensive plants. All of North Vietnam's hard-won economic progress was being risked on the gambler's throw of an intensification of the war in the south.

LAOS

Long backward and neglected, Laos in 1954 was little more than a loose collection of tribal territories strung along the middle Mekong. The efforts of its three princes, respectively 'left', 'right' and 'neutralist', to create a modern nation against the background of East-West competition for the good wishes of this supposedly strategically important new state, often appeared even to informed and sympathetic Western observers to possess many of the ingredients of classic farce.[22] Reality was tragic enough; the intervention of the powers ensured that Laos remained divided and that economic development in the part of the country controlled by the Royal Laotian Government in Vientiane was rendered abortive despite a truly enormous aid programme. At the second Geneva conference in

[22] *See, for example, Willard A. Hanna*, Eight Nation Makers: Southeast Asia's Charismatic Leaders, *St Martin's Press, New York, 1964, pp. 215–38. The sober and depressing account of Western miscalculation and incompetence in its dealings with Laos in Michael Field, op. cit., also contains much light relief.*

1962 the powers agreed on the neutrality of the Kingdom, but plans for communist participation in the Vientiane government soon came to nothing, and the Pathet Lao and its Vietminh backers remained in control of more than half the country; only the Mekong valley itself and the lower valleys of its major tributaries the Nam Ou, Nam Ngum, Se Done and Se Kong were effectively in the control of the Vientiane government in 1967, and even this area was later reduced by renewed North Vietnamese incursions.

Nevertheless, this territory represents by far the most productive part of the country and that with the greatest potential, and a stable and determined government could certainly have recorded substantial economic growth. But this Laos has never had, and, although granted with the best of motives, much of the foreign aid received by the country has produced—it is not too much to say—a negative development. Laos has been encouraged, in effect, to maintain a war economy at Western, essentially United States, expense. The Laotian army of 75,000 men and the para-military police force of over 6,000 are enormous for a country with a population of only some two million, of which perhaps less than two-thirds are under the authority of Vientiane. A large part of the young adult male population is thus maintained in unproductive employment and denied to agriculture, so that land formerly under cultivation has been abandoned. Only some 550,000 hectares were planted to lowland padi in 1968, but a further 700,000 hectares were estimated to be suitable for lowland rice production, and an additional 200,000 hectares for dry rice cultivation. The fact that Laos in the Sixties was obliged to import some 50,000 tons of rice annually from Thailand, principally of the preferred glutinous varieties, to make good its domestic deficiency cannot therefore be ascribed to a shortage of rice-land. As long as the United States is prepared, as at present, to meet all Laos' rice import bills, the will to eliminate the deficiency is seriously compromised;[23] but Laos also makes large imports of vegetables, fruits and livestock products, all of which it should be capable of producing for itself from land at present under-utilized or lying idle. The United States, it is true, has planned in its aid programme to eliminate the deficit by 1970, a target that is to be attained by the extended cultivation of superior higher-yielding varieties, which are being produced by farmers under contract in American-supervised 'multiplication centres'. The multipurpose Nam Ngum project for electricity generation and the improvement of irrigation in the Vientiane plain, will also greatly facilitate the achievement of higher yields, but this is unlikely to be completed before the middle Seventies, and in the meantime more might be done by deploying on idle land some of the labour so ineffectively employed in the defence and security forces, to say nothing of making some use of

---

[23] *Most economists now believe that food aid is a serious menace to a developing country's determination to make good a domestic food deficiency—even those from India, the principal beneficiary of food aid. A former American ambassador to Laos also thought so; see Leonard Unger, 'Laos', Focus, American Geographic Society, vol. 14, May 1964, p. 4.*

the labour of 250,000 refugees in various parts of the country, who are kept alive by American aid.

One agricultural activity has expanded, however: this is the cultivation of the opium poppy, usually the only source of cash income to mountain people such as the Miao. The swiddens of Laos probably produce about 300–400 tons of the total Southeast Asian output of raw opium of about 1,000 tons estimated by the UN Central Opium Board, a black trade with a $10,000 million international turnover, which because of its extreme profitability defies every attempt at control. But even if the cultivation of the opium poppy were illegal, which is not the case in all Southeast Asian countries, it would be impossible to prevent, not only because of the physical difficulties of detection but also because cultivation is encouraged by dissident groups for their own purposes. In Laos the trade is largely in the hands of the Pathet Lao, which has used it to finance its operations; the Shans of Burma, another branch of the Thai family of peoples, have also used it to finance their insurrection against the central government in Rangoon. Opium poppy cultivation requires freshly burnt clearings, and laborious and meticulous cultivation; about one acre of poppies is necessary for the production of a pound of raw opium, the processing of which is also a very laborious undertaking. The grower's return is small, for the big profits come nearer the point of final consumption;[24] but sooner or later this inhuman traffic must be terminated through international action, which despite all the difficulties is perhaps best accomplished at the point of origin.

To the world, opium is unquestionably Laos' most important export, and though it appears in no trade statistics anywhere, Laos itself is believed to earn only about $1·5 million of a growth industry with a world turnover of some $10,000 million, double that of 1960. About half of the value of recorded exports is accounted for by tin concentrates (*Table 9–3*) from a single French-owned mine at Phontieu, just north of Thakhek, but the output of 1,200 tons in 1967 was only half that of a decade earlier. Nevertheless, this performance was a considerable improvement on the output levels of the early Sixties, and with the planned new equipment to be installed by the company, it should be possible to raise output to some 3,000 tons in the early Seventies. However, insecurity and the lack of transport facilities have prevented the re-opening of other abandoned mines in the area, obstacles which have also enforced the abandonment of most of the estates of the Bolovens plateau, which before World War II produced high-quality coffee. Lowland smallholder coffee and timber are the only other exports of more than trifling significance, and after many years of miniscule export earnings, the increasing production of these items after 1967 was distinctly encouraging.

[24] *A pound of opium will bring the grower a return of some $10; by the time it reaches the main collecting centres in northern Thailand it will have appreciated by perhaps a hundredfold in value. Converted into heroin in Hong Kong, Beirut or Marseille, it will bring around $10,000 a pound, and three times this sum when retailed at final points of consumption in the West.*

Manufacturing in Laos is rudimentary; much of what exists has also been created through the use of aid funds, uses imported raw materials, and represents alien, principally French, Chinese and Thai enterprise. Small plants exist for the production of sawn timber, ice, matches, soft drinks, cigarettes, industrial alcohol

Table 9-3 *Laos: composition and direction of foreign trade, 1965*

Million kips

IMPORTS		EXPORTS	
Food	1,705·2	Tin	147·2
Petroleum products	1,056·0	Wood	19·1
Chemicals	436·8	Green coffee	11·1
Machinery	730·8	Benzoin	26·8
Textiles	676·8		
Transport equipment	785·0	**Total**, including others	**240·2**
Other manufactures	1,709·2		
Total, including others	**7,893·2**		

	Imports from	Exports to
Thailand	2,050·0	15·3
United States	1,981·9	0·7
Japan	638·0	—
France	422·8	2·7
Malaysia and Singapore	—	180·8
United Kingdom	683·3	—
Total, including others	**7,893·2**	**240·2**

Source: Bureau des Statistiques, *Bulletin du Commerce Extérieur*

and footwear, and there is certainly scope for the expansion of industries that could use local raw materials, sugar-milling and jute bag manufacture being obvious examples. Vientiane possesses the greater part of this limited industrial development, the balance being shared between Thakhek and Savannakhet; the former has also been selected as the site of a new cement works, which will eventually be able to supply all of the country's requirements.

The lack of transport is a major handicap to the economic development of Laos, and without major improvements the country will continue to form a collection of tiny local economies. The Mekong is the principal means of communication for the indigenous population, but the country's main supply line is the Bangkok-Nong Khai railway, by means of which most foreign aid reaches Laos; the growing congestion at Bangkok port is thus of major concern to Vientiane. Air transport, while vital for administrative purposes, is also of increasing commercial importance, but a good road system is urgently needed. At the time of independence Laos was almost entirely devoid of all-weather roads, and though large aid funds have been committed to road construction by the United States, most of these were siphoned off in fraudulent operations of varying degrees of ingenuity. After many delays, however, an all-weather road between Vientiane and Luang Prabang was completed late in 1968.

Aid has thus not been without some positive contributions to the Laotian economy, but there is a depressing catalogue to set on the other side of the ledger. The import programme, the expensive Foreign Exchange Operations Fund which props up the value of the Laotian *kip*, even the aid-financed social services as schools and clinics, most benefit the urban middle-class bureaucrats and the trading population; the great mass of the peasantry, which feeds itself, has been almost entirely untouched, a telling point in Pathet Lao propaganda. Enormous budget deficits have produced chronic inflationary pressure and new demands for additional aid. Laos' lack of exchange controls has been responsible for the growth of an exotic gold trade, in which Vientiane has become the leading centre in South-east Asia; gold is flown into the country, fabricated into crude jewellery, and smuggled out into Thailand and South Vietnam, in both of which the import of gold is illegal. Though helping to swell the demand for aid dollars, the United States has, perhaps reluctantly, condoned the trade, as no less than a quarter of government revenue is generated by the gold tax. Nevertheless there are abundant opportunities for increasing government revenue; the cost of petroleum products, all aid provided, is much lower than in Thailand, despite much higher transport costs, but all attempts at raising the tax on gasoline have been resisted by the bureaucrats, who are virtually the only consumers. Laos is a pathetic example of the inadequacy of aid to generate economic development when almost every other prerequisite is lacking.

CAMBODIA

Cambodia's physical resource basis is much richer than that of Laos, and its population is some three times as large. But the greatest advantage enjoyed by Cambodia over Laos, and indeed over both Vietnams also, has been the quality of its leadership, which has won for the country a position in the councils of the world out of all proportion to its size. Cambodian neutralism has not so far gained the frontier guarantees so persistently sought by the Chief of State,[25] and with out-breaks of *Khmer Vietminh* violence, the future of the country in the late Sixties

[25] *Perhaps in order to steal a march on a China wrecked by the excesses of the Cultural Revolution and fast alienating even its most devoted admirers, in June 1967 the USSR formally recognized the territorial integrity of Cambodia. But although North Vietnam has recognized Cambodian independence it has been silent on the boundary question. The Vietminh occupied part of the country for some time before 1954, and the Vietcong continues to use Cambodian territory as a sanctuary and a base for mounting attacks.*

appeared more obscure than at any time since independence; but it has created an environment in which economic development has been possible, and in which foreign aid has been able to make a contribution without the disruptive and corruptive influences that have been so pronounced in the Laos and South Vietnam aid programmes. Surrounded by traditionally hostile neighbours who at various times have appropriated large parts of its territory, Cambodia has felt that only through the good offices of the power that appeared able to exert the most durable influence in Southeast Asia, namely China, could the country survive, and its decision to terminate receipt of American aid in 1963, and other manifestations of apparently irrational anti-American activity, must be seen in this light. China's vicious political attacks on Burma, which has been just as neutralist as Cambodia, the strength of the American determination to resist the communist attempt at a take-take-over of South Vietnam, and Cambodia's troubles with its own communists suggest that this view may have been somewhat extreme, and after 1967 a Cambodian rapprochement with the West began to appear possible. Nevertheless, Cambodia's successful harnessing of its cultural traditions to promote political stability and economic growth represents a major accomplishment, and contrasts starkly with the political and economic disintegration which accompanied attempts at utilizing similar forces in Burma and Indonesia.

Despite its relatively good economic performance since 1954, Cambodia is still a very poor place and the estimated per capita product of $120 in 1966 is probably an over-estimate of the country's standing in Southeast Asia's levels of well-being. As in Laos, and in Thailand also until very recently, almost all occupations apart from food production are in the hands of aliens, mainly Chinese, Vietnamese or French, and the encouragement of a greater Khmer participation in non-agricultural employments is the most fundamental part of economic policy. As in Thailand also, the lack of indigenous capital and skills has led to direct government participation in many lines of industrial production and in commerce, and in the latter Cambodia has proceeded even further than has Thailand, all foreign trade and banking being nationalized in 1964. However, by retaining foreign companies as agents for the new national corporations, the disruption that attended the nationalizations of Burma has so far been avoided.

Cambodia is one of the few countries of Southeast Asia that has managed to achieve a rate of increase in food production in excess of that of population. Though not as spectacularly as in Thailand, food exports have continued to increase, rice exports in 1965 exceeding a level of 500,000 tons for the first time. However, part of Cambodia's apparent rice surplus probably represents rice smuggled across the border from South Vietnam.

Nearly all of Cambodia has a lengthy and well-defined dry season, but techniques of cultivation are primitive and much of the rice crop depends entirely on natural rainfall or flood water. Around the Tonlé Sap, in the Mongkolborey valley of Battambang province and in the bengs bordering the Mekong, floating rice is grown, and in some deeply inundated low-lying areas a quickly maturing off-season rice crop is grown by planting around the margins of the depression as the water-level falls, a practice similar to that of the *padi gogorantjah* of Indonesia. The common practice of broadcast sowing even for normal-stem varieties and the minimal use of organic manures are also contributary factors in producing a national average rice yield well below that of Vietnam, but this does not necessarily indicate that Cambodian agriculture is less efficient, because the lower yield is obtained with a substantially lower labour input. Cambodia resembles Thailand in its relatively large cattle and buffalo population, which is much used both for transport and farm purposes; the greater draft power at his disposal enables the Cambodian farmer to use a solidly built plough with a steel share, which is both more durable and efficient than the light wooden Vietnamese plough, of which the share tip alone is made of metal.

A large livestock population can be supported because there is no pressure to maximise the use of land for the production of food for direct human consumption in the Vietnamese manner. Population density is light and ricefields do not extend continuously across the plains but are much interspersed with uncultivated land and occasional dry fields devoted to subsidiary food crops; the semi-wild *thnot* (Borassus flabellifer, or Palmyra palm) is a very conspicuous feature of the landscape and supports a widespread domestic industry producing

Rice and tobacco on a joint Cambodian government—United Nations experimental farm at Prek Thnot, Cambodia.

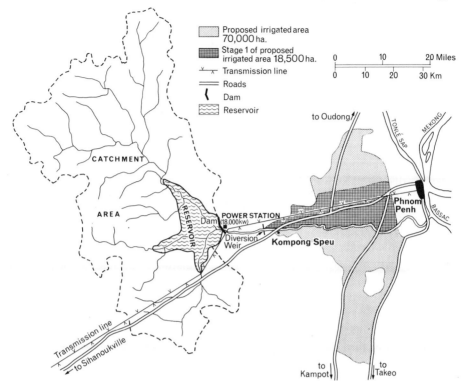

Fig. 9-3 The Prek Thnot multipurpose project, Cambodia

a non-crystalline sugar. Animals are grazed not only on the waste between the ricefields and on the stubble after the harvest, but also in the more open forests, while in some parts of the country a primitive type of ranching is practised in which the animals are allowed to run wild for part of the year. But in general, livestock receive as little attention as possible, an observation which, indeed, also applies to much of the rice crop.

The first essential in raising rice yields is improved water-control, and Cambodia's first multipurpose water project is the Prek Thnot dam near Kompong Speu (*Figure 9-3*), which will provide irrigation facilities for some 18,500 hectares, and ultimately for 70,000 hectares of rice-land; in addition to making possible a higher production in the wet season, the scheme will also encourage the cultivation of off-season cash crops such as groundnuts, soybeans and cotton, which will assist the farmer to purchase the fertilizers he now lacks. The scheme, which will also have a generating capacity of 18,000 kW, has been strongly supported by the Mekong Valley Committee of ECAFE, but unfortunately has been bogged down in financial difficulties arising from Japanese and American disagreement over the magnitude of the former's capital contribution, and by Cambodia's refusal to accept the United States as a direct contributor in the capital consortium, which also includes Israel and Australia. Several other countries have provided technical assistance, but without the capital contribution of the United States the scheme is unlikely to proceed. The proposed Tonlé Sap barrage will produce no power and its benefits will accrue mainly to South Vietnam. Its effect on the famous lake fisheries, almost entirely in the hands of Chinese operators, will need careful study, for there is considerable evidence of over-fishing and the area of the lake itself appears to have been undergoing a prolonged contraction.[26]

Cambodia is unique in Southeast Asia in having virtually no problem of agrarian organization. The average size of holdings is small, but land ownership is widely disseminated and there is very little tenancy and landlessness; moreover, as in Thailand, it has generally been possible for the villager to carve out a new holding for himself in the forest. With rapid population growth, however, the appearance of an agrarian problem in the more densely populated southeastern portion of the country between the Tonlé Sap and the South Vietnam border, where some three-quarters of the country's population is located, can be foreseen in the near future.

Cambodia's second largest export by value is natural rubber, and although its production of some 53,000 tons in 1967 is tiny in comparison with that of Malaysia or Indonesia, output has been growing steadily for several years. The industry spread into Cambodia from South Vietnam, and is still confined to the *terres rouges* and the *terres grises* of the border provinces. The 51,000 hectares planted to rubber are entirely controlled by a handful of very large French-owned estates, all members of the Socfin group, which also manages some properties which have passed to the government. The Cambodian estates have been able to press on with replanting and to introduce other technical innovations free from the difficulties that have crippled the rubber industry in South Vietnam, and they are among the most efficient in the world. Cambodia has, in fact, the highest national yield per tapped acre of any natural rubber producer, but to say this is merely to underline the total lack of either Asian-owned estate or smallholder sectors; Malaysian estates of the same size-class are just as efficient. Labour supply has long been the principal constraint to the expansion of the industry, but the failure of independent Cambodia to encourage a smallholder interest appears anomalous in the context of the country's strong economic nationalism. Khmers, however, appear to have as little interest in rubber cultivation as have the Thais, and government participation in the estate sector is apparently to be the principal means of enlarging the Khmer interest in the industry. This policy will almost certainly be followed in oil palm cultivation, a growth industry with a bright future in the country.

[26] *Presumably Angkor was constructed on the margins of the lake, which is now far distant even in the wet season. Angkor, of course, is a major source of foreign exchange earnings, and the government is well aware of the necessity of improving tourist amenities in its vicinity.*

Manufacturing accounts for scarcely as much as 10 per cent of Cambodia's GNP, and the rate of growth of industrial output in the past has been among the lowest recorded anywhere in Southeast Asia. It was inevitable that Cambodia's vigorous nationalism would endeavour to reduce this disparity, and the Five Year Plan 1960–64 provided for a much higher rate of industrial growth and for supporting infrastructural investments in power and transport facilities. Earlier plans to develop a heavy industrial foundation based on indigenous iron ores have been dropped as being totally unrealistic, and industrial policy is now to concentrate on the processing of local raw materials of agricultural or forest origin, and on a limited range of more capital-intensive industries essential for maintaining a high rate of economic growth, such as cement manufacture and petroleum refining. Most of the new industrial plants are state-owned and have been financed by foreign aid programmes, but some are joint enterprises with private capital. Phnom Penh, the capital and only real city, with a population approaching 500,000,

Table 9-4 *Cambodia: composition and direction of foreign trade, 1966*

Million riels

IMPORTS		EXPORTS	
Food and agricultural raw		Rubber	873·5
materials	233·5	Rice	846·6
Petroleum and mineral		Maize	178·1
products	413·2	Pepper	48·8
Textiles	504·5	Cattle	24·9
Chemicals and			
pharmaceutics	516·9	**Total**, including others	**2,356·2**
Metals and manufactures	1,738·0		
Total, including others	**3,887·7**		

	Imports from	Exports to
France and franc zone	1,037·1	764·2
China	622·2	198·6
Malaysia and Singapore	274·6	470·0
Japan	463·3	170·4
Hong Kong	137·9	174·1
West Germany	135·7	50·5
United Kingdom	144·3	50·8
USSR	114·7	17·9
Eastern European countries	275·4	171·7
Total, including others	**3,887·7**	**2,356·2**

Source: Banque Nationale du Cambodge, *Bulletin Mensuel*

possesses virtually all the manufacturing industries in the private sector; these are almost entirely Chinese- or French-owned, and include rice mills, sawmills, and the food, drink, footwear and building material industries, which because of the large element of natural protection they enjoy through transport costs, are encountered in all of Southeast Asia's capital cities. Inevitably also, it has attracted a substantial share of the new state-owned sector, including a paper mill, a glassworks and a tyre plant.

A second small aggregation of manufacturing, however, is evolving at Sihanoukville, the country's first and only ocean port, opened in 1956. The new port was to reduce dependence on the Mekong and South Vietnam, and to make good some of the deficiencies of Phnom Penh, which is accessible only to vessels of between 4,000 and 6,000 tons according to season. The port, built with French aid, is connected to the capital by a 230-kilometre road originally constructed by the United States, but construction was hasty and considerable repair work has proved necessary. A rail link, in which Chinese, French and West German aid have all participated, was originally scheduled for completion by mid-1967, but work was in progress two years later. The line, it is hoped, will accelerate the growth of the aid-supported capital-intensive industries located in the Sihanoukville area; these include a cement works at Chankrey Ting using imported Chinese coal, a tractor assembly works provided by Czechoslovakia (which will have to find additional employment if its equipment is to be kept working at anything like capacity), a plant for the assembly of French Berliet trucks, a French brewery which will result in diminished imports from the parent plant in Saigon, and a 500,000-ton annual capacity oil refinery, completed in 1968 and to be operated as a joint venture with French private capital. A hydro-electric plant at Kam Chay in the Elephant mountains near Kampot with a capacity of 50,000 kW was planned for construction by the USSR, but further investigations have shown that stream flow will permit utilization of this capacity for only two months of the year, and the project may not be proceeded with. As a result of this activity traffic at Sihanoukville has increased rapidly, and even by 1964 freight handled exceeded that at Phnom Penh. A long-term plan of expansion to increase the original three berths to ten by 1970 is being implemented with French assistance. As a further stimulus to the development of the port, the government in 1968 announced that it would create a Free Trade Zone, in which industrial investors would be provided with all necessary facilities, and would receive guarantees against nationalization.

Other industrial establishments have been located near their sources of raw materials; these include a cotton textile mill and a jute bag plant at Battambang, a palm-sugar mill at Kompong Speu, and a further cotton mill at Kompong Cham. The full development of all these projects, however, will still leave Cambodia with only a rudimentary industrial structure, and though the new plants are a matter of considerable national pride, the country is failing to attract the large

Battery of crepe-making machines at the Chuup estate, Cambodia, one of the world's largest rubber estates and part of the *Socfin* organization.

private capital inflow which is giving to Thailand such a bright industrial future. Indeed, the prospects of the whole private sector, outside food-producing agriculture, appear obscure. A few private industrial establishments have been established in the Sixties, and the state has continued to use French capital and expertise in joint ventures and in managerial roles, but this policy is likely to prove transitory. Despite its professed friendship with Peking, Cambodia regards its Chinese population with deep suspicion, and unless the Chinese community adopts a more obviously Khmer way of life, its activities are likely to be progressively restricted. Notwithstanding its increased reliance on the communist world for much of its aid, Cambodia's trade remains overwhelmingly oriented towards the West, particularly to France and the franc zone (*Table 9-4*). Some form of state socialism appears to be the most likely line of development of the Cambodian economy, but without private foreign capital the harnessing of Cambodia's undoubtedly large potential resources is likely to be very protracted.

IV PROSPECT

CHAPTER TEN

The destiny of Southeast Asia

With the creation in 1965 of independent Singapore, only Portuguese Timor, which comprises the eastern half of the island and the Ocussi-Ambeno enclave, remained under colonial rule. Thus in Southeast Asia as in Africa, the first great colonial power of the modern world has remained the last, but eastern Timor clearly has no future apart from close cooperation or integration with Indonesia, and this anachronism is unlikely to endure. Reinforcing an understandable anxiety to establish positions of respect and authority in the modern world, the new independent states of Southeast Asia are all committed to reducing the present great disparity in living standards between the developing and the developed worlds; but independence, of course, as many Indonesians and Burmans have discovered, in itself creates no new resources and guarantees nothing, except the ability seriously to grapple with developmental problems if the will to do so exists. Independence may or may not stimulate such a will; although independent for more than a century, Haiti and Liberia still possess living standards markedly inferior to those of neighbouring territories that have only recently thrown off colonial rule, and within the region Thailand, never a colonial possession, is poorer than either Malaysia or the Philippines. In pursuing these linked goals of national identity and economic growth the nations of Southeast Asia have adopted almost every form of political and economic organization possible, from the highly centralized and authoritarian polity and economy of North Vietnam to the largely free-enterprise political democracies of Malaysia and the Philippines, and, as has been seen, they have achieved very varying degrees of success.

Nevertheless, on the whole Southeast Asia's economic record since 1950 compares very favourably with that of the Third World of which it forms part, although 'Second World' or 'South'[1] might be more appropriate terms, as the countries concerned have made it clear that in matters of economic aid they see

---

[1] *This term is increasingly used for the mainly tropical countries responsible for the creation of the United Nations Conference on Trade and Development (UNCTAD), which from 77 at the Conference's first meeting in Geneva in 1964, had increased to 86 for the second conference at New*

little reason for distinguishing between the West and the Soviet bloc. Thus Southeast Asia might justifiably be regarded as a region of hope, where, given a reasonable period of peace, development problems although severe, will in all probability yield to a continuation of sensible national development policies. Moreover, as noted in the opening chapter, its overall performance would have made a much better showing but for the pathetic record of Indonesia, for until the disorganization of the national economy following the take-over by the Revolutionary Council in 1962, even Burma had performed rather better economically than the average for the 'developing ECAFE region', the assemblage of poor Asian countries that the United Nations Commission for Asia and the Far East uses to contrast with the three developed countries (Australia, New Zealand and Japan) that also fall within its area of interest.

Any prognosis for Southeast Asia must largely turn on the situation in Indonesia. The problems Indonesia inherited at independence were undoubtedly severe, but they have been compounded by an inept and irrational administration, which despite its interminable pontifications on the inequities of the colonial period, placed little value on economic development. Given determined leadership there appears no real reason why Indonesia should not have performed as well as, say, Pakistan, also a Muslim country and of almost equivalent population, and which though of smaller geographic extent and with what must surely be regarded as the poorer resource basis, also suffers from marked regional imbalances in the distribution of population and a great longitudinal separation of its component parts. But Pakistan's economic drive, of course, has been closely bound up with its fierce determination to match India in economic and national strength, whereas in Southeast Asia, Indonesia is so clearly without a rival in either population or potential resources that economic development has carried no such sense of urgency. Pakistan's experience is highly instructive. It has had a succession of development plans whose record of implementation has shown consistent improvement; the environment for private capital, including foreign capital, has been kept highly congenial; and to ensure a large flow of foreign aid, Pakistan has been prepared to accept a high degree of surveillance by donor countries over the implementation of its development plans and the overall conduct of the economy. This policy has paid off handsomely, for the visible fruits of foreign aid have provided the justification for requests for additional aid. Donor countries on the other hand, delighted with the demonstration that, given the right institutional and political environment, aid can be extremely effective in stimulating a higher rate of economic growth, have acceded to such requests, and they have done so despite a general tightening up since 1961 both of the flow of aid and the terms under which it has been granted.

Delhi in 1967. The term, of course, overlooks the fact that Australia and New Zealand, among the world's wealthiest nations, are also far to the south of the developed world of the northern hemisphere.

Pakistan, in short, has been an ideal aid-recipient; the contrast with Indonesia, or India also for that matter, could not be more marked. Until the Ampera government's stabilization plan, Indonesian development plans departed further and further from reality; the environment for private initiative and foreign capital grew progressively more hostile, nor was this reduction in private activity in any way compensated by enhanced enterprise in the public sector. After 1958 Indonesia for the first time began to receive a large aid inflow, but President Sukarno's fulminations against 'aid with strings' rose to a crescendo in a speech of 1964 that urged the United States to 'go to Hell' with its aid. If aid without strings is intended to imply that aid should be granted without any kind of surveillance whatever over its deployment, then such a view must be totally rejected. To grant such aid is in fact worse than useless, for it encourages expectations of improvement which cannot possibly be realized and ultimately produces in the minds of taxpayers of donor countries a profound disillusionment with the whole concept of aid as a catalyst in the development process. It is another of Indonesia's many misfortunes that its economic collapse coincided with just such a growing disillusionment in both Western and Eastern donors alike.

The problems facing Indonesia are not only on a very much larger scale than those of Burma, but they are moreover of immeasurably greater significance both to the West and to the Sino-Soviet world. Ironically enough, it is probably true, as Burma's leaders have always maintained, that theirs is potentially a very rich country, but it does not matter very much to the rest of the world if Burma continues its stubborn aloofness and allows its economy to drift into chaos. For whatever happens, Burma is unlikely to starve; it lies well off the world's major commercial arteries, and such importance as it ever had arose primarily from its function as a major rice-supplier to India, so that despite the subcontinent's heavy deficit the British Raj in South and Southeast Asia remained in overall food balance. Burma has long ceased to be the principal food supplier to India, a role that has passed to the United States, and between 1964 and 1968 the world managed to make do with progressively less Burmese rice. In meeting the emergency created by successive failures of the Indian monsoon in 1965 and 1966, which gave rise to the gloomiest forecasts of widespread mass starvation—prophecies that in the event proved entirely false—Burma played a minimal part. What has to be demonstrated is that Burma itself can manage without its customary level of rice exports; for all its efforts to seal itself off from the outside world, Burma is more dependent than ever before on the size of the exportable rice surplus. There remains to trouble the rest of the world the possibility of Chinese incursion across Burma frontiers, but such an eventuality appears remote as China can more expeditiously achieve its end by further support to Burma's Peking-oriented communist faction, and to dissident non-Burman peoples such as the Kachins.

As earlier noted, the world cannot remain indifferent to the fate of Indonesia, a fact that the Suharto administration well realizes. For the West, complete Indonesian economic collapse and a possible third-time lucky resurrection of the PKI that might follow in its train, would constitute a severe blow; but for the Eastern bloc also, recovery of the Indonesian economy is essential if it is ever to receive payment on the enormous debts owed to it by Indonesia, and the potential loss of both loans and influence is not lightly to be contemplated. For East and West alike, a chaotic and possibly fissiparous Indonesia would constitute a potentially dangerous political vacuum. Yet Indonesia has never occupied the position of importance that its size and population would appear to command, a situation that some Indonesians, and certainly ex-President Sukarno, found exceedingly irksome; and the creation of what on paper was the most formidable military machine in Southeast Asia was in part an attempt to establish such a position. The attempt was premature, for the inability of the Indonesians to handle their sophisticated Russian weapons was demonstrated during the confrontation of Malaysia. But a resuscitated Indonesia might be expected sooner or later to try again, and with Britain's decision to withdraw its forces from east of Suez, Indonesia's strategic position commanding the passages between the Pacific and Indian Oceans has increased in importance. The appearance, in 1968, for the first time of a Russian naval squadron in the Indian Ocean suggests that the British withdrawal is unlikely to signify the end of attempts by extra-regional major powers to maintain positions of influence in these waters.

Although there is little immediate prospect of any renewed attempt at creating an *Indonesia Raja* along the lines of the famous *Peta Mas* (golden map) of President Sukarno's Djakarta palace, which united south Thailand, the Malayan peninsula and the Philippines with Indonesia, the size and influence of Indonesia's armed forces continues to give rise to concern. Despite its repudiation of the PKI, Indonesia is anxious that its forces should not be enrolled in an anti-communist front such as that envisaged in ASPAC, although it may eventually prove willing to cooperate with Malaysia and Singapore in the defence of the vital Malacca Straits. While the Army is the principal safeguard against any renewed communist *coup*, economic recovery requires that the privileges of the officer class and the share of the budget consumed by the armed forces be kept to minimal levels. Yet the new regime came to power through the Army, and in view of his efforts to avoid a possible civil war sparked off by the communist underground and supporters of the deposed President Sukarno, General Suharto cannot afford to alienate too many of his fellow officers, many of whom are not professional military men but position-seeking adventurers, who early discovered that the armed forces offer excellent opportunities for personal advancement.

By mid-1968 there were some signs of improvement in the Indonesian economic situation. Although the thorny question of compensation for the earlier nationalizations remained unsettled, many of the foreign estate and manufacturing companies were preparing to resume operations in the country, and there was evidence of the adoption of more realistic pricing policies which reflected the scarcity of consumer goods; in May the price of gasoline was raised some 400 per cent. But these favourable portents hardly outweighed the heavy sense of crisis which had led General Suharto himself to proclaim that '1968 may be the year of final hope or the limit of the people's patience, which has now been exhausted'. Rising prices outraged the student population, whose opposition had finally destroyed the charismatic appeal of President Sukarno, and the administration knows that it has to achieve results quickly if it is to survive. Yet a large increase in personal consumption is not within the bounds of possibility. Unquestionably the government's most important task is to give some positive demonstration of its professional competence and of a real concern for the public welfare. This clearly requires that appointments should be made on the basis of merit and ability, and that important positions should not be filled by influential people already discharging, and ineffectively, a multiplicity of other jobs, a situation that has long been encouraged by the low salaries paid to public servants. Few Indonesians, however, believe that serious attempts are being made to curb the activities of speculators and black marketeers, and in many parts of the country there is extreme public resentment at the government's continued tolerance of the illegal levies made by members of the armed forces on almost all economic activity.

President Sukarno's excesses have often been excused on the grounds that he forged a single nation, but it was a very fragile unity that the Suharto administration inherited, and much clearly depends on the success of the economic stabilization plan. Liberalization of the so-called Export Bonus (BE) system, by which exporters are allowed to retain a larger share of the foreign exchange proceeds of their exports, and greater allocations of funds to provincial authorities, have gone some way to meeting the legitimate demands of the Provinces for a claim on the country's resources more in keeping with their contribution to the economy.

Not surprisingly, Indonesia's creditors have insisted on complete suppression of the illegal barter trade with Singapore, Malaysia and the Philippines. Yet it is striking how quickly the traditional patterns of commercial intercourse in the region of Malacca Straits, which were always east to west, re-established themselves with the creation of independent Indonesia, and the artificial division of the Malay world originating in the Treaty of London of 1824 which separated British and Dutch spheres of influence, has in large part been rejected by the peoples of east Sumatra, who, indeed, continued to carry on their barter trade even during the Malaysian confrontation. Moreover, the long-term deterioration in the terms of trade between rubber and other export crops on the one hand and rice on the other in favour of rice-producing Java, is another heavy penalty that the Outer Islands have incurred through their political link to Batavia and Djakarta. If the economy can do no better than stagger along in the manner of the past two decades, pressures for a greater measure of regional autonomy are likely to grow. Only an accelerated pace of economic development, which must inevitably involve rigorous implementation of plans to improve the efficiency of export industries, seems capable of welding together the widely scattered parts of Indonesia with their very varying cultural and economic interests, and in its absence some looser form of confederation may prove unavoidable.

The future of the Indochinese states clearly depends on the outcome of the Vietnam war, and although the Paris talks between North Vietnam and the United States begun in mid-1968 may lead to an earlier peace, it is highly likely that the struggle will be resolved one way or the other in the early Seventies. South Vietnam may eventually possess a government containing representatives of the Vietcong, or National Liberation Front, but the United States and its allies are unlikely to agree to any settlement that would enable the communists speedily to capture key ministries such as security and the armed forces, unless there is clear evidence that this is in accordance with the wishes of a majority of the population. South Vietnam, in essence, must have an economy and political organization whose orientation is either to the communist or non-communist world; it cannot be betwixt and between. Probably the most likely outcome is a Korea-type agreement guaranteed by the Great Powers—although China is scarcely likely to agree to anything supported by the USSR—perhaps involving territorial readjustments. But if the South can achieve the will to defend itself in the manner of South Korea and can enjoy some years of peaceful conditions, there is no real reason why in the Seventies it should not repeat South Korea's past economic success. While South Vietnam's military government has alienated the sympathies of many Western countries, it cannot be too strongly urged that any form of government can produce a high rate of economic growth if it so wishes; military regimes exist in Pakistan, Taiwan, South Korea and Thailand, all of which have achieved high rates of growth.

Nevertheless, the Politburo of North Vietnam considers itself heir to all Indochina, for the Vietminh also included Lao and Khmer units in its struggle against the French. Hanoi already effectively controls some two-thirds of Laos, and in the event of a communist take-over of South Vietnam, the engulfment of the remainder could take place at any time Hanoi wished. Cambodia, which has never made any secret of its profound suspicion of South Vietnam, can have little doubt that a unitary Vietnam under communist control would be no more likely to jettison Vietnamese historical traditions than China or Russia have been to repudiate theirs; hence the deference shown by Cambodia's Chief of State to Peking, which alone, so Prince Sihanouk believes, can ensure Cambodia's continuing independence. But Cambodia is no more likely to be reconciled to the loss of its Khmer people in what is now South Vietnam if a communist government rules in Saigon, than Hungary is to the loss of the Szeklers of Transylvania to Romania, where despite protestations of fraternity between the two governments, the Romanian attempt to eradicate every vestige of Hungarian influence is building up a store of animosity which will one day burst into the open. Communism, in short, has found the elimination of national antagonisms an impossible task, although it attempts to use nationalist aspirations for its own ends. Those Western political observers who, impressed with Vietnamese resistance to Chinese encroachments over the centuries, have urged that a united communist Vietnam would constitute another focus of 'polycentrism' subservient neither to Peking nor Moscow, should weigh the consequences of such an eventuality for the remaining successor states of Indochina.

Apart from poor economic performance, throughout inward-looking Southeast Asia runs a common theme. The national revolutions which led to independence were part of broader social revolutions whose aims basically were to create a new form of society: a new man in a new world in North Vietnam (although experience shows that communist societies are among the least egalitarian on earth and that privilege is even more entrenched than in the open societies of the West); 'socialisme à la Indonesia'; and *Pyidawtha*, the 'happy state'. On the face of it, these attempts in ex-colonial territories to achieve a broader measure of social justice have much to commend them; in practice, however, they have led only to frustration and disillusionment. The whole history of human society is that greater social justice follows and does not precede economic advance. Poor societies by their very nature cannot be other than highly inegalitarian, and to press on as rapidly as possible with the modernization of the economy is both a quicker and more effective way of getting to grips with the still largely unresolved problem of achieving a greater measure of social justice.

This fact appears to have been perceived in the economically more progressive countries of Southeast Asia, whose national development plans have included provisions for improving the lot of particular groups or regions broadly within the existing institutional framework. True, in both Malaysia and Thailand, this remedial investment has so far produced a disappointing return, but it has been necessary to preserve the general climate for further economic growth, and in both countries a breakthrough in resolving the problems arising from ethnic or regional imbalances in the distribution of income may be achieved in the near future. Malaysia's communal differences certainly possess a potential capacity for total disaster, but until the elections of 1969 the government had been very successful in playing down such tensions, and on the ground the situation appeared very much more encouraging than it appeared on paper. In large part this situation was the result of the very high standing of the Prime Minister, Tunku Abdul Rahman, with the non-Malay communities and his profound abhorrence of racial intolerance, and as it is inconceivable in the foreseeable future that a non-Malay could become Prime Minister of the Malaysian state, it is essential that the Tunku's successors should inherit this multiracial appeal. The Tunku's image as the tolerant and kindly supernumerary English gentleman, whose word is his bond, certainly contrasts with the smooth professionalism of most other members of the Malaysian and Singapore governments, but before mid-1969 there appeared little real reason for pessimism. In both countries there is an acute awareness that conditions into the Seventies are likely to be much less favourable for continued rapid economic growth, and that all prospects of achieving this end will be gravely jeopardized by a hardening of communal divisions. Unfortunately, the communal situation in the Malayan peninsula will also depend in some degree on what happens in neighbouring Indonesia, where the Ampera government's failure to provide adequate protection to the Chinese community contrasted starkly with its declared recognition of the vital contribution made by Chinese capital and enterprise to the national economy. Moreover, the appeal of virtually all opposition parties in Malaya is a scarcely disguised communalism, so that cooperation between them is almost impossible by definition. The lack of effective oppositions in Kuala Lumpur and Singapore makes both governments oversensitive to criticism, particularly from each other, and poses serious problems for the future of political democracy in the peninsula.

Yet the week following the federal elections of May 1969, in which although winning the election overall the Alliance lost many seats formerly held by its Malayan Chinese Association wing to Chinese opposition parties, suggested to many that in but a few days Malaysia had retrogressed from a difficult but not unpromising communal situation to one in which both major communities had passed beyond the point of no return in their rejection of mutual cooperation. The imposition in the wake of the Kuala Lumpur riots of a virtual dictatorship by the National Operations Council under the control of the Deputy Prime Minister, Tun Abdul Razak, the suspension of parliamentary and state governments and the reassertion of the absolute paramountcy of Malay interests, caused the government temporarily to forfeit all respect by the Chinese population. It is greatly to be hoped that the imposition of an all-Malay government proves short-lived, for without Chinese cooperation the Malaysian economy is doomed and the prospects of avoiding civil strife are remote.

Thailand's prospects are more closely related to the outcome of the Vietnam war than are those of Malaysia or the Philippines. But although the history of Thailand in modern times has shown the advantages of 'bending with the wind', it is scarcely conceivable that having struggled long and successfully to preserve its independence from the imperialisms of the West, the country is now prepared meekly to surrender its heritage to a new wave of imperialism from the East. Whether absolute monarchy or military dictatorship, Thailand has always been an authoritarian state. But even in Thailand the contradictions presented by an autocratic regime in a modernizing society are increasingly obvious, and possibly because it has been shamed by American insistence on some modification of the military regime in South Vietnam, whose shortcomings have cost that country much moral and material support in the West, Thailand appears slowly to be considering some more responsible government, and a beginning has been made with changes in local administration, which make provision for the first time since the early Thirties for elected representatives.

Yet responsible government, of course, is no guarantee of political and economic stability, and in some respects the Philippines presents a society in travail. The incidence of murder and other crimes of violence is distressingly high by the standards of say, Malaysia and Singapore, but it is probably little different from that of Ceylon, another country with an intense political democracy which has always stressed its peace-loving Buddhist institutions. One of the major handicaps of the Philippines has been its apparent inability to achieve continuity of administration, but the fact that no President so far has been re-elected has in part been the result of unfortunate accidents that have robbed the country of Presidents who might well have been re-elected, and President Marcos appeared in 1969 to have a reasonable chance of breaking with tradition. In 1967 the Philippines was able to dispense with net rice imports, only the second occasion since the end of World War II that this proved possible, and the prospective breakthrough in food production enhances opportunities for implementing long overdue changes in agrarian organization. The prospects of the Philippines would, of course, be greatly improved by a willingness of the Catholic church to come to terms with reality and for the Vatican to indicate its acceptance of the desirability of family limitation in poor countries. Such a pronouncement must surely come one day, and the sooner the better.

Trade, aid and regional cooperation

Aid and trade both provide foreign exchange for the prosecution of modernization plans, and Southeast Asia needs more of each. Partly for the reasons discussed earlier and partly because of a growing world liquidity problem, the flow of aid funds in real terms has remained virtually unaltered since 1961. Increasingly, bilateral aid has been tied by donors to the purchase of goods and services that create no charge on their balance-of-payments position, and it has sometimes been hard to distinguish between aid and export promotion. Moreover, aid has been granted on increasingly more severe terms; grants have become of less and less importance and loans have involved more onerous terms, so that future repayment of interest and principal may constitute a heavy charge on export earnings. The liquidity problem has had other important consequences in that the deflationary policies forced on many developed countries by the failure of world monetary reserves to expand *pari passu* with the increase in world trade, have resulted in heavy pressure on the prices of the primary products of the Third World. Thus, in spite of attempts to improve efficiency in export production, total earnings have often been reduced.

International aid to Southeast Asia is summarized in Table 10–1. On a per capita basis Southeast Asia has received much less aid than either Africa or Latin America, and much of what it has received has accrued to South Vietnam, where the developmental impact has been small. But if, as several eminent developmental economists have attempted to show, the fastest rate of economic growth is the best way to modernize, parts of Southeast Asia would appear to deserve much greater assistance than they have so far received. By concentrating aid on countries that have a good record of economic performance, pursue sensible economic policies and realistic development plans, and have competent administrations and hence a large 'absorptive capacity', these could relatively quickly be brought to the point of self-sustaining growth, whereupon aid could be switched to a second round of deserving countries, to which those countries that had attained 'take-off' could also contribute. But however attractive economically, such an aid policy is viewed with suspicion by donor countries which inevitably have to operate within rigid political constraints, and aid may be given where there is little possibility of any real developmental return. Countries with per capita incomes of $300 or more, or with large foreign exchange reserves, find it very much more difficult to obtain aid than those with incomes of $100 and minimal reserves, even though the former group of countries may be able to make very much better use of aid outlay. As the Malaysian Finance Minister, Mr Tan Siew Sin, justifiably pointed out, his country has been penalized for its economic virtue while Indonesia's profligacy is to be rewarded.

Table 10-1 *Official financial flows (disbursements) from OECD/DAC countries and multilateral agencies to Southeast Asia (million US $)*

	Average annual flow, 1960–64			1965			
	Bilateral	Multi-lateral	Total	Bilateral	Multi-lateral	Total	Aid per capita US $
Burma	28·9	3·3	32·2	16·1	−1·2*	14·9	0·6
Cambodia	22·4	1·1	23·5	8·5	2·8	11·3	1·8
Laos	39·3	0·5	39·8	67·5	0·7	68·2	34·2
Indonesia	102·3	3·9	106·2	41·2	1·6	42·8	0·4
Malaysia	15·9	3·2	19·1	20·6	13·8	34·4	4·3
Singapore	0·6	0·2	0·8	2·2	2·3	4·5	2·5
Philippines	38·8	5·4	44·2	90·9	18·3	109·2	3·2
Thailand	34·5	9·0	43·5	46·1	0·7	46·8	1·5
South Vietnam	201·0	0·2	201·2	313·4	2·2	315·6	19·6
Total	**483·7**	**26·8**	**510·5**	**606·5**	**41·2**	**647·7**	**2·9**
Africa	1,523·4	124·6	1,648·0	1,484·6	216·6	1,701·2	6·0

* Result of a loan repayment

Source: *Geographical Distribution of Financial Flows to Less Developed Countries, 1960–64;* ditto *1965,* OECD, Paris

In short, the primary consideration in granting aid so far has not been, as the economist would argue, to obtain the maximum development per unit of aid investment; but it can scarcely fail to be a consideration of progressively greater importance in the future. As there is little likelihood of an early increase in aid or of any amelioration of the terms under which it is granted, to stretch limited aid-resources further will involve greater selectivity in their allocation in favour of stable well-administered countries with good economic records. Malaysia, Thailand and Singapore are thus pre-eminently suitable candidates for additional aid; all three countries are 'credit worthy' in the eyes of the World Bank, from which each has borrowed heavily on the Bank's regular, and relatively severe, terms. Southeast Asia hopes that it will do better from the new Asian Development Bank's soft-loan wing than it has from the International Development Association (IDA), the soft-loan associate of the World Bank; nevertheless it is likely to be disappointed. Indonesia, however, appears certain to receive additional aid on relatively soft terms, both from individual donors and particularly from Japan, and from multilateral sources.

That Japan's interests in Southeast Asia can hardly fail to grow in the future, has already received comment; Asian countries look more and more to Japan, the first country in the continent to achieve a society of mass affluence, to provide the assistance to resolve their own pressing developmental problems. So far Tokyo has shown no great enthusiasm for adopting the role of leader of an Asian economic revolution, and its capital aid has largely consisted of almost bare-faced export promotion on distinctly severe terms. Its technical assistance in Southeast Asia, however, has been of high quality, although very limited in quantity. As it is becoming progressively more difficult for Japan to maintain the fiction that it is still a relatively poor nation beset with chronic balance-of-payments difficulties, an argument that Japan also uses to counter pressure for greater liberalization of its trade policy, it is virtually certain that Japanese aid will increase, and the goal of one per cent of national income which was declared the minimum target for donor nations in the UN Development Decade 1960–70, has been accepted by Tokyo as the aid target by 1970. How much of this additional aid will flow to Southeast Asia is conjectural. But despite their past disappointments, Japanese industrialists can be expected to press the claims of Indonesia, for Japan is Indonesia's largest creditor in the non-communist world.

Australia, however, is another country whose influence seems destined to grow in the region, and which will probably provide more funds for Southeast Asian development. In view of the country's wealth and high rate of economic growth, Australian aid is pathetically small, and in terms of the share of aid in GNP, Australia is one of the more parsimonious members of the group of donor countries that constitute the Development Assistance Committee (DAC) of the OECD. Despite its past discriminatory immigration policy, Australia has created a good image in Asia, and Britain's withdrawal of its east of Suez forces and the possibility that the United States may be contemplating a substantial disengagement in Southeast Asia, are compelling a major revaluation of Australia's defence needs and strategy. In this reappraisal, the situation in the 'near north' is critical; together with Britain and New Zealand, Australia has pledged assistance to enlarge the capacity of Malaysia and Singapore to defend themselves, and it is particularly anxious to remain on good terms with Indonesia, with which it shares a common frontier in New Guinea. Commercial considerations reinforce strategic needs, for it is largely to an expanding Asian market that Australia looks to find compensation for the potential loss of the preferences that its primary products have long enjoyed in the British market, should Britain succeed in its application to be admitted to the European Economic Community.

The importance of an expanding foreign trade in facilitating the developmental process has repeatedly been emphasized, but the impact of fluctuating export incomes, so the leaders of less developed countries claim, has created great difficulties for their modernization plans. Thus there has arisen a demand for some kind of compensatory financing which would provide additional funds to developing countries whenever export proceeds fell below reasonable expectations. But apart from the very great practical difficulties of drawing up and operating a general plan for compensatory financing, there is growing evidence that the fluctuations of the export earnings of developing countries are relatively no greater than those of developed countries, and the effects of such fluctuations on their national economies is less serious than has been supposed.[2] Broadly similar difficulties attend the construction and operation of International Commodity Agreements; the list of commodities that appear best suited for such agreements is not large, and few of these are of major significance to Southeast Asia.[3] The principal effects of the International Tin Agreement have probably been to encourage the development and use of substitute materials, and to maintain high-cost producers in business. On the whole it would appear very much more satisfactory to allocate aid on the basis of the record of the potential recipient's whole economy, rather than to endeavour to augment the flow of resources to developing countries through complex schemes that limit attention only to their export position.

Might not Southeast Asia be able to extract greater concessions from the developed world and greatly accelerate its own economic development through greater regional cooperation or even integration? It is worth noting that the concept of Southeast Asia, which so far has largely been a convenience for the

[2] *The case is convincingly argued in Alasdair MacBean,* Export Instability and Economic Development, *Allen & Unwin, London, 1966.*

[3] *Commodities best suited for such agreements are those which have few substitutes and which form a small part of consumer expenditure in developed countries; the price elasticity of demand should also be low. Coffee, tea, cocoa and sugar possess more of these desirable attributes than most other commodities, but the history of control schemes for these commodities is very discouraging.*

West, is slowly beginning to have significance for the peoples of the region themselves. The respective national élites on whom falls the major responsibility for
shaping its destiny, are increasingly conscious that many of their problems are
also shared by neighbours, and although what might be termed a Southeast Asian
view has yet to emerge in the councils of international organizations, its appearance
seems quite probable in the not distant future. The advantages of closer regional
integration are, on the face of it, potentially very great. Centralized plants or
facilities serving the whole of the region could achieve the economies of scale
which are necessary for competitive efficiency and are out of the question in a
national context. To expand the supply of the high-level man-power required
for the implementation of national development plans, a conference of Southeast Asian Ministers of Education and Science (SEAMES) in Kuala Lumpur
in 1966 agreed to establish a series of specialized institutions for post-graduate
training and research in Engineering, Mathematics and the teaching of English,
which would serve the whole of the region. As the greatest single impediment to
both the formulation and execution of development plans is probably the limited
supply of trained man-power, the benefits of such a development could be very
great, and it is scarcely surprising that the scheme has attracted the support of
donor countries including the United States, which in 1966 announced its intention of channelling most of its aid to Southeast Asia to undertakings that would
promote regional cooperation.

Regional cooperation in Southeast Asia is part of the wider interests of such
bodies as the Economic Commission for Asia and the Far East and its creation,
the Asia Development Bank, and involves several regional organizations such as
ASA, ASPAC, ASEAN, SEATO and the Mekong Committee of ECAFE,
some of which also include extra-regional members. Throughout much of Asia,
in fact, there is a strong desire for greater cooperation between member states of
the most populous continent, but much of this is wishful thinking which ignores
the more obvious difficulties. The primary motivation for greater Asian integration is political rather than economic. Asians ardently desire to achieve a position
in the councils of the world that they feel their populations justify, and the mood
of frustration and bitterness felt by the Third World at its powerlessness to affect
the course of events, and its inability to extract any substantial concessions from
the tiny minority of the world's population that constitutes the developed nations,
was clearly discernible at both UNCTAD conferences. But there is little reason
for believing that closer integration, even if it could be achieved, would be a
stimulus to Asian economic development at present; its more likely consequences
would be to retard the rate of growth of those countries performing reasonably
well. Asians tend to overlook the fact that the success of the European Economic
Community, the model for most regional associations, was created from states
already at a high level of economic development, and there are numerous economists who believe that a greater degree of regional economic cooperation in Asia

should follow, and indeed is likely to be a logical outcome of, a higher degree of national economic development. The place where such cooperation should begin, is quite clearly the Malayan peninsula, for Malaysia and Singapore are not only economically the most advanced states of Southeast Asia, but share a common economic heritage. Having no choice at present but to cooperate in devising a common defence policy, it is to be hoped that a way may now be found to over-come the political differences and personality clashes that have divided their leaders, and that their respective development plans can be closely co-ordinated. Such harmonization would go far to restoring the old economic unity of the peninsula, which could be further extended by close cooperation with Thailand, whose southern provinces in particular would greatly benefit from the application of much Malayan experience.

As noted in the opening chapter, cooperation between the economically advanced countries of outward-looking Southeast Asia was the broad strategy of ASA, an organization that virtually expired through differences between the Philippines and Malaysia over Sabah. On the face of it, its successor, ASEAN, appears unlikely to develop into an active and healthy progeny; no solution to the Sabah *impasse* appears in sight, and Indonesia, for whose accommodation in a regional association the new organization was largely created, must bend all its energies towards resolving its own pressing internal economic problems. Most of the regional organizations listed above have minimal secretariats and accommoda-tion, an indication of the real importance attached to them by member states. But if Southeast Asia can be granted a decade of continued economic growth and free-dom from molestation by outside powers, the prospects for closer regional inte-gration would be greatly improved.

Selected bibliography

Works of major regional as well as of national significance have been placed in section **A**, which should be consulted before the national section **B**.

(A) THE REGION

Abrams, Charles: *Housing in the Modern World*, Faber, London, 1964. (Originally published as *Man's Struggle for Shelter in an Urbanizing World*, Massachusetts Institute of Technology Press, Cambridge, Mass., 1964)

Allen, G. C. and Audrey G. Donnithorne: *Western Enterprise in Indonesia and Malaya*, Allen & Unwin, London, 1957

Angladette, A.: *Le Riz*, Maisonneuve & Larose, Paris, 1965

Asia's Economic Growth and Intra-Regional Cooperation, Asian Institute of Economic Affairs, Tokyo, 1967

Asian Development and Trade Liberalization, United Nations, Economic Commission for Asia and the Far East, New York, 1965

Asian Textile Annual, Far Eastern Economic Review, Hong Kong, periodically

Bauer, P. T.: *The Rubber Industry: A Study in Monopoly and Competition*, Longmans, London, 1948

————: *Report on a Visit to the Rubber Growing Smallholders of Malaya*, HMSO, London, 1948

van Bemmelen, R. W.: *The Geology of Indonesia*, 2 vols., Government Printing Office, The Hague, 1949

Boeke, J. H.: *Economics and Economic Policy of Dual Societies*, H. D. Tjeenk Willink, Haarlem, 1953, and Institute of Pacific Relations, New York, 1954

Breese, Gerald: *Urbanization in Newly Developing Countries*, Prentice-Hall, Englewood Cliffs, 1966

Britain and the Developing Countries: South and Southeast Asia, HMSO, London, 1966

Broek, J. O. M.: 'Diversity and unity in Southeast Asia', *Geographical Review*, vol. 34, 1944, pp. 175-95

Burkill, I. H.: *A Dictionary of the Economic Products of the Malay Peninsula*, 2 vols., Ministry of Agriculture and Cooperatives, Kuala Lumpur, 1966

Burling, R.: *Hill Farms and Padi Fields: Life in Mainland Southeast Asia*, Prentice-Hall, Englewood Cliffs, 1965

Butwell, Richard A.: *Southeast Asia Today and Tomorrow*, Frederick Praeger, New York, rev. edn., 1964

Carter, G. F. and R. L. Pendleton: 'The humid soil: process and time,' *Geographical Review*, vol. 46, 1956, pp. 488–507

Chang Jen Hu: 'The agricultural potential of the humid tropics,' *Geographical Review*, vol. 58, 1968, pp. 333–61

Coal and Iron Resources of Asia and the Far East, United Nations, Economic Commission for Asia and the Far East, Bangkok, 1952

Colombo Plan Annual Report, HMSO, London, annually

Committee for the Coordination of Investigations of the Lower Mekong Basin Annual Report, United Nations, Economic Commission for Asia and the Far East, Bangkok, annually

Conklin, H.: *Hanunoo Agriculture in the Philippines*, FAO, Rome, 1957

Continental Southeast Asia: Three Monthly Economic Review, Economist Intelligence Unit, London, quarterly

Courtenay, P. P.: 'Changing patterns in the tin mining and smelting industry of Southeast Asia,' *Journal of Tropical Geography*, vol. 25, 1967, pp. 8–17

Cowan, C. D. (ed.): *Economic Development of Southeast Asia*, Allen & Unwin, London, and Frederick Praeger, New York, 1964

Crane, David: 'Tin tabulations,' *Far Eastern Economic Review*, vol. 57, 1967, pp. 421–4

Dale, W. L.: 'Wind and drift currents in the South China Sea,' *Malayan Journal of Tropical Geography*, vol. 8, 1956, pp. 1–31

Davis, Kingsley and Hilda H. Golden: 'Urbanization and the development of pre-industrial areas,' *Economic Development and Cultural Change*, vol. 3, 1954, pp. 6–26

Development of Water Resources in the Lower Mekong Basin, Flood Control Series No. 12, United Nations, Economic Commission for Asia and the Far East, Bangkok, 1957

Dobby, E. H. G.: *Southeast Asia*, University of London Press, 1960

Dumont, René: *Types of Rural Economy*, Methuen, London, 1957

Dwyer, D. J.: 'The problem of in-migration and squatter settlement in Asian cities: two case studies, Manila and Victoria-Kowloon,' *Asian Studies*, vol. 2, 1962, pp. 145–69

East, W. G. and O. H. K. Spate: *The Changing Map of Asia*, Methuen, London, 1961

Economic Bulletin for Asia and the Far East, United Nations, Economic Commission for Asia and the Far East, Bangkok, quarterly

Economic Research Bureau, Gadjah Mada University: 'The batik industry in Central Java,' *Ekonomi dan Keuangan Indonesia*, vol. 11, 1958, pp. 345–501

Economic Survey of Asia and the Far East, United Nations, Economic Commission for Asia and the Far East, Bangkok, annually

Electric Power in Asia and the Far East 1964, United Nations, Economic Commission for Asia and the Far East, Bangkok, 1966

FAO Commodity Review, FAO, Rome, annually

FAO Monthly Bulletin of Economics and Statistics, FAO, Rome, monthly

Far Eastern Economic Review Year Book, Hong Kong, annually

Fisher, Charles A.: 'The Greater East Asia co-prosperity sphere,' *Geographical Journal*, vol. 115, 1950, pp. 179–93

——: 'Southeast Asia: the Balkans of the Orient?,' *Geography*, vol. 47, 1962, pp. 347–67

——: 'The Malaysian Federation, Indonesia and the Philippines,' *Geographical Journal*, vol. 129, 1963, pp. 311–26

————: *South-East Asia*, Methuen, London, rev. edn., 1966

Freeman, J. D.: *Iban Agriculture: A Report on the Shifting Agriculture of Hill Rice by the Iban of Sarawak*, HMSO, London, 1955

Fryer, D. W.: 'The million city in Southeast Asia,' *Geographical Review*, vol. 43, 1953, pp. 474–94

————: 'The development of cottage and small-scale industries in Malaya and in South-East Asia,' *Journal of Tropical Geography*, vol. 17, 1963, pp. 92–98

Future Population Estimates by Sex and Age, Report 3. The Population of Southeast Asia (including Ceylon and China: Taiwan) 1959–1980, United Nations, Department of Economic and Social Affairs, New York, 1958

Geertz, Clifford: *Agricultural Involution: The Process of Ecological Change in Indonesia*, University of California Press, Berkeley and Los Angeles, 1963

George, Ted: 'Tin: is the price too high?,' *Far Eastern Economic Review*, vol. 53, 1966, pp. 321–4

Ginsburg, Norton S.: 'The Great City of Southeast Asia,' *American Journal of Sociology*, vol. 40, 1955, pp. 455–62

————: *Atlas of Economic Development*, University of Chicago Press, Chicago, 1961

Gourou, Pierre (*trans.* E. D. Laborde): *The Tropical World*, Longmans, London, 1953

Grist, D. H.: *Rice*, Longmans, London, 1959

van Hall, C. J. J. and J. van de Koppel (eds.): *De Landbouw in den Indischen Archipel*, 4 vols., van Hoeve, s'Gravenhage, 1946

Hamzah Sendut: 'Contemporary urbanization in Malaysia, *Asian Survey*, vol. 6, 1966, pp. 484–92

Hanna, Willard A.: *Eight Nation Makers: Southeast Asia's Charismatic Leaders*, St Martin's Press, New York, 1964

Hauser, Philip M. (ed.): *Urbanization in Asia and the Far East*, UNESCO, Tensions and Technology Series, Calcutta, 1957

———— and Leo F. Schnore (eds.): *The Study of Urbanization*, Wiley, New York, 1965

Heeren, H. J. (ed.): 'The urbanization of Djakarta,' *Ekonomi dan Keuangan Indonesia*, vol. 8, 1955, pp. 696–736

Heine-Geldern, Robert: 'Conceptions of state and kingship in Southeast Asia,' *Far Eastern Quarterly*, vol. 2, 1942, pp. 15–30

Higgins, Benjamin: *Economic Development*, Norton & Company, New York, 1959

————: 'The dualistic theory of underdeveloped areas,' *Ekonomi dan Keuangan Indonesia*, vol. 8, 1955, pp. 58–78. (Reprinted in *Economic Development and Cultural Change*, vol. 4, 1956, pp. 99–115)

————: 'Western enterprise in the economic development of Southeast Asia: a review article,' *Pacific Affairs*, vol. 31, 1958, pp. 74–87

Hoselitz, Bert F.: 'Generative and parasitic cities,' *Economic Development and Cultural Change*, vol. 3, 1954, pp. 278–94

Industrial Developments in Asia and the Far East, 4 vols., United Nations, Economic Commission for Asia and the Far East, Bangkok, 1966

International Bank for Reconstruction and Development: *World Bank Atlas*, 3rd edn., 1969

Jackson, James C.: 'Chinese agricultural pioneering in Singapore and Johore,' *Journal of the Malaysian Branch, Royal Asiatic Society*, vol. 38, 1965, pp. 77–105

————: *Planters and Speculators: Chinese and European Agricultural Enterprise in Malaya 1786–1921*, University of Malaya Press, Kuala Lumpur, 1968

Johnson, Harry G.: *Economic Policy towards Less Developed Countries*, Frederick Praeger, New York, 1967

Jacoby, E. H.: *Agrarian Unrest in Southeast Asia*, Asia Publishing House, London and New York, 1961

Lampard, Eric E.: 'The history of cities in the economically advanced areas,' *Economic Development and Cultural Change*, vol. 3, 1954, pp. 81–136

Lebar, Frank, *et al.*: *Ethnic Groups in Mainland Southeast Asia*, HRAF Press, New Haven, 1964

Lewis, W. Arthur: *Theory of Economic Growth*, Allen & Unwin, London, 1960

MacBean Alasdair: *Export Instability and Economic Development*, Allen & Unwin, London, 1966

McGee, T. G.: 'Aspects of the political geography of Southeast Asia,' *Pacific Viewpoint*, vol. 1, 1960, pp. 39–58

————: *The Southeast Asian City*, G. Bell, London, and Frederick Praeger, New York, 1967

'Mechanization of small-scale industries,' *Ekonomi dan Keuangan Indonesia*, vol. 11, 1958, pp. 158–217

Milone, Pauline D.: 'Contemporary urbanization in Indonesia,' *Asian Survey*, vol. 4, 1964, pp. 1000–1012

Mining Development in Asia and the Far East 1945–1965, Mineral Resources Development Series no. 27, United Nations, Economic Commission for Asia and the Far East, New York, 1967

'Modernization of small industries in Asia,' *Economic Bulletin for Asia and the Far East*, vol. 11, no. 1, 1961, pp. 24–40

Mohr, E. J. C.: *Soils of the Equatorial Regions*, Edwards, Ann Arbor, 1944

Murphey, Rhoads: 'New capitals of Asia,' *Economic Development and Cultural Change*, vol. 5, 1957, pp. 216–43

Myint, Hla: 'Inward and outward looking countries of Southeast Asia and the economic future of the region,' in *Symposium on Japan's Future in Southeast Asia*, Center for Southeast Asian Studies, Kyoto University, 1963. (Reprinted in *Malayan Economic Review*, vol. 12, 1967, pp. 1–13)

Myrdal, Gunnar: *Asian Drama: An Inquiry into the Poverty of Nations*, 3 vols., The Twentieth Century Fund, New York, 1968

Onslow, Cranley (ed.): *Asian Economic Development*, Weidenfeld & Nicholson, London, 1965

Paauw, Douglas S.: 'Economic progress in Southeast Asia,' *Journal of Asian Studies*, vol. 23, 1963, pp. 69–92

Population of Southeast Asia 1950–1980, United Nations, Department of Economic and Social Affairs, New York, 1958

'Population trends and related problems of economic development in the ECAFE region,' *Economic Bulletin for Asia and the Far East*, vol. 10, no. 1, 1960, pp. 1–45

Pelzer, Karl J.: *Pioneer Settlement in the Asiatic Tropics*, American Geographic Society, New York, 1948

————: *Agriculture, Vegetation and Rational Land Utilization in the Humid Tropics*, Paper H.13, Ninth Pacific Science Congress, Bangkok, 1957 (mimeo.)

————: 'Man's role in changing the landscape of Southeast Asia,' *Journal of Asian Studies*, vol. 27, 1968, pp. 269–79

Plantation Crops, Commonwealth Economic Committee, London, annually

Preliminary Report on World Population Prospects as Assessed in 1963, United Nations, Department of Economic and Social Affairs, New York, 1964

Processing of Cassava and Cassava Production in Rural Industries, Agricultural Development Paper no. 54, FAO, Rome, 1956

Purcell, Victor: *Revolution in Southeast Asia*, Thames & Hudson, London, 1962

————: *The Chinese in Southeast Asia*, Oxford University Press, London, 2nd edn., 1965

Redfield R. and M. B. Singer: 'The cultural role of cities,' *Economic Development and Cultural Change*, vol. 3, 1954, pp. 53–73

Regional Economic Co-operation in Asia and the Far East. Report of the Second Ministerial Conference on Asian Economic Co-operation and the Asian Development Bank, United Nations, Economic Commission for Asia and the Far East, New York, 1966

'Regional trade co-operation,' *Economic Bulletin for Asia and the Far East*, vol. 11, no. 1, 1961, pp. 1–29

Report of Asian Population Conference and Selected Papers, United Nations, Department of Economic and Social Affairs, New York, 1964

Rice Report, FAO, Rome, monthly

Richards, P. W.: *The Tropical Rain Forest*, Cambridge University Press, 1957

Robequain, Charles (*trans.* E. D. Laborde): *Malaysia, Indonesia, Borneo and the Philippines*, Longmans, London, 1964

Role and Application of Electric Power in the Industrialization of Asia and the Far East, United Nations, Economic Commission for Asia and the Far East and Bureau of Technical Operations, New York, 1965

Rubber Statistics Bulletin, International Rubber Study Group, London, monthly

Sauer, Carl O.: *Agricultural Origins and Dispersals*, American Geographic Society, New York, 1952

Schaaf, C. Hart and Russell H. Fifield: *The Lower Mekong*, Van Nostrand, Princeton, 1963

Sewell, W. R. Derrick and Gilbert F. White: *The Lower Mekong: An Experiment in International River Control*, Carnegie Endowment for International Peace, New York, 1966

Sinai, I. R.: *The Challenge of Modernisation: The West's Impact on the Non-Western World*, Chatto & Windus, London, 1964

Spencer, Joseph E.: *Asia East by South*, Wiley, New York, 1955

————: *Shifting Cultivation in Southeast Asia*, University of California Press, Berkeley and Los Angeles, 1966

Staley, Eugene and Richard Morse: *Modern Small Industry for Developing Countries*, McGraw-Hill, New York, 1965

State of Food and Agriculture, FAO, Rome, annually

Statistical Yearbook, International Tin Council, London, annually

de Terra, G. J. A.: 'Farm systems in South-East Asia,' *Netherlands Journal of Agricultural Science*, vol. 6, 1958, pp. 157–81

Thomas, W. R. Jnr. (ed.): *Man's Role in Changing the Face of the Earth*, University of Chicago Press, Chicago, 1956

Timber Trends and Prospects in the Asia-Pacific Region, United Nations and FAO, Geneva, 1961

Tin Ore Resources of Asia and Australia, Mineral Resources Development Series no. 23, United Nations, Economic Commission for Asia and the Far East, New York, 1964

Trade Expansion and Economic Integration among Developing Countries, United Nations Conference on Trade and Development, New York, 1967

Umbgrove, J. H. F.: *Structural History of the East Indies*, Cambridge University Press, 1949

UNCTAD Commodity Survey, United Nations Conference on Trade and Development, New York, annually

Unger, Leonard: 'The Chinese in Southeast Asia,' *Geographical Review*, vol. 34, 1944 pp. 196–217

Vandenbosch, Amry and Richard A. Butwell: *The Changing Face of Southeast Asia*, University of Kentucky Press, Lexington, 1966

Vegetable Oils and Oilseeds, Commonwealth Economic Committee, London, annually

Wang Gungwu: *A Short History of the Nanyang Chinese*, Eastern Universities Press, Singapore, 1959

Ward, Barbara: 'Cash or credit crops,' *Economic Development and Cultural Change*, vol, 8, 1960, pp. 148–91

Water Resources Development in British Borneo, Federation of Malaya, Indonesia and Thailand, Flood Control Series no. 14, United Nations, Economic Commission for Asia and the Far East, Bangkok, 1959

Watters, R. F.: 'The nature of shifting cultivation,' *Pacific Viewpoint*, vol. 1, 1960, pp. 59–99

Wharton, Clifton R., Jnr.: 'The green revolution: cornucopia or Pandora's box?', *Foreign Affairs*, vol. 47, 1969, pp. 464–76

Wightman, David: *Towards Economic Cooperation in Asia*, Yale University Press, New Haven, 1963

Wint, Guy (ed.): *Asia: a Handbook*, Frederick Praeger, New York, 1966

Withington, W. A.: 'The Kotapradja, or King Cities of Indonesia,' *Pacific Viewpoint*, vol. 4, 1963, pp. 75–86

Wittfogel, Karl A.: *Oriental Despotism*, Yale University Press, New Haven, 1957

(B) THE NATIONS

Thailand

Andrews, J. M.: *Siam: Second Rural Economic Survey*, The Bangkok Times, 1935

Ayal, E. B.: 'Some crucial issues in Thailand's economic development,' *Pacific Affairs*, vol. 34, 1961, pp. 157–64

————: 'Thailand's Six Year Economic Development Plan,' *Asian Survey*, vol. 1, 1962, pp. 34–43

————: 'The impact of export taxes on the domestic economy of underdeveloped countries, with special reference to Thailand and Burma,' *Journal of Development Studies*, vol. 4, 1965, pp. 330–62

————: 'Private enterprise and economic progress in Thailand,' *Journal of Asian Studies*, vol. 26, 1966, pp. 5–14

Bank of Thailand Annual Economic Report, Bangkok, annually

Barton, T. E.: 'Growing rice in Thailand,' *Journal of Geography*, vol. 59, 1960, pp. 153–64

Blanchard, W. (ed.): *Thailand: Its People, Society and Culture*, HRAF Press, New Haven, 1958

Breitenbach, C. A.: *Crop Development in Thailand: A Report on Completion of Assignment*, Agency for International Development, Bangkok, 1964

Brown, L. R.: *Agricultural Diversification and Economic Development in Thailand*, USDA Foreign Agriculture Report no. 8, Washington, 1963

Cady, J. F.: *Thailand, Burma, Laos and Cambodia*, Prentice-Hall, Englewood Cliffs, 1965

Chaiyong Chuchart: *Rice Marketing in Thailand*, University Microfilms Inc., Ann Arbor and London, 1961

Committee on the Development of the Northeast: *The Northeast Development Plan 1962–66*, National Economic Development Board, Bangkok, n.d.

Coughlin, R. J.: *The Chinese in Modern Thailand*, Hong Kong University Press, Hong Kong, 1963

Credner, Wilhelm: *Siam, das Land der Thai*, J. Nagelshorn, Stuttgart, 1935

Economist Intelligence Unit: 'The rubber industry of Thailand,' *Rubber Trends*, no. 25, March 1965, pp. 13–18

FAO: *Mission to Thailand*, Washington, 1948

Fraser, Thomas F.: *Rusembilan: A Malay Fishing Village in Southern Thailand*, Cornell University Press, Ithaca, 1960

Freeman, Barbara A.: 'Reluctant planners,' *Far Eastern Economic Review*, vol. 56, 1967, pp. 415–16

Hanna, Willard A.: *Change in Chiengmai*, American Universities Field Staff, Southeast Asia Series, vol. 13, New York, 1965

Ingram, J. C.: *Economic Change in Thailand since 1950*, Stanford University Press, Stanford, 1964

———: 'Thailand's rice trade and the allocation of resources,' in Cowan, C. D. (ed.), *The Economic Development of Southeast Asia*, Allen & Unwin, London, and Frederick Praeger, New York, 1964

International Bank for Reconstruction and Development: *A Public Development Program for Thailand*, Johns Hopkins University Press, Baltimore, 1959

Janlekha, K. O.: *A Study of the Economy of a Rice Growing Village in Central Thailand*, Doctoral Dissectation Series no. 15, University Microfilms Inc., Ann Arbor and London, 1958

Judd, L. C.: *Dry Rice Agriculture in Northern Thailand*, Cornell University, Southeast Asia Program, Ithaca, 1964

Karnow, Stanley: 'Insurgency in Thailand: the looking glass war,' *Far Eastern Economic Review*, vol. 58, 1967, pp. 539–47

Kaufman, H. K.: *Bangkhuad: A Community Study in Thailand*, J. J. Augustin for the Association for Asian Studies, New York, 1960

Keyes, C. F.: *Status and Rank in a Thai-Lao Village*, Cornell University Press, Ithaca, 1964

———: *Isan: Regionalism in Northeast Thailand*, Cornell University, Southeast Asia Program, Ithaca, 1967

Kingshill, K.: *Ku Daeng, the Red Tomb: A Village Study in Northern Thailand*, The Siam Society, Bangkok, 1960

Ministry of Agriculture: *Thailand Economic Farm Survey*, Bangkok, 1953
————: *The Greater Chao Phraya Project*, Bangkok, 1957
————: *Agriculture in Thailand*, Bangkok, 1961

Moerman, Michael: 'Western culture and the Thai way of life,' *Asia*, Spring 1964, pp. 31–39

Muscat, R. J.: *Development Strategy in Thailand*, Frederick Praeger, New York, 1966

Nairn, R. C.: *International Aid to Thailand: The New Colonialism?*, Yale University Press, New Haven, 1966

National Economic Development Board: *Thailand National Economic Development Plan 1961–66*, Bangkok, 1964
————: *Thailand Second National Economic and Social Development Plan 1967–71*, Bangkok, 1966
————: *Summary of the Second Five Year Plan 1967–71*, Bangkok, 1966
————: *Evaluation of the First Six Year Plan 1961–66*, Bangkok, 1967

National Statistical Office: *Census of Agriculture 1960*, Bangkok, 1963
————: *Statistical Yearbook of Thailand*, Bangkok, annually

Nuechterlein, D. E.: *Thailand and the Struggle for Southeast Asia*, Cornell University Press, Ithaca, 1966

Nuttonson, M. Y.: *The Physical Environment and Agriculture of Thailand*, American Institute of Crop Ecology, Washington, 1963

Pendleton, Robert L.: *Thailand: Aspects of Land and Life*, Duell, Sloan and Pearce, New York, 1962

Phillips, H. P.: *Thai Peasant Personality*, University of California Press, Berkeley and Los Angeles, 1965

Report to the Government of Thailand on Internal Migration: International Labour Organization, Geneva, 1965

Riggs, Fred W.: *Thailand: The Modernization of a Bureaucratic Polity*, East-West Center Press, Honolulu, 1966

Sato, T.: *Field Crops in Thailand*, Center for Southeast Asian Studies, Kyoto University, 1966

Sharp, L. S. *et al.*: *Siamese Rice Village*, Cornell University Research Center, Bangkok, 1953

Silcock, T. H. (ed.): *Thailand: Social and Economic Studies in Development*, Australian National University Press, Canberra, 1967

Skinner, G. W.: *Chinese Society in Thailand*, Cornell University Press, Ithaca, 1957
————: *Leadership and Power in the Chinese Community in Thailand*, Cornell University Press, Ithaca, 1958

Standish, W. A.: 'South Thailand: Malay Moslim mixtures,' *Far Eastern Economic Review*, vol. 57, 1967, pp. 19–22

Starner, Frances L.: 'Northeast Thailand: troubled triangle,' *Far Eastern Economic Review*, vol. 56, 1967, pp. 659–63

Sternstein, L.: 'A critique of Thai population data,' *Pacific Viewpoint*, vol. 6, 1965, pp. 15–38
————: 'Settlement patterns in Thailand,' *Journal of Tropical Geography*, vol. 21, 1965, pp. 30–43

————: 'Aspects of agricultural land tenure in Thailand,' *Journal of Tropical Geography*, vol. 24, 1967, pp. 22–29

Textor, Robert B.: *From Peasant to Pedicab Driver*, Yale University, Southeast Asia Studies, New Haven, 1961

'The Thai rice export system,' *Far Eastern Economic Review*, vol. 34, 1961, pp. 73–74

Thisyamondol, P. *et al.*: *Agricultural Credit in Thailand*, Kasetsart University Press, Bangkok, 1965

Thompson, Virginia: *Thailand, the New Siam*, New York, 1941

US Government Printing Office: *Area Handbook for Thailand*, Washington, 1966

US Operations Mission to Thailand: *The Coordinated Program for Corn Development in Thailand*, Bangkok, 1965

————: *Thai-American Economic and Technical Cooperation*, Bangkok, 1965

Usher, D.: 'Alternative comparisons of agricultural and non-agricultural productivity in Thailand,' *Economica*, vol. 33, 1966, pp. 430–41

Van Roy, E.: 'Economic dualism and economic change among hill tribes in Thailand,' *Pacific Viewpoint*, vol. 7, 1966, pp. 151–69

————: 'The Malthusian squeeze on Thailand's rice economy,' *Asian Survey*, vol. 7, 1967, pp. 469–81

Vella, W. F.: *The Impact of the West on Government in Thailand*, University of California Press, Berkeley and Los Angeles, 1955

Watabe, T.: *Glutinous Rice in Thailand*, Center for Southeast Asian Studies, Kyoto University, 1967

de Young, J. E.: *Village Life in Modern Thailand*, University of California Press, Berkeley and Los Angeles, 1955

The Philippines

Araneta, S.: *Economic Re-examination of the Philippines*, Araneta Institute of Agriculture, Manila, 1953

Barrera, A.: 'Classification and utilization of some Philippine soils,' *Journal of Tropical Geography*, vol. 18, 1964, pp. 17–29

Berreman, Gerald D.: *The Philippines: A Survey of Current Social, Economic and Political Conditions*, Cornell University, Southeast Asia Program, Ithaca, 1956

Bureau of Census and Statistics: *Census of the Philippines 1960: Agriculture*, Manila, 1965

Castro, Alfonso B.: 'Policies and problems of the rice and corn production program,' *Economic Research Journal*, University of the East, Manila, vol. 11, 1964, pp. 29–38

Central Bank of the Philippines Annual Report, Manila, annually

Corpuz, Onofre: *The Philippines*, Prentice-Hall, Englewood Cliffs, 1965

Cutshall, Alden: 'Problems of land ownership in the Philippine Islands,' *Economic Geography*, vol. 28, 1952, pp. 31–36

————: *The Philippines: Nation of Islands*, Van Nostrand, Princeton, 1964

Dwyer, D. J.: 'Irrigation and land use problems in the Central Plain of Luzon,' *Geography*, vol. 45, 1964, pp. 236–46

Economist Intelligence Unit: *The Philippines: Three-Monthly Economic Review*, London, quarterly

Golay, Frank H.: *The Philippines: Public Policy and National Economic Development*, Cornell University Press, Ithaca, 1961

Golay, Frank H.: 'The nature of Philippine economic nationalism,' *Asia*, no. 1, 1964, pp. 13–25

Goodstein, Marvin E.: *The Pace and Pattern of Philippine Economic Growth 1938, 1948 and 1956*, Cornell University, Southeast Asia Program, Ithaca, 1962

Hart, D. V.: *The Philippine Plaza Complex: A Focal Point in Culture Change*, Yale University, Southeast Asia Studies, New Haven, 1955

Huke, Robert E.: *Shadows on the Land*, The Bookmark, Inc., Manila, 1963

Milne, R. S.: 'The role of government corporations in the Philippines,' *Pacific Affairs*, vol. 34, 1961, pp. 257–70

Multipurpose River Basin Development, Part 2A. Water Resource Development in Ceylon, China (Taiwan), Japan and the Philippines, United Nations, Economic Commission for Asia and the Far East, Bangkok, 1955

National Economic Council: *Three Year Program of Economic and Social Development 1959–60 to 1961–62*, Manila, 1962

————: Special Issue on Food and Agriculture (Coconuts, Sugar, Rice and Food), *Philippine Economy Bulletin*, vol. 2, May/June 1964

Pendleton, R. L. 'Land use and agriculture of Mindanao,' *Geographical Review*, vol. 32, 1942, pp. 180–210

Philippine Land Tenure Reform, Special Technical and Economic Mission, Mutual Security Agency, Manila, 1952

Philippine Studies Program, University of Chicago: *Area Handbook of the Philippines*, 4 vols., HRAF Press, New Haven, 1956

Polsky, Anthony: 'Politics in the Philippines: theatre of the absurd,' *Far Eastern Economic Review*, vol. 58, 1967, pp. 271–7

————: 'Murder in Manila,' *Far Eastern Economic Review*, vol. 58, 1967, pp. 409–12

Ravenholt, Albert: *Rural Reconstruction with Co-operatives*, American Universities Field Staff, Southeast Asia Series, vol. 15, no. 1, New York, 1967

————: *Miracles with Rice Technology*, American Universities Field Staff, Southeast Asia Series, vol. 15, no. 2, New York, 1967

Ronquillo, Bernadino: 'Rice—key to development,' *Far Eastern Economic Review*, vol. 56, 1967, pp. 129–34

————: 'Self sufficient,' *Far Eastern Economic Review*, vol. 58, 1967, p. 530

————: 'Unseen government,' *Far Eastern Economic Review*, vol. 58, 1967, pp. 576–7

————: 'Miracle in the Paddy,' *Far Eastern Economic Review*, vol. 59, 1968, pp. 265–6

Scaff, Alvin H.: *The Philippine Answer to Communism*, Stanford University Press, Stanford, 1955

Schul, Norman W.: 'A Philippine sugar cane plantation: land tenure and sugar cane production,' *Economic Geography*, vol. 43, 1967, pp. 157–69

————: 'Hacienda magnitude and Philippine sugar cane production,' *Asian Studies*, vol. 5, 1967, pp. 258–73

Sicat, Gerardo P. (ed.): *The Philippine Economy in the 1960's*, Institute of Economic Development and Research, University of the Philippines, Quezon City, 1964

Spencer, Joseph E.: 'Abacá and the Philippines,' *Economic Geography*, vol. 27, 1951, pp. 95–106

————: *Land and People in the Philippines*, University of California Press, Berkeley and Los Angeles, 1952

Starner, Frances L.: *Magsaysay and the Philippine Peasantry*, University of California Press, Berkeley and Los Angeles, 1961

————: 'The Huks of Central Luzon: report from Arayat,' *Far Eastern Economic Review*, vol. 58, 1967, pp. 144–9

Stifel, Laurence D.: *The Textile Industry: A Case Study of Industrial Development in the Philippines*, Cornell University, Southeast Asia Program, Ithaca, 1963

Tsutomo Takigawa: 'Land ownership and land reform problems in the Philippines,' *The Developing Economies*, vol. 2, 1964, pp. 58–77

Ullman, E. L.: 'Trade centers and tributary areas of the Philippines,' *Geographical Review*, vol. 50, 1960, pp. 203–18

Vandermeer, Canute: 'Corn cultivation in Cebu: An example of an advanced stage of migratory farming,' *Journal of Tropical Geography*, vol. 17, 1963, pp. 172–7

Venegas, Ernesto C. and V. W. Rutten: 'An analysis of rice production in the Philippines,' *Economic Research Journal*, University of the East, Manila, vol. 11, 1964, pp. 159–79

Wernstedt, Frank L.: *The Role and Importance of Philippine Interisland Trade*, Cornell University, Southeast Asia Program, Ithaca, 1957

————: 'Cebu: focus of Philippine interisland trade,' *Economic Geography*, vol. 32, 1957, pp. 336–46

———— and P. D. Simpkins: 'Growth and internal migration of the Philippine population, *Journal of Tropical Geography*, vol. 17, 1963, pp. 197–202

————: 'Migration and the settlement of Mindanao,' *Journal of Asian Studies*, vol. 35, 1965, pp. 83–103

———— and Joseph E. Spencer: *The Philippine Island World*, University of California Press, Berkeley and Los Angeles, 1967

Malaysia, Singapore and Brunei

Agricultural Policy in Sarawak and its Implementation, Government Printer, Kuching, 1963

Area Handbook for Malaysia and Singapore, Foreign Area Studies, The American University, Washington, 1965

Bank Negara Malaysia Annual Report, Kuala Lumpur, annually

Brandt, Karl *et al.*: *Policies and Measures Leading Towards Greater Diversification of the Agricultural Economy of the Federation of Malaya*, Government Printer, Kuala Lumpur, 1963

'Brunei—odd man out,' *Far Eastern Economic Review*, vol. 55, 1967, pp. 246–8

Bunting, Benjamin: *The Oil Palm in Malaya*, Ministry of Agriculture and Co-operatives, Kuala Lumpur, 1966

Caldwell, J. C.: 'Urban growth in Malaya: trends and implications,' *Population Review*, vol. 7, 1963, pp. 39–50

Clarkson, James: *The Cultural Ecology of a Chinese Village: Cameron Highlands, Malaysia*, Department of Geography, University of Chicago, Chicago, 1968

Courtenay, P. P.: 'International tin restriction and its effects on the Malayan tin mining industry,' *Geography*, vol. 46, 1961, pp. 287–315

Dobby, E. H. G.: 'The North Kedah Plain: a study in the environment of pioneering for rice cultivation,' *Economic Geography*, vol. 27, 1951, pp. 287–315

————: 'The Kelantan Delta,' *Geographical Review*, vol. 41, 1951, pp. 226–255

———— *et al.*: 'Padi landscapes of Malaya,' *Malayan Journal of Tropical Geography*, vol. 6, 1955, and vol. 10, 1957

Economist Intelligence Unit: *Malaysia, Singapore and Brunei: Three-Monthly Economic Review*, London, quarterly

Emerson, Rupert: *Malaysia: A Study in Direct and Indirect rule*, Macmillan, New York, 1937

Ferguson, D. S.: 'The Sungei Manik Irrigation Scheme,' *Malayan Journal of Tropical Geography*, vol. 2, 1954, pp. 9–16

Final Report of the Rice Committee, Government Printer, Kuala Lumpur, 1956

First Malaysia Plan 1966–1970, Government Printer, Kuala Lumpur, 1965

Firth, Raymond: *Malay Fishermen: Their Peasant Economy*, Kegan Paul, London, 1946

Fisk, E. K.: *Studies in the Rural Economy of South-East Asia*, University of London Press, Singapore, 1964

Fryer, D. W.: 'The plantation industries—the estates,' in Wang Gungwu (ed.), *Malaysia: A Survey*, Frederick Praeger, New York and London, 1964, pp. 227–45

——— and James C. Jackson: 'Peasant producers or urban planters? The Chinese rubber smallholders of Ulu Selangor,' *Pacific Viewpoint*, vol. 7, 1966, pp. 198–228

Ginsburg, Norton S. and Chester F. Roberts: *Malaya*, University of Washington Press, Seattle, 1958

Gray, B. S.: 'The potential of the oil palm in Malaya,' *Journal of Tropical Geography*, vol. 17, 1963, pp. 127–32

Greenwood, J. F.: 'Rubber smallholdings in the Federation of Malaya,' *Journal of Tropical Geography*, vol. 18, 1964, pp. 81–100

Grist, D. H.: *Agriculture in Malaya*, HMSO, London, 1936

Gullick, J. M.: *Malaya*, Ernest Benn, London, 1964

Hamzah Sendut: 'Resettlement villages in Malaya,' *Geography*, vol. 47, 1962, pp. 41–46

———: 'Patterns of urbanization in Malaya,' *Journal of Tropical Geography*, vol. 16, 1962, pp. 114–30

———: 'The structure of Kuala Lumpur: Malaysia's capital city,' *Town Planning Review*, vol. 36, 1965, pp. 125–38

Hanna, Willard A.: *The Formation of Malaysia: New Factor in World Politics*, American Universities Field Staff, New York, 1962–4

———: *The Kulai Oil Palm Scheme*, American Universities Field Staff Reports Service, Southeast Asia Series, vol. 13, no. 1, New York, 1965

Hill, A. H.: 'Kelantan padi planting,' *Journal of the Malayan Branch, Royal Asiatic Society*, vol. 24, 1951, pp. 56–76

Hill, R. D.: 'Agricultural land tenure in West Malaysia,' *Malayan Economic Review*, vol. 12, 1967, pp. 99–116

Ho, Robert: *Environment, Man and Development in Malaya*, Inaugural Lecture, University of Malaya, Kuala Lumpur, 1962

——— (ed.): *Guide to Tours*, Regional Conference of Southeast Asian Geographers, Kuala Lumpur, 1962 (mimeo.)

———: 'Land settlement projects in Malaya,' *Journal of Tropical Geography*, vol. 20, 1965, pp. 1–15

Hodder, B. W.: *Man in Malaya*, University of London Press, London, 1959

International Bank for Reconstruction and Development: *The Economic Development of Malaya*, Johns Hopkins University Press, Baltimore, 1956

Jackson, James C.: 'Smallholding cultivation of cash crops,' in Wang Gungwu (ed.), *Malaysia: A Survey*, Frederick Praeger, New York and London, 1964, pp. 246–73

————: 'Population changes in Selangor State 1850–1891,' *Journal of Tropical Geography*, vol. 19, 1964, pp. 42–57

————: *East Malaysia*, Longmans Australian Geographies, Unit 28, Adelaide, 1967

————: *Sarawak: A Geographical Survey of a Developing State*, University of London Press, London, 1968

Jackson, R. N.: *Immigrant Labour and the Development of Malaya 1786–1920*, Government Printer, Kuala Lumpur, 1961

Jones, L. W.: *Report on the Census of the Population Taken on June 15th 1960*, Government Printing Office, Kuching, 1962

Kahin, George M.: 'Malaysia and Indonesia,' *Pacific Affairs*, vol. 37, 1964, pp. 253–70

Keesing, D. B.: 'Thailand and Malaysia: a case for a Common Market,' *Malayan Economic Review*, vol. 10, 1965, pp. 102–113

Kernial Singh Sandhu: 'Emergency resettlement in Malaya,' *Journal of Tropical Geography*, vol. 18, 1964, pp. 157–83

Lee Yong Leng: 'Some factors in the development and planning of land use in British Borneo,' *Journal of Tropical Geography*, vol. 15, 1961, pp. 66–81

————: 'The population of British Borneo,' *Population Studies*, vol. 15, 1962, pp. 226–43

————: 'Agriculture in Sarawak,' *Journal of Tropical Geography*, vol. 21, 1965, pp. 21–29

————: *North Borneo (Sabah): A Study in Settlement Geography*, Eastern Universities Press, Singapore, 1965

————: 'The Dayaks of Sarawak,' *Journal of Tropical Geography*, vol. 23, 1966, pp. 28–38

Lim Chong Yah: *Economic Development of Modern Malaya*, Oxford University Press, Kuala Lumpur, 1967

Lim Tay Boh: *The Development of Singapore's Economy*, Eastern Universities Press, Singapore, 1960

———— (ed.): *Problems of the Malayan Economy*, Eastern Universities Press, Singapore, 1957

Ma, R. and You Poh Seng: 'Economic characteristics of the population of the Federation of Malaya,' *Malayan Economic Review*, vol. 5, 1960, pp. 10–45

Malaysia Official Yearbook (Buku Rasmi Tahunan) 1964, Government Printer, Kuala Lumpur, 1966

McGee, T. G.: 'The cultural role of cities: a case study of Kuala Lumpur,' *Journal of Tropical Geography*, vol. 17, 1963, pp. 178–93

———— and W. D. McTaggart: *Petaling Jaya: a socio-economic survey of a new town in Selangor, Malaysia*, Pacific Viewpoint Monograph no. 2, Wellington, 1967

Ness, Gayl D.: *Bureaucracy and Rural Development in Malaya*, University of California Press, Berkeley and Los Angeles, 1967

Neville, R. J. W.: 'The areal distribution of population in Singapore,' *Journal of Tropical Geography*, vol. 20, 1965, pp. 16–25

Ng Kay Fong *et al.*: 'Three farmers of Singapore: an example of the mechanics of specialised food production in an urban unit,' *Pacific Viewpoint*, vol. 7, 1966, pp. 169–97

Ooi Jin Bee: *Land, People and Economy in Malaya*, Longmans, London, 1963

O'Reilly, J. H.: 'An assessment of the Malayan tin mining industry in the twentieth century, *Journal of Tropical Geography*, vol. 17, 1963, pp. 72–78

Purcell, Victor: *The Chinese in Malaya*, Oxford University Press, London, 1948
————: *Malaysia*, Thames & Hudson, London, and Walker Press, New York, 1965
Puthucheary, J. J.: *Ownership and Control in the Malayan Economy*, Eastern Universities Press, Singapore, 1960
Report on Economic Aspects of Malaysia by a Mission of the International Bank for Reconstruction and Development (Rueff Report), Government Printer, Kuala Lumpur, 1963
Report on the Mission of Enquiry into the Rubber Industry of Malaya (Mudie Report), Government Printer, Kuala Lumpur, 1954
Rubber Research Institute of Malaya Annual Report, Government Printer, Kuala Lumpur, annually
Rubber Statistics Handbook, Department of Statistics, Kuala Lumpur, annually
Rutherford, John: 'Double cropping of wet padi in Penang, Malaya,' *Geographical Review*, vol. 56, 1966, pp. 239–55
Sabah Annual Report, Government Printer, Jesselton, annually
Sarawak Development Plan 1964–68, Government Printer, Kuching, 1963
Silcock, T. H.: *The Economy of Malaya*, Eastern Universities Press, Singapore, 1960
———— (ed.): *Readings in Malayan Economics*, Eastern Universities Press, Singapore, 1961
———— and E. K. Fisk (eds.): *The Political Economy of Independent Malaya*, Australian National University Press, Canberra, and University of California Press, Berkeley and Los Angeles, 1963
Singapore Annual Report 1964, Government Printing Office, Singapore, 1966
Singapore Development Plan 1961–64, Government Printing Office, Singapore, 1962
Singapore Trade and Industry, Straits Times Press, Singapore, monthly
Smith, T. E.: *Population Growth in Malaya*, Oxford University Press, London, 1952
State of Brunei Annual Report, Brunei Press, Kuala Belait, annually
Swift, M. G.: *Malay Peasant Society in Jelebu*, Athlone Press, London, 1965
Tan Ding Eing: *The Rice Industry in Malaya 1920–1940*, Malaya Publishing House, Singapore, 1963
Tan Koon Lin: *The Oilpalm Industry in Malaya*, Unpublished thesis for the degree of M.A. of the University of Malaya, Kuala Lumpur, 1965
Tregonning, K. K.: *North Borneo*, HMSO, London, 1960
Ungku Aziz et al.: *Subdivision of Estates in Malaya 1951–60*, 3 vols., Department of Economics, University of Malaya, Kuala Lumpur, 1962
Vlieland, C. A.: 'The 1947 census of Malaya,' *Pacific Affairs*, vol. 23, 1950, pp. 169–83
Voon Phin Keong: *Chinese Rubber Smallholders in Selangor*, Unpublished thesis for the degree of M.A. of the University of Malaya, Kuala Lumpur, 1967
————: 'The rubber smallholding industry of Selangor,' *Journal of Tropical Geography*, vol. 24, 1967, pp. 43–49
Wang Gungwu (ed.): *Malaysia: A Survey*, Frederick Praeger, New York and London, 1964
Ward, M. W.: 'Port Swettenham and its hinterland,' *Journal of Tropical Geography*, vol. 19, 1964, pp. 69–78
————: 'A review of problems and achievements in the economic development of independent Malaya', *Economic Geography*, vol. 44, 1968, pp. 326–42
Wheelwright, E. L.: *Industrialization in Malaya*, Melbourne University Press, 1964

Wikkramatileke, R.: 'Trends in settlement and economic development in eastern Malaya,' *Pacific Viewpoint*, vol. 3, 1962, pp. 27–50

———: 'Focus on Singapore,' *Journal of Tropical Geography*, vol. 20, 1965, pp. 73–83

Wilson, P. J.: *A Malay Village and Malaysia: Social Values and Rural Development*, HRAF Press, New Haven, 1967

Wilson, T. B.: *The Economics of Padi Production in North Malaya Part 1*, Government Printer, Kuala Lumpur, 1958

Wycherley, P. R.: 'Variations in the performance of Hevea in Malaya,' *Journal of Tropical Geography*, vol. 17, 1963, pp. 143–71

Yip Yat Hoong: 'Post war international tin control—with special reference to Malaysia,' *Kajian Ekonomi Malaya*, vol. 1, 1964, pp. 51–67

Indonesia

Admiralty, Naval Intelligence Division: *Netherlands Indies*, 2 vols., London, 1944

Bennet, Don C.: 'Three measurements of population pressure in Eastern Java,' *Ekonomi dan Keuangan Indonesia*, vol. 14, 1961, pp. 97–106

———: 'The basic food crops of Java and Madura,' *Economic Geography*, vol. 37, 1961, pp. 75–87

Bhatta, J. N.: *Regarding Internal Migration in Indonesia (with Special Reference to South Sumatra)*, Institute of Geography, Topographical Service of the Army, Publication no. 7, Djakarta, 1957

Boeke, J. H.: *The Evolution of the Netherlands Indies Economy*, Institute of Pacific Relations, New York, 1946

———: 'Indonesian economics: The concept of dualism in theory and practice', in Wertheim, W. F. and J. F. Kraal (eds) *Selected Studies in Indonesia*, vol. 6, van Hoeve, The Hague, 1961

Broek, J. O. M.: *The Economic Development of the Netherlands Indies*, Institute of Pacific Relations, New York, 1942

Castles, Lance: *Religion, Politics and Economic Behaviour in Java: The Kudus Cigarette Industry*, Yale University, Southeast Asia Studies, New Haven, 1967

Contenay, Jean: 'East Java: another Bloodbath,' *Far Eastern Economic Review*, vol. 58, 1967, pp. 357–67

———: 'The massacres in Java: heritage of blood,' *Far Eastern Economic Review*, vol. 58, 1967, pp. 509–14

Coolie Budget Commission (*trans.* Robert Van Niel): *Living Conditions of Plantation Workers and Peasants on Java in 1939–40*, Cornell University, Southeast Asia Program, Ithaca, 1956

Cunningham, Clark E.: *The Postwar Migration of the Toba-Bataks to East Sumatra*, Yale University, Southeast Asia Studies, New Haven, 1958

Davies, Derek: 'The Sultan's problems,' *Far Eastern Economic Review*, vol. 52, 1966 pp. 519–22

Dewey, Alice: *Peasant Marketing in Java*, Free Press, Glencoe, 1962

Economist Intelligence Unit: *Indonesia: Three-Monthly Economic Review*, London, quarterly

Fisher, Charles A.: 'Economic myth and geographical reality in Indonesia', *Modern Asian Studies*, vol. 1, 1967, pp. 155–89

Fryer, D. W.: 'Recovery of the sugar industry in Java,' *Economic Geography*, vol. 33, 1957, pp. 171–87

————: 'Economic aspects of Indonesian Disunity,' *Pacific Affairs*, vol. 30, 1957, pp. 195–208

————: *Indonesia: The Economic Geography of an Underdeveloped Country*, Unpublished thesis for the degree of Ph.D., University of London, 1958

————: 'Jogjakarta: economic development in an Indonesian city state,' *Economic Development and Cultural Change*, vol. 7, 1959, pp. 452–64

Furnivall, J. S.: *Colonial Policy and Practice: A Comparative Study of Burma and Netherlands Indies*, Cambridge University Press, 1948, and New York University Press, New York, 1956

Geertz, Clifford: 'Religious belief and economic behaviour in a central Javanese town: Some preliminary considerations,' *Economic Development and Cultural Change*, vol. 4, 1956, pp. 134–58

————: *Peddlers and Princes: Social Change and Economic Modernization in Two Indonesian Towns*, University of Chicago Press, Chicago, 1963

Glassburner, Bruce: 'Economic policy making in Indonesia 1950–1957,' *Economic Development and Cultural Change*, vol. 10, 1962, pp. 113–33

Hanna, Willard A.: *Bung Karno's Indonesia*, American Universities Field Staff, no. 28, New York, 1960

Hatta, Mohammed: *The Cooperative Movement in Indonesia*, Cornell University Press, Ithaca, 1957

Heeren, H. J. (ed.): 'The urbanization of Djakarta,' *Ekonomi dan Keuangan Indonesia*, vol. 8, 1955, pp. 696–736

Higgins, Benjamin: *Indonesia's Economic Stabilization and Development*, Institute of Pacific Relations, New York, 1957

———— et al.: *Entrepreneurship and Labor Skills in Indonesia: A Symposium*, Yale University, Southeast Asia Studies, New Haven, 1961

———— and Jean Higgins: *Indonesia: The Crisis of the Millstones*, Van Nostrand, Princeton, 1963

Honig, P. and F. Verdoorn (eds.): *Science and Scientists in the Netherlands Indies*, Board for the Netherlands Indies, Surinam and Curacao, New York, 1945

Humphrey, Don D.: 'Indonesia's plan for economic development,' *Asian Survey*, vol. 2, 1962, pp. 12–21

Hunter, Alex: 'The Indonesian oil industry,' *Australian Economic Papers*, vol. 5, 1966, pp. 59–106

Ismail, J. E.: 'Government purchasing of rice in East Java,' *Ekonomi dan Keuangan Indonesia*, vol. 16, 1963, no. 3, pp. 53–62

Johnson, Russell et al.: *Business Environment in an Emerging Nation: Profiles of the Indonesian Economy*, Northwestern University Press, Evanston, 1966

Kartanahardja, Ateng: 'National shipping in Indonesia,' *Ekonomi dan Keuangan Indonesia*, vol. 9, 1956, pp. 309–31

Keyfitz, Nathaniel: 'The population of Indonesia,' *Ekonomi dan Keuangan Indonesia*, vol. 6, 1953, pp. 641 *et seq.*

————: 'The ecology of Indonesian cities,' *American Journal of Sociology*, vol. 66, 1961, pp. 348–54

————: 'Indonesian population and the European Industrial Revolution,' *Asian Survey*, vol. 5, 1965, pp. 503–14

Koentjaraningrat (ed.): *Villages in Indonesia*, Cornell University Press, Ithaca, 1966

van der Kroef, Justus M.: *Indonesia in the Modern World*, 2 vols., Masa Baru, Bandung, 1954 and 1956

————: 'Economic development in Indonesia: some social and cultural impediments,' *Economic Development and Cultural Change*, vol. 4, 1956, pp. 116–33

————: 'Land tenure and social structure on rural Java,' *Rural Sociology*, vol. 25, 1960, pp. 414–30

Lev, Daniel S.: 'The political role of the army in Indonesia,' *Pacific Affairs*, vol. 36, 1963–64, pp. 349–64

Mackie, J. A. C.: 'Indonesia's government estates and their masters,' *Pacific Affairs*, vol. 34, 1961, pp. 337–60

Massachusetts Institute of Technology, Center for International Studies: *Stanvac in Indonesia*, National Planning Association, Washington, 1957

McVey, Ruth (ed.): *Indonesia*, HRAF Press, New Haven, 1963

Mears, Leon A.: *Rice Marketing in the Republic of Indonesia*, P. T. Pembangunan, Djakarta, 1961

Metcalf, John E.: *The Agricultural Economy of Indonesia*, US Department of Agriculture, Washington, 1952

Munthe-Kaas, Harald: 'The Chinese in Indonesia: the Dragon's Seeds,' *Far Eastern Economic Review*, vol. 58, 1967, pp. 282–6

National Planning Bureau: 'Some explanations of Indonesia's 1956–60 Five Year Development Plan,' *Ekonomi dan Keuangan Indonesia*, vol. 9, 1956, pp. 661–8

de Neumann, A. M.: *Industrial Development in Indonesia*, Van Dorp, Djakarta, 1955

————: 'On the promotion of indigenous Indonesian industries, with special reference to credit facilities for private business and for local government enterprises,' *Ekonomi dan Keuangan Indonesia*, vol. 9, 1956, pp. 683–728

Nugroho: *Indonesia in Facts and Figures*, Djakarta, 1967 (mimeo.)

Ormeling, F. J.: *The Timor Problem: A Geographical Interpretation of an Underdeveloped Island*, Wolters, Groningen and Djakarta, 1956

Paauw, Douglas S.: *Financing Economic Development: The Indonesian Case*, Free Press, Glencoe, 1960

———— (ed.): *Prospects for East Sumatran Plantation Industries: A Symposium*, Yale University, Southeast Asia Studies, New Haven, 1962

Palmier, Leslie H.: *Indonesia and the Dutch*, Oxford University Press, London, 1962

————: *Indonesia*, Thames & Hudson, London, and Walker & Co., New York, 1965

Panglaykim, J.: 'Some aspects of state enterprises in Indonesia,' *Ekonomi dan Keuangan Indonesia*, vol. 16, 1963, no. 3, pp. 3–18

———— and H. W. Arndt: *The Indonesian Economy: Facing a New Era?*, Rotterdam University Press, Rotterdam, 1966

———— and K. D. Thomas: 'Indonesian export performance and prospects 1950–1970,' *Bulletin of Indonesian Economic Studies*, Australian National University, *Part 1*, no. 5, October 1966, pp. 71–102: *Part 2*, no. 6, February 1967, pp. 66–89

————: 'Suharto plans again,' *Far Eastern Economic Review*, vol. 58, 1967, pp. 239–42

————: 'The road to Amsterdam and beyond: aspects of Indonesia's stabilization program,' *Asian Survey*, vol. 7, 1967, pp. 689–703

Pauker, Guy J.: 'Indonesia's Eight Year Development Plan,' *Pacific Affairs*, vol. 34, 1961, pp. 115–30

————: 'The Soviet challenge in Indonesia,' *Foreign Affairs*, vol. 40, 1962, pp. 612–26

Penny, D. H.: 'Economics of peasant agriculture: the Indonesian case,' *Bulletin of Indonesian Economic Studies*, no. 5, October 1966, pp. 22–44

Pelzer, Karl J.: 'The agrarian conflict in East Sumatra,' *Pacific Affairs*, vol. 30, 1957, pp. 151–9

Rao, K. Nagaraja: 'Small scale industry and economic development in Indonesia,' *Economic Development and Cultural Change*, vol. 4, 1956, pp. 159–70

Report of Bank Indonesia (Bank Negara Indonesia): Kolff, Djakarta, annually

Roeder, O. G.: 'Taking stock,' *Far Eastern Economic Review*, vol. 56, 1966, pp. 679–81

———: 'Anxious archipelago,' *Far Eastern Economic Review*, vol. 56, 1967, pp. 387–9

———: 'Waiting for the action,' *Far Eastern Economic Review*, vol. 59, 1968, pp. 275–7

——— and Sanjoto Sastromihardjo: 'Indonesia's economic mess,' *Far Eastern Economic Review*, vol. 52, 1966, pp. 216–8

Skinner, G. W. (ed.): *Local, Ethnic and National Loyalties in Village Indonesia: A Symposium*, Yale University, Southeast Asia Studies, New Haven, 1959

Soedjatmoko: *Economic Development as a Cultural Problem*, Cornell University, Southeast Asia Program, Ithaca, 1958

Soemardjan, Selo: *Social Changes in Jogjakarta*, Cornell University Press, Ithaca, 1962

Starner, Frances L: 'Central Java: breeding troubles,' *Far Eastern Economic Review*, vol. 57, 1967, pp. 331–5

Statistical Pocketbook of Indonesia 1963, Biro Pusat Statistik, Djakarta, 1963

de Terra, G. J. A.: 'Mixed garden horticulture in Java,' *Malayan Journal of Tropical Geography*, vol. 4, 1954, pp. 33–43

Thomas, K. D.: *Smallholders Rubber in Indonesia*, Institute for Economic and Social Research, University of Indonesia, Djakarta, n.d. (mimeo.)

Tjan Ping Tjwan, Population, 'Unemployment and economic development', *Ekonomi dan Kueangan Indonesia*, vol. 13, 1960, p. 455

Tjitrosudarmo, Sudarto: 'Government purchasing of rice in Central Java,' *Ekonomi dan Keuangan Indonesia*, vol. 16, 1963, no. 3, pp. 35–52

US Army: *Area Handbook on Indonesia*, Government Printing Office, Washington, 1964

US Economic Survey Team to Indonesia: *Indonesia: Perspective and Proposals for United States Economic Aid*, Yale University, Southeast Asia Studies, New Haven, 1963

van der Veur, Paul: 'West Irian: a new era,' *Asian Survey*, vol. 2, 1962, pp. 1–8

———: 'Political awakening in West New Guinea,' *Pacific Affairs*, vol. 36, 1963, pp. 54–73

Weatherbee, Donald E.: 'Portuguese Timor: an Indonesian dilemma,' *Asian Survey*, vol. 6, 1966, pp. 683–95

Weffert, M. Virginia: *Basic Data on the Economy of Indonesia*, World Trade Information Service, Overseas Business Reports, US Department of Commerce, Washington, 1964

Wertheim, W. F.: *The Indonesian Town*, Selected Studies on Indonesia, vol. 4, van Hoeve, The Hague, 1958

———: *Indonesian Society in Transition: A Study of Social Change*, van Hoeve, The Hague, 1959

———: 'Sociological aspects of inter-island migration in Indonesia,' *Population Studies*, vol. 12, 1959, pp. 184–201

Withington, W. A.: 'The distribution of population in Sumatra, Indonesia', *Journal of Tropical Geography*, vol. 15, 1961, pp. 203–12

————: 'The major geographic regions of Sumatra, Indonesia', *Annals of the Association of American Geographers*, vol. 57, 1967, pp. 534–49

Burma

Allen, Robert Loring: 'Burma's clearing account agreement,' *Pacific Affairs*, vol. 31, 1958, pp. 147–63

Andrus, J. Russell: *Burmese Economic Life*, Stanford University Press, Stanford, California, and Oxford University Press, London, 1947

Badgely, John H.: 'Burma's China crisis: the choices ahead,' *Asian Survey*, vol. 7, 1967, pp. 753–61

Boog, Peter: 'Burma and China: the People's War,' *Far Eastern Economic Review*, vol. 58, 1967, pp. 314–23

————: 'White flags of war,' *Far Eastern Economic Review*, vol. 58, 1967, pp. 373–7

Burma Facts and Figures, Longmans Burma Pamphlets no. 9, Orient Longmans, Bombay, 1946

Burma Rice, Longmans Burma Pamphlets no. 4, Orient Longmans, Bombay, reprinted 1956

Butwell, Richard A.: *U Nu of Burma*, Stanford University Press, Stanford, 1963

Cressey, Paul: 'The ecological organization of Rangoon, Burma,' *Sociology and Social Research*, vol. 11, 1956, pp. 166–9

'Dependence on none,' *Far Eastern Economic Review*, vol. 59, 1968, pp. 510–11

Economic and Engineering Development of Burma, Knappen, Tippetts, Abbett & McCarthy, in association with Pierce Management, Inc., and Robert R. Nathan Associates, 2 vols., n.p., 1953

Fairbairn, Geoffrey: 'Some minority problems in Burma,' *Pacific Affairs*, vol. 30, 1957, 1957, pp. 299–311

Fisher, Charles A.: 'The Thailand-Burma Railway,' *Economic Geography*, vol. 23, 1947, pp. 85–97

'Fruit between thorns,' *Far Eastern Economic Review*, vol. 59, 1968, p. 444

Goodstadt, L. F.: 'Dismal tidings,' *Far Eastern Economic Review*, vol. 58, 1967, pp. 12–13

————: 'Cultural backlash,' *Far Eastern Economic Review*, vol. 57, 1967, pp. 49–50

————: 'Peasants' Parliament,' *Far Eastern Economic Review*, vol. 57, 1967, pp. 573–5

Guyot, James F.: 'Bureaucratic transformation in Burma,' in Braibanti, Ralph J. *et al.*, *Asian Bureaucratic Systems Emergent from the British Imperial Tradition*, Duke University Press, Durham, 1966, pp. 354–443

Hagan, Everett E.: *The Economic Development of Burma*, National Planning Association, Washington, 1956

Holmes, Robert A.: 'Burmese domestic policy: the politics of Burmanization,' *Asian Survey*, vol. 7, 1967, pp. 188–97

Huke, Robert E.: 'Burma,' *Focus*, vol. 10, October 1960

Katsu Yanahaira: 'Problems of the rice trade between Burma and Japan,' *The Developing Economies*, vol. 2, 1964, pp. 58–77

Koop, John Clement: *The Eurasian Population in Burma*, Yale University, Southeast Asia Studies, New Haven, 1960

Langtry, Lionel: *Burma: The Land and the People*, J. B. Lippincott Company, Philadelphia, 1968

Leach, G. R.: *Political Systems of Highland Burma: A Study of Kachin Social Structure*, G. Bell, London, 1954

Lewis, Norman: *Golden Earth*, Jonathan Cape, London, 1952

Lockwood, Agnese W.: *The Burma Road to Pyidawtha*, Carnegie Endowment for International Peace, New York, 1958

Ministry of Finance and Revenue: *Economic Survey of Burma 1960*, Office of Development Finance and Private Enterprise, AID. Photocopy distributed by Clearing House for Federal Scientific and Technical Information, US Department of Commerce, Washington, n.d.

Ministry of National Planning: *Second Four Year Plan for the Union of Burma 1961–62 to 1964–65*, Government Printing and Stationery, Rangoon, 1961

Morehead, F. T.: *The Forests of Burma*, Longmans Burma Pamphlets no. 5, Orient Longmans, Bombay, 1944

Mya Maung: 'Cultural values and economic development of Burma,' *Asian Survey*, vol. 4, 1964, pp. 757–65

————: 'The social and economic development of Burma,' *Asian Survey*, vol. 4, 1964, pp. 1182–91

————: 'The elephant-catching co-operative society of Burma: a case study on the effect of planned socio-economic change,' *Asian Survey*, vol. 6, 1966, pp. 326–38

Myaung Kyaw: 'Land utilization of the Insein district,' *Malayan Journal of Tropical Geography*, vol. 2, 1954, pp. 56–61

Nash, Manning: *The Golden Road to Mandalay*, John Wiley, New York, 1965

Pye, Lucian W.: *Politics, Personality and Nation Building: Burma's Search for Identity*, Yale University Press, New Haven, 1962

Pyidawtha—The New Burma. Report on long-term programme for Economic and Social Development, Rangoon, 1954

Redick, Richard W.: 'A demographic and ecological study of Rangoon, Burma, 1953,' in Burgess, Ernest W. and Donald J, Bogue, *Contributions to Urban Sociology*, University of Chicago Press, Chicago, 1954, pp. 31–41

Silverstein, Josef: 'First steps on the Burmese way to socialism,' *Asian Survey*, vol. 4, 1964, pp. 716–22

————: 'Problems in Burma, economic, political and diplomatic,' *Asian Survey*, vol. 7, 1967, pp. 117–25

Sinai, I. R.: *The Challenge of Modernization*, Chatto & Windus, London, and Norton & Co., New York, 1964, pp. 108–79

Spate, O. H. K.: 'The beginnings of industrialization in Burma,' *Economic Geography*, vol. 17, 1941, pp. 75–92

————: *Burma Setting*, Longmans Burma Pamphlets no. 2, Orient Longmans, Bombay, 1942

————: 'The Burmese village,' *Geographical Review*, vol. 35, 1945, pp. 523–43

———— and L. W. Trueblood: 'Rangoon: a study in urban geography,' *Geographical Review*, vol. 32, 1942, pp. 56–73

Stamp, L. Dudley: 'The Irrawaddy River,' *Geographical Journal*, vol. 95, 1940, pp. 329–59

de Terra, Hellmut: 'Component geographic factors of the natural regions of Burma,' *Annals of the Association of American Geographers*, vol. 34, 1944, pp. 67–96

Tinker, Hugh: *The Union of Burma*, Oxford University Press, 3rd edn., London, 1960

Trager, Frank N.: *Building a Welfare State in Burma 1948–1956*, Institute of Pacific Relations, New York, 1958

————: 'Burma 1967: a better ending than beginning,' *Asian Survey*, vol. 8, 1968, pp. 110–19

US Government Printing Office: *Area Handbook for Burma*, Washington, 1968

U Tun Wai: *Economic Development of Burma from 1800 till 1940*, Department of Economics, Rangoon University, 1961

Walinsky, Louis J.: *Economic Development in Burma 1951–1960*, The Twentieth Century Fund, New York, 1962

Vietnam, Laos and Cambodia

Admiralty, Naval Intelligence Division: *Indo-China*, London, 1943

Agricultural Problems, Foreign Languages Publishing House, Hanoi, 1964

Asian Survey, Special issue on Vietnam, vol. 7, no. 8, August 1967

Brodrick, Alan Houghton: *Little Vehicle: Cambodia and Laos*, Hutchinson, London, 1947

'Cambodia's Chinese: friendship with frictions,' *Far Eastern Economic Review*, vol. 56, 1967, pp. 623–7

Canada, Department of Mines and Technical Surveys: *Indo-China, a Geographical Appreciation*, Foreign Geography Information Series no. 6, Ottawa, 1953

Cambodia, Ministère du Plan: *Annuaire Statistique Retrospectif du Cambodge 1958–61*, Phnom Penh, n.d.

Child, Frank C.: *Towards a Policy for Economic Growth in Vietnam*, Michigan State University Advisory Group, Saigon, 1962

Close, Alexandra: 'Laos: land of twilight,' *Far Eastern Economic Review*, vol. 57, 1967, pp. 643–9

Davies, Derek: 'What price peace at Paris?,' *Far Eastern Economic Review*, vol. 59, 1968, pp. 473–6

Delvert, Jean: *Le Paysan Cambodgien*, Mouton & Co., Paris, 1961

Devereaux, George: 'The potential contributions of the Moi to the cultural landscape of Indochina,' *Far Eastern Quarterly*, vol. 6, 1947, pp. 390–5

Dumont, René: *La Culture du Riz dans le Delta du Tonkin*, Société d'Éditions Géographiques, Maritimes et Coloniales, Paris, 1935

Fall, Bernard B.: 'The political religious sects of Viet-Nam,' *Pacific Affairs*, vol. 28, 1955, pp. 235–53

————: 'The international relations of Laos,' *Pacific Affairs*, vol. 30, 1957, pp. 22–34

————: 'South Viet-Nam's internal problems,' *Pacific Affairs*, vol. 31, 1958, pp. 241–60

————: *Le Viet-Minh: La République Democratique du Viet-Nam 1945–1960*, Armand Colin, Paris, 1960

————: *The Two Vietnams*, Frederick Praeger, New York and London, 2nd rev. edn., 1967

Far Eastern Quarterly, Special Number on French Indochina, vol. 6, August, 1947

Field, Michael: *The Prevailing Wind: Witness in Indo-China*, Methuen, London, 1965

Fisher, Charles A.: 'The Vietnamese problem in its geographical context,' *Geographical Journal*, vol. 131, 1965, pp. 502–15

Foreign Area Studies, The American University: *Area Handbook for Cambodia*, Government Printing Office, Washington, 1968

————: *Area Handbook for Laos*, Government Printing Office, Washington, 1967

————: *Area Handbook for North Vietnam*, Government Printing Office, Washington, 1967

————: *Area Handbook for South Vietnam*, Government Printing Office, Washington, 1967

Gittinger, J. Price: 'Communist land policy in North Vietnam,' *Far Eastern Survey*, vol. 28, 1959, pp. 113–26

————: 'A note on the economic impact of totalitarian land tenure change: the Vietnamese experience,' *Malayan Economic Review*, vol. 5, 1960, pp. 81–84

Gourou, Pierre: *L'Utilisation du Sol en Indochine Française*, Centre d'Études de Politique Étrangère, Presses Universitaires de France, Paris, 1940. English edition: *Land Utilization in French Indochina*, Institute of Pacific Relations, New York, 1945

————: 'Land utilization in upland areas of Indochina,' in *Development of Upland Areas of the Far East*, vol. 2, Institute of Pacific Relations, New York, 1951, pp. 24–52

————: *Les Paysans du Delta Tonkinois*, Mouton & Co., Paris, 1965

Halpern, Joel M.: *The Economy and Society of Laos*, Southeast Asia Studies, Yale University, 1964

Head, Simon: 'Pacification in South Vietnam: unhappy harbingers,' *Far Eastern Economic Review*, vol. 56, 1967, pp. 495–8

Hendry, James B.: 'Land tenure in South Vietnam,' *Economic Development and Cultural Change*, vol. 9, 1960, pp. 27–44

————: *The Small World of Khanh Hau*, Aldine Publishing Co., Chicago, 1964

————: *Study of a Vietnamese Rural Community Economic Activity*, Michigan State University Press, East Lansing, 1959

Hickey, Gerald Cannon: *Village in Vietnam*, Yale University Press, New Haven, 1964

Honey, P. J.: 'Pham Van Dong's tour,' *China Quarterly*, no. 8, 1961, pp. 42–44

————: *North Vietnam Today*, Frederick Praeger, New York and London, 1962

————: *Communism in North Vietnam*, Massachusetts Institute of Technology Press, Cambridge, Mass., 1963

————: 'Food crisis in North Vietnam,' *Far Eastern Economic Review*, vol. 41, 1963, pp. 493–5

Jones, P. M. H.: 'The industry of North Vietnam,' *Far Eastern Economic Review*, vol. 29, 1960, pp. 656–60

Kaye, William: 'A bowl of rice divided: the economy of North Vietnam,' *China Quarterly*, no. 9, 1962, pp. 82–93

Kinloch, R. J.: 'Industrialization in Cambodia,' *Pacific Viewpoint*, vol. 7, 1966, pp. 236–7

Le Chau: *Le Viet Nam Socialiste*, Francois Maspero, Paris, 1966

Lebar, Frank M. and Adrienne Suddard (eds.): *Laos: its People, its Society, its Culture*, HRAF Press, New Haven, 1963

Lewis, Norman: *A Dragon Apparent*, Jonathan Cape, London, 1951

Lindholm, Richard W. (ed.): *Vietnam: The First Five Years*, Michigan State University Press, East Lansing, 1959

Osborne, Milton E.: *Strategic Hamlets in South Viet-Nam*, Southeast Asia Program, Cornell University, Ithaca, 1965

Republic of Vietnam, Department of National Education and National Commission for UNESCO: *Viet-Nam Past and Present*, Saigon, 1957

————, National Institute of Statistics: *Viet-Nam Statistical Yearbook 1966–67*, Saigon, 1968

Robequain, Charles: *Le Thanh Hoa: Étude Géographique d'une Province Annamite*, Van Oest, Paris, 1929

————: *The Economic Development of French Indo-China*, Oxford University Press, London, 1944

————: *L'Indochine*, Armand Colin, Paris, 1952

Salisbury, Harrison E.: *Behind the Lines—Hanoi*, Harper & Row, New York, 1967

Scigliano, Robert G.: *South Vietnam: Nation Under Stress*, Houghton Miflin, Boston, 1963

Shabad, Theodore: 'Economic developments in North Vietnam,' *Pacific Affairs*, vol. 31, 1958, pp. 36–53

Starner, Frances L.: 'Pacification in South Vietnam: a "real new life"?,' *Far Eastern Economic Review*, vol. 57, 1967, pp. 456–60

Steinberg, David J. *et al.*: *Cambodia: Its People, its Society, its Culture*, HRAF Press, New Haven, rev. edn., 1959

Taylor, Milton C.: 'South Vietnam: lavish aid, limited progress,' *Pacific Affairs*, vol. 34, 1961, pp. 242–56

Thompson, Virginia M.: *French Indo-China*, Allen & Unwin, London, and The Macmillan Company, New York, 1937

Ton That Thien: 'South Vietnam's economy: better than nothing,' *Far Eastern Economic Review*, vol. 56, 1967, pp. 459–60

Toye, Hugh: Laos: *Buffer State or Battleground*, Oxford University Press, London, 1968

Warner, Denis: *The Last Confucian*, The Macmillan Company, New York, 1963

Willmot, William E.: *The Chinese in Cambodia*, Publications Centre, University of British Columbia, Vancouver, 1967

Yoshinori Nakano: 'Economic conditions in North Vietnam,' *The Developing Economies*, vol. 1, no. 2, 1963, pp. 218–31

Zasloff, J. J.: 'Rural resettlement in South Vietnam: the Agroville Program,' *Pacific Affairs*, vol. 35, 1962–63, pp. 327–40

Index

475